INNOVATION AND CHANGE IN READING INSTRUCTION

Officers of the Society
1967-68
(Term of office expires March 1 of the year indicated.)

EDGAR DALE
(1968)
Ohio State University, Columbus, Ohio

JOHN I. GOODLAD
(1969)
University of California, Los Angeles, California

W. C. KVARACEUS
(1970)
Tufts University, Medford, Massachusetts

HERMAN G. RICHEY
(1968) *(Ex-officio)*
University of Chicago, Chicago, Illinois

HAROLD G. SHANE
(1968)
Indiana University, Bloomington, Indiana

RALPH W. TYLER
(1970)
Center for Advanced Study in the Behavioral Sciences
Stanford, California

PAUL A. WITTY
(1969)
Northwestern University, Evanston, Illinois

Secretary-Treasurer
HERMAN G. RICHEY
5835 Kimbark Avenue, Chicago, Illinois 60637

INNOVATION AND CHANGE IN READING INSTRUCTION

The Sixty-seventh Yearbook of the National Society for the Study of Education

PART II

By
THE YEARBOOK COMMITTEE
and
ASSOCIATED CONTRIBUTORS

Edited by

HELEN M. ROBINSON

Editor for the Society

HERMAN G. RICHEY

Distributed by THE UNIVERSITY OF CHICAGO PRESS • CHICAGO, ILLINOIS 60637

The responsibilities of the Board of Directors of the National Society for the Study of Education in the case of yearbooks prepared by the Society's committees are (1) to select the subjects to be investigated, (2) to appoint committees calculated in their personnel to insure consideration of all significant points of view, (3) to provide appropriate subsidies for necessary expenses, (4) to publish and distribute the committees' reports, and (5) to arrange for their discussion at the annual meeting.

The responsibility of the Society's editor is to prepare the submitted manuscripts for publication in accordance with the principles and regulations approved by the Board of Directors.

Neither the Board of Directors, nor the Society's editor, nor the Society is responsible for the conclusions reached or the opinions expressed by the Society's yearbook committees.

Published 1968 by
THE NATIONAL SOCIETY FOR THE STUDY OF EDUCATION
5835 Kimbark Avenue, Chicago, Illinois 60637
Copyright, 1968, by HERMAN G. RICHEY, Secretary
The National Society for the Study of Education

No part of this Yearbook may be reproduced in any form without written permission from the Secretary of the Society.

First printing, 10,000 Copies

Printed in the United States of America

The Society's Committee on Reading

JEANNE CHALL
Professor of Education
Harvard University
Cambridge, Massachusetts

EDGAR DALE
Professor of Education
Ohio State University
Columbus, Ohio

DOLORES DURKIN
Professor of Education
University of Illinois
Urbana, Illinois

HELEN M. ROBINSON
(Chairman)
William S. Gray Research Professor of Reading
Department of Education
University of Chicago
Chicago, Illinois

GEORGE D. SPACHE
Professor of Education
University of Florida
Gainesville, Florida

Associated Contributors

MARY C. AUSTIN
Professor of Education
Western Reserve University
Cleveland, Ohio

ASSOCIATED CONTRIBUTORS

THEODORE W. CLYMER
Professor of Elementary Education and Educational Psychology
University of Minnesota
Minneapolis, Minnesota

WILLARD J. CONGREVE
Director, Urban Education Development Project
University of Chicago
Chicago, Illinois

ALBERT J. HARRIS
Director, Office of Research and Evaluation
Division of Teacher Education
City University of New York
New York, New York

HELEN HUUS
Professor of Education
University of Missouri
Kansas City, Missouri

CONSTANCE M. MCCULLOUGH
Professor of Education
San Francisco State College
San Francisco, California

HARRY W. SARTAIN
Professor of Education and
Director, Falk Laboratory School
University of Pittsburgh
Pittsburgh, Pennsylvania

MILDRED LETTON WITTICK
Professor of English
Paterson State College
Wayne, New Jersey

Editor's Preface

The National Society has published, over a period of nearly fifty years, a number of yearbooks which have contributed to and reflected the remarkable development of reading as an area of instruction and a field of research.

In 1921, the *Report of the Society's Committee on Silent Reading* (Horn) appeared, followed by the *Report of the National Committee on Reading* (Gray) in 1925, *The Teaching of Reading* (Gray) in 1937, *Reading in High School and College* (Gray) in 1948, *Reading in the Elementary School* (Gates) in 1949, *Adult Reading* (Clift) in 1956, and *Development in and through Reading* (Witty) in 1961.

Late in 1964, the Board reviewed the proposals and suggestions for a yearbook in reading that had been received after the preparation of *Development in and through Reading* had been approved. These proposals suggested the need for a critical examination of new concepts and theories and of innovative practices in the field. Edgar Dale was asked to confer with several reading specialists and to report to the Board their views concerning the need for a new yearbook on reading and the feasibility of bringing out such a book only some seven or eight years after the publication of the Society's last yearbook on reading.

In February, 1965, Mr. Dale—after conferring with Jean Chall, Theodore Clymer, Arthur S. Gates, Helen M. Robinson, and others —reported their suggestions and recommendations and presented a tentative proposal for a yearbook. He recommended that a committee, with Mrs. Robinson as chairman, be appointed to formulate a final proposal for the yearbook and to prepare it for publication in 1968.

Mrs. Robinson called a meeting of committee members and other specialists (see *Introduction*) at which time the plans for the yearbook were revised and perfected. The Committee's proposal was approved in February, 1966, and has been only slightly modified since that time.

The high quality of the Committee and of the contributing authors is attested to by the yearbook. Their intelligent and well-directed efforts have produced a yearbook that is timely, readable, and of great value—not only to scholars in the field but to teachers, parents, and many others who need assurance that, although the right road to reading has not been nor is likely in the foreseeable future to be charted, research and innovative practices are combining to give intelligent direction toward the goals that are sought by teachers, pupils, and the greater society.

HERMAN G. RICHEY
Editor for the Society

Table of Contents

	PAGE
OFFICERS OF THE SOCIETY, 1967-68	ii
THE SOCIETY'S COMMITTEE ON READING	v
ASSOCIATED CONTRIBUTORS	v
EDITOR'S PREFACE	vii

INTRODUCTION, *Helen M. Robinson* 1

CHAPTER

 I. WHAT IS "READING"?: SOME CURRENT CONCEPTS, *Theodore Clymer* 7
  Introduction. Some Current Definitions. A Comprehensive Skills Model: Gray and Robinson. A Concluding Statement.

 II. WHEN SHOULD CHILDREN BEGIN TO READ? *Dolores Durkin*   30
  Introduction. When Should Reading Instruction Start? When Should a Child Begin To Read? When To Begin: A Final Summary.

 III. INNOVATIONS IN READING INSTRUCTION: FOR BEGINNERS, *Mildred Letton Wittick* 72
  Introduction. Major Current Innovations in Methods and Materials. The Research Evidence. Innovations in Testing at the Beginning Stages of Reading. Summary and Conclusions.

 IV. INNOVATIONS IN READING INSTRUCTION: AT LATER LEVELS, *Helen Huus* 126
  Introduction. The Situation in 1960. The Innovations and Changes. A Look to the Future.

 V. DIAGNOSIS AND REMEDIAL INSTRUCTION IN READING, *Albert J. Harris* 159
  Terminology. A Brief Historical Review. Causes of Reading Disability. Diagnostic Procedures. Organization of Corrective and Remedial Instruction. New Methodology and Materials. The Results of Remedial Reading. Possible Future Developments.

 VI. ORGANIZATIONAL PATTERNS OF SCHOOLS AND CLASSROOMS FOR READING INSTRUCTION, *Harry W. Sartain* 195
  Establishment of Multiple Standards. An Evaluation of Major Organizational Patterns. Changing Organizational Patterns.

TABLE OF CONTENTS

CHAPTER   PAGE

VII. CONTRIBUTIONS OF ALLIED FIELDS TO THE TEACHING OF READING, *George D. Spache* 237
    Introduction. Sociology. Social Psychology. Child Development. Linguistics, Psycholinguistics, and Language Development. Educational Psychology. Optometry and Opthalmology. Clinical Psychology. Concluding Statement.

VIII. IMPLEMENTING AND EVALUATING THE USE OF INNOVATIONS, *Willard J. Congreve* 291
    Introduction. Instituting Desirable Change. Evaluating Innovations. Concluding Statement.

IX. BALANCED READING DEVELOPMENT, *Constance M. McCullough* 320
    Introduction. Historical Contributions to the Concept of Balance. Available Materials for Balance. Current Innovations and the Concept of Balance. Final Statement.

X. PROFESSIONAL TRAINING OF READING PERSONNEL, *Mary C. Austin* 357
    Impetus for Change. Teacher Preparation. Administrators and Reading. Reading Consultants. College Teachers. Researchers in Reading. Training for Paraprofessionals. Looking Ahead.

XI. THE NEXT DECADE, *Helen M. Robinson* 397
    Introduction. Unsolved Problems. Experiment and Research. Future Experimentation and Research. New Materials and Services. Programs for Illiterates and Poor Readers. National and International Assessment. Needs and Expectations.

INDEX 431

CONSTITUTION AND BY-LAWS i

MINUTES OF THE ANNUAL MEETING OF THE SOCIETY ix

SYNOPSIS OF THE PROCEEDINGS OF THE BOARD OF DIRECTORS OF THE SOCIETY FOR 1967 xi

REPORT OF THE TREASURER OF THE SOCIETY xiii

LIST OF MEMBERS xv

INFORMATION CONCERNING THE SOCIETY

LIST OF PUBLICATIONS OF THE SOCIETY

Introduction

HELEN M. ROBINSON

The theme of this yearbook evolved from the discussion of a number of specialists in reading, called together to consider the desirability of returning to the topic of reading so soon after the publication (in 1961) of the Society's yearbook, *Development in and through Reading*. It was evident, in view of the many changes and new developments which had occurred since 1960, that an assessment of the field was timely. The entire group supported the decision to prepare this yearbook.

Innovation and Change in Reading Instruction was chosen as the title because innovation and change appeared to characterize the last decade, the period being surveyed. *Innovation* is defined in the dictionary as a change from established custom—a new idea, method, or device. An examination of research and practice in reading revealed many changes from what generally had been accepted in the past. Even though many of the methods and devices being described as new in the 1960's were adaptations or variations of methods or devices reported earlier, they were appearing in the context of a new era. Consequently, those practices and materials which represented marked changes from custom have been identified as innovations.

To imply that, except for such innovations, reading instruction and materials of the sixties were unchanged from those of the fifties would be a mistake. Therefore, the word *change* was included in the title to mean gradual movement from one state of being to another, variation, or refinement. It is anticipated that the many changes reported in this yearbook may contribute to the improvement of instruction of children and youth in reading and to greater accomplishment on their part. However, neither the innovations nor the changes have had sufficient trial to be called improvements.

INTRODUCTION

The title, then, indicates precisely the intent of the committee to deal as objectively as possible with the major attempts directed toward the improvement of reading.

Changes resulted from the increase in number and complexity of the aims and goals of teaching reading during the first half of the twentieth century. These changes were due, in part, to the research which supported the conclusion that instruction in one aspect of reading, such as oral reading, did not insure equal growth in another aspect, such as silent reading. In part, the changes were due to evidence which made it clear that competent reading in one subject area was not necessarily accompanied by equal achievement in another area. Furthermore, as the education of youth was extended upward, heavier demands were made on students to read more widely and with greater discernment.

Continued research in reading and related fields, combined with new insights into the interests of individual children, has led to gradual changes in instructional materials and methods. However, there were no radical changes and few innovative experiments before the advent of Sputnik in 1957, which brought the nation's leaders to a realization of the value of education and the need for improving it. Since that time, pressures both inside and outside the profession have been exerted to improve all education and particularly to improve reading instruction.

In addition to these pressures, the increased availability of funds to support research and experimentation in the schools has encouraged many persons to "do something different." In fact, change probably characterizes the sixties as conformity did the forties and fifties. The effects of most innovations and of many changes cannot be evaluated at this time.

The committee members and the authors of each chapter are keenly aware of the many unsolved problems in and unanswered questions about reading instruction. At the same time, they are cognizant of the need to bring out sharply the fundamental issues related to reading instruction, especially the innovations and changes of the sixties. Available research has been surveyed, and numerous references are offered to the reader.

Most chapters present a brief historical background, selected to provide an understanding of current problems. The limitations of space make it impossible to include any other than the most important or representative research related to each topic. Recommendations for practice based on the accumulated research are presented. In addition, principles for evaluating research and practice are set forth to guide practitioners in making future decisions. Each chapter concludes with the author's description or discussion of developments anticipated in the near future.

A survey of the field reveals that a number of different theories of learning and models of the reading process have been published during the last decade. Some of the models resulted from the research of increasingly concerned allied professional groups, especially linguists and psychologists. Other models were constructed by curriculum specialists who were attempting to build a logical taxonomy that would be useful in developing instructional procedures and materials. Additional models grew out of the combined research, experience, and insight of teacher-researchers in the field of reading. It is anticipated that such analyses will influence the construction of reading tests, bringing them in closer harmony with curricular goals.

Chapter i of this volume presents a summary of the theories and an analysis of the models most relevant to the current scene. A model is designed to bring together the knowledge in a field, to show how the various parts fit together, and finally to chart areas which are relatively unexplored. Some of the models confuse intellectual process with reading behavior and with procedures for instruction. Others consider only a portion of what has been included under the rubric of reading in the past. As Clymer points out, the model that an administrator or teacher adopts, either consciously or unconsciously, markedly affects the curriculum, the selection of materials, the instructional procedures, and the evaluation of progress and competence. Although a single comprehensive theory or model is not anticipated in the near future or even in the distant future, it seems likely that, as co-operative interprofessional research becomes more conclusive and the reading process is better understood, sharp differences among models will be less prevalent.

Following chapter i, fundamental questions relating to specific innovations have been examined. In chapter ii, Durkin considers the question, "When Should Children Begin To Read?" During the sixties, this question has become a vital issue, with some writers advocating teaching infants to read. Although it is known that some children in the past have read before age six and although studies have shown that others could be taught to do so, extensive experimentation with early reading is a change from custom, hence an innovation. The author has examined the assumptions on which the custom of beginning instruction at age six has developed, so as to place in proper perspective the questions being asked in the sixties. On the basis of an examination of available research, she has indicated the nature of the experimentation that is yet needed and has suggested how tentative judgments can be made.

In chapter iii, Wittick has identified various innovations in beginning reading and placed them against a background of the gradual changes which have characterized methods and materials. This is the level at which linguists and psychologists have experimented. Furthermore, a greater volume of research has been reported at the primary-grade level than for later levels. Tentative conclusions concerning the present status of methods and materials for beginning reading are very important for most schools.

Even though the beginning levels have had public prominence and have been subjected to a larger part of the research in the field, professionals in reading are aware of the importance of later stages of instruction. In chapter iv, Huus has explored innovations in teaching the skills beyond word recognition at the middle- and upper-grade levels of the elementary school, in high school and college, and to adult illiterates. A number of innovative efforts are in progress. Some are just on the horizon, and their effects can only be anticipated at present.

In chapter v, Harris has given special attention to the contributions of psychologists, neurologists, and the staff members of medical centers to the understanding of reading disability. New diagnostic procedures are explained and evaluated in relation to possible causes of retardation. Innovations in remedial instruction as well as older procedures are examined. Some predictions concerning directions of development complete this chapter.

In addition to making changes in the methods and materials of instruction, many schools have altered their organizational patterns in an attempt to meet the needs of an increasing and divergent school population. During the past decade, a number of conflicting reports on the effectiveness of inter- and intraclass organizations have been made. Efforts to individualize instruction have been made in some schools, while attempts have been made in others to change the graded pattern. In chapter vi, Sartain has examined the values and limitations of various organizational patterns of schools and classrooms. His criteria for evaluating various patterns and his examples, which combine the strengths and minimize the weaknesses of different patterns, should be quite useful to the reader.

As mentioned earlier, one special contribution of the sixties has been the combination of research, materials, and suggestions for practice emanating from allied professional groups. In chapter vii, Spache has considered the contributions of sociology, social psychology, child development, linguistics and psycholinguistics, educational psychology, optometry and ophthalmology, and clinical psychology to the field of reading. The author has pointed out sharp differences in conclusions, based on differing concepts of learning and teaching. He has also presented ideas and techniques through which educators may arrive at broader understanding and research.

If innovations and changes in reading practices are to become effective in the schools, administrators must be prepared to exert leadership in their schools. In chapter viii, Congreve, an administrator, has (*a*) suggested criteria for selecting innovations to be introduced in the schools, (*b*) described ways of introducing them and giving them a fair chance to demonstrate their worth, and (*c*) indicated the importance of evaluating the effects of an innovation on the total curriculum.

As suggested earlier, most innovations apply to a small segment of the total reading program. If such a segment is overemphasized or if all others are neglected, it seems likely that the reading program will be unbalanced. Therefore, chapter ix, written by McCullough, sets forth the important factors to consider in making certain that accepted goals are attained. With particular emphasis on the learner and on language and the learning process, she shows how attainments in reading may be properly assessed.

With all due regard to the importance of innovations in reading instruction, it is agreed that the teacher is still, without question, one of the most potent forces in reading instruction. In order to improve reading instruction, new insights must be gleaned through research and experimentation. But, to have any effect, research must be translated into practice. Hence the importance of chapter x, by Austin, which deals with the training of reading personnel, including not only teachers but also administrators, supervisors, consultants, researchers, and others involved directly or indirectly with reading instruction.

Finally, the last chapter offers criteria for evaluating research, suggests problems in need of immediate investigation, and points to what appears to be the beginning of future trends.

The plans for this yearbook were ambitious and could only have been realized through the tremendous efforts of many people—committee members, consultants, and contributing authors.

In addition to the members of the committee, the following people contributed to the initial planning: A. Sterl Artley, Mary C. Austin, Theodore Clymer, and Margaret Early. Their ideas helped to determine the general direction of the volume.

The members of the committee on the yearbook have given generously of their time in planning, reading critically, and completing the manuscripts. The writer wishes to express deep appreciation to each member. Finally, the authors of each chapter labored diligently, gave careful attention to the criticism and suggestions of the committee, and revised their chapters in the interest of eliminating duplications and of producing a volume which would meet the highest standards of scholarship.

Without the valuable help of so many people, the 1968 yearbook would not have been completed.

CHAPTER I

What Is "Reading"?: Some Current Concepts

THEODORE CLYMER

Introduction

During the last two decades, increased attention has been given to definitions and explanations of reading. The influence of these definitions and explanations on instructional procedures in the classroom may not be immediately apparent, but an examination of a few definitions in action will serve to indicate the impact of prevailing descriptions of reading on how and what we teach and on how we assess what our pupils have learned in reading.

Recently a mother accosted an intermediate-grade teacher with this question: "Why haven't you let my girl read this week?" The bewildered teacher thought through the busy school schedule and, while he could not immediately recall all of the activities in his classroom that week, he knew that the girl had been reading and working on an independent project. At this point the mother provided a clue to her concept of reading by adding, "She hasn't read to you once this week!" It was now clear that this parent's definition of reading was an incomplete one so far as the teacher's program was concerned. To this mother, "reading" was oral reading. So narrow a concept of reading would result in an instructional program which neglects many of the desirable outcomes of a modern program.

In an interview with a capable boy who was having reading problems, the author asked, "Why do you think you have trouble reading?" Without hesitation, this bright child of ten responded, "Oh, I read all right, it's just the words that bother me." His diagnosis was a good one. He was a bright, perceptive child with a fairly good stock of sight words and an excellent technique of gaining general significance from his reading, but he had no word-analysis skills. His definition of reading was getting the gist of the author's message, and this he could do; but he lacked some other abilities which might be involved in a broader definition of reading. His concept of reading prevented him from seeing clearly his shortcomings as an effective reader.

Definitions of reading which give a unique or limited emphasis or focus to the reading program are not restricted to pupils or to their parents. The statement from Flesch, "I don't understand it; I just read it," presents in capsule form one of the real controversies in the definition of reading. Does reading involve only the translation of printed symbols to the spoken word, or does reading involve understanding of those words as well? If concern for understanding is eliminated from our definition of reading, obvious and sweeping changes are mandatory in our instructional programs and in the ways we evaluate our success in instruction. Instructional programs which deal with "nonsense" words, pay little attention to backgrounds for understanding, and spend the major portion of time on word-analysis skills are logical outcomes of reading defined as translation of printed symbols to the spoken word.

These brief and selective illustrations of the impact of the definition of reading on instructional procedures will have served their purpose if the reader is alerted to carefully assess the material which follows for its implications on reading instruction. A clear concept of reading is not just an "academic" concern. A teacher's definition of reading influences every action he takes in the classroom.

The difficulty in formulating a comprehensive and satisfactory definition of reading is also apparent. The areas of perception, psychology of learning, linguistics, social psychology, and language learning are a few of the fields contributing to an understanding of the reading process and the reading program.

Some Current Definitions

As Spache points out, a clear definition of reading is essential to planning the goals of the instructional program.[1] The lack of attention in reading textbooks to a definition of reading is, therefore, surprising. It is the unusual text which devotes much attention to the definition of reading. An examination of all types of pro-

---

1. George D. Spache, *Reading in the Elementary School* (Boston: Allyn & Bacon, 1964), p. 4.

fessional literature reveals few systematic attempts to define the reading process in any comprehensive fashion.

SOME PARTIAL DEFINITIONS

Walcutt presents a simplified and assured definition of reading.[2] The title of his article seems to imply that anyone who disagrees with him is using a non-professional definition. And who could admit to that? His definition is three-pronged: (*a*) Reading is "decoding the printed visual symbol into a spoken word." (*b*) Reading is "understanding language." (*c*) Reading is appreciation of great literature and the cultural heritage it represents. From his discussion, it is clear that he believes the reading program has special responsibilities in the areas of decoding symbols and appreciation, but that "understanding language" is not really within the province of the reading program. He makes this clear when he states that understanding language "is not really reading at all."

Thus, to Walcutt, reading is decoding and literary appreciation in the highest and finest sense. How the child is helped to bridge the gap between these two important goals of the curriculum is not indicated.

The linguists have been active in defining reading in terms of their concern for oral language. To some linguists, reading is "talk written down," as Tinker and McCullough point out.[3] The impact of such a description on instruction, if it is accepted as a total definition, is clear: the major job of the reading program will be the teaching of "decoding skills."

Reed raises a serious objection to what he calls extreme statements of the primacy of speech over writing.[4] He notes that the newer grammars move from syntax to speech and writing rather than vice versa. He also questions the defining of writing as a secondary representation of speech, for to do so would render us un-

---

2. Charles C. Walcutt, "Reading—a Professional Definition," *Elementary School Journal*, LXVII (April, 1967), 363-65.

3. Miles A. Tinker and Constance M. McCullough, *Teaching Elementary Reading* (New York: Appleton-Century-Crofts, 1962), p. 11.

4. David W. Reed, "A Theory of Language, Speech and Writing," *Elementary English*, XLII (December, 1965), 845-51.

able to explain deaf-mutes who read or skilled readers who read with far greater speed than the most rapid speaker can speak.

In some cases, this primacy-of-speech concept impels the linguist to specify the type of word-analysis program which should be provided. Here the writer sometimes feels like the graduate student who said, "I can understand what they say. It's just the material that comes after the 'therefore' that troubles me." Fries indicates that, while reading is not a simple process, it can be summed up in a simple statement. "One can 'read' insofar as he can respond to the language signals represented by graphic shapes as fully as he has learned to respond to the same language signals of his code represented by patterns of auditory shapes."[5] The crucial word here is "respond." Evidently, triggering the oral response which is represented by the print produces reading.

The type of word recognition typically associated with the linguistic approach is that which is based on the regular consistency of letter and sound. Fries carries the matter further and places emphasis upon "spelling patterns" or, in other words, upon larger visual units. His basic approach, however, is the same as that of Bloomfield, who states that the child should be presented with carefully programed material in teaching the orthographic-phonic regularities of English.[6]

This consistency approach is challenged by interpretations of research completed by Levin and his co-workers.[7] The results of Levin's work suggest that beginning a task with a list of words containing variable grapheme-phoneme relationships creates an expectation of variability of correspondences which transfers to a second situation and facilitates learning. A "set for diversity" may, therefore, be a valuable aid in the transfer of learned relationships to new

---

5. Charles C. Fries, *Linguistics and Reading* (New York: Holt, Rinehart & Winston, Inc., 1963), p. 131.

6. Leonard Bloomfield, "Teaching Children To Read," in Leonard Bloomfield and Clarence L. Barnhart, *Let's Read: A Linguistic Approach* (Detroit: Wayne State University Press, 1961).

7. Harry Levin and J. Watson, "The Learning of Variable Grapheme-to-Phoneme Correspondence," in *A Basic Research Program on Reading* (Cornell University Cooperative Research Project No. 639 [Ithaca, N.Y., 1963]).

situations. If this evidence is verified in other settings, the consistency theory is clearly challenged.

Gibson is representative of the experimental child psychologists who have taken an interest in reading. Gibson's research in the perception of children has lead her naturally to some of the initial problems of visual discrimination in the prereading period. Her work also reflects the work of the Cornell group, including Hockett and Levin. She characterizes reading behavior as (*a*) receiving communication, (*b*) making discriminative responses to graphic symbols, (*c*) decoding graphic symbols to speech, and (*d*) obtaining meaning from the printed page.[8]

Gibson does not concern herself with the communication aspects of reading, because she believes the child has mastered this by the time he begins to learn to read. Reading instruction, then, includes attention only to the other three aspects of reading behavior listed in the preceding paragraph.

Unfortunately, Gibson's discussion of her research is restricted almost entirely to material on making discriminations and on decoding. Obtaining meaning is given little attention in her widely quoted article.

Betts and a number of his students have defined reading as a thinking process.[9] Admittedly, thinking is involved in even the narrowest definition of reading, but such a definition seems to provide no real avenue to understanding, for as Robinson points out, the nature of thought is complex and obscure.[10] There is undoubtedly value in considering thinking as one aspect of the reading process if such a position emphasizes the need for broader goals of a reading program.

SOME MODELS OF READING

Beyond the brief and relatively unstructured definitions of read-

---

8. Eleanor J. Gibson, "Learning To Read," *Science*, CXLVIII (May 21, 1965), 1066-72.

9. Emmett A. Betts, "Reading: Psychological and Linguistic Bases," *Education*, LXXVI (April, 1966), 454-58.

10. Helen M. Robinson, "The Major Aspects of Reading," chap. iii in *Reading: Seventy-Five Years of Progress*, ed. H. Alan Robinson ("Supplementary Educational Monographs," No. 96 [Chicago: University of Chicago Press, 1966]), pp. 22-32.

ing sampled in the earlier section of the chapter are the models which attempt to set forth in more depth and with greater detail the nature of reading. Some of these models stress process, others skills. The use of models in reading research has been discussed by Kingston.[11] He regards the use of a model as a method of specifying the components with which we must deal and as a technique for generating testable hypotheses. Constructing a model forces the investigator to organize facts and to set them against a rational framework; at the same time, it provides a technique for testing these facts and for generating more hypotheses for testing.

Robinson points out the confusion created by models and partial models now available in reading.[12] She traces much of the difficulty to the failure to differentiate clearly among (a) the processes required to read, (b) the skills and abilities used in reading, and (c) the procedures used to teach reading. All three are important to an eventual understanding of reading, but Robinson stresses the importance of clearly separating these three as models are considered.

The discussion up to this point may suggest a much greater specificity in reading models than actually exists and a greater number than have been published. Only the barest beginnings have been made. None appear to be fully satisfactory, as all leave important factors unaccounted for. A model will have served its purpose, however, if it calls attention to missing pieces and if it brings about its own revision, refinement, development, or eventual discard.

The substrata-factor theory, as developed by Holmes and his students, attempts to relate ideas of the function of the brain to the reading process.[13] Brain cells may respond not only singly but in groups as well. These groups of cells, called subsystems by some

---

11. Albert J. Kingston, "Introduction: Current Interest in the Concept of Model in Scientific Research," in *Use of Theoretical Models in Research*, ed. Albert J. Kingston (Highlights of the Pre-Convention Institutes, Institute V [Newark, Del.: International Reading Association, 1966]), pp. 3-5.

12. Robinson, *op. cit.*, pp. 22-32.

13. Jack A. Holmes, "Factors Underlying Major Reading Disabilities at the College Level," *Genetic Psychology Monographs*, XLIX (January-June, 1954), 3-95; and "Basic Assumptions Underlying the Substrata-Factor Theory," *Reading Research Quarterly*, I (Fall, 1965), 4-28.

investigators, may have certain parallels in the level of complexity of the various reading skills and how they relate to each other, according to Holmes.

Using a statistical procedure which is an adaptation of the multiple-regression technique, Holmes specifies the relationship of the results of certain tests to his outcome measurements in reading. In addition, he calculates further relationships among the results of tests he administers, and he attempts by this process to determine the "subfactors" in reading. How accurately this procedure shows relationships which parallel brain functions can only be surmised. What is known is that the Holmes procedure results in interesting, complex, and seemingly very precise determinations of subfactors in reading.

While some of Holmes's results appear to be consistent with other findings in reading research, several points should be kept in mind in evaluating the Holmes model. First, another set of tests might easily produce quite different results. This would be true even if the tests carried the same name. Would another speed-of-reading test permit us to duplicate his results? Probably not. Second, Sparks and Mitzel have seriously challenged the statistical assumptions on which the Holmes analysis is based.[14] Until their challenge is met by Holmes or his students, the result of his detailed analysis should be accepted very tentatively. Third, the Holmes analysis does not permit statements of cause-and-effect relationships. Holmes demonstrates only that certain measurements vary together, nothing more. Fourth, the Holmes theory is a model or theory only in limited degree, since it fulfils only some of the functions of a model, as Sparks and Mitzel point out. The Holmes theory does not, for example, generate testable hypotheses.

Smith and Carrigan have also offered a model for the reading act based on neurological considerations.[15] Successful reading, to them, is based upon efficient synaptic transmission. Children with difficulty in reading are said to have faulty synaptic transmission

---

14. Jack A. Sparks and Harold E. Mitzel, "A Reaction to Holmes's 'Basic Assumptions Underlying the Substrata-Factor Theory,'" *Reading Research Quarterly*, I (Spring, 1966), 137-45.

15. Donald E. P. Smith and Patricia M. Carrigan, *The Nature of Reading Disability* (New York: Harcourt, Brace & Co., 1959).

due to imbalance of acetylcholine (ACh) and cholinesterase (ChE). The major report of these investigators is so marred by flaws in their tables, by omission of subjects at strategic points, and by far-reaching generalizations that the study, while intriguing, cannot be considered helpful in establishing their model of synaptic transmission.

Strang provides a model in which she carefully distinguishes among the three areas of confusion as identified by Robinson.[16] In addition, Strang adds another area—prerequisites. Her listing becomes: (*a*) products (the skills and abilities used in reading); (*b*) prerequisites (the traits and experiences necessary for successful reading); (*c*) the reading process (the chemistry, physiology, and psychology of the reading process); (*d*) procedures (the techniques and conditions of instruction). While Strang gives only a partial analysis of each of these four aspects of a reading model, her four-part division is helpful in organizing our thinking about reading. Her description of the model includes several interesting insights into reading which were derived from informal interviews.

COMPREHENSION MODELS

Guilford's famous model of the structure of the intellect, reproduced in Figure 1, has important applications to the teaching of reading.[17] As Guilford points out, the reading teacher has a wealth of opportunity to stimulate thinking. If the teacher has no idea of what constitutes the products, contents, or operations of intellect, he can do only a partial job of fulfilling his obligations.[18] While not all of the cells within Guilford's model have relevance for reading comprehension, Spache has demonstrated how the model can be applied (see Fig. 2).[19]

---

16. Ruth Strang, "The Reading Process and Its Ramifications," in *Invitational Addresses, 1965* (Newark, Del.: International Reading Association, 1965), 49-74.

17. Joy P. Guilford, "Three Faces of Intellect," *American Psychologist*, XIV (August, 1959), 469-79.

18. Joy P. Guilford, "Frontiers in Thinking That Teachers Should Know About," *Reading Teacher*, XIII (February, 1960), 176-82.

19. George D. Spache, *Toward Better Reading* (Champaign, Ill.: Garrard Publishing Co., 1963), p. 67.

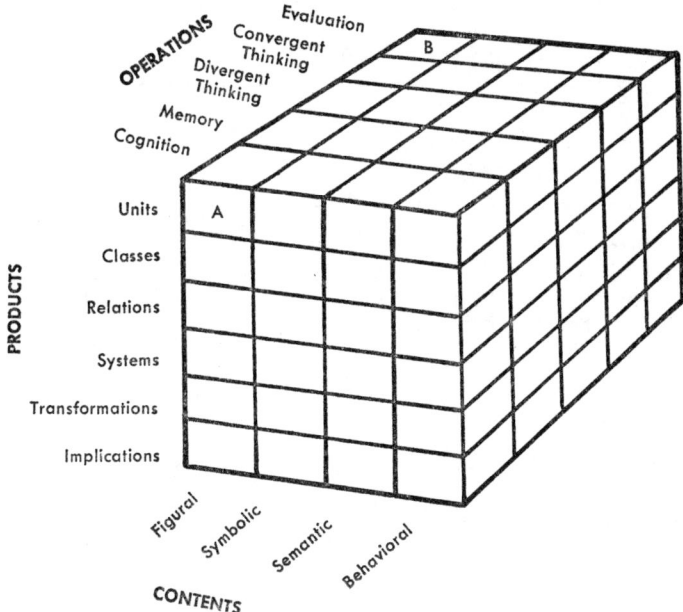

FIG. 1.—"Three Faces of Intellect"

His chart shows reading behavior in "semantic content" for all of Guilford's "products" (across the top of the chart) and for all of Guilford's "operations" (left-hand margin). Spache cautions the reader that there is not necessarily a hierarchy from cognition to evaluation. Individual differences in the background of the reader as well as the concreteness of the material are pointed out as influencing the order of difficulty of the operations.

McCullough takes a different approach to much the same problem. Her "Schema of Thought Patterns" has some factors in common with Guilford's analysis.[20] Again, no hierarchy of difficulty is intended by the ordering of items and no order of events is implied by placement in the last three rows. Indeed, McCullough's point is that thought patterns are or should be flexible and fluid. A part-whole relationship might contribute to the development of a generalization, which might in turn extend a definition or focus attention on a sequential relationship. Real comprehension, accord-

20. See chap. ix of this yearbook.

	UNIT	CLASS	RELATIONS	SYSTEMS	TRANSFORMATIONS	IMPLICATIONS
Cognition (recognition of information)	Recognition that word has meaning	Recognition of sentence as complete thought	Recognition of paragraph meaning (literal idea of paragraph)	Recognition of types of relationships within structure of paragraph	Underline key words of paragraph	Recognize that there are implications in author's main idea
Memory (retention of information)	Recall specific word meanings	Recall of thoughts of sentence (reverberations)	Comprehend main idea as summation of sentences (reverberation)	Summarize facts of paragraph in own words with due attention to structure	Combine recall with own associations	Choose possible implications from given alternates
Divergent Production (logical, creative ideas)	Meaning from context by inference	Selecting implied meaning of sentence	Choosing implied main idea	Analyze author's reasons for structure	Construct rebus of paragraph; offer new titles for paragraph	Amplify author's implications and ideas in free association
Convergent Production (conclusions, inductive thinking)	Meaning from structure of context, (i.e. appositive sentence)	Combining ideas into literal meaning of sentence	Evolving main idea as extension of topic sentence	Categorize structure of paragraph; outline it	Choose among alternate titles or statements of main idea	Suggest future applications of author's ideas
Evaluation (critical thinking)	Acceptance or rejection of author's diction	Acceptance or rejection of meaning of sentence, as fact-opinion	Acceptance or rejection of main idea as fact or opinion; check author's sources; compare with own experiences and beliefs	Look for fallacies in logic, appeals to reader's emotions, overgeneralizations, omissions, distortions	Identify author's viewpoint and purpose; compare with other viewpoints; explore the ultimate outcomes of acceptance of author's viewpoint	Check author's background as basis for viewpoint; react to author's value judgments; examine author's basic assumptions and inferences from these

FIG. 2.—Reading behaviors in semantic content (meanings, ideas)

ing to McCullough, can occur only when the reader understands the ideas and thought patterns of the authors.

Extending some work of Deighton,[21] McCullough demonstrated the reader's need to maintain a "mental flexibility" as he reads.[22] Using a complicated sentence, McCullough shows how the reader must constantly sift meanings and search for understandings as one word after another is taken into consideration. Her analysis brings us very close to observing the thought patterns of a reader.

Several other models of reading comprehension are available in the literature. Kingston presents a model, which he describes as tentative, in which he includes level of abstraction, experiences, developmental level, and linguistic symbols as variables.[23] He provides a set of postulates which flow from his model and which can be subjected to objective tests. Cleland has also offered a comprehension model in which he has specified some of the major processes which constitute reading.[24]

Barrett, in an unpublished paper, identifies two misconceptions which teachers face in instruction in comprehension.[25] These misconceptions are: (*a*) considering comprehension a single unitary skill and (*b*) assuming that comprehension contains so many separate skills as to be unmanageable. To provide both a manageable and understandable means of teaching comprehension, Barrett has developed the "Taxonomy of the Cognitive and Affective Dimensions of Reading Comprehension" that is presented later in

---

21. Lee C. Deighton, "The Flow of Thought through an English Sentence," in *Vistas in Reading*, ed. J. Allen Figurel (Proceedings of the Eleventh Annual Convention, Vol. XXI, Part 1 [Newark, Del.: International Reading Association, 1967]), pp. 322-26.

22. Constance M. McCullough, "Linguistics, Psychology and the Teaching of Reading," *Elementary English*, XLIV (April, 1967), 353-62.

23. Albert J. Kingston, "A Conceptual Model of Reading Comprehension," in *Phases of College and Other Adult Reading Programs*, ed. Emery P. Bliesmer and Albert J. Kingston (Milwaukee: National Reading Conference, 1961), pp. 100-107.

24. Donald L. Cleland, "A Construct of Comprehension," in *Reading and Inquiry*, ed. J. Allen Figurel (Conference Proceedings, Vol X [Newark, Del.: International Reading Association, 1965]), pp. 59-64.

25. The discussion and material which follow are drawn from Thomas C. Barrett's unpublished paper, "Taxonomy of Cognitive and Affective Dimensions of Reading Comprehension" and are used by permission.

this chapter. In developing the taxonomy, Barrett drew heavily from the work of Bloom,[26] Sanders,[27] Letton,[28] and Guszak.[29] Reading comprehension, as treated in the taxonomy, is divided into five major skill categories or levels: (a) literal comprehension; (b) reorganization; (c) inferential comprehension; (d) evaluation, and (e) appreciation. Within each of these categories Barrett provides examples of specific types of tasks, in the form of purposes for reading, which the teacher might utilize. The five major categories have been ordered to move from the easy to the difficult in terms of the requirements each category appears to demand. To a certain extent, the same thing has been attempted with the tasks in each of the major categories. Of course, some literal comprehension tasks may be more demanding than some inferential or evaluative tasks. The same observation applies to tasks within categories.

There are several useful applications that such a system of categorization may have for teachers. First, teachers may use the taxonomy as a basis for developing purposes and questions for guiding children's reading. Second, teachers may apply the taxonomy to questions presented in basal manuals to determine what types of comprehension are emphasized in the selections.

In both of these cases, as Barrett indicates, teachers must be familiar with the reading selections upon which the purposes or questions are based. This is so because some questions may appear to require a higher level of thought than they actually do. Questions which on the surface may seem to fall in the inferential or evaluative categories may belong in the literal category if the author has stated the answers in the selection. Further, knowledge of the selection will help the teacher in judging the relative difficulty of questions falling within the same category.

26. Benjamin S. Bloom et al., *Taxonomy of Educational Objectives*, Handbook I, *Cognitive Domain* (New York: Longmans, Green & Co., 1956).

27. Norris M. Sanders, *Classroom Questions* (New York: Harper & Row, 1966).

28. Mildred C. Letton, "Evaluating the Effectiveness of Teaching Reading," in *Evaluation of Reading*, ed. Helen M. Robinson ("Supplementary Educational Monographs," No. 88 [Chicago: University of Chicago Press, 1958]), pp. 76-82.

29. James Guszak, "Reading Comprehension Solicitation Response Inventory" (unpublished paper, University of Wisconsin, 1965).

Several observations may be made about the Barrett taxonomy. As is true with all taxonomies, the orderly presentation of the categories may suggest a greater precision than the classification system really possesses. Also, the system of categories fails to take into account the overlap which may exist in certain types of questions. Most important of all, perhaps, the taxonomy cannot take into account the background which the reader brings to the comprehension tasks. Background must in many cases be a deciding factor in the type or level of comprehension required by the question. The type of comprehension demanded and the difficulty of the task is a product of (*a*) the selection, (*b*) the questions, and (*c*) the reader's background. The taxonomy in its usual application can take only the first two into account. Barrett's presentation of his taxonomy follows:

THE BARRETT TAXONOMY
COGNITIVE AND AFFECTIVE DIMENSIONS
OF
READING COMPREHENSION

1.0 *Literal Comprehension.* Literal comprehension focuses on ideas and information which are *explicitly* stated in the selection. Purposes for reading and teacher's questions designed to elicit responses at this level may range from simple to complex. A simple task in literal comprehension may be the recognition or recall of a single fact or incident. A more complex task might be the recognition or recall of a series of facts or the sequencing of incidents in a reading selection. Purposes and questions at this level may have the following characteristics.

1.1 *Recognition* requires the student to locate or identify ideas or information *explicitly* stated in the reading selection itself or in exercises which use the explicit ideas and information presented in the reading selection. Recognition tasks are:

1.11 *Recognition of Details.* The student is required to locate or identify facts such as the names of characters, the time of the story, or the place of the story.

1.12 *Recognition of Main Ideas.* The student is asked to locate or identify an explicit statement in or from a selection which is a main idea of a paragraph or a larger portion of the selection.

1.13 *Recognition of a Sequence.* The student is required to locate or identify the order of incidents or actions explicitly stated in the selection.

1.14 *Recognition of Comparison.* The student is requested to locate or identify likenesses and differences in characters, times, and places that are explicitly stated in the selection.

1.15 *Recognition of Cause and Effect Relationships.* The student in this instance may be required to locate or identify the explicitly stated reasons for certain happenings or actions in the selection.

1.16 *Recognition of Character Traits.* The student is required to identify or locate explicit statements about a character which helps to point up the type of person he is.

1.2 *Recall* requires the student to produce from memory ideas and information *explicitly* stated in the reading selection. Recall tasks are:

1.21 *Recall of Details.* The student is asked to produce from memory facts such as the names of characters, the time of the story, or the place of the story.

1.22 *Recall of Main Ideas.* The student is required to state a main idea of a paragraph or a larger portion of the selection from memory, when the main idea is explicitly stated in the selection.

1.23 *Recall of a Sequence.* The student is asked to provide from memory the order of incidents or actions explicitly stated in the selection.

1.24 *Recall of Comparisons.* The student is required to call up from memory the likenesses and differences in characters, times, and places that are explicitly stated in the selection.

1.25 *Recall of Cause and Effect Relationships.* The student is requested to produce from memory explicitly stated reasons for certain happenings or actions in the selection.

1.26 *Recall of Character Traits.* The student is asked to call up from memory explicit statements about characters which illustrate the type of persons they are.

2.0 *Reorganization.* Reorganization requires the student to analyze, synthesize, and/or organize ideas or information explicitly stated in the selection. To produce the desired thought product, the reader may utilize the statements of the author verbatim or he may paraphrase or translate the author's statements. Reorganization tasks are:

2.1 *Classifying.* In this instance the student is required to place people, things, places, and/or events into categories.

2.2 *Outlining.* The student is requested to organize the selection into outline form using direct statements or paraphrased statements from the selection.

2.3 *Summarizing.* The student is asked to condense the selection using direct or paraphrased statements from the selection.

2.4 *Synthesizing.* In this instance, the student is requested to consolidate explicit ideas or information from more than one source.

3.0 *Inferential Comprehension.* Inferential comprehension is demonstrated by the student when he uses the ideas and information explicitly stated in the selection, his intuition, and his personal experience as a basis for conjectures and hypotheses. Inferences drawn by the student may be either convergent or divergent in nature and the student may or may not be asked to verbalize the rationale underlying his inferences. In general, then, inferential comprehension is stimulated by purposes for reading and teachers' questions which demand thinking and imagination that go beyond the printed page.

3.1 *Inferring Supporting Details.* In this instance, the student is asked to conjecture about additional facts the author might have included in the selection which would have made it more informative, interesting, or appealing.

3.2 *Inferring Main Ideas.* The student is required to provide the main idea, general significance, theme, or moral which is not explicitly stated in the selection.

3.3 *Inferring Sequence.* The student, in this case, may be requested to conjecture as to what action or incident might have taken place between two explicitly stated actions or incidents, or he may be asked to hypothesize about what would happen next if the selection had not ended as it did but had been extended.

3.4 *Inferring Comparisons.* The student is required to infer likenesses and differences in characters, times, or places. Such inferential comparisons revolve around ideas such as: "here and there," "then and now," "he and he," "he and she," and "she and she."

3.5 *Inferring Cause and Effect Relationships.* The student is required to hypothesize about the motivations of characters and their interactions with time and place. He may also be required to conjecture as to what caused the author to include certain ideas, words, characterizations, and actions in his writing.

3.6 *Inferring Character Traits.* In this case, the student is asked to hypothesize about the nature of characters on the basis of explicit clues presented in the selection.

3.7 *Predicting Outcomes.* The student is requested to read an initial portion of the selections and on the basis of this reading he is required to conjecture about the outcome of the selection.

3.8 *Interpreting Figurative Language.* The student, in this instance, is asked to infer literal meanings from the author's figurative use of language.

4.0 *Evaluation.* Purposes for reading and teacher's questions, in this instance, require responses by the student which indicate that he has made an evaluative judgment by comparing ideas presented in the selection with external criteria provided by the teacher, other authorities, or other written sources, or with internal criteria provided by the reader's experiences, knowledge, or values. In essence evaluation deals with judgment and focuses on qualities of accuracy, acceptability, desirability, worth, or probability of occurrence. Evaluative thinking may be demonstrated by asking the student to make the following judgments.

4.1 *Judgments of Reality or Fantasy.* Could this really happen? Such a question calls for a judgment by the reader based on his experience.

4.2 *Judgments of Fact or Opinion.* Does the author provide adequate support for his conclusions. Is the author attempting to sway your thinking? Questions of this type require the student to analyze and evaluate the writing on the basis of the knowledge he has on the subject as well as to analyze and evaluate the intent of the author.

4.3 *Judgments of Adequacy and Validity.* Is the information presented here in keeping with what you have read on the subject in other sources? Questions of this nature call for the reader to compare written sources of information, with an eye toward agreement and disagreement or completeness and incompleteness.

4.4 *Judgments of Appropriateness.* What part of the story best describes the main character? Such a question requires the reader to make a judgment about the relative adequacy of different parts of the selection to answer the question.

4.5 *Judgments of Worth, Desirability and Acceptability.* Was the character right or wrong in what he did? Was his behavior good or bad? Questions of this nature call for judgments based on the reader's moral code or his value system.

5.0 *Appreciation.* Appreciation involves all the previously cited cognitive dimensions of reading, for it deals with the psychological and aesthetic impact of the selection on the reader. Appreciation calls for the student to be emotionally and aesthetically sensitive to the work and to have a reaction to the worth of its psychological and artistic elements. Appreciation includes both the knowledge of and the emotional response to literary techniques, forms, styles, and structures.

5.1 *Emotional Response to the Content.* The student is required to verbalize his feelings about the selection in terms of interest, excitement, boredom, fear, hate, amusement, etc. It is concerned with the emotional impact of the total work on the reader.

5.2 *Identification with Characters or Incidents.* Teachers' questions of this nature will elicit responses from the reader which demonstrate his sensitivity to, sympathy for, and empathy with characters and happenings portrayed by the author.

5.3 *Reactions to the Author's Use of Language.* In this instance the student is required to respond to the author's craftsmanship in terms of the semantic dimensions of the selection, namely, connotations and denotations of words.

5.4 *Imagery.* In this instance, the reader is required to verbalize his feelings with regard to the author's artistic ability to paint word pictures which cause the reader to visualize, smell, taste, hear, or feel.

A Comprehensive Skills Model: Gray and Robinson

Few comprehensive models of reading have appeared in the literature. The most detailed model was presented by Gray[30] and has been updated and amplified by Robinson.[31] In the material which follows, the model presented by Gray and Robinson is summarized and evaluated.

The Gray-Robinson model is essentially a skills model. While Gray gives some attention to the process of reading, his model is primarily a catalog of skills required for the various aspects of reading. He gives some (rather incomplete) attention to the process of reading. Gray stated that an analysis of the evidence available showed that the understandings, skills, and attitudes common to most reading activities can be classified under four headings. These headings are:

1. Word perception, including pronunciation and meaning
2. Comprehension, which includes a "clear grasp of what is read"
3. Reaction to and evaluation of ideas the author presents
4. Assimilation of what is read, through fusion of old ideas and information obtained through reading

While each of these aspects is discussed separately, Gray makes it abundantly clear that these aspects operate simultaneously and that reading must be considered a "unitary act."

The four major aspects of reading were illustrated and their

---

30. William S. Gray, "The Major Aspects of Reading," in *Sequential Development of Reading Abilities,* ed. Helen M. Robinson ("Supplementary Educational Monographs," No. 90 [Chicago: University of Chicago Press, 1960]), pp. 8-24.

31. Robinson, *op. cit.,* pp. 22-32.

relationships revealed by Gray's diagram (Fig. 3). Word perception is at the center of the diagram, for, without the skills for this aspect of reading, communication cannot take place. The first concentric band represents "comprehension." Gray's definition of comprehension includes three levels or types of understandings. The first of these is "literal" comprehension, which involves a "clear grasp of what is read." The second level is determining implied

FIG. 3.—Major components of reading (Gray)

meanings. The third level focuses on the implications and significance of the author's ideas beyond those things actually stated. In popular terms, these three levels are described by Gray as "ability to read the lines, to read between the lines, and to read beyond the lines."[32]

32. His quoted words are a paraphrase of an earlier statement by Edgar Dale in "The Art of Reading," *News Letter* (Ohio State University), XI (February, 1946), 1.

FIG. 4.—Five major aspects of reading (Helen M. Robinson's revision of William S. Gray's model)

The second concentric band, identified as "reaction," seems to be what many authors have called "critical reading." This aspect of reading, according to Gray, involves an inquiring attitude, standards or criteria of judgment, reaching conclusions, and emotional responses to content. How some of the skills involved in reaction differ from the third level of comprehension is not made clear by Gray.

Assimilation or fusion of ideas, represented by the outer band, comes about, according to Gray, through the exercise of critical judgment, of creative thinking, and of combining information secured from reading with one's previous experiences. Again Gray does not clearly demonstrate how the skills involved in this aspect of reading are differentiated from the skills involved in his other aspects—reaction, for example. The differences appear to be of degree rather than of kind.

Gray provided four elaborate diagrams, each explaining to some extent one of the four aspects of reading. In addition, he attempted to describe how these four major aspects operated in a diagram entitled "Composite View of the Reading Act." Gray attempted also to show how each of the four aspects of reading is involved in reading in the content field and in reading for different purposes. These diagrams are not reproduced here, for Gray did not provide a complete explanation of his visual representations. In addition, his paper represented a first version of a model which undoubtedly he would have revised and extended.

Robinson, in a thoughtful analysis of Gray's model, drew upon the research literature in an attempt to validate the major aspects of reading.[33] Included in Robinson's discussion are evaluations of "substrata-factor theory" research, several theoretical models of reading, and a number of relevant experimental analyses of the reading act. Robinson carefully indicated that her concern was with the skills dimension of reading, not with the process of reading or the techniques of reading instruction.

Robinson's diagram of the major aspects of reading is presented as Figure 4. She retained the four major aspects as given by Gray—word perception, comprehension, reaction, and fusion. The design

---

33. Robinson, *op. cit.*, pp. 22-28.

of her diagram differs, however. Two reasons are presented for this change: accommodation of a fifth aspect, rates of reading, and demonstration of the limitless opportunities for growth in the four aspects.

In her descriptions of the aspects of reading, Robinson sharpens the definitions of each of the first three aspects. She sees word perception as composed of word-recognition skills and word meanings. Comprehension, the second aspect, is divided into literal and implied meanings. Intellectual judgments and emotional responses are given as the two divisions of reaction. Unfortunately, Robinson does not supply a new description of assimilation, which might have more clearly differentiated this aspect from reaction and from comprehension.

Speed or rate is an important aspect of Robinson's revised model. She notes that rate of reading must be flexible and adjusted to the reader's purpose and the nature of the material. She illustrates the use of various rates in meeting different demands and conditions and thereby shows the close relationship of rate to the other major aspects of reading.

The Gray-Robinson model is a useful tool for examining some of our current concepts concerning reading. The comments below summarize some of the major observations which can be made about the model:

1. The emphasizing of the need to clearly differentiate *skills, processes,* and *instructional procedures* is a major contribution of the model. While these three factors are related and interdependent, a distinction among these factors is essential for thoughtful and productive analysis of reading.
2. Robinson has properly centered her attention on the skills as the area most likely at present to produce fruitful results.
3. A careful analysis of process is vital to further understanding of reading, but, at present, the analysis might better be made on a part of the process, such as word perception or one type of comprehension, rather than on the total process of reading. Gray's attempts to depict the total process with all its interrelationships resulted in such elaborate systems of representation that his work is perhaps most useful for stimulating further analysis of certain parts of the process. There is no question, however, of the major value of Gray's first efforts to catalogue the reading process and its function.
4. Robinson's refinement of the model has clarified word perception

and comprehension; but, to this writer, further delineation and description of the skills in assimilation and reaction are important future developments which probably must await additional evidence from basic and applied research.
5. The model, especially as refined by Robinson, clearly recognizes the interrelationships among the major aspects of reading, while at the same time it attempts to determine the specific details of the four aspects: word perception, comprehension, assimilation, and reaction. Reading can be viewed as a totally unified or global trait which denies analysis. Reading can also be defined as a long list of independent skills. The model as revised by Robinson steers a reasonable middle course between these two points of view.
6. The model will be a useful tool for stimulating further discussion, writing, and research.

A Concluding Statement

The range of definitions and descriptions of reading is great, as this chapter has attempted to demonstrate. To some authors, reading is responding orally to printed symbols. At the other end of the continuum, reading is viewed as resulting in a changed view of life which produces corresponding changes in behavior. While most thoughtful persons would assign this latter outcome to the goals of education, not all would consider it a responsibility of the reading program.

The principle which is sometimes applied, especially by some of the linguists, is that, unless the outcome is unique to reading and cannot take place in other types of communication, the outcome is not properly assigned to reading. Application of this principle places only word-perception skills within the special province of reading outcomes.

Most educators with special interest in reading assign relatively broad goals or outcomes to reading instruction. The implied principle seems to be that, if reading instruction can make an important contribution to an outcome, even if it is not necessarily a unique contribution, the outcome is a legitimate objective of the reading program. This view places a broad range of outcomes within the province of the reading program.

What are the outcomes or goals which are customarily assigned to reading, and how much agreement on these goals does the literature reveal? The answer to this question is not easily obtained. While the following statements may be oversimplified, it seems that four relatively separate but major outcomes or goals of the reading program can be listed. The reader will recognize some parallel between these four outcomes and the four aspects of the Gray-Robinson model. The four outcomes might be listed as (*a*) decoding, which corresponds to the Gray-Robinson aspect labeled "word perception"; (*b*) grasping the author's meaning, which corresponds to Barrett's "literal interpretation"; (*c*) testing and recombining the author's message with the understanding and background of the reader; (*d*) application of ideas and values to decisions and actions and extension of author's ideas to new settings. The third outcome involves not only the higher-level comprehension skills of Barrett but also certain aspects of reaction as defined by Robinson. The fourth outcome carries us to courses of action determined, in part, on the basis of information, goals, and attitudes obtained through reading. This fourth outcome includes assimilation, as defined by Robinson. Applications and extension encompass the actions of the highest level of maturity in reading, as defined by Gray and Rogers.[34]

These outcomes differ greatly in their complexity, with decoding the least complex and application and extension the most complex. The characteristic of complexity seems to bear a direct relationship to the agreement in the literature that the outcome is a legitimate concern of the reading program. (These relationships are illustrated in Figure 5). The less complex the outcome, the more general agreement in the literature on its inclusion as an objective for reading. The broad goals are often excluded from the reading program by some specialists, such as linguists, psychologists, and others.

This chapter has attempted to explore and to evaluate critically many of the current concepts of reading. In some ways the exploration and evaluation are unsatisfying, because so much remains to be learned about what reading is and how the process functions. Much of what we need to know must await further developments in basic and applied research.

---

34. William S. Gray and Bernice Rogers, *Maturity in Reading: Its Nature and Appraisal* (Chicago: University of Chicago Press, 1956).

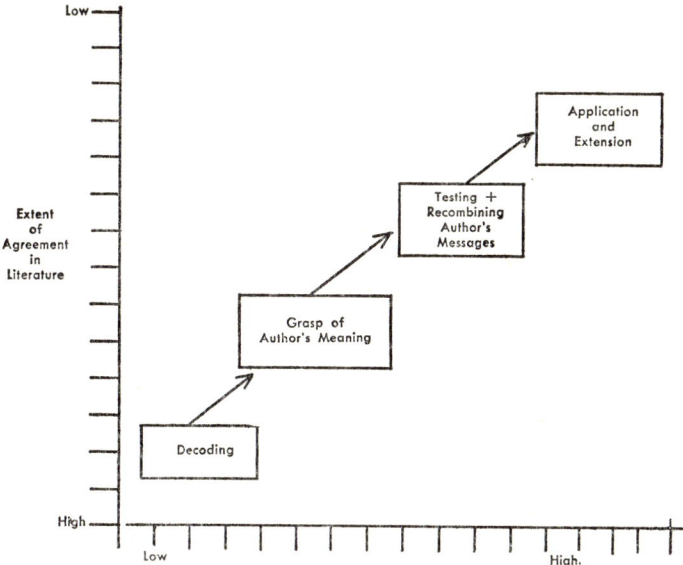

Fig 5.—The relationship between complexity of reading outcomes and extent of agreement in the literature.

The lack of definite information on all factors should not obscure one fact of enormous importance to teachers and educators: our definition of reading and the outcomes we hold for the reading program have immediate and important implications for how we teach reading and what we teach in it. There is no question more important to ask than: "What is reading?" Because of its implications for the instructional program, this question deserves and must have thoughtful attention.

CHAPTER II

When Should Children Begin To Read?

DOLORES DURKIN

Introduction

To study the question that is the title of this chapter is to experience the frustration of dealing with the complex. But with this question there is still another source of frustration: the current popularity of simple answers. To be sure, these simple answers are not identical. In fact, they are in some instances radically different in what they propose. A few illustrations will bear this out.

When visits to schools are used to identify current answers about "when to begin," it is possible to find first-grade classrooms preserving the belief that six-year-olds are not ready to read until they have had a reading readiness program, generally of a fixed duration with fairly fixed content for all. Yet, the message to be found in the practice of other schools is that kindergarten children *are* ready to read and the way to teach them is through whole-class use of workbooks and drill.

When literature on the teaching of reading is used to identify current answers about "when to begin," diversity and oversimplification again are characteristic. For example, some writers in the 1960's still support the idea that a mental age of 6.5 years is a prerequisite for success in reading.[1] Other writers, to the contrary, urge us to believe that children are ready to read as soon as they have an oral command of the language or even that children as young as ten months are ready, provided their mothers are "very clever" in how they teach reading.[2]

---

1. Helen Heffernan, "Significance of Kindergarten Education," *Childhood Education*, XXXVI (March, 1960), 313-19.
2. Glenn Doman, G. N. Stevens, and R. C. Orem, "You Can Teach Your Baby To Read," *Ladies' Home Journal*, LXXX (May, 1963), 62 ff.; Charles C. Fries, *Linguistics and Reading* (New York: Holt, Rinehart & Winston, 1962).

On the assumption that "readiness" is more complex than some would have us believe, this chapter will consider the question of "when to begin" by focusing separately on two questions. The first asks: "When should reading instruction start?" Here the focus will be on the school and the groups of children for which it has a responsibility to teach reading. The second question—"When should a child begin to read?"—will deal more specifically with the individual child, his preschool years, and the role of the family in teaching reading.

Since the artificiality of separating these questions is recognized, the concluding part of the chapter will deal with the two concerns in combination.

When Should Reading Instruction Start?

A HISTORICAL PERSPECTIVE

In American schools a close association has existed between first grade and the beginning of reading instruction.[3] Because the chronological age of six has been the common criterion for admission into first grade, it is natural that a parallel development was the expectation that "being six" and "starting to read" occur simultaneously.

Using the beginning of this century as the starting point, a study of the professional literature concerned with reading quickly identifies some well-known scholars who voiced early objection to the idea that entrance into first grade should mean the start of reading instruction. Dewey is among them, and so is Huey, probably best known for his 1908 text, *The Psychology and Pedagogy of Reading*.[4] In this text the author quotes Dewey as recommending the age of eight as an appropriate time to begin instruction in reading. But he also emphasizes that Dewey was objecting as much to the mechanical and passive way in which the schools taught reading as he was to the time when they initiated their instruction. Huey's own objections were also directed as much to the nature of school

---

3. Nila B. Smith, *American Reading Instruction* (New York: Silver Burdett Co., 1934); "What Have We Accomplished in Reading?" *Elementary English*, XXXVIII (March, 1961), 144-45.

4. Edmund B. Huey, *The Psychology and Pedagogy of Reading* (New York: Macmillan Co., 1908).

instruction as to the time when it began. He especially complained about the "unnatural" ways in which the schools were introducing children to reading.

While these well-known educators did speak out against the practice of initiating school instruction in reading when the child was six and starting first grade, it still must be concluded from a study of the literature that the two decades following 1900 were relatively quiet about "when to begin." However, the start of the 1920's and the decades that followed stand out in contrast, as books and journals became heavy with questions and answers about the best time to begin school instruction in reading. Why the change?

One important though indirect cause was the new interest in the "scientific" measurement of a child's behavior, including his achievements in school.[5] Among the results of what became almost a "craze to measure" was the appearance of school surveys. Of special relevance to this chapter is a finding common to many of the survey reports: Large numbers of children were failing first grade, the most frequent cause being insufficient achievement in reading.[6]

Within a short time, concern about this finding became as widespread as the finding itself, and for at least two reasons. Successful teaching of reading, then as now, was considered uniquely important among elementary-school responsibilities. In addition, the failures that were occurring resulted in first-grade classrooms being populated by many "over-age" children. Behavior problems blossomed, and so did the concern about why so many first-graders were having difficulty learning to read.

Logically, it would seem, a study of reading problems—at any grade level and in any period of time—would look to such multiple and common-sense causes as inadequate teacher preparation, poor instruction, inappropriate instructional materials, overly crowded classrooms, low IQ's among the children, or, perhaps, a lack of

---

5. Robert L. Thorndike and Elizabeth Hagen, *Measurement and Evaluation in Psychology and Education* (New York: John Wiley & Sons, 1961).

6. Virgil E. Dickson, *Mental Tests and the Classroom Teacher* (New York: World Book Co., 1923); Margaret C. Holmes, "Investigation of Reading Readiness of First-Grade Entrants," *Childhood Education*, III (January, 1927), 215-21; Mary M. Reed, *An Investigation of Practices in First Grade Admission and Promotion* (New York: Bureau of Publications, Teachers College, Columbia University, 1927).

motivation on their part. However, in the study of beginning reading problems that was made in the 1920's and 1930's, the factor given singular attention is to be found in a pronouncement appearing with great frequency in the professional literature of that period: First-graders had difficulty learning to read because they were not ready when the instruction began.[7] Why reading difficulties were attributed so exclusively to a lack of readiness and, in addition, why postponing instruction was proposed as a solution to the problem can be understood only when the broader psychological and educational setting of the 1920's and 1930's is brought into focus.

One quick yet accurate way of characterizing the prevailing psychological beliefs of the period is to describe the publications of Gesell and his students and especially to highlight the underlying assumptions of their work at the Gesell Institute. Whether the publication was, for instance, *The Mental Growth of the Preschool Child*, appearing in 1925, or *Infancy and Human Growth*, published in 1928, Gesell's emphasis was on a description of the maturation process interpreted in terms of developmental stages.[8] What is especially important to point out in this chapter is that Gesell's description and also his explanation of progressive growth stages referred not to such influential factors as learning and practice but, instead, to sources like "neural ripening" and "intrinsic growth."

Such a concept of development, the literature shows, found support in the earlier writings of Thorndike, in which readiness for learning was discussed with reference to brain physiology and the behavior of neurones.[9] Gesell's position also found support in empirical studies of animals in which, typically, the animal was quite low on the phylogenetic scale. Probably the best known of these studies were those done by Coghill in the 1920's on the development of

---

7. Dickson, *op. cit.*; Holmes, *op. cit.*

8. Arnold Gesell, *The Mental Growth of the Pre-School Child* (New York: Macmillan Co., 1925); *Infancy and Human Growth* (New York: Macmillan Co., 1928); *The First Five Years of Life* (New York: Harper & Bros., 1940); Arnold Gesell and Frances L. Ilg, *The Child from Five to Ten* (New York: Harper & Bros., 1946).

9. E. L. Thorndike, *The Psychology of Learning* (New York: Teachers College, Columbia University, 1923).

behavior in amblystoma.[10] Commenting on Coghill's animal studies, Hunt has recently written:

> These [studies] demonstrated that behavioral development, like anatomical development, starts at the head-end and proceeds tailward, starts from the inside and proceeds outward, and consists of progressive differentiation of more specific units from general units. From such evidence Coghill and others inferred the special additional notion that behavior unfolds automatically as the anatomical basis for behavior matures.[11]

An emphasis on automatic and unfolding behavior also appeared in studies of children done in the 1920's and 1930's.[12] Of these, the widely publicized research of McGraw is representative, both in its findings and in the way those findings were interpreted and applied.[13] In her research McGraw studied the effect of practice on the development of selected motor skills during infancy. The subjects in the research were twin boys. Over time, one twin was given opportunities to practice such motor skills as crawling, while the other twin was not. Findings in the study regarding the age at which each twin mastered the various motor skills led McGraw to conclude that practice does not hasten the developmental process. Or, to use the terminology of Gesell and his followers, neural ripening seemed to remain uninfluenced by environmental factors.

Throughout the 1920's and the 1930's, the literature shows, McGraw and other researchers studying motor development in children commonly used their data to counteract the extreme environmental position of Watson and his school of behaviorism.[14] How-

---

10. G. E. Coghill, *Anatomy and the Problem of Behavior* (Cambridge: Cambridge University Press, 1929).

11. J. McVicker Hunt, "The Psychological Basis for Using Preschool Enrichment as an Antidote for Cultural Deprivation," *Merrill-Palmer Quarterly*, X (July, 1964), 209-48 (see p. 213).

12. Arnold Gesell and Helen Thompson, "Learning and Growth in Identical Twin Infants," *Genetic Psychology Monographs*, VI (July, 1929), 1-124; Josephine Rohrs Hilgard, "Learning and Maturation in Pre-School Children," *Journal of Genetic Psychology*, XLI (September, 1932), 36-56.

13. Myrtle B. McGraw, *Growth: A Study of Johnny and Jimmy* (New York: D. Appleton–Century Co., 1935).

14. John B. Watson, *Behaviorism* (New York: W. W. Norton & Co., 1924); *Psychological Care of Infant and Child* (New York: W. W. Norton & Co., 1928).

ever, they also used their data on the development of motor skills to explain the development of intellectual skills.[15] Resulting from this highly questionable merger was the idea—and this was supported by the Progressive Education movement—that time is the remedy for a lack of readiness to learn. Or, to use the words of another writer as he characterizes a basic tenet in the Progressive Education point of view, ". . . the educational environment facilitates development best by providing a maximally permissive field that does not interfere with the predetermined process of spontaneous maturation." [16]

THE READING READINESS CONCEPT

Even with this sketchy description of historical background, it is easy to understand how a concept like "reading readiness," especially when interpreted in terms of a need to postpone reading instruction, fitted very naturally into the Progressive Education setting of the 1920's and 1930's, and into the thinking of influential researchers like Gesell and McGraw. Yet, such a portrayal of the times would be both incomplete and misleading were it to overlook those in the minority who still gave explicit attention to the dependence of readiness on prior learnings and experiences. For instance, in the Twenty-Fourth Yearbook of the National Society for the Study of Education, published in 1925, the recommendation is made that schools develop a "period of preparation" for reading. The yearbook states: "This period includes the pre-school age, the kindergarten, and frequently the early part of the first grade. Its primary purpose is to provide the training and experience which prepare pupils for reading." [17]

How did the educational world respond? To be concluded from

---

15. David P. Ausubel, "Viewpoints from Related Disciplines: Human Growth and Development," *Teachers College Record*, LX (February, 1959), 245-54; J. McVicker Hunt, *Intelligence and Experience* (New York: Ronald Press Co., 1961).

16. David P. Ausubel, "Learning by Discovery: Rationale and Mystique," *Bulletin of the National Association of Secondary-School Principals*, XLV (December, 1961), 18-58.

17. *Report of the National Committee on Reading* (Twenty-fourth Yearbook of the National Society for the Study of Education, Part I [Chicago: Distributed by the University of Chicago Press, 1925]), p. 24.

a study of the whole of the literature of the 1920's is that the N.S.S.E. emphasis on the need for special, early experiences to insure more successful reading was overshadowed by the more popular view emphasizing time as the remedy for problems. Also to be concluded is that the theme of the N.S.S.E. recommendation was superseded by a mental set that was very much engrossed in measuring and testing.

As was pointed out earlier, the decade of the 1920's was a "boom period" in test development. Among the results of the new enthusiasm for "objective" measurement were many group intelligence tests.[18] Evidence of the use of these tests quickly appeared in the literature concerned with the time when school instruction in reading ought to begin. As early as the year 1920, for instance, one writer was emphasizing that the children who were failing first grade had mental ages of less than six years.[19] Subsequently, other authors in the 1920's moved toward proposals that would establish a certain mental-age level as a requirement for starting school instruction in reading.[20] Arthur, for example, writing in 1925, maintained that a mental age of 6.0 to 6.5 years was "necessary for standard first-grade achievement."[21]

The kind of thinking about readiness for reading that is reflected in these various articles of the 1920's seems to have been crystallized in a report about first-grade reading published by Morphett and Washburne in 1931.[22] In this report the writers proposed a mental age of 6.5 years as a prerequisite for success. Although many ques-

18. Thorndike and Hagen, *op. cit.*

19. Virgil E. Dickson, "What First-Grade Children Can Do in School as Related to What Is Shown by Mental Tests," *Journal of Educational Research*, II (June, 1920), 475-80.

20. Grace Arthur, "A Quantitative Study of the Results of Grouping First-Grade Classes According to Mental Age," *Journal of Educational Research*, XII (October, 1925), 173-85; Holmes, *op. cit.*; Theodore A. Zornow and L. A. Pechstein, "An Experiment in the Classification of First-Grade Children through the Use of Mental Tests," *Elementary School Journal*, XXIII (October, 1922), 136-46.

21. Arthur, *op. cit.*, p. 179.

22. Mabel Vogel Morphett and Carleton Washburne, "When Should Children Begin To Read?" *Elementary School Journal*, XXXI (March, 1931), 496-503.

tions should have been raised about the general applicability of the Morphett-Washburne research, their findings, implying the need to postpone and to wait, were a "natural" for the 1930's. Perhaps this, combined with the status of Washburne as a leader in the Progressive Education movement, was what led to such ready support of a mental-age concept of readiness by professional educators. That the support was widespread and amazingly long-lasting is made unequivocally clear in the numerous professional texts on reading that were to appear in the next two decades.

READING READINESS TESTS

A description of early ideas about readiness cannot omit attention to the development of reading readiness tests. Whether they were the product of disenchantment with the power of mental age to predict success in reading or the product of an era that was unusually enthusiastic about developing "scientific" and "objective" measurements, readiness testing appears in the literature in the latter part of the 1920's.[23] Portions of an editorial in the January, 1927, issue of *Childhood Education* portray the era in capsule form:

> In the field of reading it is essential that a joyous attitude of success shall be cultivated from the first. This necessitates a stage of development in which the learner is capable of getting meaning from the crooked marks which symbolize ideas. When does this period come? . . . In which direction shall we look to discover the truth regarding this confused situation? Fortunately the scientific method points the way toward the solution of this as of other baffling problems. The first steps have been taken. First, the problem has been recognized. Second, a name has been coined for the characteristic which is sought, Reading Readiness, a term not only alliterative but meaningful. Third, tests are in process of developing which shall be applicable to any young child. . . . So we may look forward to the day when the measure of readiness will rest in objective tests and parent and teacher will both be governed thereby.[24]

The reading readiness tests that were soon described in the litera-

23. Frances M. Berry, "The Baltimore Reading Readiness Test," *Childhood Education*, III (January, 1927), 222-23; Nila B. Smith, "Matching Ability as a Factor in First Grade Reading," *Journal of Educational Psychology*, XIX (November, 1928), 560-71.

24. Frances Jenkins, "Beginnings in Reading" (editorial), *Childhood Education*, III (January, 1927), 209.

ture and soon widely used in classrooms were followed by many studies attempting to evaluate their effectiveness as predictors of success in reading. One of the best and most comprehensive of the studies was done by Gates and his associates.[25] This particular study, begun in 1934 and published five years later, was designed "to test the value of practically every type of test, rating, examination, or other means of appraisal which has been suggested, or which the authors could think of, as a means of predicting reading progress." One of its conclusions is particularly well worth repeating here: "It should be noted that among the tests of little or no predictive value are many tests and ratings widely recommended in books and articles on reading readiness testing and teaching." [26]

This negative note—and there were many more to come—had some effect on the content of subsequent readiness tests but little effect on the number published. In fact, together with reading readiness workbooks, the tests became a routine part of the beginning materials in basal-reader series.

It should be pointed out here that studies questioning the predictive value of readiness tests were not the only kind to receive scant acclaim in the 1930's. Again, the research of Gates and his students is illustrative. Certain of their studies focused on the relationship between varied methods of instruction and first-grade achievement. Reported at a time when a mental age of 6.5 years generally was accepted as a requirement for success in beginning reading, the findings are especially interesting. One research report, for example, described four different methods of teaching reading and the achievement that resulted.[27] Commenting on the findings, Gates wrote:

Reading is begun by very different materials, methods, and general procedures, some of which a pupil can master at the mental age of five

---

25. A. I. Gates, G. L. Bond, and D. H. Russell, *Methods of Determining Reading Readiness* (New York: Bureau of Publications, Teachers College, Columbia University, 1939).

26. *Ibid.*, p. 54.

27. Arthur I. Gates, "The Necessary Mental Age for Beginning Reading," *Elementary School Journal*, XXXVII (March, 1937), 497-508.

with reasonable ease, others of which would give him difficulty at the mental age of seven.[28]

In another research report, Gates wrote:

> Correlations of mental age with reading achievement at the end of the year were about 0.25. When one studies the range of mental ages from the lowest to the highest in relation to reading achievement, there appears no suggestion of a crucial or critical point above which very few fail and below which a relatively large proportion fail.[29]

The same report concluded: "the optimum time of beginning reading is not entirely dependent upon the nature of the child himself, but it is in a large measure determined by the nature of the reading program." [30]

From these studies, of course, a concept of reading readiness emerged which emphasized the very special importance of the kind of reading instruction that was offered a child rather than the unique significance of mental age or of maturation. It should not be surprising, therefore, that relatively little attention was given to the Gates studies at the time of their publication in the late 1930's. The findings simply did not move with the stream of popular thought. Nor, it seems, were the studies able to redirect the current of the stream; for the reading readiness literature throughout the 1940's and even into the 1950's continued to be concerned with maturation, mental age, postponement of instruction, and assessment by reading readiness tests. During these decades the psychological literature most frequently quoted pertained to the Gesell studies, still very popular and being continued by Gesell's students.[31] Another psychologist popular among educators was Olson, who throughout this period was describing the development of a child

28. *Ibid.*, p. 508.

29. Arthur I. Gates and Guy L. Bond, "Reading Readiness: A Study of Factors Determining Success and Failure in Beginning Reading," *Teachers College Record*, XXXVII (May, 1936), 679-85 (see p. 680).

30. *Ibid.*, p. 684.

31. Louise B. Ames and Frances L. Ilg, "Developmental Trends in Writing Behavior," *Journal of Genetic Psychology*, LXXIX (September, 1951), 29-46; Frances L. Ilg and Louise Bates Ames, "Developmental Trends in Reading Behavior," *Journal of Gentic Psychology*, LXXVI (June, 1950), 291-312.

in terms of "organismic age."[32] Havighurst also became well known as he discussed the growth of an individual in terms of "developmental tasks."[33]

Occasionally, of course, there was a dissenter. One of the most vocal critics in education was McCracken, who, in the early 1950's, began writing protests against the use of the readiness concept to de-emphasize the ineffectiveness of school instruction in reading.[34] Had McCracken's complaints been calm and carefully substantiated, they might have been taken more seriously. As it was, McCracken's articles and his subsequent book, *The Right To Learn,* seem to have been viewed more as the writings of a crank than as a reason for serious re-examination of the school's interpretation and use of the readiness concept.[35] So, as the literature clearly shows, questions and discussions about reading readiness—even in the 1950's—continued to focus on maturation, mental age, and readiness testing. Too often overlooked was the likelihood that changes in instruction affect a child's readiness to begin to read.

A NEW ERA

Professional educators whose careers spanned the latter part of the 1950's witnessed an era of marked educational change. In fact, it is more realistic than dramatic to describe those years as a revolutionary period for which it would be difficult to stipulate whether the amount or rate of change was the more unusual.

While no revolution ever begins suddenly on one certain day, it has become the practice to designate the beginning of this mid-century educational revolution by citing the date when the Russians

---

32. Willard C. Olson, *Child Development* (Boston: D. C. Heath & Co., 1949); Willard C. Olson and Byron O. Hughes, "Concepts of Growth," *Childhood Education,* XXI (October, 1944), 53-63.

33. Robert J. Havighurst, *Human Development and Education* (New York: Longmans, Green, & Co., 1953).

34. Glenn McCracken, "Have We Overemphasized Readiness?" *Elementary English,* XXIX (May, 1952), 271-76; "The New Castle Reading Experiment," *Elementary English,* XXX (January, 1953), 13-21; "The New Castle Reading Experiment," *Elementary School Journal,* LIV (March, 1954), 385-90.

35. Glenn McCracken, *The Right To Learn* (Chicago: Henry Regnery Co., 1959).

launched Sputnik I: October 4, 1957. As would be expected, the successful launching of a satellite by a foreign power produced a variety of repercussions in the United States. Easily heard among the clamor was a criticism that pounced on public school education, increasing the tempo of the already existing debate about the quality of instruction in American schools.[36] Now the debate stressed the inferiority of our educational endeavors compared to those of Soviet Russia.[37]

Resulting from this furor was the creation of an atmosphere characterized by the cry, "Let's teach more in our schools and, too, let's teach it earlier!" Such an atmosphere, as time has demonstrated, fostered rapt attention to some new emphases and concerns. Of particular relevance to this chapter are those that highlighted the learning potential of young children and the unique importance of a child's early years to his future intellectual development.

New emphases in psychology.—One of the first books to receive the friendly blessing of the post-Sputnik era came from a 1959 conference called by the National Academy of Sciences. This book, *The Process of Education*, by Bruner, was a psychologist's account of a ten-day meeting "to discuss how education in science might be improved in our primary and secondary schools."[38] In the account, special attention was given to the importance of the "structure of a discipline" in teaching that discipline to others. More specifically emphasized, however, was that the "fundamental character" of a discipline enables one "to narrow the gap between 'advanced' knowledge and 'elementary' knowledge."[39] This claim was then followed by a chapter on "Readiness for Learning." And introducing the chapter was a statement that was to be quoted with great frequency: "We begin with the hypothesis that any subject can be

---

36. Arthur E. Bestor, *Educational Wastelands, the Retreat from Learning in Our Public Schools* (Urbana: University of Illinois Press, 1953).

37. William Benton, *This Is the Challenge* (New York: Associated College Presses, 1958); see also unsigned editorial, "Crisis in Education," *Life*, XLIX (March 24, 1958), 26-35.

38. Jerome S. Bruner, *The Process of Education* (Cambridge: Harvard University Press, 1960), p. vii.

39. *Ibid.*, p. 26.

taught effectively in some intellectually honest form to any child at any stage of development."[40]

Those who read all of *The Process of Education* found this statement to have a meaning that was not startling. In fact, it was really only urging, but in a new way, that schools take another look at how they organized and presented their instruction in fields such as science and mathematics. However, when the pronouncement was quoted out of context—and it often was—it sometimes fostered what only could be called wishful thinking about the learning potential of young children.[41]

That was the beginning. Later, in 1961, a book by another psychologist became unusually popular. This one, *Intelligence and Experience*, was written by Hunt.[42] Essentially the book was a review and also a reinterpretation of earlier research dealing with the effect of training and practice on learning. One result of the reinterpretation was a renewal of interest in the special importance of environmental factors to a child's development.

The unique importance of the early years was the theme of still another book from which it became fashionable to quote. This one, *Stability and Change in Human Characteristics*, appeared in 1964 and was written by Bloom.[43] Like Hunt's book, it was a detailed re-examination of earlier research—in this instance, of longitudinal studies concerned with the development of certain measurable characteristics including intelligence and achievement. Stressed in the conclusions of this text was the crucial importance of a child's early environment, based on the assumption that the most rapid period for the development of many characteristics, including intelligence, is in the first five years of life.

New social concerns.— It was in the beginning of the 1960's— and so in the midst of this renewed excitement about the special importance of early environmental factors—that another interest

---

40. *Ibid.*, p. 33.

41. Millie Almy, "Wishful Thinking about Children's Thinking," *Teachers College Record*, LXII (February, 1961), 396-406.

42. Hunt, *op. cit.*

43. Benjamin S. Bloom, *Stability and Change in Human Characteristics* (New York: John Wiley & Sons, 1964).

developed, again with amazing speed. In this case it was a new interest in an old problem: Children from the lowest socioeconomic levels start school with disadvantages that preclude adequate achievement. Why this concern became so vocal and widespread at this particular period of time is to be found in factors that were political, social, and economic in nature.[44] But why the concern evolved into plans for prekindergarten schooling for "culturally disadvantaged" children—plans later formalized in "Head Start" programs—was clearly related to the psychological climate of the times.

For instance, it was not by chance or accident that the author of *Intelligence and Experience* (Hunt) was a participant in one of the earliest endeavors indicating concerned interest in the educational problems accompanying poverty. This was a conference on "Pre-School Enrichment of Socially Disadvantaged Children," held in December of 1962, "to explore . . . the possibilities of accelerating the cognitive development of young children, beyond what might be expected from a standard nursery school situation." [45] Later, at another conference in 1963, it was not by accident that references were being made to studies testing the assumption that "early intervention by well-structured programs will significantly reduce the attenuating influence of the socially marginal environment." [46] And still later, in 1966, it was not by accident that the Educational Policies Commission of the National Education Association published a statement supporting earlier schooling not just for the "culturally disadvantaged" but for all children.[47] Portions of the introduction to the Commission's statement serve well in characterizing this "new era" in both psychology and education:

A growing body of research and experience demonstrates that by the

44. Frederick Shaw, "The Changing Curriculum," *Review of Educational Research*, XXXVI (June, 1966), 343-52.

45. Martin Deutsch, "Papers from the Arden House Conference on Preschool Enrichment," *Merrill-Palmer Quarterly*, X (July, 1964), 207-8.

46. Martin Deutsch, "The Disadvantaged Child and the Learning Process," in *Education in Depressed Areas*, ed. A. Harry Passow (New York: Bureau of Publications, Teachers College, Columbia University, 1963).

47. *Universal Opportunity for Early Childhood Education* (Washington: Educational Policies Commission, National Education Association, 1966).

age of six most children have already developed a considerable part of the intellectual ability they will possess as adults. Six is now generally accepted as the normal age of entrance to school. We believe that this practice is obsolete. All children should have the opportunity to go to school at public expense beginning at the age of four.[48]

New thoughts about reading readiness.—It would be unusual, given the circumstances of the 1960's, not to have new questions about the meaning of "reading readiness" and its effect on school practices. Actually, what was soon to become widespread questioning had its beginnings in the latter part of the 1950's. At that time three independent happenings began to get attention—attention that might not have existed at some other period.

One was the revival of Montessori education in the United States. Of particular interest in the 1950's was the Whitby School in Connecticut, which was demonstrating how three- and four-year-olds can learn to read, write, and spell when Montessori materials and curriculum were used.[49] At about the same time, the work of O. K. Moore began to get national attention.[50] In his project children were also learning to read and write at early ages, but with the use of computerized typewriters. At about the same time, too, but in another part of the country, other related research was underway. In this instance it was a longitudinal study of preschool children who learned to read at home.[51]

With the arrival of the 1960's more reports about reading at earlier ages became available. Some were observational accounts of reading in individual kindergartens.[52] One report, however, per-

48. *Ibid.*, p. 1.

49. O. Burke, "Whitby School," *Jubilee*, VI (February, 1959), 21-27.

50. "O.K.'s Children," *Time*, LXXVI (November 7, 1960), 103.

51. Dolores Durkin, "A Study of Children Who Learned To Read Prior to First Grade," *California Journal of Educational Research*, X (May, 1959), 109-13.

52. Edith Appleton, "Beginning with Enthusiasm," *Education*, LXXXVI (February, 1966), 347-49; "Kindergarteners Pace Themselves in Reading," *Elementary School Journal*, LXIV (February, 1964), 248-52; Lucille Mayne, "An Individual Study of the Reading Acceleration of Two Kindergarten Children," *Elementary English*, XL (April, 1963), 406-8; Marjorie Hunt Sutton, "Readiness for Reading at the Kindergarten Level," *Reading Teacher*, XVII (January, 1964), 234-40; Edith K. Van Wie and Donald M. Lammers, "Are We Being Fair to Our Kindergartners?" *Elementary School Journal*, LXII (April, 1962), 348-51.

tained to a study supported by the Denver public school system.[53] In this case reading was introduced in the kindergarten, and, in addition, a parent-education program was developed with a focus on the preschool child and with a theme of "Preparing Your Child for Reading."[54]

In other instances there were parental accounts of children who were reading at the age of two.[55] Also available were articles in nonprofessional magazines in which the authors questioned the suitability of traditional kindergarten programs for the "sophisticated, TV-indoctrinated five-year-old."[56]

During this period of time, too, the U.S. Office of Education convened a conference of educators and psychologists to consider the question of "Teaching Young Children To Read."[57] As it turned out, the conference papers presented widely different opinions both about the time to begin instruction and the way it ought to be carried out. Meanwhile the *Reading Teacher*, a publication of the International Reading Association, was presenting "Preschool and Beginning Reading" as its theme for October, 1964. Included in this issue of the journal were: an interim report of the Denver kindergarten reading project showing positive results;[58] an article about possible implications for the kindergarten of findings from longi-

---

53. Joseph E. Brzeinski, "Beginning Reading in Denver," *Reading Teacher*, XVIII (October, 1964), 16-21.

54. G. M. Hurd and E. L. Rimmel, *Preparing Your Child for Reading* (Denver: Denver Public Schools, 1961).

55. Mayme Cohan, "Two and a Half and Reading," *Elementary English*, XXXVIII (November, 1961), 506-8; William Fowler, "Teaching a Two-Year-Old To Read: An Experiment in Early Childhood Learning," *Genetic Psychology Monographs*, LXVI (November, 1962), 181-284.

56. Rosemary Hillman, "In Defense of the Five-Year-Old," *Saturday Review*, XLVI (November 16, 1963), 77 ff.; M. L. Kelly, "When Are Children 'Ready' To Read?" *Saturday Review*, XLVI (July 20, 1963), 58 ff.; Virginia C. Simmons, "Why Waste Our Five-Year-Olds?" *Harper's Magazine*, CCXX (April, 1960), 71-73.

57. *Teaching Young Children To Read*, ed. Warren G. Cutts (Washington: United States Department of Health Education, and Welfare, Office of Education Bulletin 1964, No. 19).

58. Brzeinski, *op. cit.*

tudinal studies of preschool readers;[59] and an article by an ophthalmologist who stated that children's eyes are efficient enough for reading at twelve months.[60]

Of course, a portrayal of the 1960's must not overlook those who took a stand against the possibility of earlier reading. In 1962, for instance, the Association for Childhood Education International (ACEI) published a collection of articles generally discouraging moves to include reading instruction in the kindergarten.[61] This position was also supported by individual articles in the ACEI journal, *Childhood Education*,[62] and in articles in other journals written by educators closely associated with ACEI.[63] Generally the themes gave continued support to a kindergarten child's need for social and emotional development and voiced objection to "formal" instruction that would "push" five-year-olds.

During the 1960's, too, the "Gesell group" published a text called *School Readiness*.[64] Though carrying a 1964 copyright date, the book showed the typical Gesell point of view on maturation and "developmental expressions of age." Other voices in the 1960's also could be heard giving singular attention to the maturational aspect of readiness. For instance, one speaker at the 1963 meeting of the International Reading Association was still referring to the Morphett-Washburne proposal about a mental age of 6.5 years being a prerequisite for reading and still commenting that "Read-

---

59. Dolores Durkin, "Early Readers—Reflections after Six Years of Research," *Reading Teacher*, XVIII (October, 1964), 3-7.

60. Jules H. Shaw, "Vision and Seeing Skills of Preschool Children," *Reading Teacher*, XVIII (October, 1964), 33-36.

61. *Reading in the Kindergarten?* ed. Margaret Rasmussen (Washington: Association for Childhood Education International, 1962).

62. Heffernan, *op. cit.*; James L. Hymes, Jr., "More Pressure for Early Reading," *Childhood Education*, XL (September, 1963), 34-35; Nila B. Smith, "Early Reading: Viewpoints," *Childhood Education*, XLII (December, 1965), 229-41.

63. James L. Hymes, Jr., "Changes in Preparing Five-Year-Olds for Reading," *Parents Magazine*, XXXVI (September, 1961), 45 ff.; Lucille Lindberg and Mary W. Moffitt, "The Program and the Child," *National Elementary Principal*, XL (September, 1960), 50-125.

64. Frances L. Ilg and Louise Bates Ames, *School Readiness* (New York: Harper & Row, 1964).

ing, like walking and talking, is a developmental task." [65] At the same meeting, however—and this typifies the conflicting beliefs of the 1960's—another speaker was saying that the emphasis of the past on the maturational aspect of readiness had led to the "indoctrination of the teacher that time, not she herself, is in charge of readiness." [66]

THE CURRENT SCENE

A review of the literature that concludes with references to conflicting beliefs about the basic nature of "readiness to read" provides an appropriate introduction to this attempt to portray the current scene. For today, too, diversity prevails as ideas are presented about the optimum time to begin reading instruction.

Let it be emphasized, though, that a review of the literature offers much more than an explanation of the present in terms of developments in the past. In this instance a knowledge of the past could be very valuable in suggesting guidelines for creating a future that deals more adequately with the question of when to start reading instruction.

For example, the 20/20 vision of hindsight clearly outlines the need to avoid extreme positions in the nature-nurture controversy—and the interpretation of readiness *is* one dimension of this classical debate. In the past, as the literature shows, the concept of readiness applied to reading was swept along by individuals and groups who gave their support to the primary importance of nature and, therefore, of maturation to the development of both motor and intellectual skills. Over a period of time, it would seem, this support was fashioned more in the form of an emotional allegiance to a position than of a questioning concern about possible flaws in it. The result was (*a*) a widespread and long-lasting belief that readiness occurs at a given point in time and, therefore, that "it" will "happen" with the passing of time; and (*b*) a tendency to by-pass any research which suggested contrary ideas—for instance, that a child's readi-

---

65. Sue Moskowitz, "When Should Reading Instruction Begin?" in *Reading as an Intellectual Activity*, ed. J. A. Figurel (Conference Proceedings, Vol. VIII, 1963 [New York: International Reading Association, 1963]), p. 220.

66. Agatha Townsend, "Readiness for Beginning Reading," in *Reading as an Intellectual Activity, op. cit.*

ness to read is affected by the quality of instruction offered him.[67]

The literature still shows some remnants of the maturational concept of readiness, but, as a whole, articles and books are now dominated by the opposite conception highlighting the contribution of environmental factors. Or, to put this characterization of the current scene into the framework of the nature-nurture debate, today the spotlight happens to be on nurture and so, quite typically, there is a neglect of nature through underemphasis. Moving the scene more specifically to reading, today the spotlight is on the benefits to be derived from earlier instruction and almost totally away from the possibility that there might be some children for whom later teaching—even later than the age of six—would be more productive in the long run.

Of course the inevitability of myopic thinking when extreme positions prevail is not the only lesson to be learned from a study of how the readiness concept has been interpreted at different periods of time. For instance, clearly apparent in the current scene is the lesson that one extreme does not react against another in such a way that a more balanced position emerges. But, here, a specific illustration from the present will outline more graphically the lesson in question.

One has only to live in these times to know that it is becoming almost commonplace to hear about researchers—most often not specialists in reading—who set out to teach reading to a group of, let us say, four-year-olds, even though they have little empirical justification for beginning at this age. Now, what has been the reaction to such a practice? Again, one has only to live in these times to know that, all too frequently, the responses have been steeped in equally extreme but opposite beliefs. Here reference is made to such rebuttal as: "We have a mountain of evidence to prove that a perfectly 'normal' child—I.Q. 100—cannot learn to read until he is about six years six months old." [68] ". . . there is nothing special you can do to speed up readiness." [69]

---

67. Gates, "The Necessary Mental Age for Beginning Reading," *op. cit.*

68. Heffernan, *op. cit.*, p. 316.

69. Hymes, "Changes in Preparing Five-Year-Olds for Reading," *op. cit.*, p. 128.

Surely, unfounded claims like these, made in the 1960's, offer little help in the development of a more balanced and flexible position about the optimum time to begin reading instruction. But what will help? What can be done in the present to insure a future that makes the best possible use of the readiness concept?

READING READINESS: A RECAPITULATION

Because the use of the readiness concept is so directly related to the way it is interpreted, initial efforts ought to go in the direction of coming to terms with the meaning of "readiness," in this instance applied to learning to read.

Meaning of readiness.—Traditionally, the literature shows, attempts to define "readiness" have viewed it as a product. For instance, in the beginning, readiness to read was assumed to be the product of maturation. Viewing readiness as a product is defensible, but current knowledge indicates that a child's readiness to learn to read or, more generally, his capacities for learning are the product both of maturation (nature) and of environmental factors (nurture). Within this framework, then, reading readiness can be defined as various combinations of abilities which result from nature and nurture interacting with each other.

Viewing readiness as a product is helpful, but viewing it only as a product is incomplete. What must be added to the definition of readiness seen as a product is that dimension which brings into focus the relationship between a child's particular capacities and the kind of learning opportunities made available to him. Within this framework readiness is still a product, but a product in relation to a given set of circumstances. Or, to use Ausubel's words, readiness is "the adequacy of existing capacity in relation to the demands of a given learning task." [70]

Assessment of readiness.—Outlining the two dimensions of readiness—readiness as a product and readiness as a relationship—brings into focus some obvious implications for school assessments of a child's readiness to begin to read. Clearly apparent, for instance, is the oversimplification of assessments which use a single-factor criterion such as chronological age or, as was once commonly sug-

---

70. Ausubel, "Viewpoints from Related Disciplines," *op. cit.*, p. 247.

gested, mental age. Equally apparent, though, is the inadequacy of any attempt to assess readiness apart from the kind of reading instruction that will be available.

But, it might be asked here, what about the positive implications of this view of readiness? What positive suggestions does it offer to elementary-school administrators and teachers who must deal with the question, "When should reading begin?" First, if a chronological age of six is no longer defensible as *the* criterion for starting instruction and if it is likely that particular combinations of maturation and environmental factors produce high learning capacities in some five-year-olds, then one positive implication is that the kindergarten year is the time to begin school efforts in assessing readiness. Second, if readiness can only be established in relation to "the demands of a given learning task," then another positive implication is that an assessment of readiness during the kindergarten year will be most reliable when it comes from the combination of (*a*) a situation offering varied opportunities to learn to read; and (*b*) a knowledge of what individual children are able to learn from the opportunities offered.

Examples of assessments.—To insure specific understanding of the kind of diagnostic situation that has just been proposed, it might be helpful at this point in the discussion to include a few illustrations of "kindergarten opportunities to learn to read." Of course, one immediate difficulty in choosing illustrations is the lack of realism in thinking about kindergarten in terms of a single kind of program. To be sure, there is always the temptation to believe that kindergarten is still comprised of the experiences we ourselves had as five-year-olds; but visits to schools in the 1960's show anything but one kind of program. Some kindergartens, for instance, have swung over to an imitation of the first grade in their use of reading workbooks and basal readers. And of course it is just this kind of wholesale, unimaginative swing that has engendered opposition to reading during the kindergarten year—opposition, it must be added, which rarely distinguishes between a method that might be inappropriate but a timing that might be just right, at least for some kindergartners.

Regardless, though, of these variations in particular programs, it still is realistic to assume that certain procedures go on in every kindergarten. For instance, it is safe to assume that time is given to the task of taking attendance. Mundane and routine though it is, attendance-taking can provide the opportunity for five-year-olds to recognize their names "written down"—though here it must be emphasized that some children at age five will already be far beyond just knowing the written form of their names. Nonetheless, the simple routine of beginning with the showing of names by a teacher and concluding, later in the school year, with the children indicating their presence by selecting their name card and putting it on an attendance board, could teach children to read their names and probably other names as well. Also—and this is the point to be emphasized—this kind of situation could also help a teacher identify those particular children who have difficulty even in remembering a word that is as personal as their own names.

Another safe assumption about kindergartens today is that art activities are still a part of the curriculum. Without diminishing their value as forms of free expression, finished products in art provide a timely opportunity to offer kindergarten children the chance to learn to sign their names, to write their own captions, and to read those composed by others. At the same time, however, this situation may be the teacher's opportunity to identify children for whom writing and spelling might be the easiest way into reading, to identify those who remember whole words with a minimum of exposure to them, and also to become aware of children for whom the motor skill of writing is a formidable task or for whom it is very difficult to compose even the briefest of captions.

Still another activity that is to be found in kindergartens is that of reading to the children. Generally, it is assumed, this is done for enjoyment or, perhaps, for gathering information to answer questions that were raised when magnets were being discussed or when conflicting ideas appeared in a spontaneous conversation about the stars being out at night but not in the daytime. Periodically, as part of this reading, the kindergarten teacher might write a word like "Magnet" on the chalkboard, identify it, and then ask, "Does anybody know the name of this first letter?" or, perhaps, "Does anybody have a name that starts with this same letter?" or—after "Marcy," "Michael," and "Matthew" have been written—state, "I'm going to say all of these words to show you that they not only begin with the same letter but also with the same sound." And then later she may ask, "Can you think of other words that begin with the same sound as "Magnet?" Obviously, with this kind of questioning, a kindergarten teacher can identify children who seem to know the alphabet as well as those who have skill in making visual and auditory discriminations. But, too, she is becoming aware of other children who appear to have no acquaintance even with a few letters of the alphabet or, more likely, no understanding of what is meant by the description "begin with the same sound."

Perhaps these few ordinary illustrations of very ordinary kindergarten activities are sufficient to give specific meaning to the procedure recommended for assessing a child's readiness to read—give him opportunities to begin. Implied even in the few illustrations, however, are some basic assumptions which seem important enough to merit explicit attention.

Assumptions inherent in the recommendation.—One obvious and important assumption underlying the illustrations is that the assessment of readiness and the teaching of reading can result from the same situation. For instance, the teacher's use of written names in attendance-taking was proposed as a way of collecting diagnostic information about the readiness of the children; but, in addition, for the individual children who were in fact "ready," it could be the start of learning to read—in this instance, learning to read children's names.

A second assumption that ought to be made explicit is that the same situation can be not only readiness instruction but also instruction in reading itself. For example, the use that was made of the word "magnet" in one of the illustrations could result in beginning learnings in phonics for some children. For other less ready children, however, the teacher's questions about a particular group of words would be only the first step in a series of steps which will finally result—perhaps during the kindergarten year—in their understanding that some words "sound the same at the beginning." For these latter children, the kindergarten teacher was carrying on readiness instruction. Yet, with other children who were ready to grasp the association between the letter "m" and a certain sound, reading instruction was taking place.

Still another assumption that is basic to what has been proposed as a way of assessing readiness relates to the nature of the learning opportunities that will be offered children. What must be assumed is that these opportunities will be high in quality and broad in scope. Otherwise, the proposal made for determining readiness could result in diagnostic and teaching situations which would transplant us right back to the 1920's and the 1930's in our basic conception of readiness. More specifically, if the learning opportunities offered to children turned out to be uninteresting, routine, and, therefore, not at all productive of some achievement in reading, then there would be the temptation to conclude—as happened on a wide scale back in the 1920's and 1930's—that the children did not learn because they were not ready. Of course, what this suggests is that, in any situation in which readiness is being assessed in relation to responses to learning opportunities, careful attention must always be given to the quality of the opportunities. Otherwise it becomes impossible to judge whether the shortcomings lay with the child or with the kind of instruction that was available.

READINESS AND BEGINNING READING

The very close connection between "getting ready" and "reading" that has been stressed throughout the previous sections of the chapter offers an interesting conclusion to the consideration of "when to begin reading instruction." What the close connection does, of course, is to point out that this long-debated question about the time to teach reading can also be a misleading one in its subtle inference that "getting ready to read" and "beginning to read" occur at separated points on some time line. It is within just such a framework that readiness programs have been separated from reading programs and kindergartens from first grades. And it is within the same framework that there always is the temptation—and the 1960's seem to have succumbed—to spend far too much time debating "when to begin" and far too little on finding imaginative answers to "how to begin."

In contrast, if future endeavors concentrated on the dependent relationship between "when" and "how," then it would be realistic to expect more concerted efforts to identify the many different ways in which beginning reading might be taught. Were such efforts then followed by attempts to identify which of these possible methods best match the capacities and interests of particular children, then it would also be realistic to expect not only higher achievement but also greater insight into the nature of the question, "When should reading instruction start?"

A VERY BRIEF SUMMARY

Thus far in this chapter attention has been given only to the time when schools ought to begin to teach reading. With this as the focus, the recommendation was made that the kindergarten year can be the beginning of readiness assessments. Emphasized in this recommendation, however, was the close association between the assessments and readiness instruction itself. Emphasized, too, was the fact that, for ready children, these assessments became forms of reading instruction that could lead to a beginning of reading on their part.

In all of this discussion, it was assumed but not stated that the recommendation made for kindergartens would apply to the first-grade year in those school systems in which kindergarten classes still do not exist. However, in the first grade it could be presumed that the combination of (*a*) older children and (*b*) much more school time for reading would lead to more immediate assessments, to more ready children, and, therefore, to more reading instruction.

What must not be lost in any of this discussion about "when to begin" are two ideas that comprise the framework for what has been said in the concluding parts of this section of the chapter. The first is the reminder that the answer to "when to begin" will be affected by the kinds of reading instruction that can be made available to children. This reminder simply restates the dependent relationship between the "when" and the "how" of instruction. It emphasizes, again, that a child's readiness to read is a reflection not only of his own capacities and interests but also of the degree to which a school's instruction is able to accommodate both.

A second idea that frames the context in which the major section of the chapter has been written is that most kindergarten or first-grade children are probably neither totally unready nor totally ready to begin to read. When children come to school—either to kindergarten or first grade—it is likely that some are ready to remember the written forms of whole words, but not yet ready to grasp the concept of letter-sound relationships. On the other hand, though, there might be some children who enjoy playing with the sounds of language and who would also enjoy finding objects whose names begin with the same sound or thinking of words that rhyme with "man" and "ran." It might be, too, that still other children come to school with little desire to read *per se* but very ready and eager to learn how words are spelled so that they might print these words themselves.

Suggested in these sample variations, of course, is the important reminder that "readiness" is not one particular combination of abilities. What the variations also suggest, however, is the need for both schools and reading specialists to give increased attention to identifying instructional forms which match the various capacities and interests of young children. The end result of such matching could only be a much better understanding of the problem that has been the focus of this chapter thus far: "When should reading instruction start?"

When Should a Child Begin To Read?

Early in the chapter, it was mentioned that this discussion about the time to begin reading would initially concentrate on the school and the groups of children for which it has a responsibility to teach reading. With the question, "When should a child begin to read?" it was also stated that the chapter would shift its focus to the individual child, the preschool years, and the role of the family in teaching reading.

Why the preschool years require attention in an N.S.S.E. yearbook can be explained in various ways. The most compelling reason, of course, is the possibility that some preschoolers are ready to read. However, another reason relates to the fact that the popular press, if only by the sheer quantity of articles, is quickly becoming the dominant source of both information and misinformation about preschool reading. With this in the background, to write an N.S.S.E. chapter that deals with the time to begin reading and that omits attention to current questions about the role of the family in teaching it would be to side-step a professional responsibility. And so it is to deal with some of the more basic of these questions that this section of the chapter has been written.

SOME HISTORICAL PERSPECTIVES

As seems to be true of all significant questions in education, the one about the role of the family in teaching reading has a long history. In fact, even a mere acquaintance with descriptions of the earliest education in the United States makes it clear that beginning reading was taught more often in the kitchen than in the classroom.[71] Over a period of time, though, as educational opportunities came to be viewed as the heritage of all rather than the privilege of a few, the job of teaching reading to large groups of children was transferred to the school. And, as the review of the literature in this chapter has already shown, it was not long before a close association developed between being in first grade and learning to read. Also developing, however, was the belief that attempts to teach reading earlier than the school years would result not in achievement but in problems. Certainly it is relevant to ask: "How and why did such a belief emerge?"

What seems clear, first of all, is that the psychological views which prevailed in the 1920's and 1930's and which supported the idea that a postponement of school instruction would minimize reading problems also gave impetus to the corollary belief that preschool instruction given at home would surely maximize them. Because both beliefs were related to the uniquely important role assigned to maturation, it was only natural that the more specific arguments opposing preschool reading would dwell on such concerns as the immaturity of the young child's eyesight.[72]

As time passed, the literature shows, the belief that preschool reading would be injurious to a child's vision became just one part of a more encompassing point of view which, in retrospect, might be called "traditional viewpoints" about reading that begins before

---

71. Fries, *op. cit.*; Smith, *American Reading Instruction, op. cit.*

72. Matthew Luckiesch and Frank K. Moss, "The Task of Reading," *Elementary School Journal*, XLII (March, 1942), 510-14; Arthur L. Rautman, "Your Child Begins To Read," *Parents Magazine*, XX (September, 1945), 21 ff.; Wilda Rosebrook, "Preventing Reading Deficiency," *Elementary School Journal*, XXXVI (December, 1935), 276-80; Charles A. Smith and Myrtle L. Jenson, "Educational, Psychological, and Physiological Factors in Reading Readiness," *Elementary School Journal*, XXXVI (April, 1936), 538-94; W. B. Townsend, "When To Start Reading Activities," *Instructor*, XLIV (October, 1935), 18 ff.

a child starts school. Included in the broader perspective was the idea that teaching reading requires a training not generally found among parents, that a head start in reading provides only a temporary advantage, and that it even results in confusion or boredom once school instruction begins.[73] Although neither confirmed nor contradicted by research findings, this whole collection of ideas appears to have been handed down to parents through articles in professional journals and, most of all, through the media of P.T.A. meetings, school bulletins, and parent-teacher conferences.[74]

THE MORE CURRENT IDEAS

Because of traditional beliefs about the dangers of preschool reading, reports in the 1950's highlighting earlier beginnings in reading came as something of a shock.[75] In this instance, though, the shock was soon cushioned by the avalanche of psychological texts and articles which, as previous sections in the chapter pointed out, created great excitement both about the potential of young children and the unique importance of their preschool years. A subsequent development not impeded by this excitement was widespread attention to the topic of earlier reading. It is unfortunate that the attention has been more productive of emotion than of facts.

This being the case, what are some possible ways to deal with the issue of preschool reading? One productive possibility, it seems, is to try to distinguish between what is and is not known. To do this, the following sections of the chapter will deal briefly with objections to preschool reading raised in past decades and then with some of the optimistic claims now being made by those who foster an earlier start.

---

73. Board of Education, City of New York, "Question Box," *Curriculum and Materials*, VI (January, 1952), 6; Lester D. Crow and Alice Crow, *Introduction to Education* (New York: American Book Co., 1947); Helen P. Niegosch, "Interpreting the Reading Program to Parents," *National Elementary Principal*, XVII (July, 1938), 608-22; Olson, *op. cit.*; Angelo Patri, *How To Help Your Child Grow Up* (Chicago: Rand McNally & Co., 1948); Helen T. Wooley, "Pre-School Education," *American School*, VIII (June, 1922), 173-76.

74. Dolores Durkin, *Children Who Read Early* (New York: Teachers College Press, Columbia University, 1966).

75. Burke, *op. cit.*; Durkin, "A Study of Children Who Learned to Read Prior to First Grade," *op. cit.*; "O.K.'s Children," *op. cit.*

TRADITIONAL OBJECTIONS TO PRESCHOOL READING

Three persistent objections to preschool reading were identified in the review of the literature in this chapter. Each will be stated, and each statement will be followed by some reactions. Because in this instance actual facts are so few, the reactions generally will be in the form of questions and reminders. What ought to emerge, therefore, is not definitive answers but, rather, some clarification of what is and is not known about reading that begins before a child enters school.

Preschool reading will be injurious to a child's vision.—In discussions of early reading it still is common to hear objections stated in the form of, "But won't it be harmful to the child's eyesight?" Like so many of the questions about preschool reading, this one has no factual answer. In this instance the lack of facts may be especially surprising because, in earlier decades of this century, when both physical and intellectual growth were interpreted as dimensions of maturation, it was relatively common to hear that a child's eyesight was "too immature" for reading during the preschool years.[76] In some instances, as part of the maturational concept of reading readiness, the warnings also included the first-grade year.[77] But these early concerns, it must be emphasized, were not supported by research data. Nor were they voiced by medical personnel even though the question of vision and preschool reading is, first of all, a medical one.

Although many years have passed since the warnings about vision were first heard, relevant research has not been accumulating. In fact, when the more current professional literature is studied, the lack of research dealing with preschool reading and vision is very apparent. Indirectly related research is gradually becoming available—for instance, there is a series of studies in progress designed

---

76. Lukeisch and Moss, *op. cit.*; Rautman, *op. cit.*; Calvin T. Ryan, "Should He Read at 5?" *Better Homes and Gardens*, XXV (October, 1946), 95.

77. Luella Cole, *The Improvement of Reading* (New York: Farrar & Rinehart, 1938); Rosebrook, *op. cit.*; W. B. Townsend, *op. cit.*; Paul A. Witty and David Kopel, "Preventing Reading Disability: The Reading Readiness Factor," *Educational Administration and Supervision*, XXII (September, 1936), 401-18.

to examine the effect of environmental factors on fundamental aspects of visual development.[78] However, until other research is productive of facts dealing specifically with early reading and its effects on vision, there probably is the need to adopt a somewhat conservative position when questions about preschool reading are raised. As a result of discussions with ophthalmologists, this writer believes that such a position can be defined by two statements. First, preschool children who show an interest in written language are probably visually ready for reading. On the other hand, however, parents who are eager to teach their preschoolers to read even though the children themselves show no interest ought to keep in mind the dearth of facts about the effect of early reading on vision and, in turn, see in this lack a message of caution.

Parents are not trained to teach reading.—Another traditional opposition to preschool reading is based on two assumptions: (*a*) the teaching of reading requires special training, and (*b*) few parents have this training.[79] To consider the validity and thus the significance of this type of concern, initial attention must be given to the meaning of "teaching reading" at the preschool level and then to the question that asks whether it requires special preparation.

Because ability to read does not happen in some spontaneous fashion, it must be assumed that any child who reads before entering school learned this skill and so in some sense was "taught." That is, something or someone in his preschool environment gave him the chance to learn to identify written words. For example, findings from two longitudinal studies of preschool readers have indicated that productive help comes from sources like television commercials or, for instance, labels attached to pictures found in picture dictionaries and alphabet books.[80] The research also shows that other successful help can come in the form of a parent answering a pre-

78. Harold Haynes, B. L. White, and R. Held, "Visual Accommodation in Human Infants," *Science*, CXLVIII (April 23, 1965), 528-30; B. L. White and R. Held, "Plasticity of Sensorimotor Development in the Human Infant," in *The Causes of Behavior: Readings in Child Development and Educational Psychology*, ed. Judy A. Rosenblith and Wesley Allinsmith (2nd ed.; Boston: Allyn & Bacon, Inc., 1966).

79. Patri, *op. cit.*; Wooley, *op. cit.*

80. Durkin, *Children Who Read Early, op. cit.*

schooler's questions about written words or, sometimes, of an older sibling "playing school" at home with a younger brother or sister.

What this same research also emphasizes, however, is the dependent relationship between the productivity of these varied learning opportunities and the child's interest. Such a relationship is very relevant, for it is the factor which requires that distinctions be made when the need for training is brought into discussions of early reading. If children of a preschool age *are* interested in such things as the identification or the spelling of certain words, the "teaching" of reading with them is simply a response to questions or requests for help. No decisions have to be made about matters like sequence and continuity or even instructional materials. In this instance both "correct" and "successful" teaching is dependent more on qualities like common sense and patience than on some special kind of training.

In the case of uninterested children, however, the contention that training is required assumes more validity; for with these children important questions like "when to begin" and "how to begin" have no obvious answers. Also without answer, however, is the most important question a parent of a disinterested child must consider: "*Should* I try to teach him to read?"

Preschool reading leads to problems of boredom or confusion when school instruction begins.—Still another traditional concern about a preschool start in reading is the likelihood of future problems linked to boredom or confusion.[81] Actually, the little research that is available tends to give credence to the prediction of boredom, especially for early readers who are both bright and fairly advanced in reading at their entrance into first grade.[82] However, such a problem is an indictment not against an early start but, rather, against the inability of schools to accommodate their instruction to the disparities among children who happen to be of the same chronological age. This problem of possible boredom is a serious one, certainly; but it should be used to raise questions about first-grade reading programs, not preschool beginnings in reading.

81. Board of Education, City of New York, *op. cit.;* Crow and Crow, *op. cit.;* Niegosch, *op. cit.*

82. Durkin, *Children Who Read Early, op. cit.*

The prediction of confusion for early readers is more nebulous, for it has never been explicitly outlined by those who cite confusion as a reason to discourage preschool reading. How the problem has generally been stated is reflected in the following excerpt from a 1952 curriculum bulletin:

> Parents are asked not to teach their children to read because there are many methods of teaching reading. A child is taught by one method in school and his parents, by introducing another method, may serve only to confuse him.[83]

One way of considering the validity of this particular prediction is to examine possible ways to teach beginning reading and then see whether some form of contradiction might be inherent in them.

Essentially, reading in its initial stages is concerned with word identification. Toward this end, attention can be given to the whole of words. Or, on the other hand, the focus might be on letter-sound relationships with the intent of blending sounds into words or of using sounds to identify existing but unfamiliar words. Research with preschool readers also indicates that reading which begins at home sometimes originates with spelling and writing.[84]

Within the context of these various approaches, what are the roots of possible confusion? For instance, does some kind of contradiction exist if a child learns to read whole words at home, even though first-grade instruction begins with attention to letter-sound relationships? In addition, will these differences in approach cause confusion? As of now, empirical evidence for such a cause-and-effect relationship cannot be found; and, in the opinion of this writer, such a relationship would be difficult to establish by any kind of logical analysis. In fact, it might be easier and more realistic to conclude that a beginning reading vocabulary learned at home adds concrete meaning to the more abstract letter-sound relationships stressed in school.

But, it might now be asked, what about the preschool child who begins to read because of some attention that was given to letters and sounds? Will this—assuming it was the only kind given—help

---

83. Board of Education, City of New York, *op. cit.*, p. 6.

84. Durkin, *Children Who Read Early, op. cit.*

cause confusion if the identification of whole words is stressed in the instructional program of the school?

In answer, it might seem logical to suggest that a child who has been focusing on parts of words at home might have extra difficulty attending to whole words in school. However, were such a claim made, it would be necessary to ask whether children really do "look at the whole word," even when instruction employs the so-called "whole-word" approach. What is more likely, research suggests, is that the child looks at certain letters or letter combinations, which are then used as cues for recalling the whole.[85]

Perhaps even this small amount of questioning is sufficient to show that the likelihood of confusion for preschool readers is hardly supported either by research or logical analysis. This being so, it is only natural to wonder how such pessimism originated, especially when so little factual information about preschool reading has been available. In this instance the literature does not identify the origin with certainty, but it does suggest the possibility of its connection with the idea that there is one best way to teach beginning reading.

More specifically, from about the 1930's and extending into the 1950's, it was commonly believed that the "whole-word" approach was the best way to introduce children to reading.[86] With such a belief would it not be tempting to append still more beliefs—for example, that other approaches are incorrect and that the use of multiple approaches is confusing?

If, in the past, there really were these connections, then it would seem that present beliefs require re-examination of the traditional idea that preschool reading results in confusion. For, today, we have advanced to the realization that there is no single method of teaching beginning reading that is best for all children. Within such a framework there is much room for eclectic approaches and, perhaps, no room at all for the notion that confusion is to be the fruit

---

85. Gabrielle Marchbanks and Harry Levin, "Cues by Which Children Recognize Words," *Journal of Educational Psychology*, LVI (April, 1965), 57-61.

86. Guy L. Bond and Eva Bond, *Teaching the Child To Read* (New York: Macmillan Co., 1943); Edward W. Dolch, *Teaching Primary Reading* (Champaign, Ill.: Garrard Press, 1941); Kathleen B. Hester, *Teaching Every Child To Read* (New York: Harper & Bros., 1955); Clarence R. Stone, *Better Primary Reading* (St. Louis: Webster Publishing Co., 1936).

of reading that begins at home. At least this is a possibility meriting consideration in current discussions of the question, "When should a child begin to read?"

CLAIMS SUPPORTING PRESCHOOL READING

Future texts recording the history of educational thought will surely describe positive and even enthusiastic reactions to preschool reading as a phenomenon of the 1960's. What they will also have to record, however, is that these reactions were hardly bolstered by research data; that, in fact, preschool reading was an aspect of development that remained practically untouched by researchers. It may be that these historians will record, too, that it was this very lack of facts which promoted myth-making, first in the form of exaggerated fears and then in the form of wishful expectations.

As a way of introducing this brief discussion of some of the current claims about earlier beginnings in reading, it might be helpful to consider a few factors that account for these new and more positive reactions. Why have views about preschool reading changed from pessimistic concerns to optimistic claims?

Certainly one factor encouraging the shift is the current emphasis on the importance of learning opportunities to a child's development and, more especially, their unique importance during the early years. It is only natural that such emphasis would have repercussions in a field like reading, particularly with the question of when its teaching ought to begin.

However, the idea that reading might start at home rather than in school was a possibility that received encouragement even earlier than the advent of this new psychological climate. For example, in 1955, in the widely circulated book, *Why Johnny Can't Read*, Flesch not only criticized the schools for omitting phonics instruction but also urged parents to start teaching phonic skills at home, preferably before their children started school.[87] The same twofold message was repeated in another though less influential book, *Reading: Chaos and Cure*, appearing in 1958.[88]

---

87. Rudolph Flesch, *Why Johnny Can't Read* (New York: Harper & Bros., 1955).

88. Sibyl Terman and Charles Child Walcutt, *Reading: Chaos and Cure* (New York: McGraw-Hill Book Co., 1958).

By the early 1960's, linguists had joined in criticizing the methodology employed by schools in teaching beginning reading. What is especially relevant to notice, however, is that their counter-recommendations also were accompanied by teaching proposals that involved the parent and the preschool child.[89]

In the early 1960's, too, books written directly to parents made their way into the marketplace. For instance, in 1961 the Denver Public Schools published *Preparing Your Child for Reading* which, with its lessons, phonic cards, and exercises, went far beyond mere "preparation."[90] Later, in the May, 1963, issue of the *Ladies Home Journal*, an article offered teaching suggestions for use with very young children.[91] Accompanying this widely discussed article was an advertisement for a teaching kit; and following it, in 1964, was a book extending the suggestions, called *How To Teach Your Baby To Read*.[92]

Resulting from this broad collection of new ideas and, in some instances, new heights in wishful thinking, are certain specific claims about the possibility and also the advantages of earlier beginnings in reading. For example, the possibility of a preschool start is supported not only by the identification of early readers but also by the claim that children who have learned to speak their native language ought to be able to learn to read it. In the case of the advantages of an earlier beginning, the claim might be, "The younger the child, the easier it is to teach him to read" or, perhaps, "The child who gets a head start will maintain his lead over children who do not begin early."

At this point, it is relevant to ask: "What about these claims?" Do they have a validity that merits their being considered in serious discussions about the optimum time for a child to begin to read?

A child who has demonstrated ability in oral language ought to be able to begin to read.—Since learning the native language is

---

89. Leonard Bloomfield and Clarence L. Barnhart, *Let's Read* (Detroit: Wayne State University Press, 1961); Fries, *op. cit.*

90. Hurd and Rimmel, *op. cit.*

91. Doman, Stevens, and Orem, *op. cit.*

92. Glenn Doman, *How To Teach Your Baby To Read* (New York: Random House, 1964).

generally well established by age three or four, this particular claim can easily be interpreted as signaling the message that reading ought to be initiated at these same ages. However, with careful and searching consideration it seems more accurate to say that the claim often reflects not so much a desire to move toward earlier reading as it does a reaction almost of awe at the language-learning capacities of preschool children.[93] Back in 1954, for instance, before earlier starts in reading became so fashionable, Gates said:

> There are factors which suggest that most children could learn to read in their fourth year. They learn to understand spoken language quite well by their second year, and psychologically there is little difference between learning, as it were, "to read" spoken words and learning to read printed words. . . . The main reason they learn to understand spoken words first is merely that it is more convenient for parents and others to use them than to present printed material. As far as the present writer is aware there is no evidence that printed words are more difficult to perceive or distinguish than spoken words.[94]

More recent interest in the impressive language-learning capacities of young children has branched out to include efforts in analyzing their acquisition of oral language as a way of identifying better ways to teach them to read its written form.[95] In a 1966 article, for example, Carroll speculates:

> That such complex learning occurs with apparent ease tempts us to think that the process of native language learning is in some sense an "ideal" learning process, and that it might be worthy of imitation when we try to arrange the conditions for other kinds of learning. Might it not be possible for a child to learn to read in somewhat the same "natural" way that he learns his native language? Could reading perhaps be "acquired" through conditions and experiences analogous to those by which the child acquires his native language, rather than by the slow,

---

93. John B. Carroll, "Some Neglected Relationships in Reading and Language Learning," *Elementary English*, XLIII (October, 1966), 577-82; Arthur I. Gates, "Unsolved Problems in Reading: A Symposium," *Elementary English*, XXXI (October, 1954), 331-34; Arthur W. Staats and Carolyn K. Staats, "A Comparison of the Development of Speech and Reading Behavior with Implications for Research," *Child Development*, XXXIII (December, 1962), 831-46.

94. Gates, "Unsolved Problems in Reading: A Symposium," *op. cit.*, p. 334.

95. Carroll, *op. cit.*; Staats and Staats, *op. cit.*

careful teaching processes which we have thought necessary.[96]

If concerted interest in the kind of analysis proposed by Carroll and others continues, it seems realistic to anticipate some new understanding about ways to teach beginning reading. What could only result from this, as was pointed out in earlier sections of the chapter, is new understandings about optimum times for starting it.

The younger the child the easier it is to teach him to read.—The somewhat startling message of this claim has been heralded primarily in a popular magazine article and, subsequently, in a book by one of the writers of that article.[97] In its most extreme form, the message can be summarized by a quotation from the magazine article:

> The best time to teach your child to read with little or no trouble is when he is about two years old. Beyond two years of age, the teaching of reading gets harder every year. If your child is five, it will be easier than it will be when he is six. Four is still easier, and three is even easier. If you are willing to go to a little trouble, you can begin when your baby is 18 months old or—if you are very clever—as early as 10 months.[98]

Reactions to claims like these could take a variety of forms. For instance, the claims could be automatically dismissed as mere nonsense. Or their wording could be used in an exercise in logic leading to questions like: If less age makes for more ease, why does a parent have to be "clever" when the child is ten months but only "go to a little trouble" when the child is eighteen months? Then, too, there is the simple response of, "But where is your evidence?"

However, there is another possible reaction, assuming the reader of the article can contain his justified anger long enough to entertain it. This reaction would give serious consideration to the possibility of there being some element of truth underlying the idea of "the younger, the easier to teach reading." For example, it is not at all nonsensical to ask whether there might be something about the nature and interests of children younger than six that would make beginning reading easier for a three- or four-year-old child, let us

---

96. Carroll, *op. cit.*, p. 577.

97. Doman, Stevens, and Orem, *op. cit.*; Doman, *op. cit.*

98. Doman, Stevens, and Orem, *op. cit.*, p. 62.

say, than it sometimes is for a six-year-old. Actually, this very kind of question has been raised by Kohlberg in a paper characterized by a conservative and even cautious position regarding the benefits to be derived from preschool programs.[99] Within the context of careful caution he still writes:

> A good deal of learning to read and to write in the elementary school is a tedious task for the six to eight year old, requiring drill, repetition, self-correction and considerable insecurity in comparing the child's own performance with that of other children in the classroom. Because reading and writing (especially reading) are relatively low level sensori-motor skills, there is nothing in the cognitive structure of the reading task which involves any high challenge to the older child. In contrast, the identification of letters and words can be challenging fun for younger children.[100]

With this statement, too, there is room for a variety of reactions. Some reading specialists, for example, might argue with the implied definition of beginning reading. But another and perhaps more fruitful reaction is the recognition that, as far as is now known, there is nothing about six-year-old children that makes this age level the very best time for beginning reading. Even now the idea that the start of reading and six years of age go together is based not on any defined system of matching a learning task with a given set of skills and interests but, rather, on an educational system that continues to use a chronological age of six as the criterion for starting school and, consequently, for beginning reading.

While nobody would want to give even the hint of support to the idea that mothers ought to be working on reading with their ten-month-old children, nobody, either, should discourage future research efforts to see whether there are characteristics of children younger than six that might provide a match for the requirements of beginning reading. What must be pointedly emphasized is that these efforts will be helped neither by outlandish claims about infants nor by sentimental views of childhood.

Preschool readers will maintain their lead over children who do not begin to read until the first grade.—It would be difficult to quar-

---

99. Lawrence Kohlberg, "Early Education: A Cognitive-Developmental View" (unpublished manuscript, University of Chicago, n.d.).

100. *Ibid.*, p. 40.

rel with the idea that a preschool child's interest in reading is enough to warrant an early start. However, there are those who prefer to find justification in the positive effect preschool beginnings have on later achievement.[101] Here the problem is the lack of substantial and realiable information about preschool reading, including the effect it has on future achievement. This writer has completed two longitudinal studies of early readers, both showing continuing advantages for the subjects; but two studies of small groups of children are hardly sufficient basis on which to issue proclamations.[102] What the studies can do, however, is to issue the warning that other research efforts to assess the future value of a head start must make a distinction between early readers who are treated in first-grade classes as if they had not yet begun to read, and early readers whose achievements are matched by appropriate school instruction. Surely what is or is not done with early reading is one of the factors that will have an effect on how it comes to be viewed in the decades that lie ahead.

When To Begin: A Final Summary

That the truth is likely to be a long story and that it is also likely to be inconclusive has certainly been borne out by this chapter. Dealing with the question of the optimum time to initiate reading, the various sections have shown that it is, in fact, a complicated question having nothing like a single, unequivocal answer. And perhaps it never will have. However, much still must be learned about both children and reading before such a conclusion is warranted.

At the preschool level, for instance, very little is known about why some young children are so curious about written language, while others—perhaps brothers or sisters—are obviously disinterested. One tempting explanation, of course, is that the more curious are the more intelligent; but it happens that, among groups of preschool readers, high I.Q's are not always evident.[103]

There are other unanswered questions too. For example, what

---

101. Doman, *op. cit.*; Ruth Moss, "By Fifth Grade, Early Readers Can Be Two Years Ahead of Their Classmates," *Chicago Tribune*, November 13, 1966, Sec. 5, p. 1.

102. Durkin, *Children Who Read Early, op. cit.*

103. *Ibid.*

will be the effect of preschool reading that occurs not because of a child's own interest in learning but because of parental concerns, ambitions, insecurities—or whatever it is that can turn a home into a school? With this particular question there might be the temptation to react negatively even before the facts are in; consequently, what must be emphasized is the reminder that intentional instruction by a parent is not necessarily undesirable instruction. Given the setting of a home, there is always the possibility of a teaching-learning situation that is far more personal and private than even the best of classrooms can ever hope to be. The problem, of course, is to communicate to parents the important difference between forced instruction and what Gates once referred to as "easy-going guidance."[104] As it happens, in the 1960's this job of communicating what might be called the "common sense" of preschool reading is especially difficult because of complications created by popular press articles and advertisements. Almost without exception these communications portray earlier reading—regardless of how it is achieved—as something that is both easy and desirable. As part of the thrust to sell an idea, differences among children are minimized or simply ignored; and parents are made to feel that neglecting a matter like reading is to be an irresponsible parent.

In response to this "Madison Avenue" treatment of preschool reading, professional educators have done little to combat the oversimplification and misinformation. And, with the little that has been written in publications likely to be seen by parents, the tendency has been to restate the fears about preschool reading that were so prevalent in earlier decades of this century.[105]

Obviously, a different kind of article for parents would be more helpful. But what is really needed are parent-education programs sponsored by individual schools, designed to communicate what is and is not known about preschool reading. What these programs can offer parents, too, is some help in making distinctions between their role and the role of a teacher both in preparing a child for

104. Gates, "Unsolved Problems in Reading: A Symposium," *op. cit.*

105. Bruno Bettelheim, "The Danger of Teaching Your Baby To Read," *Ladies' Home Journal*, LXXXIII (September, 1966), 38-40; Hymes, *op. cit.;* Eda J. LeShan, "The Anxious Child Can Learn—but What?" *PTA Magazine*, LXI (December, 1966), 8-10.

reading and in actually teaching him. In some communities, what will also have to be emphasized is the educational significance of parents' reading to preschool children, talking with them, and certainly answering their questions. In other communities, however (and this underscores the need for individual programs), the urgent need is to help parents realize the important difference between a home that is intellectually stimulating and one that is intellectually smothering.

The school must enter more directly into discussions about earlier reading in other ways, too. Certainly one question meriting careful study has to do with the function of the kindergarten year. More and more, statistics show, kindergarten is becoming a part of the school life of a child.[106] Yet, very little has been done on a broad scale to re-examine the traditional program of the kindergarten to see whether functions once thought essential continue to be so for children who are living in a world that is very different from the one surrounding the earliest of the kindergartens. In any re-examination, it seems, the first question must *not* be one that asks about the possible place of reading instruction—this would be a piecemeal approach. Rather, the initial questioning ought to deal with the function of the whole of the kindergarten program and only later with such specific questions as the possible contributions reading might make. In any such discussions, too, as much attention should be given to the ways reading might be taught as to the best time for teaching it. Otherwise, if objections to kindergarten reading are heard, it would be difficult to know whether they stemmed from stereotyped concepts of instruction or from factual descriptions of children living in the 1960's.

Meanwhile, though, an unquestionable responsibility of all schools is to insure that any child who enters first grade already able to read finds instruction that reflects his achievement. For far too many years, primary reading programs have been based on the assumption that beginning first-graders are unable to read anything. In the 1960's, if only because of television and the easy availability

---

106. Samuel Schloss, "Enrollment of 3-, 4-, and 5-year-olds in Nursery Schools and Kindergarten" (Bureau of Educational Research and Development, OE-200079 [Washington: United States Department of Health, Education, and Welfare, Office of Education, June, 1965]).

of books and magazines, this assumption is inaccurate. However, to dispute the assumption is not to overlook the fact that some entering first-graders not only will not be reading; they might not even be ready to begin. With these children, though, the immediate solution is not to postpone instruction but to look for ways of teaching reading that might match their particular skills and interests. In the process of searching, much can be learned about the readiness of these children—much more, it is suggested, than can ever be gleaned from reading readiness test scores.[107]

To summarize, then, this question of when to begin reading is, indeed, a very complicated one. Essentially, it is concerned with the fact of differences among children of the same chronological age. For the schools, these differences have always created both challenges and problems—challenges and problems that will take many years to resolve because, as new adaptations and solutions are found, new and more subtle differences among children will be identified. The road to success is a long one, to be sure; but as the old Chinese proverb reminds us, "Even in a thousand mile journey one must take the first step."

107. Robert Dykstra, "The Use of Reading Readiness Tests for Prediction and Diagnosis: A Critique," in *The Evaluation of Children's Reading Achievement*, ed. Thomas Barrett ("Perspectives in Reading," No. 8 [Newark, Del.: International Reading Association, 1967]), pp. 35-52.

CHAPTER III

Innovations in Reading Instruction: For Beginners

MILDRED LETTON WITTICK

Introduction

Probably no ten-year period in the development of American reading instruction has witnessed as many and as varied efforts to innovate in the teaching of beginning reading as has the past decade. Some of the innovations involve fragments of older methods or combinations of the best of several. Some contain the elements of earlier ones but change the order of their presentation. Some innovations represent interpretations of newer learning theories or efforts to implement psychological studies.

The history of reading instruction in preceding periods helps the reader understand the broader context in which current innovations appear. Matthews surveyed the course of reading instruction from the invention of the alphabet,[1] while Smith restricted herself to reading in America, with emphasis upon the more recent period.[2]

By 1900, series of readers were carefully graded; colored illustrations had appeared; enrichment materials were in use. Standardized tests and scientific studies of reading, which appeared between 1910 and 1935, began the shift of emphasis to the investigation of the reading process and the application of this research to classroom methods and materials. During this period, experience charts were introduced. Ability grouping became more common, and assignments and materials which provided for individual differences received more attention, partly through publicity surrounding the Dalton and the Washburne (or Winnetka) plans. It was also dur-

1. Mitford M. Mathews, *Teaching To Read* (Chicago: University of Chicago Press, 1966).

2. Nila Banton Smith, *American Reading Instruction* (Newark, Del.: International Reading Association, 1965).

ing this period that the concept of reading readiness was accepted, vitalized at last by Dewey after almost two hundred years of occasional mention in the writings of philosophers and educators.

Chall found that reading programs in wide use between the 1930's and 1965 were in general agreement on the following basic points: (*a*) Major goals of reading included, from the beginning, word recognition, comprehension, interpretation, appreciation, and application of the facts to the study of personal and social problems. (*b*) The child started with "meaningful reading" of whole words, sentences, and stories geared to his experiences and interests. (*c*) He learned a sight vocabulary of about fifty words and then began, through a process of word analysis, to identify new words. This instruction included the use of picture and meaning clues and structural analysis as well as phonics. (*d*) Such instruction extended over the six years of elementary school with major emphasis on phonics in Grades II and III. (*e*) Phonics were not drilled or practiced in "isolation" but rather were treated as an integral part of meaningful reading. Sounds were not isolated. (*f*) Especially in the primary grades, the vocabulary of basal readers was controlled and repeated often, using a meaning-frequency principle. (*g*) A readiness period was recommended for all children, a longer one for those judged "not ready." [3] Chall concluded:

The above principles, based partly on research, partly on theory, partly on experience, and partly on belief, have become, since about 1930, the "conventional wisdom" of beginning reading instruction. Since the middle 1950's, however, one after another aspect of this conventional wisdom has been vehemently challenged. Out of these challenges have come new programs and approaches, some resembling rather closely the older programs discarded like the "modern" programs of the 1930's. As in the past, most current innovators claim that theirs is "the new," "the natural," "the logical," and "the true." One additional claim has been added—that theirs is "the most scientific." [4]

The most vocal criticism of beginning reading instruction in the

---

3. Jeanne Chall, "Innovations in Beginning Reading," *Instructor Magazine*, LXXIV (March, 1965, 67, 91 ff; reprinted in *Reading '65: An Overview of Current Practices*, guest ed. Helen M. Robinson (*Instructor* Supplement, March, 1965).

4. *Ibid.*, p. 67.

United States began with *Why Johnny Can't Read*[5] (1955) and was augmented by *Reading: Chaos and Cure*[6] (1958) and *Tomorrow's Illiterates*[7] (1961). In 1956, Daniels and Diack published their experimental report in England. All of these authors were in general agreement that (*a*) the "sight reading" method was inefficient and incorrect and (*b*) some variation of the phonics approach was the most effective method to use in beginning reading. All examined some research. Some of these authors had reached their conclusions from an analysis of the performance of limited samples of subjects and others from observations of a few children as they learned to read. Criticism of education in general and of reading programs in particular was almost routine in American life, so these voices might have been less heeded except for the launching of Sputnik in 1957. Critics found the press eager to give them space, and their audience widened to include the general public. Best coverage was usually given to innovations that differed most from reading methods and materials with which the public was already familiar or to suggestions that the schools return to the practices of the "good old days."

Major Current Innovations in Methods and Materials

The tremendous amounts of federal money now available to local schools through the National Defense Education Act and Title I of the 1966 Elementary and Secondary Education Act (which authorized more than one billion dollars) have attracted many newcomers to the publishing field. The major buyers of the publishing houses have been the large communications companies—Xerox, R.C.A., I.B.M., Fairchild Camera, and the like. With a certain market for their materials, such companies have been able to spend large sums on experimental materials and, among these, some truly effective innovations may appear.

To examine some of the current systems of teaching reading to

---

5. Rudolf Flesch, *Why Johnny Can't Read and What You Can Do About It* (New York: Harper & Bros., 1955).

6. Sibyl Terman and Charles C. Walcutt, *Reading: Chaos and Cure* (New York: McGraw-Hill Book Co., Inc., 1958).

7. Charles C. Walcutt (ed.), *Tomorrow's Illiterates* (New York: Little, Brown, & Co., 1961).

beginners, Robinson developed a design for analysis.[8] She found that both methods and materials involved simplification and sequence. In this discussion of major current innovations, the Robinson framework will be used.

A careful examination of experimental methods designed to teach young children to read reveals efforts to simplify the initial steps so that the young child will not be overwhelmed by learning tasks that are too numerous or too complicated. The differences among the methods seem to involve primarily what is simplified —stories, sentences, words, phonemes, or letters. All methods require control of some of these elements and repetition of those introduced.

Simplification at the beginning implies later introduction of many aspects of reading. Hence, the sequence of teaching skills differs from one beginning method to another. In most instances, more complicated phases of the initial emphasis are accompanied by the gradual introduction and development of other skills and abilities to promote competency in reading.

Of special interest is the fact that little research has been done to determine the most effective learning sequences, regardless of the method used. Sequences have been produced logically rather than psychologically. Adult perceptions of what is most or least difficult may differ from children's difficulty or ease in learning; evidence needs to be secured from chidren's learning to determine the most appropriate order of developing the various facets of reading. Certain methods may be found more effective than others chiefly because the sequence is better programed or better suited to the way children learn.

Tyler suggests three contributions which sequence makes to effective learning:

(1) By providing new features to each new learning situation the pupil is required to give attention to it and thus to be reacting intelligently rather than repeating previous behavior without real involvement in it. (2) By building on previous learning, each sequential learning experience carries the pupil to a higher level of understanding, or skill, or appreciation, or some other objective. (3) Because each new

---

8. Helen M. Robinson, "Beginning Reading," in "News and Comments," *Elementary School Journal*, LXIII (May, 1963), 417.

learning situation incorporates features of earlier learning, the amount of meaningful practice and satisfaction of basic concepts, skills, values and the like is greatly extended, thus leading to greater permanence in the learning involved.[9]

The eclectic programs embodied in basal readers, as described earlier by Chall, appeared to be in common use in the early sixties. Austin reported:

> Among the sixty-five school systems in both field studies, thirty-nine used a completely basal reader approach, eighteen combined experience charts and basal reading materials, six introduced a separate phonics program before or with basal reading books, one employed the language-experience approach, and one school system was totally committed to individualized reading.[10]

The phonics systems that are a part of the basal reader programs vary from one series to another. In most, the reading readiness period (with emphasis upon language ability) precedes work in phonics, and other techniques of word recognition—picture clues, context clues, and structural analysis—are taught along with the phonics. In recent revisions of the major series, emphasis has shifted to earlier attention to the teaching of sounds and letters. The skills needed for phonics analysis have appeared in the basal reader programs for many years. The major change that has taken place is to introduce these earlier and, in some instances, in a different sequence. Most programs place strong emphasis on auditory skills and early independence in word attack.

Current innovations in methods and materials for beginning readers may be placed in four categories: (*a*) the stronger "decoding" programs; (*b*) programs stressing greater individualization of instruction, self-pacing, and more self-direction; (*c*) programs in which revamped or new subject-matter content and illustrations

---

9. Ralph W. Tyler, "The Importance of Sequence in Teaching Reading," in *Sequential Development of Reading Abilities*, ed. Helen M. Robinson ("Supplementary Educational Monographs," No. 90 [Chicago: University of Chicago Press, 1960]), p. 4.

10. Mary C. Austin and Coleman Morrison, *The First R: The Harvard Report on Reading in Elementary Schools* (New York: Macmillan Co., 1963), p. 21.

constitute the change; and (d) extensions of technology.[11]

The plan of presentation of innovations in this chapter is first to present a general description of the group. If materials and methods have unique characteristics, these will be noted briefly. This will be followed by a generalization about the efforts to achieve simplification and sequence. In order to reduce duplication, the evidence from research is combined in a later section entitled "The Research Evidence."

THE STRONGER "DECODING" PROGRAMS

Decoding is a term that has been commonly used in reading during the past ten years to describe the act of mastering the relationship between sounds and symbols. Among such programs are: (a) the special phonics systems to be used in conjunction with a conventional basal series; (b) new phonics-oriented basal reading programs; (c) methods and materials based on a linguistic approach; (d) Initial Teaching Alphabet (i.t.a.; ITA), Unifon, and others employing changes in medium, with or without concomitant changes in methods and materials.

The special phonics systems.—Numerous separate phonics systems, mostly in workbook form, have been on the market for more than thirty years. These materials also often appear in preprinted carbon masters for liquid duplicating or in the form of transparencies, filmstrips, pictorial charts, recordings, and tapes. They are frequently designed for use with all basal reading series.

Simplification in the special phonics systems is achieved by limiting the number of new words introduced at the initial period of instruction. Sequence is provided by continuous introduction and practice in word perception as a means of acquiring meaning from printed language. These programs usually proceed deductively. Durkin points out that they begin "with generalizations about the sounds of letters which are then applied to the pronunciation of specific syllables and words." [12] The process is synthetic, concen-

---

11. Jeanne Chall, "Approaches to Beginning Reading: What Is New in America," in *Reading Instruction: An International Forum*, ed. Marion D. Jenkinson (Newark, Del.: International Reading Association, 1967), pp. 155-66.

12. Dolores Durkin, *Phonics and the Teaching of Reading* (New York: Teachers College, Columbia University, 1962), p. 11.

trating at first on parts of words, later combining these into whole words.

Phonics systems tend to be more alike than different. Only a few can be mentioned here. The "Economy Program," although proposed and tried before 1960, probably has had the greatest impact; it has been widely argued and studied. Among others of the well-known early programs were those developed by Hay and Wingo [13] and the Phonovisual method.[14]

In the past decade, new programs have appeared and older ones have been brought up to date. For example, *Breaking the Sound Barrier* [15] is a phonics handbook to be used directly with children or by the teacher as a guide for organizing his own phonics lessons. *Phonics We Use* [16] is comprised of seven books for use in the first six grades. *Speech-to-Print Phonics: A Phonics Foundation for Reading* [17] is primarily a reading readiness program. *New Phonics Skilltexts* [18] consists of four workbooks designed to study the sound and structure of words.

Phonics-oriented basal readers.—At least two basal reading programs which emphasize a stronger phonics approach are currently available. Both series begin with the study of letters and sounds. Both have a larger vocabulary load, especially in the primary grades. *Basic Reading* [19] introduces letter names and sounds with readiness. The program, according to its publisher, works toward the twin goals of recognition and comprehension and uses both analytic and

---

13. Julie Hay and Charles E. Wingo, *Reading with Phonics* (Philadelphia: J. B. Lippincott Co., 1960).

14. Lucille D. Schoolfield and Josephine B. Timberlake, *Phonovisual Method* (rev. ed.; Washington: Phonovisual Products, Inc., 1960).

15. Sister Mary Caroline, I.H.M., *Breaking the Sound Barrier* (New York: Macmillan Co., 1960).

16. *Phonics We Use* (Books *A* through *G* [Chicago: Lyons & Carnahan, 1966]).

17. Donald D. Durrell and Helen A. Murphy, *Speech-to-Print Phonics: A Phonics Foundation for Reading* (New York: Harcourt, Brace & World, Inc., 1964).

18. Rachel G. Brake, *New Phonics Skilltexts* (Books *A* through *D* [Columbus, Ohio: Charles E. Merrill Books, Inc., 1963]).

19. Glenn McCracken and Charles C. Walcutt, *Basic Reading* (Philadelphia: J. B. Lippincott Co., 1963-65).

synthetic approaches. The *Open Court Series* [20] delays the reading of stories until a considerable amount of phonic knowledge is mastered. It also concentrates on literature as early as the first grade, with the introduction of folk and fairy tales.

Linguistic approaches.—In the reading field, as on the political scene, some figures emerge "ahead of their times," so that their ideas and contributions fall on deaf contemporary ears; it is only somewhat later that the public becomes aware of what such individuals were saying. This seems to have been the fate of some linguists in relation to their comments on the reading process.

Smith [21] found the first discussion of linguistics as applied to reading in a chapter titled, "Acquiring of Word-Ideas in Reading," in a book by O'Shea [22] published in 1927. The most-quoted article, however, written by Bloomfield, appeared in 1942.[23] In this, the author discussed the application of linguistics to the teaching of reading. In the late 1950's and the 1960's, films, professional books, and articles on the topic appeared. Three linguists—Bloomfield,[24] Fries,[25] and Henry Lee Smith, Jr.,[26]—have entered the field of reading with publications for teachers or children or with films. Barnhart developed experimental materials based on Bloomfield's theory.

Strickland, commenting on two viewpoints of reading, points out that the linguist's concept of reading is not that commonly held

---

20. Arthur Trace and Priscilla McQueen, *Open Court Basic Readers* (La Salle, Ill.: Open Court Publishing Co., 1963).

21. Nila Banton Smith, *op. cit.*, pp. 386-87.

22. M. V. O'Shea, *Linguistics in Education* (New York: Macmillan Co., 1927), chap. vii.

23. Leonard Bloomfield, "Linguistics and Reading," *Elementary English Review*, XIX (April, 1942), 125-30, and (May, 1942), 183-86.

24. Leonard Bloomfield and Clarence L. Barnhart, *Let's Read, A Linguistic Approach* (Detroit: Wayne State University Press, 1961).

25. Charles C. Fries, *Linguistics and Reading* (New York: Holt, Rinehart & Winston, Inc., 1963).

26. Henry Lee Smith, Jr., *Language and Linguistics* (a series of films produced by the University of Buffalo in conjunction with the National Educational Television and Radio Center; titles related to reading include: *The Alphabet, Language and Writing*, and *Linguistic Science and the Teaching of Reading*).

by teachers and reading specialists—that reading is getting meaning from the printed page. The linguist proposes that, since the graphic symbols represent speech, reading is achieved when the child "can recognize symbol-sound correspondence to the point that he can respond to the marks with appropriate speech."[27] The remainder of what the school calls teaching reading is actually teaching *thinking*, according to some linguists' point of view.

Anastasiow and Hansen point out that, although "linguistic-based programs vary among themselves and fail at times clearly to establish relationships between their programs and linguistic facts or theories, there are relevant criteria that clearly differentiate the 'linguistic approaches' from the more traditional reading approaches."[28] As proposed by the authors, the six distinguishing characteristics of the linguistic approach are: (*a*) the children are taught a systematic decoding system at the beginning of their reading experience rather than after the acquisition of a sight vocabulary; (*b*) the introduction and patterning of consonant and vowel combinations are systematically controlled; (*c*) letters, letter names, and corresponding sounds are introduced early; (*d*) the major part of the learning activities are focused on decoding behaviors; (*e*) morphological rules and syntactic concepts are explicitly introduced; and (*f*) picture and content clues are not considered part of the decoding system, although some linguistic approaches introduce them as separate skills.

The first reading material for children based on the linguistic approach was *Let's Read*,[29] published in 1961. A single volume contained an introduction for parents, one for the teacher, teaching instructions, and the child's material, which included 245 lessons introducing about 5,000 words. Later, in an experimental edition, it was divided into smaller books with accompanying teachers' manuals.

27. Ruth G. Strickland, *The Contribution of Structural Linguistics to the Teaching of Reading, Writing, and Grammar in the Elementary School* (Bulletin of the School of Education, Indiana University, Vol. XL, No. 1 [Bloomington: Indiana University, 1964]), p. 10.

28. Nicholas J. Anastasiow and Duncan Hansen, "Criteria for Linguistic Reading Programs," *Elementary English*, XLIV (March, 1967), 231.

29. Leonard Bloomfield and Clarence L. Barnhart, *Let's Read* (experimental ed.; Bronxville, N.Y.: Clarence L. Barnhart, Inc., 1963-66).

The child begins by learning: (*a*) the alphabet; (*b*) lists of words having similar sound patterns; (*c*)sentences containing these words; and (*d*) irregular symbol-sound correspondences. He reads orally only at first. He reads paragraphs after he has mastered the initial material. Emphasis is upon association of sound and spelling patterns.

Fries was the senior author of one of the first graded series of basal readers designed to apply linguistics theory. In 1966 the series, which earlier had been called *A Basic Reading Series Developed upon Linguistic Principles*, appeared as the *Merrill Linguistic Readers*.[30] The series begins with *My Alphabet Book*, followed by six readers, each with an accompanying skills book; all are for the primary grades. Pictures, considered distractors, are excluded in the readers; those appearing in the skills books are used to check on correctness of reading. Stories have ordinary settings and present realistic experiences and characters.

First, the child engages in many oral language activities while he learns the alphabet, first capital and then lower-case forms. He learns certain word patterns and uses them in carefully organized sentence sequences. He has early practice in writing. He learns a "spelling-pattern" approach and applies his knowledge of major spelling patterns. He masters a limited number of high-frequency words (sight words) that do not conform to spelling patterns developed early in the series in order that he may use material containing normal sentence patterns. He reads for meaning and has practice in interpreting, recalling, organizing, and drawing conclusions.

The *SRA Basic Reading Series*[31] is the decoding portion of Science Research Associates' *Comprehensive Reading Series* for Grades I through VI. The basic series is designed to be finished by the end of Grade II or extended into Grade III, according to pupil progress. The beginner learns the alphabet and the regular sounds of the language through the pattern of words with a common sound-spelling relationship. He learns the effect of altering one

---

30. Charles C. Fries, Rosemary Green Wilson, and Mildred K. Rudolph, *Merrill Linguistic Readers, A Basic Program for Primary Grades* (Columbus, Ohio: Charles E. Merrill Books, Inc., 1966).

31. Donald Rasmussen and Lynn Goldberg, *SRA Basic Reading Series* (Chicago: Science Research Associates, Inc., 1964, 1965).

element of the sound-spelling relationship at a time, advancing from simple consonant-vowel-consonant patterns to less frequently encountered patterns. He reads stories which emphasize the patterns he has learned.

The *Visual-Linguistic Basic Reading Series*[32] begins with *Alphy's Show-and-Tell Book*. There are accompanying transparency originals for use with the overhead projector and copying machine. In this program the child learns the names, not the sounds, of the letters of the alphabet and to recognize both capital and lower-case letters. He learns the shapes of the letters, letter discrimination, and alphabetical sequence. He learns to write the letters of the alphabet as well as left-to-right perception and orientation. At the time this chapter was written, no other information was available to suggest what direction the series would take from this point.

The *Structural Reading Series*[33] is described by its publisher as based on a modified linguistic approach. The revised edition continues the synthetic approach to phonics and emphasizes that words in groups must have significant meaning.

The phonetic and linguistic methods of teaching beginning reading achieve simplification in the initial stage by (*a*) limiting the number of sounds introduced, (*b*) using only monosyllabic words or nonsense syllables that involve known sounds, and (*c*) limiting words to those that follow phonetic rules. Sequence is achieved by the gradual introduction of the remainder of the sounds of letters and letter combinations and the exceptions to phonetic rules.

The modified alphabets.—At present, at least four modified alphabets are being used in the United States: the "Initial Teaching Alphabet" (i.t.a.), "Diacritical Marks System" (DMS), "Unifon Sound Alphabet," and "Words in Color" (modified by color in early presentation). The first and most popular is the "Initial Teaching Alphabet" designed by Sir James Pitman in England. His grandfather had devised an earlier form which was used in St. Louis,

---

32. James I. Brown, *Visual-Linguistic Basic Reading Series* (St. Paul: Education Services Press, Visual Products Division, Minnesota Mining and Manufacturing Co., 1966).

33. Catherine Stern, *The Structural Reading Series* (rev. ed.; Syracuse, N.Y.: L. W. Singer Co., Inc., 1966).

Missouri, and in Massachusetts. The present form was revised to provide easier transfer to the traditional orthography (t.o.; TO). The first experiment to determine whether i.t.a. was easier for young children than the traditional orthography began in 1961 and was conducted by Downing.[34]

The present i.t.a. has forty-four characters, each representing a single phoneme. The conventional alphabet has been augmented by additional characters for those phonemes which have no letter of their own in traditional orthography. In this way, spelling is made as regular as possible. There is only one form of the alphabet, and this is designed in lower-case letters, since these forms appear more often in reading than upper-case letters.

In 1964, Downing reported that the British teachers had used an eclectic approach and that there was no evidence to support a phonetic approach to instruction.[35] He emphasized that i.t.a. is a medium or orthography and not a method of teaching. The *Downing Readers*[36] begin by teaching sight words, but phonics can be introduced earlier than with other types of readers because the children seem to be ready for phonics in the consistent alphabet.

In contrast, the *Early-To-Read i/t/a Program*,[37] which appeared in the United States in 1963, begins with *My Alphabet Book* and places early emphasis on phonics. The readers include fanciful as well as realistic narratives to extend the child's world far beyond his immediate environment. In addition, children have many language arts experiences involving spelling and handwriting.

A second modified alphabet, the "Unifon Sound Alphabet," was developed by Malone, a consulting economist and executive director of the Foundation for a Compatible and Consistent Alphabet.

---

34. See John A. Downing, *The Initial Teaching Alphabet Reading Experiment* (Chicago: Scott, Foresman, & Co., 1964), pp. 3-58.

35. *Ibid.*, p. xvi.

36. John A. Downing and Faith Graham, *The Downing Readers* (London: Initial Teaching Publishing Co., Ltd., 1964).

37. Albert J. Mazurkiewicz and Harold J. Tanyzer, *Early-To-Read i/t/a Program* (New York: i/t/a Publications, Inc., 1963-64, rev. 1966).

The Alphabet was copyrighted in 1962.[38] Unifon, also called the "Single-Sound Alphabet," consists of a forty-phoneme alphabet without lower- and upper-case distinctions. Nine English spelling rules explain its use. It is designed as a synthetic adjunct spelling of English and seven other languages, including Russian.

It should be remembered that Unifon was designed to reform spelling and not for the teaching of beginning reading, though some teachers of reading believe that it may be useful. At present there are relatively few materials published in Unifon.[39]

The reader must learn the forty-symbol alphabet, the sounds for which each symbol stands, and the nine rules. While this has not proven too difficult for adults, children have needed considerable time, spaced repetition, and practice with written materials. As with i.t.a., readers begin personal writing early in the program.

The third modification is called the "Diacritical Marking System" (DMS) and was designed by Fry. Its purpose is to regularize orthography for beginning reading instruction by adding marks to regular letters to preserve basic word form. Later the marks can be eliminated as the reading habit is established. The DMS can be used with or without any special phonics instruction.[40] There are seven basic rules plus special treatment of *R*, of *Y*, and of consonant digraphs. The marks, which can be made on any typewriter, can also be overprinted on any printed material. DMS may be used with basal reader material.

The fourth modified alphabet was devised by Gattegno, who developed "Numbers in Color," based on the Cuisenaire rods, and then put "Words in Color" on the market in 1962.[41] For the entire class, there are twenty-one colored charts which use forty-seven sounds of English; each sound is in a different color. There are also eight charts in color called "Phonic Code," a systematic organiza-

---

38. John R. Malone, "The Larger Aspects of Spelling Reform," *Elementary English*, XXXIX (May, 1962), 441.

39. See Western Publishing Educational Services, Whitman Publishing Co., Racine, Wis.

40. Edward Fry, "A Diacritical Marking System To Aid Beginning Reading Instruction," *Elementary English*, XLI (May, 1964), 526.

41. Caleb Gattegno, *Words in Color* (Chicago: Learning Materials, Inc., Encyclopaedia Britannica Press, 1962).

tion of the signs (spelling) occurring in English, and "Word Cards" which introduce words representing different parts of speech.

The author uses color to make English regular without changing traditional spellings. The reader learns that a sound is always represented by *one* color regardless of its spelling. He reads the colored images, writes in black and white, and reads what he has written. He learns to spell as an integral part of the program. He uses an over-all multisensory approach. Toward the end of the program, he learns the names of the letters. The program is designed to be completed in about eight weeks.

The modified alphabets achieve simplification in several ways: the alphabet is redesigned to provide essentially a one-to-one correspondence between the most common printed symbols and their sounds; only one set of letters, usually lower-case, is used; or the regular alphabet is kept, but it is altered for pronunciation purposes through the use of color or superimposed markings.

The sequence, except for "Words in Color" and the *Early-To-Read* series, is often the same as that in basal readers, but the modified alphabets are generally adaptable to a phonetic or linguistic approach as well. All involve the additional step of transfer from the modified alphabet materials to those of conventional print.

The early letter emphasis approach.—The early letter emphasis approach is, as its name suggests, one in which the child learns the letters early in the reading readiness program. It is a visual-auditory approach in which he begins with visual discrimination of letters. Interest in this approach has been heightened by evidence from the research of Barrett,[42] Durrell,[43] and Kingston [44] indicating that letter knowledge may be a predictor of reading success. Durrell identified several levels of letter knowledge: ability to (*a*) directly match letters, upper and lower case; (*b*) match letters shown, upper and

---

42. Thomas C. Barrett, "Visual Discrimination Tasks as Predictors of First Grade Reading Achievement," *Reading Teacher*, XVIII (January, 1965), 276-82.

43. Donald D. Durrell and Helen Murphy, "Boston University Research in Elementary School Reading, 1933-1963," *Journal of Education* (Boston University), CXLVI (December, 1963), 3-53.

44. Albert J. Kingston, Jr., "The Relationship of First Grade Readiness to Third and Fourth Grade Achievement," *Journal of Educational Research*, LVI (October, 1962), 61-67.

lower case; (c) identify letters shown, upper and lower case; (d) name the letter, upper and lower case; (e) relate upper- to lower-case letters; and (f) write letters.[45]

In situations in which the early letter emphasis has been used, programs generally include non-symbol activities, oral language activities, and letter experiences associating grapheme and phoneme. The child receives direct instruction in puzzle completion, beginning with a few large individual pieces and solving more difficult ones with as many as fifty-four pieces as he gains skill.

Simplification is based on the single emphasis on recognition of letters and some sounds. Sequence is structured by orderly progression through seven levels of visual and auditory discrimination ability.

O. K. Moore's "Responsive Environment" has been a popular topic for feature writers in recent years. His work, done with three- and four-year-olds who learn to read by using automated typewriters, is based on the theory that early reading experiences are beneficial for the general intellectual development of the child. Experiments are continuing with children, including five-year-olds, at the Responsive Environments Foundation in Hamden, Connecticut, and elsewhere. Chall describes his program thus:

> Methods and materials used by Moore depart significantly from conventional approaches. The child starts by learning letters; then he proceeds to words and sentences. As he explores and strikes a key, the automated typewriter calls out the name of the letter or symbol that was struck. This goes on until the child learns the names of the letters. Then gradually a teacher, called by Moore a 'boothgirl,' takes him through a series of steps in which he reproduces on an electric typewriter the letter that is presented to him on a television-like screen. Later the child types words and sentences. He also reads from various books, including basal readers, and writes words, sentences, and stories." [46]

Simplification is achieved by initial attention to the letters of the alphabet. In the sequence, the child goes to words, then sentences. The method of word identification is to spell out words

---

45. Donald D. Durrell et al., "Success in First Grade Reading," *Journal of Education* (Boston University), CXL (February, 1958), 2-47.

46. Jeanne Chall, "Innovations in Beginning Reading," *op. cit.*, p. 94.

first learned rather than to study sound-letter relationships. Later emphasis is on meaning and application.

The Montessori method, briefly popular in the United States about the time of World War I, had a revival beginning in the 1950's. Like Moore, Montessori's initial concern was with the learning of preschool children. In *The Montessori Method*,[47] which focuses on the child from three to six, the author describes teaching materials that were and still are imaginative and interesting to the young child. Using materials designed to be self-correcting, the child proceeds at his own rate and sees his mistakes quickly. Montessori believed all the senses should be involved in the learning process. Long before Fernald experimented with the kinesthetic method, the child in the Montessori school was developing tactile senses as he handled letters of the alphabet cut from sand-paper. The pupil learned to name and write the letters of the Latin alphabet and to sound the letters heuristically; he learned to blend the sounds into words for objects that were familiar. There were games for the reading of words and for the reading of phrases. Reading was described as the interpretation of an idea from written signs, and the child had opportunities to learn to write the words he was learning to read.

The contribution of Montessori is reflected in the present curriculum of some nursery schools, in educational toys, in the content of readiness programs, and most recently in the methods and materials developed for use with the culturally disadvantaged child.

Simplification is achieved by beginning at the child's developmental level and allowing him to pace himself. Sequence is from what is considered simple (i.e., learning the alphabet) to the more complex ideas involving meaning.

INNOVATIONS STRESSING GREATER INDIVIDUALIZATION OF INSTRUCTION

Individualized reading.—In the late 1950's, attention focused on the individual, his ability for self-pacing, and his need for greater self-direction. The proponents of individualized reading were pub-

---

47. Maria Montessori, *The Montessori Method* (1965 ed.; Cambridge, Mass.: Robert Bentley, Inc., 1965).

lishing widely and their audience was large.[48] Initially, this program was suggested for readers who had mastered some of the basic skills. Later programs were developed for use as early as Grade I.

The materials for individualized reading are fiction and nonfiction. The reader uses whatever available books appeal to him and are at a reading level he can handle. The classroom in which such a program is used must have many books, including a great variety of titles and encompassing several levels of reading difficulty. One of the real contributions that this program has made to the teaching of reading is to focus upon and to emphasize interesting, challenging content.

The child participating in an individualized reading program usually begins by selecting a book he wants to read. He has an individual conference with the teacher, who records on his card what he is reading, his level of performance, and his strengths and weaknesses. Later, he has occasional individual conferences at which he may read aloud and answer comprehension questions based on his book. If there is need, he may meet with a group working to improve a particular reading skill.

The idea of individualized instruction is very old indeed. In America it was a characteristic of the dame schools. Throughout our history, emphasis on such instruction has reappeared at intervals. Nila Banton Smith explains that the present concept of individualized instruction in reading extends far beyond the earlier plans of permitting children to progress at their own rates. "It is interested not only in a child's reading achievement but also in his interest in reading, his attitude toward reading, and his personal self-esteem and satisfaction in being able to read." [49]

The growing interest in dynamic psychology has called attention to the importance of motivation and levels of aspiration in learning activities. Olson made several studies of growth, behavior,

---

48. Jeannette Veatch, *Individualizing Your Reading Program* (New York: G. P. Putnam's Sons, 1959); Alice Miel (ed.), *Individualizing Reading Practices* (New York: Teachers College, Columbia University, 1958); Russell G. Stauffer (ed.), *Individualizing Reading Instruction* (Proceedings of the 39th Annual Education Conference [Newark, Del.: University of Delaware, 1957]); Helen Fisher Darrow and Virgil M. Howes, *An Approach to Individualized Reading* (New York: Appleton-Century-Crofts, 1960).

49. Nila Banton Smith, *op. cit.*, p. 378.

and development of children from which he then synthesized the results into three terse terms: *seeking, self-selection,* and *pacing.*[50]

Groff also discusses the modern view of individualization and considers some of its special values for the child in reading: (*a*) it shows respect for the child as an individual; (*b*) it helps him develop self-management, and he sees that reading is done for one's own purposes; (*c*) he brings his own motivation to the reading activity; (*d*) with guidance he learns to select appropriate reading materials that fit his abilities and needs; and (*e*) with success comes pleasure in reading and a desirable attitude toward reading.[51]

The simplification in individualized reading as a method for teaching beginning readers is achieved by the child himself when he selects his own book. The one-to-one relationship between pupil and teacher likewise is aimed to eliminate extraneous and unneeded material. Sequence is provided as the reader, with guidance, moves from easy to increasingly difficult selections.

The language-experience approach.—The language-experience approach represents the integration of the four facets of the language arts. Experience represents the total background the individual brings to each new situation. In this approach there is no predetermined, rigid control over vocabulary; and the teacher, in order to provide sequence, needs to be consistently aware of how, in each learning experience, to enrich the child's knowledge of words. Allen has been the chief proponent of this approach to reading.[52]

In the early 1960's the best seller, *Teacher*, by Sylvia Ashton-Warner echoed the logic of concentrating on the pupil's own words and experiences for beginning reading material. She found that, to teach the Maoris in New Zealand, she needed to begin with such words as "truck," "beer," "police," and "mummy" because these

---

50. Willard Olson, "Seeking Self-Selection and Pacing in the Use of Books by Children," in *The Packet* (Boston: D. C. Heath, 1962), pp. 3-10.

51. Patrick Groff, "Individualized Reading in First Grade," in *First Grade Reading Programs*, ed. James F. Kerfoot ("Perspectives in Reading," No. 5 [Newark, Del.: International Reading Association, 1965]), pp. 7-27.

52. R. V. Allen, "Language Experience Approach," *Current Approaches to Teaching Reading*, ed. Helen K. Mackintosh (N. E. A. Elementary Instructional Service Leaflet [Washington: Department of Elementary-Kindergarten-Nursery Education, National Education Association, 1965]).

words were in the children's speaking vocabularies and represented pleasurable or frightening experiences.

In the language-experience approach the child begins by dictating "stories" to the teacher who records them, sometimes on charts for the group to talk about and read, then on paper for the author to learn to read. At this time the child's attention is called to letter forms and words that are alike or begin or end in the same way. He learns to read his story to the teacher and may read it to other children. He will probably illustrate it. He goes through some of the same steps that he would in individualized reading, except that he reads the material he has created. As he gains skill in handwriting and spelling, he begins to write his own stories, asking for help and instruction as he needs it. The teacher corrects errors in usage and spelling and points out the relationship between sounds and letters. Later the child takes into account problems of punctuation and capitalization. As he gains more experience with language, his writing becomes more mature. Stauffer gives some suggestions for starting a language-experience approach in the first grade, including a dictating cycle for the children, methods for vocabulary building, and word recognition training.[53]

Simplification in the language-experience approach is based on the child's own limitations in the production of materials to be "read" back to the teacher. Sequence comes with growth in the child's production and the transfer from reading his own productions to reading what other children have written. Still later he reads from conventional books.

Programed instruction.—Many early educators explored the problems of providing self-instruction and self-corrective practice materials. However, in discussing the historical setting of programed instruction, Dale observes that "the first use of the term *programed instruction* is associated with B. F. Skinner, with computers and *teaching machines*."[54] How programed instruction may affect the

---

53. Russell G. Stauffer, "A Language Experiences Approach," in *First Grade Reading Programs, op. cit.*

54. Edgar Dale, "Historical Setting of Programed Instruction," chap. ii in *Programed Instruction,* ed. Phil C. Lange (Sixty-sixth Yearbook of the National Society for the Study of Education, Part II [Chicago: Distributed by the University of Chicago Press, 1967]), p. 30.

curriculum is suggested by Lange: "... the nature of programing and the nature of schooling as we now know them are such that programed instruction can be absorbed in a small way without making much difference in school organization. Introduced in a big way it becomes a major innovation." [55]

The programed materials for beginning readers that have been developed up to this time use the phonic or phonic-linguistic approach. Some rely on programed texts, while others must be used with a machine. *The Teachall Reading Course* [56] uses a Teachall machine with 180 cards to teach 48 nouns. *First Steps in Reading* [57] is a primer designed for use by parents. It may or may not be used in a machine. *Dialogue I* [58] is a programed book to be used with tape recordings. The child learns phonics in an aural-oral course. *Lift Off to Reading* [59] consists of three cycles, with a teacher's manual for each cycle. Early in the program the child learns the capital letters, studies compounds (i.e., *ea, ow, ir*), learns the effect of final *e* on the pronunciation of internal vowels, learns alphabetical letter names, and learns the alphabet in order. Somewhat later he recognizes the uses of capitalization and punctuation, begins to use a dictionary, spells words related to reading material, and shows comprehension of stories.

Programmed Reading [60] is a series for Grades I through VI. It employs a linguistic approach. In the beginning stages, this series uses letters, discrete words and sentences, and simple, amusing illustrations, without a story content. The Sullivan materials include fourteen basic books and workbooks to be used with a special

55. Phil C. Lange, "Administrative and Curricular Considerations," chap. vi in *Programed Instruction, op. cit.*, pp. 147-48.

56. *Teachall Reading Course* (Washington: Publishers Co., Inc., 1962).

57. *First Steps in Reading* (Teaching Machine Course TM-002 [New York: Teaching Materials Corporation, Grolier, Inc., 1962]).

58. Andrews Brogan and Emily Hotchkiss, *Dialogue I, An Aural-Oral Course in Phonics* (Chester, Conn.: Chester Electronic Laboratories, Inc., 1963).

59. Myron Woolman, *Lift Off to Reading* (Chicago: Science Research Associates, Inc., 1966).

60. Sullivan Associates (Cynthia Dee Buchanan, program director), *Programmed Reading* (Manchester, Mo.: Webster Division, McGraw-Hill Book Co., Inc., 1963-66).

crayon the marks of which disappear in about twenty minutes, a feature which makes the workbooks reusable.

Simplification is attained by beginning with single and concrete tasks. Stories are introduced later, when emphasis shifts to comprehension skills. Sequence is controlled by moving from simple to more complex elements in very short, logical, and related steps.

INNOVATIONS IN SUBJECT-MATTER CONTENT AND ILLUSTRATIONS

Multi-ethnic programs received their impetus from widespread interest in the culturally disadvantaged child. By 1960, the Great Cities School Improvement Project headed by Marburger was well under way in Detroit. The original project involved 7 schools, 420 school personnel, and 10,400 children and their families. The budget was provided in part by Board of Education funds and in part by funds from the Ford Foundation.

Whipple [61] reported that among many materials designed to increase the child's chances for success in reading were those developed by the Writers' Committee selected to prepare new curricular materials for use with immigrants. After completing four studies related to the problem, the committee began the construction of preprimers. Later these materials were published commercially.[62] Both vocabulary and sentence patterns are controlled, and there is emphasis on phonics. There are tests of word recognition and planned oral reading, and attention is given to comprehension skills. The child has many language experiences. The lessons are similar in plan to those in good basal readers. Their content is related to the out-of-school activities of children who come from many different ethnic groups.

The *Miami Linguistic Reader Series* [63] was developed in Dade County, Florida, as a beginning reading program for bilingual chil-

---

61. Gertrude Whipple, "The Culturally and Socially Deprived Reader," in *The Underachiever in Reading*, ed. H. Alan Robinson ("Supplementary Educational Monographs," No. 92 [Chicago: University of Chicago Press, 1962]), pp. 129-36.

62. Writers' Committee of the Great Cities Schools Improvement Program of the Detroit Public Schools, *City Schools Reading Program* (Chicago: Follett Publishing Co., 1962-66).

63. Ralph F. Robinett, Production Director, *Miami Linguistic Reader Series* (Miami, Fla.: Board of Public Instruction, 1963-66).

dren. There are twenty-one pupils' books, accompanying seatwork, booklets, and teachers' manuals in the series. The materials were first used with Spanish-speaking pupils and were later employed in six other states and Puerto Rico as a part of a nation-wide Ford Foundation Project directed by Pauline M. Rojas. The series has been developed around ten major premises [64] that relate to the child's experiential background, his language patterns, interests, and need for success in reading. In beginning reading materials, focus is on the development of skills rather than on the use of reading. As the title suggests, the content is linguistically oriented.

The Bank Street Readers [65] are an "urban-centered basal reading program for the primary grades." The authors point out that they break with tradition in three ways: the city is their setting; in style they turn to children's literature; and the format for each selection depends upon its subject. Major emphasis is upon language experience. The books are not especially designed for culturally disadvantaged children, but they are planned for city children, regardless of ethnic group.

The first year of the *Multimedia Chandler Reading Program* [66] is aimed at urban children of a variety of racial and socioeconomic backgrounds. One of its unique features is its use of photographs of real children in real life situations.

Representative of recent specially oriented editions of conventional basal readers is a multi-ethnic edition of *The New Basic Reading Program* of the *Curriculum Foundation Series*.[67] Pictures and stories present members of many different ethnic groups as they participate in daily activities in the United States. Aside from this change in content and illustrations, such multi-ethnic series rely on the same organization, vocabulary controls, and methods

---

64. Ralph F. Robinett, "A 'Linguistic' Approach to Beginning Reading for Bilingual Children," *First Grade Reading Programs, op. cit.*, pp. 132-49.

65. Bank Street College of Education, *The Bank Street Readers* (New York: Macmillan Co., 1965, 1966).

66. *The Multimedia Chandler Reading Program* (San Francisco: Chandler Publishing Co., 1966).

67. Helen M. Robinson, Marion Monroe, and A. Sterl Artley, *The New Basic Reading Program* (Chicago: Scott, Foresman, & Co., 1965).

characteristic of the established edition of the basal readers to which they are related.

Simplification and sequence are attained in the multi-ethnic programs in the same general way that they are attained in the programs to which they are related, whether they are basal, language experience, or linguistically oriented.

INNOVATIONS IN TECHNOLOGY

The idea of using mechanical devices as teaching aids is not an innovation in the field of reading. For many years, both clinics and classrooms have supplemented printed materials with such audiovisual aids as films, film strips, recordings, tapes, overhead projectors, closed- or open-circuit television, tachistoscopes, and reading rate accelerators. These devices may be used with individuals or groups.

Among the advantages of teaching machines designed for individual use are: the learner can work independently; he proceeds at his own rate; and he has each response to questions checked immediately, so that errors are corrected at once. Numbers of these machines were designed for use with programed materials. Some are simple boxes which house rolls of "framed" questions and answers; these are usually rolled from the top to the bottom of the box, one question at a time, by a simple knob arrangement. A second turn of the knob reveals the correct response and perhaps the next question. When this idea first became popular, it was not unusual to find classrooms in which teachers or pupils were designing their own materials to put in candy or shoe boxes. Commercial machines are precision-made and generally require an electrical outlet.

There are numerous instruments now available which are designed for use by beginning readers. These may be grouped generally as teaching machines, quick exposure devices, tape recorders, computers, or combinations of two or more of them. Two such instruments that have received considerable publicity will be discussed in the following paragraphs.

The "talking typewriters" developed by Moore, in use at the Responsive Environments Foundation in Hamden, Connecticut, can flash a picture on a screen, identify it by saying the word aloud, and guide the child into spelling the word on a typewriter keyboard. A transparent partition separates the picture, the typing mechanism, and the typed copy from the curious hands of the child who has produced it. When the machine shows the picture of a dog and spells D-O-G, all the letters on the keyboard lock except the *D*. When the child hits the *D*, the letter appears on the paper in the typewriter. The keyboard continues to lock in proper sequences until the child has spelled out the word *dog*.

The IBM 1500 computer was first used on November 1, 1966, in a new first-grade room of the Brentwood Elementary School at East Palo Alto, California.[68] It is a windowless room with individual booths. Many of the one hundred subjects of the one-semester experiment (terminating in June, 1967) would be described as culturally disadvantaged. Half of the first-grade children in the school took all of their arithmetic and the other half took most of their reading instruction from the computer. The IBM Corporation has invested about thirty million dollars to develop computer-based instruction. The cost of the Brentwood first-grade experimental program was about one and one-half million dollars. During the experiment, there were more programers and machine proctors on hand than there were regular staff members.

In this program, the child wears earphones, observes images on a television-like screen and uses a light-projecting pen with which he is told to touch certain images as they appear, as a dog or snail. When he touches the correct image the voice says, "Good." If the child is incorrect, the voice says softly, "No," and repeats the original instruction. If a child makes several consecutive mistakes or does not respond at all, the computer sets up a distress signal on a monitor, and the teacher comes to help.

Computerized exercises and word games have been designed to teach the child how to read. He learns his own name at the start, hears words enunciated clearly, and proceeds at his own rate. The program is based on the concept of individualizing instruction.

The cost range for teaching machines is very wide. Some simple devices may be had for twenty-five or thirty dollars, while the

---

68. Ezra Bowen, " 'Hello, Jimmy,' said the machine, 'I've been waiting for you,' " *Life Magazine*, LXII (January, 1967), pp. 70-81.

most complex may reach thirty thousand dollars. Many companies have been attracted to the field by the government money the schools have to spend. The design and production of these instruments are in their infancy; the development and testing of materials for them have hardly begun.

Umans points out some of the limitations of machines. "Booklets and textbooks have the advantage of being portable. They may be carried to the library, to the classroom, or home. This cannot be done with a machine. A student can work from a textbook whenever he has free time; but he can use a machine only when it is available." [69]

As has been suggested by Burns, we now have the essential tools and new technical developments for improving the quality of education.[70] He notes the availability of centralized tape libraries, closed-circuit TV systems, electronic teaching machines, programed learning systems, computers for a variety of uses, and a flexible open-circuit educational TV network. Interestingly enough, most of these techniques and tools have been used, at least in a limited way, in the teaching of reading. The next steps are to determine the best uses of such devices and to improve the quality of content of those tools which are teaching instruments.

The Research Evidence

The results of innovations in beginning reading must be evaluated. Are current changes achieving better results than the older, conventional methods and materials for the beginning reader? Or will we find once again that there is no simple solution? Certainly this yearbook can offer no conclusive evidence, if for no other reason than that many projects are still in progress at this moment. There are several difficulties in obtaining reliable evidence to answer the foregoing questions, the strong and often extravagant claims made by proponents of innovative methods notwithstanding. Similar excessive claims have been made in the past for the very methods from which various groups are now changing. In

---

69. Shelley Umans, *New Trends in Reading Instruction* (New York: Teachers College, Columbia University, 1963), p. 114.

70. John L. Burns, "Our Era of Opportunity," *Saturday Review*, L (January 14, 1967), pp. 38-39.

chapter xi, Robinson discusses the inadequacy of answers found in published research and some of the reasons for this dilemma.

THE RESEARCH EVIDENCE: ITS NATURE

The most thorough-going recent study of the research on beginning reading instruction was reported by Chall.[71] She reviewed much of the research from 1910 to 1965 from several sources: the experimental research from classroom and laboratory, the findings from correlational studies, and the evidence from several well-known clinical studies of children who have failed to learn to read. As was to be expected, Chall found that many studies lacked at least some of the information that was needed in order to judge them: "why was it [the study] made; how the author defined 'reading'; what methods and materials were being compared; what the size, age, grade level, and other characteristics of the population studied were; how the author defined reading 'success'; what care was taken to assure comparability of the groups studied; and so on."[72]

In analyzing the studies she decided to give "priority to the authors' findings rather than their conclusions, and for a very good reason: Many authors drew conclusions that seemed to go counter to their own findings. . . . To counter this tendency, it is necessary to consider the author's conclusions in terms of both his findings and his assumptions."[73]

Chall concluded that the first step in learning to read one's native language is to learn the printed code for speech. She did not find that any one code-emphasis method (e.g., systematic phonics) was better than the others. She reported no evidence that either a code or a meaning emphasis produced greater "love of reading" or was more interesting to children. She noted, however, that the two kinds of emphases did produce different learning patterns. Chall cited some experimental evidence to show that children of below average and average intelligence as well as those of lower socio-economic background did better with an early code emphasis. She

---

71. Jeanne Chall, *Learning To Read: The Great Debate* (New York: McGraw-Hill Book Co., Inc., 1967).

72. *Ibid.*, p. 100.

73. *Ibid.*, p. 102.

also believes, on the basis of clinical reports she analyzed, "that a stronger code emphasis would help prevent reading failure, although never eliminate it entirely: There is sufficient evidence to show that such failure stems also from personal characteristics of the learner." [74]

While Chall took into account other methods and materials, she appeared to have special interest in the phonics-meaning debate. Her efforts to re-examine the data rather than to accept the researchers' own interpretations sometimes led her to conclusions which differed from those of the original investigators.

SOURCES OF RESEARCH EVIDENCE

Evidence from phonics stuides.—Many other studies have examined the use of phonics in teaching beginning reading. In 1958, Morrone reviewed 198 articles on phonics for a doctoral study. He found that no incontrovertible evidence was provided by scientific investigations of phonics in reading and spelling. Morrone noted: "Disagreement exists as to the approach and amount of phonic instruction teachers should utilize in reading; however, most of the scientifically accurate experiments show that phonics has considerable value to the learner in the reading process." [75]

Rudisill, investigating the interrelationships among phonics knowledge, reading achievement, spelling achievement, and mental age, found that a knowledge of phonics made a substantial contribution to achievement in reading.[76] In 1964 she reported that first-grade children, taught by a newly-developed combination phonics and sight-context-reading approach, vastly increased spelling and reading achievement as compared to children taught by "usual methods." [77]

Duncan's study compared two approaches to beginning reading

---

74. *Ibid.*, p. 84.

75. Victor Eugene Morrone, "A Critical Analysis of Scientific Research in Phonics" (unpublished Doctor's dissertation, University of Pittsburgh, 1958).

76. Mabel Rudisill, "Interrelations of Functional Phonic Knowledge, Reading, Spelling, and Mental Age," *Elementary School Journal*, LVII (February, 1957), 264-67.

77. Mabel Rudisill, "Sight, Sound, and Meaning in Learning to Read," *Elementary English*, XLI (October, 1964), 622-30.

instruction. He used two first-grade groups of more than a thousand pupils, equated on several variables.[78] The experimental classrooms used the phonics-first approach and the basal reader as a supplementary program. Control classes used the basal reading program only. All differences, based on the results of standardized tests given at the end of Grades II and III, favored the experimental group. Major differences were found in groups of average and above average ability.

Cleland and Miller compared the reading achievement of an experimental group of 112 first graders who used a basal reader in conjunction with a separate phonics series with the reading achievement of 112 first-graders who used the basal reading series only.[79] At the .01 level of confidence, the investigators found no significant differences between total scores of the two groups on a primary battery of the *Metropolitan Achievement Test*, although experimental boys scored significantly higher (.05) in "Word Knowledge."

Gurren and Hughes re-analyzed the data from the Cleland-Miller study and found that, in seven of the eight comparisons made, the analytic phonics approach was significantly superior to the eclectic method.[80]

Sweeney compared the effectiveness of the "phonovisual" method of teaching phonics with the basal-series-guidebook method of phonics instruction in Grade II.[81] He concluded that the former method was superior for improving spelling and word-attack skills.

From the U.S. Office of Education first-grade studies.—In the school year 1964-65, twenty-seven first-grade reading studies were begun, sponsored by the U.S. Office of Education. The co-ordinat-

---

78. Roger L. Duncan, "What's the Best Way To Teach Reading?" *School Management*, VIII (December, 1964), 46-47.

79. Donald L. Cleland and Harry B. Miller, "Instruction in Phonics and Success in Beginning Reading," *Elementary School Journal*, LXV (February, 1965), 278-82.

80. Louise Gurren and Ann Hughes, "The Cleland-Miller Study on Phonics," *Elementary School Journal*, LXVI (November, 1965), 87-91.

81. John R. Sweeney, "An Experimental Study of the Phonovisual Method of Teaching Phonics," *Ontario Journal of Educational Research*, VII (Spring, 1965), 263-72.

ing center for this co-operative research program was located at the University of Minnesota and served two functions: to maintain communication among project directors and to collect, organize, analyze, and interpret the common data from the projects. The study was designed to explore three basic questions:

(1) To what extent are various pupil, teacher, class, school, and community characteristics related to pupil achievement in first grade reading and spelling? (2) Which of the many approaches to initial reading instruction produces superior reading and spelling achievement at the end of the first grade? (3) Is any program uniquely effective or ineffective for pupils with high or low readiness for reading? [82]

All the studies were carried on for approximately 140 school days. All used the *Metropolitan Readiness Test*, Form A, and the *Pintner-Cunningham Test of General Ability*, Form A, in the fall. Many studies also included all or parts of the following tests, administered in the fall: the *Murphy-Durrell Diagnostic Reading Readiness Test* and the *Thurstone Pattern Copying and Identical Forms Test*.

The criterion tests for May achievement included parts or all of the following: the Word Reading, Word Study Skills, Paragraph Meaning, Vocabulary, and Spelling subtests of the Stanford Achievement Test (SAT), Primary I, Form X; the Gates Word Pronunciation Test; the Phonetically Regular Words Oral Reading Test; the Gilmore Oral Reading Test, Form A; the Gates Word Recognition Test; and the Fry Oral Reading Test of Phonetically Regular Words. The SAT appears to have been given to all pupils. Many of the other tests, when reported as having been used, were given only to a random sample of children involved in the particular project.[83]

In addition, some studies included the *San Diego County Inventory of Reading Attitudes*. Bond made four tentative observations at the end of the first year of these studies:

---

82. Guy L. Bond and Robert Dykstra, *Coordinating Center for First-Grade Reading Instruction Programs* (Final Report, Project No. X-001, Contract No. OE-5-10-264, U.S. Department of Health, Education, and Welfare [Minneapolis: University of Minnesota, February, 1967]), p. 205. This volume lists the twenty-seven studies.

83. Helen M. Robinson, Samuel Weintraub, and Helen K. Smith, "Summary of Investigations Relating to Reading, July 1, 1965, to June 30, 1966," *Reading Research Quarterly*, II (Winter, 1966-67), 63.

(1) There is no one method that is so outstanding that it should be used to the exclusion of the others.
(2) The effectiveness of any one approach appears to be increased when it is broadened by addition of other instructional components. For example, a basic program's effectiveness is increased when writing experiences are added, or a phonetic approach appears to profit from the addition of audio and visual instructional aids, etc.
(3) Specific approaches to first-grade reading instruction appeared to increase children's achievement in certain instructional outcomes but are weak in other outcomes. Another method may develop different patterns of growth. This observation gives hope to the possibility that we may find combinations of approaches that will encourage over-all balanced reading growth.
(4) As would be expected, there was greater variation between the teachers within the methods than there was between the methods. This again points up the importance of the teacher's role in learning.[84]

This latter point raises the important question as to whether the methods debate is of consequence and implies, perhaps, that pupil-teacher interaction should receive major consideration. The answers to the three major questions posed at the beginning of the study, as revealed by the data obtained from all studies, are reported by Bond and Dykstra.[85]

Data related to the first question indicated that there was sufficient uniformity in the relationships to conclude that no single method of reading instruction would by itself overcome the limitations imposed on children by deficiencies in any characteristic measured in the study. Likewise, no method was found to be singularly effective for pupils who scored well on any of the premeasures. At the end of first grade, reading is considered to be a unitary accomplishment based on accurate word recognition and associated meanings, unless the reading tests are incapable of differentiating different abilities. Class size, which varied little, bore no relationship to achievement. While younger children read somewhat better than their older classmates, the results may have been related to selective admissions to school. Teacher experience and efficiency

---

84. Guy L. Bond, "First-Grade Reading Studies: An Overview," *Elementary English*, XLIII (May, 1966), 465.

85. Bond and Dykstra, *op. cit.*, pp. 205-17.

ratings were only slightly related to pupil achievement. A fair amount of variation in pupil success could be attributed to pupil capabilities, such as visual and auditory discrimination, intelligence, and pre-first-grade familiarity with print.

The second question, which dealt with evaluation of methods, was answered by the conclusion that no one approach was so distinctly superior in all situations and respects that it should be considered the one best method or the one to be used exclusively. However, it was found that programs which introduced words more rapidly tended to enhance pupils' word-recognition abilities. Furthermore, it was found that a writing component is likely to be an effective addition to a primary reading program. The relative success of the non-basal reading programs compared to basal programs suggests that reading instruction can be improved. "Perhaps an instructional program which incorporated the most important elements of all the approaches used in the study would be a more effective method of teaching than any currently in use." [86] The achievement of girls was superior to that of boys, on the average, regardless of the beginning reading approach—perhaps because boys appeared to be less ready than girls when they entered school. Of special interest was the finding that pupils in some school systems became better readers than those in other school systems when all measured pupil characteristics were controlled statistically. It seems to follow that factors other than those investigated in the studies account for this difference.

The third question dealt with reading readiness as it related to methods of instruction. The conclusion was reached that there was no indication that approaches operated differentially for pupils with high or low auditory discrimination or with high or low ability to recognize letters. Of special interest was the conclusion that "a teacher who is successful with a given instructional program will be successful with that approach for pupils of varying degrees of readiness and capability." [87] The recurring emphasis on the importance of the teacher is of current interest in these studies as in others.

The U.S. Office of Education extended fourteen of the studies

86. *Ibid.*, p. 212.
87. *Ibid.*, p. 215.

through the second and third grades. Such continued investigations should be especially valuable, since one of the great weaknesses of general research in reading has been that too often it was characterized by a proliferation of bits and pieces looked at in isolation rather than as a part of the sequential development of the individual's reading pattern.

From the modified alphabet studies.—Thus far results of research on i.t.a. are inconclusive. The first formal reports were made by Downing, who summarized and reviewed i.t.a. research in Britain in 1964 and 1965.[88] Among his findings: "One-and-a-half school years after starting to learn to read the new alphabet, the i.t.a. pupils achieve significantly superior scores on tests *printed in the traditional alphabet and spelling*. The children who began with i.t.a. and later transferred to t.o. have read the latter with greater accuracy and comprehension than children who have been learning with t.o. from the outset." [89]

Mazurkiewicz compared the reading achievement of two groups, of about four hundred children each, taught to read, respectively, by using ITA and TO (t.o., traditional orthography).[90] He found the ITA population achieved significantly better on the "Word Reading" subtest of the *Stanford Achievement Test*, but no significant differences were found on the "Paragraph Meaning" and "Word Study Skills" subtests. When the study was extended into second grade, Mazurkiewicz reported the general confirmation of the earlier research.[91] The investigator found that the superiority of the ITA group in word recognition was not retained at the end of the third year. No differences in the use of the mechanics of reading were found between the two groups, and achievement in comprehension on a standardized test did not differ in the two populations.

In four of the U.S. Office of Education first-grade studies which

---

88. Downing, *op. cit.*

89. *Ibid.*, p. xxviii.

90. Albert J. Mazurkiewicz, "ITA and TO Reading Achievement When Methdology Is Controlled," *Reading Teacher*, XIX (May, 1966), 606-10.

91. Albert J. Mazurkiewicz, "ITA and TO Reading Achievement When Methodology Is Controlled—Extended into Second Grade," *Reading Teacher*, XX (May, 1967), 726-29.

evaluated the ITA medium, the conclusions were: no differences compared to other methods tests; results not always consistent; inconclusive at the end of Grade II; useful in combination with other materials. The real test is whether, by Grades IV and V, pupils who have used ITA can be identified as better readers than those children exposed to other methods.

Experiments using Unifon have been carried on in the public schools of Chicago and St. Louis and the Principia Lower School, St. Louis. However, the chief research which tested Unifon as a method of introducing beginning reading is in progress in the Detroit Public Schools from 1965 to 1968. It is being compared with five other widely different methods. One criticism of this study is that Unifon was not developed for the purpose for which it was evaluated. The author designed it as a permanent spelling reform. In using this alphabet in beginning reading instruction, the teacher must devise methods for making the transition to the conventional English alphabet. Unifon was not especially designed, as was i.t.a., for the reader to move from it to traditional orthography.

Fry's study comparing his Diacritical Marking System (DMS), described earlier, with unmarked books and with the Initial Teaching Alphabet (ITA) was carried out in twenty-one New Jersey first grades during the school year 1964-65.[92] The ITA group used the *Early-To-Read* series, while the traditional orthography group used the Sheldon readers (Allyn and Bacon) and the DMS classes used the same readers with diacritical marks superimposed on the words.

Among Fry's findings were that there was no statistically significant difference between the mean scores of any of the subtests of the post-test, the *Stanford Achievement Test*, and the *Gilmore Oral Reading Test* for any of the three groups. No method was better for boys or for girls, or for younger first graders or for older first graders. The variation between classrooms was much greater than the variations between methods. When this study was

---

92. Edward Bernard Fry, "First Grade Reading Instruction Using Diacritical Marking System, Initial Teaching Alphabet, and Basal Reading System," *Reading Teacher*, XIX (May, 1966), 666-69; "Comparing the Diacritical Marking System, I.T.A., and a Basal Reading Series," *Elementary English*, XLIII (October, 1966), 607-11.

extended to second grade, results were about the same as those of the first-grade study.[93]

From studies comparing other methods of teaching reading. —Much of the current research has focused on the comparison of two or more methods of teaching reading. However, it is very difficult to demonstrate that one method is better than another since, in any classroom situation, numerous extraneous factors operate during any period in which data are being collected. Reporting, even in doctoral dissertations, may omit kinds of observations and information that have, in truth, altered the situation. Careful supervision is needed to see what actually happens in the classroom.

In 1961, Allen reported a three-year study carried on in the San Diego area.[94] Three methods were compared: the basic reading approach, the individualized method, and language-experience approach. Each teacher who participated selected the approach that he understood best and that he had the materials to teach. Each teacher had a supportive in-service program. Allen reported that, when language-experience teachers ruled out all other approaches, they found their children made at least as much progress in skills measured by standardized reading tests as did children who had direct teaching of skills. He found that dealing with basic sight vocabulary on an individual basis, from oral language to written language to recall of written language, "usually results in recognition of high frequency words as a result of repetition. . . . Ceilings are lifted for all children at all grade levels." [95] This agrees with suggestions made by Bond and Dykstra in the final report of the Coordinating Center for First-Grade Reading Instruction Programs.[96]

Groff found relatively little research which compared the individualized reading approach with other methods of instruction

---

93. Edward Bernard Fry, "First Grade Reading Instruction Using Diacritical Marking System, Initial Teaching Alphabet, and Basal Reading System —Extended to Second Grade," *Reading Teacher*, XX (May, 1967), 687-93.

94. R. Van Allen, "More Ways Than One," *Childhood Education*, XXXVIII (November, 1961), 108-11.

95. *Ibid.*, p. 99.

96. Bond and Dykstra, *op. cit.*, p. 211.

or grouping in the primary grades.[97] Bohnhorst and Sellers carried on a study at first-grade level with one class.[98] The subjects were taught using the basal reader-ability grouping for three months; they then engaged in individualized reading the second three months. The investigators concluded that the basal reader-ability grouping produced significantly greater gains in reading than did individualized reading. However, they pointed out that growth in reading ability is usually greater during the first few months of the school year, whatever the method used.

Studies by Adams,[99] Braidford,[100] Izzo,[101] and Roston[102] yielded no significant differences between the reading achievement of subjects using ability grouping and those using individualized reading. Sperry[103] and Hilson and Thomas[104] reported that individualized reading was superior to ability grouping in Grade I. However, in the second study, the superiority was slight, and no testing for the significance of the differences of the scores was reported.

Bliesmer and Yarborough compared the results of a reading test given to 484 children distributed among twenty first-grade

97. Patrick Groff, "Individualized Reading," in *First Grade Reading Programs*, ed. James F. Kerfoot ("Perspectives in Reading," No. 5 [Newark, Del.: International Reading Association, 1965]), pp. 20-23.

98. Ben A. Bohnhorst and Sophia Sellers, "Individualized Reading vs Textbook Instruction," *Elementary English*, XXXVI (March, 1959), 185-90.

99. Phyllis S. Adams, *An Investigation of an Individualized Reading Program and a Modified Basal Reading Program in First Grade* (unpublished Doctor's dissertation, University of Denver, 1962).

100. Margaret Braidford, *A Comparison of Two Teaching Methods, Individual and Group, in the Teaching of Comprehension in Beginning Reading* (unpublished Doctor's dissertation, New York University, 1960).

101. Ruth K. Izzo, *A Comparison of Two Teaching Methods, Individualized and Group, in the Teaching of Word Identification in Beginning Reading* (unpublished Doctor's dissertation, New York University, 1960).

102. Sylvia W. Roston, *An Individualized Reading Program in a First and Second Grade* (Master's thesis, National College of Education, 1962).

103. Florence Sperry, *The Relationship between Reading and Achievement and Patterns of Reading Instruction in the Primary Grades* (unpublished Doctor's dissertation, University of Southern California, 1961).

104. Helen H. Hilson and Glenn G. Thomas, "Individualized Reading in First Grade," *Educational Leadership*, XVI (February, 1959), 319-22.

classes after receiving ten different initial reading programs.[105] Only two teachers taught pupils by each program. Five programs were analytic, five were synthetic approaches to word recognition. Individualized reading was one of the analytic approaches. When the mean scores of the synthetic program groups were compared with those of the analytic program groups, the majority of differences among means were found to be statistically in favor of the synthetic groups. Of fifty comparisons made among the analytic approaches, only six significant differences were found, all of which favored individualized reading.

Skolnick found no significant differences between the reading achievement of six second-grade classes given individualized reading and six involving ability grouping. Nor did he find, using the two approaches, any significant difference in reading achievement between high-anxiety and low-anxiety children.[106] Gordon and Clark found that reading was significantly superior in one second grade compared to another when both used individualized reading.[107]

After examining research in 1965, Groff concluded: "From this evidence the validity of the claim that individualized reading will bring on *greater* gains in reading than will ability-grouping does not seem to be substantiated. There can be little doubt, on the other hand, that the available evidence on approach has shown it to produce *as much* achievement in reading as does ability-grouping. Whether individualized reading develops better oral reading apparently has not been investigated." [108]

The first large-scale experiment in reading made with the aid of ESEA (Elementary and Secondary Education Act) funds began in the Detroit schools in 1966, after a year of pilot studies.[109] Six

105. Emery P. Bliesmer and Betty H. Yarborough, "A Comparison of Ten Different Beginning Reading Programs in First Grade," *Phi Delta Kappan*, XLVII (June, 1965), 500-504.

106. Sidney Skolnick, *A Comparison of the Effects of Two Methods of Teaching Reading on the Reading Achievement of High and Low Anxiety Children* (unpublished Doctor's dissertation, University of Connecticut, 1963).

107. Ira J. Gordon and Christine H. Clark, "Experiment in Individualized Reading," *Childhood Education*, XXXVIII (November, 1961), 112-13.

108. Groff, *op. cit.*, pp. 22-23.

109. "A Long Hard Look at Reading," *Grade Teacher*, LXXXIV (September, 1966), 110-13, 156.

very different reading systems are being tested over a three-year period. More than 2,200 children and 70 teachers began the program. The six systems under study include: Ginn's basal reader; Pitman's ITA; Harper and Row's linguistics; Lippincott's phonics; McGraw-Hill's programed reading; and Western Publishing Company's Unifon. Each began in first-grade classes in three schools in the city. Mahar, the director of the project, said, "We expect success with all six methods. Each has valuable ideas to contribute to our reading program. What we hope to do is identify the basic success factors and establish guidelines so that we can train teachers in the skills needed to enrich the language experiences of our pupils." [110] If the project achieves its stated goals, the contribution will be greater than that deriving from a mere comparison of methods. At the time of this publication, results of the study were not available.

During the academic year 1964-65, Sister M. Marita used thirty-two classrooms of first-grade children to compare reading achievement, using three classroom organizational patterns: Treatment One—a modified individualized pattern; Treatment Two—a three-to-five group pattern; and Treatment Three—a whole-class language-experience pattern.[111] One of the limitations of the 140-day study, pointed out by the investigator, was that the groups were not well matched, as shown by the pretests. But no other arrangement was feasible. Results include the following: There were no significant differences between Treatment One and Treatment Three on any subtests. Treatment One and Treatment Three were significantly higher than Treatment Two on "Word Meaning," "Word Study Skills," and "Arithmetic." There were no significant differences between treatment groups with subjects of mental age above seventy-seven months. With those of mental age below seventy-seven months, differences, in most instances, were in favor of Treatment One and Treatment Two. Differences in attitude toward reading were not significant among treatment groups.

110. *Ibid.*, pp. 110-12.

111. Sister M. Marita, A Comparative Study of Beginning Reading Achievement under Three Classroom Organizational Patterns: Modified Individualized, Three-to-Five Groups, and Whole Class Language Experience (mimeographed; Cooperative Research Project No. 2659, Office of Education, U.S. Department of Health, Education, and Welfare. [Milwaukee: Marquette University, 1965]).

Hayes and Wuest extended into the second grade their comparisons of ITA and three other approaches to reading: a basal reading program; a combination "whole word–phonic program with ability grouping, using a basal reader supplemented with phonics material; the phonic, filmstrip, whole-class approach; and the Early to Read ability-grouping program of ITA." [112] In the last program, children who used ITA in Grade I moved to the *Treasury of Literature Series* (Charles E. Merrill Books, Inc.) after completing the transition to traditional orthography.

The investigators found that results were not always consistent. For the low I.Q. level the basal reader program compared favorably with the other three programs. On "Paragraph Meaning" as measured by the *Stanford Achievement Test*, the basal reader group of the low I.Q. level was one-third of a grade higher at the end of Grade II than each of the other three groups at this level. The phonics, filmstrip, whole-class approach appeared to have a consistent advantage in the area of "Word Study Skills," except when compared with ITA for the high I.Q. level. The results for spelling generally favored both the whole-class approach and ITA. (Note: During the second year, about two-thirds of the ITA subjects were tested in ITA.) The results on "Paragraph Meaning" indicated that the whole-class approach and ITA programs were more successful than the basal reader program with high I.Q. pupils. Replicative and longitudinal evidence is needed to find out which of these methods of teaching beginning reading in best for which children. The investigators are continuing this research.

The purpose of the CRAFT (Comparing Reading Approaches in First-Grade Teaching) Project was to compare, over a three-year period, the effectiveness of two major approaches of teaching reading to disadvantaged urban children in New York City: the skills-centered approach and the language-experience approach. Each of these was tried with two variations, making four methods in all. These were described by Harris, the project director, as follows: (*a*) a skills-centered method using basal readers, with close adherence to the instructions contained in the teacher's manuals;

---

112. Robert B. Hayes and Richard C. Wuest, "ITA and Three Other Approaches to Reading in First Grade—Extended into Second Grade," *Reading Teacher*, XX (May, 1967), 694-97.

(*b*) a skills-centered method utilizing basal readers but substituting the phonovisual method of teaching word-attack skills for the word-attack lessons accompanying the basal reader; (*c*) a language-experience method, in which the beginning reading materials were developed from the oral language of the children; and (*d*) a language-experience method with heavy supplementation of audio-visual procedures.

The investigators,[113] in the introduction to the second-grade study, summarized the findings of the first-grade research in this way: ". . . comparisons between the two approaches (skills-centered vs. language-experience) and among the four teaching methods (basal reader, phonovisual, language-experience, language-experience audio-visual) were inconclusive. Instructional time was found to be an important variable related to results, and differences among the teachers in any one method were much larger than average differences between methods." [114]

At the end of the second year of the study, the investigators stated tentatively that the differences in the results of the two approaches and four methods will continue to be small and of doubtful significance. The wide variations in means of achievement within each method far exceeded the differences between the groups using the methods. The investigators concluded: "The second grade results reinforce the recommendations made in the first CRAFT report, that the characteristics that distinguish the teachers who obtain superior results from those who obtain mediocre results deserve to be studied intensively." [115]

A comparison of a linguistic approach and a basal reader approach was extended into second grade by Schneyer.[116] He reported, "At the end of the second year of this three-year investigation, the major conclusion is that when the two treatment groups are consid-

---

113. Albert J. Harris, Blanche L. Serwer, and Lawrence Gold, "Comparing Reading Approaches in First Grade Teaching with Disadvantaged Children—Extended into Second Grade," *Reading Teacher*, XX (May, 1967), 698-703.

114. *Ibid.*, p. 698.

115. *Ibid.*, p. 703.

116. J. Wesley Schneyer, "Reading Achievement of First Grade Children Taught by a Linguistic Approach and a Basal Reader Approach—Extended into Second Grade," *Reading Teacher*, XX (May, 1967), 704-710.

ered as a whole neither of the two reading approaches produced significantly higher spelling or reading achievement that was consistent at all ability levels." [117]

Sheldon, Nichols, and Lashinger also studied the use of basal readers, modified linguistic materials, and linguistic readers in Grades I and II.[118] The authors found all three of the approaches to primary reading instruction effective at second-grade level. None of the approaches was shown to be superior in all aspects of reading, although some significant differences were noted in some of the subskills. "When average achievement scores are considered, each of the three groups was shown to be reading at an acceptable level at the end of grade two." [119]

Ruddell extended into second grade a study begun in 1964-65.[120] He used twenty-four first-grade classrooms in the Oakland, California, Unified School District, representing a wide range of socioeconomic levels, to test the effectiveness of four reading programs. Program B consisted of a basal reader series. Program B+, developed by the investigator, was designed to stress language structure as related to meaning and supplemented Program B. Program P consisted of a basal reader series, different from Program B in that phonic training was introduced earlier and followed a different pattern from phonic instruction in Program B. Program P+, also developed by Ruddell, was designed to stress language structure as related to meaning, supplementing Program P. Attention was given to controlling as many variables as possible, and an attempt was made to reduce the Hawthorne effect. The investigator concluded, "Paragraph Meaning and Sentence Meaning achievement of second grade subjects at the end of grade two are a function of the control which the subjects exhibit over designated aspects of (*a*) their

---

117. *Ibid.*, p. 710.

118. William D. Sheldon, Nancy J. Nichols, and Donald R. Lashinger, "Effect of First Grade Instruction Using Basal Readers, Modified Linguistic Materials and Linguistic Readers—Extended into Second Grade," *Reading Teacher*, XX (May, 1967), 720-25.

119. *Ibid.*, p. 725.

120. Robert B. Ruddell, "Reading Instruction in First Grade with Varying Emphasis on the Regularity of Grapheme-Phoneme Correspondences and the Relation of Language Structure to Meaning—Extended into Second Grade," *Reading Teacher*, XX (May, 1967) 730-39.

morphological language system and (b) their syntactical language system at the beginning of first grade. A similar conclusion was drawn at the end of grade one." [121] He suggested that, possibly, the inclusion in readiness tests of items designed to measure the morphological and syntactical control of children's oral language would enhance the predictive validity of such instruments.

Wyatt, in a study of sex differences in reading achievement at first-grade level, concluded that neither the linguistic, the typical basal reader approach with ability groups, nor the sex-grouping approach was better for boys for any reading skill except word reading.[122] Girls achieved higher scores than boys only on the test of paragraph meaning. This was true in each of the three approaches. The researcher noted, "Although the differences were not significant, the sex-grouping approach seemed more effective for boys than the control approach (basal reader with ability grouping). The advantage was small but consistent. For girls, however, the sex-grouping approach seemed detrimental. Girls in the sex-grouping approach sometimes had lower scores on the achievement tests than girls in the control approach." [123]

From other studies in the primary grades.—Chall and Feldmann [124] explored the question: Within one given reading method, does the teacher make a difference in the reading achievement of her pupils? If so, what is it that she does that makes the difference? Although the investigators were well aware of the limitations of the study, they found several teacher characteristics significantly associated with reading achievement at the end of the first grade. "There was some evidence that teacher competence, a thinking approach to learning, a sound-symbol emphasis in reading, and using appropriate

---

121. *Ibid.*, p. 738.

122. Nita M. Wyatt, "The Reading Achievement of First Grade Boys versus First Grade Girls," *Reading Teacher*, XIX (May, 1966), 661-65; "Sex Differences in Reading Achievement," *Elementary English*, XLIII (October, 1966), 596-600.

123. *Ibid.*, (second item), p. 600.

124. Jeanne Chall and Shirley Feldmann, "First Grade Reading: An Analysis of the Interactions of Professed Methods, Teacher Implementation and Child Backgrounds," *Reading Teacher*, XIX (May, 1966), 569-75; see also Shirley C. Feldmann, "A Study in Depth of First-Grade Reading," *Elementary English*, XLIII (October, 1966), 573-76.

level of lessons were positively related to reading achievement for this particular sample of children and teachers." [125]

A factor analysis of the eighty-three teacher measures used gave five meaningful factors: (*a*) an "excellence in teaching" factor which was independent of reading method emphasis: (*b*) a factor describing a meaning approach to teaching reading, similar to the approach described in many basal reader series; (*c*) a factor describing a meaning approach to reading, with some mixture in emphasis (i.e., there was a sound-symbol approach mixed with the meaning approach); (*d*) a factor describing an inconsistent and confused approach to reading instruction; and (*e*) a factor which described an authoritarian teacher who used a spelling approach to teaching reading.[126]

Dykstra, probing the relationships between prereading measures of auditory discrimination and reading achievement at the end of first grade, found girls significantly superior to boys in the seven auditory discrimination skills measured.[127] They were also superior in reading achievement after a year of instruction. His study also indicated that the same auditory discrimination skills were related to the future reading ability of boys and girls.

Spache *et al.* sought to determine the effect of an intensified and extended reading readiness program upon first-grade reading achievement.[128] They reported: "The results indicated that the greatest achievement was attained (*a*) by girls, (*b*) by white pupils, (*c*) by control pupils [those not given extended readiness instruction] among white groups, and (*d*) by experimental pupils among Negro groups." [129]

Two major implications are "that the experimental readiness program was of significant value to Negro pupils, and that the achievement in the experimental and control groups was quite

---

125. Chall and Feldmann, *op. cit.*, p. 574.

126. *Ibid.*, p. 573.

127. Robert Dykstra, "Auditory Discrimination Abilities and Beginning Reading Achievement," *Reading Research Quarterly*, I (Spring, 1966), 5-34.

128. George D. Spache *et al.*, "A Longitudinal First Grade Reading Readiness Program," *Reading Teacher*, XIX (May, 1966), 580-84.

129. *Ibid.*, p. 583.

similar, despite the delay in the introduction to formal reading of the majority of experimental pupils." [130] The investigators also noted that the program seemed to have an insignificant effect upon those pupils who were mature enough to read early in the school year, and their participation in it was actually limited.

The *Frostig Developmental Test of Visual Perception* was designed to establish age-level norms for the early detection and diagnosis of difficulties in visual perception as well as to differentiate between visual-motor and perceptual functions. Olson used a population of seventy-one second-grade children to determine whether the Frostig test predicted specific reading difficulties (i.e., paragraph comprehension, word recognition, hearing sounds in words, visual memory, using reversible words in context correctly, and synthesizing words in context).[131] "The Frostig test of visual perception was of little value in predicting the specific reading abilities of the students tested in this study. The Frostig test of visual perception seems to have little relationship to either mental age or chronological age." [132] However, he reported that the coefficient of correlation (.386) between results on the "Position in Space" subtest and a test of reversible words in context suggests that this subtest has specific values.

Denny and Weintraub analyzed the responses of 111 first-grade children to three questions: Do you want to learn how to read? Why? What must you do to learn how to read? One-fourth of the children could give no meaningful reason for wanting to learn to read, while almost one-third of the responses were categorized as intrinsic, or learning in order to perform the act. About one-third of the group could give no meaningful reply to what one must do to learn to read. Approximately one-half of the answers were categorized as either obedience-oriented or self-directed.[133]

Robbins evaluated the program advocated by Delacato, using

---

130. *Ibid.*

131. Arthur V. Olson, "The Frostig Developmental Test of Visual Perception as a Predictor of Specific Reading Abilities with Second-Grade Children," *Elementary English*, XLIII (December, 1966), 869-72.

132. *Ibid.*, p. 872.

133. T. Denny and S. Weintraub, "First-Graders' Responses to Three Questions about Reading," *Elementary School Journal*, LXVI (May, 1966), 441-48.

three groups of second-grade subjects.[134] The experimental group used a Delacato-type program, the second group a placebo program, and the third group a traditional control program. Pretests measured each subject's achievement in arithmetic, creeping, general intelligence, laterality, and reading. As part of post-tests, all three groups took a reading test. Members of the experimental group were also tested in arithmetic and laterality. The findings revealed that the Delacato-type program did not enhance either lateral or reading development of the subjects and that the postulated relationship between neurological organization and reading could not be supported.

GENERAL COMMENTS ON RESEARCH

In the past decade, much of the research carried on in the primary grades has dealt with methods of teaching reading. The number has been bolstered by the USOE "First Grade Reading Studies" and their extensions into second grade. New questions have been raised about the appropriateness of reading readiness programs. Modified alphabets have been invented and are continuing to be evaluated. Research on programed reading materials and computer-based plans is in its infancy.

The research picture is not altogether an encouraging one. Barton and Wilder, in a study of (*a*) investigators engaged in reading research and (*b*) the results of their research, found that, while there was a great quantity, the quality was poor and it was non-cumulative.[135] Most observers have pointed out that one can, without too much difficulty, locate evidence to support almost any point of view, particularly in the area of methodology in the teaching of reading.

Little of the research in recent years has been conclusive; one study refutes another; the Hawthorne effect continues to plague projects; many of the studies are carried out (*a*) with a relatively

---

134. Melvyn Paul Robbins, "The Delacato Interpretation of Neurological Organization," *Reading Research Quarterly*, I (Spring, 1966), 57-78.

135. Allen H. Barton and David E. Wilder, "Research and Practice in the Teaching of Reading: A Progress Report," in *Innovations in Education*, ed. Matthew B. Miles (New York: Teachers College, Columbia University, 1964), p. 397.

small number of subjects, (*b*) over a short time span, and (*c*) with teachers often inexperienced in participating in research and sometimes poorly trained in the particular phase of the reading program under scrutiny. When an enthusiastic investigator becomes "emotionally involved" in evaluating a pet theory, he may fail to remain objective and uncommitted.

How then is a teacher or school to choose the methods and materials for beginning reading programs? He may need to look for the answers to several queries.

Is the problem under investigation one with which we are concerned? Has the plan been given a fair and adequate appraisal? That is, has more than one carefully designed study been completed? Have results been assessed by dependable tests and informal devices? Has the research been carried on over a long period of time, so that the superiority of its methods or materials are clearly established? What has been written about the plan in professional reading journals which would suggest its strengths and weaknesses? It may well be a waste of time for schools to adopt beginning reading programs that are clearly in an experimental stage.

What are the unique characteristics of the methods or materials that make them different from those of our school's present program? Does the new plan suggest that a change of objectives or school policy may be needed to put it into operation? Is this desirable or feasible? Can our school system meet the requirements of personnel, materials, and scheduling which the research plan requires? Are the subjects, geographic location, and socioeconomic factors in the study representative of those of the local situation? Must the plan be modified in order to use it in our situation? If so, will this alter its effectiveness? For what kind of child is this plan best? In order to meet the needs of a certain group of children, does this plan penalize other groups?

In general, decisions to use methods and materials that have been the subject of research studies should be based upon (*a*) the effectiveness of the plan as measured by adequate, carefully interpreted, objective data (for some investigations these data should have been collected longitudinally); (*b*) generally favorable analyses by reading experts; (*c*) appropriateness in terms of the school's objectives; (*d*) appropriateness for use with the particular school population;

(e) feasibility of putting the plan into operation, including adequacy of materials, space, and personnel; and (f) ability to provide for suitable, continuous evaluation of the plan during the time it is in use.

Innovations in Testing at the Beginning Stages of Reading

According to Davis, the three major roles that testing plays in reading instruction are: (a) to assess an individual's performance in reading at a given time; (b) to assess changes in the reading of individuals or groups over a period of time; and (c) to estimate the degree to which individual or group potential for reading has been realized.[136]

Harris has discussed the clinical tests which generally measure various components of the mechanics of reading (see chap. v). Some diagnostic tests, such as those by de Hirsch and by Slingerland, are designed to identify potential failures. De Hirsch, Jansky, and Langford, interested in predicting reading failure, carried on a study to determine the combination of tests, administered at kindergarten age, that will most effectively predict reading, writing, and spelling achievement at the end of the second grade.[137] The "Predictive Index" was developed to forecast reading and spelling but not writing achievement. The index includes a test of pencil use, a test involving a count of the number of words used in telling a story, a test requiring children to produce class names for three groups of objects, and tests involving word recognition and word reproduction as well as the *Bender Visuo-Motor Gestalt Test*, the *Wepman Auditory Discrimination Test*, the *Horst Reversals Test*, and the *Gates Word Matching Test*. The authors suggested that a letter-naming test also showed promise of having value.

The Slingerland tests are designed to screen out children of average to high intelligence who show indications of specific lan-

---

136. Frederick B. Davis, "The Role of Testing in Reading Instruction," in *Reading: Seventy-five Years of Progress*, ed. H. Alan Robinson ("Supplementary Educational Monographs," No. 96 [Chicago: University of Chicago Press, 1966]), pp. 178-89.

137. Katrina de Hirsch, Jeannette Jefferson Jansky, and William S. Langford, *Predicting Reading Failure, A Preliminary Study* (New York: Harper & Row, 1966).

guage difficulties in reading, handwriting, spelling, and speaking.[138] In the first test, there are eight subtests which check visual and auditory skills. The manual and supplement must be used to interpret the scores, for there never was an intention to develop norms.

Other tests measure the child's readiness for learning. The *Anton Brenner Developmental Gestalt Test of School Readiness*,[139] designed to be administered by the teacher, is predictive of reading readiness and number readiness, according to the author. It consists of five subtests: "Number Producing," "Number Recognition," "Ten Dot Gestalt," "Sentence Gestalt," and "Draw-a-Man." Administration time is, on the average, about five minutes. Being almost "culture free," it can be used in testing non-English-speaking children. It is most predictive when used with five- and six-year-olds.

Reading readiness tests.—An analysis by Harris showed that current reading readiness tests tend to include measures of three or more factors: visual perception, verbal comprehension, auditory perception, ability to identify letters of the alphabet and digits, ability to recognize words taught in sample lessons, and ability to draw or copy a drawing.[140] He commented on the relative inconsistency in the research as to which of these abilities are the most vital or essential. "As new tasks of a particular nature are developed, the usefulness of that kind of test may be found to have increased. For example, there has been considerable recent research interest in tests of auditory perception and visual perception, including new types of tests which require individual administration." [141]

What is the trend in reading readiness? Schools continue to use the tests of the fifties with adaptations or revisions. Among those in wide use are: the *Murphy-Durrell Diagnostic Readiness Test*

---

138. Beth H. Slingerland, *Screening Tests for Identifying Children with Specific Language Disability* (Grade I and Beginning Grade II; Grade II and Beginning Grade III; Grades III and IV [Cambridge, Mass.: Educators Publishing Service, 1962, 1964]).

139. Anton Brenner, *The Anton Brenner Developmental Gestalt Test of School Readiness* (Beverly Hills, Calif.: Western Psychological Services, 1964).

140. Albert J. Harris, "Evaluating Reading Readiness Tests," in *Problem Areas in Reading—Some Observations and Recommendations*, ed. Coleman Morrison (Rhode Island College Reading Conference Proceedings, 1965 [Providence, R.I.: Oxford Press, Inc., 1966]), p. 11.

141. *Ibid.*

(Harcourt, Brace and World, Inc.), the *Revised Metropolitan Readiness Test* (Harcourt, Brace and World, Inc., the *Lee-Clark Reading Readiness Test* (California Test Bureau), and the *Lippincott Reading Readiness Test* (J. B. Lippincott). The *Gates-MacGinitie Readiness Skills* (Teachers College Press, Columbia University) is one of the newest, with a 1967 copyright.

The *Steinbach Test of Reading Readiness* (Scholastic Testing Service, Inc.) measures ability to identify capital and lower-case letters, memory of word forms, auditory discrimination, and language ability in terms of comprehension and interpretation.

The Murphy-Durrell test can be used to measure achievement in distinguishing beginning sounds from one another and in distinguishing letter forms from one another. The Lee-Clark instrument tests visual discrimination in matching letters and words, vocabulary, and following directions. The Metropolitan instrument tests following directions, visual discrimination of forms, and number readiness.

The effect of early introduction of the alphabet has been to make letter readiness a large part of some of the reading readiness tests. For example, the Lippincott test uses four tasks as predictors of reading achievement in first grade: (*a*) identifying capitals shown: (*b*) identifying upper-case letters named; (*c*) identifying lower-case letters named; and (*d*) writing letters dictated at random.

Silvaroli sought to determine which combination of several readiness factors would predict success in first-grade reading.[142] He found that the measure of letter identification was the single factor most predictive of first-grade reading success.

In 1965, Barrett reviewed the literature on visual discrimination and its predictive relationship to first-grade reading.[143] He asked several questions. (*a*) Is a child's ability to see likenesses and differences in letters more significant than his ability to see likenesses and

---

142. Nicholas J. Silvaroli, "Factors in Predicting Children's Success in First Grade Reading," in *Reading and Inquiry*, ed. J. A. Figurel (Proceedings of the International Reading Association, Vol. X [Newark, Del.: International Reading Association, 1965]), pp. 296-98.

143. Thomas C. Barrett, "The Relationship between Measures of Prereading Visual Discrimination and First-Grade Reading Achievement: A Review of the Literature," *Reading Research Quarterly*, I (Fall, 1965), 51-76.

differences in words? He could not propose an answer from the evidence he located. (*b*) Are pictures and geometric designs valid content for reading readiness tests? The non-verbal visual discrimination tests examined appeared to be relatively good predictors of first-grade reading. At least this area warrants further study. (*c*) Do pure visual discrimination tasks have a higher degree of relationship with early reading achievement than tasks which combine visual discrimination with cognition or motor skills? Research on this problem is lacking. However, two researchers had reported that early reading achievement correlated at a much higher level with tasks that required visual discrimination and knowledge of letters than it did with letter-matching exercises. (*d*) Is there an optimum combination of visual discrimination tests for predicting first-grade reading achievement? Again, though studies were meager, the evidence suggests that there may be such a combination.

After examining readiness measures for predicting reading achievement, Weintraub concluded, "Various factors interact in the development of readiness for reading. It is unlikely that any one measure will be an accurate predictor." [144] This agrees with Johansson's findings in a study made in Sweden. Weintraub suggests that next steps involve (*a*) the development of better measures or batteries of measures, (*b*) the thorough investigation of the areas of attention and of oral lanugage, and (*c*) learning from children themselves how they reach readiness for reading. He believes careful, observational, longitudinal case studies may give the best clues.

Diagnostic reading tests.—The diagnostic tests are designed to determine correctable weaknesses; among such tests are Spache's *Diagnostic Reading Scales* (California Test Bureau), the *Gates-McKillop Reading Diagnostic Tests* (Teachers College, Columbia University), the *Roswell-Chall Diagnostic Test of Word Analysis Skills* (Essay Press), and the *Durrell Analysis of Reading Difficulty* (Harcourt, Brace & World, Inc.).

Other group tests, such as the *Phonics Knowledge Survey* (Teachers College, Columbia University) by Durkin and Meshover and the *McCullough Word-Analysis Tests, Primary Level*

---

144. Samuel Weintraub, "What Research Says to the Reading Teacher," *Reading Teacher*, XX (March, 1967), 557.

(Personnel Press) measure progress in specific skills. The *Standard Reading Inventory* is an individual reading test for measuring a child's frustration, instructional, and independent reading levels. It appraises reading performance in Grades I through VI. It measures four areas of reading: recognition vocabulary, oral errors, comprehension, and speed.

Designed as a predictive as well as a diagnostic instrument, the *Reading Prognosis Test* is individually administered to measure skills in language and perceptual discrimination. Weiner and Feldmann, in validation studies, reported that beginning reading and perceptual discrimination subtests were better predictors than the language area of the *Reading Prognosis Test*.[145]

Oral reading tests.—The two standardized oral reading tests in wide use are the *Gilmore Oral Reading Test* (Harcourt, Brace & World, Inc.) and the *Gray Oral Reading Tests* (Bobbs-Merrill Co., Inc.). The Gilmore test yields scores in accuracy, comprehension, and rate. The two major functions of the Gray test are to provide an objective measurement of growth in oral reading from early first grade to college and to aid in the diagnosis of oral reading difficulties. The test checks eight types of errors and provides suggestions for observations by the examiner.

Standardized reading achievement tests.—By the end of the first grade, what tests are used? Mostly the old familiar ones like the *California Reading Tests*, the *Metropolitan Reading Tests*, and the *Stanford Achievement Reading Tests* appear. They have been revised in the sixties with slight changes in content and format. The primary batteries of the Metropolitan and Stanford tests include other areas, such as arithmetic and spelling. In Grade III and above, the standardized tests often include vocabulary, reading-study skills, rate, locating information, and comprehension.

Among the newer tests are: the *Gates-MacGinitie Reading Tests* (Teachers College Press, Columbia University); the *New Developmental Reading Tests* and the *SRA Achievement Series: Reading* (Science Research Associates). The vocabulary tests generally

---

145. For discussion of the two tests, see M. Weiner and Shirley Feldmann, "Validation Studies of a Reading Prognosis Test for Children of Lower and Middle Socio-Economic Status," *Educational and Psychological Measurement*, XXIII (Winter, 1963), 807-14.

sample the child's ability to recognize or analyze isolated words. Comprehension tests usually measure the child's ability to understand sentences and paragraphs.

Tests to accompany basal reader series.—In the past ten years, there has been an increasing number of tests designed to accompany basal readers and to determine the level of mastery of what has been taught at several points, usually at the pupils' completion of each book in the series.

The tests that accompany the basal readers at the primary level often check the pupil's knowledge of letter-sound associations, his ability to note similarities and differences in letter sounds, his comprehension of paragraph meaning, and his reading aptitude.

Summary and Conclusions

This chapter has attempted to describe the major innovations in beginning reading. Most of them are too new to have been thoroughly evaluated, and the writer believes the answers are not yet clearly evident in the research that has been done. The most gratifying statement that can be made at this time is that many studies are being extended into two- and three-year investigations. If this marks a definite trend toward longitudinal studies, it is a firm step forward.

One characteristic of research carried on at the end of Grade I seems to be that the experimental group does better than the control group on tests of the particular skills which have been taught. Aside from the Hawthorne effect, such progress seems logical. The real test, however, is whether, in Grades IV, V, or VI, members of the experimental group maintain their level of performance or are superior in over-all reading achievement to members of the control group. Or are they superior in certain aspects of reading in the middle grades? Few studies of such longitudinal design have been reported, although Loban has shown that the plan is feasible.[146]

Many investigators have reached the same conclusion: there is no *one* method that can be used to teach *all* children to read. Investigators have established that wide differences are to be found

---

146. Walter D. Loban, *The Language of Elementary School Children* (Champaign, Ill.: National Council of Teachers of English, 1963).

within most of the individual approaches to teaching reading. For example, the variations in phonics systems are well known. Similar variations appear in the language-experience and the linguistic approaches. Proponents of individualized reading may combine work with basal readers and workbooks and devote frequent periods to group instruction. These combinations contaminate the findings of attempts to test a single method. Also, the variation between classrooms is frequently much greater than is the variation between methods.

New directions in research.—It appears that steps which should be taken to increase our knowledge of beginning reading include the following:

1.) New research must be designed at the primary grade level to explore a variety of methods with *all* types of children.
2.) Longitudinal studies should be designed to cover a minimum of five years.
3.) Further study of the sex differences in the reading achievement of beginning readers should be made, with special attention to teacher-pupil interaction and factors other than grouping which may prove significant. Wyatt's study of sex differences in reading achievement of beginning readers should be (*a*) replicated, (*b*) redesigned using another group of methods of teaching reading, or (*c*) perhaps extended as a longitudinal study. We need to know whether the sex-grouping approach would be consistently detrimental to girls, whether this difference would disappear in Grades II or III, and whether continued sex-grouping would be advantageous for boys in these grades. It is possible that such grouping would allow the boys to use reading materials which appeal more to male interests, such as stories involving adventure, space, science, and communication.
4.) Continuing research should investigate *combinations* of approaches that will encourage over-all balanced reading growth.
5.) The teacher's role in the learning-to-read situation should be evaluated. The questions asked by Chall and Feldmann in their exploratory study of the relationship of teacher characteristics and reading practices in the classroom should be asked again, and answers should be sought through more elaborate research. Little is known about such relationships, despite the fact that many investigators have frequently suggested that it is the teacher rather than the particular method that accounts for some of their findings. In the beginning reading situation, objective evidence should be acquired about classroom climate, the teacher's own enthusiasm, his expectations for the

pupil's success, his confidence in the child's ability, and his knowledge of how to help the child learn to read.

6.) Ways should be found for identifying children who learn best by different methods. Weintraub proposes, ". . . if more than lip service is to be given to the concept of individual differences, we must begin to explore ways of identifying which children learn best by which approaches. To this point, research has not addressed itself to any great extent." [147]

7.) Studies should be made which show the effects of various reading programs on the interest of beginning readers in learning to read and on their attitudes toward reading.

8.) In the next decade, it will be crucial for educators to develop evaluative procedures for judging the effectiveness of the "hardware" being developed to use with beginning readers.

New directions in practice.—The directions classroom practice in the teaching of beginning reading will take are not easy to predict. However, with the great variety of materials and methods available to the reading teacher, it appears certain that during the next decade:

1.) Basal readers will continue to be used in many primary classrooms. The content will change somewhat, probably in the direction of multi-ethnic material. Methods will be refined and more attention will be given to the early introduction of letter identification and letter-sound association.

2.) Teachers will make increased use of machines as they develop auditory and visual discrimination skills.

3.) Classrooms will build larger collections of library books for individualized or recreatory reading. Dictionaries for every child in the primary grades will be the rule.

4.) Interest in the linguistic approach for teaching beginning reading will continue, and the influence will extend beyond the level of word perception.

5.) Teachers will re-examine the reading readiness program in the light of new evidence, reconsidering its content, length, and relationship to success in beginning reading.

6.) Classroom experimentation with modified alphabets will continue on a limited scale.

7.) Programed instructional materials, in instances in which they are effectively designed and appropriate, will be used for the development of some reading skills.

147. Samuel Weintraub, "A Critique of Review of Phonic Studies," *Elementary School Journal*, LXVII (October, 1966), 39.

8.) More attention will be given to spelling in the initial stages of reading instruction.
9.) Expanded language experiences will become an integral part of most programs.
10.) Teachers will examine more objectively their own attitudes, their informal comments, and the general atmosphere of their classrooms and will be increasingly more aware of how these affect individual pupils as well as the group.

And, most assuredly, the teacher of reading will find himself adaptable to change, able to move in new directions thus far unexplored, flexible in using innovative ideas and materials, and undismayed because the easy, never-failing method of teaching reading remains yet undiscovered.

CHAPTER IV

Innovations in Reading Instruction: At Later Levels

HELEN HUUS

Introduction

This chapter of the yearbook focuses on the innovations and changes in reading instruction that apply to "later levels," which here include the fourth, fifth, and sixth grades of the elementary school, the junior and senior high schools, and the college. It also focuses on adult programs for the teaching of reading, including literacy training. The innovations are in the nature of approaches, methods, and materials which have not hitherto been used at these various levels for the teaching of reading. The changes include shifts in sequence and emphasis, as well as the use of various combinations of old approaches, old methods, and old materials as they have been applied to current needs. Unfortunately, few innovations appeared during the last decade.

In the 1950's, the methods and materials in the later elementary grades were not noticeably different from those of the later thirties. Interest in extending the teaching of reading into high schools and colleges was growing, with more attention to the latter than to the former. Programs for out-of-school adults were emerging as the awareness of the need for them developed, and programs in government offices were sparked by the Air Force Reading Laboratory in the Pentagon, which had become the prototype for others in the armed forces. Impetus to adult programs was given by the retooling of industry to peace-time purposes and by the increased interest in personal improvement as a necessary means of keeping up with the growing technology and of attaining a higher standard of living.

The excitement caused first by *Why Johnny Can't Read* and then by *What Ivan Knows That Johnny Doesn't* resulted in critiques, "then and now" comparisons, and considerable soul-searching by the schools. Modifications and changes in method followed, though not always in the directions advocated by the extremists. Anxious parents became concerned with college entrance while their children were still in elementary school. Professors of linguistics evinced interest in the contribution of their discipline to elementary-school instruction, just as their colleagues in science and mathematics had done before them.

Team teaching, which utilized groups of various sizes for different types of activities, was introduced. This necessitated adaptation of instruction and a shifting of teacher schedules. The new interest stimulated a reconsideration of grouping in general, and several plans evolved (see chapter vi). Experimentation with television teaching, programed instruction, and teaching machines began, and a few current innovations stem directly from this research. Sociological and anthropological research in communication and culture emphasized the influence of mass media, and the shift in the role of the federal government in relation to education resulted in the appropriation of funds for all levels of education, for the retraining of adults, for the upgrading of the disadvantaged, and for the development of libraries. And so, in the sixties, a few new approaches, new methods, and new materials were introduced into the schools, while many methods previously found effective were adapted and refined.

Following a brief description of the status of reading instruction at the beginning of this decade, the innovations and changes are described in three sections, indicating the direction of change (*a*) toward improvement of basic skills, (*b*) toward higher levels of thinking and learning, and (*c*) toward individual work.

The Situation in 1960

In the early sixties, the typical pattern of reading instruction at later levels was not very different in kind from the pattern before World War II. According to the Harvard-Carnegie study of 1961-62, the basal reading series and their accompanying workbooks continued to be the chief materials for teaching reading in the elementary grades.[1] The methods, as outlined in several reading series, empha-

---

[1] Mary C. Austin, "Reading Instruction in the Public Schools of the U.S.A.," in *Reading as an Intellectual Activity*, ed. J. Allen Figurel (Conference Proceedings, Vol. VIII [New York: International Reading Association, 1963]), pp. 244-46.

sized fundamental skills of word recognition, comprehension, and study, with slight variations among the series. The teaching of these skills comprised the basic program, and, at higher levels, the skills were adapted to the learner and the material. In addition, the total developmental program at the elementary and secondary levels was intended to include special help for retarded or accelerated readers, the application of reading skills to other school subjects, the use of library and supplementary readers, and a continuous evaluation of pupil progress.

The word-recognition skills taught in the primary grades were reviewed and extended in the later elementary years, with teachers giving practice in multisyllabic words, accent, prefixes, suffixes, roots, and dictionary usage. In the junior high school, pupils increased their competence in the use of context, structure, phonics, and the dictionary in order to become independent readers, and high-school students who could not apply the recognition skills in pronouncing needed words were given additional help. The same was true at college and adult levels; if needed, the skills of recognition were taught but adapted to the maturity of the student.

Literacy training, a special aspect of adult reading, necessarily included elementary word-recognition skills. By 1960, the Foundation for World Literacy had begun experimentation with television as a medium for reaching some of the ten million adults, ages twenty-five and over, who had not completed as much as four full years of schooling.

At the same time, the comprehension skills were analyzed variously by reading experts, and it was suggested that different levels of meaning could be obtained from the same material. Gray defined three levels of comprehension as (*a*) the literal, at which the reader determines "what the book says"; (*b*) the interpretive, at which a fuller and more penetrating grasp is obtained because the reader recalls related experiences, senses implied meanings, recognizes and questions the type of material, and identifies the author's purpose, mood, and attitude; and (*c*) the level at which the significance and implications of the author's ideas are grasped. Gray pointed out that the complete reading act also includes the evaluation of and reaction to the author's ideas and manner of presentation and the assimilation of these ideas with previous knowledge, resulting in "new insights, fresh ideas, and new organizations or patterns of thought." [2]

Reading authorities suggested incorporating all levels of comprehension skills into classroom instruction, but the fact remained that many teachers still focused on the lower levels—the literal and the interpretive—with less attention to the higher aspects of evaluation and assimilation.

The basic reading program at the beginning of the sixties had as its third essential the application of reading skills to the study of content subjects. The study skills included locating appropriate sources and material within these sources, selecting and evaluating the material located, noting salient points, synthesizing material from several sources, recalling what was read, and following directions.

Under conditions like those already described, many students learned to read, but there were still those who needed more individual attention than they had received, those who could profit from wider reading than they had been given the opportunity to do, and those who achieved well according to their grade placement but less well according to their potential. This was the situation when the decade of the sixties began, a situation in which the climate was favorable for innovation and renovation.

The Innovations and Changes

The most surprising fact, perhaps, is that there have been so few real innovations at these later levels. The new developments are more in the nature of adaptations than of radical departures from previous practice. The changes that have occurred tend to fall into three categories: (a) those which extend or refine the teaching of basic skills; (b) those which lead to higher levels of thought; and (c) those which adapt instruction to individual learning.

THE IMPROVEMENT OF BASIC SKILLS

The basic skills are the central focus of a sound reading pro-

---

2. William S. Gray, "The Major Aspects of Reading," in *Sequential Development of Reading Abilities*, ed. Helen M. Robinson ("Supplementary Educational Monographs," No. 90 [Chicago: University of Chicago Press, 1960]), pp. 13-19.

gram. Research to find better ways of improving these skills is crucial to progress, not only in reading but also in other subjects dependent upon learning from print. Aspects of comprehension, rate, and study skills as well as literacy (which is a special problem of adult reading) are treated in the following pages.

Comprehension.—Current developments in improving comprehension are basically an implementation of the aspects described by Gray. The reports of research and practice seem to focus on four factors: (*a*) the influence of linguistics as it relates to structure and grammar; (*b*) context as an aid, with the use of the "cloze" procedure as an instructional device; (*c*) the types of questions posed; and (*d*) the purposes for reading.

The first development includes emphasis on the structure of our language and on individual language patterns. It stands to reason that children will find it easier to read material similar to their own oral language patterns than material which is dissimilar. Ruddell's experiment with fourth graders bore out this hypothesis.[3] But should reading material be written at the child's level of speaking —using his grammatical constructions, his word usage, his sentence structure—or should it be written at a somewhat more complex level and the child be expected to grasp it (provided, of course, that the distance between the two is not too great for him to span)? How will a child learn to understand successively more complex levels of language patterns if he is kept at the level of his current knowledge? These questions can also be raised regarding the use of colloquial English, dialects, or substandard language in reading materials.

Other aspects of language patterns have also been studied to determine their effect on comprehension. Bormuth's recent readability studies show that both the length and the complexity (grammatical structure) of an independent clause affect the difficulty of comprehension. He found that the complexity or depth depends upon the number of grammatical facts the reader must hold in mind

---

3. Robert Ruddell, "The Effect of Oral and Written Patterns of Language Structure on Reading Comprehension," *Reading Teacher*, XVIII (January, 1965), 270; see also "An Investigation of the Effect of the Similarity of Oral and Written Patterns of Language Structure on Reading Comprehension," in Edward G. Summers and Billie Hubrig, "Doctoral Dissertation Research in Reading Reported for 1963," *Journal of Reading*, IX (May, 1966), 392-93.

until he completes the unit, as indicated by the number of word separating a word or phrase and its modifiers. Parts of speech also influence comprehension, and Bormuth found that the ratio of pronouns to conjunctions and nearly all ratios involving interjections were good predictors of difficulty. He also pointed out the need to measure attributes of prose style as they affect difficulty and to find features of language that influence comprehension in segments of text longer than the independent clause or sentence.[4]

Long words have often been thought to be more difficult than short words. The research of Coleman has corroborated this premise, for he found high correlations between difficulty and number of letters, number of syllables, and number of affixes, stems, and inflectional morphemes.[5]

Just what teachers can do to improve comprehension by giving attention to the features of the language being studied has not yet been demonstrated; research is needed to indicate the instructional procedures that will apply the contributions of linguistics to improve understanding in reading.

The second development is the recent attention given to context as an aid to comprehension, primarily because of the interest in the cloze procedure (see chap. vii for a description of this procedure). Cloze exercises are given to the pupils to complete and are then returned to them for study after being corrected by the teacher. Only a few studies have been made using the cloze approach to instruction, and results are inconsistent. Bloomer found that an experimental group which used the exercises made statistically significant gains in comprehension and grade-point average but not in rate.[6] This finding is understandable, for the exercises are more

---

4. John R. Bormuth, "Readability: A New Approach," *Reading Research Quarterly*, I (Spring, 1966), 79-132.

5. E. B. Coleman, "Developing a Technology of Written Instruction: Some Determiners of Complexity of Prose," in *Symposium on Verbal Learning Research and the Technology of Written Instruction, 1966* (unpublished manuscript cited by John Bormuth in "New Data on Readability," an unpublished paper presented at a meeting cosponsored by the American Educational Research Association and the International Reading Association in Seattle, May 4, 1967).

6. R. H. Bloomer, "The Cloze Procedure as a Remedial Reading Exercise," *Journal of Developmental Reading*, X (Spring, 1962), 173-81.

related to comprehension than to rate.

Ames found that clues for the missing words came from elements of experience, parts of speech, vocabulary selection, and the organizational pattern of the paragraph read;[7] and Schneyer, on the basis of his experiment, suggested that pupils apparently need to verbalize the reasons for their choices if the exercises are to function as an instructional device.[8]

The cloze technique seems to have possibilities for diagnosis and instruction that have not been explored. For example, asking an individual student why he filled in an incorrect word may enable the teacher to provide the kind of instruction that he needs. Instructional possibilities include the teaching of synonyms to fill a particular deletion and the provision of opportunities to learn clues for the selection of the most appropriate of these synonyms. Comprehension may be improved by attention to syntax and other clues to the selection of correct words to fill the deletions. The cloze procedure has elements similar to those of programed instruction, and adaptations could be made so that the cloze exercises would become self-teaching.

The third development is the renewed interest in types of comprehension questions, including an evaluation of the most effective sequence for presenting them.

One part of a co-operative reading project carried out by representatives of twelve school districts in Pennsylvania was focused on formulating types of questions which would require reading the material at various levels of comprehension.[9] Questions of three types were prepared for selections chosen from compositions submitted by junior-high-school students in the districts involved. The types consisted of (*a*) simple fact questions ("what the book says"), (*b*) questions requiring interpretation ("what the book

---

7. Wilbur Ames, "The Development of a Classification Scheme of Contextual Aids," *Reading Research Quarterly*, II (Fall, 1966), 57-82.

8. J. Wesley Schneyer, "Use of Cloze Procedure for Improving Reading Comprehension," *Reading Teacher*, XIX (December, 1965), 174-79.

9. South Penn School Study Council Reading Committee (Helen Huus, consultant), *A Handbook of Developmental Reading* (a publication of the Educational Service Bureau, University of Pennsylvania [Danville, Ill.: Interstate Printers and Publishers, 1961]), pp. 90-103.

means"), and (c) questions necessitating the reader's application of or reaction to what has been read ("what the book means to this particular reader"). Teachers who have used these questions informally suggest that they stimulate better reading.

The third type of question just noted was developed on the assumption that pupils need guidance in applying what they read to the solution of their own problems. This hypothesis should be tested to determine if such questions lead to changed behavior.

The relation between pupil response and type of question has been shown in an unpublished study by King *et al.*, based upon 144 observations in 24 classrooms. The authors' report concluded as follows:

> The teachers' expectations of pupils, as communicated through their questions, especially, strongly influence the intellectual effort expended by the pupils when responding. The interpreting, analyzing, applying, and evaluating questions tended to bring higher levels of response from children in both groups than the specific fact or clarifying questions. The experimental teachers asked more analyzing, summarizing, and evaluating questions than the control teachers and their children responded more frequently with higher levels of thinking.[10]

Ballard compared the effectiveness of guiding questions with that of motivating questions and the effectiveness of both types with that of reading without any questions.[11] He found that guiding questions were best for fourth- and fifth-grade pupils in understanding the entire selection and that motivating questions were no better than no questions at all.

Little has been done regarding the optimum sequencing of questions for discussion, although programed instruction must of necessity take the progression of questions into account. There still is insufficient evidence, but additional information regarding the

---

10. Martha King *et al.*, "Observations of Teacher-Pupil Verbal Behavior during Critical Reading Lessons," ("Occasional Paper Series," mimeographed [Columbus, Ohio: School of Education, Ohio State University, n.d.]), p. 13.

11. Grady Lee Ballard, "The Effect of Guiding and Motivating Questions upon the Reading Comprehension of Fourth and Fifth Grade Pupils" (unpublished Doctor's dissertation, University of Maryland, 1964), in Edward C. Summers and James Laffey, "Doctoral Dissertation Research in Reading for 1964: Part I," *Journal of Reading*, X (December, 1966), 175-76.

types of questions and their best sequence should be forthcoming in the near future.

A fourth development relates to studies of reading for different purposes. Good teachers have generally given pupils purposes for reading, but Anderson emphasizes the "unseen question," which remains unknown until the material has been read.[12] In meeting this challenge the reader prepares himself for reading by assuming an inquiring attitude, which not only aids in comprehension but contributes to his independence as well.

Smith conducted an elaborate study to determine the effectiveness of direct, planned instruction in reading for ninth-grade students who did not adapt their reading to purposes related to details, main idea, comparison and contrast, sequence, cause and effect, generalization, anticipation of outcome, sensory imagery, mood, characterization, and fact and opinion.[13] Those who received the instruction gained more in reading and in identifying appropriate purposes for reading than did those who were subjected to the incidental procedures commonly used in English classes.

The abilities to recognize purpose and to adjust rate to different purposes are essential to the mature reader. More attention must be paid to the development of these abilities if readers are to cope with the great amount of printed material that is constantly being published.

Though the developments to improve comprehension are more basic than startling, the work on linguistics, cloze, questioning, and purpose should be continued and expanded in the future in order that evidence may be obtained to indicate the best applications for instruction.

Rate of reading.—In the past, the improvement of rate has generally been confined to secondary, college, and adult programs in reading, for, until basic skills have been acquired, there seems to be little value in increasing the rate. However, the writer believes that

---

12. A. W. Anderson, "Directing Reading Comprehension," *Reading Teacher*, XIII (Feburary, 1960), 206-7, 211.

13. Helen K. Smith, "Instruction of High School Students in Reading for Different Purposes" (Project No. 1714, mineographed; University of Chicago, March, 1966).

even elementary-school children must read with enough speed that sentences and paragraphs hang together and that a selection can be seen as a whole rather than piecemeal.

Speed of reading can be increased merely by putting on pressure to read faster. Maxwell found this to be true in a recent experiment in which she instructed students to read faster on a test.[14] The gains were statistically significant. Her study suggests that speed on a reading test increases with strong motivation and that reported gains in speed may actually be the result of forcing. A second finding was that students could increase their reading speed in three or four periods of practice. This implies that speed may be improved in a shorter amount of time than previously thought. Further investigations of maximal effects of minimal instruction and of the permanency of gains are needed.

Another development in rate of reading concerns the need for flexibility. McDonald [15] and Sister Theophemia [16] have previously pointed out the need for flexibility in reading. Flexibility implies (*a*) adapting the method and rate to the style and theme of the author and to the background and purpose of the reader; (*b*) varying the rate *within* a selection; and (*c*) improving such skills as skimming and previewing, using format clues (spacing, italics, boldface headings), and using transitional words.

Braam reported that seventy-one college-bound seniors improved in flexibility as the result of attending a reading camp for six weeks.[17] He found a higher degree of relationship between famili-

---

14. Martha J. Maxwell, "An Experimental Investigation of the Effect of Instructional Set and Information on Reading Rate," in *The Philosophical and Sociological Bases of Reading*, ed. Eric L. Thurston and Lawrence E. Hafner (Fourteenth Yearbook of the National Reading Conference [Milwaukee: National Reading Conference, Inc., 1965]), pp. 181-87.

15. Arthur McDonald, "Flexibility in Reading," in *Reading as an Intellectual Activity*, op. cit., p. 82.

16. Sister Mary Theophemia, "Testing Flexibility in Reading," in *Challenge and Experiment in Reading*, ed. J. Allen Figurel (Conference Proceedings, Vol. VII [New York: International Reading Association, 1962]), p. 138.

17. Leonard Braam, "Developing and Measuring Flexibility in Reading," *Reading Teacher*, XVI (January, 1963), 247-51.

arity and speed than between difficulty and speed for flexible readers. However, he did not describe the methods which were used to attain the results.

In teaching for flexibility, it is important that pupils be given a variety of types of material to read (not just fiction), that various purposes be set up consciously by the pupils and the teacher in order to provide practice, that discussion following the reading focus on factors that influence rate and comprehension, and that checks of progress be made in order to tailor instruction to fit individual needs. McDonald has constructed a test of flexibility; Braam constructed two tests for his study; and Letson [18] has described some informal tests which teachers can adapt to their own situations.

The problem of flexibility is only beginning to be studied as greater depth in reading is expected and promoted. Whether this skill is primarily a matter of rate, comprehension, purpose, or higher levels of thinking can be debated. Certainly, all these factors are involved. This topic was arbitrarily placed in this section in order to call attention to the fact that merely increasing speed will not produce all aspects of reading improvement at later levels.

A radical departure that has caused considerable controversy, especially in the adult field, is the "Reading Dynamics" program, which focuses on speed reading.[19] Men and women in the professions, in business, and in industry need to be able to read quickly the large amount of material that crosses their desks daily, and many of them are seeking ways to become more proficient at this task.

The Reading Dynamics classes, which cater to this need, have had a phenomenal growth. The technique involves using the hands as pacers in training the eye to take in the ideas on an entire line of the page and to make vertical rather than horizontal movements of the eyes. In addition to class time, an hour a day must be spent in practice. Several evaluations of the program have been

---

18. Charles Letson, "The Relative Influence of Material and Purpose on Reading Rate," *Journal of Educational Research*, LII (Feburary, 1959), 240.

19. Evelyn N. Wood, "Breakthrough in Reading," *Reading Teacher*, XIV (November, 1960), 115-17.

made, including those by Liddle,[20] Taylor,[21] Thalberg and Eller,[22] and Spache.[23] In general, substantial gains in reading rate have been made, but, in controlled studies, the comprehension of the speed readers has not been superior to that of the control groups. Spache analyzed the physiological limits of eye movements and reached the conclusion that nine hundred words per minutes is the top speed possible if comprehension is to be maintained.

Adams, however, claimed that twelve students whose records were selected from the files of the National Reading Research Foundation read over fifteen hundred words per minute with comprehension at 70 per cent or more.[24]

It is difficult to make evaluations of speed reading because of the variation in the level of difficulty of the materials, the format in which the material is presented, the motivation and purposes for reading, the quality of the comprehension questions used, the standards of comprehension accepted, and the background of the subjects. There is a place for rapid reading and also for skimming, but the two are not synonymous. The research to date does not discriminate sufficiently between them. Furthermore, follow-up studies to determine permanency of gains have not been reported; therefore, until more information is available, claims of fantastic gains must be viewed cautiously.

---

20. Reported by Russell G. Stauffer, "Speed Reading and Versatility," in *Challenge and Experiment in Reading, op cit.*, pp. 208-9.

21. Stanford E. Taylor, "An Evaluation of Forty-One Trainees Who Had Recently Completed the 'Reading Dynamics' Program," in *Problems, Programs and Projects in College-Adult Reading*, ed. Emery P. Bliesmer and Ralph C. Staiger (Eleventh Yearbook of the National Reading Conference [Milwaukee: National Reading Conference, Inc., 1962]), pp. 41-56.

22. Stanton P. Thalberg and William Eller, "A Comparison of Two Widely Differing Methods of Teaching Reading Efficiency," in *New Developments in Programs and Procedures for College-Adult Reading*, ed. Ralph C. Staiger and Culbreth Y. Melton (Twelfth Yearbook of the National Reading Conference [Milwaukee: National Reading Conference, Inc., 1963]), pp. 112-17.

23. George D. Spache, "Is This a Breakthrough in Reading?" *Reading Teacher*, XV (January, 1962), 259-60.

24. R. Buchanan Adams, "The Phenomenon of Supernormal Reading Ability," in *New Developments in Programs and Procedures for College-Adult Reading, op. cit.*, pp. 133-42.

Study skills.—Attention has been given to study skills as well as to comprehension and rate. Beginning in the middle grades, pupils today are faced with a sharp increase in the number of texts and supplementary books they are expected to read, and, by the time college is reached, the reading-study load becomes extremely demanding. The pressure for academic excellence, the attention to greater depth in learning, the increase in the amount and availability of materials, and changes in the curriculum have accentuated the current need to improve reading-study skills.

The skills required have been redefined by several procedures. Textbook content has been analyzed, and the skills needed for mastery have been inferred;[25] tapes made by children who "thought out loud" when solving social-studics problems have been studied;[26] and logical deduction has been used. Only one new skill has been identified: adjusting rate to the purpose and the nature of the material.

The tremendous growth of school libraries has given impetus as early as the middle grades to the initiation of "research" papers. For such papers, pupils need to become increasingly proficient in locating information, a study skill that has long been recognized but not applied so much in previous years as it is at present.

The consistent application of a study-skills program in a high school becomes the concern of all teachers, and descriptions of all-school programs, such as that reported by Severson, emphasize the importance of having all teachers emphasize the same skills.[27] Herber confirmed this importance; when study exercises were given to students in both history and science, there was statistically significant growth in reading, but there was no such growth when exercises were used in history alone.[28] However, there is still resistance

25. Nila Banton Smith, "Patterns of Writing in Different Subject Areas, Part I," *Journal of Reading*, VIII (October, 1964), 31-37; "Part II," VIII (November, 1964), 97-102.

26. H. Alan Robinson, "Reading Skills Employed in Solving Social Studies Problems," *Reading Teacher*, XVIII (January, 1965), 263-69.

27. Eileen E. Severson, "A Reading Program for High School Students," *Reading Teacher*, XVI (November, 1962), 103-6.

28. Harold L. Herber, "An Experiment in Teaching Reading through Social Studies Context," in *Changing Concepts of Reading Instruction*, ed. J.

on the part of some content teachers who prefer to have these skills taught by the English or reading teacher.

Some study skills are common to all content areas, while others are unique to one area. In mathematics, for example, the technical vocabulary must be understood; the rate must be adjusted to a pace that allows for deliberation; the mathematical symbols must be translated; attention must be given to all the details; the relationships among words and between groups of words must be determined; and the graphic and tabular material must be interpreted. Students can draw pictures, construct models, and make charts, graphs, and tables in order to clarify their thinking. In this connection, Summers has presented a comprehensive treatment of the use of maps, charts and diagrams, tables and graphs, and pictures and cartoons as aids in reading.[29] While no research is cited, his analysis and suggestions may be useful to teachers at any of the later levels.

There is little research to identify the methods for improving study skills. Berg and Rentel, who made a survey of the literature on this topic, found that the materials they analyzed contained "preachments based apparently on opinion rather than research" and that both successful and unsuccessful students used similar methods.[30] However, their survey did indicate an advantage for those receiving instruction over those depending on trial-and-error approaches.

Some of the questions still to be answered, however, include: What skills should be taught? In what order and with what content should they be taught? Which methods are best for students

---

Allen Figurel (Conference Proceedings, Vol. VI [New York: International Reading Association, 1961]), pp. 122-24; see also "Teaching Secondary School Students to Read History," in *Reading Instruction in Secondary Schools*, ed. Margaret J. Early ("Perspectives in Reading," No. 2 [Newark, Del.: International Reading Association, 1964]), p. 82.

29. Edward G. Summers, "Utilizing Visual Aids in Reading Materials for Effective Learning," in *Developing Study Skills in Secondary Schools*, ed. Harold L. Herber ("Perspectives in Reading," No. 4 [Newark, Del.: International Reading Association, 1965]), pp. 97-135.

30. Paul Berg and Victor H. Rentel, "Improving Study Skills," *Journal of Reading*, IX (April, 1966), pp. 343-48.

of different intellectual levels? What is the place of individual and of group activities? How much and what kind of guidance is necessary? How is motivation for study developed?

Literacy training for adults.—At several periods in the history of our country, literacy training has been emphasized. As new waves of immigrants arrived and wished to become citizens, literacy training was often combined with the programs of Americanization classes. The current emphasis, however, has a broader scope, for, although new arrivals are fewer, vast numbers of citizens need retraining and upgrading in order to obtain jobs as automation increases and the need for unskilled labor decreases. Other reasons for the national concern with literacy stem from its relation to crime and to social welfare and from recognition of the fact that illiteracy breeds illiteracy. Furthermore, the need for literacy training in the emerging nations around the world has created an international demand that is unprecedented in scope.

"Operation Alphabet" represents an innovation in the use of television as the medium of instruction. This program to teach functional illiterates, identified as those not possessing fourth-grade reading ability, was developed in Philadelphia.[31] It was put on video tape, and, because the production was financed by grants, the tape was offered free to other stations. The program consisted of one hundred half-hour lessons, to be presented five days a week for twenty weeks. A study aid *(Home-Study Book)* was provided. An eclectic method was used, beginning with a sight vocabulary, and the level of reading approximated that of the first and second grades. According to reports of listener interest, ten thousand adults in a fifty-mile radius of Philadelphia listened to it. The program has since been shown in over one hundred cities across the nation.

The success of the program in Philadelphia has been judged informally by the number of copies of the *Home-Study Book* sold, by the reports of listener interest, by the number who sent in the tests included in the book, and by the unsolicited letters written to the television station. A doctoral study evaluating the success of "Operation Alphabet" in Florida was made by Bunger, who surveyed

---

31. *A Guide to "Operation Alphabet"* (mimeographed; Washington: National Association of Public School Adult Educators, 1963).

the work of 243 adults, 31 volunteer teachers, and 10 directors of adult education programs.³² She concluded that the program was not successful in meeting the criteria set up, that group work seemed more beneficial than individual work, that regularity of viewing did not assure improvement, and that the series did not seem to affect enrolment in literacy or adult elementary-education classes.

The problem of evaluation of "Operation Alphabet" is a knotty one, for, like other voluntary programs, it too has its dropouts, slow learners, and unmotivated. The lack of direct contact with students, the inability to pace instruction to individual needs (the *Home-Study Book* does attempt to reinforce the skills presented in the programs), and the lack of choice of time for viewing are other difficulties inherent in this type of offering.

Still other problems arise from the facts that the illiterates cannot read advertisements and thus learn about the course and that many adults are reluctant to admit their lack of ability to read. In order to overcome this obstacle, "Operation Alphabet" was advertised by radio and television, by displaying placards in stores, churches, and community agencies, and by placing advertisements in newspapers inviting readers to call the program to the attention of non-readers.

The level reached on the successful completion of the first series is only Grade II, which is scarcely high enough to allow much practice with materials easily available. "Operation Alphabet II," which has recently been released, is designed to extend literacy, for it encompasses the levels from Grades III to V. Upon completion of this series, new readers may begin to cope with parts of some newspapers and periodicals.

Until controlled studies have been made, it is difficult to assess the actual contribution of the program, but, according to the informal measures, it has had some success.

Another departure in literacy training is represented by "Operation Second Chance," which was an eight-week intensive program

---

32. Marianne Bunger, "A Descriptive Study of 'Operation Alphabet' in Florida and an Evaluation of Certain Procedures Employed" (unpublished Doctor's dissertation, Florida State University, 1964), in Summers and Laffey, *op. cit.*, p. 179.

conducted for approximately three hours a day, five days a week, by the New York City Bureau of Community Education during the summer of 1963. The method used for teaching reading involved basically an "experience approach," using discussion, key words written on the board, practice with word and sound recognition using these words, and making a story "edited" by the teacher and read by the class. Later, the story was duplicated and given to each student for his workbook. Teachers used topics which arose in the class, such as "Application Blanks," "Getting Along with Others," "Social Security," "Vacations," "Unions," and "Taxes."

At the end of the program, all of the eighteen illiterates had learned to read common signs, the questions on job-application forms, and simple sentences. The one hundred twenty originally classed as functionally illiterate (those not reading up to fifth-grade level) "made excellent progress, reading the equivalent of six-grade material, writing letters, and original compositions. Forty-nine received elementary school diplomas . . . . One hundred ten were screened for high school equivalency." [33] The report does not indicate the number who were accepted for or engaged in programs at the high-school level.

Public libaries are assuming a new role by sponsoring literacy programs. Two examples are LARK (Literacy for Adults and Related Knowledge), which was operating in seventeen states, and LIFT (Literacy Instruction for Texas), which had twenty-nine centers near Dallas as of 1965.[34]

New materials are being devised by many publishers, and lists of books for adult classes and new literates are distributed by the American Library Association's Adult Services Division.[35] These are but a few of the developments in a rapidly growing field.

This section has described some of the departures from previous practice and a few innovations relating to improvement in the basic

---

33. Gladys Alesi and Mary C. McDonald, "Teaching Reading to Illiterate Adults," in *College-Adult Reading Instruction*, ed. Paul D. Leedy ("Perspectives in Reading," No. 1 [Newark, Del.: International Reading Association, 1964]), p. 95.

34. Bernice MacDonald, "Libraries and Literacy Activities," *Wilson Library Bulletin*, XL (September, 1965), 48-50.

35. American Library Association, 50 E. Huron St., Chicago, Ill. 60611.

skills of comprehension, rate, and study and has described types of programs for adult illiterates. These skills form the foundation of a reading program, but, if the program ends at this point, it falls short of developing an individual's highest potential and thus reduces his ultimate contribution to the larger society. The next section deals with some of the current activities pointed towards the development of the higher mental processes in relation to reading.

THE DEVELOPMENT OF HIGHER LEVELS OF THINKING

In the past, the intellectual aspects of reading have sometimes been submerged by an immediate concern for techniques to upgrade students having low levels of proficiency. In the sixties, attention to higher levels of thinking in reading has been directed toward the fundamental processes of acquiring word meanings and of interpreting and judging content.

While most of the ideas are not innovative, it is the emphasis on the higher thought processes, the analysis and experimentation to define the aspects and to find the applications for instruction, that forms the departure. This section describes contemporary thinking in regard to the ways concepts are formed, vocabulary is developed, and critical thinking is applied.

Development of concepts.—Concepts have been variously defined: by Vinacke as "cognitive organizing systems which serve to bring pertinent features of past experience to bear upon a present stimulus-object"; [36] by Carner and Sheldon as "a construct which is the result of experience [and] may be fixed by a word or an idea, and [which] has a functional value to the individual in his thinking or behavior"; [37] and by Carroll as "recognized classes of experience" (with or without words). Concepts become associated with words through learning and socialization, and thus "meanings" of words

---

36. W. Edgar Vinacke, "Concept Formation in Children of School Ages," *Education*, LXXIV (May, 1954), 527.

37. R. L. Carner and W. D. Sheldon, "Problems in the Development of Concepts through Reading," *Elementary School Journal*, LV (December, 1954), 226.

become the accepted concepts.[88] In other words, concepts appear to be developed when past experiences are applied to a new object or situation in order to make sense from it and the idea, understanding, or general notion that results is given a label or name.

Carner and Sheldon described five types of concepts: concrete, chronological, spatial, numerical, and social.[39] They pointed out that the effectiveness of learning through reading is dependent upon the extent to which relations in or among the types of concepts are grasped and utilized by the reader.

The influence of experience was pointed out by Vinacke in his description of how concepts are learned.[40] The child builds up experiences with objects and learns to deal with them in terms of their properties by manipulation, observation, or use. At the younger ages, inductive procedures are superior, in which several experiences with an object lead the child to classify into groups, to hypothesize, to identify, and to define. Later, when he is exposed to the ingredients, he can generalize, symbolize, and apply. Still later, when he shifts from inductive to deductive methods, he can recognize the particulars in relation to the generalization and can apply generalizations appropriate to new situations. Important in this process is the acquisition of the vocabulary necessary for the manipulation and communication of ideas.

The first task of the teacher in concept formation is to provide concrete experiences by arranging many and varied opportunities for children to meet new situations at first hand. In instances in which vicarious experiences are required, they should be as vivid as the whole gamut of visual materials can make them.

The second teaching task is helping pupils learn to abstract from their images and experiences, by first noting differentiating properties, then classifying them into groups on the basis of similar properties, and finally labeling the groups. Verbalization at this level is necessary and should be encouraged.

The third task is the development of the ability to generalize

---

38. John B. Carroll, "Words, Meanings, and Concepts," *Harvard Educational Review*, XXXIV (Spring, 1964), 178-202.

39. Carner and Sheldon, *op. cit.*

40. Vinacke, *op. cit.*, pp. 532-34.

from the abstractions, to associate and make connections between known abstractions which pupils can then apply to new situations.

But the sequence is not complete until the student can apply what he has learned (generalizations) to new situations. When he has learned how to apply concepts, he can continue developing his own concepts independently.

While this is a rather sketchy outline, the possibilities of a sequence should be clear. Intuitively good teachers have devised instructional procedures in the past; today attempts to analyze strategies are being made in order that sequential steps to learning can be facilitated.

Vocabulary development.—The contemporary emphasis on vocabulary development is especially apparent at the high-school level, as students prepare for college entrance; some high schools have set up special classes for vocabulary improvement. The need is twofold: (*a*) to increase the size of the vocabulary and (*b*) to improve the precision with which words are used.

At the elementary level, too, it is important to extend the vocabulary of pupils. This raises the question of vocabulary control in textbooks for this level. The strictly controlled middle-grade readers have been criticized as limiting, yet the new-word load of any book cannot exceed the reader's ability to gain meaning from it. To what extent should control be maintained, and how many new words can pupils learn? Should vocabulary control be used in technical subjects like mathematics and science as well as in literature, and how can the optimal level of vocabulary increase be established?

Methods for improving vocabulary have been outlined by many writers in the field who suggest that instruction is essential for improvement. For those who wish practical suggestions, the comprehensive bibliography compiled by Dale and Razik contains references to 3,125 research studies and articles, including 375 references to studies on methods for developing vocabulary.[41]

In spite of the number of vocabulary studies that have been reported, the testing of earlier views still needs to be done, and

---

41. Edgar Dale and Taher Razik, *Bibliography of Vocabulary Studies*, (2nd rev. ed.; Columbus, Ohio: Bureau of Research and Service, Ohio State University, 1963).

innovations need to be introduced that will improve instruction in this vital area.

Critical reading.—The need for critical reading in our contemporary culture has not been questioned. But there has been little agreement concerning the attributes of critical reading, and the term has been confused with vague descriptions of creative and interpretive reading.

Definitions of critical reading include those by Smith, who defined it as "the kind of reading done when personal judgment and evaluation are involved"; [42] by Huus, who viewed it as requiring "evaluation of the material, comparing it with known standards and norms, and concluding or acting upon the judgment"; [43] and by Ennis, who described it as the "correct assessing of statements." [44] Common to all of these is an appraisal of worth, value, or truth that goes beyond mere recognition or interpreted information.

Ellinger and her colleagues indicated three components of critical reading (and the several subskills involved in each) in a classification as follows: (*a*) judging the reliability of information, detecting material fallacies, discovering unstated premises, recognizing persuasive uses of words, and drawing conclusions (semantics and logic); (*b*) selecting relevant information, comparing information from multiple sources, evaluating qualifications of the author, and recognizing adequacy of information (general authenticity); and (*c*) interpreting figurative language, evaluating use of literary devices, evaluating characterization, theme, and plot, and developing criteria for evaluating form (literary analysis).[45] This schema formed the basis for developing tests of critical reading.

Another approach to an analysis of critical reading is presented by Schick in his report on the reading program at DePaul Univer-

42. Nila Banton Smith, "Reading for Depth," in *Reading and Inquiry*, ed. J. Allen Figurel (Proceedings of the Annual Convention, Vol. X [Newark, Del.: International Reading Association, 1965]), p. 118.

43. Helen Huus, "Critical and Creative Reading," *ibid.*, p. 115.

44. Robert H. Ennis, "A Concept of Critical Thinking," *Harvard Educational Review*, XXXII (Winter, 1962), 81.

45. Bernice D. Ellinger *et al.*, "Development and Refinement of a Test of Critical Reading Ability of Elementary School Children" ("Occasional Papers Series," No. 67-102, mimeographed [Columbus, Ohio: School of Education, Ohio State University, February, 1967]).

sity.⁴⁶ Five levels of thinking-skills, each with accompanying clues, were designated: (*a*) recognizing the author's deductive conclusions or inferring them when facts are presented inductively with clues to alert the reader, like *therefore, hence, thus, so, then,* and *in conclusion*; (*b*) recognizing statements of positive judgment given in negative form, in a kind of reverse cause-effect; (*c*) recognizing the contrary proposition, using *but*; (*d*) recognizing the contradictory proposition, using *however*; and (*e*) recognizing the dilemma or paradox, using *since, because,* or *nevertheless*. Learning the linguistic relationships imposed by these and other connectives is one step in the development of critical reading.

Even these few examples of analysis suggest that critical reading is a complex process and imply that various aspects must be considered if it is to be taught. Strang, McCullough, and Traxler pointed out five errors that occur in critical thinking: (*a*) going beyond the facts in making unwarranted generalizations, (*b*) depending on a single source, (*c*) attributing results to a single cause, (*d*) oversimplifying a situation by describing it as "either/or" or as all black or all white, and (*e*) not recognizing the different meanings that words have in different contexts.⁴⁷

The literature provides few guidelines and little assistance for developing instructional procedures. However, a recent study was conducted by Wolf and her colleagues at Ohio State University to determine whether or not children in grades one to six could learn to read critically.⁴⁸ For the experimental group, twelve units were prepared on skills of critical reading, identified under such headings as semantics, logic, authenticity, literary criticism, and the like. For the second group (the children's literature group), lessons also were prepared, using a wide variety of children's books in social studies, mathematics, creative arts, science, and literature. Tests

---

46. George D. Schick, "Diversity in College Reading Programs," in *College-Adult Reading Instruction, op. cit.,* pp. 21-22.

47. Ruth Strang, Constance McCullough, and Arthur E. Traxler, *The Improvement of Reading* (New York: McGraw-Hill Book Co., Inc., 1961), pp. 385-86.

48. Willavene Wolf *et al.,* "Teaching Critical Reading to Elementary School Children" ("Occasional Papers Series," No. 67-101, mimeographed [Columbus, Ohio: School of Education, Ohio State University, 1967]).

of critical reading were developed (see Ellinger, footnote 45), and pre- and post-test scores were compared. The conclusions indicate, in general, that the groups receiving instruction in critical reading did better than the children's literature group, that teaching children to apply the rules of logic is an effective means of increasing critical reading ability, and that there were no statistically significant differences in general reading between the groups except in Grade I, in which the critical reading group did better than the children's literature group at a marginal level of significance.

A report by Howards indicates some instructional procedures for use in the higher grades.[49] To teach propaganda techniques, he used magazine, newspaper, and television ads, then had the students write some ads of their own. Another technique, which he utilized during a presidential campaign, involved newspaper analysis. Each student in the class subscribed to one newspaper for thirty days, tabulated the amount of news space, feature space, editorial space, and picture space alloted to each candidate, then analyzed the results. In the group, twelve different newspapers from different parts of the country were included. The biases of the papers were inferred and compared with the election returns from the area covered by each newspaper.

Burton showed how the acquisition of the higher levels of skill requires a mastery of the prior levels.[50] He analyzed three sets of abilities needed for the reading of literature, which he defined as "those genres which have reference to the world of imagination, of fiction." The first set, needed for "imaginative entry into work," can be promoted by selecting for study those works which allow students to use their experiences as the "touchstone," by helping students think about their experiences as related to the work, and by helping them understand the functions of literary forms. The establishment of time and place setting, the general context, the characters, and the tone may present obstacles that must be overcome by the students.

---

49. Melvin Howards, "Ways and Means of Improving Critical Reading Skills," in *Reading and Inquiry, op. cit.*, p. 126.

50. Dwight L. Burton, "Teaching Students to Read Literature," in *Reading Instruction in Secondary Schools, op. cit.*, pp. 87-100.

The second set of abilities, needed for "perception of meaning and central purpose," includes those that enable the student to organize the work, to proceed from its particulars to the universal, and to develop hypotheses relating to individual parts, the total allegorical or symbolic framework, and the point of view.

In the third set are those needed for "perception of artistic unity and significance," and students must be led to see the similarity to life (not life itself) of characters, descriptions, and plots and to recognize discordance in the unity of the total work.

The complexity of skills needed for this penetration into reading lessons, propaganda, and literature requires intelligent planning and logical arrangement of learning activities by teachers. The development of higher-level skills begins with concrete experiences basic to concept formation and with labels for these experiences that accumulate to form the vocabulary; it culminates with the evaluation of the truth, value, or worth of the material read.

THE EMPHASIS ON INDIVIDUAL WORK

The emphasis on methods, materials, and machines for individual learning is one of the innovations arising from the self-teaching courses designed during World War II for the United States Armed Forces Institute (USAFI), from the interest in how-to-do-it programs, and from the development of individualized reading.

The advantages of individual work lie in its adaptation to individual interests and to individual rate and level of learning and in the flexibility allowed in the case of students who must interrupt their education because of illness, economic considerations, or other factors.

The materials have usually been developed to be followed in a specific manner, such as checking comprehension, reinforcing the learning of a word-recognition skill, giving practice in reading new words at sight, and the like. Included in this group are workbooks accompanying the basal texts, skill-texts independent of another book, kits of various types, trade books, teacher-made materials, programed courses, and computer programs.

There is little that is innovative in the printed materials except for refinement of purposes, an improvement in the quality of exercises, and, in one skill-text, the introduction of a unit approach with a story serving as the springboard to related selections in social studies, science, and mathematics.[51] For each selection, skills appropriate to the type of content are developed; interspersed between units are exercises on the common reading skills. The comprehension exercises emphasize interpretation, critical and creative reading, and specific skills for the content areas (*e.g.*, classifying, explaining processes, and problem-solving in science.)

Library books.—An all-school program at any level should include not only attention to the basic reading skills and to their application to the various subjects but also to the students' reading of library books for personal purposes, including that of enjoyment. It is interesting that greater motivation for outside reading is needed at the junior-high-school level than at the elementary. This situation may arise from the increased independence of adolescents, which allows more competition for their time; therefore, more emphasis must be placed on enticing them to read than is needed in the case of younger children. Reading may have less status, perhaps, than more active and social types of recreation. Furthermore, those students who find it difficult to make sense of what they are given or encouraged to read may reject reading in favor of activities in which they can be successful. Nor have some schools adapted the themes, characters, locale, and level of difficulty of the materials to the students.

There are differing points of view regarding the place and purpose of literature and reading in separate instructional periods. At one time, the slogan was "learn to read" first, then "read to learn." While the two activities are obviously related, there is still something to be said for accomplishing the "learning to read" part of reading with material that is especially adapted to instruction, rather than through the use of artistic masterpieces of literature which require such detailed analysis that the enjoyment and appreciation of seeing the work as a whole is missed. To apply the skills of analysis and interpretation while reading literature may "sharpen the students' apprehension," but to stop at every figure of speech and analyze it word by word, idea by idea, and line by line kills the work forever for many students.

51. "Be a Better Reader: Foundations A" (New York: Prentice-Hall, Inc., 1966 [brochure]).

So often has the work of Shakespeare been treated thus that many students never afterwards read his plays. It is better that figures of speech be learned with sentences or selections of less high quality and that the literature period be used for dealing with ideas, characters, events, the logic and development, or the style as adapted to the purpose. Analysis of these aspects as a reflection of life itself presupposes the reader's ability to deal with what some might call the "mechanics" of the material, but the basic reading skills certainly must be mastered before the ideas can be evaluated or manipulated.

Students also need to hear prose and poetry read aloud. This affords the teacher the opportunity to present to the class stories or works that some of the students would be unable or unlikely to read for themselves. The teacher's oral reading should present a pattern that students can emulate.

Students need to read books completely through on their own, without having to report or discuss them with anyone if they prefer not to do so. However, many readers want to share and check their ideas with others who have read the same book. In so doing, they verbalize their thoughts and learn to analyze and defend their points of view. Literature should focus on the total, and students should "see life" as they read, not necessarily life itself but "like life," and acquire the ability to recognize subtle modifiers, apt figures of speech, faithful delineation of characters, and plausible action. Different types of content will require other criteria for use in judging and analyzing them, but the important learning is that of the techniques which allow the students to read fully and to understand at the highest level possible. To keep them reading, especially after they leave school, requires that they have confidence in their ability to read, that they have had an opportunity to read many and varied materials, and that they have found enjoyment and pleasure in reading.

Three recent developments in addition to individualized reading have promoted the use of library (trade) books for independent reading both in and out of formal class situations. The first is the revision or creation of materials based on a realistic recognition of existing interests and needs. Several publishers have produced "easy reading" books, which can be read by first graders with only limited reading skills, and books on topics of interest to adults and young adults with reading levels from Grades IV to IX. While the latter have been designed especially for new literates, they should also prove useful in secondary schools.

Other publishers have recognized the integrated and multi-ethnic character of the schools. They have revised illustrations and texts to include Negro, Puerto Rican, Mexican, and Oriental children along with the Caucasians. Some of the changes are patently superficial, while others have been done with consideration and real understanding.

The phenomenal growth of the paperback industry in the last decade has meant that materials hitherto unavailable because of expense have been placed within the reach of secondary-school and college students. The printing of such books for the elementary school is just beginning, but several companies are now reprinting even picture books in paperback, though occasionally with some abridgment in text or illustration.

Unusual success in the use of paperbacks with delinquent boys and adolescents who had resisted reading has been reported by Fader.[52] His approach was to get the boys to read something by deluging them with paperbacks and then letting them read whatever they wished. In his report he includes a list of the five hundred best books as selected by his teenage readers.

A second development, paralleling the availability of inexpensive materials, is the establishment of book clubs for various age levels. These clubs usually dispense a limited number of paperbacks throughout the year. Schools need to consider the quality, recency, and cost (assuming this is borne by the school, with teachers doing the bookkeeping) of paperbacks in comparison with the costs and other characteristics of more permanent materials. In those instances in which students pay for the books themselves, the question should be raised as to whether the bookkeeping involved is a proper activity for teachers or whether the parent association or some other group should assume the responsibility for their distribution. But, certainly, the availability of lower-priced books has led many to read and to purchase books for their own libraries.

---

52. Daniel N. Fader, *Hooked on Books* (New York: Berkeley Publishing Co., 1966).

The third development is that of making library books accessible through federal funds. While good books have been written on nearly every topic at different levels, their accessibility has been limited by the lack of adequate library service in some schools and communities. Now that additional funds have been allocated for library development, the problem becomes one of selection and distribution. There are many indexes and bibliographies to aid teachers in making selections. In the future, more books should be available which fit the interests and reading levels of their readers.

These developments should result in much more independent reading than in the past, and, as students develop the reading habit in school, there is hope that they will continue reading throughout their lifetimes. However, with government money easily available, there is a danger that schools will purchase ready-made kits and complete sets of materials without careful evaluation and cost analysis. McCullough has formulated an excellent list of criteria for selection of materials (see chap. ix). It should be helpful in many situations.

Teacher-made materials.—A recent development is to combine materials made by teachers with commercially prepared materials into a modified self-teaching plan for high-school and college reading programs. Sherbourne prepared courses similar to correspondence courses for use in a college reading clinic.[53] She also noted the laborious work entailed in writing the courses. Noall devised a similar plan to make the reading clinic for senior-high-school students "automatic."[54] After diagnosing each student's difficulties, she made individual folders containing exercises and directions designed to meet the needs of each student.

This pattern of combining published materials with those devised especially for an individual or group seems a logical plan for individual teaching, and it contains elements similar to programed instruction. The chief difficulty lies in the number and variety of lessons that must be prepared to put the program into operation.

---

53. Julia Florence Sherbourne, "A Method of Combining Individual and Group Instruction," in *New Developments in Programs and Procedures for College-Adult Reading, op. cit.,* pp. 42-45.

54. Mabel S. Noall, "Automatic Teaching of Reading Skills in High School," *Journal of Education,* CXLIII (February, 1961), 1-73.

Programed instruction and teaching machines.—Programed instruction dates back to 1926, when Pressey's first teaching machine was developed,[55] but the idea did not take hold until after Skinner reported in 1954 on his work in the same area.[56] Since that time, many machines and many programs have been developed. The big expansion, however, came in the early sixties.

Whether a program is written for a teaching machine or whether it is put into a book, it is individual, self-teaching, and provides instant reinforcement, for a student knows immediately whether or not his answer is correct. The subject matter is presented in small, discrete, sequential steps or "frames" containing a question or instructions. The student responds to the directions, then checks to see if his answer is correct before proceeding to the next frame.

The two chief types of programs are the linear and the branching. The linear program requires the learner to recall or construct the answer and write the missing word or phrase, or to recognize and choose the correct alternative in a multiple-choice question. If his response is correct, the learner then proceeds to the next question and continues forward until all of the questions are answered. Each student completes the items in the same order throughout the program. The adaptation for individuals is in terms of the time required for the mastery of the programed lesson.

The teaching machine is adapted to linear programing, for it presents the reader with a stimulus situation (a question or a direction) to which he responds by writing the answer or pushing the proper button or key. Once his answer has been given, the lever is pushed that exposes the correct answer and, at the same time, places his answer under a plastic plate so that it is still exposed but cannot be changed. In some cases where buttons are pushed, the machine will not record until the correct answer has been chosen. Rankin and Smith describe four somewhat similar machines and point out

---

55. S. L. Pressey, "A Simple Apparatus Which Gives Tests and Scores—and Teaches," *School and Society*, XXIII (March 20, 1926), 373-76.

56. B. F. Skinner, "Science of Learning and the Art of Teaching," *Harvard Educational Review*, XXIV (Spring, 1954), 86-97.

that Pressey favored the multiple-choice type of question.[57]

The "striped book" is another example of a linear program. In working on this type of program, the learner completes the first stripe at the top of the right-hand page, turns the page, and finds the correct answer in the left-hand portion of the stripe at the top of this right-hand page. He thus proceeds through the book, reading only the top stripe on the right-hand pages. When this is finished, he returns to the front of he book and reads all the second stripes on the right-hand pages. When all stripes have been completed, he then reverses the book and reads all the left-hand pages in the same manner, making appropriate responses when directed.

The second type of program, the branching, scrambled, or intrinsic type, requires the learner to read a short unit of text material and then respond to a question, usually multiple-choice. Each alternative is numbered. If the answer chosen is the correct one, the learner goes on to the next item. If it is not correct, he turns to the page the number of which is set beside the alternative he has chosen and reads the directions given there. Directions may send him to another page to see why his choice was wrong, or they may send him to a book to get more background. He then returns to the original question and, when it has been answered correctly, moves on to the next item.

Though the number of programs prepared for schools is increasing rapidly each year, there are still relatively few in the field of reading, particularly for levels above the primary grades. The programs that have been developed include linear programs in phonetic analysis, structural analysis, comprehension skills, contextual clues, and vocabulary and branching programs in reference skills, following directions, interpretation, and vocabulary.[58] It is important to note that most programs currently available deal with lower-level

---

57. Earl Rankin and Donald E. P. Smith, "Teaching Machines and the Reading Program," in *Phases of College and Other Adult Reading Programs*, ed. Emery P. Bliesmer and Albert J. Kingston, Jr. (Tenth Yearbook of the National Reading Conference [Milwaukee: Reading Center, Marquette University, 1961]), pp. 74-84.

58. For information on current programs with planned supplements through 1968, see Carl H. Hendershot, "Programmed Learning, A Bibliography of Programs and Presentation Devices," 4114 Ridgewood Drive, Bay City, Michigan (looseleaf).

skills and with those which are developed by practice rather than by analysis. The technique, however, is in its infancy, and the future should bring expansion and development. There is not now enough data to determine the effectiveness of programed instruction, and the Hawthorne effect is difficult to eliminate.

There are advantages in having self-instruction for those who need supplementary work or an additional course, who have missed classes, and who are motivated by this unique method. However, information is needed regarding the optimum gradation of steps for slow and fast learners, the proper balance between right and wrong answers, the transfer of learning to other subjects, the long-term retention of material learned, and the best ways to incorporate programed learning into the total curriculum of the school so that the procedure can be used for those aspects to which it is best suited.

Laboratory programs.—Another outgrowth of programed materials and teaching machines is their use to complement each other in planned laboratory programs. Some schools are just beginning to build individual learning carrels, which include closed circuit television, a tape recorder, an 8-mm. projector, and a variety of other teaching machines. These devices can be used individually or in combination. For example, the Coatesville (Pennsylvania) public schools are experimenting with the use of moving pictures, 35-mm. slides, filmstrips, and video tapes which have been placed in a "bank." The teacher dials the number of the visual aid she desires at a given moment, and the appropriate picture then appears on the screen in the classroom. Materials are prepared by a local staff, and video tapes are also obtained from educational television stations. At present, the program is being used in secondary English literature and business education classes, but expansion to other levels and in other fields is planned. It has even been suggested that home television sets be hooked up with the system so that pupils can have assistance needed in doing their homework.

The Philadelphia public schools, under a contract with the Philco Corporation, are devising a computer program in remedial reading for the junior high school, entitled "Project Grow." In this program, each pupil response is scanned by the computer and appropriate help is given through a branching technique. The program was introduced so recently that no report of its operation is available.

A simpler type of program features a receiver headset that can be used with any tape recorder because it receives by wireless induction. Still another combines the use of recordings on tapes or disks with that of projection machines so that the student can listen and see.

All of the innovations designed to lead towards individual work point to a greater assumption of responsibility by the learner, a more careful sequencing of learning steps, and a consideration of the role of reinforcement in learning. The mechanical and electronic devices are still too new for much careful testing to have been completed, and they are constantly being refined to become even more automatic and self-teaching.

A Look to the Future

This decade has seen the beginning of some changes in reading instruction. These changes have not yet been in operation long enough for their worth to have been determined, but, on the basis of what has been accomplished, the following predictions are made for the future.

More attention will be paid to defining purposes of reading and to developing flexibility in method and rate to meet specific purposes.

General basic skills will be upgraded, and comprehension will be improved through utilization of the knowledge of linguistic principles and through direct teaching of the various skills of critical reading. Illiteracy will decline in the next generation, and remedial programs will be gradually phased out as basic skills are better taught and as instruction is programed to deal with specific problems or aspects of reading, permitting individuals to correct their difficulties with a minimum of direct teacher assistance.

Computer programs that allow a student to respond to items on the machine, then wait while the computer scans the response and provides him with the proper program for overcoming the difficulties that have come to light, will free the teacher to work with students on analysis of content, evaluation and comparison of ideas, and other higher-level thinking skills as they relate to reading.

Libraries and books will be available to all, and, with basic skills well developed, reading should become a real pleasure. Students will work on individual projects—on those that are not class assignments as well as on those related to class work—and methods for research will be learned and used at earlier levels than formerly.

While much of the practice required in reading will be left to the individual, it does not follow that all instruction will be independent of the group. Opportunities to share, to question, to compare, to evaluate one's own ideas against those of the group, and to learn to support one's points of view will need to be provided. The combination of individual and group instruction will require a much more flexible schedule than is found in today's schools. Hopefully, ways will be found to bridge the gap between school and after-school years so that students will carry into their adult life both the competencies and the interests that will insure the continued use of reading.

CHAPTER V

Diagnosis and Remedial Instruction in Reading

ALBERT J. HARRIS

The study of reading disability and its correction has been a very active field in the past few years. There have been major new developments in diagnostic procedures, in teaching approaches, and in the organization of instructional programs. Some particularly significant new trends are: (*a*) progress in the differentiation of groups of retarded readers differing with respect to causation and to treatment needs; (*b*) the emergence of major concern for the special learning problems of the disadvantaged; (*c*) development of programs for reaching larger proportions of those who need special help in reading; and (*d*) movement toward greater interprofessional co-operation among the several professions engaged in working on these problems.

Terminology

The words used to describe individuals whose achievement in learning to read is unsatisfactory vary from one investigator to another, and definitions offered have not yet resulted in any definitive terminology. Thus, a particular child may be labeled a case of reading disability or deficiency, a retarded reader, an underachiever in reading, a case of specific or developmental dyslexia, or a case of specific language disability. While authors vary in their preferences for and in the meanings they attribute to a particular term, it is desirable to be clear about the usual meaning of each of these terms and about the variant meanings that have been used.

Reading retardation is a term which originally was used to designate the condition of all children whose reading was significantly below age and grade norms, regardless of the children's potential or intelligence. Recently it has been used by many writers (unfortunately, in the opinion of this writer) as a synonym for the term "reading disability."

Reading deficiency "is a mild to severe retardation in learning to read, which is disparate with the individual's general intelligence and with his cultural, linguistic and educational experience." [1] This term is also often used as if it were synonymous with reading disability.

Reading disability is the term used in referring to retarded readers whose mental ability should enable them to read considerably better than they do.[2] In general, this term is used synonymously with reading deficiency.

Underachiever in reading is a designation which preferably should be restricted to indicate those whose reading performance is not below age and grade standards but who are judged to be functioning significantly below their own potential level in reading. However, the term is sometimes used more broadly to designate the slow learner, the disabled reader, the bright underachiever, the reluctant reader, and the culturally or socially deprived pupil.[3]

Dyslexia "means defective reading. The reading defect may represent loss of competency following brain injury or degeneration; or it may represent a developmental failure to profit from reading instruction." [4] Dyslexia is often qualified as *developmental* (a general failure in learning) or as *specific* (in contrast to general learning failure). The term is often used to denote a severe reading disability in an individual who is free from mental defect, serious primary neurotic traits, and all gross neurological deficits. "This syndrome of developmental dyslexia is of constitutional and not of environmental origin, and it is often—perhaps even always—genetic-

---

1. E. Gillet Ketchum, "Neurological and Psychological Trends in Reading Diagnosis," *Reading Teacher,* XVII (May, 1964), 589-93.

2. Albert J. Harris, *How To Increase Reading Ability* (4th ed.; New York: David McKay Co., Inc., 1961), p. 17.

3. Helen M. Robinson, "Characteristics of the Underachiever," in *The Underachiever in Reading,* ed. H. Alan Robinson ("Supplementary Educational Monographs," No. 92 [Chicago: University of Chicago Press, 1962]), pp. 9-18.

4. John Money, "Dyslexia: a Post-conference Review," chap. i in *Reading Disability: Progress and Research Needs in Dyslexia,* ed. John Money (Baltimore: Johns Hopkins Press, 1962), p. 9.

ally determined." [5] Dyslexia, then, is a term used primarily by medical specialists to define a subgroup within the group referred to by the term "reading disability."

Primary and *secondary reading retardation* are terms proposed by Rabinovitch.[6] "Primary reading retardation" is a term referring to a severe impairment of capacity to learn to read which, although there is no brain damage, is based on a constitutional pattern of disturbed neurological organization. In contrast, "secondary reading retardation" refers to a reading disability for which the causation is mainly environmental or external. He also proposes a third category, "brain injury with reading retardation."

Specific language disability, a term much used by the Orton Society, denotes a concept like that of dyslexia but broadened to include spelling, handwriting, and speech problems presumably of similar constitutional origin.

The one common element among these terms is agreement that there exists a group of children whose progress in reading is unsatisfactory when compared to their potential. Beyond this, there still are wide disagreements not only concerning terminology but also on the significance of different causative factors and on the efficacy of various methods of treatment.

Help given to children with reading problems is usually classified as "corrective" or "remedial." The term "corrective" usually refers to help given within the regular classroom to an individual or small group, although it sometimes refers to that given to a reading class of less than usual size and made up of children with milder form of reading retardation. The term "remedial" usually refers to instruction outside the regular classroom, given individually or to small groups, by a teacher who has had some special training for such work; it may occur within or outside the school. Corrective and remedial instruction have many similarities in objectives and procedures. As regular classroom instruction becomes successfully adapted to individual needs, the differences between developmental

5. Macdonald Critchley, *Developmental Dyslexia* (London: William Heinemann Medical Books, Limited, 1964), p. 19.

6. Ralph D. Rabinovitch, "Dyslexia: Psychiatric Considerations," chap. v in *Reading Disability: Progress and Research Needs in Dyslexia, op. cit.*, pp. 73-79.

teaching of reading on the one hand and corrective and remedial instruction on the other become smaller and smaller.

A Brief Historical Review

According to Critchley, the first report of a case of reading disability was made by Dr. W. Pringle Morgan in 1896. It described a fourteen-year-old boy who could not learn to read although he seemed intelligent. The term "congenital word-blindness" was used and continued to be popular in Europe for many years.[7] Most prominent among the early investigators in Great Britain was Hinshelwood, a Glasgow eye surgeon, whose 1917 monograph attracted international attention.[8] The early attention to reading problems by medical men in Great Britain attracted relatively little notice from psychologists and educators.

The first attempt in the United States to diagnose individual reading problems and prescribe treatment was by Uhl in 1916.[9] In 1922, the first two American books on reading disabilities, by Clarence T. Gray [10] and William S. Gray,[11] were published. Meanwhile, a practical phonic method for teaching non-readers had been described by Schmitt,[12] and the kinesthetic method had been presented by Fernald and Keller.[13] The first battery of tests for the intensive diagnosis of reading disabilities was published by Gates, and these

---

7. Critchley, op. cit., chap. ii.

8. James Hinshelwood, *Congenital Word-Blindness* (London: H. K. Lewis, 1917).

9. W. L. Uhl, "The Use of the Results of Reading Tests as Bases for Planning Remedial Work," *Elementary School Journal*, XVII (December, 1916), 266-75.

10. Clarence T. Gray, *Deficiencies in Reading Ability: Their Diagnosis and Remedies* (Boston: D. C. Heath & Co., 1922).

11. William S. Gray, *Remedial Cases in Reading: Their Diagnosis and Treatment* ("Supplementary Educational Monographs," No. 22 [Chicago: University of Chicago Press, 1922]).

12. Clara Schmitt, "Developmental Alexia: Congenital Word-Blindness, or Inability To Learn To Read," *Elementary School Journal*, XVIII (May and June, 1918), 680-700, 757-69.

13. Grace M. Fernald and Helen Keller, "The Effect of Kinesthetic Factors in Development of Word Recognition in the Case of Non-Readers," *Journal of Educational Research*, IV (December, 1921), 355-77.

tests, in subsequent revisions, are still widely used.[14] Other psychologists whose contributions to the diagnosis and treatment of reading disabilities were influential during the 1930's were Monroe [15] and Betts.[16]

The first clinics specializing in reading difficulties were begun under the auspices of graduate schools of education and included the reading clinics at the University of Chicago and Boston University. These became centers for the training of reading specialists and remedial teachers, and college reading clinics now number in the hundreds.

The first large-scale remedial reading program in a public school system was begun in New York City in the mid-1930's. It was financed by the Works Progress Administration and other antidepression agencies of the federal government. Several hundred unemployed college graduates were given brief training and were placed in public schools to teach small groups of retarded readers. Special materials (including a series of eighty graded unit-books) were written for their use, and a substantial corps of supervisors was developed. The program lasted until World War II. The number of school systems providing corrective and remedial help in reading and the number of positions for reading specialists have consistently grown at a faster rate than have the training programs in the universities.

American medical men were later than their European counterparts in paying attention to reading difficulties. Samuel T. Orton, a neurologist, began to study reading problems in 1925 and published his major work in 1937.[17] While he recognized multiple causes for delay in learning to read (including visual and hearing defects, dullness, and emotional disturbances), Orton was mainly

---

14. Arthur I. Gates, *The Improvement of Reading: A Program of Diagnostic and Remedial Methods* (New York: Macmillan Co., 1927 [2nd ed., 1935; 3d ed., 1947]).

15. Marion Monroe, *Children Who Cannot Read* (Chicago: University of Chicago Press, 1932).

16. Emmett A. Betts, *The Prevention and Correction of Reading Difficulties* (Evanston, Ill.: Row, Peterson & Co., 1936).

17. Samuel T. Orton, *Reading, Writing, and Speech Problems in Children* (New York: W. W. Norton Co., 1937).

interested in cases of "*the* reading disability." He considered the primary symptom to be a severe reversal tendency, explained this as based on a failure to establish clear-cut dominance of one cerebral hemisphere over the other, coined the term *strephosymbolia* ("twisted symbols") as a preferred name for the condition, and recommended a systematic sounding-blending phonics-teaching procedure. Books by Orton's followers detailing methods of teaching all present a synthetic phonics approach in which sounding the parts of a word and blending the parts together is stressed.[18] The Orton Society is an interdisciplinary group started by Orton's followers. While Orton's theoretical formulation has never achieved wide acceptance, the teaching methods used by his followers provide one approach that can be used with severe reading disabilities.

In his writing, Orton ignored the professional literature of American education and educational psychology; in turn, his influence has been largely restricted to some private schools and clinics. Current neurological theory regards his theoretical formulations as outdated, although his pioneering contributions are greatly respected.

Throughout the fifty years since the publication of Hinshelwood's *Congenital Word-Blindness*, there have been two opposed tendencies in theoretical explanations of reading disability. Neurologists have postulated a basic constitutional condition, often hereditary and usually accompanied by other communication difficulties (in speech, spelling, handwriting, composition). Among the major recent contributors, in addition to those already mentioned, have been Hallgren [19] and Hermann.[20] While admitting that such cases may

---

18. Margaret A. Stanger and Ellen K. Donohue, *Prediction and Prevention of Reading Difficulties* (New York: Oxford University Press, 1937); Anna Gillingham and Bessie Stillman, *Remedial Training for Children with Specific Disability in Reading, Spelling, and Penmanship* (6th ed.; Boston: Educators Publishing Service, 1960); Sally B. Childs and Ralph deS. Childs, *Sound Phonics* (Boston: Educators Publishing Service, 1962).

19. Bertil Hallgren, *Specific Dyslexia ("Congenital Word-Blindness"): A Clinical and Genetic Study* ("Supplement 65," 1950, *Acta Psychiatrica et Neurologica* [Stockholm, 1950]).

20. Knud Hermann, *Reading Disability: A Medical Study of Word-Blindness and Related Handicaps*, trans. from Danish (Springfield, Ill.: Charles C. Thomas, 1959).

be a small proportion of all reading disabilities, they have preferred to concentrate on this group.

Educational and experimental psychologists, on the other hand, have tended to be impressed by the wide range of physical, psychological, emotional, sociological, and educational handicaps that may be found in a group of poor readers and have tended to favor a pluralistic theory of causation. Support for this point of view has come from many sources; among the major contributors have been Gates,[21] Monroe,[22] Robinson,[23] Vernon,[24] and Malmquist.[25] Without denying the possibility of specific subgroups, they have emphasized the wide range of handicaps to be found in school and clinic populations and the continuity of problems from mild to most severe disabilities.

For about a twenty-year period (1935-55), psychoanalysts and clinical psychologists sought to explain reading disability as a symptom of emotional disturbance and to suggest psychotherapy as a preferred mode of treatment.[26] There is little doubt that the great majority of children with reading deficiencies who come to the attention of psychologists and psychiatrists have emotional problems. This writer has described ten patterns of emotional behavior to be found in children with reading disabilities.[27] In individual cases, however, it is often very difficult to determine whether the emotional problem is a cause of reading difficulty or a result of it. Psychotherapy seems to be an adequate method of treatment only in a small minority of cases. Because many poor readers improve in

21. Gates, *op. cit.*

22. Monroe, *op. cit.*

23. Helen M. Robinson, *Why Pupils Fail in Reading* (Chicago: University of Chicago Press, 1947).

24. M. D. Vernon, *Backwardness in Reading* (Cambridge: Cambridge University Press, 1957).

25. Eve Malmquist, *Factors Related to Reading Disabilities in the First Grade of the Elementary School* (Stockholm: Almqvist & Wiksell, 1958).

26. Gerald H. J. Pearson, "A Survey of Learning Difficulties in Children," *Psychoanalytic Study of the Child*, VII (1952), 372-86.

27. Harris, *How To Increase Reading Ability, op. cit.*, pp. 264-69.

personality adjustment as they become able to succeed in school, it is often desirable to postpone consideration of the need for psychotherapy until the effects of remedial teaching are evident.

Since 1955, there has been an accelerating interest in reading disabilities in the United States. This interest has resulted in a vast expansion of remedial programs and in an upsurge in research by medical personnel and by psychologists working within medical or clinical settings. This is due in part to increased government support. A great many reading teachers have been able to attend institutes under provisions of the National Defense Education Act. A great many school systems have been able to begin, expand, or improve their remedial reading programs with funds from Title I and Title III of the Elementary and Secondary Education Act. Research projects on reading disability have received support from the National Institute of Health as well as from the U.S. Office of Education and from private foundations.

Another trend is toward more discussion and co-operative effort among representatives of the various professional groups engaged in studying reading problems. For example, a 1961 conference on dyslexia at Johns Hopkins University was initiated by an opthalmologist and included participants trained in psychiatry, neurology, optometry, speech, and clinical, experimental, and educational psychology.[28] Since 1966, the Institute for Applied Linguistics has sponsored an effort at interprofessional co-operative planning of research on reading disability.

Recognition of the vast amount of reading retardation among children of the economically, socially, and educationally disadvantaged is very recent. Research on the psychology and education of disadvantaged children dates mainly from 1960; few relevant publications appeared earlier than 1962. It is now evident that there is a strong interrelationship between social class and reading progress. According to Barton, "the norm for upper middle-class children is a year ahead of 'grade level' from the end of first grade on; while the norm for lower working-class children (the poorer and more culturally deprived part of the working class) is to fall back

---

28. *Reading Disability: Progress and Research Needs in Dyslexia, op. cit.*

until they are a year or more behind by the time they reach fourth and fifth grade." [29]

As part of the "War on Poverty," federal funds in unprecedented amounts have recently been poured into projects for improving the education of the disadvantaged. One major effort is the Head Start program, providing preschool education for thousands of disadvantaged youngsters.[30] A second major effort has been the allocation of hundreds of millions of dollars under Title I of the Elementary and Secondary Education Act of 1965 for innovative educational programs for the disadvantaged; many of these projects have centered around remedial reading. A third effort, supported through the Office of Economic Opportunity, has provided a variety of programs which stress literacy training for unemployed adolescents and adults. These efforts are so new and so vast that it is impossible as yet to discern the full size and shape of the total effort or to evaluate its results.

Causes of Reading Disability

PRIMARY READING DISABILITY OR DYSLEXIA

Rabinovitch has explained his concept of primary reading retardation as follows:

"Capacity to learn to read is impaired without definite brain damage being suggested in the case history or upon neurological examination. The defect is in the ability to deal with letters and words as symbols, with resultant diminished ability to integrate the meaningfulness of written material. The problem appears to reflect a basic disturbed pattern of neurological organization. Because the cause is biological or endogenous, these cases are diagnosed as *primary reading retardation*." [31]

Critchley's description of dyslexia is very similar. He says:

---

29. Allen H. Barton, "Reading Research and Its Communication: The Columbia-Carnegie Project," in *Reading as an Intellectual Activity*, ed. J. Allen Figurel (International Reading Association Conference Proceedings, VIII, 1963), pp. 246-50.

30. Operation Head Start is described in several articles in the February, 1966, issue of the *Reading Teacher*, and many Title I reading projects are described in the January, 1967, issue.

31. Rabinovitch, *op. cit.*, p. 74.

"There is a small hard core of cases where the tendency to the learning defect is inborn and independent of any intellectual inadequacies, emotional factors, educational or linguistic shortcomings which may happen to co-exist." [32]

Rabinovitch and Critchley are both opposed to the rather widespread current fashion of ascribing severe reading disabilities to "minimal brain damage." They are more sympathetic to Bender's concept of a *maturational lag*, or slowness in certain specialized aspects of neurological development.[33]

Recognizing that at present the diagnostic differentiation of maturational lag from minimal brain damage is difficult and uncertain, Clements has proposed the term "minimal brain dysfunction syndrome," which begs the question.

"These aberrations may arise from genetic variations, biochemical irregularities, perinatal insults or other illnesses or injuries sustained during the years which are critical for the development and maturation of the central nervous system, or from unknown causes. The definition also allows for the possibility that early severe sensory deprivation could result in central nervous system alterations which may be permanent. During the school years, a variety of learning disabilities is the most prominent manifestation of the condition which can be designated by this term." [34]

Although fully accepting Clements' concept, this writer greatly prefers the term "delayed and irregular neurological development" as both conveying the central idea more clearly and being far less threatening to children, parents, and teachers. This term was first suggested to him by Dr. Alfred L. Abrams, a psychiatrist.

The integrative difficulties which seem to be close to the heart of the problems of primary reading disability are not completely specific to reading; they can be found in related aspects of perception and cognition. The problem lies not so much in the perception

---

32. Critchley, *op. cit.*, p. 74.

33. Lauretta Bender, "Specific Reading Disability as a Maturational Lag," *Bulletin of the Orton Society*, VII (1957), 9-18.

34. Sam D. Clements, *Minimal Brain Dysfunction in Children: Terminology and Identification* ("National Institute of Neurological Diseases Monograph," No. 3, Public Health Service Publication No. 1415, 1966 [Washington: Government Printing Office, 1966]).

or grasp of one unit by itself but, rather, in the ability to deal with relationships. Thus, there is likely to be difficulty in comparing parts within wholes in both visual and auditory perception, difficulty in clearly distinguishing figure from background, difficulty in achieving closure (filling in missing parts), difficulty in grasping sequential arrangement, directional difficulty with reversals in reading and writing, difficulty in integrating (blending) parts into a recognizable whole, and difficulty in establishing associations between sensory modalities—the sound of a word with its visual appearance or the "feel" of a cut-out or traced letter with its visual appearance. In short, the child with primary reading disability shows deficient ability to deal with the Gestalt aspects of perception and cognition.[35]

According to such Europeans as Hallgren, Hermann, and Critchley, the tendency for dyslexia to run in families is strong, and they consider the presence of similar difficulties in other members of the family to be an important factor in diagnosis.

In practice, the identification of primary reading disability is complicated by two problems. The first is that some (but not all) of the described symptoms are present in a given case, and there is no invariable common core except for the learning difficulty. The second is that "pure" cases are hard to find. Rabinovitch said: "Despite the neatness of all our attempted theoretical formulations, I must confess that in practice our group not infrequently arrives at a diagnosis such as "secondary retardation with a touch of primary disability."[36] Since some of the symptoms thought to indicate primary disability are usually found along with some of the causal factors included under secondary disability (see following section), differential diagnosis is not easy; and skepticism about the reality of constitutional specific dyslexia, such as that expressed by

---

35. Albert J. Harris, "Perceptual Difficulties in Reading Disability," in *Changing Concepts of Reading Instruction*, ed. J. Allen Figurel (International Reading Conference Proceedings, VI, 1961), pp. 281-90; Katrina deHirsch, "Psychological Correlates in the Reading Process," in *Challenge and Experiment in Reading*, ed. J. Allen Figurel (International Reading Association Conference Proceedings, VII, 1962), pp. 218-26; A. L. Drew, "A Neurological Appraisal of Familial Congenital Word-Blindness," *Brain*, LXXIX (1956), 440-60.

36. Rabinovitch, *op. cit.*, p. 76.

Malmquist, remains a tenable scientific position.[37] The opposite view, that all reading disabilities are due to maturational lag, with severity extending through a continuum from mildest to most severe, cannot at present be disproved, although it is not widely held.[38]

A distinctively different explanation of reading disability is that put forth by Delacato.[39] He places emphasis on attainment of developmental stages in neurological maturity and ascribes importance to immature patterns of movement and posture which are attributable to the medulla and spinal cord, the pons, the mid-brain, and the cerebral cortex. Of those at the cortical level, failure to achieve clear dominance of one cerebral hemisphere over the other is considered to be the basic cause of reading disability. Major emphasis in treatment is on promoting neurological organization and hemisphere dominance.

There is widespread skepticism about Delacato's ideas among psychologists and neurologists. There are as yet only two independent published reports of research using the Delacato procedures, both by Robbins.[40] Neither demonstrated superior results, either with second-grade pupils or with retarded readers.

Another effort to provide a unifying theory to explain reading disability is the chemical-balance hypothesis of Smith and Carrigan.[41] They predicted specific symptoms that might result from excess or deficiency in the acetylcholine-cholinesterase balance in the brain and compared them with symptom patterns in groups of poor readers. Until additional evidence is available, their ideas should be regarded as interesting hypotheses. It is possible, although not yet

37. Malmquist, *op. cit.*, pp. 34-44.

38. Lauretta Bender, *Psychopathology of Children with Organic Brain Disorders* (Springfield, Ill.: Charles C. Thomas, 1956).

39. Carl H. Delacato, *The Treatment and Prevention of Reading Problems* (Springfield, Ill.: Charles C. Thomas, 1959); *The Diagnosis and Treatment of Speech and Reading Problems* (Springfield, Ill.: Charles C. Thomas, 1963).

40. Melvyn P. Robbins, "Delacato Interpretation of Neurological Organization," *Reading Research Quarterly*, I (Spring, 1966), 57-78; *Influence of Special Programs on the Development of Mental Age and Reading* (Cooperative Research Project No. S-349, U.S. Department of Health, Education, and Welfare, Office of Education, 1965).

41. Donald E. P. Smith and Patricia M. Carrigan, *The Nature of Reading Disability* (New York: Harcourt, Brace & Co., 1959).

demonstrated, that the kind of severe learning disability called primary reading disability or dyslexia is mediated through some irregularity or peculiarity in brain chemistry. A predisposition for such a peculiarity could be hereditary in some families and could be a result of illness, malnutrition, or obscure factors in other cases.

Brain damage in children is often accompanied by severe learning disabilities. There is a growing literature on diagnosis and treatment, for which Clements' report provides a good bibliography.[42] Among the books of particular relevance for remedial reading are those of Strauss and Kephart[43] and of Cruikshank.[44] As noted, the question of the importance of minimal brain damage in the causation of reading disability is still far from solution.

SECONDARY READING DISABILITY

Following Rabinovitch, the term "secondary" may be used as a differentiating term for cases of reading disability in which the major causation is not attributable to dysfunction or delayed development of the brain. The large number of factors which have been studied cannot be adequately reviewed in this chapter. Instead, the summary provided by Robinson[45] will be supplemented by reference to evidence that has appeared since her summary was written.

Sensory and other physical factors.—In vision, Robinson indicated that poor readers are apt to be farsighted and to have difficulties with eye co-ordination. Rosborough[46] and Taylor[47] have

42. Clements, *op. cit.*

43. A. A. Strauss and Newell C. Kephart, *Psychopathology and Education of the Brain-Injured Child*, (2 vols.; New York: Grune & Stratton, 1955).

44. W. M. Cruikshank et al., *A Teaching Method for Brain-Injured and Hyperactive Children* (Syracuse: Syracuse University Press, 1961).

45. Helen M. Robinson, "Corrective and Remedial Instruction," chap. xx in *Development in and through Reading* (Sixtieth Yearbook of the National Society for the Study of Education, Part I [Chicago: Distributed by the University of Chicago Press, 1961]), pp. 362-66.

46. Pearl M. Rosborough, *Physical Fitness and the Child's Reading Problem* (New York: Exposition Press, 1963).

47. Earl A. Taylor, *The Fundamental Reading Skill as Related to Eye-Movement Photography and Visual Anomalies* (2nd ed.; Springfield, Ill.: Charles C. Thomas, 1966).

presented case studies pointing up the significance of visual inefficiency in some reading disability cases. Calvert and Crome reported that, of the 20 per cent of their remedial reading students not responding to help, over 90 per cent had fine oculomotor spasms that could be seen in eye-movement photographs and that drug treatment for this condition both stopped the spasms and improved learning.[48] These studies raise a question as to whether reading clinics should routinely use an eye-movement camera as part of the diagnostic process.

There has been no important new research on hearing as related to reading disability. Undetected or uncorrected loss of hearing may interfere with auditory discrimination and learning of phonics as well as, more generally, with language development.

The importance of general physical fitness and co-ordination has been stressed by some writers. Rosborough has reported a high incidence of postural and skeletal difficulties among reading disability cases and recommends including an osteopath in the diagnostic team.[49] Taylor reports cases responding favorably to a combination of endocrine treatment (chorionic gonadotrophin) and visual training.[50] Kephart has emphasized the importance of basic motor skills and eye-hand co-ordination in slow learners and has described a diagnostic and treatment program in these areas of functioning.[51]

Dominance and directionality.—The significance of sidedness or lateral dominance for reading is still a controversial issue. Zangwill, in a recent review of the literature, concluded:

"On balance, the evidence suggests that an appreciable proportion of dyslexic children show poorly developed laterality and that there is commonly evidence of slow speech development. . . . If poorly developed laterality can be linked with incomplete cerebral dominance, it might be said that these patterns of disability reflect faulty establish-

---

48. James J. Calvert and George F. Crome, "Oculomotor Spasms in Handicapped Readers," *Reading Teacher*, XX (December, 1966), 231-36, 241.

49. Rosborough, *op. cit.*

50. Earl A. Taylor, *Meeting the Increasing Stresses of Life: A Multiple-Therapy Approach in Education* (Springfield, Ill.: Charles C Thomas, 1963).

51. Newell C. Kephart, *The Slow Learner in the Classroom* (Columbus, Ohio: Charles E. Merrill Books, Inc., 1960).

ment of asymmetrical (i.e., normally lateralized) functions in the two hemispheres." [52]

He left unsolved such questions as why some poor readers are fully right-sided; why some poorly lateralized children learn to read well; and the relationship between laterality, early brain injury, delayed maturation, and vulnerability to stress.

There continue to be contrasting findings in studies of clinical groups of severely disabled readers [53] and surveys of school populations, such as the one by Balow.[54] The former tend to find relatively strong relationships between laterality and poor reading while the latter usually find no relationship. It may be that the per cent of children with primary reading disability is too small a part of the total school population to make a discernible impression on group averages. According to this writer's findings, directional confusion is shown by one-quarter of children with severe reading disability at the age of nine.[55] Differences in ages of populations and in methods of testing also tend to prevent clear interpretation of apparently conflicting results.

INTELLECTUAL FACTORS

Specific mental abilities.—The *Illinois Tests of Psycholinguistic Abilities* (ITPA) has attracted considerable attention through its promise of specifying particular areas of functioning in which a

52. O. L. Zangwill, "Dyslexia in Relation to Cerebral Dominance," chap. vii in *Reading Disability: Progress and Research Needs in Dyslexia, op. cit.*, pp. 103-13.

53. Lillian Belmont and Herbert G. Birch, "Lateral Dominance, Lateral Awareness, and Reading Disability," *Child Development*, XXXIV (1965), 257-71; Arthur L. Benton, "Dyslexia in Relation to Form Perception and Directional Sense," chap. vi in *Reading Disability: Progress and Research Needs in Dyslexia, op. cit.*, pp. 81-102; Archie A. Silver and Rosa A. Hagin, "Specific Reading Disability: Follow-up Studies," *American Journal of Orthopsychiatry*, XXXIV (1964), 95-102.

54. Irving H. Balow, "Lateral Dominance Characteristics and Reading Achievement in First Grade," *Journal of Psychology*, LV (April, 1963), 323-28.

55. Albert J. Harris, "Lateral Dominance, Directional Confusion, and Reading Disability," *Journal of Psychology*, XLIV (1957), 283-94.

child with a language problem may be weak.[56] These tests measure nine aspects of visual, auditory, and motor functioning considered important in the development of language in children and are already used in a number of reading clinics. Since they do not cover such areas as verbal comprehension and problem-solving, they supplement but do not replace such tests as the *Stanford-Binet* or the *Wechsler Intelligence Scale for Children*.

Perception.—Barrett, in a thorough review of the value of visual perception tests in predicting first-grade reading, concluded that: (*a*) visual discrimination of letters and words has a somewhat higher value than visual discrimination of geometric designs and pictures; and (*b*) several tasks requiring discrimination of geometric designs and pictures have predictive possibilities and warrant additional study.[57] Among the latter may be mentioned the *Bender Visual-Motor Gestalt Test*,[58] the *Frostig Developmental Test of Visual Perception*,[59] and the Beery *Geometric Form Reproduction Test* (GFR).[60] The Frostig test has five parts: eye-hand co-ordination, figure-ground, form constancy, position in space, and spatial relations. Olson found the total test to have fair ability for predicting third-grade reading, but two of the subtests (figure-ground and position in space) did not have significant correlations. He concluded that his results did not support Frostig's postulates concerning the

---

56. Samuel A. Kirk and J. J. McCarthy, "The Illinois Test of Psycholinguistic Abilities—An Approach to Differential Diagnosis," *American Journal of Mental Deficiency*, LXVI (November, 1961), 399-412; Dorothy J. Sievers et al., *Selected Studies on the Illinois Test of Psycholinguistic Abilities* (Madison, Wis.: Photo Press, Inc., 1963).

57. Thomas C. Barrett, "The Relationship between Measures of Pre-Reading Visual Discrimination and First-Grade Reading Achievement: A Review of the Literature," *Reading Research Quarterly*, I (Fall, 1965), 51-76.

58. Lauretta Bender, *A Visual-Motor Gestalt Test and Its Clinical Use* ("Research Monograph," No. 3 [New York: American Orthopsychiatric Association, 1938]); Elizabeth M. Koppitz, *The Bender-Gestalt Test for Young Children* (New York: Grune & Stratton, 1964).

59. Marianne Frostig, Welty Lefever, and John R. B. Whittlesey, *Administration and Scoring Manual for the Marianne Frostig Developmental Test of Visual Perception* (Palo Alto, Calif.: Consulting Psychologists Press, 1964).

60. Keith E. Beery, *Geometric Form Reproduction: Developmental Studies of Visual-Motor Integrity* (mimeographed; San Francisco: San Francisco Medical Center, 1964).

relationship between data yielded by her subtests and specific reading difficulties.[61]

This writer has suggested that, if the child's reading problem is secondary and results from emotional conflicts, social conditions, or inappropriate educational experiences, the child's perception in reading may be poor but his perceptual functioning should not be faulty in tasks unrelated to reading; a more general impairment of perception is suggestive of primary disability.[62]

Auditory discrimination is also significantly related to success in learning to read. Dykstra reported that the auditory-perception parts of various tests of reading readiness vary considerably in predictive value;[63] the "Making of Auditory Discriminations" section of the *Harrison-Stroud Reading Readiness Test* predicted comparatively well.[64] Favorable validity data for distinguishing between reading disability cases and normal readers have been reported for the *Wepman Auditory Discrimination Test*[65] and an auditory blending test.[66] Deutsch has also shown that poor auditory discrimination is frequent among disadvantaged children.[67]

There is growing evidence that difficulty in integrating one area of functioning with another may be a major problem in many cases of reading disability. Beery, in discussing visual-motor performance,

---

61. Arthur V. Olson, "School Achievement, Reading Ability, and Specific Visual Perception Skills in the Third Grade," *Reading Teacher*, XIX (April, 1966), 490-92.

62. Albert J. Harris, "Perceptual Difficulties in Reading Disability," in *Changing Concepts of Reading Instruction, op. cit.*, pp. 282-90.

63. Robert Dykstra, "Auditory Discrimination Abilities and Beginning Reading Achievement," *Reading Research Quarterly*, I (Spring, 1966) 5-34.

64. M. Lucile Harrison and J. B. Stroud, *Harrison-Stroud Reading Readiness Profiles* (Boston: Houghton Mifflin Co., 1956).

65. Dorothy Christine and Charles Christine, "The Relationship of Auditory Discrimination to Articulatory Defects and Reading Retardation," *Elementary School Journal*, LXV (November, 1964), 97-100.

66. Jeanne Chall, Florence G. Roswell, and Susan H. Blumenthal, "Auditory Blending Ability: A Factor in Success in Beginning Reading," *Reading Teaching*, XVII (November, 1963), 113-18.

67. Cynthia P. Deutsch, "Auditory Discrimination and Learning: Social Factors," *Merrill-Palmer Quarterly of Behavior and Development*, X (July, 1964), 277-96.

emphasized the importance of the connection between the "visual" and the "motor" aspects.[68] Katz and Deutsch found that poor readers had difficulty in shifting their attention between auditory and visual stimuli.[69] Thus, there seem to be children for whom the development of associations between sensory modalities (especially relating sights to sounds) is particularly troublesome.

SCHOOL PRACTICES

The twenty-seven co-operative studies of first-grade reading supported by the U.S. Office of Education in 1964-65 showed, with almost complete unanimity, that differences in results were far greater among the classes of teachers using the same method than were the differences between the averages resulting from contrasting methods of instruction.[70] This dramatically shows how powerful an effect teachers have on the progress of beginning readers. It follows that many a poor reader might have done much better if he had been luckier in his first- and second-grade teachers.

It has long been known that frequent changes of school, excessive absence, and insensitive teaching can slow progress. Continued exposure to excessively difficult, frustrating reading materials often prevent a child who has fallen behind from making progress in reading.

Nevertheless, it is probably true that, if a child's constitutional predisposition toward reading disability is strong enough, he is likely to become a severely retarded reader in almost any school setting.

SOCIOCULTURAL DISADVANTAGE

By the time children growing up in conditions of severe cultural and educational disadvantage reach the seventh grade, they are

---

68. Beery, *op. cit.*, p. 18.

69. Phyllis A. Katz and Martin Deutsch, "Relation of Auditory-Visual Shifting to Reading Achievement," *Perceptual and Motor Skills*, XVII (October, 1963), 327-32.

70. Guy L. Bond and Robert Dykstra, "The Cooperative Research in First-Grade Reading," *Reading Research Quarterly*, II (Summer, 1967), 122-24.

likely to be two or more years retarded in reading.⁷¹ The nature of their disadvantage is a pervasive one, starting very early in childhood. It involves the lack of non-verbal as well as verbal abilities and tends to increase rather than decrease during the elementary-school years.⁷² The long-time effects of prekindergarten and kindergarten programs specifically designed to alleviate this disadvantage are not yet known; such programs have not been in operation long enough. Yet the alternative to such programs is to continue a situation in which the majority of little children in certain neighborhoods will continue to enter school so lacking in language development, in information and ideas, and in habits of social living as to be foredoomed to the role of slow learners.

Although the long-term effects of efforts at the preschool level are still to be determined, there is evidence to support the common-sense assumptions that such measures as small classes, rich provision of materials, expert consultation, and in-service training for first-grade teachers can substantially improve the learning of disadvantaged children in the first grade.⁷³ Thus, with further improvement of school practices, it does not seem too optimistic to expect a lessening of the massive retardation currently shown by the majority of disadvantaged children.

PERSONALITY MALADJUSTMENT

There is relatively little significant new evidence on the relation of personality maladjustment to reading disability. Recent reports confirm the frequent expression of feelings of discouragement, inadequacy, and nervousness by poor readers.⁷⁴ However, as

---

71. Gertrude Downing *et al.*, *The Preparation of Teachers for Schools in Culturally Deprived Neighborhoods (The BRIDGE Project)* (U.S. Office of Education Co-operative Research Project, No. 935 [New York: Department of Education, Queens College, 1965]).

72. Martin Deutsch, "The Role of Social Class in Language Development and Cognition," *American Journal of Orthopsychiatry*, XXXV (January, 1965), 78-88.

73. Marjorie S. Johnson and Roy A. Kress, "Philadelphia's Educational Improvement Program," *Reading Teacher*, XVIII (March, 1965), 488-92.

74. G. N. Allebrand, "Personality Characteristics and Attitudes toward Achievement of Good and Poor Readers," *Journal of Educational Research*, LIX (September, 1965), 28-31.

already noted, there has been a recent tendency to assume that, in the most severe reading disabilities, the emotional problems are not causal but are either concommitant symptoms of the underlying neurological condition or the result of frustration and failure. In milder cases, on the other hand, there is far greater readiness to ascribe causal significance to patterns of emotional maladjustment and particularly to disturbed parent-child relationships. Reading disability occurs with high frequency among child schizophrenics and delinquents as well as among children with a variety of psychoneurotic patterns and milder forms of character disorder.[75] Observation and interview are preferable to personality tests in studying the personal adjustment of poor readers.

Diagnostic Procedures

IDENTIFYING THE DISABLED READER

The general agreement that a disabled reader is one who is both retarded in reading and functioning below his potential runs into problems when acted upon.

The first problem is that of how to measure potential. In clinical practice, individual intelligence tests such as the *Revised Stanford-Binet* and *WISC* are still preferred. For large-scale testing in schools, however, the problem is more difficult. Group I.Q. tests that require the taker to read the questions are obviously unsuitable. Group tests of a non-reading type tend to utilize pictures and geometric designs, which may penalize the child with a perceptual difficulty, and their correlations with reading (and their predictive value) are not high.

Cleland and Toussaint found that, for pupils in Grades IV, V, and VI, results on group tests of listening comprehension correlated with measurements of silent reading at least as well as did scores on individual or group I.Q. tests.[76] The combination of *STEP Listening* and *Primary Mental Abilities* tests gave a multiple correlation of .76 with reading. The *STEP 4a Listening* section did slightly

75. Harris, *How To Increase Reading Ability, op. cit.,* pp. 2, 264-73.

76. Donald L. Cleland and Isabelle Toussaint, "The Interrelationship of Reading, Listening, Arithmetic Computation, and Intelligence," *Reading Teacher,* XV (January, 1962), 228-31.

better than the *Durrell-Sullivan Reading Capacity Test*, another listening comprehension test. Wider use of listening tests seem justified. They may, however, give unduly low ratings to children characterized by foreign-language or dialect backgrounds, hearing defects, or inability to maintain sustained attention.

Assuming one has chosen a reasonably satisfactory measure of reading capacity or potential, the simplest way to compare reading performance with capacity is to compare reading grade with capacity grade (or reading age with capacity age). There is a difference of approximately five years between these two grades or ages. Woodbury recommended a difference between the two of at least one standard deviation.[77] This deviation he translated into a minimum difference of one year and five months at fourth-grade level. A re-examination of his data, however, reveals that, when underachievers reading less than a year below grade level are eliminated, 12 per cent are found to be a year or more below both grade placement and mental age—a quite reasonable finding. The formulas proposed by Bond and Tinker, Monroe, Torgerson and Adams, and others involve arithmetic which has discouraged remedial teachers from applying them.[78]

Otto and McMenemy have recommended a short, individual I.Q. test for use with retarded readers because it involves no reading, can be administered by teachers, takes only two minutes per child, and came within 10 points of the WISC I.Q. in 54 per cent of their cases.[79]

There is some resistance to using I.Q. or M.A. (mental age) as a criterion for the selection of children for remedial reading help. Chansky and Frost have both found relatively low correlations between mental ability and rate of improvement in a remedial program and question the use of a minimum mental-ability score in

---

77. Charles A. Woodbury, "The Identification of Underachieving Readers," *Reading Teacher*, XVI (January, 1963), 218-23.

78. Harris, *How To Increase Reading Ability, op. cit.*, pp. 288-302.

79. Wayne Otto and Richard A. McMenemy, "An Appraisal of the Ammons Quick Test in a Remedial Reading Program," *Journal of Educational Measurement*, II (December, 1965), 193-98.

selecting remedial pupils.[80] Evidence of potential for improvement is preferable to an arbitrarily chosen minimum I.Q.

DETERMINING LEVEL OF DIAGNOSIS NECESSARY

In practical situations, it is wasteful to attempt to make diagnostic differentiations that are not necessary for the decisions that have to be made. Diagnosis at a simple level is carried on by many classroom teachers as they use standardized and teacher-made tests to form instructional groups and look over record cards for health handicaps, measures of potential, and achievement in previous grades. This diagnosis usually results in the selection of a few pupils for more analytical study.

A more analytical diagnosis can be carried out by a reading specialist on the school staff or by a teacher with special training. It concentrates on more detailed testing of specific aspects of reading skill—such items as sight vocabulary, structural and phonic skills, knowledge of word meanings, sentence and paragraph comprehension, and rate. In the upper grades, study skills may be included, and comprehension of several kinds of material, including content textbooks, may be tested. There has been a trend toward greater use of book samples, often called an "informal reading inventory." This is a quite useful procedure, particularly when it is not excessively formal and long.[81] Many reading specialists prefer to use tests with standardized directions, printed forms for pupil and examiner, and grade norms.[82]

When a child does not respond satisfactorily to corrective or remedial instruction, an intensive case study should be undertaken. This can best be carried out in a clinical setting in which the re-

---

80. Norman M. Chansky, "Age, I.Q., and Improvement of Reading," *Journal of Educational Research*, LVI (1963), 439; Barry P. Frost, "The Role of Intelligence 'C' in the Selection of Children for Remedial Reading," *Alberta Journal of Educational Research*, IX (June, 1963), 73-78.

81. Marjorie S. Johnson and Roy A. Kress, *Informal Reading Inventories* (Newark, Del.: International Reading Association, 1965); Mary A. Austin, Cliford L. Busk, and Mildred H. Huebner, *Reading Evaluation* (New York: Ronald Press Co., 1961).

82. Recent tests include two important revisions: *Gray Oral Reading Tests*, by William S. Gray, ed. Helen M. Robinson (Indianapolis: Bobbs-Merrill Co., 1963); *Gates-McKillop Reading Diagnostic Tests*, by Arthur I. Gates and Anne S. McKillop (New York: Bureau of Publications, Teachers College, Columbia University, 1962), a revision of the *Gates Reading Diagnostic Tests*.

sources of several professions can be brought to bear on the problems of the child. In such a case study, major emphasis is placed on analyses of the handicaps or casual factors, past and present. A comprehensive case study may involve a social case worker, clinical psychologist, speech pathologist, psychiatrist, neurologist, pediatrician, opthalmologist or optometrist, and so forth. The findings of their examinations are put together to form a comprehensive picture resulting in recommendations for any forms of treatment that may be indicated. Most clinics do not have all relevant professions represented on their staffs and refer to other community resources for special examinations that seem to be needed.

Diagnosis does not have to be comprehensive in every case. For example, if no suspicions of neurological problems are reported from a psychological examination and general medical check-up, a thorough neurological study is likely to be wasteful of time, money, and limited professional resources. Also, vision and hearing screening tests can reduce greatly the number to be referred to vision and hearing specialists.

When a significant handicap is discovered, correcting it becomes as important a part of the treatment program as teaching the child reading skills. In a given case, this may involve one or more of the following: parent counseling, play therapy, orthoptic training, medication, perceptual or motor training, and so on.

PREDICTION OF READING DISABILITY

Malmquist has described a program involving small classes, careful testing, and adaptation of instruction to individual characteristics designed to prevent the development of reading disabilities among first-graders in Sweden.[83]

A careful longitudinal study by deHirsch, Jansky, and Langford has explored the possibility of predicting later reading disability through testing and clinically examining preschool children.[84] In the main study, fifty-three children were examined when

---

83. Eve Malmquist, "Organizing Instruction To Prevent Reading Disability," in *Reading as an Intellectual Activity, op. cit.,* pp. 36-39.

84. Katrina deHirsch, Jeannette J. Jansky, and William S. Langford, *Predicting Reading Failure: A Preliminary Study* (New York: Harper & Row, 1966).

in kindergarten and given reading tests at the end of first and second grades. The children were predominantly lower middle class, 60 per cent white. Of thirty-seven tests given, nineteen were significantly related to second-grade reading, twenty to spelling, and sixteen to writing. The study permitted some differentiation of the eight failing readers from a group of "slow starters." The useful tests included measures of visual and auditory perception, visual-motor performance, reversals, letter recognition, oral vocabulary, and I.Q. and clinical ratings of hyperactivity and ego strength. No evidence of hereditary background factors was found; of ten family-background variables, none was significantly correlated with outcomes. Perfect prediction was not achieved; a low "Predictive Index" identified ten of eleven failures and also four "false positives." Since most of the tests required individual administration, considerably more work will be needed to translate this approach into one widely usable with school beginners.

A much simpler predictive procedure has been described by McLeod.[85] A "Dyslexia Schedule" of twenty-three items, based mainly on a parental report of a child's preschool experience and history, identified twenty of twenty-three dyslexic children and only one out of twenty-three non-dyslexic children. McLeod recommends his schedule as one that could be routinely filled out at the time that a child enters school.

An accurate group screening device which can be used to identify potential failures, who may thus be given special attention from the beginning, should be extremely useful in reducing the frequency and severity of reading disability.

Organization of Corrective and Remedial Instruction

IN PUBLIC SCHOOLS

Positions for reading specialists have increased in number much faster than the output of graduate training programs. As a result, many school systems have placed competent teachers with little or no special training in reading-specialist positions. A great variation

---

85. John McLeod, "Prediction of Childhood Dyslexia," *Bulletin of the Orton Society*, XVI (1966), 14-23.

exists in the specific duties performed and in the distribution of effort among such major activities as diagnosing children, teaching corrective classes or remedial groups, providing in-service training for teachers, serving on curriculum committees, and the like. Remedial teachers are likely to spend most of their time teaching small groups of retarded readers, usually for one period a day, two or three times a week. The remedial teachers often work in two schools. Reading consultants generally advise the classroom teacher on methods and materials for the retarded reader instead of working directly with the child. Both kinds of services are desirable.

The development of reading clinics or reading centers within school systems has been increasing. In New York City, the eleven clinics of the Special Reading Services employ multidisciplinary staffs, each with reading teachers, a psychologist, a social worker, and a part-time psychiatrist.[86] An increasing number of states are providing financial support for remedial reading; sometimes this is organized on a county-wide basis. Under Titles I and III of the Elementary and Secondary Education Act of 1965, many new kinds of remedial programs have been organized.

Remedial reading programs have been increasing in number at secondary- as well as at elementary-school levels. A lack of trained personnel has militated against the quality of many of these laudable efforts. Generally, the remedial reading work takes the place of periods of English. Secondary programs tend toward larger groups and less diagnosis and individualization than is common in elementary remedial programs and usually should be called "corrective" rather than "remedial."

IN COLLEGES

It is an exceptional junior college, senior college, or university today that does not provide special help in reading for some of its students. This help may be provided through one or more optional reading-improvement courses, or it may be more clinical and individualized.

The most common pattern takes the form of a multipurpose

---

86. Stella M. Cohn, "Upgrading Instruction through Special Reading Services," *Reading Teacher,* XVIII (March, 1965), 477-81.

reading clinic. Many of these clinics provide reading help to the institution's own students, offer diagnosis and limited remedial help to public school students from near-by communities, serve as training centers for reading specialists, and serve as research laboratories.[87]

IN PRIVATE ORGANIZATIONS

There is a small but increasing number of schools that offer full-time schooling to children with severe reading disabilities.[88] Centers or individual tutors who offer remedial help to children and adults can be found in most cities. One should be cautious about making referrals to organizations that stress speed and utilize high-pressure advertising. A statement of minimum standards for staff qualifications and professional ethics has been promulgated by the International Reading Association.

New Methodology and Materials

The most common approach to remedial reading is an eclectic one, in which many methods and materials are considered useful and the guiding principle is to choose for each child the approach, materials, pace, motivation, and so forth that seem to offer the greatest promise of success for the individual.[89]

Within the past few years, many exciting innovations in remediation have appeared, some of which are based on the use of new materials. Most of these innovations have not been available long enough for careful, comparative evaluations to have been completed and published. Space does not allow more than a brief listing, with reference to evaluative research in instances in which it exists.

---

87. Albert J. Harris (ed.), *Some Administrative Problems of Reading Clinics* ("Institute Highlights," No. 3 [Newark, Del.: International Reading Association, 1965]); Roy A. Kress and Marjorie S. Johnson, *Reading Clinics* (International Reading Association, 1964 [annotated bibliography]).

88. Among them may be listed the Hawthorne Center, Northville, Michigan; Fryeburg Academy, Fryeburg, Maine; Marianne Frostig Center of Educational Therapy, Los Angeles, California; and the McGlannan School, Miami, Florida.

89. Harris, *How To Increase Reading Ability, op. cit.*; Florence Roswell and Gladys Natchez, *Reading Disability: Diagnosis and Treatment* (New York: Basic Books, Inc., 1964).

NEUROLOGICAL PATTERNING

The Delacato approach, briefly described earlier (see footnote 39), emphasizes readiness activities which are supposed to eliminate specific types of neurological immaturity and develop unilateral dominance. In individual cases, this program may involve practice in crawling and creeping, sleeping in a particular position, preventing the use of the preferred eye, and so on. The only published independent research on the Delacato approach reported no support for any of the Delacato hypotheses that were tested (see footnote 40).

A somewhat related but more limited procedure is Leavell's stereoscopic procedure for correcting crossed dominance by training the non-dominant eye when it is on the opposite side from the dominant hand.[90] Yarborough failed to find significantly greater reading gains in a group of poor readers with crossed dominance (after training by this procedure) than were found in the control group.[91]

MOTOR AND PERCEPTUAL TRAINING

Kephart, developing his principles out of a background of work with brain-injured children, stressed the importance of developing mastery over simple tasks before tackling more complex performances. His program includes procedures for diagnosing mastery of basic motor and perceptual skills. Training procedures include sensory-motor training, chalkboard training, training for directionality, training ocular control, and training form perception.[92] Although the program seems to be oriented primarily to work with brain-injured or mentally retarded children, it has been incorporated into some remedial programs.[93] No research on the value of these

---

90. Ullin W. Leavell, *Leavell Language-Development Service* (Meadeville, Pa.: Keystone View Co., 1958).

91. Betty H. Yarborough, "A Study of the Effectiveness of the Leavell Language-Development Service in Improving the Silent Reading Ability and Other Language Skills of Persons with Mixed Dominance" (unpublished Doctor's dissertation, University of Virginia, 1964).

92. Kephart, *op. cit.*

93. Clifford J. Kolson and George Kaluger, *Clinical Aspects of Remedial Reading* (Springfield, Ill.: Charles C. Thomas, 1963).

procedures in the treatment of reading disability has come to this writer's attention.

Frostig has developed materials for improving the five aspects of visual perception measured by her test.[94] So far these seem to be used more to develop readiness in inmature, disadvantaged children than in remedial programs. As has been noted earlier, Olson's results do not support the claims that the test is accurately diagnostic (see footnote 61).

A major effort to study the value of specific training to overcome deficits in visual and auditory perception has been reported by Silver, Hagin, and Hersch.[95] They matched two groups of boys with reading and behavior problems. In one group, specific perceptual training based on each boy's perceptual profile was given for six months, followed by six months of tutoring in reading; the other group had remedial reading followed by perceptual training. A follow-up will be conducted through 1968. Preliminary results suggest that "where perceptual defects are first trained out, reading instruction at intermodal and verbal levels will have a better chance of success." The alternative of building perceptual training into the reading instruction was not involved in the study.

MULTISENSORY APPROACHES

The kinesthetic techniques developed by Fernald remain in wide use in remedial reading programs, although little has been done to separate the specific word-learning procedures (tracing, writing from memory) from the other features, such as reliance on pupils' oral productions for reading content.[96] Some recent variations on the Fernald program include Johnson's description of VAKT (visual-auditory-kinesthetic-tactual) and VAK (without tracing)

---

94. Marianne Frostig and David Horne, *The Frostig Program for the Development of Visual Perception* (Chicago: Follett Publishing Co., 1964).

95. Archie A. Silver, Rosa A. Hagin, and Marilyn F. Hersch, *Specific Reading Disability: Teaching through Stimulation of Deficit Perceptual Areas* (mimeographed; Department of Psychiatry and Neurology, New York University Medical Center, 1965).

96. Grace M. Fernald, *Remedial Techniques in Basic School Subjects* (New York: McGraw-Hill Book Co., 1943).

procedures used at Temple University.[97] Other variants have been described by Frostig [98] and by McCarthy and Oliver.[99] An interesting but untested method proposed by Blau is to block off vision when using a kinesthetic-tracing method; the learner is blindfolded and three-dimensional letters are employed.[100] The rationale is that this allows the child to learn through reasonably intact channels without interference or shortcircuiting from a deficient channel.

Ofman and Shaevitz compared two tracing methods with "look and say" in learning nonsense syllables. Tracing with the eye was as effective as tracing with the finger. They speculated that enforced attention to detail in sequence rather than tactual-kinesthetic sensation is the significant aid to learning.[101]

Commercial packages have begun to appear which combine tape recordings, film-strips, and reading materials. As in the case of so many recent developments in reading, there is as yet no evidence that these contribute to superior results in remedial programs.

USE OF MODIFIED ALPHABETS

The years since 1960 have seen intense interest generated in the possibilities of simplifying the task of learning to read English by using printed symbols that eliminate the inconsistency of the relationship between sound and printed symbol. Two main approaches have emerged: the use of transitional alphabets requiring special type fonts and the use of color.

The "Initial Teaching Alphabet" (i/t/a) devised by Sir James

---

97. Marjorie S. Johnson, "Tracing and Kinesthetic Techniques," chap. ix in *The Disabled Reader: Education of the Dyslexic Child*, ed. John Money (Baltimore: Johns Hopkins Press, 1966), pp. 147-60.

98. Marianne Frostig, "Corrective Reading in the Classroom," *Reading Teacher*, XVIII (April, 1965), 573-80.

99. W. McCarthy and J. Oliver, "Some Tactile-Kinesthetic Procedures for Teaching to Slow-Learning Children," *Exceptional Child*, XXXI (April, 1965), 419-21.

100. Harold Blau and Harriet Blau, *A Theory of Learning To Read by "Modality Blocking" or "Non-Visual" AKT* (mimeographed; Jamaica, N.Y.: Long Island Reading Institute, 1966).

101. William Ofman and Morton Shaevitz, "The Kinesthetic Method in Remedial Reading," *Journal of Experimental Education*, XXXI (March, 1963), 319-20.

Pitman has been widely studied since its introduction a few years ago. Providing an almost perfect correspondence between morpheme and grapheme, this forty-four-symbol alphabet also allows a relatively easy transition to the traditional alphabet. Its value in remedial work rests at present on reports of school tryouts with small groups rather than on controlled research.[102]

Another new alphabet, "Unifon," has been studied far less than i/t/a.[103] Fry did not find any advantage in using an alphabet with diacritical markings; users of basal readers in the traditional alphabet did as well as those of either i/t/a or diacritically marked materials in his first-grade study.[104]

Two color schemes that deserve serious consideration are Gattegno's "Words in Color" and Bannatyne's "Color Phonics System," neither of which has been subjected to comparative evaluation as yet.[105] In both systems, color is used to indicate which sound a particular printed symbol represents; the regular alphabet is used. "Words in Color" has a separate color for every sound, consonant as well as vowel; the Bannatyne system uses special colors only for symbols that can represent more than one sound. Both systems rely on color vision, ability to make auditory discriminations, and ability to use a synthetic blending procedure. Both stress integration of reading with writing and spelling.

PHONIC AND LINGUISTIC APPROACHES

June L. Orton has provided a useful description of the development and methodology of the synthetic phonics-blending method followed by Orton's disciples (see footnote 17) and particularly

---

102. *i/t/a bulletin*, IV (Winter, 1967), 2 (New York: Initial Teaching Alphabet Publications, Inc.).

103. Published by the Western Publishing Educational Services, Racine, Wis.

104. Edward B. Fry, "First Grade Reading Instruction Using Diacritical Marking System, Initial Teaching Alphabet and Basal Reading System," *Reading Teacher*, XIX (May, 1966), 666-69.

105. Caleb Gattegno and Dorothy Hinman, "Words in Color," chap. xi in *The Disabled Reader, op. cit.*, pp. 177-91; Alex D. Bannatyne, "The Color Phonics System," chap. xii in *The Disabled Reader, op. cit.*, pp. 193-214.

by Anna Gillingham.[106] Although this method has been in use for many years, this writer has not been able to find any comparative research on it.

The notion that reading problems can be prevented or cured by restricting beginning reading vocabulary to phonetically regular words has been advocated by Daniels and Diack [107] in Great Britain and by Barnhart [108] and Fries [109] in the United States. Instruction begins with words in lists and moves into sentences like "A fat cat ran." Opinions differ on the absence of meaningful content in the early stages; in the same volume Joos was sharply critical while Edwards accepted it.[110] Research data on the use of such materials in remedial reading are not yet available.

The "Progressive Choice Method" devised by Woolman has been developed mainly for use in programs for adult illiterates.[111] It is basically a synthetic sounding-blending method very much like Gillingham's. Bloomer reported that student clinicians learned to teach faster with it and that their pupils gained more as compared to "various standard techniques." [112] This study is open to the suspicion of a very strong Hawthorne effect.

PROGRAMED INSTRUCTION

In an unusually stimulating presentation, Goldiamond and Dyrud have clarified the point of view toward reading disability of those developing programed instructional procedures. Basically, the attitude is that, if the child fails to learn, something is wrong with the

---

106. June L. Orton, "The Orton-Gillingham Approach," chap. viii in *The Disabled Reader, op. cit.*, pp. 119-45.

107. J. C. Daniels and Hunter Diack, *Progress in Reading in the Infant School* (Nottingham: Institute of Education, University of Nottingham, 1960).

108. Leonard Bloomfield and Clarence L. Barnhart, *Let's Read: A Linguistic Approach* (Detroit: Wayne State University Press, 1961).

109. Charles C. Fries, *Linguistics and Reading* (New York: Holt, Rinehart & Winston, Inc., 1963).

110. See *The Disabled Reader, op. cit.*, pp. 92, 356.

111. Thomas J. Edwards, "The Progressive Choice Reading Method," chap. xiii in *The Disabled Reader, op. cit.*, pp. 215-28.

112. Richard H. Bloomer, "Progressive Choice Reading Techniques in a Remedial Reading Clinic," *Journal of Educational Research*, LVII (1964), 486-89.

teaching program. "What might normally have been permanent impairment was permanent only in the absence of the appropriate behavorial technology."[113] They point out many implications of such concepts as small steps, shaping, fading, and varying reinforcement schedules for remedial teaching.

Ellson has reported a series of studies based on conventional beginning reading materials, in which reinforcement theory has been applied to the careful specification of the procedures used in individual tutoring. Subjects included mentally retarded children and slow learners in the first grade.[114] The procedure seems applicable to a wide variety of materials and methods. The per cent failing to learn was unusually low, and the program is now being tried with a sizable disadvantaged first-grade population.

Sullivan has developed a beginning reading program in the form of programed workbooks, following a linguistic approach to some extent but teaching separate sounds and blending. These are now being advertised as remedial materials.[115] As with other very new materials, no evaluation studies are yet available.

USE OF NON-TEACHING ACCESSORY PROCEDURES

Many remedial teachers have longed for a magic button that could be pushed to lessen restlessness, lengthen attention span, sharpen concentration, cut down distractibility, and thereby increase the poor reader's ability to profit from his remedial opportunities.

One possibility lies in the use of hypnosis. Krippner reported on nine children with willing parents for whom hypnosis decreased tension, increased motivation, fostered interest, maintained attention, "facilitated revisualization and aided reauditorization."[116] An-

---

113. Israel Goldiamond and Jarl E. Dyrud, "Reading as Operant Behavior," chap. vii in *The Disabled Reader, op. cit.,* pp. 93-115.

114. Douglas G. Ellson et al., "Programmed Tutoring: A Teaching Aid and a Research Tool," *Reading Research Quarterly,* I (Fall, 1965), 77-127.

115. M. W. Sullivan, *Programmed Reading* (Palo Alto, Calif.: Behavior Research Laboratories, 1965).

116. Stanley Krippner, "The Use of Hypnosis with Elementary and Secondary School Children in a Summer Reading Clinic," *American Journal of Clinical Hypnosis,* VIII (April, 1966), 261-65.

other favorable report on hypnosis, based on a single case, was made by McCord.[117]

Another possibility lies in the use of mind-influencing medication. Smith and Carrigan reported greater gains in fourteen cases in which drugs were prescribed and taken than in six other cases in which the medication was prescribed but not taken.[118] Six different drugs were used, in varying doses. The results are obscured by presumed differences in motivation and by failure to follow the double-blind procedure usually employed in studies of drug effects. Staiger tried out Deanol with retarded readers and found no improvement in reading comprehension, although speed of perception seemed to show a gain.[119] There are now drugs known to be effective as tranquilizers, energizers, antidepressants, and so forth. Logically, there should be some value for remediation in the use of drugs which control interfering symptoms, although verification of such an expectation is not yet available. Further research is needed in this area.

Psychotherapy as a treatment for reading disability was more actively studied in the 1940's than in the 1960's. Studholme reported a pilot study of group guidance for mothers of adolescent boys in a remedial program.[120] Roman found that delinquent adolescents responded more favorably to a "tutorial-group-therapy" approach than to a straight instructional approach.[121] While, unquestionably many poor readers have been treated by psychotherapy, reports about such treatment have not been getting into print.

USE OF NON-PROFESSIONAL HELP

Under the pressure of finding help for thousands of youngsters

---

117. Hallack McCord, "Improving Reading Ability through Combined Tutoring and Hypnotherapy," *Journal of Developmental Reading*, (Winter, 1964), 142-43.

118. Smith and Carrigan, *op. cit.*

119. Ralph C. Staiger, "Medicine for Reading Improvement," *Journal of Developmental Reading*, V (Autumn, 1961), 48-51.

120. Janice M. Studholme, "Group Guidance with Mothers of Retarded Readers," *Reading Teacher*, XVII (April, 1964), 528-30.

121. Melvin Roman, "Tutorial Group Therapy and Remedial Reading," *High Points*, XLIII (January, 1961), 29-31.

who cannot be reached by available trained remedial personnel, many ventures in the use of untrained helpers have been launched. A pioneer was the Public Education Association in New York City, which provides professional training and supervision to college graduates willing to be volunteer tutors in public schools. After-school programs staffed by well-meaning volunteers abound, but most of them provide help with homework rather than instruction to overcome deficiencies in skills.

An interesting study of tutoring has been reported by Cloward.[122] Disadvantaged secondary-school students (including some retarded readers) were trained by "Mobilization for Youth" to act as reading tutors to disadvantaged elementary-school students. Those seen once a week failed to show more gain than a control group, but those seen twice a week showed significant gains. The tutors in general made more growth in reading than the tutored, and most gain was made by the poorer readers among the tutors. The tutored group did not improve significantly in school marks, school behavior ratings, attitudes, or aspirations.

In the light of Cloward's findings, one may well question the widely held belief that any help, no matter how inexpert, is better than no help at all. Unless volunteers are trained and supervised, their efforts may be fruitless.

The Results of Remedial Reading

There is, finally, a partial answer to the question, "What happens to the remedial pupil afterward?"

Two studies have reported long-time follow-up of cases given intensive remedial treatment for as long as they seemed to need it. Robinson and Smith checked on forty-eight clients who received help at the Reading Clinic of the University of Chicago in 1948.[123] The majority had graduated from college, and some were still in school. Rawson reported on fifty-six private school boys given remedial help during the period 1930-47 and followed up in 1964-

---

122. Robert D. Cloward, *Studies in Tutoring* (mimeographed; New York: Research Center, School of Social Work, Columbia University, 1966).

123. Helen M. Robinson and Helen K. Smith, "Reading Clinic Clients—Ten Years After," *Elementary School Journal*, LXIII (October, 1962), 22-27.

65.[124] Their median I.Q. was 131. Of the fifty-six, forty-eight had Bachelor's degrees, and three were still in college. Five had earned doctorates. The group included six research scientists and three professors. These two studies are in agreement that remedial reading, if continued as long as needed, enables the intellectually competent to be successful in higher education.

The results of short-term remediation are, however, disappointing. Remedial pupils tend to gain at better than a normal rate (and far better than their own previous rate) while receiving help. When the help lasts for a school year or less, the average remedial pupil fails to maintain his rate of progress and gradually falls behind again.[125]

Balow provided evidence that continuing to maintain contact with pupils may be an important factor in their later progress. Those children from the University of Minnesota Reading Clinic who did not receive supportive follow-up failed to continue to gain, while those who received it continued to gain at three-quarters of the normal rate of growth.[126]

These studies tend to show that remedial reading can have very favorable outcomes but that the gains may be lost if the remediation is stopped too soon. Even a very occasional contact may help a pupil to maintain his momentum.

Possible Future Developments

Some speculation about trends in the next decade may be ventured. One trend already evident is toward recognition of remedial reading as a field of special education, requiring trained practitioners and deserving special financial support comparable to

---

124. Margaret B. Rawson, "After a Generation's Time: A Follow-up Study of Fifty-six Boys," *Bulletin of the Orton Society*, XVI (1966), 24-37.

125. J. E. Collins, *The Effects of Remedial Education* ("Educational Monographs," No. 4 [Edinburgh: Oliver & Boyd, 1961]); K. Lovel, C. Byrne, and B. A. Richardson, "A Further Study of the Educational Progress of Children Who Had Received Remedial Instruction," *British Journal of Educational Psychology*, XXXIII (February, 1963), 3-9; L. R. Johnson and D. Platts, "A Summary of a Study of the Reading Ages of Children Who Had Been Given Remedial Teaching," *British Journal of Educational Psychology*, XXXII (February, 1962), 66-71.

126. Bruce Balow, "The Long-Term Effect of Remedial Reading Instruction," *Reading Teacher*, XVIII (April, 1965), 581-86.

that given for speech correction, teaching the mentally retarded, and the like. Certification for reading specialists is likely to be adopted in many states, and federal and state support for remedial programs is likely to be strengthened. Thus, a higher percentage of disabled readers is likely to receive competent help than at present.

In differential diagnosis, there will be further study of the validity of existing diagnostic procedures and of promising new ones. In this connection, financial support is needed for a co-ordinated, large-scale, multidisciplinary research program. Planning for the first steps of such a program has already begun.

The competing claims of a variety of new materials will be subjected to objective evaluation. Innovations and revised versions, however, are likely to come out faster than research workers can conduct the needed evaluations.

The solutions of many unsolved problems relating to the organization and administration of remedial programs are waiting for appropriate research to be conducted. A guess may be ventured that not much progress will be made in this area and that a wide variety of plans will continue to be based more on personal judgment than on research evidence.

CHAPTER VI

Organizational Patterns of Schools and Classrooms for Reading Instruction

HARRY W. SARTAIN

During the colonial period, reading, the cornerstone of religious training, was taught in the dame schools, in the village reading and writing schools, or in tutorial style in homes and churches.[1] Increased enrolments led to the introduction of the monitorial system and to a rather broad sectioning of children by general levels of progress in the early decades of the nineteenth century.[2]

Concerned about the poor quality of instruction in district schools in the 1830's, Horace Mann left a promising political career to devote all his efforts to improving education, and, after traveling in Europe, he recommended that American schools adopt as a major organizational innovation the highly graded plan of Prussia.[3] This type of organization spread throughout America until it became the typical plan in urban areas.

At first, graded organization appeared to make teaching more effective than it had previously been, but, in time, it became evident that the system did not make allowances for either qualitative or quantitative differences in children's talents and accomplishments. Consequently, sensitive educators began in the late nineteenth century to urge changes that would break the "lock step" in which they found their pupils trapped. Attempts were made to differentiate progress rates, to differentiate curriculums, and to add subject-

---

1. William M. French, *America's Educational Tradition: An Interpretive History* (Boston: D. C. Heath & Co., 1964), p. 14.

2. *Grouping in the Elementary School*, ed. Ann Morganstern (New York: Pitman Publishing Corp., 1966), p. 5.

3. French, *op. cit.*, p. 100.

matter specialists and other personnel to supplement the work of the classroom teacher.[4] Among these were forerunners of special plans currently used in many schools.[5]

In response to many factors—increased awareness of individual differences (caused by more extensive and improved intelligence and achievement testing), increasing enrolments, the "explosion" of knowledge, pressures engendered by public reaction to the first Sputnik, and so forth—the schools have continually broadened and extended their objectives and have adopted a long series of innovations, including various forms of departmentalization, non-grading, team teaching, and many other organizational patterns. Occasionally, school administrators have made careful preliminary studies of such organizational patterns before adopting them, but, too often, they have instituted changes hastily and imprudently in the name of "progress."

This chapter presents criteria to be considered in judging proposed organizational patterns and then applies them to various patterns in use today. Because most research projects have not been designed to measure and control halo effects and all of the many variables involved, few of their findings have been conclusive. Most available research is best used to indicate trends rather than to supply answers. Consequently, the philosophically derived criteria offered in this chapter are considered to be fully as significant as the results of the research for judging the patterns of school and classroom organization.

Although the discussion focuses directly upon reading instruction, it cannot be entirely limited to what happens during "reading periods"; most authorities agree that reading must be taught in all areas of study. Thus, organizational procedures must be considered in relation to the whole school operation, not to reading periods alone.

---

4. *Elementary School Organization: Purposes, Patterns, Perspective*, published as entire issue of *The National Elementary Principal*, XLI (December, 1961), 52-55.

5. Rose Koury, "Elementary School Organization . . . What Direction Shall It Take?" *Education Briefs*, No. 37 (January, 1960), 15.

Establishment of Multiple Standards

Too often, a newly conceived organizational pattern has been initiated in a school because of a single obvious strength and without adequate consideration of possible adverse effects upon the pupils or upon the curriculum. As a result, organizational structures adopted in some schools often have created as many problems as they have solved.

In order to be effective, school-organization changes should be planned with consideration for total value systems, for the type and structure of the content to be studied, for the principles of child growth, for the psychology of teaching and of learning, and for the intricacies of daily classroom instruction. Planners must recognize that most Americans value the individual person more than all else. Goodlad says that the humanistic conception of education ". . . values each student simply because he is a human being." [6] In accordance with this view, school systems should place high value on the rights and dignity of individuals.

The curriculum should be planned to develop the unique talents of each individual in order that he may become personally and vocationally self-fulfilling as well as socially effective. Methods and organizational patterns should enable the teacher to know children as social and intellectual individuals and to guide their growth according to each unique set of interests and capabilities. This will foster both the development of creative thinking [7] and the acquisition of fruitful habits of independent study.

School organizational changes should be based on the fact that, often, the learning of significant concepts is enhanced not only by the logical structure of the content [8] but also by its gradual intro-

---

6. John I. Goodlad, "Directions of Curriculum Change," *NEA Journal*, LV (December, 1966), 37.

7. Pauline Snedden Sears, *The Effect of Classroom Conditions on the Strength of Achievement Motive and Work Output on Elementary School Children* (U.S. Office of Education, Co-operative Research Project No. 873 [Stanford, Calif.: Stanford University, 1963]), as quoted by Robert L. Spaulding, "Peer and School Influences," *Review of Educational Research*, XXXIV (December, 1964), 592-94.

8. *Ibid.*

duction, by its integration into a complex of related knowledge, and by the closeness of the concepts to be learned to the experience of the learner. Because structures and sequences must be those that can be perceived by the child, they may not always be those seen by the adult academician who remembers imperfectly his own experiences and behavior during the early stages of childhood learning.

Modern organizational patterns should be based on the recognition that the child's self-concept is of vital importance in motivating learning and in setting ceilings on learning. The child who has attained an inadequate self-concept because of frequent criticisms or because of an inflexible curriculum that has constantly marked him as a failure is just as handicapped as he imagines himself to be. And most children perform less well for a teacher who is seen as a threatening stranger than for one who is seen as supporting the learner.[9] A teacher who knows the child as a person, not merely as a pupil having certain academic strengths and deficiencies, is viewed as a trusted friend.

Schools create their own dropouts and other problems by trying to force some children into educational programs in which they feel unrewarded either because of lack of success or lack of stimulation. Since no one program, even a three-track system, will provide for all human variability, it is essential that school-organization changes lead to increased flexibility in curriculum.

The teacher, too, must be considered as a person. The organizational pattern should enable him to be as successful as his knowledge and skill permit. It should encourage him to adapt his teaching in the ways that, for him, are most productive, and it should not place more demands upon him than can be met by a person of his capability.

In view of these and related considerations, a number of criteria can be offered for judging the merits of various patterns of school and classroom organization. Thoughtful educators will consider all of these criteria instead of only one or two when planning for innovation.

---

9. Spaulding, *op. cit.*, p. 594; C. M. Christensen, "Relationships between Pupil Achievement, Pupil-Affect-Need, Teacher Warmth, and Teacher Permissiveness," *Journal of Educational Psychology*, LI (June, 1960), 169-74.

CRITERIA FOR EVALUATING ORGANIZATIONAL PATTERNS [10]

Factors related to curriculum content and structure.—The organizational patterns of schools and classrooms should contribute to the effectiveness of curricular planning and experiences. In view of the purposes of modern education, the recommended curriculum plan:

1. Places special value upon the uniqueness of each learner.
2. Provides both balance of content and opportunity for correlations among the various areas of study.
3. Structures the expected outcomes in continuous developmental growth sequences that include provision for spaced review.
4. Expands or contracts its offerings in depth and breadth to fit the varying capabilities and purposes of learners at different times.
5. Provides a variety of types of learning experiences to capitalize upon learners' different interests and modes of learning.

Factors related to the personal success of the learner.—In order to enhance the child's opportunities to become an increasingly adequate person, the modern school:

1. Develops a warm, supportive teacher-pupil relationship.
2. Helps various pupils, in accordance with their different capabilities, to set somewhat different academic goals that provide challenge and stimulation.
3. Provides experiences which will help the learner see himself as a worthy, adequately capable person.
4. Provides experiences which encourage the child to interact with others in ways that strengthen his social understanding and habits as well as his academic competencies.
5. Facilitates the placement of responsibility for learning on the pupil, making him an intellectually active participant rather than a passive observer.
6. Develops habits of constructive self-direction through increasing opportunities for purposeful independent work.
7. Offers a consistent work load rather than one which fluctuates greatly from day to day and week to week.

---

10. Harry W. Sartain, "Applications of Research to the Problem of Instructional Flexibility," in *Progress and Promise in Reading Instruction*, ed. Donald L. Cleland and Elaine Vilscek (Report of the Twenty-second Annual Conference on Reading [Pittsburgh: School of Education, University of Pittsburgh, 1966]).

Factors related to teacher effectiveness.—A desirable pattern of school and classroom organization:

1. Makes the teacher fully aware of the extent and types of individual differences among children.
2. Provides for frequent evaluation of each pupil's general progress in terms of individual capacity rather than of class standards.
3. Enables teachers to do individual diagnostic appraisals and corrective teaching for most children who encounter temporary difficulties.
4. Makes fairly comprehensive pupil records readily available for adding notes about significant behaviors and for use in examining and analyzing problems and progress.
5. Provides enough flexibility of scheduling to permit teachers to readily change or extend daily time blocks and to alter curriculum plans in order to capitalize upon various types of learning opportunities.
6. Utilizes the special capabilities of teachers as fully as possible.
7. Makes efficient use of teacher time, providing the maximum amount of learning possible for the amount of instructional time and effort expended.
8. Is reasonably economical with respect to teacher-pupil ratio and utilization of school facilities.

An Evaluation of Major Organizational Patterns

In this section, four generally inclusive features of most organization plans are discussed. Following that discussion, a number of specific plans are briefly described.

GENERAL PATTERNS

Each system of school and classroom organization can be classified according to its degree of polarity on one or more of the following four continuums of characteristics:

1. One-teacher ⟵⟶ Multiple-Teacher Instruction
2. Heterogeneous ⟵⟶ Homogeneous Sectioning
3. Differentiated ⟵⟶ Uniform Instruction within the Classroom
4. Independent ⟵⟶ Directed Study

As mentioned previously, because the research evidence on the comparative values of these characteristics is not adequate, one must also evaluate organizational patterns in terms of the criteria listed in the preceding section.

One-Teacher ⟵⟶ *Multiple-Teacher Instruction.*—The one-teacher pattern of organization is necessarily that of the self-contained classroom, whether it houses children of one age level or several. The multiple-teacher feature is found in a number of different patterns.

Single-teacher plans have long been defended because the person who teaches one group in all or almost all subjects can learn a great deal about each individual, can adjust the curriculum and the time schedules easily, and can interrelate academic and social experiences in an optimum manner. The rationale most often given for adopting a multiple-teacher system is that it utilizes the special capabilities of teachers as fully as possible—staff members may specialize in teaching subjects in which they are best prepared or, with a different type of competence, in teaching children of certain ability levels. Some teachers believe they save time and effort under the multiple-teacher plan because it permits them to concentrate on a limited area of in-service study and to use the same lesson plans with more than one group or class. There is also the possibility that long-term curriculum planning can be better structured if done by specialists rather than by generalists, especially if the latter are given inadequate consultant assistance.

In a multiple-teacher organization, however, the teacher must meet with a number of classes—perhaps as few as two in modified teaming or as many as six or eight in a fully departmentalized situation. This means he must attempt to teach many more different children each day than are taught by a teacher under a one-teacher arrangement, and he must fit his plans to the schedule of pupil movements from room to room. Because the teacher in this situation may work with fifty to two hundred children daily, he usually finds it impossible to become well acquainted with most of his pupils. Without outside help, he is generally unable to provide the individual diagnostic testing and to make the detailed observations that are needed to adjust the curricular goals and experiences to the unique pattern of capabilities of each pupil and to offer individual corrective work needed to overcome his temporary problems. Even the teacher's general-progress evaluations are seldom related to the inherent capability of the child; in fact, a parent too often may find that the teacher is even uncertain of the child's name. Records, if kept in a central location, are not readily used because of their relative inaccessibility.

Not only does individualization suffer when a pupil has too

many teachers, but flexibility in arranging curricular experiences is lost. As the number of pupil movements from room to room increases, the less likelihood there is of correlation among subject fields. This is especially deleterious in reading because, for best results, reading skills must be taught in all subject fields, and the child who needs special help or special stimulation should receive it throughout the day instead of only during a language-arts period. In addition to a lack of consistent challenge or assistance, children frequently are subjected to unreasonable work expectations when several teachers give heavy assignments at one time. Such experiences certainly will not help most of them acquire effective independent study habits or learn to see themselves as capable persons.

When classes move by the bell, there is a lack of flexibility that makes it almost impossible for the teacher to extend a period in order to complete activities of special value, such as the pursuit of newly awakened interests in independent reading, the preparation of a puppet show related to group reading, or participation in a field trip to gain certain concepts needed for depth of comprehension.

While multiple-teacher organization may be necessary for adequate specialization at the secondary levels, it would appear that, at the elementary level, the number of teachers a child faces each day should be limited in order to provide optimal learning situations. Moreover, competent teachers who are college graduates, even though they lack a highly specialized education, usually find it possible to challenge the brightest pupils in the lower and intermediate grades.

Heterogeneous ⟷ Homogeneous Sectioning.—These terms distinguish between situations in which pupils are assigned to classes somewhat randomly and situations in which the assignments are made on the basis of ability. The word "sectioning" is used in this chapter instead of "grouping" to avoid confusing intraclass with interclass grouping.

The Joplin Interclass Grouping Plan and the Dual Progress Plan both require homogeneous sectioning. Other common plans of organization—self-contained, departmentalized, and team teaching—may involve either heterogeneous or homogeneous class sectioning.

Every teacher is aware that there is some range of accomplishment among his pupils, but many fail to perceive the full range of differences in pupil capability. Cook and Clymer, after analyzing several studies, noted significant facts about the ranges of general intelligence and achievement as follows:

> When intelligence is measured and converted into age units, the range among first-graders (6-years-old) is 4 years. At the seventh-grade level (12-year-olds) the range is 8 years. The typical range of ability in any grade (disregarding the 2 per cent of pupils at each end of the distribution) is equal to two-thirds the chronological age of the median pupil in that grade.
>
> When achievement in the various subjects is measured at each grade level, the range of achievement is found to be approximately the same as that for intelligence as described above.[11]

Using newly devised instruments for measurement, educational leaders during the first two decades of the twentieth century became increasingly aware of the extent of pupil differences, and some advocated homogeneous sectioning as a convenience in differentiating the curriculum and as a means of conserving teacher effort. Usually it was assumed that, if the three or four classes at a given level in a school were sectioned on the basis of mental age or achievement, the number of instructional groups needed for adequately differentiated work in each room would be greatly reduced. Consequently, some schools assigned pupils to classrooms on the basis of mental age, average reading-achievement score, or average mathematics-achievement score, and the teacher usually gave the same materials and assignments to all the pupils in his room. This practice is followed in many schools today.

In the secondary schools which provide many class sections and a variety of course options, class sectioning on the basis of achievement may be defended. At the elementary level, at which children often stay with the same class section all day, a complete commitment to homogeneous sectioning infers the assumptions (a) that a single index of ability is an adequate estimate of a child's potential in all required fields of study or in all components of any single field and (b) that every child in a homogeneous class will progress

---

11. Walter W. Cook and Theodore Clymer, "Acceleration and Retardation," chap. ix in *Individualizing Instruction*, (Sixty-first Yearbook of the National Society for the Study of Education, Part I [Chicago: Distributed by the University of Chicago Press, 1962]), pp. 206-7.

at the same rate, thereby maintaining the initial homogeneity throughout the school term.

The fallacy of these assumptions is easily shown by examining the average and subtest scores of individual pupils on a standard achievement battery given in any classroom in the United States. A look at results of a second battery administered at another time will reveal a large number of differences in achievement and in patterns of special ability.

Each pupil varies in his capability in different phases of the curriculum. Studies by Hull [12] in 1927 and Burr [13] in 1931 revealed that, after pupils had been sectioned into three classes on the basis of general ability, the range of *individual* achievement scores in each class was at least 80 per cent as great as the range of scores for the entire group before the classes were sectioned. These and later studies tended to discourage homogeneous sectioning for a number of years. During the last two decades, however, public pressures have caused administrators to return to homogeneous sectioning in numerous schools. Doubts about the likelihood of its success are reinforced by past research reports summarized by Ekstrom; [14] Keliher; [15] Borg; [16] Goldberg, Passow, and Justman; [17] and others.

Although a few studies, especially older ones, have seemed to support homogeneous sectioning, Borg's careful analysis of experiments at both the elementary and the secondary levels shows that

12. Clark L. Hull, "Variability in Amount of Different Traits Possessed by the Individual," *Journal of Educational Psychology*, XVIII (February, 1927), 97-106.

13. Marvin A. Burr, *A Study of Homogeneous Grouping*, ("Teachers College Contributions to Education," No. 457 [New York: Teachers College, Columbia University, 1931]).

14. Ruth Ekstrom, "Experimental Studies of Homogeneous Grouping," *School Review*, LXIX (Summer, 1961), 222.

15. Alice Keliher, "The Grouping Question—1930-1962: 1930 Research on Homogeneous Grouping Compared with More Recent Studies," in *Toward Effective Grouping* (Washington: Association for Childhood Education International, 1962), pp. 17-24.

16. Walter R. Borg, *Ability Grouping in the Public Schools* (Madison, Wis.: Denmar Educational Research Services, 1966), pp. 11-21.

17. Miriam L. Goldberg, A. Harry Passow, and Joseph Justman, *The Effects of Ability Grouping* (New York: Teachers College, Columbia University, 1966), pp. 1-22.

those favorable to homogeneous sectioning almost invariably were faulty in design or failed to provide appropriate statistical treatment of data.[18] A possible exception is the study by Simpson and Martinson involving only superior students; such students at both the elementary and secondary levels made significantly greater gains in reading and other subjects when sectioned by ability.[19] From his own three-year study, Borg concluded that, in general, superior pupils achieved slightly more in homogeneous than in heterogeneous classes, but in reading (measured at only the elementary level) differences did not consistently favor either form of organization.[20]

In a brief but well-designed study described by Hartill, 1,374 intermediate-grade pupils were instructed by the same teacher during successive half-years. The children made greater over-all achievement gains while assigned to heterogeneous classes.[21] Edmiston and Benfer found that, when curriculum patterns were not specifically differentiated, fifth- and sixth-graders in groups having an I.Q. range of 41 points did not make less reading progress than pupils in groups having an I.Q. range of 29 points.[22] Goldberg, Passow, and Justman, investigating the progress of more than 2,000 fifth- and sixth-grade pupils grouped in fifteen different combinations on the basis of ability, found that ". . . narrowing the ability range in the classroom on the basis of some measure of general academic aptitude will, by itself, in the absence of carefully planned adaptations of content and method, produce little positive change in the academic achievement of pupils at any ability level."[23] They also observed that pupil achievement was less affected by the pattern of organization than by assignment to a particular teacher; some teachers were

---

18. Borg, *op. cit.*, pp. 12-15.

19. R. E. Simpson and Ruth A. Martinson, *Educational Programs for Gifted Pupils* (Sacramento: California State Department of Education, January, 1961).

20. Borg, *op. cit.*, p. 27.

21. R. W. Hartill, *Homogeneous Grouping* (New York: Teachers College, Columbia University, 1936).

22. R. W. Edmiston and J. C. Benfer, "Relationship between Group Achievement and Range of Abilities within Groups," *Journal of Educational Research*, XLII (March, 1949), 547-48.

23. Goldberg, Passow, and Justman, *op. cit.*, p. 167.

consistently more successful than others regardless of types of grouping.[24]

Borg's experiment compared achievements of homogeneous and heterogeneous sections of several hundred elementary and secondary students. Most homogeneous classes except the slowest groups made greater progress during the first year, when homogeneous sectioning was novel. Elementary-school data in succeeding years were available for only the classes which began in fourth grade. Reading achievement for these classes during the second year was significantly higher in heterogeneous sections, but during the third year there was no significant difference. On the *California Study Methods Survey*, administered to these pupils when they were in seventh grade, the heterogeneously sectioned classes were significantly superior to those sectioned homogeneously at all three levels of ability represented by the homogeneous sections.[25]

In a recent study involving sectioning at the high-school level, the factor of teacher skills was well controlled by having eight ninth-grade instructors teach both ability-grouped and heterogeneously grouped sections during different periods of the day. They planned together the procedures to be used in differentiating instruction to suit individual needs in both types of sections. T-test analyses of the scores of tests administered at the beginning and at the close of the experiment revealed that the type of organization did not make a significant difference in growth in reading comprehension.[26]

As implied previously, homogeneous-sectioning plans have failed to produce better results because human variability is too complex to be extensively modified by any simple one-dimensional change in school organization. Support for this statement is found in the results of Balow's study of ninety-four fifth-grade pupils sectioned into four so-called homogeneous classes on the basis of their grade-equivalent score averages on eight tests of various reading skills. Prior to sectioning, average scores of individual pupils on the

24. *Ibid.*, p. 62.

25. Borg, *op. cit.*, pp. 22-31.

26. E. M. Drews, "The Effectiveness of Homogeneous Ability Grouping in Ninth Grade English Classes with Slow, Average, and Superior Students" (unpublished manuscript, Michigan State University, 1962), summarized by Borg, *op. cit.*, pp. 18-19.

reading tests ranged from 2.0 to 9.0, but the ranges of average scores for each class after sectioning were only 2.0—3.6, 3.6—4.6, 4.6—5.6, and 5.7—9.0. Thus, it would appear that homogeneous sectioning had greatly reduced the amount of differentiated teaching required to help members of each class make rapid growth in reading.[27] However, when Balow analyzed the scores of the individual pupils in each of the four "homogeneous classes" on the eight different tests of reading skills, he found that the individual-score variation within each class often was almost as great as the variation in the entire group before it was separated into classes. For example, in Class B, for which the range of average scores was only 4.6—5.6, the ranges of scores of individual pupils on four tests were: rate, 1.8—12.7; comprehension, 2.5—11.1; word meaning, 1.8—7.9; and alphabetizing, 3.1—12.4. Balow clearly had every reason to conclude that the practice of homogeneous grouping did not provide homogeneous groups.[28] In Tyler's words, "A limited range in average grade equivalent is no guarantee of equally narrow ranges in the grade equivalents used to derive the average." [29]

Researchers have been concerned also with the social-emotional effects of homogeneous sectioning on pupils. Borg found that superior students received the largest number of sociometric choices in heterogeneous classes, while average and slower pupils were most favored in homogeneous classes. Apparently the bright pupils are most admired in whichever class sections they are included; therefore, average and slow pupils receive sociometric choices more often when bright pupils are not present to compete. However, the self-concept scores of pupils on the *Index of Adjustment and Values* consistently revealed more favorable self-concepts in heterogeneous classes.[30] In one report of their study, Goldberg and Passow concluded:

... In general, self-attitudes seemed rather more sensitive to grouping

---

27. Irving Balow, "Does Homogeneous Grouping Give Homogeneous Groups?" *Elementary School Journal*, LXIII (October, 1962), 28-32.

28. *Ibid.*

29. Fred T. Tyler, "Intraindividual Variability," chap. x in *Individualizing Instruction, op. cit.*, p. 171.

30. Borg, *op. cit.*, pp. 76-84.

than did the other nonacademic variables, but the effects of narrowing the range or separating the extreme levels was to *raise* the self-assessments of the slower pupils, *lower* the initially high self-ratings of the gifted, and leave the intermediate levels largely unaffected. The slow pupils also showed greater gains in their "ideal image" when the gifted were absent than was true when they were present.[31]

Through the years, homogeneous sectioning has been recommended because it was credited with fulfilling the organizational criteria of providing for individuals and of making teaching less difficult. The research available shows that it does neither. Pupils differ in every aspect of academic growth and with respect to their backgrounds of experience; this complexity of human differences makes it impossible to form a class that is homogeneous in more than one area of skill development, and that homogeneity is only temporary.

As implied previously, achievement sectioning in secondary schools may be appropriate if entirely different curricular experiences are provided for students having different educational and vocational goals. At the elementary levels, homogeneous sectioning, with the possible exception of the sectioning of enrichment groups and special education classes, appears to be of little value. It can even be dangerous in that it may deceive many teachers into concluding that they can give uniform instruction to all in a class. Cook explains: "The harm resulting from homogeneous grouping is inherent in the assumption that the group is homogeneous and that instructional materials and procedures can be adjusted to the needs of the whole group—that, in other words, a problem has been solved before it has been understood." [32]

Goldberg, Passow, and Justman likewise warn that, without carefully planned curriculum variations, ability sectioning can be ". . . at best, ineffective, at worst, harmful."

It can become harmful when it lulls teachers and parents into believing that because there is grouping, the school is providing differentiated education for pupils of varying degrees of ability, when in reality

---

31. Miriam L. Goldberg and A. Harry Passow, "The Effects of Ability Grouping," in *Grouping in the Elementary School, op. cit.,* p. 34

32. Walter W. Cook, *Grouping and Promotion in the Elementary Schools* (Minneapolis: University of Minnesota Press, 1941), p. 33.

that is not the case. It may become dangerous when it leads teachers to underestimate the learning capacities of pupils at the lower ability levels. It can also be damaging when it is inflexible and does not provide channels for moving children from lower to higher ability groups and back again. . .[33]

Finally, in Greene's words, "We cannot disregard the basic law of human nature that each child is a 'custom-made job.' "[34]

Differentiated ⟷ Uniform Instruction in the Classroom.—Whole-class teaching is most often practiced with interclass grouping, while differentiated instruction is an inherent feature of individualized reading, non-graded classes, the Continuous Progress Plan, and Individually Prescribed Instruction. The work in both self-contained and departmentalized classes may be highly differentiated or completely undifferentiated.

All those criteria of effective school organization listed in the first section of this chapter that deal with valuing uniqueness, supportive teacher-pupil relationships, individualized academic goals, individualized appraisal, and corrective instruction require highly differentiated teaching. It has been shown that systems for sectioning classes by ability do not produce homogeneous groups and, therefore, are usually inadequate as a means of differentiating work for most children.[35] If classes are self-contained, differentiation must be practiced *within* the classroom.

Elsewhere it has been explained that whole-class teaching leads pupils to form habits of inattention and to waste time waiting for the teacher while he is occupied with other children.[36] Moreover, children become bored listening to the teacher's voice; this may be the reason why excessive teacher talk is associated with mediocre

---

33. Goldberg, Passow, and Justman, *op. cit.*, p. 168.

34. John D. Greene, quoted by June Franseth and Rose Koury, in "A Guide to Research and Informed Judgment on Grouping Children," *Education Briefs*, No. 40 (May, 1964), 11.

35. Balow, *op. cit.*; Burr, *op. cit.*; Hull, *op. cit.*

36. Harry W. Sartain, "Classroom Carrels Improve Study," *Public School Digest* (Tri-State Area School Study Council, University of Pittsburgh), XIX (Autumn, 1966), 4-6.

achievement.[37] When instruction is properly differentiated within the classroom, children in each group are ready to learn the next concept or skill with reasonable effort and speed. After such learning, they have time to read independently while the teacher instructs other groups.

Small-group teaching makes it possible for the teacher to become well acquainted with the pupils as individuals, to perceive and diagnose their difficulties, to provide corrective instruction, or to modify the instructional goal. Such teaching is conducive to superior pupil progress. Jones found that children in rooms in which intraclass (within-class) grouping was practiced during one school year made academic gains that, on the average, were 2.5 months in excess of the gains made by children in rooms in which whole-class teaching at one level was practiced.[38] Likewise, Walker, working with three equivalent heterogeneous seventh-grade classes for only six weeks, found that significant progress was made by the lower halves of two classes using two separate plans for differentiated work, but the progress of comparable pupils in the class that was taught as a whole on one level was not significant.[39]

Despite the obvious need for differentiated instruction, it is not always provided. Tens of thousands of teachers persist in using inadequate whole-class activities because they do not know how to differentiate or because they are not convinced that the results are worth the effort required to make diagnostic appraisals and to plan learning experiences on several levels. At the opposite extreme can be found a number of zealous teachers who teach each child separately in a totally individualized reading program. While some teachers can succeed in the latter program, one must question whether the procedure results in the maximum amount of learning possible for the amount of instructional time and effort expended. Surely, in every classroom there are a few children who are progress-

---

37. Ned A. Flanders, *Teacher Influence, Pupil Attitudes, and Achievement* (Final Report, U.S. Office of Education, Co-operative Research Project No. 397 [Minneapolis: University of Minnesota, 1960]).

38. Daisy M. Jones, "Experiment in Adaptation to Individual Differences," *Journal of Educational Psychology*, XXXIX (May, 1948), 257-72.

39. Frederick R. Walker, "Evaluation of Three Methods of Teaching Reading, Seventh Grade," *Journal of Educational Research*, LIV (May, 1961), 356-58.

ing at rates similar enough to permit grouping them together for the introduction to basic skills, thereby reducing instructional repetition and giving the teacher time to teach more thoroughly.

It seems evident that whole-class teaching is usually indefensible, that fully individualized teaching is often impractical, and that teaching in small, flexible groups is essential for excellence.

Independent ⟷ Directed Study.—Educators have shown increased concern for independent study in recent years. The rapid growth of knowledge and the conditions of modern life require that people continue to be active learners after their formal education is completed. The importance of independence in learning has been expressed by Dale:

> The goal of all learning is to develop the independent learner—the individual who no longer needs the protective counsel and guidance of the school or college. We may well expect, therefore, that instructional materials and methods will be used to decrease dependent learning and increase independent learning.
>
> Every individual must be prepared to meet new developmental tasks. He must be able to read, listen, and view critically and thoughtfully. He must be able to use a library of books, films, and recordings. He must have methods of study and attitudes which will enable him to learn and relearn at all age levels. . .[40]

Bond and Wagner emphasize that, "It is important to inculcate early and to develop throughout the reading program the attitude of independently establishing purposes for reading."[41] Detailed lists of study habits and skills that are reinforced through independent study have been formulated by a number of writers.[42]

Although all types of reading programs purport to include some kind of provision for independent study, they vary greatly with

---

40. Edgar Dale, "Instructional Resources," chap. iv in *The Changing American School*, ed. John I. Goodlad (Sixty-fifth Yearbook of the National Society for the Study of Education, Part II [Chicago: Distributed by the University of Chicago Press, 1966]), pp. 108-9.

41. Guy L. Bond and Eva Bond Wagner, *Teaching the Child To Read* (New York: Macmillan Co., 1966), p. 311.

42. Paul A. Witty, Alma M. Freeland, and Edith H. Grotberg, *The Teaching of Reading* (Boston: D. C. Heath & Co., 1966), pp. 221-24; Robert A. Karlin, *Teaching Reading in High School* (Indianapolis: Bobbs-Merrill Co., 1964), pp. 138-66; Nila B. Smith, *Reading Instruction for Today's Children* (Englewood Cliffs, N.J.: Prentice-Hall, Inc., 1963), pp. 305-52.

respect to the amount of such study actually found in practice. Teachers in whole-class instructional situations are prone to spend too much time plodding through the directed reading, vainly expecting that study habits and skills will be developed by unguided, assigned homework.[43] When classes are divided into small groups, teachers usually provide independent assignments for pupils to complete while groups other than their own are being taught. Such assignments may challenge the child to read widely and thoughtfully to fulfil worthwhile goals, or they may be unstimulating, narrowly conceived seatwork that does little to develop capability to think and act independently.

Non-grading, individualized reading, and individually prescribed instruction make independent study a prime feature. However, while research leaves little doubt that independent study can be effective under certain conditions,[44] poorly motivated or immature learners may not profit from it. Spache found that some children felt no need for reading.[45] Moreover, overreliance on independent work was shown in at least one individualized reading situation to produce inferior results in reading-vocabulary growth for below-average achievers, although not for able readers.[46]

Apparently the plan of organization should give children enough independent reading time to enable them to attain habits of self-direction, fluency in their use of skills, expanded understandings, and refined literary tastes. Independent activities should be balanced by directed study in which children are introduced to different kinds of reading material and receive needed guidance, especially in setting initial purposes, in attaining preliminary skills proficiency, and in using high-level thought processes when reading.

Evidently the proportions of directed and independent study

---

43. Harry W. Sartain, "How Children and Youth Learn To Study," *Educational Leadership*, XVI (December, 1958), 155-60.

44. Robert M. W. Travers and Kent E. Meyers, "Efficiency in Rote Learning under Four Learning Conditions," *Journal of Educational Research*, LX (September, 1966), 10-12.

45. George D. Spache, "Personality Patterns of Retarded Readers," *Journal of Educational Research*, L (February, 1957), 461-69.

46. Harry W. Sartain, "The Roseville Experiment with Individualized Reading," *Reading Teacher*, XIII (April, 1960), 277-81.

should vary with differences in circumstances and pupil-growth patterns. The amount of time spent on independent study probably should be somewhat greater for the high achiever than for the low achiever. The anxious child and the pupil from a deprived area appear to profit most from a rather highly structured curriculum,[47] which suggests that they, like the low achiever, need more direction than other pupils.

SPECIFIC PATTERNS OF CURRENT INTEREST

The effects of innovation and change in organizational patterns of American schools have been under examination for a long time. However, in spite of its obvious shortcomings, an innovation of more than a century ago, the graded school, still may be found side by side with the newest innovations of the atomic era. Many plans, old or new, are characterized by more than one of the general features described in the preceding paragraphs. The better-known plans are discussed in the following pages.

Intraclass grouping within the self-contained classroom.—The self-contained classroom, found only at the elementary level, has one inherent weakness for which it is much criticized—it requires all things of each teacher, thereby failing to capitalize on his special capabilities. At the same time, it can be rated positively on almost every other criterion for good organization listed in the first section of this chapter. Because he handles all or most curricular fields, a competent elementary teacher can provide systematic structure, intercorrelations, variety in learning experiences, and a consistent work load. Because he teaches the same children all day, he can maintain an entirely flexible schedule, come to understand each child well enough to appreciate his uniqueness and to offer a supportive relationship, help the child build an adequate self-image, and maintain and utilize comprehensive individual records.

If he groups the children appropriately within the room, the professionally well-prepared teacher is able to make effective general

---

47. Jesse W. Grimes and Wesley Allinsmith, "Compulsivity, Anxiety, and School Achievement," *Merrill-Palmer Quarterly*, VII (October, 1961), 247-71; David P. Ausubel and Pearl Ausubel, "Ego Development among Segregated Negro Children," in *Education in Depressed Areas*, ed. A. Harry Passow (New York: Teachers College, Columbia University, 1963), pp. 109-41.

and diagnostic appraisals, adapt the curriculum to each member of the class, offer needed corrective instruction, and provide the guidance that each child should have in strengthening his reading skills in relation to every school subject. By grouping, he can make the most efficient use of his own time. He can also provide adequately for pupil interaction. Such interaction within groups is helpful in refining comprehension abilities. According to Stauffer, ". . . It is here—in the reading-thinking situation directed by a wise teacher—that pupils can acquire the attitudes of honest thinking, so that later in life they will always desire to be enlightened and informed, rather than blind and unreasoning. . ."[48]

At least eight types of grouping have been described: ability, achievement, special needs, interest, research, social, tutorial, and invitational.[49] For this discussion, they are reclassified into three general types: reading-power groups, skills-refinement groups, and reading-activity groups.

The *reading-power group* may be described as the developmental or the basal instruction group. The child is assigned to it because he can recognize approximately 95 per cent of the vocabulary in instructional materials at a given level without assistance and he can perceive the literal meanings of 60 to 75 per cent (depending on the difficulty) of the ideas. After instruction, he can recognize practically all of the vocabulary and comprehend most of the literal ideas as well as the more subtle meanings that require interpretive thinking. Grouping can be based on performance on specially prepared tests.[50] The type of informal inventory offered by Betts is also a suitable tool for initially dividing children into small power groups.[51] The number of groups will vary according to the capabil-

---

48. Russell G. Stauffer, "The Role of Group Instruction in Reading," *Elementary English*, XLI (March, 1964), 231.

49. Josephine T. Benson, "Grouping for Individual Differences," *Individualizing Reading Instruction*, ed. Donald L. Cleland and Elaine C. Vilscek (Report of the Twentieth Annual Conference on Reading [Pittsburgh: University of Pittsburgh Press, 1964]), pp. 123-29.

50. George D. Spache, *Diagnostic Reading Scales* (Monterey: California Test Bureau, 1963).

51. Emmett A. Betts, *Handbook on Corrective Reading for the American Adventure Series* (Chicago: Wheeler Publishing Co., 1956); additional sug-

ity of the teacher and the diversity within the body of students, but rarely will the traditional three-group plan be adequate.

Usually, it is recommended that primary power groups meet twice and intermediate power groups meet once daily for some phase of their work. Incidentally, individual and small-group instruction should not be restricted to the self-contained classroom. It should be provided for elementary and secondary pupils regardless of the organizational pattern.

Since children progress at different rates, several may be expected to move from one power group to another each year. One investigator found that these changes occurred more often in the early part of the term, when teachers were becoming acquainted with their pupils; it was implied that more changes should have been made, but evidence was not supplied to support this view.[52]

For years, writers have asserted that grouping for reading instruction must be kept flexible.[53] Wilt says, "In grouping for teaching reading, flexibility is probably the major condition." [54] However, the classroom teacher sees no logic in moving an individual pupil into a power group for which his vocabulary and comprehension background are not suitable. Such a practice almost certainly would result in arrested progress; the child would be either inadequately challenged or overwhelmed. But, while the organized, systematic introduction of new skills and vocabulary can be provided in developmental power groups, there are occasions for setting up

---

gestions by Lester E. Wheeler and Edwin H. Smith, "A Modification of the Informal Reading Inventory," *Elementary English*, XXXIV (April, 1957), 224-26; similar instruments provided by Nila Banton Smith, *Graded Selections for Informal Reading Diagnosis, Grades 1 through 3* [*1959*] and *Grades 4 through 6* [*1963*] (New York: New York University Press); also Mary C. Austin, Clifford L. Bush, and Mildred H. Huebner, *Reading Evaluation* (New York: Ronald Press Co., 1961), pp. 235-46.

52. Patrick J. Groff, "A Survey of Basal Reading Grouping Practices," *Reading Teacher*, XV (January, 1962), 232-35.

53. Robert E. Martin, "The Teacher's First Step: Discovering and Planning for Individual Needs in Reading," *Reading Teacher*, X (December, 1956), 77-81.

54. Miriam E. Wilt, "Grouping for Reading or for Reading Instruction?" *Educational Leadership*, XXIV (February, 1967), 451.

". . . small reading groups in which neither age nor ability level are the major determiners but rather 'Who can profit from the experience.' "[55] This means the formation of *skills-refinement groups* and *reading-activity groups.*

Although a half-dozen children may have approximately the same general reading power, each may lead or lag behind others in learning some specific skills, such as recognizing certain prefixes, adapting rate to purpose, reading to detect propaganda, or using a particular reference book. Regardless of their power-group membership, all children who are ready for extra help with a specific skill, whether the help is needed for acceleration or as corrective reteaching, may be brought together for additional small-group instruction. Such a skills-refinement group should meet for ten to twenty minutes once, twice, or as many times as necessary. After this group work has served its purpose, a new skills-refinement group may be formed to include those children who need help with another skill.

Frequently during the year, children may be regrouped on the basis of their own preferences for such experiences as sharing their independent reading, participating in choral reading, working on unit projects, or dramatizing stories read. Membership in these *activity groups* is flexible and temporary, as in the skills-refinement groups. In such groups, children may read extensively in dozens of books and become fluent readers by applying skills that have been introduced systematically in power groups.

Although space permits the description of only the simplest types of grouping, the writer recommends that skillful teachers vary their arrangements for group and individual reading to permit work in language experience, topical reading, and other instructional units.[56] The teacher who fails to provide organizational flexibility in one form or another is failing to follow a practice which is in accord with the best thought of today.

55. *Ibid.*

56. Arthur W. Heilman, *Principles and Practices of Teaching Reading* (Columbus, Ohio: Charles E. Merrill Books, Inc., 1961), pp. 273-82; David H. Russell, *Children Learn To Read* (Boston: Ginn & Co., 1961), pp. 409-51; Bond and Wagner, *op. cit.*, pp. 116-27; Paul McKee with William K. Durr, *Reading, A Program of Instruction for the Elementary School* (New York: Houghton Mifflin Co., 1966), pp. 197-200.

Because its success depends entirely on the capability and industry of the individual teacher, the self-contained classroom is slowly giving way to other plans. It is recommended, however, that school administrators be extremely cautious and not adopt a less adequate form of organization merely for the sake of change. Where self-contained classrooms are continued, teachers can be substantially aided by additional staff—special instructors for art, music, physical education, and so on. Also, an increased number of specialized consultants can help teachers learn diagnostic-corrective techniques and can keep them informed of new materials and curriculum improvements.

Departmentalization.—Because teachers are prepared as subject specialists, departmentalization at the senior-high-school level has not been seriously challenged except by occasional moves toward eliminating departmental organization while retaining its major feature—teacher specialization. Recently, team teaching has been advocated as a means of lowering departmental walls and increasing teacher co-operation.[57]

Many junior high schools have adopted core and block plans, wherein developmental reading is taught by a teacher who has the class for at least two hours for work in social studies and the language arts. Such innovative modifications of departmentalization substantially increase opportunities of the competent teacher to relate reading instruction to content study and, at the same time, to provide increased classroom diagnostic and corrective assistance. Some of the research comparing fully departmentalized and core programs has been equivocal, but other studies suggest increased progress in reading through core organization.[58]

Elementary-school departmentalization, which advanced and then sharply declined earlier in this century, has attracted renewed attention during the movement of the sixties toward a content-

---

57. Carl H. Peterson, *Effective Team Teaching: The Easton Area High School Program* (West Nyack, N.Y.: Parker Publishing Co., 1966).

58. William A. Reiner, *A Third Report on the Evaluation of Pupil Growth in the Core Program of Two Academic High Schools 1953-1954* (New York: City Board of Education, 1955); Arthur C. Kelly and Robert E. Beatty, "Here's Proof that Core Program Students Learn Basic Skills," *School Executive*, LXXII (February, 1953), 54-55.

centered curriculum. It has the obvious advantage of permitting full use of the teachers' special capabilities, and, in these days of teacher shortage, administrators have observed that it gives children a better chance of avoiding placement with a weak teacher all day. It has, however, all of the shortcomings previously ascribed to multiple-teacher plans, and most teachers in such situations apparently feel that each group is with them too short a time to permit instructional grouping within the room.[59] The hourly movement of pupils from one room to another makes it practically impossible for teachers to become intimately familiar with each child or to deal effectively with the personal problems that may affect his reading growth.

Although a 1954 study of semidepartmentalized sixth grades relates improved progress in reading to departmentalization [60] and a recent study suggests that some teachers are more effective in one or two fields than in all fields,[61] most careful experiments have failed to demonstrate that full departmentalization offers advantages for reading instruction. Investigations by Otto,[62] Rouse,[63] Jackson,[64] and Spivak [65] have indicated that pupils in departmentalized programs do no better and sometimes not so well as pupils in self-contained rooms. Recently the school system of Montgomery County, Maryland, undertook an experiment with departmentalization in

---

59. Margaret Rouse, "A Comparison of Curriculum Practices in Departmental and Nondepartmental Schools," *Elementary School Journal*, XLVII (September, 1946), 34-43.

60. Charles T. Hosley, "Learning Outcomes of 6th Grade Pupils under Alternate Grade Organization Patterns" (unpublished Ph.D. thesis, Stanford University, 1954), quoted by Harold G. Shane and J. Z. Polychrones, *Encyclopedia of Educational Research*, ed. Chester W. Harris (New York: Macmillan Co., 1960), p. 426.

61. Goldberg and Passow, *op. cit.*, p. 28.

62. Summarized by Koury, *op. cit.*, pp. 3-4.

63. Rouse, *op. cit.*

64. Joseph Jackson, "The Effect of Classroom Organization and Guidance upon the Personality Adjustment and Academic Growth of Students," *Journal of Genetic Psychology*, LXXXIII (September, 1953), 159-70.

65. Monroe L. Spivak, "Effectiveness of Departmental and Self-Contained Seventh and Eighth Grade Classrooms," *School Review*, LXIV (December, 1956), 391-96.

fourth, fifth, and sixth grades. Although many pupils reported they had more stimulating learning activities in certain departmentalized courses, test results did not show superior achievement. In fact, the pupils in self-contained classrooms as a rule scored higher in reading and in arithmetic than did those in departmentalized classes; pupils in the lower I.Q. range (75-89) achieved better in all subjects in self-contained rooms.[66]

The Joplin Interclass Grouping Plan.—This plan, sometimes called redeployment, cross-class, or interclass grouping, requires that teachers of several classes follow identical daily schedules. During the reading period, children are assigned to different rooms according to general reading level, and, at the beginning of each succeeding hour, they may be reassigned to rooms according to general achievement in other subjects. Balow has shown that this redeployment into presumably homogeneous sections reduces the range of pupils' specific-skills differences very little,[67] but Austin and Morrison found "most teachers equated a reduction in range of ability with homogeniety. The result was they usually had all children reading from the same page of the same book. . ."[68]

Under this plan, interclass grouping may embrace all the weaknesses of so-called homogeneous sectioning plus those of departmentalization (in fact, departmentalization without teacher specialization). Although it recognizes that a pupil's capabilities may not be the same in different subjects, it does not recognize, unless it also includes grouping within classes, that an individual child's various skills in reading may be developed at entirely different levels. In schools where redeployment does include within-class grouping for diagnostic and differentiated instruction, the hourly change of classes seems to be an impediment to the teacher's success in relating reading to other areas of the curriculum.

Although interclass grouping without intraclass grouping is only

66. Fred M. King, "A Corner on Research," *Curriculum Leadership* (Minnesota Association for Supervision and Curriculum Development), III (October, 1965), 28-29; also summarized in "Instructor News Front," *Instructor*, LXXV (September, 1965), 2.

67. Balow, *op. cit.*

68. Mary C. Austin and Coleman Morrison, *The First R* (New York: Macmillan Co., 1963), p. 73.

a half-measure in providing adequately for individual differences, even this plan may represent a slight improvement over whole-class teaching at a single level. A few studies have shown it to produce better results.[69] More experiments have shown interclass grouping to have no significant effect [70] or to have a negative effect on pupil achievement at some or all levels of ability.[71] The inconsistency of experimental results suggests that the administrative plan is not as crucial as the action taken by the teacher. After finding very small differences in results yielded by an experiment comparing cross-class grouping with individualized and intraclass grouping, Ramsey concluded, "Given the good teacher other factors in teaching reading tend to pale to insignificance." [72]

The Dual Progress Plan.—The dual-progress plan, developed by Stoddard for the elementary school, combines some of the features of the earlier semidepartmentalized platoon system, the Joplin plan, and the secondary-level core curriculum.[73] During one-half of the day, the children are heterogeneously sectioned in a graded manner

69. Donald C. Cushenbery, "The Intergrade Plan of Grouping for Reading Instruction as Used in the Public Schools of Joplin, Missouri" (unpublished Ph.D. dissertation, University of Missouri, 1964); Elmer F. Morgan, Jr., and G. R. Stucker, "The Joplin Plan of Reading vs. a Traditional Method," *Journal of Educational Psychology,* LI (April, 1960), 69-73; Donald M. Green and Hazel W. Riley, "Intraclass Grouping for Reading Instruction in the Middle Grades," *Journal of Experimental Education,* XXXI (March, 1963), 273-78.

70. William F. Morehouse, "Interclass Grouping for Reading Instruction," *Elementary School Journal,* LIV (February, 1964), 280-86; Wallace Ramsey, "An Evaluation of a Joplin Plan of Grouping for Reading Instruction," *Journal of Educational Research,* LV (August, 1962), 567-72; Roy M. Carson and Jack M. Thompson, "The Joplin Plan and Traditional Reading Groups," *Elementary School Journal,* LXV (October, 1964), 75-77; William F. Koontz, "A Study of Achievement as a Function of Homogeneous Grouping," *Journal of Experimental Education,* XXX (December, 1961), 249-53.

71. David H. Russell, "Inter-class Grouping for Reading Instruction in the Intermediate Grades," *Journal of Educational Research,* XXXIX (February, 1946), 462-70; William R. Powell, "The Joplin Plan: An Evaluation," *Elementary School Journal,* LXIV (April, 1964), 387-92.

72. Wallace Ramsey, "An Evaluation of Three Methods of Teaching Sixth Grade Reading," in *Challenge and Experiment in Reading,* ed. J. Allen Figurel (International Reading Association Conference Proceedings, Vol. VIII, 1962), p. 153.

73. George D. Stoddard, *The Dual Progress Plan* (Evanston, Ill.: Harper & Row, 1961).

while they are instructed in the language arts and social studies by one teacher and take physical education from another. During the other half-day they are sectioned by achievement levels in each subject, as under the Joplin plan, to study mathematics, science, music, and art with different subject specialists.

While this plan gives the children at least two consecutive hours to get to know each other and to receive individualized guidance, it still incorporates many of the shortcomings of other multiple-teacher and homogeneous grouping plans. Heathers reported that, after two years of an experiment involving Grades III-VIII, pupil achievements under the plan showed no definite superiority except that the ablest pupils appeared to have advanced more rapidly in mathematics and science. Pupils appeared to like the plan, but teachers' opinions were divided. Their criticisms focused on difficulties encountered in getting to know pupils well, in teaching low-ability groups adequately, and in dealing with emotional and conduct problems.[74] The plan has been adopted by relatively few school systems.

Co-operative teaching (team teaching).—Anderson, who has participated actively in the development of team teaching, describes the team and the co-operative teaching situation as follows:

> A teaching team is a group of several teachers (usually three to six) with joint responsibility for planning, executing, and evaluating an educational program for a specified number of children, which is usually 25 to 30 times the number of teachers in the team. At the elementary level, the team may include pupils of the same age or grade level or of adjoining age or grade levels. In general, each teacher in an elementary team teaches all subjects taught in her grade and works at one time or another with every child in the group. Each teacher might, however, have special competency and interest in a curriculum area, so that the total team would include a number of specialists (e.g., one in science-mathematics, one in language arts, one in social studies, one in the creative arts), each capable of taking leadership for the planning and perhaps for a major share of the teaching in his area. However, because all teachers are involved in the total instructional program, there would not be departmentalization in the usual sense.[75]

---

74. Glen Heathers, "Dual Progress Plan," *Educational Leadership*, XVIII (November, 1960), 89-91.

75. Robert H. Anderson, "Organizing Groups for Instruction," chap. xiii in *Individualizing Instruction, op. cit.*, p. 257.

At the secondary level, teams may be formed either within subject fields or across subject lines. Both elementary and secondary teams usually have a leader who co-ordinates planning and an aid or "team mother" who is employed to do clerical and other nonprofessional work.

Among the major advantages given for co-operative teaching is its provision for altering group sizes for different types of instruction. In a team of six or seven teachers, two may offer reading instruction to very large groups while the others work with smaller groups on advanced or corrective lessons. Team meetings are held, usually once a week, to discuss pupil progress, to plan groupings, and to determine each teacher's responsibilities for future lessons.

Teachers of the large groups in elementary schools mention two serious problems: (*a*) maintaining class control and (*b*) finding an appreciable number of assignments which can be studied as appropriately at one level with fifty to one hundred children as in small differentiated groups. If groups are too large or change teachers too often, it is extremely difficult to make diagnostic observations and to provide sympathetic personal support for any except those who stand out strongly as being either very advanced or in great difficulty.

Team organization gives inexperienced teachers an excellent opportunity to learn from capable, experienced persons. This advantage occasionally is partly neutralized by personality conflicts, but even so, some professional growth accrues through team meetings. When teachers having different academic majors or minors are assigned to a team, each can function as a valuable resource person for a different aspect of curriculum planning. However, if this specialization results in one person's teaching all classes in his favorite field, co-operative teaching will become nothing more than departmentalization.

Although numerous schools have adopted the co-operative teaching plan, little objective evaluative evidence on its results has been published. Probably the lack of evidence is attributable to the great difficulty involved in equating all factors in experimental and control situations. One reviewer of the limited research states, "The reports offer assurance that team teaching does at least as well as conventional plans with respect to ouctomes measured by standardized tests."[76] A recent study comparing progress of primary and intermediate team classes with the progress of pupils in self-contained classes favored the latter during the first year of the study but found teamed classes gaining more during the second year.[77]

Co-operative teaching in elementary schools is to be highly recommended if the grouping permits a child to remain with one teacher a large part of the day and if team and class sizes are kept small enough to permit the teachers to become thoroughly familiar with each child's personal and academic characteristics. If, however, teams consist of more than three or four teachers and if they function as in departmentalization, all the weaknesses of older multiple-teacher plans may be evident, and the differentiation of instruction will be seriously limited.

Individualized reading.—Although numerous variations are being utilized today, individualized reading is usually considered to be a procedure in which each child chooses a book he wants to read from a large selection and is given needed instruction in individual conferences with his teacher each week. The child progresses at his own rate; little assistance is provided outside the conference. Detailed discussion of individualized reading have been presented by Veatch and others.[78]

Because individualized reading requires differentiation only within the classroom, it can be undertaken regardless of the school's over-all organization. Programs of individualized reading provide for abundant independent study but sometimes have been criticized for their failure to provide enough directed work to insure that all pupils learn skills in the most meaningful sequences. Research has shown

---

76. Glen Heathers, "Research on Team Teaching," in *Team Teaching*, ed. Judson T. Shaplin and Henry F. Olds, Jr. (Evanston, Ill.: Harper & Row, 1964); and "Research on Implementing and Evaluating Co-operative Teaching," *National Elementary Principal*, XLIV (January, 1965), 27-33.

77. Philip Lambert et. al., "A Comparison of Pupil Achievement in Team and Self-Contained Organizations," *Journal of Experimental Education*, XXXIII (Spring, 1965), 217-24, as summarized by Helen Robinson et. al., *Reading Research Quarterly*, I (Winter, 1965), 69, 104.

78. Jeanette Veatch, *Individualizing Your Reading Program* (New York: G. P. Putnam's Sons, 1959).

some teachers to be successful with individualized reading [79] and others to be very unsuccessful.[80] In a careful analysis of the procedure, Robinson pointed out that teachers who adopt individualized reading should have exceptional knowledge of the skills program, should be excellent diagnosticians, and should be thoroughly familiar with the hundreds of basal and trade books that children may read.[81]

Two of the first-grade studies sponsored by the Office of Education during 1964-65 dealt with special adaptations of individualized reading. In one, children were given a concentrated preliminary series of lessons on word analysis, and then both word-analysis and sight-vocabulary lessons were taught individually, in small and large groups, and in pupil-team activities during the months when children were reading from books individually. Many new books and extra in-service work for teachers were provided.[82] It is not surprising that this vigorously instituted combination program of group and individualized instruction produced better results than were produced by a standard basal program having few of the extra embellishments.

The second experiment compared progress of the pupils using the same basal readers (a) in an individual-conference program and (b) in a small-group program. Except that attitudes in individualized classes were more favorable to reading and high-readiness pupils in grouped classes achieved higher test scores than their counterparts, few differences were noted.[83]

Few experiments in individualized reading have been carefully controlled with respect to instructional time, instructional materials,

79. Rodney H. Johnson, "Individualized and Basal Primary Reading Programs," *Elementary English*, XLII (December, 1965), 902-4, 915.

80. Alton L. Safford, "Evaluation of an Individualized Reading Program," *Reading Teacher*, XIII (April, 1960), 266-70.

81. Helen M. Robinson, "News and Comment—Individualized Reading," *Elementary School Journal*, LX (May, 1960), 411-20.

82. Doris U. Spencer, "Individualized First Grade Reading versus a Basal Reader Program in Rural Communities," *Reading Teacher*, XIX (May, 1966), 595-600.

83. James B. Macdonald, Theodore L. Harris, and John S. Mann, "Individual versus Group Instruction in First Grade Reading," *Reading Teacher*, XIX (May, 1966), 643-46, 652.

and teacher capability. But, on the basis of available evidence, it can be concluded that some teachers, especially the more enthusiastic and experienced ones, can teach individualized reading successfully. Many children, especially the more capable ones, make adequate progress in individualized reading programs. The less capable students are less likely to progress satisfactorily in an individualized situation because they are not able to work independently for long periods of time.[84]

In some situations, the personal conference between the student and teacher seems to have great motivational value for the child; this is not invariably true, perhaps because of the lack of teacher-pupil rapport. Most children read more books in a program of individualized self-selection with conferences than in a basal program with supplementary books, unless the teachers of the basal program make a special effort to promote extension reading. The additional amount of individualized reading practice does not always result in proportionately greater attainment of skills—perhaps because not every teacher can give enough help during the short conferences.[85]

Individualized reading has reawakened teachers to the fact that children should read far beyond basal books. Basal materials can serve to introduce reading skills systematically, but these skills must be practiced in many other books if the child is to become a fluent reader. The best features of individualized reading can be combined with basal-group reading by completing basal books early in the year and continuing with individualized reading, by doing group reading in the morning and individualized reading in the afternoon, by following several days of group work with several days of individualized extension reading, or by including both in broad language-arts units on a specific literary theme.

Individually Prescribed Instruction.—A program of individually prescribed instruction has been demonstrated since 1964 in the suburban Oakleaf School by the staff members of the Baldwin-White-

---

84. Adapted from Harry W. Sartain, "Individualized Reading," in *Recent Developments in Reading*, ed. H. Alan Robinson ("Supplementary Educational Monographs," No. 95 [Chicago: University of Chicago Press, 1965]), p. 85; and Sartain, *The Place of Individualized Reading in a Well-Planned Program*, ("Contributions in Reading," No. 28 [Boston: Ginn & Co., 1964]).

85. *Ibid.*

hall schools and the Learning Research and Development Center of the University of Pittsburgh under a grant from the Office of Education. Non-graded courses in reading, mathematics, and science are planned in carefully developed sequences of numbered lessons spanning the first six years of school. These lessons, which may be in programed form or taken from books and workbooks, are filed on shelves and on library carts in a materials center that connects several rooms. Lessons may call for use of tapes, recordings, library books, packets of materials for first-hand experiences, or for a face-to-face reading session with the teacher.

On four mornings of the week, the child looks in his personal folder to find the lesson assignments that his teacher has prescribed for him for the half-day given to individually prescribed instruction. (At present, children study other subjects in regular graded-room situations the other half-day.) He locates the required lesson sheets, goes to his desk or to a special audio-visual station, and proceeds to study independently, making the written or oral responses that are called for at each step. He works at his own rate, signaling the teacher for help when needed. Items responded to are scored, objective items by the pupil or an aide and subjective items by the teacher. Then the teacher studies the results to decide what the next lesson should be and prescribes it for the following day. Although some lessons call for group work, each pupil progresses quite independently. Readiness, achievement, and diagnostic tests are used frequently to determine whether the child has mastered the work at one stage and is ready to move to the next. A lesson may be skipped if a readiness test shows that the child has already learned it incidentally.

During one half-day a week, the pupils meet in ordinary whole-class groups for "seminar" sessions. Sometimes these sessions may be broken into smaller group meetings. In the seminar session, the pupils share experiences, ask questions about work in progress, or listen to and observe the teacher's presentations of concepts and processes that cannot be learned readily from planned written material.

Children and parents seem to like the program. The lack of unfair competition and pressures and the feeling of continuous success and progress are probable reasons for the school's better-than-average attendance record. Test results indicate that the range of achievement in classes is approximately that found in situations in which teachers divide children into several instructional groups. Although general achievement averages are about the same as in other schools, children score higher on tests of specific knowledge which teachers in other situations might overlook because of the pressures of time or inadequate preparation.[86]

Because of its emphasis on personal involvement in learning and on individualized work, this plan fulfils more of the previously listed organizational criteria than do most traditional procedures. It may be criticized for the somewhat limited opportunities it offers for pupil interaction in small groups and for the lack of adequately differentiated work on the fifth day—work which seems out of step with that of other days. Teacher aids are provided, and, once the prodigious task of curriculum development has been completed (with expert outside help), the teacher has a marvelous fund of resources to make teaching effective. This feature may, however, present problems; it may tend to make teaching so mechanical and the teacher so dependent on the content programers that he may be led to forfeit his prerogative of making intelligent decisions about instructional approaches that should be used with children having different types of backgrounds and perceptual capabilities.

Pupil-team study.—Durrell has urged that pupils be paired to lead each other in certain practice experiences.[87] Reading activities for pairs might involve word analysis and recognition, shared oral reading, storytelling, dictionary use, and checking workbooks. Experimental results in one situation in which pupil-team study was utilized for a year showed over-all average achievement (compared with the prior year's achievement) to be six months higher in Grade

---

86. John O. Bolvin and C. Mauritz Lindvall, "One Approach to the Problem of Individual Differences" ("Learning Research and Development Working Paper," No. 8 [Pittsburgh: School of Education, University of Pittsburgh, 1966]); also Lindvall and Bolvin, "Programed Instruction in the Schools: An Application of Programing Principles in Individually Prescribed Instruction," chap. viii in *Programed Instruction*, ed. Phil C. Lange (Sixty-sixth Yearbook of the National Society for the Study of Education, Part II [Chicago: Distributed by the University of Chicago Press, 1967]).

87. Donald Durrell, "Implementing and Evaluating Pupil Team Learning Plans," *Journal of Educational Sociology*, XXXIV (April, 1961), 360-65; and "Pupil Team Learning," *Instructor*, LXXIV (February, 1965), 5.

VI, four months higher in Grade V, but higher only in spelling in Grade IV. An instrument for rating teacher practices showed that classroom adjustments to individual differences had improved "one hundred per cent," with the most effective application of the team-study technique being in reading.[88] Psychological research cautions that children in teams must exchange roles, because the one in the pupil role learns and retains substantially more than the one in the teacher role.[89]

If experiences are appropriately selected, planned, and supervised, pupil-team study can be recommended as a classroom procedure in keeping with the criteria for effective organization.

Non-graded classes.—Within the non-graded organization, children of either a narrow or a wide age-span are assigned to classrooms with little regard for academic capability and are guided at their own rates (individually or in small, flexible groups) through planned learning sequences of several years' duration. (In some places, homogeneous sectioning is erroneously called non-grading.) The age span in a non-graded class may be one year or several, but the mixing of several age levels has been shown to have academic value,[90] and such mixing permits pleasant adjustment within a wide range of differences in social growth. In primary and intermediate units, non-grading often is employed only for reading and arithmetic, the other subjects being taught at a single broad level.

Some children may take more or fewer years than the average to complete a given non-graded block of learnings, but progress is differentiated and continuous, with no artificial end-of-the-year promotions and no forced repetition of hastily covered work. When a child responds to a challenge to make progress beyond his own current level of achievement instead of being obliged to compete with classmates having different capabilities, it is believed that he will acquire a wholesome feeling of success instead of the feelings

---

88. *Ibid.*

89. Kent E. Meyers *et. al.*, "Learning and Reinforcement in Student Pairs," *Journal of Educational Psychology*, LVI (April, 1965), 67-72.

90. Walter Rehwaldt and Warren W. Hamilton, "An Analysis of Some Effects of Interage and Intergrade Grouping in an Elementary School" (mimeographed; Torrance, Calif.: Unified School District, 1965).

of defeat or smugness that often result from being judged on the basis of uniform expectations.

One-third of the school systems responding to a National Education Association survey in 1965 reported that they were trying some form of non-grading.[91] Detailed explanations of these procedures at both elementary [92] and secondary levels [93] are available.

Research on non-grading like most research on organization, has produced conflicting results. Carbone found progress to be significantly greater in graded schools.[94] Hopkins found that reading achievement was not significantly different in graded and non-graded schools but that teachers of non-graded classes, on the whole, expressed more satisfaction.[95] Skapski [96] and Ingram [97] both concluded that non-graded primary classes made significantly greater gains than ability-grouped classes. In a matched-pairs experiment continuing for three years, Hillson found that non-graded classes scored significantly higher than graded classes (at .01) on standard reading tests.[98] Uncertainties about the researchers' interpretation of non-grading make it inadvisable to mention additional studies which ap-

91. "Nongraded School Organization," *National Education Association Research Bulletin*, XLIII (October, 1965), 93-95.

92. John I. Goodlad and Robert H. Anderson, *The Nongraded Elementary School* (rev. ed.; New York: Harcourt, Brace and World, Inc., 1963); Lillian Glogau and Murray Fessel, *The Nongraded Primary School: A Case Study* (West Nyack, N.Y.: Parker Publishing Co., 1967).

93. B. Frank Brown, *The Nongraded High School*. Englewood Cliffs, N.J.: Prentice-Hall, Inc., 1963.

94. Robert F. Carbone, "The Non-Graded School: An Appraisal," *Administrators Notebook* (Midwest Administration Center, University of Chicago), X (September, 1961).

95. Kenneth D. Hopkins, O. A. Oldridge, and Malcom L. Williamson, "An Empirical Comparison of Pupil Achievement and Other Variables in Graded and Ungraded Classes," *American Educational Research Journal*, II (November, 1965), 207-15.

96. Mary Skapski, "Ungraded Primary Reading Program: An Objective Evaluation," *Elementary School Journal*, LXI (October, 1960), 41-45.

97. Vivien Ingram, "Flint Evaluates Its Primary Cycle," *Elementary School Journal*, LXI (November, 1960), 76-80.

98. Maurie Hillson et. al., "A Controlled Experiment Evaluating the Effects of Non-Graded Organization on Pupil Achievement," *Journal of Educational Research*, LVII (July-August, 1964), 548-50.

pear to favor this type of organization.

The non-graded plan is to be recommended because it proposes to make differentiated progress the rule rather than the exception. Administrators must be cautioned, however, that, in order to prevent misunderstandings and a haphazard development of concepts, it is important that non-graded curriculum sequences, achievement-marking systems, pupil records, and progress-reporting procedures should be carefully planned to reflect the philosophy of individualization. In instances in which preparation for the change has not been adequate, the result has been (*a*) confusion, (*b*) a continuation of the same old rigid practices under a new name, or (*c*) the introduction of some new form of lock-step arrangement.

Continuous Progress Plan.—The continuous-progress plan represents a refinement of non-grading that has been developed in a few university laboratory schools. As instituted in the Falk School (located on the campus of the University of Pittsburgh),[99] it features a combination of organizational innovations—non-grading, multi-age heterogeneous sectioning, and modified team teaching—a combination which has been recommended by some authorities.[100] Elementary-school classes are designated as "primary," "midgroup," and "intermediate," each embracing an age range of at least two years but more often of three or four years. Within any room, children usually are divided into four to seven power groups for reading and into three to six groups for other fields of study to accommodate an I.Q. range sometimes from 80 to 180. Children of various ages participate in the group that offers intellectual challenge, and they make friends in the room with those at compatible stages of physical and social development.

A team usually consists of no more than two homeroom teachers and the special teachers in art, music, and physical education who have the children part of the time. The two homeroom teachers belonging to the team plan class schedules that are almost identical. Together they discuss the progress of the twenty-five children in

---

99. Harry W. Sartain and the Falk School Faculty, *The Continuous Progress Plan at Falk School* (mimeographed; Pittsburgh: School of Education, University of Pittsburgh, 1966).

100. Robert W. Anderson, "Some Types of Cooperative Teaching in Current Use," *National Elementary Principal*, XLIV (January, 1965), 22-26.

each room and determine at which instructional levels there may be too few children in either room to make a small working group. Then they arrange for these pupils to exchange rooms at certain times of the day to fit into groups in the other room. Once a week the two team teachers meet, sometimes with student teachers and special teachers, to discuss the progress of groups and individuals. Through this meeting, the homeroom teacher is kept informed about his "exchange" pupils. Teachers also do general planning together and schedule occasional field trips, audiovisual experiences, and auditorium activities in which all fifty children participate.

Homeroom teachers get to know children and their learning traits very well because most pupils stay in a room two years, the older ones leaving and younger ones moving in each term. A few remain longer, and others may leave after a shorter period. When any child has progressed beyond the top group in his team and is mature enough to fit socially with younger children in the next higher team section, he is moved. This occurs fairly frequently, preferably during the year rather than at the end of the term.

Because of teacher specialization involved at the junior-high-school level and the very small size of the enrolment at that level in the Falk School, it is not possible to provide as much schedule flexibility as at the elementary level. However, within three class sections in each field there are usually between six and eighteen small groups for differentiated instruction.

The continuous-progress plan at Falk School differs from most non-graded plans especially with respect to the structure of its curriculum. In each broad field, there are several planned sequences of basic learnings, each sequence developing some concept or set of related concepts and skills. These streams of educational outcomes are divided into sequential "develoblocks" of increasing difficulty. The several develoblocks at the same level for the different conceptual streams in any one field of study are called an "incline." In any field, there may be between ten and twenty inclines in the continuum of growth from kindergarten through junior high school. The teaching unit planned for each develoblock in the content fields indicates expected outcomes and experiences and lists readings at four general levels—minimal, basal (which may be further differentiated), horizontal enrichment (study in depth of the same topic), and vertical enrichment (study at the level of the next higher incline in the sequence). These "levels" broaden to provide for the entire range of capability in a class. Reading-skills units include both introductory basal reading and extensive individual reading. Consequently, great quantities of books of different literary types and varied content must be made available.

Many of these books are shelved in individual study carrells provided for all pupils in intermediate rooms and for the more mature children in midgroup rooms. When children are not working with the teacher in a small group at the instruction table in a corner of the room, they may study and write independently in their carrells, or they may go to an alcove to work in pairs or as a committee on unit activities.

This organization was developed gradually over a period of several years. Therefore, it has not been possible to arrange an objective "before-and-after" evaluation. The range of scores on standard achievement tests is wide enough to suggest that even the brightest children are challenged. An individual test of sight vocabulary in reading, given in the spring of 1965 and again in the spring of 1966, showed that the brightest pupils in their first year beyond kindergarten were able to recognize more than five thousand words and third-year pupils nearly ten thousand words.

After the first year of multi-age grouping, teachers were asked to list the pupils whose social and academic adjustment had been especially aided by the plan; most teachers listed between 10 and 30 per cent of their children.

Because its whole purpose is to focus attention on individuals in a structured but flexible manner, this plan fulfills most of the organizational criteria. Its chief disadvantage is that it requires highly competent, dedicated teachers. These are in short supply. Perhaps such intellectually challenging plans will attract more persons of outstanding capability into the teaching profession.

Changing Organizational Patterns

GENERALIZATIONS FROM THE HISTORY OF CHANGE IN SCHOOL ORGANIZATION

Research reports suggest that pupil growth depends on teacher effort and capability more than on such factors as school-organization patterns and methods. While investigators have not been able to identify the teaching behavior that will always produce good results, there is evidence that different teachers do produce different results. In considering reasons for the contradictory findings of the co-operative first-grade reading studies of the Office of Education, Stauffer says, "The widest variation among these uncontrolled variables was shown by the teachers involved." [101] In their investigation of reading in deprived areas, Harris and Serwer found that certain teachers consistently produced better results than others.[102] Gibb and Matala, summarizing a study on the teaching of science and mathematics, concluded that "Good teachers are effective regardless of organization." [103] Similar conclusions from two other studies have already been mentioned.[104]

Because human variability is extremely complex, the administrative structures of a school cannot provide for individual differences in reading growth; this can be done only by the teacher in the classroom. While clumsy school organization impedes the teacher's efforts, excellent organization removes the blocks to teaching-learning effectiveness by providing the flexibility teachers need in order to marshal all available resources for stimulating learning.

It is not likely that research will soon show clear and consistent achievement-test results favoring one organizational pattern over another, because pupil achievement is so much affected by teacher performance, curriculum structure, and other factors that may differ in schools having the same form of organization. Moreover, tests do not measure important aspects of personal adjustment that should be considered. Consequently, each faculty must determine

---

101. Russell G. Stauffer, "The Verdict: Speculative Controversy," *Reading Teacher*, VIII (May, 1966), 563.

102. Albert J. Harris and Blanche L. Serwer, *Comparison of Reading Approaches in First Grade Teaching with Disadvantaged Children* (U.S. Office of Education, Co-operative Research Project No. 2677 [New York: Office of Research and Evaluation, Division of Teacher Education, City University of New York, 1966]).

103. E. Glenadine Gibb and Dorothy C. Matala, "Study on the Use of Special Teachers of Science and Mathematics in Grades 5 and 6," *School Science and Mathematics*, LXII (November, 1962), 565-85.

104. Goldberg, Passow, and Justman, *op. cit.*, p. 62; Ramsey, *op. cit.*

the type of school and classroom organizational patterns that appear likely to be most helpful in its schools.

Owing to the lack of objective answers to some questions and the disparity among opinions held by today's leaders, one may wonder what the direction of organizational innovation and change will be in the future. Probably, for a few years, there will continue to be a certain amount of grasping for panaceas, as administrators grope for some kind of change that will produce increased quantities of what it takes to get a child admitted to the college of the parents' choice. This willingness to settle for a simplified, ready-made, new-looking, assembly-line approach will be abetted by the unhappy fact that teachers' organizations recently have become militant in their efforts to obtain fair economic rewards for teaching. Under these circumstances, unfortunately, a significant minority of teachers are likely to become so involved in issues concerning what they are getting that they will overlook the importance of what they are giving in the way of instruction tailored to individual needs within the classroom.

Still, there will be many dedicated teachers who will continue to try unstintingly to provide quality work in the classroom, regardless of the over-all school organization. They will practice various types of intraclass grouping and individual guidance, thus discovering new ways of using pupil-team study, independent reading guides, and programed materials. Eventually their belief in highly differentiated work within the classroom will prevail, for three reasons: (*a*) educators will rediscover the fact that improved achievement will not result from the mere initiation of an over-all administrative organization plan; (*b*) parents will see that their children are most comfortable and successful when working with teachers who show the greatest personal interest in them; and (*c*) the cyclical swing from a primary public concern for academic achievement to a primary concern for well-rounded child development will dictate a renewed interest in procedures that individualize and integrate learning experiences.[105] In time, those schools that have adopted organization plans which enhance the efforts of individual teachers to personalize teaching—some types of teaming, individually pre-

---

105. Goodlad, *op. cit.*

scribed instruction, non-grading, multi-age sectioning, and continuous-progress planning—will be considered to have been moving in the right direction.

In the meantime, the development of more and better diagnostic instruments, of computerized instruction equipment, and of other technological aids will give teachers the tools they need to make the task of fully differentiated teaching seem less formidable than it is at present. Finally, research will supply more adequate answers to questions on organization, but these answers will be complex, many-sided, and subject to various conditions rather than the simple "either-or" type of answers that are usually sought today.

RECOMMENDATIONS FOR PLANNING ORGANIZATIONAL INNOVATIONS

In order to avoid repeating earlier errors, school administrators are urged to consider the following recommendations:

1. Involve all staff members in planning for change to obtain the benefit of their combined experience and knowledge and to give them an opportunity to learn about plans being developed.
2. Consider *all* the goals of the school and how their fulfilment will be affected by different styles of organization.
3. Evaluate proposed organization plans by the application of an adequate number of criteria, such as those offered in the first section of this chapter, instead of considering them in relation to only one or two obvious values. Then avoid the adoption of organizational schemes which have fundamental weaknesses that make them only insufficient half-measures.
4. Recognize that it may be desirable to have more than one organizational plan in operation in any school or classroom. Owing to their earlier experiences, some children need to learn to read in a situation that is more formally structured than that required for others. Likewise, different teachers may succeed best in somewhat different organizational patterns. For these reasons the traits of teachers and pupils should be considered in assigning children to homerooms.
5. Recognize that no very effective plan will make teaching easier. Excellence in all fields of endeavor, including teaching, requires concentrated effort.
6. Make changes gradually, adapting curriculum plans as needed and educating parents, teachers, and pupils for such changes. Otherwise there may be a change in organizational name only, with no improvement in educational practice.
7. Provide adequate psychological and reading-consultant services to

aid the teacher in diagnosing pupil difficulties and sometimes in offering remediation. No organizational plan gives the classroom teacher enough time to analyze the most serious reading problems.
8. As teachers engage in innovative procedures to successfully individualize reading instruction, provide them with generous psychological (if not financial) rewards in the form of encouragement, recognition, and favorable publicity.
9. Regardless of organizational plan, keep the class size small enough to make excellent teaching of reading possible.[106] Some studies of achievement in relation to class size have been misleading, because the common failure of mediocre teachers to improve their teaching when class size decreases neutralizes the improved achievement attained by good teachers. An industrious teacher can regularly provide the best of differential work and sensitive personal counseling for no more than twenty-five or thirty children.[107]
10. Withhold final judgment on the value of the innovative organizational procedure until there has been time for the novelty effect to wear off and for a thorough evaluation of the results to be made. When assessing results, look for ways in which pupil success is related to specific combinations of teaching behavior and features of school and classroom organization.

Current trends indicate that traditional plans of school and classroom organization for teaching reading are gradually being replaced by various innovative plans. Careful preparation and evaluation will insure the initiation of effective patterns rather than the resurrection of plans found to be inadequate in the past.

106. Jack R. Frymier, "The Effects of Class Size upon Reading Achievement in First Grade," *Reading Teacher*, XVIII (November, 1964), 90-93.

107. Bernard H. McKenna and James B. Pugh, Jr., "Performance of Pupils and Teachers in Small Classes Compared to Large," *Institute of Administrative Research Bulletin*, IV (February, 1964), 1-4.

CHAPTER VII

Contributions of Allied Fields to the Teaching of Reading

GEORGE D. SPACHE

Introduction

To report comprehensively the contributions of other disciplines to the field of reading would require much more space than that which can be allotted to such a task in a yearbook of this sort. At best, one can but sample some of the research and writings of a half-dozen fields and point out their more obvious implications for reading instruction.

In some respects, reading specialists are very fortunate that so many other experts are concerned with parallel or related problems. Many research studies and clinical insights emanating from other disciplines offer significant information for the reading specialist. It is also true that researchers in some disciplines see much more application of their studies to reading than is seen by reading specialists. However, it should be noted that the research of the past seventy-five years in the psychology of reading is sometimes as unfamiliar to experts of other disciplines as their innovative research is to reading experts.

Another obstacle that retards the exchange of information is that of terminology. Each discipline, including reading, has tended to evolve its own esoteric vocabulary, often known only to its own group. Some groups even have their own distinctive terms for the basic components of reading (graphemes, phonemes, phonemics, morphemes, T-unit, and so on) and for the various processes in the reading act (grapheme-phoneme translation, encoding-decoding, and many more). Some disciplines have their own interpretations of the learning process (reinforcement, insight-discovery, reward-punishment). Even the child experiencing reading difficulties is categorized by one or more of a half-dozen ill-defined labels (reading disability, dyslexia, minimum cerebral dysfunction, learning disability, and the like). This use of different terms to describe conditions or concepts which are often quite similar is a deterrent to the ready exchange of information and to ultimate progress.

A third obstacle to the ready application of discoveries offered by various disciplines is the variation in type and depth of the research. Reading specialists are inclined to insist that such studies involve relatively large numbers of cases, objective testing instruments for evaluation, realistic conditions, and a determined attempt to control most of the variables known to affect the outcomes of studies involving human reaction and behavior. Many other disciplines routinely study very small populations, employ subjective personal judgments as evaluation criteria, and make little attempt to control all but one or two significant variables. The validity and reliability of professional observations or generalizations are widely assumed in some disciplines. The effects of biased sampling, nearly always present in very small-scale studies or in studies of populations drawn from clinical or private practice or from laboratory situations which differ markedly from normal classrooms, are often ignored. In other studies, the need for broad-scale standardization of the measuring instruments or criteria and for statistical control of such factors as intelligence, regression to the mean, initial reading ability, age, socioeconomic status, and the interactions of these factors are unrecognized. Certainly, much of the research in reading is also faulty, but the absence of many of the basic elements of scientific research in some of the seemingly relevant studies made in other disciplines is a hindrance to their acceptance by the reading specialist. In time, it is hoped, the obstacles to a ready interchange of research findings among the disciplines will be removed.

Sociology

In its emphasis upon the social groups and forces which constitute our society, the field of sociology continues to offer significant contributions to the science of reading instruction. To their audience, sociologists have pointed out the interactions of mass media with their users, the cultural and socioeconomic factors which influence educational efforts, and the effects of peers, the community, the school, and the family upon the pupil's academic success.

MASS MEDIA AND THE PUBLIC

Both sociologists and reading specialists are concerned with the effects of mass media upon social groups. It is important for both to learn whether one's information, beliefs, or attitudes can be modified by various media and, if they can be changed, to learn the most effective procedures for producing these changes.

Longitudinal studies offer some support to the idea that opinions and attitudes are affected through the use of such media. For example, Healy recently demonstrated that early negative attitudes toward reading and authority figures could be modified by special reading programs of an extended nature.[1] In addition, behavioral changes were observed in the recreational use of books and other manifestations.

One medium which has been a particular source of interest and a subject of evaluation is television. Witty has made an annual study of the influences of this medium upon school children.[2] In general, although there has been a decided decrease since the first appearance of television, it continues to monopolize a large part of the school child's day, ranging from about sixteen hours weekly in the first grade to twenty-four hours in the fifth grade and declining to twelve hours for secondary students. This medium has largely replaced radio, decreased movie attendance, and, in the opinion of some, similarly intruded upon the time for recreational reading.

A large-scale study (directed by Schramm) of the effects of television appears to offer very significant observations.[3] This study indicated that bright children are heavy televiewers until about eleven, at which age they tend to shift their interest to books. Schramm and his co-workers noted that the average child spends as much time televiewing during his first sixteen years as he does in school. From this viewing there is some incidental learning, as is

---

[1]. Ann Kertland Healy, "Effects of Changing Children's Attitudes toward Reading," *Elementary English*, XLII (March, 1965), 269-72.

[2]. Paul A. Witty, assisted by Lloyd Melis, "A 1964 Study of TV: Comparisons and Comments," *Elementary English*, XLII (February, 1965), 134-41.

[3]. Wilbur Schramm, Jack Lyle, and Edwin B. Parker, *Television in the Lives of Our Children* (Stanford: Stanford University Press, 1961).

indicated by the fact that school entrants who are avid television viewers temporarily exhibit somewhat larger vocabularies than other children. A number of factors, such as mental ability, sex, age, and social class, determine children's use of television.

Other sociological studies of the mass media have been concerned with readership preferences or interest of various age groups. The general indications of such studies are that readership is enhanced by simpler versions, by more obvious organization of material, or by more readable formats. Factors of interest, background, and beliefs also enter into comprehension, readership, and reactions to communications. Whether the reader or listener can learn to deal critically with all types of propaganda or communications, even when prewarned or given instruction in critical reactions, has not been entirely demonstrated.[4] Many short-term studies seem to indicate that he can do so, but long-range experiments with results of any great breadth or depth are still lacking.

Since reading instruction is the foundation for the reader's interaction with certain of the mass media, research involving these media has great significance for reading teachers. They must follow carefully the implications of sociological research in assessing the impact of mass media. They must also study ways and means of dealing with these influences as they impinge upon instructional practices. Teachers, like sociologists, must continue to study effective methods of helping school children of all ages deal constructively with the influences of mass media and learn how to use these media to further their own personal and educational goals.

CULTURAL AND SOCIOECONOMIC FORCES

At the moment, there is a tremendous upsurge of concern about the educational handicaps imposed upon various segments of the population by cultural and socioeconomic deprivations. Federal, state, and local governmental agencies are linked in a massive effort to eradicate these obstacles to self-realization. Spurred by this governmental interest and aided by the financial support now available in large volume for the first time in our national history, school

---

[4]. Charles A. Kiesler and Sara B. Kiesler, "Role of Forewarning in Persuasive Communications," *Journal of Abnormal and Social Psychology*, LXVIII (May, 1964), 547-49.

systems are engaged in an all-out effort to break down these barriers to the accomplishment of educational goals by all pupils.

Much of the information for identifying cultural and socioeconomic forces which militate against universal education has been available from the field of sociology for some time. Sociologists have long noted the relationships between academic success and such factors as parental attitudes, income, and occupational level; deviant cultural or language patterns; and racial, ethnic, and social-class group patterns of behavior and thought which conflict with common middle-class-oriented educational goals.[5] The interference of these factors with desired levels of academic achievement is demonstrated in many studies. Hill and Giammatteo, for example, have reported high correlations between socioeconomic levels and achievement.[6] Negative parental attitudes toward reading success, low-level language development, and restriction of the normal freedom of childhood experiences continue to exert retarding influences upon pupil achievement throughout a child's school career.[7] Parents who conceive of themselves as educational, marital, or vocational failures tend to transmit their feelings of frustration and hopelessness to their children.[8] Even in attempting to convey their concepts of an appropriate sex role to their sons, some male parents lead boys to

---

5. Philip H. Ennis, "Recent Sociological Contributions to Reading Research," *Reading Teacher*, XVII (May, 1964), 577; Robert C. Ziller, "The Social Psychology of Reading," *Reading Teacher*, XVII (May, 1964), 583-88.

6. Edwin H. Hill and Michael C. Giammatteo, "Socio-economic Status and Its Relationship to School Achievement in the Elementary School," *Elementary English*, XL (March, 1963), 265-70.

7. Homer L. J. Carter, "A Study of Attitudes toward Certain Aspects of Reading Expressed by Parents of Inferior and Superior College Readers," in *The Philosophical and Sociological Bases of Reading*, ed. Eric L. Thurston and Lawrence E. Hafner (Fourteenth Yearbook of the National Reading Conference [Milwaukee: National Reading Conference, Inc., 1965]), pp. 188-202; Dorothy P. MacDonald, "An Investigation of the Attitudes of Parents of Unsuccessful and Successful Readers," *Journal of Educational Research*. LVI (April, 1963), 437-38.

8. M. G. Grunebaum et al., "Fathers of Sons with Primary Neurotic Learning Inhibitions," *American Journal of Orthopsychiatry*, XXXII (April, 1962), 462-72; Hazel G. Seigler and Malcolm D. Gynther, "Reading Ability of Children and Family Harmony," *Journal of Developmental Reading*, IV (Autumn, 1960), 17-24.

reject success in reading as a feminine accomplishment.[9] Reading achievement is closely related to peer-group standards and peer status, irrespective of the socioeconomic level of the school community.[10]

Yet, some research indicates that there are wide individual differences among the members of any deprived group and that, therefore, efforts to break down cultural and socioeconomic barriers may be successful. For example, in a study of library usage by low-income families, Peil found no constant cultural or socioeconomic factors.[11] Despite lower income, Negro mothers in this group tended to read more books and magazines than white mothers even when the significant factors of age and education were controlled. Mothers who used the library bought more books for their children, and the extensiveness of the use of the library by their first-grade children was definitely related to the frequency of use by the mothers.

In any culturally handicapped group, there may be as many upwardly mobile members who show positive and constructive attitudes and behavior toward educational goals as there are who exhibit indifference, ambivalence, or outright negativism. No matter what cultural or socioeconomic deprivations are present, they do not impinge equally upon all members of the group. The sociological research has been precise in describing the characteristics of the deprived group and in pointing out the negative forces operating to that group's detriment. This research must now be implemented by efforts to identify the individual differences in motivation and self-identification within the group and to capitalize upon these differences or to modify them toward constructive educational goals. This obligation rests as heavily (or even more heavily) upon teachers of reading as upon other educators because of the foundational nature of these teachers' instructional efforts.

9. Albert J. Mazurkiewicz, "Social-Cultural Influences and Reading," *Journal of Developmental Reading*, III (Summer, 1960), 254-63.

10. O. V. Porterfield and Harry F. Schlichting, "Peer Status and Reading Achievement," *Journal of Educational Research*, LIV (April, 1961), 291-97.

11. Margaret Peil, "Library Use by Low-Income Chicago Families," *Library Quarterly*, XXXIII (October, 1963), 329-33.

THE TEACHER AND CLASS STRUCTURE

Social and cultural forces affect teachers, just as they do all members of a society, and in affecting teachers these forces impinge upon the learning process. The average teacher is most likely to belong to a middle-class family, although her ambitions tend to make her upwardly mobile. This characterization is, of course, an overstatement if construed to apply to the entire population, for there are systematic variations from the mode related to differences in the social composition of groups of teachers in different teaching situations. Age, social class, and sex distributions of teaching personnel vary considerably in different geographic regions (as between rural and urban school districts), from elementary to secondary schools (and within the latter), and from one teaching field to another.

Some social anthropologists and sociologists are inclined to believe that social environment shapes the value orientations of its members and that, in the case of teachers, their middle-class value systems are transmitted through them to their pupils. This transmission of values occurs not so often by direct teaching as by example, precept, and the reward-and-punishment system inherent in schools.

Whether teachers externalize value orientations that are unique to the middle class, to which we earlier assumed most of them belong, is still a debated issue. Early studies of the classroom behaviors which teachers tended to disapprove seemed to reflect a value system which decried sexual behavior, aggressiveness, obscenity, and the like, or to reflect, perhaps, the puritanical morality of a traditional value system. More recent replications of this research reveal, however, a shift to teacher concern with such problems as sullenness, unhappiness, and resentfulness—reflecting a mental-hygiene viewpoint rather than a social-class position.

Certain studies of the interactions between teachers and children of various social classes and of the consequent handling of favors, privileges, and punishments seem to show an influence of the teacher's social-class position on her attitudes and behavior toward her pupils. In a group of middle-class teachers, more "domination-with-conflict" contacts were observed with lower-class children than with children of a higher social class. The poorer the achievement of the children, the more the attention of the teacher was needed, but it was given largely in a negatively charged relationship. Other studies show that, when teachers counsel with the parents of lower-class children, the emphasis seems to be upon discipline problems. Paradoxically, counseling sessions with upper-class parents stress school work, even though the children in question are the better achievers. Some interpreters of this and similar studies have suggested that the teachers' behavior reflects attitudes toward pupil achievement rather than toward pupil social class, since the same discriminatory behavior has been observed to be directed against boys from higher-class families who exhibit low achievement.

An accurate interpretation of the influence of the social-class attitudes of teachers is complicated by the fact that academic achievement is highly conditioned by the pupil's social-class position. Every type of favorable accomplishment, reward, or success that can be found in the framework of the school is readily gained by the pupils of the higher social class in disproportionate share. To some observers, it would appear that the school is structured to produce only frustration, punishment, and failure for the pupil of the lower social class.[12] It would hardly be fair, however, to say that the concern of the middle-class teacher with the value system of her social class is the major cause of the maladaptation of lower-class pupils to school life. Certainly this situation also reflects the values imposed upon the teacher from administrative heights and by the community, as well as her internal frustration in dealing with pupils whose failure seems to disprove her professional competence.

Two other forces which impinge upon the social interaction of the classroom are the real or imagined community restraints and pressures as they are perceived by teachers and the teacher's perceptions of the role expected of her by parents and by other teachers. There is ample evidence, particularly in the field of reading, that communities may exert pressures and induce changes in

---

12. Allen H. Barton, "Social Class and Instructional Procedures in the Process of Learning to Read," in *New Developments in Programs and Procedures for College-Adult Reading*, ed. Ralph C. Staiger and Culbreth Y. Melton (Twelfth Yearbook of the National Reading Conference, [Milwaukee: National Reading Conference, Inc., 1963]), pp. 167-74.

school curriculums and instructional procedures. The teaching of phonics is a strident example of an instructional procedure which has been the core of numerous conflicts between community pressure groups and school personnel. There is no question that, upon occasion, such groups may impose their value systems on educational institutions, regardless of the academic outcomes. Some schools and teachers feel these pressures and restraints more acutely than others. In all probability, however, teachers actually interpret the feelings of parents and community as more prudish and restrictive than they really are. They similarly perceive their administrators as more authoritarian than those persons believe themselves to be.

The implication of this examination of the impact of the teacher's social class and value systems upon her pupils is obvious—particularly in the area of reading, in which so many materials deal with social concepts and values. Social scientists and others have severely criticized the white middle-class orientation of reading instruction texts.[13] It is unneccessary to repeat their scathing comments in detail at this time, but certain questions must be asked. How can the reading teacher expect the lower-class child to enjoy or even succeed in the process of learning to read when he cannot possibly identify with the characters or social life portrayed? How can one expect academic motivation among children constantly exposed to materials which deal with an almost unknown—if not phantasmal-appearing—way of life? How can one expect the lower-class pupil to perceive the ultimate personal and vocational values of reading skill when he finds so little reading material that is cast in terms of life as he understands it?

There is now widespread recognition of the fact that many instructional materials are in conflict with reality as lower-class pupils experience it. Many texts are now being prepared which avoid the middle-class bias, and a few are already in use in many classrooms. Reading teachers are becoming alert to the need for the use of basic and recreational texts which deal with life as lower-class pupils of various ethnic and racial groups know it. As a result of this new awareness, perhaps, the psychological mechanisms (such

---

13. Otto Klineberg, "Life Is Fun in a Smiling, Fair-Skinned World," *Saturday Review*, XLVI (February 16, 1963), 75-77, 87.

as identification, insight, strengthening of the self-concept, and empathy) which are essential to enjoyment and lasting impressions from reading may also be made available to lower-class pupils.

Reading teachers may even come to recognize that reading well and widely, particularly in "good" literature, may itself be a middle-class status symbol. They may seriously question whether their standards of skill and their selections of "appropriate" materials are not reflections of their own middle-class values. Reading instruction may even be perceived as training in a tool which is to be used to achieve the pupil's own goals and social and vocational aims rather than as training in a skill which should be possessed to a maximum degree by all pupils.

Social Psychology

Social psychology offers perhaps its most pointed applications and implications for the field of reading in its research on learning as a group process. Borrowing freely from other areas, these studies emphasize social interaction in the classroom, social climate, group dynamics, the interaction of teacher-pupil verbal and non-verbal behaviors, social organization of classroom groups, and the relevance of teacher attitudes and understanding of child development to learning in an instructional situation. As indicated in this brief review of the research, the studies and their implications have pyramided from simple observations of single variables affecting learning into complex investigations of mental health, group dynamics, and learning—all involving concepts of the classroom environment as a constantly changing process.

An early, sterile search for simple, easily measured criteria of teaching effectiveness gradually gave way to study of the interaction of the behaviors of teacher and child. Descriptions of teacher behavior or of classroom climate were generalized as democratic-authoritarian, laissez faire, dominative-integrative, permissive-directive, or active-traditional, and the impact of these upon child behavior was noted.[14] Other studies explored the effect upon the learning process of teacher perceptions of pupil characteristics and

---

14. R. K. White and R. Lippitt, *Autocracy and Democracy: An Experimental Inquiry* (New York: Harper & Bros., 1960).

needs. Methods of observing and recording verbal and physical behaviors of pupils and teachers were evolved in this attempt to describe and analyze the social milieu of the classroom. At the same time, borrowing from the studies of group dynamics, social psychologists became concerned about the interactions of pupils—about their *esprit*, cohesiveness, leadership roles, problem-solving orientation, and goal-defining activities.

As such research progressed, the emphasis upon global judgments of classroom climate and teacher effectiveness became more concrete and pointed more directly toward behavioral referents. It became apparent that the research was not dealing with single factors but rather with an ongoing social process of constant change in a variety of patterns. Among these interacting factors might be teacher behavior–pupil behavior, pupil behavior–group interaction, and group behavior–teacher behavior. Furthermore, it was realized that each of these interrelationships tends to induce change in or to be changed by its interacting forces. Thus, currently, the research in social psychology attempts to study operationally the patterns or sequences of behavior resulting in learning which involve not only the teacher but also the individual pupils, the class as a group, and the class as a collection of groups.[15]

This dynamics research has obvious implications not only for the general classroom situation as a learning center but even more particularly for that remedial work which attempts to deal with pupils who have failed to learn. In most cases of reading disability, there is the implication of a breakdown in the classroom communication–learning process, of the failure of the pupil and his teachers to adapt or adjust and relate to each other. Despite this implication, remedial teachers often attempt to find a single procedure or device which will correct the disability. They tend to seek this ameliorative factor in a new teaching approach (individualized, language-ex-

---

15. Jacob W. Getzels and H. A. Thelen, "The Classroom Group as a Unique Social System," in *The Dynamics of Instructional Groups*, ed. Nelson B. Henry (Fifty-ninth Yearbook of the National Society for the Study of Education, Part II [Chicago: Distributed by the University of Chicago Press, 1960]), pp. 53-82; John Withall and W. W. Lewis, "Social Interaction in the Classroom," in *Handbook of Research in Teaching*, ed. N. L. Gage (Chicago: Rand McNally & Co., 1963), pp. 683-714.

perience, kinesthetic, phonic, and so on), a fresh set of reading materials (recreational or basal), the repair of a suspected developmental lag (visual training, perceptual training, visuo-motor skills), more intensive drill in specific skills (vocabulary, word analysis, comprehension), a self-motivating device (a kit, game, or machine), or in some combination of these which by its sheer variety will induce greater learning.

General results seem to recommend these approaches—in fact, each approach in almost equal degree—perhaps largely because of the Hawthorne effect. And undoubtedly there are reading cases in which any one or several of these techniques will contribute in a mechanical sense to development of the reader's skills. But the rationale of remedial reading has failed to come to grips with what is probably, in many cases, the basic underlying cause—the disruption of the dynamic interaction of teacher-pupil-group relationships that produce successful learning in the retarded reader.

Social psychology has long since demonstrated that the authoritarian, highly teacher-directed learning situation does support learning in some children, particularly in those who are anxious, withdrawn, and non-self-directing. But this climate also promotes tensions, hostilities, and aggression among pupils and between pupils and teacher. Classroom climates that permit some self-selection, self-direction, and self-pacing (with the assistance of rather than constant direction by the teacher) are more conducive to learning and to wholesome relationships among pupils and between pupils and teacher as well. Children who are isolated socially or physically by their peers tend to react in ways that further isolate them from the learning activities of the group. Groups may develop an *esprit* or goal antagonistic to learning because of the attitudes of their leaders. Groups may fail to achieve educational goals because their composition is determined by the teacher rather than through natural selection. These are but a few possible examples of disruption of the teacher-pupil-group relationships which, if intact, should promote learning.

In the not too distant future, as this facet of research in social psychology influences reading teachers, we may see some modification of the remedial reading process. Teachers may better analyze and understand (*a*) their impact upon the pupil and his consequent behaviors, (*b*) his interactions with the peer group and its effects upon him, and (*c*) the significance of his self-concept as a person and particularly as a reader. The teacher will experiment in assuming various roles and relationships, in modifying group reactions, and in adapting to the perceived needs and feelings of the pupils— observing, meanwhile, the effects upon pupil learning of these changes in the teacher's physical and verbal behavior.

Someday, teachers may perceive that the more significant aspect of the teacher-pupil relationship is the interaction of the personalities involved—that this interaction is more important than methodology or instructional materials, as shown by the recent study of Feldmann.[16] Teachers will recognize that a child may learn to read better only as learning takes on greater significance in relation to his self-concept. Moreover, they will realize that the pupil's growth in reading may progress only in proportion to the supportive and reinforcing effects provided by the teacher and the peer group.

Another possible application of the research in social interaction to the field of reading would seem to be in the comparison of the effectiveness of various instructional approaches. Studies of the individualized or the language-experience methods, for example, may frequently indicate a superiority of these techniques that is merely the result of the types of teacher-pupil interaction they promote rather than because of any inherent superiority in the procedure. Both of these approaches emphasize more pupil planning, permissiveness in selecting reading materials, more and closer teacher-pupil relationships, more frequent small-group activities (often based on common interests), and other procedures and conditions known to provide a more successful learning climate. Yet reports of comparative studies not only treat widely varying teacher-definitions of a method as equivalent, but also seldom even employ observational techniques to determine whether the teacher is actually using the basic elements of the method claimed.

It is not surprising that these comparative studies are often either inconclusive or of doubtful validity. Too often, no attempt is made

---

16. Shirley C. Feldmann, "A Study in Depth of First-Grade Reading," *Elementary English*, XLIII (October, 1966), 573-76.

to define, to implement, or to observe the dynamic facets which actually might distinguish these experimental methods from more traditional approaches. It is time that experimenters claiming to compare classroom procedures in teaching reading report on such items as (*a*) the basic differences in daily practices, (*b*) their analysis of the verbal behavior of the teacher, (*c*) the type, variety, and tone of pupil-teacher-group interactions, (*d*) a sociometric analysis of the social interactions in the group, (*e*) the teacher's perceptions of her pupils and her efforts to implement these perceptions, and (*f*) the extent of the success of the teacher in making the learning process a problem-solving, goal-oriented series of situations. There are ample tools and techniques now available to facilitate study of these well-recognized factors in learning in the classroom milieu.[17] Until these tools of social research are utilized to determine the significant effects of various instructional approaches upon the teacher-pupil-group learning process, the comparative values of these methods will remain in doubt.

Child Development

The field of child development originated as an interdisciplinary interest and grew as a result of the continued contributions of scientists of a half-dozen fields. Today there is a significant body of theory and research which concerns itself with the phenomenon of child growth and development, and it has many implications for persons in the field of reading. An attempt to review these implications is particularly appropriate in view of the contemporary surge of interest in the works of Piaget and Montessori.[18]

THE GOALS OF EARLY CHILDHOOD EDUCATION

A major area of contemporary interest in child development is found in the attempt to define the goals of preschool, kindergarten, and primary education. One group of specialists conceives of this period as one of opportunity for group experience largely intended

---

17. Donald M. Medley and Harold E. Mitzel, "Measuring Classroom Behavior by Systematic Observation," in *Handbook of Research in Teaching, op. cit.,* pp. 247-328.

18. See chapter ii of this yearbook for a historical review of the interrelatedness of child-development science and reading readiness.

as preparation for later schooling. By learning health habits, social habits and skills, and consideration for the rights of others, the children develop in their ability to conform to the demands of the group (society). Thus, routines in connection with naps, toileting, music time, play time, dressing, and the like are imposed or directed by the teacher. Gesell's monumental work in the study of the sequential development of language and of motor and social skills probably contributed greatly to this philosophy, which emphasizes group experience and natural development as the fundamental bases of child development.

Another school of thought of very recent vintage places its major emphasis upon the shifting downward into the nursery and kindergarten of some aspects of training in formal school skills. It has been claimed by the representatives of this school of thought that it is essential for our country's welfare that formal training begin as early as possible and that progress in such areas as reading, science, and mathematics should be accelerated by the earlier introduction of skills and concepts. The fact that some children can and do learn to read prior to formal entrance to school, seemingly without great harm, is drawn out of context and used as an argument that most children can or should be introduced to reading during the preschool period.

It is argued by some that early stimulation of the child's cognitive abilities would be achieved by the downward shifting of school content into the nursery ages. However, no justification has come to the attention of this writer for the assumption that formal lessons in reading, spelling, arithmetic, and the like constitute the best or even an acceptable approach to the stimulation of early cognitive development. In fact, Dawe's work indicates that the desired development of certain cognitive abilities can also be effected by *informal* programs specifically designed for that age group.[19] Furthermore, to accept the argument for the downward shifting of school content, one would have to assume, contrary to Piaget, that acceleration of cognitive development of preschool children is entirely feasible

---

19. Helen C. Dawe, "A Study of the Effect of an Educational Program upon Language Development and Related Mental Functions in Young Children," *Journal of Experimental Education*, XI (1942), 200-209.

within the framework of school learning tasks. However, no definitive research is available to show that the use of school content, particularly in the highly teacher-directed fashion commonly employed, is to be preferred as a way of stimulating early cognitive development. Nor is there evidence that such programs actually result in accelerated growth in cognition, unless this is perhaps considered synonymous with growth in school skills.

Research on nursery and kindergarten groups which pursued the group-experience goal drastically undermined many of its assumptions. The studies demonstrated, for example, that the imposition of routines stimulated aggressive behavior among the children, that the training did not have lasting or transfer effects, and that a great deal of the desired social learning was of an incidental, imitative nature. The variations in individual attention span, the need for bodily activity, and the inability of a small child to share an adult with others became apparent in many observational studies, thus casting further doubts on the group-experience program. Spurred by the implications of this research, the goals of child development shifted toward emphasis upon development of the individual. It is apparent that the implications of this research are not clear to proponents of more formal preschool training.

Nursery schools, kindergartens, and primary schools that act upon these research implications de-emphasize teacher-directed routines and attempt rather to develop social skills, increase skill in interpersonal relationships, enhance emotional development, and provide ample opportunity for all facets of language development in a relatively individualized self-directing program. Attention is also given to the child's need for developing his self-identification. It is believed by proponents of this program that learning occurs within a relationship between the stimulation of the environment and the child's fundamental needs as a feeling, responding individual.

In moving away from the idea of sequential, relatively fixed developmental patterns among children toward greater recognition of individuality, child-development science does not completely deny that some learning is sequential nor that its development cannot sometimes be stimulated. Dawe's work with deprived orphanage children demonstrated that a special program intended to improve language development resulted in significant gains in vocabulary, in information about home living and science, in greater readiness, and in increases in verbal I.Q. Milner has shown the importance of manipulating the social climate among preschoolers by the finding that children with more verbal and affectionate relationships with their mothers achieved higher readiness scores.[20]

However, the trend toward a highly directed, structured preschool and kindergarten environment persists. Some appear to believe that, with judicious selection of modes of presentation, it should be possible to teach anything at any age. Apparently the goal of child-development specialists should be simply the devising of ways and means of presenting skills and facts so that they may be readily learned, whether or not they are essential to the child's life or development or needs.

In a sense, the philosophy of Piaget seems to include both of these basic concepts of child development.[21] His experiments emphasize the sequential development of the child's thinking through distinct stages from sensori-motor to perceptual to abstract operations. He apparently believes that these stages are reflections of stable modes of functioning or stages of logic that are not easily altered by training. Thus, Piaget appears to confirm the concept of development in sequences or stages as suggested by Gesell and, at the same time, to refute assumptions of contemporary theorists that this development can be accelerated. Piaget's defense of naturalistic development is supported in several experiments which failed to show that such a principle of thinking as conservation, the ability to recognize the basic properties of objects even when arrangements or order are changed, was amenable to training.

These observations of the evolution of the goals of the education of young children are certainly pertinent to reading instruction. Questions about early reading analogous to those that the child-development specialists have labored with are: "What is reading readiness—a series of sequential learnings which respond to training or a gradually unfolding development which proceeds at its own

---

20. *Ibid.*; Esther Milner, "A Study of the Relationship between Readiness in Grade One School Children and Patterns of Parent-Child Interaction," *Child Development*, XXII (1951), 95-112.

21. John H. Flavell, *The Developmental Psychology of Jean Piaget* (New York: D. Van Nostrand Co., Inc., 1963).

naturalistic pace?" "Is reading readiness basically a cognitive development, closely related to mental age and ability, or is it composed of a group of skills which may be taught?" [22]

Observation of current practices in school admissions and primary education demonstrate that school administrators and reading personnel accept diametrically opposed answers to the questions just posed. Despite the overwhelming evidence that carefully planned readiness programs definitely promote early success in reading, there is widespread use of mental or chronological age as the major criterion for school admission. Similarly, in their use of brief and often highly structured readiness programs, teachers fail to implement the belief that readiness is trainable; for, if these programs are not obviously successful, training tends to cease while the solution of the problem is left to natural forces toward development. The individual rate of development characteristic of young children is forgotten, and the possible values of extended or intensive training as determined by careful diagnosis are often ignored.[23]

There is ample research which demonstrates that readiness is not entirely a cognitive or a chronological development insured by the process of natural development. Among the recognized components are visual discrimination, auditory discrimination, auditory comprehension, language development, and verbal intelligence. All of these abilities are readily improved or increased by specific training procedures, provided that they are directly related to the child's individual needs and that the duration of training is extended to that point at which development is adequate for the purposes intended. Perhaps some teachers and administrators need to repeat the evolutionary thinking which child-development specialists have shown in moving gradually away from highly structured, group-oriented programs and dependence upon naturalistic development toward those centered upon the needs and characteristics of the individual child.

There is strong evidence that some reading specialists have

22. See chapter ii for a detailed review of conflicting concepts of readiness.

23. George D. Spache et al., *A Study of a Longitudinal First-Grade Reading Readiness Program* (U.S. Office of Education, Co-operative Research Project No. 2742 [Tallahassee: Florida State Department of Education, 1965]).

moved away from structured, group-oriented instructional programs. There are those, for example, who emphasize the values of individualized reading in keeping with Olson's principles of self-selection, self-pacing, and seeking (intrinsic motivation). While certain uses are made of group instruction in this approach, the rationale stresses the fitting of instruction to the individual child's needs and rate of growth rather than the use of teacher-determined sequences of reading materials and the pacing of child development in reading.

Another group of reading experts supports a language-experience approach to beginning reading in which the child creates much of the reading material as his communication skills develop. Again, the child's own language development guides instruction and reading practice, while the teacher, rather than directing or pacing this growth, supports and promotes it by providing stimulating experiences and materials.

COGNITIVE DEVELOPMENT

Closely allied with the research relating to the definition of goals in child development but with much wider implications is the current research in cognitive development. This area is concerned with the information-processing system of the human, his strategies or programs of thinking. Piaget, for example, distinguishes a preoperational stage which extends to the age of seven, and a concrete-operations stage which extends to adolescence. These stages are distinguished by the learning of principles of logic or of thought—conservation, centration, decentration, and the like.

Other students have approached cognitive development through the child's development of language, again distinguishing a sequence of stages characterized by certain plans or strategies for forming utterances.[24] Still another group has suggested that this system of information processing is composed of (a) memories, (b) operations for acting on memories and on incoming stimulation, and

---

24. *The Acquisition of Learning: Report of the Fourth Conference Sponsored by the Committee on Intellectual Processes Research of the Social Science Research Council*, ed. Ursula Bellugi and Roger Brown ("Monographs of the Society for Research in Child Development," Vol. XXIX, No. 1, Serial No. 92, [Lafayette, Ind.: Child Development Publications, 1964]).

(c) rules for combining operations into larger programs for processing information.[25] Some writers emphasize the role of experience in intellectual development, pointing out the possibilities of fostering or retarding it by varied environments. This viewpoint, as well as that of the theorists who stress the importance of the learning set, is based largely on the related experiments of transfer in animal learning.[26] Numerous studies of intellectual changes in mental retardates, institutionalized children, and culturally deprived children as they move from one environment to another relate to this view.[27]

Some research on cognitive development has attempted to distinguish styles of thinking, such as analytic-synthetic, objective-subjective, field dependent–field independent, and others.[28] The point here is that the individual's cognitive style influences his information-processing system and hence his learning and intellectual development. Related to this concept of cognitive style are the studies in convergent and divergent (creative) thinking by Getzels,[29] Torrance,[30] and others.

Since comprehension is generally recognized as a cognitive or information-processing system, direct application of much of this research to the teaching of this process is possible. There is the distinct possibility that comprehension develops through a series

25. Allen Newell, J. C. Shaw, and Herbert A. Simon, "Elements of a Theory of Human Problems Solving," *Psychological Review*, LXV (May, 1958), 151-66.

26. Joseph McVickers Hunt, *Intelligence and Experience* (New York: Ronald Press Co., 1961).

27. Benjamin S. Bloom, *Stability and Change in Human Characteristics* (New York: John Wiley & Sons, 1964).

28. Riley W. Gardner, Douglas N. Jackson, and Samuel J. Messick, "Personality Organization in Cognitive Controls," *Psychological Issues*, II, Monograph 8 (1960); H. A. Witkin *et al.*, *Psychological Differentiation: Studies of Development* (New York: John Wiley & Sons, 1962).

29. Jacob W. Getzels, "Creative Thinking, Problem-solving and Instruction," chap. x in *Theories of Learning and Instruction*, ed. Ernest R. Hilgard (Sixty-third Yearbook of the National Society for the Study of Education, Part I [Chicago: Distributed by the University of Chicago Press, 1964]), pp. 240-67.

30. E. Paul Torrance, *Guiding Creative Talent* (Englewood Cliffs, N.J.: Prentice-Hall, Inc., 1962).

of what are as yet unrecognized stages. Some of these might involve strategies of logic, such as those we now label word recognition, main ideas, details, inferences, critical reading, and the like. The first research step, of course, would be to define these behaviors operationally, perhaps at several levels of performance, and then to study carefully the chronology of their appearance. For example, it may be that the ability to comprehend main ideas is simply an extension of noting details—of selecting, combining, and recombining these into major generalizations. A second step suggested by the implications of the research in cognitive development is the exploration of the programing of the child's learning or development of comprehension—the appropriate chronology of presentation, the best training sequences, and the most efficient modes of presentation. Somewhere in this research program, we should include a careful study of cognitive styles in comprehension as well as of the influence of personality traits and the set of the reader.

Some reading specialists may attempt to point out that much of this research has already been completed. They may point to the impressive lists of reading skills enumerated by various authors and to the sequences of skill training outlined in many sources. In answer to them, it may be shown that the skills now taught were defined arbitrarily by a priori thinking rather than after careful observations of their actual development or of their constituent behaviors. Similarly, the tests used to measure their development contain completely abstract, arbitrary labels. Moreover, no researcher has been able to demonstrate that these labels are valid—that the tests and subtests actually measure different facets of the comprehension process. Despite these lists and tests, not much is known about the discriminative differences between good and poor comprehenders—differences in strategies of thought or logic. If repetitive drill in answering certain types of questions (which can be described more accurately as practice in retaining or arriving at certain types of facts to which we attach labels) fails, there is no further remedial recourse, for no clear knowledge of the process is available. In the area of cognitive styles and the relationships among personality, set, and comprehension, the necessary research is being initiated, perhaps because of the realization of the inability of educators to predict gains from reading-improvement efforts and of the difficulty in understanding the variations in reading performances among individuals apparently given the same training.[31]

If its significance is recognized, the research in the area of child development and cognitive development can help give direction to efforts in the field of reading, ranging from readiness levels upward to adolescence.

Linguistics, Psycholinguistics, and Language Development

One of the major complexities in interpreting the significance of linguistic science for the teaching of reading is the diversity of schools of opinion within that science. One group, the phonologists, attacks current methods of teaching phonics as the unnatural and distorted representation of the basic sounds of our language, (which they call phonemes).[32] Another group, the structural linguists, proposes that knowledge of their branch of the field, sentence structure, must be conveyed to children to insure comprehension. The whole-word approach, which they believe to be the most common current method of teaching reading, as well as that based on phonics or even on phonemes are all decried by this school of linguists.[33] Still another group studies the structure of morphemes (combination of sounds) and suggests the importance of this knowledge of word structure for reading instruction. And yet another group, the semanticists, emphasizes the importance of shades of meanings in words and of their relation to the experiential background of the reader.[34] As a result, the statements of linguists as well as the instructional materials for reading that some have prepared appear to the reading professional as quite confusing and even contradictory. As Hull has noted in her efforts to react to linguistics-based readers, "The

---

31. Earl F. Rankin, Jr., "Reading Test Performance of Introverts and Extroverts," in *New Developments in Programs and Procedures for College-Adult Reading, op. cit.*, pp. 158-66.

32. Leonard Bloomfield and C. L. Barnhart, *Let's Read* (Detroit: Wayne State University Press, 1961); Charles C. Fries, *Linguistics and Reading* (New York: Henry Holt & Co., 1963).

33. Robert L. Allen, "Better Reading through the Recognition of Grammatical Relations," *Reading Teacher*, XVIII (December, 1964), 194-98.

34. Philip B. Gove, "Reading from the Lexicographer's Viewpoint," *Reading Teacher*, XVIII (December, 1964), 199-201.

theory as to how linguistic knowledge relates to reading programs varies from linguist to linguist." [35]

Another major problem for the average teacher is the fact that most of the knowledge he has absorbed regarding the language development of children (from studies prior to 1960) is being challenged or vitiated by studies employing techniques of language-analysis quite different and obscure, couched in new and unfamiliar terms and yielding results almost incomprehensible to members of non-linguistic disciplines.

Recent normative and developmental studies, such as those of Strickland, Loban, and Francis, are apparently superior to the early language studies of McCarthy, Davis and Templin, and Irwin because the later studies emphasize the new approaches to analysis of syntax in the speech and writing of children. Measures used earlier, such as length of sentence, development of correct articulation, analysis of types of sentences, and the use of various parts of speech and subordinate clauses as indications of language development are no longer adequate for this purpose, according to the linguists. The implications of all this earlier research, which until now has seemed quite meaningful, appear to be ignored in this new view of language development.[36]

Similarly, the early language research on the development of babbling and speech sounds, phonemes, consonant-vowel ratio, and the like are to be discarded because, in the opinions of some linguists, "these phenomena have little specific significance for the development of true language." [37]

Some who review the new offerings receive the distinct impression that the linguists are declaring that true language and, consequently, scientific study of language development can be begun only after the child speaks in complete sentences, because only this kind of language can be analyzed by their techniques. The observed

---

35. Lorene Hull, "Linguistic Reading in First Grade," *Elementary English*, XLII (December, 1965), 883-88 (quotation from p. 883).

36. John B. Carroll, "Linguistics and the Psychology of Language," *Review of Educational Research*, XXXIV (April, 1964), 119-26.

37. Dorothea McCarthy, "Research in Language Development: Retrospect and Prospect," *Child Development Monographs*, XXIV, 5 (1959), 3-24 (quotation by John B. Carroll from p. 11).

effects of physical nurture, feeding experiences, institutionalization, and lack of warm relationship or "mothering" upon infant speech during the first six months of life and their subsequent relationships to later language development as observed in different cultures and social classes are given little attention by the linguists. The effects upon language development of parental personality patterns, marital relationships, and emotional tone of the home also appear to be ignored in the effort to evolve a technique of analysis of the internal structure of spoken and written speech.[38]

In contrast to earlier studies, some modern linguists employ a "phonological unit" which, despite the number of so-called sentences in it or its interminable run-on nature, is now considered synonymous with a sentence. A phonological unit ends only when the speaker shows by falling intonation or silence that he has reached a terminal point. Some research employing this new system of classifying children's speech has reported that children tend to speak in phonological units that are longer than the sentences contained in the readers now being offered, an observation obviously predicated upon the researchers' new definition of a sentence. The assumption drawn from the Strickland study that it is unsound for readers to present sentences of lesser complexity than those used by pupils remains untested. Both the unique definition of a sentence used in this study and the lack of evidence of harmful effects in attempting to read in simple language leave this assumption unsupported. Other criticisms of the so-called normative studies of Strickland and Loban are their use (*a*) of adult-child interaction only, (*b*) of a set pattern of picture stimuli at all ages, and (*c*) of their unique definition of a sentence.

Other linguists subscribe to a system of analysis termed "transformational grammar" which attempts to interpret the manipulation of syntactic units, as by expansion, reduction, or rearrangement of basic or kernel utterances or by the combining of several sentences into one. One study by Hunt attacked the fundamental problem of the

---

38. Frank May, "The Effects of Environment on Oral Language Development, I," *Elementary English*, XLIII (October, 1966), 587-95; Ellis G. Olin, Robert D. Hess, and Virginia C. Shipman, "Role of Mothers' Language Styles in Mediating Their Preschool Children's Cognitive Development" (paper read at the American Educational Research Association, Chicago, 1966).

identification of the basic unit of expression, often termed a sentence.[39] He evolved a "T-unit," a single independent predication with its complements and all the modifiers that may be embedded or otherwise grammatically attached to it. Hunt's final results show this description of a complete utterance to be a better index of maturity in writing than were those techniques that he discarded. O'Donnell, Griffin, and Norris, employing a similar technique, also succeeded in demonstrating the discriminative nature of this T-unit.[40] Interestingly enough, this later study tends to confirm some of the significance given to growth in the use of subordinate clauses as an indicator of maturity in language that had been indicated by the early language-development studies.

The only purpose in this rather lengthy contrasting of linguistic schools, techniques of language analysis, and older studies of language development is to point out the obvious inference that linguistics is an emerging science. Linguistics is still refining techniques and methodology from which there will undoubtedly arise, perhaps in the near future, some new and fresh insights into language development containing possible implications for reading instruction. It is also hoped that linguistic scientists will begin to use previous work in related disciplines. It would be profitable at this time to review, if only superficially, some of the basic linguistic principles which may prove to have some significance for reading instruction.

LINGUISTIC CONCEPTS AND PRINCIPLES

Many linguists ascribe to the belief that speech is the primary language function and that writing or reading are secondary or are even derived from oral language. From this assumption deductions such as the following are drawn: (*a*) simple, normal power of speech is all that a child needs as readiness for the act of reading; (*b*) reading is highly dependent upon auditory memories; and (*c*) compre-

39. Kellogg W. Hunt, *Differences in Grammatical Structures Written at Three Grade Levels, the Structures To Be Analyzed by Transformational Methods* (U.S. Office of Education, Co-operative Research Project No. 1998 [Tallahassee: Florida State Department of Education, 1964]).

40. Roy C. O'Donnell, William J. Griffin, and Raymond C. Norris, *A Transformational Analysis of the Language of Kindergarten and Elementary School Children* (mimeographed; Nashville, Tenn.: George Peabody College for Teachers, 1965), p. 122.

hension depends upon the reader's ability to hear (to think) the written word in its normal inflection and to hear the combination of stress, tone, pitch, and junctures of the sentence as he reads.

Only a few linguists, such as Reed, have questioned this principle by pointing out that such exceptional children as deaf-mutes (or the foreign-born, bilingual, or hard-of-hearing, it might be added) learn to read and write without adequate auditory memories for spoken language.[41] In addition to this refutation offered by Reed, other evidences of the lack of parallelism between spoken and written language may be cited. In an early study, Harrell showed that the length of written stories lags behind oral composition for both boys and girls, but that written stories are composed in more complicated sentences, as indicated by the index of subordinate clauses.[42] Recent studies employing the techniques of transformational grammar again indicated that oral compositions showed significant differences from written language in structural elements at various grade levels.

Other major differences between spoken prose (reading aloud) and conversation are noted by Marquardt.[43] Among these are (*a*) the highly standardized intonation patterns of spoken prose, (*b*) its even tempo, (*c*) the relationship of pauses to grammatical structure in spoken prose as contrasted with the unpredictability of such pauses in conversation, (*d*) the lack of meaningfully filled silences in spoken prose in comparison with the frequency of these (plus gestures and grimaces) in conversation, (*e*) the fewer phonetically different speech sounds in spoken prose, (*f*) the repetitive, structurally incomplete nature of conversation, as well as its constant use of meaningless words and phrases that serve as mechanisms of rapport or as silence fillers. Marquardt's emphasis upon these differences between conversation and spoken prose applies with equal cogence

---

41. David W. Reed, "A Theory of Language, Speech and Writing," *Elementary English*, XLII (December, 1965), 845-51.

42. Lester E. Harrell, Jr., *A Comparison of the Development of Oral and Written Language in School-Age Children* ("Monographs of the Society for Research in Child Development," Vol. XXII, No. 3, Serial No. 66 [Lafayette, Ind.: Child Development Publications, 1957]).

43. William F. Marquardt, "Language Interference in Reading," *Reading Teacher*, XVIII (December, 1964), 214-18.

to a comparison of oral speech and reading materials. Certainly these studies and observations imply that the relating of spoken to written language, the act of reading, is not as simple an act as some linguists suggest.

Many linguists offer as a second principle in their interpretation of the reading process the theory that reading is a simple decoding of the written graphemes (letters) into their equivalent phonemes (sounds). This concept of the reading process as a phonemic-graphemic matching is exemplified in the instructional materials now offered by various linguists.[44] Acceptance of this concept has led to the following assumptions: (*a*) learning the names of the letters of the alphabet is of primary value in beginning reading; (*b*) the words offered for beginning reading must be phonemically consistent—i.e., offer only one consistent grapheme for each phoneme or follow certain spelling patterns; (*c*) the interpretation of the meaning of printed materials is secondary to the process of learning to read as linguists define it; (*d*) a conscious learning of syntax patterns or sentence patterns is a significant aid to reading; (*e*) pictures related to the text should be eliminated in early materials because children may use them as clues to word form: (*f*) word recognition occurs by the decoding of each successive grapheme, not by recognition of word form, word length, configuration, context clues, or the like; (*g*) the letter groups used in beginning reading need not be real words provided they parallel such words in phonemic consistency; (*h*) it is a fallacy of the whole-word method to confuse reading and understanding (one may read without being able to understand or comprehend);[45] (*i*) early emphasis upon recognition or reading of structural units (phrases, clauses) might, according to some writers, help solve those problems of narrow eye-span which may be psycholinguistic rather than physical.

The research evidence to support these assumptions is not entirely convincing. Marquardt strongly refutes the assumption that speech is simply a sequence of phonemes and that reading is an

---

44. Rose Sabaroff, "Breaking the Code: What Method? Introducing an Integrated Linguistic Approach to Beginning Reading," *Elementary School Journal*, LXVII (November, 1966), 95-103.

45. Karl U. Smith, Richard Cambria, and James Steffan, "Sensory-Feedback of Reading," *Journal of Applied Psychology*, XLVIII (October, 1964), 275-86.

equivalent sequence of graphemes. In fact, he feels strongly that the child's conversation experiences are so different from the language experiences he will encounter in reading aloud that a great deal of special preparation in listening to spoken prose is needed to make the transition from conversation to reading.

Miller attacks some linguistic assumptions by pointing out that (*a*) not all significant features of speech have a physical representation and that (*b*) the descriptions of a language and a language-user must be kept distinct, because the later employs techniques of information storage and information processing as well as the linguistic rules of language.[46]

The confusion between the spelling process and the reading process apparent in linguistic writings is remarked upon by the Hannas.[47] As they and many others point out, spelling is a synthetic process of arranging letters in conventionalized patterns, as contrasted to the fundamentally analytic act of reading. On this same point, Bloomer and others have demonstrated that the lengths of words and their frequency of occurence determine the difficulty of words in spelling, while the multiplicity of meanings, not the order of letters or the degree of phonemic regularity, is the determinant in reading.[48] Letter order, phonemic consistency (or the regularity of "spelling patterns"), length of word, and the like may be significant for spelling progress, but it appears doubtful that they are appropriate criteria for the selection of the vocabulary of readers, as a number of linguistis have assumed.

As for the hypothesis that word recognition depends almost entirely upon the order of the letters and, therefore, that all other clues

---

46. George A. Miller, "Some Preliminaries to Psycholinguistics," *American Psychologist*, XX (January, 1965), 15-20.

47. Paul R. Hanna and Jean S. Hanna, "Applications of Linguistics and Psychological Cues to the Spelling Course of Study," *Elementary English*, XLII (November, 1965), 753-59.

48. Richard H. Bloomer, "Concepts of Meaning and the Reading and Spelling Difficulty of Words," *Journal of Educational Research*, LIV (January, 1961), 178-82.

should be controlled, both Levin [49] and La Pray [50] have experimentally demonstrated the contrary. Words are learned more slowly at first if some are phonemically inconsistent, but on new tasks there is greater transfer. Moreover, better beginning readers do utilize configuration clues, word length, and the like as significant aids in word perception.

Even those experiments employing materials based on the linguistic assumptions about the reading process, such as that of Goldberg and Rasmussen,[51] reveal that children readily learn irregularly spelled or irregular phonemic words when they have meaningful associations and that unreal or nonsense words are not well understood or learned, despite their phonemic regularity. Finally, Karlsen [52] and Bateman and Wetherell [53] point out the dependence of the linguistic concept of reading upon an automatic rather than a reasoned association between letters and sounds, upon the naive dependence upon the names of the letters as an aid to identification of their sounds, and upon the obviously inadequate consideration of methodological, instructional, and learning problems in this rationale.

Of all the linguistic interpretations of the reading process that have been noted, the only assumption supported by definitive research evidence is that of the significance of the child's comprehension and use of language for his success in beginning reading. The breadth of the child's language experiences, auditory and oral, and the maturity of the sentence structures that he can use in speaking and can listen to comprehendingly are certainly related to early

---

49. Harry Levin, "Reading Research: What, Why and for Whom" (Talk delivered to National Conference on Research in English, February 12, 1965).

50. Margaret Helen La Pray, "An Investigation of the Linguistic Approach to Beginning Reading with Respect to Word-Perception" (unpublished Ph.D. dissertation, Cornell University, 1961).

51. Lynn Goldberg and Donald Rasmussen, "The Use of Linguistics in the Beginning Reading Program of the Miquon School," *Elementary English*, XL (March, 1963), 242-47, 254.

52. Bjorn Karlsen, "Children's Reading and the Linguistic Structure of Languages," *Reading Teacher*, XVIII (December, 1964), 184-87.

53. Barbara Bateman and Janis Wetherell, "A Critique of Bloomfield's Linguistic Approach to the Teaching of Reading," *Reading Teacher*, XVIII (November, 1964), 98-104.

success in reading.[54] Volumes of studies attest to the handicaps imposed by the inadequate language experiences of the bilingual, the culturally deprived, or the foreign-born child. Dozens of contemporary experimental programs are engaged in the exploration of effective ways of strengthening or promoting the language development of such children. Some of these are employing linguistic concepts and materials with favorable results.[55]

PSYCHOLINGUISTICS

In his review of the psychology of language, Carroll mentions a variety of studies in what might be characterized as psycholinguistic research.[56] Such research involves the application of techniques and concepts of psychology to language research. Among those cited are reports of recent experiments in verbal learning involving serial items or paired associates, recall, and memory decay; experiments in the roles of feedback environments, reinforcement, learner set, and frequency of occurrence of words in language behavior; studies of verbal learning as an "all-or-none" or gradual-increment process; and studies in the psychology of grammar. However, large areas of psycholinguistic research are absent from Carroll's review as well as from other contemporary descriptions of linguistic science (see Fries).[57]

Some idea of the breadth of this research (apparently not considered by some linguists) is made evident in a paper by Weaver.[58] In this paper, Weaver refers to current studies of the relationship between the predictability of words in context and the reader's pauses, the relationship between rate of reading and function-word position, the interaction of semantic and structural constraints in decoding or interpreting the language of another, the cognitive

---

54. Robert B. Ruddell, "The Effect of Oral and Written Patterns of Language Structure on Reading Comprehension," *Reading Teacher*, XVIII (January, 1965), 270-75.

55. David C. Davis, "Phonemic Structural Approach to Initial Reading Instruction," *Elementary English*, XLI (March, 1964), 218-23.

56. Carroll, *op. cit.*

57. Fries, *op. cit.*

58. Wendell W. Weaver, "Theoretical Aspects of the Cloze Procedure," in *The Philosophical and Sociological Bases of Reading, op. cit.*, pp. 115-32.

activities underlying encoding or generating of language, and the basic differences between encoding and decoding. Other studies alluded to by Weaver include those dealing with the dimensions of our language—from left to right, the temporal sequence from first to last, and the "choice" of possible meanings within each language unit in the sentence.

Space does not permit recounting all the details of these many psycholinguistic efforts, but it is possible to point out briefly some of their obvious implications for reading instruction. It appears that a sentence is interpreted in a general way in segments of perhaps four or five words before it is actually differentiated into the words to be uttered or read. At the same time, interpretation of an unknown word or the identification of a missing word as in the cloze procedure tends to proceed from the possibilities offered by the context to the general incorporation of the meaning into the thought of the sentence. In reading terms, this is an exploration of the manner in which a reader derives meaning of the word from context.

Does he derive the meaning from the words to the left or to the right or from both? Or does he derive it from the structural unit in which the word is embedded, as structuralists seem to imply? Or from an overall, general interpretation of the entire thought? Weaver believes that his own research and the other studies he cites indicate that derivation of meaning from context is, of course, aided by the placement of the unknown word in the context but that, when there is bilateral context (context on either side of the unknown or missing word) the five words immediately before and the five words after the unknown word are most crucial to the reader's success in dealing with it. Meaning is supported strongly by the lexical rather than by the structural words in these portions of the bilateral context. The implication is to be noted that, in attempting to teach students to use the context for meaning clues, they should be taught not to stop at a difficult word but to interject a "guess" or to skip it and read on in the sentence. Furthermore, in an effort to lead students to make the fullest use of the limited redundancy of textbooks, the additional tactic of extending the search for meaning through the remainder of the paragraph or other integrated segment of the text is suggested.

Weaver suggests that there is considerable evidence from the studies of aphasics, who have been classified by some speech pathologists as syntactic aphasics and semantic aphasics, for the support of the dichotomizing of language into structural and lexical categories. The first of the two types of aphasics is characterized by its misuse or omission of function words and grammatical inflections, the second by similar difficulties with substantive, lexical words. Syntactic aphasics retain substantive words (nouns and some verbs) and certain well-practiced phrases and routine sentences; semantic aphasics, although exhibiting the usual characteristics of speech-flow, melody, pitch, intonation, and grammatical structure, lack the substantives, except for the most frequent or general ones. Weaver's own experiments in supplying missing words in a given context indicate much greater volume of responses for words determined by semantic constraint than for those determined by structural pattern or syntactic constraint. From these two types of observation of language behavior, he suggests that the learner stores lexical (meaningful) elements mentally in much greater variety and depth than he does structural or functional elements. Structural elements are probably stored in a fashion to function as cues for the mass of stored substantive or semantic words. Entire language units or structures, Weaver suggests, are not stored but recoded, or "chunked," as it were.

In other words, Weaver hypothesizes that the stored high-frequency structural words are matched to the language input in decoding and used again in generating or encoding the response. The lexical or substantive terms used in the response are drawn from the large stored bank of such terms and tend to be determined by the structural constraints. This interpretation is supported by the fact that the function words offered in recall of such material as a story tend to be similar to the individual's own spontaneous productions while the lexical elements agree very closely with those in the original materials, conforming to the semantic constraints of the context.

Other facts that Weaver introduces to point up the differences between language production and interpretation are: (*a*) input language sequences are not maintained intact, for they cannot be reproduced in that form; (*b*) if input sequences were maintained intact, individual speaking styles could not or would not develop; and

(c) long messages of more than eight or nine digits or twenty-five words cannot remain intact because they exceed the memory capacity and must be processed as parts of the sequence.

Structural elements are learned very clearly, as shown by a number of studies, but are not recalled or decoded very readily. This fact has two possible implications for reading instruction. Early training should emphasize building a large bank of substantive words or concepts—nouns and main verbs—to enable the reader to deal with or process a wide variety of ideas. At the same time, there should be ample exposure to varying structural patterns or writing styles to permit quick reactions to variations in sentences. This last premise is further supported by the longer latencies of response observed in instances in which the structural elements are confusing to the reader. From Weaver's viewpoint (shared by many reading specialists), these two emphases are not mutually exclusive but, rather, are probably complementary.

One other major area of psycholinguistic research, apparently familiar to only a small group of reading and language specialists, is that concerned with the cloze procedure. The technique involves simply the deletion of words from printed passages, the reader being expected to supply the exact word that is missing. The deletions may be every fifth, tenth, or n^{th} word, constituting what is termed a structural or "any-word" deletion, or there may be a selected deletion of specific parts of speech (as noun-verb), a lexical deletion. These basic types were first distinguished by Rankin.[59] The cloze test may be administered before the reading by the subjects of the unmutilated text—a pre-cloze test—or after they have read the original text—a post-cloze test. Most of the research referred to in this summary used the "every-fifth-word" deletion pattern in a pre-cloze procedure.

The cloze technique has been used in a great many studies. First and most frequently, it has served to measure the reading difficulty of passages or even of foreign languages. When used to measure comprehension, its results correlate substantially, in many instances, with those yielded by common standardized tests at levels ranging from

---

59. Earl F. Rankin, Jr., "The Cloze Procedure—A Survey of Research," *ibid.*, pp. 133-50.

fourth grade to college. The cloze test may serve to measure specific or detailed comprehension or the comprehension of main ideas, according to the type of test used, or to provide an estimate of prereading as well as of post-reading knowledge. One or two studies used it to diagnose and analyze the reader's reasoning processes. Despite these related applications, the cloze procedure is not simply a parallel to or an alternative for ordinary reading tests; for, despite the substantial relationships, it appears to measure facets of the reading process other than those sampled by reading tests. It certainly measures redundancy-utilization as well as the other recognized factorial components of reading (e.g., the vocabulary or word factor and the word-relationship factor).

Other studies employed the cloze procedure to measure listening. From this application, Weaver found that structural meaning is conveyed better by silent reading than by listening, while lexical meaning or substantive content is conveyed equally well by either medium.

The technique has served to measure proficiency in a second language. It has also been used in a number of studies of learning, motivation, and personality. Bloomer used the technique as a teaching device, with significant improvement in comprehension and college grades but not in reading rate or vocabulary.[60] Roosinck perfected a series of programed cloze exercises for improving comprehension,[61] and Friedman experimented with cloze exercises in an attempt to improve the comprehension of foreign-born college students.[62]

To add to all these applications, Hafner [63] is exploring the use of the cloze procedure (a) in field testing of all types of instructional materials; (b) in providing a breadth of experiences with word meanings and concepts and thus stimulating vocabulary growth;

60. Richard H. Bloomer, "The Cloze Procedure as a Remedial Reading Exercise," *Journal of Developmental Reading*, V (Spring, 1962), 173-81.

61. P. L. Roosinck, *A Method for Improving Reading Comprehension* (Master's thesis, University of Michigan, 1962).

62. Mildred Friedman, "The Use of the Cloze Procedure for Improving the Reading Comprehension of Foreign Students at the University of Florida" (unpublished Ph.D. dissertation, University of Florida, 1964).

63. Lawrence E. Hafner, "Implications of Cloze," in *The Philosophical and Sociological Bases of Reading, op. cit.*, pp. 151-58.

(c) in analyzing the role of reasoning in reading—detecting and eliminating incongruencies in students' reasoning and analyzing their interpretation of information in the context or in the pattern of the sentence; (d) in the further study of variant deletion patterns, such as of letters; (e) in evaluating student reading abilities and their possible relationships to personality; and (f) as a possible technique for studying language creativity, intelligence, concept development, and the dynamics of thinking.

In a large-scale experiment, Bormuth used cloze-technique data along with a variety of linguistic variables, such as the frequency of independent clause patterns, word depth (the number of syntactic relationships among the words and phrases in a sentence as found for each word), letters per word, and the like.[64] He also utilized older variables, such as parts-of-speech ratios; syllables per word, clause or sentence; sentence length in number of words; and prepositional-phrase ratios. Employing a series of cloze tests which tested systematically every single word in each passage, he studied the foregoing linguistic variables at the word level, the independent-clause level, and the entire passage level as measures of readability. Many of his new variables, including letter counts, words or syllables per independent clause, and pronoun-conjunction and verb-conjunction ratios, demonstrated some value as readability measures. Despite the breadth of this study, Bormuth considers this approach to the analysis of the comprehensibility of language to represent only the initial steps in a long-range program.

As Hafner and Weaver both imply, the cloze procedure may present an opportunity to examine closely the syntactic and semantic effects of context on language units and their basic differences. Furthermore, problem-solving strategies or cognitive styles and the human information-storage and information-retrieval systems may be illuminated.

While much of this psycholinguistic research is in its preliminary stages, its values for reading instruction are manifest. The experiments may well have direct implications for vocabulary teaching,

---

64. John R. Bormuth, *Relationships between Selected Language Variables and Comprehension Ability and Difficulty* (U.S. Office of Education, Cooperative Research Project No. 2082 [Los Angeles: University of California, 1964]).

for analyzing the development of the cognitive processes underlying comprehension, for the extent and kind of training upon words of structural or lexical function, for adapting instruction to our knowledge of the fundamental differences between the encoding processes, for new methods of evaluating the reading difficulty of many types of instructional and other materials, for further study of the process of deriving meaning from context, for new approaches to the measurement of comprehension, and for many other facets of reading.

Educational Psychology

As is true of so many other scientific disciplines, the field of educational psychology has developed into a wide variety of areas of special interest which are barely encompassed by its rubric. The relationship between reading instruction and educational psychology is no longer a single direct line along which new ideas about methodology, classroom organization, and testing procedures move from the psychological experimenter to the reading teacher. Today, educational psychologists are adding to this flow of information a host of implications for reading instruction by their experimental study of new techniques, devices, and media of instruction, of theories of learning, and of theoretical models of skills and processes as well as by their investigations of learning modes and of cognitive and noncognitive variables which influence achievement. Space will permit only an overview of the many fresh lines of communication between these closely related disciplines.

MEDIA OF INSTRUCTION

The values and relationships of various audiovisual materials, television, the teaching machine, programed materials, and other media to classroom instruction are a major area of interest to educational psychologists. They have initiated large-scale studies of the educational effects of television upon students—for example, the study directed by Schramm.[65] Borrowing from the work of the animal experimentalists, they have flooded educational institutions with teaching machines, programed materials, and an accompanying

---

65. Schramm, Lyle, and Parker, *op. cit.*

theory of learning that should eventually have a great impact upon school practices.[66] They have studied the methods and values of audiovisual materials and have been seriously concerned when their guidelines have been ignored in naive classroom use of such materials.[67]

Presently, educational psychologists have shifted their research interests away from simple comparisons of the results of programed courses with those taught conventionally. The comparisons were seldom clear-cut or even essential to intelligent use of these new media. Currently the experimental emphasis is upon the refinement of these tools—their internal characteristics-of-response mode, the use of prompts and confirmation, and sequencing arrangements. Present research is concerned with demonstrating how, with whom, and when this new instructional approach may be used rather than with proving it superior to older methods. The recent reports of Ellson et al. are illustrative of this careful attempt to learn the principles of effective use of a programed approach among children of varying intellectual levels.[68] Among the facets explored in this series of experiments were duration of presentation, retention after various procedures, alternation of programed and classroom procedures, the extent of learning of various reading skills, and the values for young and old mental retardates, normal pupils, and slow learners.

Some generalizations of significance for reading instruction may be made at this time. It is apparent, for example, that (*a*) under certain conditions, programed learning may have great value in the teaching of mental retardates, slow learners, or even normal children;[69] (*b*) the development of certain skills, the acquisition and

66. Wilbur Schramm, Jack Lyle, and Edwin B. Parker, *Programmed Instruction: Today and Tomorrow* (New York: Fund for the Advancement of Education, 1964).

67. K. A. McRobbie, "An Interim Report on Experiments in Several Ontario Schools with the New Castle Textfilm Method of Teaching Reading in the Primary Grades," *Ontario Journal of Educational Research*, III (April, 1961), 191-97.

68. D. G. Ellson et al., "Programmed Tutoring: A Teaching Aid and A Research Tool," *Reading Research Quarterly*, I (Fall, 1965), 77-127.

69. Leslie F. Malpass et al., *Comparison of Two Automated Teaching Procedures for Retarded Children* (U.S. Office of Education, Co-operative Research Project No. 1267 [Washington: U.S. Department of Health, Education and Welfare, 1963]).

maintenance of which are aided by a high degree of repetition, such as word recognition, word analysis, spelling, and perhaps the acquiring of meaning (vocabulary), may be particularly promoted by selective use of programed materials and teaching machines;[70] (c) many aspects of programed learning, such as individual variations in learning rate, size of unit, length of session, reduction of repetition, alternation of prompts and confirmation, type of reinforcement—verbal, visual, or even none—and the sequence and inter-relatedness of skills, remain to be defined and described more objectively.[71]

BEHAVIOR ANALYSIS

Among the tangential areas of research and theory stimulated by the development of programed instruction is that of behavior analysis. This involves the analysis of behavior into terms of stimulus, response, and reinforcement. Analysis of data is based on reinforcement schedules and rate-of-response curves obtained from a small number of subjects; statistical controls and group procedures are unnecessary because of the close similarity of these observations from one individual to another. Smith[72] and Raygor[73] have described and employed this approach, the former in creating instructional materials based on beginning reading as discrimination and the latter in an analysis of the reading rate and comprehension of college readers.

Behavior-analysis research has been employed in a number of studies of the influence of various methods of presentation at beginning and at higher levels of reading. Studies by Muehl and his associates have demonstrated the interfering effects of learning letter names upon later learning of words containing these letters and

---

70. Gerhard Eichholz and Richard Barbe, "An Experiment in Vocabulary Development," *Educational Research Bulletin*, XL (January, 1961), 1-7, 28.

71. John D. McNeil and Evan B. Keislar, "Value of the Oral Response in Beginning Reading: An Experimental Study Using Programmed Instruction," *British Journal of Educational Psychology*, XXXIII (June, 1963), 162-68.

72. Donald E. P. Smith, "Learning To Read as a Discrimination Process," in *College and Adult Reading* (Third and Fourth Annual Yearbooks of the North Central Reading Association, 1965), pp. 28-51.

73. Alton L. Raygor, "Behavior Analysis: The New Look in Reading Research," in *The Philosophical and Sociological Bases of Reading, op. cit.*, pp. 224-36.

the effectiveness of discrimination practice with words to be learned as opposed to transfer of learning from practice with other words or forms.[74] Ofman and Shaevitz cast doubts on any assumption that kinesthetic tracing has greater value than visual tracing or simple pronunciation among retarded readers,[75] while, for a similar population, Otto also concluded that additional reinforcement by combinations of visual, auditory, or kinesthetic clues did not influence retention once mastery of a list of words had been achieved through a single mode of presentation.[76] Budoff and Quinlan found that both normal and retarded second-grade readers learned paired associates better by aural than by visual presentation,[77] while Lockard and Sidowski found differences in the effectiveness of the mode of presentation when the response was overt (visual or visual-auditory were found superior to auditory), with no differences in covert response groups.[78] Marchbanks and Levin reaffirmed the primary significance of the first and last letters as discrimination cues for both long and short words in kindergarten and first-grade.[79] Zigler and Kanzer discovered that, for lower-class children, reinforcement by some tangible reward or praise was most effective, while middle-class children needed only to know that their responses were correct to

---

74. Siegmar Muehl, "The Effects of Visual Discrimination Pretraining on Learning To Read a Vocabulary List in Kindergarten Children," *Journal of Educational Psychology*, LI (August, 1960), 217-21.

75. William Ofman and Morton Shaevitz, "The Kinesthetic Method in Remedial Reading," *Journal of Experimental Education*, XXXI (Spring, 1963), 317-20.

76. Wayne Otto, "The Acquisition and Retention of Paired Associates by Good, Average, and Poor Readers," *Journal of Educational Psychology*, LII (October, 1961), 241-48.

77. Milton Budoff and Donald Quinlan, "Reading Progress as Related to Efficiency of Visual and Aural Learning in the Primary Grades," *Journal of Educational Psychology*, LV (October, 1964), 247-52.

78. Joan Lockard and Joseph B. Sidowski, "Learning in Fourth and Sixth Graders as a Function of Sensory Mode of Stimulus Presentation and Overt or Covert Practice," *Journal of Educational Psychology*, LII (October, 1961), 262-65.

79. Gabrielle Marchbanks and Harry Levin, "Cues by Which Children Recognize Words," *Journal of Educational Psychology*, LVI (April, 1965), 57-61.

be reinforced in their learning.[80]

At this point in behavior-analysis research, there are perhaps only a few generalizations that may be drawn. Among these is, first, the desirability of continuous and immediate reinforcement for the desired response, whatever form that reinforcement may take. Although widely accepted, this generalization still needs further examination, for certain recent studies indicate that negative reinforcement may sometimes be as effective as positive and that continuous or even immediate reinforcement is not always essential.

Second, when the desired behavior is achieved, only a periodic reinforcement is necessary to maintain a high level of responses with resistance to extinction. One implication of this principle for reading instruction is that use should be made of shorter and more frequent practice periods with a consequent higher incidence of reinforcements of the desired behavior, as in word recognition, rate improvement, and perhaps even in improvement of comprehension.

It is apparent that additional research is needed on the influence of the mode of presentation in beginning reading as related to the type of expected response and on the significance of types of reinforcement among pupils of varying intelligence and motivational sets. In instances in which the learning conditions and desired behavioral responses are carefully designed to reproduce or parallel faithfully some aspect of the reading process, behavior-analysis research will continue to make significant contributions. It is to be hoped that these studies will soon begin to explore the relationship of the effectiveness of various modes of presentation among children who vary not only in intelligence and social-class status but also in visual and auditory discrimination, thus determining the extent to which these abilities are trainable and respond to logical approaches or whether compensatory emphasis is more desirable.

LEARNING THEORY AND THEORETICAL MODELS

As Holmes and Singer pointed out in their review of reading

---

80. Edward Zigler and Paul Kanzer, "The Effectiveness of Two Classes of Verbal Reinforcers on the Performance of Middle- and Lower-Class Children," *Journal of Personality,* XXX (June, 1962), 157-63.

research in 1964,[81] there are two current trends in research in the psychology of reading: (a) the tendency toward studies which attempt to analyze the reading process in very small units, as already noted, and (b) that toward the development of new models and theories which will better explain the reading act and its components. Among these models and theories are: the teaching-machine model, the synaptic-transmission model of Smith and Carrigan,[82] the mixed-dominance theory, the substrata-factor theory of Holmes and Singer, the "Initial-Teaching-Alphabet" model, and the structural-linguistic theory. Of these, only the substrata-factor theory is not discussed elsewhere in this chapter. Briefly, Holmes and Singer have attempted to determine the significant elements of the reading process by the use of successive analyses by regression equations at three descending levels of significance of the matrices of the intercorrelations of some fifty-four variables.[83] This research is dealt with in chapter i, and the underlying assumptions have been reviewed by Sparks and Mitzell.[84] The studies by Holmes and Singer represent examples of the trends in psychology which have significance for reading instruction.

Whatever may be the strengths and weaknesses of this substrata-factor model, it presents significant implications for reading instruction which must be explored further. The research reports give evidence that boys and girls, good and poor readers, and groups of varying ages or intelligence differ in the manner in which they employ or depend upon subskills for power or speed in reading. Certain components, such as vocabulary, range of information, and listening comprehension, appear to be of basic importance for all groups. These findings carry obvious implications for plans for reading instruction.

81. Jack A. Holmes and Harry Singer, "Theoretical Models and Trends toward More Basic Research in Reading," *Review of Educational Research*, XXXIV (April, 1964), 127-55.

82. Donald E. P. Smith and Patricia M. Carrigan, *The Nature of Reading Disability* (New York: Harcourt, Brace & World, 1959).

83. See chapter i.

84. Jack N. Sparks and Harold E. Mitzell, "A Reaction to Holmes' Basic Assumptions Underlying the Substrata-Factor Theory," *Reading Research Quarterly*, I (Spring, 1966), 137-46.

Other theories and models have appeared in the literature subsequent to the 1964 review. Among these are the models of beginning reading as a visual-auditory discrimination process, as suggested by Smith [85] and by Clark.[86] Clark's model is based on the well-known Guilford structure of intellect which differentiates, in one part, between convergent and divergent thinking. Using a number of Guilford's tests, Clark found that input in reading is discriminated or processed differently according to these two modes of thinking. Convergent readers, according to Clark, should be relatively slow, with good mastery of detail but poor comprehension of the overall message or its implications. Divergent readers should exhibit the converse of these performances: that is, they should be less dependent upon word recognition than upon context and show greater ability to master the logic and inferences of the content. A factor analysis of Clark's test data was interpreted as supporting his hypothesis of a convergent-divergent continuum. The use of information theory in the analogy drawn by Clark in studying facets of the reading process has already been alluded to in the earlier discussion of the cloze procedure as it is viewed by Rankin [87] and Weaver.[88] Still other writers have attempted to apply information theory to the function of perception as it occurs in the reading act.[89] These trends toward analysis of the reading process in minute units, as in behavior analysis and programed learning, and toward a variety of models and theories explaining segments of the process are healthy developments toward the improvement of reading instruction. It is true that the trends are probably at opposite ends of a continuum of finiteness, yet they complement each other, for how shall researchers know how or what to study in detail unless they hypothesize the place of each unit in the overall picture?

85. Smith, *op. cit.*

86. Philip Clark, "Reading Comprehension as Information Processing," in *College and Adult Reading, op. cit.*, pp. 96-105.

87. Rankin, *op. cit.*

88. Weaver, *op. cit.*

89. F. Attneave, "Some Informational Aspects of Visual Perception," *Psychological Review*, LXI (1954), 183-93.

VARIABLES INFLUENCING READING ACHIEVEMENT

One of the major lines of communication between the fields of educational psychology and reading instruction has been research findings regarding variables that influence reading instruction. Remedial reading itself, with its practice of detailed diagnosis of poor readers and related use of corrective techniques, was originally stimulated largely by the efforts of such educational psychologists as Gates and Buswell, who were concerned with the factors that interfere with reading achievement. This type of psychological research continues to appear and to influence reading practices.

For convenience, the research investigations may be grouped as studies of non-cognitive or non-intellectual variables and of cognitive variables. In the area of non-cognitive variables, the differences between the reading achievement of boys and girls and the possible reasons for these differences continue to be of interest. Gates found that, in general, girls excelled boys in reading in Grades II through VIII.[90] The persistence of the degree of superiority of girls he interpreted as reflecting an environmental rather than a hereditary or sexual influence. Preston's comparison of the reading of American and German children indicated that German boys were superior to girls, an observation which seems to support Gates' conclusions.[91] Some further study of the trends toward greater social conformity and overachievement among girls and of the influence of the concept of reading as a feminine activity upon boys' achievement is most desirable, as indicated by the work of Sinks and Powell [92] and of Mazurkiewicz.[93] Despite this evidence of sex differences in reading achievement, few authors of reading tests offer differentiated sex norms; thus, they tend to promote the continuation of the overestimation of reading success among girls and a

---

90. Arthur I. Gates, "Sex Differences in Reading Ability," *Elementary School Journal*, LXI (May, 1961), 431-34.

91. Ralph C. Preston, "Reading Achievement of German and American Children," *School and Society*, XC (October 20, 1962), 350-54.

92. Naomi B. Sinks and Marvin Powell, "Sex and Intelligence in Reading in Grades Four through Eight," *Journal of Genetic Psychology*, CVI (March, 1965), 67-79.

93. Mazurkiewicz, *op. cit.*

converse underestimation of the achievement of boys. Studies of the interaction of family interrelationships, sex, and reading achievement, as explored in the work of Barwick and Arbuckle [94] and of Morrow and Wilson,[95] should eventually add more understanding to this area.

Another area of investigation deals with the interaction of method of instruction, reading achievement, and pupil personality traits, such as anxiety and compulsivity.[96] Preliminary evidence indicates a significant relationship between anxiety and teaching methods, with high anxiety and compulsivity among pupils seeming to enhance achievement in highly structured programs. The implications of this type of study reinforce this writer's earlier emphasis upon the importance of the interactions of pupil personality, social climate, and teaching method. Studies which attempt only to contrast teaching methods or materials must yield inconclusive results, for they do not indicate for what type of child or under what classroom climates a method is superior.

Among the cognitive variables which educational psychologists continue to explore are the relationships among reading, intelligence, and cognitive styles. It appears that the manner of handling stimuli, of organizing and processing them, is related to some traditional measures of intelligence, to sex and age, perhaps, to the nature of the task, and even to the type of school or community.[97] As implied earlier, this work is based largely on the developmental concepts of Piaget, which indicate that strategies of thinking differ among individuals of different ages. As yet, this research is concerned largely with evolving adequate tests of cognitive style, with distinguishing and defining types of thinking, and with the be-

---

94. Janice M. Barwick and Dugald S. Arbuckle, "A Study of the Relationship between Parental Acceptance and the Academic Achievement of Adolescents," *Journal of Educational Research*, LVI (November, 1962), 148-51.

95. William R. Morrow and Robert C. Wilson, "Family Relations of Bright High-Achieving and Under-Achieving High School Boys," *Child Development*, XXXII (September, 1961), 501-10.

96. Jesse W. Grimes and Wesley Allinsmith, "Compulsivity, Anxiety and School Achievement," *Merrill-Palmer Quarterly*, VII (October, 1961), 247-71.

97. Carson McGuire, "Sex Role and Community Variability in Test Performances," *Journal of Educational Psychology*, LII (April, 1961), 61-73.

ginning steps of determining how the different types influence an individual's learning. Further studies should contribute to the understanding of the nature of the process of comprehension and, therefore, to the techniques for its development.

Optometry and Ophthalmology

Specialists in the fields of both optometry and ophthalmology have exhibited an increasing interest in the relationships of their research to reading achievement. One group of studies, for example, has been concerned with the perceptual behavior of children in English and other languages as it differs with respect to their directionality.[98] There does not appear to be an obvious effect upon accuracy of perception in the right or left hemifield of vision by school training in reading from left to right. Preschool and school children and college students as well showed a tendency to favor targets to the left of the fixation point. A subsequent parallel study with readers in Hebrew, however, did seem to show the influence of the directionality of that language by a tendency to right-to-left responses.[99] Still another study of this type seemed to indicate that prereading set probably out-weighed any neurological differences in right-left fields.[100] The implication of such studies is the possible need for special training in perception in view of the directionality of the language or of the neurological differences in perception in the visual fields.

Other studies have explored a variety of visual characteristics and their implications for reading and perception. Walton and Schubert studied myopia in relation to size of print and suggested

---

98. Dorothy W. Dyer and E. Rae Harcum, "Visual Perception of Binary Patterns by Preschool Children and by School Children," *Journal of Educational Psychology*, LII (June, 1961), 161-65; E. Rae Harcum and Dorothy W. Dyer, "Monocular and Binocular Reproduction of Binary Stimuli Appearing Right and Left of Fixation," *American Journal of Psychology*, LXXV (March, 1962), 56-65.

99. E. Rae Harcum and Stephen M. Friedman, "Reversal Reading by Israeli Observers of Visual Patterns without Intrinsic Directionality," *Canadian Journal of Psychology*, XVII (December, 1963), 361-69.

100. Wilma Winnick and Rhea L. Dornbush, "Pre- and Post-Exposure Processes in Tachistoscopic Identification," *Perceptual and Motor Skills*, XX (February, 1965), 107-13.

some standards for the latter at far point.[101] Eames redemonstrated the retarding effects of anisometropia, unequal vision in the eyes, upon reading achievement.[102] In a more extensive study, Spache and Tillman found that a significantly greater proportion of retarded readers failed the near-point acuity test or showed differences in near-point acuity in the left eye.[103] Ong, Schneider, and Moray found no differences in the peripheral visual fields in the right versus the left eye, in fast or slow readers, in powerful or non-powerful readers, or in high- or low-I.Q. groups.[104] Smith, Cambria, and Steffan investigated the variations in time required for reading and in the number of errors made in different reading materials presented in various orientations to left- and right-handed subjects. The angle of the reading material or its inversion or reversal all seemed to influence the performances of the readers.[105]

Another group of studies has been concerned with the relations between motor co-ordination and reading ability, as exemplified in the investigation of Grattan and Matin.[106] They found no significant relationships among reading distance, motor skills, and certain visual skills demanding neuromuscular co-ordination. This study should certainly be carefully replicated on a larger scale, for it raises some doubts about the effectiveness of certain programs emphasizing motor-skill training for the improvement of reading skills.

101. Howard N. Walton and Delwyn N. Schubert, "Induced Myopia and Far Point Perception," *American Journal of Optometry and Archives of American Academy of Optometry*, XLII (May, 1965), 311-14.

102. Thomas H. Eames, "The Effect of Anisometropia on Reading Achievement," *American Journal of Optometry and Archives of American Academy of Optometry*, XLI (December, 1964), 700-702.

103. George D. Spache and Chester E. Tillman, "A Comparison of the Visual Profiles of Retarded and Non-Retarded Readers," *Journal of Developmental Reading*, V (Winter, 1962), 101-9.

104. Jin Ong, Kenneth Schneider, and Kenneth Moray, "Reading Ability and Perimetric Visual Field," *California Journal of Educational Research*, XI (March, 1960), 61-67.

105. Smith, Cambria, and Steffan, *op. cit.*

106. Paul E. Grattan and Milton B. Matin, "Neuro-muscular Coordination versus Reading Ability," *American Journal of Optometry and Archives of American Academy of Optometry*, XLII (August, 1965), 450-58.

Longitudinal studies of children's vision, studies of the incidence of various defects at various ages, studies of visual problems of children and their relationships to success in school and life, and studies of other anatomical and physiological aspects of children's vision have been collected in an excellent symposium edited by Hirsch and Wick.[107] The effects of training in spatial orientation and visual skills upon school achievement has been demonstrated in a number of reports, such as that of Cox and Stewart.[108] This particular study again emphasized the interrelatedness of visual skills, for only those children who showed improvement in all skills practiced evidenced great gains in achievement.

All this research in vision and related factors has had some dramatic values for and effect upon reading instruction. The demonstrated correlation between visual defects or poorly functioning visual skills and poor achievement has stimulated reading specialists to more careful and thorough vision screening at near-point. The research has promoted exploration of the effects of specific visual training procedures designed to correct functional difficulties and has stimulated trial-and-error experimentation with a wide variety of hand-eye and other motor-skill training procedures. Much more attention is being given to the perceptual habits and difficulties of children and to corrective and training procedures, even though the research in these areas is still fragmentary and unco-ordinated.

There still remains the need to implement the findings of the longitudinal studies of the developmental variations in children's vision in order to adjust to classroom conditions and to choose instructional materials and procedures.[109] Much more needs to be learned about the process of perception and the factors which may influence it, such as attentional set, physical posture, the nature of the symbols, cognitive style of the learners, and variations in eye-

---

107. *Vision of Children: An Optometric Symposium*, ed. Monroe J. Hirsch and Ralph E. Wick (Philadelphia: Chilton Press, 1963).

108. Brian J. Cox and Colin Stewart, "The Effect of Certain Specific Factors in Optometric Care upon the Scholastic Performance of Underfunctioning Students in Junior High School in Their Response to Remedial Teaching," *Canadian Journal of Optometry*, XX (December, 1957), 31-41, 42-46, 53.

109. Monroe J. Hirsch, "The Longitudinal Study in Refraction," *American Journal of Optometry and Archives of American Academy of Optometry*, XL (March, 1964), 137-41.

movement patterns in scanning objects. Further studies will have to be made of the relationships of perceptual behavior and the reading process at various stages and ages and in different languages.

On the negative side, the tangential studies of the inter-relatedness of reading, eyedness, cerebral dominance, and the like are gradually disappearing under the weight of accumulated research which indicates that these areas do not yield significant findings for reading instruction. Similarly, although they persist in many places, there is growing recognition of the uselessness of training procedures which attempt to improve reading behaviors by influencing the visual span. The physiological limits of retinal vision, the lack of any real increase in span, and the failure to produce permanent changes in reading or vision by these methods, plus the demonstrated similarity in span among good and poor readers, have all tended toward the non-acceptance of this type of training approach.[110]

Clinical Psychology

Probably the strongest interaction between the fields of reading instruction and clinical psychology occurs in the area of common interest—learning disabilities. Clinical psychologists are vitally concerned with children who exhibit visuomotor disturbances, brain damage or dysfunction, emotional disturbances, and perceptual deficits. Reading specialists are equally interested in these deviations to the degree that they touch upon reading disabilities.

Among the major problems plaguing both disciplines are the lack (a) of an adequate definition of learning disability, (b) of a definitive or even descriptive categorization of types of learning problems, (c) of a clear understanding of etiology, and (d) of valid and reliable diagnostic instruments. Confusion regarding appropriate remediation also represents a serious problem. Moreover, as pointed out earlier in the discussions of the concepts of the reading process held by various disciplines, the lack of comprehensive definition of reading is a handicap to co-ordinated research.[111]

In addition to these practical problems, there is still evident a

---

110. Joanne Lambeth, *What Optometry and Related Fields Have To Offer the Reading Teacher* (Duncan, Okla.: Optometric Extension Program, 1966).

111. See chapter v of this yearbook for a detailed review of the difficulties in integrating viewpoints of various disciplines.

trial-and-error process underlying the efforts to evolve the framework of an etiology-diagnosis-remediation continuum. For example, Bateman proposes a three-dimensional frame involving (a) type of problem, (b) emphasis upon etiology, diagnosis, or remediation, and (c) the viewpoint of a discipline, such as medical, psychological, or educational.[112] Rabinovitch sees no value in postulating a discrete diagnostic entity of learning disability.[113] He classifies reading problems as of three types: (a) secondary, in which capacity is handicapped by environmental factors, (b) primary, in which there is a disturbance of neurological organization, and (c) the type represented by the brain-injured retarded reader, in whom clear-cut neurological deficits are present. Rabinovitch interprets the greater frequency of retardation among boys as indicating a hereditary, sex-linked factor — an interpretation that would need to discount the reversal of this ratio in German schools as revealed in Preston's study.[114]

Single-factor theories of learning disorders include the cerebral-dominance hypothesis, the chemical-imbalance theory of Smith and Carrigan, the maturational-lag theory of Bender,[115] the dyslexia syndrome of Bryant,[116] and many others. Multifactor explanations were offered by Robinson[117] and several other writers, such as Holmes and Singer. Unfortunately, most etiological and classificatory theories have not been validated by replications of the original research studies.

112. Barbara Bateman, "Learning Disorders," *Review of Educational Research*, XXXVI (February, 1966), 93-119.

113. Ralph D. Rabinovitch and Winifred Ingram, "Neuro-psychiatric Considerations in Reading Retardation," *Reading Teacher*, XV (May, 1962), 433-38.

114. Preston, *op. cit.*

115. Lauretta Bender, "Problems in Conceptualization and Communication in Children with Developmental Alexia," in *Psychopathology of Communication*, ed. Paul H. Hoch and Joseph Zubin (New York: Grune & Stratton, 1958), pp. 155-176.

116. N. Dale Bryant, "Reading Disability: Part of a Syndrome of Neurological Dysfunctioning," in *Challenge and Experiment in Reading*, ed. J. Allen Figurel (Conference Proceedings, Vol. VII, October 7, 1962 [New York: International Reading Association, 1962]), pp. 139-43.

117. Helen M. Robinson, *Why Pupils Fail in Reading* (Chicago: University of Chicago Press, 1946).

As Cohn has observed,[118] this confusion is likely to persist for at least two reasons: (a) a relationship between minimal clinical signs of neuropathology and actual minimal brain pathology has not been demonstrated; and (b) the group of clinical signs found reflects the nature of the test battery and the philosophy of the researcher. To these criticisms, one might add (a) the lack of consistency in the criteria used to define a reading disability; (b) the attempt to establish an artificial dichotomy—heredity versus environment—in studying learning difficulties; (c) the use of several naive statistical procedures, such as combining tests of unknown homogeneity and interpreting correlations as indicating cause and effect; (d) the use of extremely small samples to obtain very detailed results; and (e) the assumption of high reliability of observational and subjective techniques.

It is also appropriate to note that the neuromuscular development of visuomotor skills needed for the act of reading has not yet been defined. How can studies emphasizing neuromuscular development, laterality, and motor co-ordination be meaningful if no one knows what levels or stages of neuromuscular development are essential to reading or even how to recognize or describe precisely these developmental stages?

Eventually, the replications of these diagnostic efforts may result in a core group of reliable and objective symptoms, even taking into account the frequent methodological and statistical faults of many of the studies. By the time this result is achieved, it is to be hoped that some clear-cut interpretation of the nature of the reading process at various ages or stages will appear to help in relating diagnostic symptoms to learning problems.

Like reading specialists, clinical psychologists have been struggling with the relationship of remediation to diagnosis as well as with the problem of evolving a rationale of remedial treatments. Some authors hold that patterns of modality strengths and weaknesses should indicate teaching methods, i.e., visual methods for good visualizers, auditory methods for those strong in auditory

---

118. Robert Cohn, "Neurological Concepts Pertaining to the Brain-Damaged Child," in *Speech and Language Therapy with the Brain-Damaged Child*, ed. William T. Daley (Washington, D.C.: Catholic University Press, 1962), pp. 13-36.

skills, a combination of these methods for pupils strong in both, and a multiple approach, including the kinesthetic, for children weak in both visual and auditory abilities. Others, such as Kirk and McCarthy, have proposed directing remediation to the improvement of any perceptual, cognitive, or linguistic deficits.[119] Still others apparently use identical remedial techniques with all retarded readers, regardless of diagnostic variations.

Some clues to this dilemma may be found in the data of follow-up studies, particularly those in which an effort has been made to follow a consistent and planned remedial approach keyed directly to the initial diagnosis. Cruikshank *et al.* used a very carefully planned program for brain-injured and hyperactive children, but the gains, which were largely in the perceptual area, disappeared during the second year of the training.[120] Gallegher achieved some improvement in verbal skills and verbal I.Q. in a similar population in a two-year program, but these gains were largely lost in subsequent years.[121] Silver and Hagin [122] and Balow [123] failed to find that their remedial cases had been corrected by short-term intensive instruction. The age at which remediation was attempted, the presence of developmental rather than organic difficulties, and the extent of the retardation seemed to be significant factors in some of these studies. As a result, several of these authors suggested that remedial reading must be conceived as a prolonged supportive program rather than as a temporary corrective treatment.

Perhaps the most comprehensive program of diagnosis and treat-

---

119. Samuel A. Kirk and James J. McCarthy, "The Illinois Test of Psycholinguistic Abilities—An Approach to Differential Diagnosis," *American Journal of Mental Deficiency*, LXVI (November, 1961), 399-412.

120. William M. Cruikshank, *A Teaching Method for Brain-Injured and Hyperactive Children: A Demonstration—Pilot Study* (Syracuse: Syracuse University Press, 1961).

121. James J. Gallegher, *The Tutoring of Brain-Injured Mentally Retarded Children* (Springfield, Illinois: Charles C. Thomas, 1960).

122. Archie A. Silver and Rosa A. Hagin, "Specific Reading Disability: A Twelve-Year Follow-up Study," *American Journal of Orthopsychiatry*, XXXIII (March, 1963), 338-39.

123. Bruce Balow, "The Long-Term Effect of Remedial Reading Instruction," *Reading Teacher*, XVIII (April, 1965), 581-86.

ment is the one outlined by Llorens.[124] Under her proposed plan, nine areas of cognitive, motor, and perceptual functions would be investigated by current diagnostic tests, and recognized training procedures would be undertaken to repair deficiencies. This program has not been widely tested experimentally, nor has its rationale for remediation been demonstrated. But it is a comprehensive plan for studies which could be readily replicated.

CLINICAL STUDIES IN PERCEPTION

The significant areas of visual and auditory perception have been greatly emphasized in recent psychological research, and many findings of importance for diagnosis, remediation, and ordinary classroom instruction in reading are being offered. Gibson and others have conducted a series of experiments in the behavior-analysis fashion of analyzing the perceptual performances of a small group of pupils in some minor facet of the reading process.[125] Graham, Berman, and Ernhart have pursued a similar program of repeated research in visual perception and have labored with the problem of the definition of the skill as well as the validity of its measurement in such ill-defined groups as the brain-injured or perceptually disturbed.[126] Following the lead of Piaget, many researchers, including Elkind, Larson, and Van Doorninck, are studying the development of visual perception.[127]

As of the moment, a number of tentative observations seem to be indicated by this research in visual perception. It is apparent that the ability is not a unitary trait readily measured by one or two simple tests or even by a battery of such tests. Performances are seen to vary according to the nature of the task (geometric forms,

---

124. Lela A. Llorens et al., "Cognitive-Perceptual-Motor Functions," *American Journal Occupational Therapy*, XVIII (September-October, 1964), 202-8.

125. Eleanor J. Gibson et al., "The Role of Grapheme-Phoneme Correspondence in the Perception of Words," *American Journal of Psychology*, LXXV (1962), 554-70.

126. Frances K. Graham, Phyllis W. Berman, and Clair B. Ernhart, "Development in Pre-School Children of Ability To Copy Forms," *Child Development*, XXXI (1960), 339-60.

127. David Elkind, Margaret Larson, and William Van Doorninck, "Perceptual Decentration Learning and Performance in Slow and Average Readers," *Journal of Educational Psychology*, LVI (February, 1965), 50-56.

letters, words, and so on); the administration of the test (immediate reproduction or recall) and the time limits of exposure of the target; the set of the learner; pretest instructions; intelligence and age of the testees; and the cognitive style and self-concept of the pupils. There is even some evidence that social class, preschool experiences, personality, and emotional reactions may play some part in visual perception. More research on the development of the various facets of visual perception, their individual significance for reading success, the possibilities of stimulating their development or compensating for their lack, the interrelatedness of perceptual skills, and the effect of varying instructional procedures is certainly needed.

In the area of auditory perception, a number of similar questions continue to be explored. Auditory perception may be measured in a half-dozen ways, some of which seem quite unrelated to the others. Certain of these measures are significant for reading achievement, while others are of minor importance, as shown by Dykstra [128] and by Birch and Belmont.[129] Approaches to auditory skills through a psycholinguistic instrument, the ITPA, reaffirm the significant relationship with reading ability of the rote or automatic-sequential auditory function, as contrasted to the meaningful or representational linguistic functions. In this connection, it is significant to note that instructional approaches to reading, such as the basal reading or phonics method, differ in their demands for various auditory skills and thus alter the significance of these skills for reading achievement.

Until the research in auditory perception similar to that suggested for visual perception has been extended, reading teachers must continue, in their own best way, to assess their pupil's needs and abilities in both these areas, to attempt to relate these assessments to the demands inherent in their instructional practices, and to aid their pupils in compensating for or overcoming deficits in their perceptual abilities.

128. Robert Dykstra, "Auditory Discrimination Abilities and Beginning Reading Achievement," *Reading Research Quarterly*, I (Spring, 1966), 5-34.

129. Herbert G. Birch and Lillian Belmont, "Auditory-Visual Integration in Normal and Retarded Readers," *American Journal of Orthopsychiatry*, XXXIV (October, 1964), 852-61.

Concluding Statement

Each section of this chapter has pointed out the past and potential contribution of the research in allied fields to the knowledge essential for teaching reading.

It seems clear that allied fields have both specialized knowledge of and their own techniques for approaching problems in reading. Both the techniques and the knowledge can make a contribution to research in reading and eventually to procedures and materials for teaching and learning.

Researchers are challenged to keep abreast of all contributions of allied fields and to evaluate them in the context of other types of knowledge. Indeed, the team approach to research may be essential in the future, combining talents and skills so as to conserve time and gain the greatest rewards for the efforts expended.

CHAPTER VIII

Implementing and Evaluating the Use of Innovations

WILLARD J. CONGREVE[*]

Introduction

DISJUNCTION BETWEEN RESEARCHER AND PRACTITIONER

This chapter is being written from the point of view of a practicing principal for several reasons. Practicing educators have fallen short of their responsibilities to experiment with new ideas and to search for better ways of operating their schools. While there is a shred of truth in the assertion that "ivory tower" researchers fail to communicate with teachers and principals, there is a concomitant and perhaps even more valid assertion that principals and teachers make little or no effort to become knowledgeable about the work of the researcher.

As a result, there exists a serious gap in the educational arena between the researcher and the practicing educator. Much research in education meets the standards of precision set by rigorous research designs. The sample studied has been carefully selected and the experimental manipulations strictly controlled. The results are valid, to be sure, for the conditions set up for the research. The only problem is that it is often impossible to find any situation in a school setting which is similar to the research setting. *Ergo*, the rare practicing educator who does become aware of the research findings frequently dismisses them from his mind on the grounds that the experimental conditions represent a distortion of reality to the extent that the results have no relevance to practice. This response on the part of the practitioner is unfortunate. Taken one by one, the con-

[*] The author is indebted to Ellen Lamar Thomas, Reading Consultant, University of Chicago Laboratory High School, for her contributions of examples and for her assistance in other ways in the preparation of this chapter.

tribution of each research project may be quite small. But the cumulative effect of several projects, especially when they have been done sequentially, as has been the case in several areas in reading, can be quite formidable.

BRINGING THE RESEARCHER AND THE PRACTITIONER TOGETHER

It is apparent that something must be done to fill the void between research and practice. Teachers are confronted daily with problems which have a meaningful relationship to those with which the research scholar deals. The researcher studies them, using rigorous designs, matched subjects or control groups, and carefully worked-out measuring procedures. Such studies often lead to the discovery of important new knowledge. But, to be useful in education, this new knowledge must be applied to situations where students come in groups, where teachers are confronted with a myriad of variables, where the total complexity of the natural daily life of students and teacher often bears little resemblance to the research situation. It is here that this new knowledge must be applied, that newly developed theories must be tested, that teacher behavior and attitudes must be changed, and that new organizational structures must be created. And it is here that the creative role of the teacher comes into play.

Teachers must become active agents in bringing about the essential development and subsequent conversions in the real-life situation necessary to make new knowledge productive. They must become partners with the researcher by translating research findings into practice. This co-operative role can operate in at least two ways. In the manner just described, the teacher takes research findings and uses them to improve practice or as a basis for changing practice. It is also quite possible for teachers to initiate an innovative program which seems to improve effectiveness of learning and then for the researcher to develop techniques for studying the new program to ferret out the variables which contribute to this new achievement.[1] But, in either method, the appropriate results will be achieved only if teachers are willing to accept the researcher as a vital partner in carving out the educational program.

1. E. A. Enstrom, "Wanted: Unbiased Answers," *Elementary English*, XLIV (January, 1967), 47-49.

Failure to look upon the teacher and principal as essential ingredients in the process of innovation and change has been largely responsible for the extreme resistance to the introduction of productive methods, materials, and organizational schemes into our schools.[2] To be sure, one can point to attempts to improve curriculum. Goodlad recently summarized nation-wide curriculum movements and programs.[3] Among the better known programs are the physics program of the Physical Science Study Committee (PSSC), the mathematics programs of the School Mathematics Study Group (SMSG) and the University of Illinois Committee on School Mathematics (UICSM), and the biology program of the Biological Science Curriculum Study (BSCS). Many creative innovations have been introduced into schools throughout the country, among them being programed instruction, non-graded organization, team teaching, flexible scheduling, and independent learning.

However, one must ask, "What impact have these movements actually had upon the learning of youngsters?" Of course, it is clear that content has been upgraded, concepts refined, sequences reordered, and emphases shifted and that new materials and equipment have been added to our resources. All these improvements are noteworthy and should not be depreciated. But one must stop and ponder such comments as the one overheard at a recent conference on mathematics innovation—that, despite the best intentions of the people who sparked the mathematics revolution, the ideas become distorted and the final product bears little resemblance to what was hoped for. When one examines a team-teaching situation (which in form replicates quite accurately the model designed by Trump and his colleagues) and finds many students inattentive or sleeping during large-group instruction and a sizable number of lost, apathetic students, usually coupled with an unhappy, frustrated teaching team, one begins to ask such questions as "Why such blind allegiance to a popular innovation?" and "Is the innovation merely a response to the desire to stay on the bandwagon?" Team teaching as it presently

---

2. Willard J. Congreve, "The Role of the Principal in School Improvement," *Bulletin of the National Association of Secondary School Principals*, XLVIII (March, 1964), 3-9.

3. John I. Goodlad, *School Curriculum Reform in the United States* (New York: Fund for the Advancement of Education, March, 1964).

exists in many schools would best be described as "take-your-turn" teaching.

Instituting Desirable Change

THE NEED FOR A RATIONALE FOR CHANGE

It does not take much awareness to recognize that vast technological and sociological changes are shaking our society at its very foundations. It is highly doubtful that any school which was conceived before the advent of these changes and has not been updated can possibly educate today's youth to live as adults in tomorrow's world. Almost everyone agrees that schools must be changed.

In fact, change has become so much a part of our current thinking that some people now are beginning to believe that it is sinful to do anything the same way twice. This cry for unending change is pushing many schools into new programs for which they are ill prepared; they reject tried-and-true procedures for new ones and find faculty and students frustrated with the resulting chaos.[4] At the same time, this doctrine of change is having the opposite effect. Many school people, seeing what has happened to their neighbors who were panicked into change, have decided to stand stolidly, refusing to consider anything new, not even those innovations which give promise of considerable improvement in their schools.[5]

It is quite apparent that some rationale for change must be developed to protect the schools from irresponsible change and, at the same time, to encourage them into sensible innovative activities. Schools must be helped to take advantage of the several opportunities for improvement which are, indeed, emerging from the work of technologists and responsible scholars who are engaged in educational research.

A FIVE-POINT RATIONALE FOR SENSIBLE CHANGE

Often the question is asked, "When should schools move toward change?" This question implies that the more common state of

4. Erven Brundage, "Our Love Affair with Change," *Theory into Practice*, V (April, 1966), 91-95.

5. Jennelle Moorhead, "Who's Blocking Educational Change," *PTA Magazine*, LX (March, 1966), 2-3.

schools should be characterized by *status quo* operations. Such is not the case. The good school is one which is constantly studying its programs, evaluating their effectiveness, making the necessary adjustments, and subsequently studying and evaluating these changes. A good school resists the oft-expressed (but really never wanted) human desire for an unrocked boat. The words, "continuous sensible innovation," describe the state of affairs in a good school. The results of the "Eight-year Study" support this position by clearly identifying the sensibly innovative secondary school as the one which provides the best preparation for students who move on to college.[6] But what are the dimensions of the sensibly innovative school?

Faculty commitment to quality education.—First and foremost, the faculty is committed to designing and implementing learning programs which meet the special instructional needs of all the students enrolled. The reading program, for example, involves careful diagnosis, insures teacher and student mutual understanding of need, and provides rich and varied instructional opportunities using a variety of materials and approaches.

Resistance to current fads.—Second, and fully consistent with the first commitment, the faculty and administration are unalterably opposed to quick adoption of fads. Wholesale adoption of any innovation without careful regard for its implications for the total instructional program cannot be justified even though the innovation seems to promise excellent results.[7] Just as all children tend to be somewhat different, so do schools. While an innovation may result in some improvement, it may also detract from other quality programs in the school. There are times when schools should not change. Certainly, strong programs should not be discarded for or jeopardized by new ones just because they are new. To be sure, the sensibly innovative school should consider programs which have been developed elsewhere. Careful study of new programs, followed by appropriate custom-fitting adoption, is defensible. But to team-

---

6. Dean Chamberlin et al., *Did They Succeed in College? The Follow-up Study of the Graduates of the Thirty Schools* ("Adventures in American Education," Vol. IV [New York: Harper & Bros., 1942]), p. 182.

7. John I. Goodlad, "Beyond Survival for the Elementary Principal," *National Elementary Principal*, XLIV (September, 1966), 15.

teach, for example, because every one else seems to be team-teaching is an instance of the blind following those who see poorly.

Continuous institutional self-study.—Third, the faculty and administration should constantly study the school as it is. School people should take on the role of the responsible critic in educational reform.[8] They should keep the school's objectives current and carry on a continuous assessment of its operational aspects (methods, materials, and organization) designed to reach these objectives. Continuous feedback should give a current picture of strengths and weaknesses. Under these circumstances, the school will not be tempted to abandon hastily a part of its program for something thought to be better. Rather, it will be in a position to engage, experimentally, a small portion of the students and faculty in a new program, even in an area of strength. The program can be studied and tested, and a decision can be made as to its value as a continuing part of the curriculum. Often it will be discovered that some aspects of the new can be incorporated into the established program, with the outcome better than that resulting from the adoption of either program alone.

Public pressures of various sorts, such as those that resulted from the book *Why Johnny Can't Read*[9] and from certain speed-reading techniques which have recently been in the national spotlight, can be dealt with best by schools which persist in self-study. Such schools can provide their public with sound data and can make sensible decisions quite readily about just how to respond to these pressures. Such schools would not find themselves caught up in the overstressing of phonics instruction which has occurred so often when the uninformed have been stirred up. Nor would they find themselves enthroning speed in their high-school reading programs as so many did when national TV demonstrations convinced parents that all college-bound students must read at fantastic speeds.

In some cases, the data will neutralize the pressure; in others, possible experiments with the newly suggested materials and procedures will be suggested. But, in every case, the structure for study

---

8. Paul Woodring, "The Role of Responsible Criticism in Educational Reform," *Education Digest*, XXXI (December, 1965), 1-4.

9. Rudolph Flesch, *Why Johnny Can't Read—and What You Can Do about It* (New York: Harper & Bros., 1955).

and evaluation of the practice will be so built into the school program that "riding off in several directions at the same time" will be avoided.

Awareness of innovative alternatives.—Fourth, when the need for change has been defined, the school should accept the responsibility of becoming aware of the various innovations available which might correct the weaknesses. In developing this awareness of alternatives, the faculty should study each carefully.[10] This study must delve into the various aspects of the innovation to determine how they are related to the specific instructional needs of the school into which it will be introduced. Claims for success must be especially examined. Something that has been designed for and that works in one school may not be transferable to another. In fact, when it has been transferred and made workable, it may bear little resemblance to its original form.

It is extremely important that the school examine various alternatives, not just one. In the process, school personnel should not bemuse themselves into believing that one innovation can be used to solve all problems, although each may contribute something. It is quite possible that the innovation which one school adopts will be a custom-tailored composite of several alternatives. To date, experience with varying methods and organizational structures clearly points out that probably no one method or single organization will ever be found which will cure all educational ills.[11] Therefore, the school that is looking for *the* panacean innovation is doomed to disappointment and frustration.

Responding sensibly to outside pressures.—The development of technology and the concomitant push by commercial enterprises to have this technology incorporated into school systems place considerable pressure upon school personnel. Many teachers have resisted using new teaching aids in the belief that they are designed to eliminate the teacher.

10. William W. Brickman, "Educational Innovation and the Individual," *School and Society*, XCV (January 21, 1967), 38.

11. See John I. Goodlad, "Individual Differences and Vertical Organization of the School," in *Individualizing Instruction* (Sixty-first Yearbook of the National Society for the Study of Education, Part I [Chicago: Distributed by the University of Chicago Press, 1962]).

The new technology is not designated to take the place of the teacher as stimulator, catalyst, and resource in the intellectual process. But technology and programed learning can impart knowledge and aid in skill development. Should technology be found capable of playing these two roles, the basic innovation confronting the school is not the use of technology but, rather, that of reconverting its teachers to accept the truly professional role which cannot be taken over by the machine.

In addition to the pressures for change mounted by technologists, the school is faced with pressures arising from many other sources in the community. Each of these pressures must be met with willingness to inquire into the suggestions offered. If change is recommended for an area in which there has been little study or evaluation, the school must undertake to study that aspect of its school program to determine whether the recommended innovation is worth a trial. Failure to accept these pressures as a challenge to study the school is an evasion of responsibility on the part of school personnel.

Schools should not become so completely occupied in responding to outside pressures that they fail to maintain the continuous institutional self-study referred to earlier. Systematic examination of all aspects of the program will reveal weaknesses not in the public eye which, nevertheless, deserve innovative attention. Because the school is not responding to outside pressures in these areas, the innovations can be planned carefully and introduced under circumstances more conducive to study and evaluation.

A sensible rationale toward innovation and change in schools embodies several dimensions. First, the faculty commits itself to the best educational program possible for the children and youth in the school. Second, they take a lifelong vow against blindly following every new idea. Third, they commit themselves to a continuing study of the school program in order to be aware of strengths and weaknesses at all times. Fourth, as they consider courses of action, they become aware of the many alternatives available, they become knowledgeable about the effectiveness of such innovations as they have been practiced in other situations, and they incorporate study and evaluation as part of introducing the innovation. Finally, the faculty does not give its exclusive attention to those aspects of the curriculum which seem to be getting attention from outside sources. Some innovations should arise out of weaknesses apparent only to the school personnel. This rationale, which views *teachers* as the principal actors in the innovation drama, should provide a school with the strength to resist unwarranted pressures for change, the strength to conduct inquiry into areas in which innovation may be needed, and the integrity to keep the entire school program balanced and at as high a level of efficiency and effectiveness as can be managed in our imperfect society.

INVOLVING THE PARENTS AND COMMUNITY IN INNOVATIONS

Innovations are doomed to slow acceptance or rejection if the parents and the community are not somehow involved in the early stages of the planning. Schools can take steps to avoid parental discontent, which can "torpedo" an innovation as well as make it difficult for other innovations to be introduced into the school. Before initiating the change, the school should describe the innovation as fully as it can to the parents of the children to be involved in the program. The parents should be guided through the same line of argument and discussion that the faculty has gone through in coming to the decision to try out the new idea. They should understand the questions being asked and the hopes for the alternatives being tried out. They should be helped to realize that some difficulties may be encountered in launching the program in the way it is designed. Even the Navy has its shakedown cruise for every new vessel, including those that are just like others which are already at sea. Furthermore, parents should be helped to accept the fact that the results of an innovation cannot be fully predicted until the experiment has been tried out.

EXAMPLES OF INNOVATION AND CHANGE IN READING: A CASE STUDY

Reading, the subject of this yearbook, is an area which lends itself particularly well to the application of the five-dimension rationale already described. Language skills are deeply embedded within a person's entire personality and, as such, are not likely to be changed without intensive instruction. Yet, because reading skill is absolutely essential to self-instruction and personal inquiry, it has often become the target at which proposed panacean techniques (along with the concomitantly generated public pressure for the adoption of these techniques) have been aimed.

The faculty of the University of Chicago Laboratory High School, a school with an enrolment of 675 students, has, like other faculties, been bombarded with demands to follow several currently popular reading innovations. The faculty and administration adopted the rationale for change just outlined with some exciting and satisfactory results. Space permits only a brief description of what has occurred, but the history of these efforts may document and support the rationale. It was faculty commitment to quality education that gave rise to teacher concern about the achievements of the students in reading. This concern led the faculty and principal into a consideration of what should be done. It soon became apparent that a specialist was needed to help the teachers study reading problems and to find ways of meeting student needs revealed by such inquiry.

The decision to engage a full-time reading consultant.—But what should this person be? Should a reading teacher be added who would work with a handful of students? Or should someone be found who could help all teachers become creative in improving reading instruction? For teachers who wanted help in learning how to improve reading rather than substitutes who would take over this responsibility, the latter alternative made the most sense. A reading consultant (even though no one knew for sure at that time just what such a person could do) might be able to alert an entire school to its needs, share insights, and perhaps enlist the entire high-school faculty in a drive to improve the reading of all students.[12] Getting all or a major portion of such a faculty concerned about reading and somewhat better prepared to help their students meet the diverse reading requirements of the varying subject areas appeared to be quite an innovation.

The consultant joined with colleagues who were well seasoned in determining the instructional programs for their particular disciplines. Therefore, she did not come to direct but, rather, to help. It was recognized from the onset that any attempt to establish a

---

12. H. Alan Robinson and Sidney J. Rauch, *Guiding the Reading Program: A Reading Consultant's Handbook* (Chicago: Science Research Associates, Inc., 1965).

role for the consultant which might be viewed by the faculty as reducing their decisions-making role with regard to the curriculum would be met with resistance and perhaps doomed to failure. Upon arrival, therefore, the consultant, stocked with all sorts of helping materials, became available to serve on request.

Involving the consultant in teachers' concerns.—No fanfare accompanied her arrival. Generally, the data concerning students looked good—average I.Q. of 128, median reading score at the 89th percentile, a large percentage of the students reading two to three levels above actual grade placement. One could ask, "Why did she come?"

It was not long before the consultant became involved in teachers' concerns. "Some students just never read the textbook. I'm beginning to wonder if they can," declared one teacher. A study of students' achievement in reading by the consultant suggested why. Test scores revealed that at each grade level there was a range in reading achievement of at least seven full years. There were problems of the kind no one in University High School had ever before fully realized. The impact of these data suggested a great need for innovations of a sort that were not to be found in other schools.

The increased awareness about the spread in reading levels created a demand on the consultant to help teachers adjust their teaching to take into account this variability among students. While a compressed discussion of what took place in the six years that followed does injustice to the work of the consultant and to a description of the evolving new roles of the teachers, a summary of what happened during this period suggests that far-reaching strides forward have been made.

Contrary to the findings of Austin and Morrison, more teachers came to realize that, even in high school, the improvement of reading is every teacher's responsibility.[13] When presented with evidence that study-reading is complex, not one general skill, teachers in several subject areas expressed interest in and willingness to develop the skills needed to include reading instruction as an integral part of their daily learning experiences. For example, the mathematics

---

13. Mary C. Austin and Coleman Morrison, *The First R: The Harvard Report on Reading in the Elementary Schools* (New York: Macmillan Co., 1963), pp. 181-91.

teachers asked, "How can we do more with reading in our classes?" With such readiness expressed, the teachers and the reading consultant sat down together and exchanged insights. The consultant was invited to watch the mathematics teachers hold "how-to-do-it" sessions. One such teacher became so expert that he made a presentation of his technique to a national conference and published an article in a major reading journal.[14] In the past six years, conversions to an active interest in reading have been effected in every subject area.

Further examination of reading scores revealed that students were not doing as well in vocabulary development as in the areas of speed and comprehension, a weakness not to be expected in a highly academic school where students verbalized adult-sounding words with ease in class discussions. English teachers accepted this challenge by deciding that vocabulary activities needed to be incorporated into the English curriculum. The consultant made specific suggestions about appropriate materials and assisted the teachers in designing methods for developing dictionary skills and for teaching students to use Latin and Greek roots as aids in reasoning out the meaning of new words. In addition, the vocabularies of students were enriched by helping them use context clues and by engaging them in direct study of selected words. As a result of these and other efforts, an instructional sequence in vocabulary development was created and integrated into the English curriculum throughout all grade-levels in the high school.

Teachers who were unfamiliar with methods for teaching vocabulary invited the consultant to come to their classes to give demonstration lessons. Students were provided with self-help materials and launched into summer vocabulary programs on their own. Teachers recommended to students that they become their own personal "word collectors," and provided them with an abundant supply of specially designed word-collector's slips. Evaluation of this major effort to correct a serious vocabulary weakness already indicates that progress has been made.

14. Richard H. Muelder. "Helping Students Read Mathematics," in *Corrective Reading in the High School Classroom*, ed. H. Alan Robinson and Sydney J. Rauch ("Perspectives in Reading," No. 6 [Newark, Del.: International Reading Association, 1966]).

Evolution of four methods of encouraging and facilitating innovations in reading.—As the principles embodied in the rationale described earlier were observed and since the appropriate participation of the faculty was never jeopardized, four activities for encouraging and facilitating innovations (improvements) in reading through the use of the consultant evolved: (*a*) meetings with groups, (*b*) conferences with individuals, (*c*) classroom visits to give reading instruction in the presence of the teacher, and (*d*) the creation of a reading resource center.

Group meetings were characterized by question-raising on the part of the faculty: "What are our reading weaknesses?" "How can all teachers help all students become better readers?" These meetings aroused interest and gave the consultant an opportunity to offer assistance and to present data which stimulated action.

Individual conferences focused on the specific problems which a teacher was having and often led to a visit of the consultant to demonstrate reading instruction in the teacher's classroom. Undergirding the activities mentioned above was a comprehensive resource center filled with sample diagnostic materials, books, workbooks, and kits collected from publishers, as well as specially tailored homemade materials developed on the scene by the consultant and by teachers striving to solve reading problems.

The volume of these specially tailored homemade materials has grown steadily. Self-instructional-type materials have been created for students who wish to work independently to improve vocabulary. For example, a lesson series called "The Teen-Age Vocabulary Builders" has been developed. This series introduces new words in context clues close to teen-age life, e.g., attending the prom, buying a car, going off to college. A complete word-attack kit for teacher use, accompanied by folders containing multilevel materials on each of many phonetic and structural principles, has been worked out, and a comprehensive package, replete with overhead transparencies, entitled "A Research-Designed Approach to the Reading of Primary Sources in Social Studies," has been designed for classroom or individual student use. With such an array of rich alternatives readily available, even the most reticent teacher sometimes found it easy to try out at least one new idea, especially if it had worked before in this school with these children.

Little steps forward result in major consequences.—Effort to innovate in the field of reading, designed to enlist every teacher in improving reading, has not been a spectacular show. Progress has been made slowly but surely. The consultant clung to the counsel in *The Shoes of the Fisherman*: [15] "We must do the small possible rather than chase the great impossible." She found that, over a period of time, many half-steps made a giant step. In each case, teachers were expected to pick up the innovative ball and run with it. From the beginning the consultant was advised, "Don't intrude or tell our teachers what to do. Be non-directive yet catalytic." Teachers' requests for assistance developed so rapidly that the consultant has never been lacking for something to do.

While it is true that some other curricular innovations, such as the one launched by the Physical Sciences Study Committee, were spectacular overhauls of an entire program, experience suggests that slow progressive changes, each one building on the one before, can also produce significant and lasting improvements. By adhering to a sensible rationale for change, University High School is currently more reading-minded than it was six years ago. Six years may seem to be a long time, but many of the innovations introduced during this period have now become established practices. Of course, not all of University High School's present concern can be credited to the all-school drive, because some competent teachers would have moved ahead anyway.

As pointed out earlier, commitment to quality education caused the teachers to question the effectiveness of the school's reading program in a thoughtful scholarly fashion. Unwilling to respond spuriously to outside pressures and recognizing the need for specialized assistance, the teachers welcomed the arrival of the full-time reading consultant and turned to her for (*a*) demonstration lessons given in their classrooms, (*b*) assessment of specific reading needs, and (*c*)special assistance in developing and using appropriate instructional materials. As a consequence of their own growing enthusiasm about and involvement in reading instruction and spurred on by the effective catalytic action of the consultant, teachers in a

---

15. Morris Langlo West, *The Shoes of the Fisherman* (New York: William Morrow & Co., 1963).

wide variety of areas have developed and adopted a large number of alternative innovative approaches to reading instruction:

1. At the beginning of each year, comprehensive reading data are now used to plan for the reading needs of the students.
2. An impressive collection of reading aids in almost every subject area is available to assist teachers in dealing with reading problems. These aids have been created by teachers and tested in actual class sessions. They have been reproduced in quantities through the use of facilities normally available in schools and are readily accessible in the resource-room file cabinets.
3. Reading has become important in areas in which it was hardly considered heretofore. Two physical education teachers are now maintaining collections of fascinating sports fiction and irresistible "how-to-do-it" books in specific sports areas, which they are using to encourage some of the less active readers to explore areas in which they have shown an interest. An art teacher has intensified his efforts to encourage reading in his classes.
4. Teachers have devised a number of ways in which to individualize instruction: (a) The librarians are supplied with a diagnostic reading-level file card for every student which they can refer to when assisting a child to select materials suited to his reading and learning needs. To make this program operable, teachers and librarians worked together diligently to create a library collection which provides multilevel materials. (b) When preparing book lists, teachers make sure that there are enough books and enough selections at the lower as well as at the higher levels of difficulty. (c) Multilevel texts are used in the same classroom to help students achieve success by using a book closely in line with the achievement level of each and thus allowing each to participate fully in the classroom discussion. (d) Assignment sheets with broad lists of study questions, accompanied by references representing varying levels of reading difficulty, were passed out to students with such comments as "If the first book does not appear to help with this question, try the one below it." A report from one social-studies teacher illustrates what is occurring more frequently: "In our unit on the early colonial period in Africa, we have a core of readings all of which are beyond the poor readers. I make it a point to see that there 'happens to be' a need for special investigators for related topics. I have selected topics that are appropriate in difficulty and interest for handicapped readers, who are guided in conference to references they can handle. They share their findings with others in the class. Through class discussions, slides, and the opaque projector, the 'reporters' get some of the information they missed through not completing the assigned readings.

Gifted readers, too, make special investigations and complete highly challenging assignments."[16]

5. Other innovative techniques have been designed to encourage the less able and reluctant readers. (a) One teacher observed that her less able readers were struggling with primary source materials. Arranging advanced work for others in the class, this teacher brought these less able students together for a "how-to-do-it" reading session followed by supervised practice. (b) Other teachers are finding ways to "trap" youngsters into reading more difficult documents. One high-school teacher uses the fascinating, fact-packed (but admittedly partisan) film, *Martin Luther*, to make the reading of difficult documents on Martin Luther less difficult. With informational background strengthened through this highly interesting film, less efficient readers can sometimes "crack a difficult assignment." Efficient readers can comprehend it better. (c) An elementary teacher tape-recorded lengthy introductions of books, interjecting explanations along the way. The child listens to the tape while he reads the introduction. This plan has proved invaluable to less efficient readers, who usually find it difficult to "get into" a book.

In addition to developing and implementing innovative reading programs, the teachers have begun to report their activities to others. Recently, individual articles have been published by an art teacher and by a mathematics teacher, and twenty-four teachers have played a part in writing articles with the consultant. When a teacher becomes expert in conducting classroom lessons that help students develop efficient reading techniques, the consultant asks the teacher if she might visit and tape these lessons. These "on-the-spot" recordings of lessons are then made available to other teachers who are interested in improving their teaching skills. Tapes are available on (a) teaching depth reading of difficult primary source materials in social studies, (b) procedures for teaching students to read difficult expository passages in mathematics, (c) teaching difficult technical terms in science through the use of Greek and Latin roots, and (d) developing study habits and skills for studying freshman science.

The compendium of innovative activities in reading which have been developed at the University of Chicago Laboratory Schools suggests that the rationale presented earlier can lead to substantial

---

16. Unpublished report by Margaret Fallers, Social Studies Teacher, University of Chicago Laboratory High School.

changes and lasting improvements. Progress throughout the school has been uneven, but scores on standardized reading tests have inched upward. The median total score on the *Cooperative Reading Test* has advanced from a national percentile of 89 to one of 92.5, and the imbalance between the vocabulary score and the scores in speed and comprehension has become less marked. It would be gratifying to claim that this improvement is a result of the all-school program, but it may be revealed that reading is just keeping pace with other factors not yet studied. Nevertheless, the enthusiastic involvement of the teachers is encouraging, while the caution of a realistic teacher keeps us ever mindful of the magnitude of our task: "Let no reading person give the impression that adjusting materials and methods to a variety of reading needs is easy. *Years of searching go into finding the appropriate instructional combination for each child. No one should be discouraged when instant attainment of the ideal does not prove possible.*" [17]

Evaluating Innovations

THE NEED FOR BETTER EVALUATION OF ALL EDUCATIONAL PROGRAMS

Lack of appropriate evaluation is undoubtedly one of the greatest weaknesses in the entire field of education today. This indictment applies to education in general as well as to innovations which have been introduced and are being introduced on an increasingly rapid scale. Many innovators have declared openly that they will not be concerned with evaluation because the process of studying the effects of the innovation, using a rigorous research design, interferes with the creative process.[18] Some have argued that the innovation should not be required to shoulder a burden of proof which goes beyond that which has been placed upon the existing program. They have declared that when education generally submits itself to rigorous evaluation, the innovations introduced will fall naturally under this scrutiny.

17. *Ibid.*

18. James W. Brown, "The Process of Innovation," *Educational Screen and TV Guide*, XLV (November, 1966), 18-19.

Minimizing evaluation or overlooking it completely seems to be a historic fact in education. No sophisticated evaluation devices were required to assess the goals of reading and ciphering as taught in the early schools. But, as new programs were introduced, schools took on more complicated goals. Great effort was directed toward developing learning activities, but almost none was directed toward measuring their effectiveness or their outcomes. Some educators observed that since the child spends only 18 per cent of his waking hours in school, one cannot really tell what effect the school is having on him. So, subjective opinions were used in deciding whether or not a program was worthwhile.

THE BASIC ELEMENTS TO BE EVALUATED

Confusion about the basic elements to be evaluated seems to cloud the issue for most practicing educators. For some reason, they have found it difficult to distinguish between process and outcomes, to find ways to assess each of these elements separately, and then to explain the relationships between them.

Measurement of outcomes.—Measurement of outcomes has advanced steadily. With the advent of standardized testing, great strides have been made in defining desirable learning outcomes [19] and in finding ways to assess them. A teacher can use standardized reading test to determine the range in reading skills (vocabulary, comprehension, and speed) among his students, to obtain gross clues as to the instructional emphases needed to improve these skills, and to rank the individual students on national scales. If more knowledge is desired, standardized diagnostic tests will provide insight into the reading needs of individuals. Standardized tests can also be administered at the beginning and again at the end of an instructional period to assess over-all gains of a class (and, less accurately, of the individuals within the class).

Assessment of process (or program).—Many practicing educators have made surprising interpretations of the results of standardized tests. To some of these educators, standardized tests results in-

---

19. Benjamin S. Bloom *et al., Taxonomy of Educational Objectives, Handbook I: Cognitive Domain* (New York: David McKay Co., Inc., 1956); David R. Krathwohl *et al., Taxonomy of Educational Objectives, Handbook II: Affective Domain* (New York: David McKay Co., Inc., 1964).

dicating that 50 per cent of the children in their school are doing as well as or better than 50 per cent of those throughout the country are sufficient evidence that the process (or program) contributing to this outcome is sound.[20] If the results do not reflect such a favorable result, a great effort (usually ill-defined as to process) is often launched to "get students up to grade level."

This interpretation of standardized tests reveals lack of understanding. Standardized tests cannot measure well the effectiveness of a local school curriculum as it facilitates learning in its peculiar population and, more specifically, in an individual child. All they can do is to assess the level of achievement (outcome) of a student as compared with that of other students of similar grade or age level throughout the country.

The process that contributes to the outcome as assessed by the standardized test is another matter. To be sure, part of the outcome results from the personal learning equipment of the child, part from his own involvement in the learning process, and part from his environmental experiences. But that part of the outcome which should be of major interest to the innovator who is concerned with improved educational practice is the part which results from the explicitly defined process (methods, materials, organization, and teacher behavior) in which the school engages to bring about the outcome desired. The goal of the innovator should be to find ways to analyze the process that produced the outcome and to determine relevant cause-and-effect relationships.

DESIGNING THE EVALUATION COMPONENT OF AN INNOVATION

Planning for the assessment of outcomes.—Thus, in designing the evaluation component of an innovation, it is important to clearly distinguish between process and outcomes and to design evaluation procedures which will measure either or both of these dimensions. If the innovation is designed to bring about outcomes already universally defined (as is the usual situation with regard to reading skills), available assessment devices for measuring these outcomes can be used. If, however, the outcome has not already been well defined (e.g., attitudes) or if assessment instruments for the out-

---

20. Austin and Morrison, *op. cit.*, p. 147.

comes as defined are not available, the innovator faces the problem of explicit definition of desired outcomes in behavorial terms and the construction of appropriate measurement devices. This can be a formidable task which may require the assistance of an evaluation expert.

Planning for the assessment of process.—The problem with respect to assessing process is a much more difficult one. It is here that such matters as student-teacher interaction, attitudes, interest, enthusiasm, and environmental stimuli of various sorts compound the learning situation. Even with the best measurement techniques and under the most controlled conditions, it is often impossible to sort out precisely the many complex variables in a child's environment which impinge upon the educational process. However, better techniques, such as observation, interaction analysis, and student reporting, are being developed by the evaluation experts.[21] These techniques, coupled with better and better research designs, offer hope for more reliable and valid assessment in the future. Again, the innovator will probably find it advisable to call upon the evaluation expert for assistance in designing techniques to measure process.

Taking into account the Hawthorne effect.—One element which complicates the assessment of process in any innovation is the Hawthorne effect, which can be defined as that learning or student productivity which results simply because the program is new and presents to some students and teachers a special opportunity for personal recognition to be achieved by exerting a little more effort. Because this effect is related to the newness and special attention which is an integral part of every innovation, the innovation will have to be continued over several years, and assessments will have to be made regularly to determine if the achievement level recedes when the excitement surrounding innovation has disappeared.

Perhaps one goal we seek in introducing innovations in our schools is a kind of permanent Hawthorne effect.[22] For some innovations, perhaps, their main value lies in the fact that they facili-

---

21. See, for example, Ned A. Flanders, *Interaction Analysis in a Classroom* (Ann Arbor: University of Michigan Press, 1964).

22. Sister M. Jacqueline Grennan, "Rationale for Changes in Education," *North Central Association Quarterly*, XXXIX (Spring, 1965), 309.

tate a Hawthorne reaction. This appears to be valid reason to experiment.

But a word of caution about the Hawthorne effect is in order. An innovation which appears to be effective in one school could be realizing its positive results simply because of the Hawthorne effect. When it is transferred to another school, the conditions (excited teachers, enthusiastic students) which produced the extra effort and positive results might not exist, and for that reason the results would be disappointing. Therefore, even though the Hawthorne effect is difficult to assess, a school which is considering adopting an innovation developed in another school should be aware of this possibility, should try to obtain dependable evidence, and should be prepared for less favorable results.

Consideration of process can expand the teacher's view of his role.—Designing evaluation devices which measure process and outcomes separately can do much to expand the narrow view of education which is held firmly by too many teachers. It is appalling to note the number of times teachers lay the full blame for learning failure directly upon the child himself, never giving a thought to the possibility that the problem might lie in the methods used to teach him. Methods can fail for several reasons, none of which can be placed at the feet of the learner. Material can be inappropriate, teacher language incomprehensible, explanations inadequate, or interest-catching techniques ineffective. Including assessment of process as an integral part of evaluation can do much to eliminate this shortsighted and potentially damaging view held by some teachers.

PRACTICAL VIEW OF EVALUATING INNOVATIONS

Up to this point, the discussion of evaluation of innovations has been somewhat idealistic. To be sure, it would be utopian if all innovations could be planned, executed, and evaluated by carefully designed, valid procedures. But many innovations seemingly are not capable of being so well worked out. Several years of just tinkering about may be necessary before the precision of thought necessary for a well-worked-out effort can be developed. Often, for this reason, the innovator simply dismisses evaluation as unimportant.

The lack of good instruments and precise planning does not constitute a valid reason for no evaluation. In any situation, some forms of measurement can be used which will provide at least hunches as to the effectiveness of programs. As the evidence is accumulated over a period of years, one may legitimately come to have greater faith in the reliability of the measuring instruments. Furthermore, as attempts are made to measure new and differing procedures in the educational process over a period of time, instruments which are initially crude can be refined with each replication. In addition, if the innovation can be tried out in several places at one time and if the mass of evidence accumulated in different schools points to the same conclusions, a reasonable amount of faith in these results is justifiable.

The recent national drive to provide special summer programs for disadvantaged youth provides one example of how mass accumulation of evidence can lead to justifiable hunches. While, at this writing, no precise means have been developed to measure the processes being used to bring about change in the enthusiasm of these students for learning, evidence repeatedly and consistently comes out of interviews, self-reports, and reports from home schools which indicates that over half the students involved are being redirected toward positive educational activities. Furthermore, the process consistently identified as being responsible for bringing about this change is the exposure of these youth to and their immersion in an environment made up of a large number of adults who are excited about learning, who can transmit this excitement to the young people, and who obviously care about the directions in which the youth are going.[23]

To be sure, conclusions are based on extremely imprecise data. One could ask, "How many teachers and other adult types are essential to immersion?" "What kinds of behavior represent excitement about learning?" "What teacher behaviors stimulate students to learn?" "How does one communicate concern and care to children?" Furthermore, inasmuch as these students voluntarily subject themselves to a special summer program, one might ask, "Could it not be true that they were already finding and redirecting

23. *Summer Education for Children of Poverty* (Report of the National Advisory Council on the Education of Disadvantaged Children, U.S. Department of Health, Education, and Welfare, OE-37006 [Washington: Government Printing Office, 1966]).

themselves and might possibly have done as well, or almost as well, without the special summer project?"

One must accept the present limitations of evaluation and recognize that coarse evaluative techniques which lead to defensible hunches will leave unanswered many more precise questions. But, as the innovation is replicated and refined and as research continues, better methods of measurement as well as better procedures of teaching will be devised. By involving a skilled researcher, the innovator has a better chance of identifying more precisely the cause-and-effect relationships inherent in an innovation.

At the practical level, lack of availability of entirely adequate means for evaluation is no reason for not using the means which are available and for not searching for better ones. All educational devices can be considered exploratory, and all should be seen as being in the process of developing. We should be constantly trying out, testing, refining, and trying out again. Inasmuch as there are as yet no laws of learning, just learning theories,[24] we should not be uncomfortable with the innovative, exploratory state of education. Rather, we should accept it, thrive on it, and push it ahead as fast as possible.

It must be made clear that, even in instances in which the ideal cannot be reached, we should not settle for undirected, hit-or-miss approaches to evaluation. Regardless of the stage of an innovation, it is imperative that innovators build several steps into their new programs to insure the best evaluation possible at each given stage:

1. A comprehensive review of the literature (reports of previous research) must be undertaken to become knowledgeable about what has been done and what devices have been used to measure process and outcomes. This review should be undertaken with full awareness of the strengths and weaknesses of such reports.[25]
2. Much work has been done in the past few years by scholars in the field of tests and measurements. The innovator should be fully aware

---

24. Brundage, *op. cit.*, p. 95.

25. For an excellent guide to assessing research reports, see Helen M. Robinson, "Assessing the Experimental Evidence for Various Beginning Reading Plans," *Modern Educational Developments: Another Look* (Report of the Thirteenth Educational Conference [New York: Educational Records Bureau, 1966]), pp. 167-73.

of their accomplishments,[26] or he should engage an expert to work with him.
3. Evaluation should be in terms of the purposes of the innovation and should focus on both process and outcomes.
4. Before launching the innovation, the innovator should construct as completely as possible the rationale for and instruments to be used in measuring process and outcomes. All aspects of the innovation should be considered, and all those of which some assessment can be made should be provided for in the evaluative plan.
5. Innovators should accept responsibility to report in detail the results of their efforts, both successes and non-successes, so that other innovators may profit from them. Information about the latter is as important as that about the former to those who are pushing ahead the boundaries of knowledge.

EVALUATING INNOVATIVE READING PROGRAMS

It would be comforting to be able to report that innovations at the University of Chicago High School have met the conditions set forth in the previous section. But that school's faculty and principal are also in the state of becoming more expert in evaluation. Some ways in which the members of the faculty are seeking to evaluate their innovations in reading are described. Evaluation was attempted in light of two broad objectives—that students will use reading effectively to gain information and that they will turn to reading for enjoyment.

While improvement as measured by results of general standardized reading tests has been accomplished, no published tests are available which measure how well students read to gain information in specific courses. An examination of the literature reveals that correlations between scores on standardized reading tests and reading achievement in specific subject areas are not impressively high. It appears that the reading power of a student may differ markedly from one discipline to another.[27] Therefore, *general* reading tests are limited in value.

26. For a systematic discussion of practical measurement and evaluation procedures, see James M. Bradfield and H. Stewart Moredock, *Measurement and Evaluation in Education* (New York: Macmillan Co., 1957).

27. Miles A. Tinker, "Speed *versus* Comprehension in Reading as Affected by Level of Difficulty," *Journal of Educational Psychology*, XXX (February, 1939), 81-94; James M. McCallister, "Reading Difficulties in Studying Content Subjects," *Elementary School Journal*, XXXI (November, 1930), 191-201.

University High School social-studies teachers, concerned about the rigorous reading demands facing seniors, constructed their own test, a task which they found neither difficult nor forbidding. They simply asked students to read a primary-source selection typical of those to be assigned, then perform a few sample tasks of the type that would confront them all year: selecting and expressing the main idea, grasping clearly expressed details, grasping unwritten meanings, drawing sound conclusions, making deep interpretations, and the like.

Results of the test were quickly recorded on a "Reading Needs Chart" for each class. Names of students were listed down the right side; types of reading skills across the top. A check mark indicated a special need. A glance *down* the chart revealed instruction needed by the entire class. A glance *across* it revealed special help needed by individuals. In some classes the test became a teaching exercise as teacher and class held a "how-you-should-have-read-it" session. In all classes there was some reading instruction and supervised practice tailored to the needs revealed. Did the innovation of testing and instruction on actual course materials facilitate learning? *Did the behavior of students change?*

Later, students took a matching test on a document approximately equal in difficulty, and improvement was recorded on the "Reading Needs Chart." Teachers could make a before-and-after comparison of the competencies of the class and of individuals.

A physics teacher, probing to learn how his students actually studied their physics, approached his class: "Just what did you do when you read your assignment last night? Just pretend there was a little mouse in the room watching—what would he have seen? Please write down exactly what you did. I'm purposely not asking any leading questions. If *I* get a questionnaire, I tend to answer the questions in the way I think the person wants me to—so no leading questions. So that I can help you study better, I'm snooping a little into your study habits."

The introspective reports, which were most revealing, were supplemented by a teacher-made test, which was not difficult to make or administer. Using a short passage from the regular textbook, the teacher probed for a few skills he considered indispensable for effective reading in science. As the test was given, he made clear to the class the nature of each skill being measured so that the students were inwardly assessing themselves. Papers were returned to the students with strengths and weaknesses evaluated in the margin by a simple points system. A matching test can be developed to measure progress.

Efforts to measure change in attitudes present special problems. The reader will recall an earlier reference to a reading program undertaken by two physical-education teachers. Since they were popular with the students, these teachers felt that they could influence reluctant readers to capture the fervor for reading and to practice it through "real fun sports books." Having assembled libraries of colorful, attractive books and having involved the reluctant readers by sharing their own enthusiasm about the materials, these teachers now find students who were infrequent readers taking home books on their favorite sport.

Will this innovation change the attitudes of these reluctant readers? If it does, how will this change be assessed? The teachers are asking each student to respond to a before-and-after questionnaire, "Please Tell Us," which contains questions about the amount of time the student devotes to reading, the extent of his reading during the past vacation period, and his likes and dislikes about subjects at school which require reading. The teachers are also using Strang's "Incomplete Sentence Technique."[28] The school librarians have contributed their insights into the students' attitudes. The before-and-after data will help these teachers assess the change in attitude toward reading. Admittedly, this assessment will be coarse, in view of the fact that there will be no control of other factors which may be influencing the student's attitudes.

Observation is often one of the best methods for assessing change which comes about as a result of innovative activities. The reader will recall the all-school drive to make every teacher sensitive to individual differences and fully active in considering the reading needs of his students. The basic questions to ask are: "Has teacher behavior changed?" "Are teachers attempting to structure experiences which will facilitate learning in the field of reading?" There

---

28. Ruth Strang, *Diagnostic Teaching of Reading* (New York: McGraw-Hill, Inc., 1964), pp. 256-57.

was a major effort to bring the "right reading" and the "right child" together. Some day-to-day observations about teacher behavior are:

1. A young teacher, previously not fully aware of reading diversity, pored over the reading achievement of his students, then prepared a list of science biographies with reading-level requirements indicated for each reference.
2. Librarians use their "Instant Reading Level File" constantly and study their "Class Reading Placement Sheets" as they make reference lists for teachers.
3. Carts are seen trundling books from the elementary-school library to the high-school building to be used by poor readers.
4. As students approach the mythology unit (and other units), their teachers assemble classroom libraries containing something that every child can use.
5. Three teachers who have classroom libraries have asked that reading difficulty be coded in all the books.
6. A teacher of the history of music, dissatisfied with one textbook for all and the survival of the fittest, made an exhaustive search through music libraries to find textbooks and reference materials which the poorest of his students can read successfully.

We recognize the above as limited observations, but, when properly recorded and sufficiently replicated, these data do provide an assessment of teacher behavior. If these reports coincide with improvements in achievement in reading as well as with an increased enthusiasm for reading, it appears reasonable to conclude that these innovations are bringing about desired changes in teacher performance.

Concluding Statement

It is apparent that schools are on the threshold of a long period of innovation and change. Practicing educators must come to accept this fact. Meaningful change is brought about by developing a consensus among teachers and administrators about educational needs and by innovations arising from within the school. Findings from research, experimentation, and innovative programs in other schools can shed light on local school problems, but they must be incorporated cautiously and evaluated continuously to insure that they have relevance and value in dealing with both the specific problem and the total school.

It is probable that considerable time will pass before schools generally develop systematic processes for innovating and changing, for evaluating and feeding back into the system, and for establishing meaningful and productive relationships with research scholars. While it is probably true that "educational programs should be changed by educators," [29] the roles of the primary actors within the schools must be reviewed if this is to be realized.

In the foregoing pages, an attempt was made to identify and describe ways in which a sensible program of innovation and change in reading could be carried on systematically. It is apparent that each school needs a competent person, such as a reading consultant, to carry on a continuous examination of learning needs in reading and to serve as a stimulator, catalyst, and resource person to teachers and students in improving reading performance. It is quite obvious that few school principals have either the time or the *expertise* to perform these vital functions. Furthermore, an effective reading program within a school will not be realized unless all teachers and administrators accept reading as their legitimate professional concern and involve themselves actively in its improvement. Such a commitment requires the leadership of a competent reading consultant.

But the mere employment of a consultant does not automatically insure that the many aspects of the process of change described earlier will be carried on. Lerner summarizes succinctly the task lying before educators if schools are to benefit from the new agents of change and other opportunities which are now available.

The attempt to develop a quality reading program within a school throws the reading consultant or whoever undertakes this challenge into such problem areas as educational change, communication patterns within the school system, personality conflicts, goal perception differences, role ambiguity, power struggles, and organizational disequilibrium. Therefore, the structure of the organization and the patterns of administrative behavior have a direct and strong impact on the direction of the developmental reading program.[30]

It is clear that administrators are crucial to the introduction of

---

29. Brundage, *op. cit.*, p. 95.

30. Janet W. Lerner, "A New Focus in Reading Research: The Decision-making Process," *Elementary English*, XLIV (March, 1967), 239.

innovations. Administrative policy and in-service education must support innovative activities if present efforts (however valiant) to improve instructional practice in reading as well as in other areas are not to fail. Teachers' legitimate roles in the decision-making and creative processes must be recognized. If teachers and administrators accept new leadership roles, find ways to work through the complex interrelationships involved, and use a sound rationale for introducing and evaluating change, the future of public education generally and of reading specifically will be exciting indeed.

CHAPTER IX

Balanced Reading Development

CONSTANCE M. MC CULLOUGH

Introduction

DEFINITION

Balanced reading development is reading development which does not neglect one essential avenue of learning to read or one aspect of the reading process in favor of another but maintains an offering which, at any level of instruction, produces the optimal achievement and versatility of the individual reader.

If most children achieved the goals of reading instruction and guidance regardless of the kind of teaching, kind of program, availability of materials, and time devoted to reading, there would be little point in being concerned about balance. But one has only to note the volume of research on reading retardation and disability and on maturity in reading to become aware that what the home, school, and larger environment offer the child can and does make a difference. Children become cripples in word attack, in comprehension, in study skills, in oral or silent reading, in reading a given type of material for a particular purpose, in ability to interpret and use what they have read; all kinds of patterns of competence and incompetence and all kinds of blind spots and active dislikes appear. Some of these shortcomings are highly individual, while others can be traced to the failure of the home situation, neighborhood, school, or teacher.

With the many aids to instruction, the many methods, the many materials, and the many types of organization of the reading program now available to the teacher, choices become important. What should be done? When? How much? How often? For whom? Balance apparently is important. But what balance?

This chapter will attempt to show the facets of balance which might be considered in designing and administering a reading program. The reader is invited to measure the ideas expressed in the chapter against his own experience and convictions and to create his own concept of a balanced program.

THE PROBLEM

The concept of balance is affected by the conceptions of the reading act and of the goals of reading instruction. Reading development in some countries means development in the learning of the symbols which represent sounds in the language and the application of this knowledge to the oral reading of various types of selections.[1] In keeping with this concept, the reading act represents the ability to sound out all the letters, blend them successfully into words, and read aloud accurately, imitating the teacher's expression. The goal is effective oral reading.

The teaching method in such a country is typically that of dictation. The teacher tells what the letter "says," and the children repeat and learn to write it and to "say" its sound. What the teacher says is the child's only means of discovery. There is no discussion of the meaning of what is read, because the purpose is accurate oral reading, and the teacher dictates the way it is to be expressed. To an outsider, this emphasis upon dictation and this denial of the child's own initiative seems to be a case of imbalance, but in a society which wants unthinking obedience and imitation of fixed models it is not even questioned.

The material that is given the child to read is typically unrelated to the child's life or to the present. It may be adult content extolling the nation's past. So, even if the child does try to think of the meaning of what he repeats, he finds little satisfaction in doing so. From our point of view, this constitutes an imbalance.

In such a situation, reading is a ritual of sounds that have no meaning to the child, a ritual difficult to learn partly because it has no meaning. All of his reading experiences are oral; therefore, included in his conception of reading is the idea that it is saying something to others who are listening for mistakes. It is not sur-

1. William S. Gray, *The Teaching of Reading and Writing* (Chicago: Scott, Foresman & Co., 1956).

prising that a large percentage of children entering first grade in such a country do not stay through the year.[2]

Balanced reading development in the United States at this time involves more than a single program or simple alterations in it. Historical developments in American education, research in the field of reading and in related disciplines, the wealth of children's literature from all over the world, and the growing awareness of the complexity of the reading process and of its supporting skills—all contribute to a different and more comprehensive interpretation of balance. As new discoveries are made about the reading process and about learning and as the culture makes new uses of reading, the number of components subject to instruction is increased, and new relationships are sought in the learning. Thus, balanced reading development is a growing, changing concept. The problem is that it can be described only for today, only within the limits of present knowledge and goals. What is considered excellent today may be found wanting tomorrow because of some elements or arrangements or relationships which previously had been overlooked.

The problem is that of planning a balanced program for individuals of many backgrounds who are more or less strangers to "book English" and who are variously motivated and equipped to meet the task of reading.[3] Hence, a balanced program for one is not necessarily a balanced program for another; rather, each program varies from a standard or ideal to compensate for individual weaknesses and strengths.

Furthermore, in the beginnings of learning to read, the child has a great struggle with decoding the printed symbols into sounds, and so this decoding of symbols is given an amount of attention out of proportion to its relative importance in the entire process of (*a*) decoding symbols, (*b*) decoding meanings, (*c*) interpreting meanings, and (*d*) using the resultant ideas. Balance in beginning reading,

---

2. Constance M. McCullough, "Illiteracy in India: Problems and Progress," *Reading Teacher*, XIX (November, 1965), 83-90.

3. Sarita G. Schotta, *Teaching English as a Second Language* ("Davis Publications in English," No. 3 [Davis: University of California, Spring, 1966]); Richard Corbin, Muriel Crosby, and associates, *Language Programs for the Disadvantaged* (Champaign, Ill.: National Council of Teachers of English, 1965).

therefore, may look quite different from balance in middle-grade or upper-grade reading, in which the grasp of meanings, their interpretation, and their use become more difficult.

Historical Contributions to the Concept of Balance

THE COMPONENTS: WHAT SHOULD BE BALANCED?

American educators have been made aware of various components of reading during periods of emphasis upon one or another component. There are quotations throughout Smith's *American Reading Instruction* expressing the dissatisfaction of one educator or another as he viewed the current problems engendered by overemphasis on the different goals of and approaches to reading.[4] For example, an emphasis upon oral reading appeared to produce slow silent reading; an emphasis upon silent reading tended to produce poor oral reading.

The "cee-a-tee-cat" spelling approach to word analysis failed to strengthen the child's knowledge of the sounds the letters represented in the words. The ca-t analysis created a blending problem at the end of a word, while c-at analysis created a blending problem at its beginning. (Apparently it had occurred to no one to stretch the *a* to affect both consonants: ca-at, cat.)

The synthetic approach (sounds to words) discouraged children by its long delay in providing meaningful content. The sentence method left the child in a quandary about the identity of a particular word, and the word method left him almost helpless in solving new words. Both the phonics method and the word method made a "bead-stringer" of the child if no attempt was made to clarify word relationships and the meaning of what was read. Stress upon speed was another blow to comprehension.

After reading clinics began to appear in the 1920's, specialists were able to give more than passing attention to reading problems, and the factors involved in reading success became more carefully delineated. Although some children had a general reading disability, others had "blind spots" in their complement of skills, some of which could be traced directly to omissions in instruction. Robinson's

---

4. Nila Banton Smith, *American Reading Instruction* (rev. ed.; Newark, Del.: International Reading Association, 1965).

study on the causes of failure in reading gave strong support to the notion of multiple causation for reading failure (e.g., that retarded readers may have difficulty in aspects of reading other than word recognition) and to the idea that reading instruction should deal with many components.[5]

McCallister's study of student difficulties with science and social-studies textbooks produced nine types of paragraph organization which needed to be mastered if the students were to follow the thinking of the authors of those books.[6]

Russell's *The Dimensions of Children's Meaning Vocabularies in Grades Four through Twelve* extended the teacher's idea of her responsibility for vocabulary development.[7]

Over a forty-year period, American reading instruction has passed from the practice of dealing with three components called vocabulary, comprehension, and speed to that of dealing with a multitude of skills and subskills. Indexes of teachers' manuals list as many as two hundred such items.[8] And along with this increased complexity has come the realization that no letter, no word, no sentence, no paragraph is an island; that the interpretation of sound and meaning is relative, because context determines what sound a letter shall be given and what meaning a word or phrase or sentence or paragraph shall have.[9]

While the temptation to view the task simply and to find an easy answer remains, many educators today are beginning to appreciate something of the child's struggle to decode the meanings as well as to decode the written symbols of book language.[10]

5. Helen M. Robinson, *Why Pupils Fail in Reading* (Chicago: University of Chicago Press, 1946).

6. James M. McCallister, "Reading Difficulties in Studying Content Subjects," *Elementary School Journal*, XXXI (November, 1930), 191-201.

7. David H. Russell, *The Dimensions of Children's Meaning Vocabularies in Grades Four through Twelve* ("Publications in Education," XI, No. 5 [Berkeley: University of California Press, 1954]).

8. For example, see David H. Russell and Mabel Snedaker, *Manual for Teaching "Wings to Adventure"* (Boston: Ginn & Co., 1950), pp. 384-88.

9. Constance M. McCullough, "Linguistics, Psychology, and the Teaching of Reading," *Elementary English*, XLIV (April, 1967), 353-62.

10. Wilbur S. Ames, "The Development of a Classification Scheme of Contextual Aids," *Reading Research Quarterly*, II (Fall, 1966), 57-82.

There is good reason to believe that there are many components of the reading process, that they can be fostered or taught, and that to neglect one or more of them is to create an imbalance which, because of their interrelatedness, affects the whole. However impossible it may be to achieve balance, not to try is to fail to heed the warnings of history.

THE INFLUENCE OF DISCIPLINES

Literature.—The contributions of various fields of knowledge to the teaching of reading pose problems of balance. The field of literature presents innumerable possibilities, and choices must be made.[11] If one is, indeed, a product of all his experiences, the choice of types of materials for the classroom or school library is of great significance. The factual, the fictional; the realistic, the fanciful; the humorous, the serious; the variety of literary forms—the letter, the poem, the drama, the story, the topical article or essay (persuasion or exposition), the news item, the advertisement, the announcement—all of these types of material have a place in a balanced program.

Two pieces of writing can be dramatically different in effectiveness and should be studied for the elements which make them so. Beauty of expression, in a language so rich in examples of it, surely should be considered in choice of materials. Materials should reflect all the interests the children bring to school as well as those which they may later acquire.[12] The school library should contain books and magazines covering a broad spectrum of interests, exploring them at different levels of reading difficulty and from different points of view. Reference materials and graphic aids should be on hand to assist the development of topics and concepts. A classroom collection is tailored to the children. The highly able reader is challenged. The child who finds reading a difficult and slow process can find easier material that will enable him to maintain some fluency. Each child should be able to find something he

---

11. *1966 Curriculum Projects in English: A Report on 172 Projects in 35 States* (Champaign, Ill.: National Council of Teachers of English, 1966).

12. Helen Huus, "Interpreting Research in Children's Literature," in *Children, Books, and Reading* ("Perspectives in Reading," No. 3 [Newark, Del.: International Reading Association, 1964]), pp. 123-45.

can read (even though it is only pictures) for special reports and assignments in the content fields.

In addition to making all of these materials available and giving children the opportunity to use them, a balanced program certainly brings to the reader's attention the characteristics of the different forms which have been perfected in English literature.[13] At the present time, there is renewed concern that children should become acquainted with some pieces of classic children's literature, "books too good to miss."[14] Some, perhaps, should be read aloud to the children rather than read by them. It is anticipated that "a good story" will be discussed for its good attributes, so that gradually good judgment will develop.

A perennial concern is the reading fare for boys as opposed to girls—what will hold them and what they will tolerate. For many years, also, studies have revealed the preferences of the bright, the dull, the able reader, and the retarded reader. Bibliotherapy has been an interest of some researchers since the 1940's; they have searched for material which would meet the deeper, personal concerns of children and adults.[15]

Now the focus is upon the so-called disadvantaged child and the development of his self-concept, partly through the use and support of literature which features people of backgrounds like his own.[16] Obviously, the value of this kind of reading experience is such that it should be a consideration in the reading experience of every child. The question which has no ready answer is: "How much of a person's reading material should be focused on his own kind?" Sooner or later he can acquire the satisfaction of identification with all life and learn much of personal value from it.

Linguistics.—Up to the time of this writing, the main contribution of linguists to the teaching of reading has been proposals for changes in the way in which children are taught the decoding

---

13. Miles A. Tinker and C. M. McCullough, *Teaching Elementary Reading* (New York: Appleton-Century-Crofts, 1962), pp. 24-34.

14. May Hill Arbuthnot *et al., Children's Books Too Good to Miss* (3d rev. ed.; Cleveland: Western Reserve University Press, 1966).

15. David H. Russell, "Some Research on the Impact of Reading," *English Journal*, XLVIII (October, 1958), 398-413.

16. Corbin and Crosby and associates, *op. cit.*

of printed symbols and for orientation in basic sentence types.[17] The teaching materials which have come out of this proposal are varied and show the lack of agreement among specialists; but what the reading teacher may eventually learn from the linguist will affect the decoding of meaning and will profoundly influence the teaching of comprehension skills. When as much is known about the subskills of comprehension and interpretation as is now known about the subskills of word analysis, a more balanced program can be offered.

Balance in the linguistic offering for the development of the child as a reader of English takes into account some of the following: [18]

1. The history of English
2. The sounds and patterns of "book English"
3. Different ways of expressing the same idea
4. Alteration of ideas by substitution of words or transposition of words within a sentence
5. The identification of structure words
6. The multiple meanings of structure words
7. Occasions when "signal words" do not give the expected signal (not only . . . but also=both . . . and)
8. Signals to the continuation of an idea or change of subject
9. The effect of context upon letter sounds and the meaning of words, phrases, and larger units (lead [verb] or lead [noun])
10. Analysis of lengthy sentences into basic sentences
11. Construction of longer sentences from basic sentences
12. Patterns and irregularities in English spelling
13. Signals to tense in different classes of verbs
14. Signals to number and gender in different classes of nouns and in pronouns
15. Expected position and form of parts of speech.

In the learning of some of the foregoing items, listening, speak-

---

[17] C. C. Fries, *Linguistics: The Study of Language* (New York: Holt, Rinehart, & Winston, Inc., 1962); Carl LeFevre, *Linguistics and the Teaching of Reading* (New York: McGraw-Hill Book Co., 1964).

[18] H. A. Gleason, Jr., *Linguistics and English Grammar* (New York: Holt, Rinehart, & Winston, Inc., 1965); Robert A. Hall, Jr., *Sound and Spelling in English* (New York: Chilton Co., 1961); Archibald Hill, *Introduction to Linguistic Structures* (New York: Harcourt, Brace & Co., 1958); Verna Newsome, *Structural Grammar in the Classroom* (Oshkosh, Wis.: Wisconsin Council of Teachers of English, 1962).

ing, and writing activities will be employed. Programs will have to compensate for the difficulties arising from the different sentence order in the mother tongue of the child who speaks a language other than English and from the fact that some of the sounds and sequences of sound in English are foreign to him and require, therefore, both ear and speech training.[19] Certain Negro dialects which do not use the "complete" sentences of "book English" must be considered if reading-readiness activities and beginning reading are not to prove inefficient and even ineffectual.[20] Eventually, perhaps, such provision will be made for children of every background as is now made for Spanish-speaking children in Lancaster's *Introducing English*.[21]

Some teachers take dictation in the dialect of a pupil and write the language so that he can learn to read it. Others add "book English" to his speech before they record anything to be learned. One view is that the child should improve his own dialect before he adds another language, but improvement of his dialect requires a teacher or native speaker capable of effecting this change. This creates a problem for the teacher who has children from three or more language backgrounds in her classroom and has only one or two languages at her command. There are so many conflicting firm opinions about the best procedure for initiating instruction with such pupils that, at the present time, teachers can only do what seems to make the best sense to them. A clear-cut answer sometime soon would be welcome.

Sociology.—The field of sociology offers suggestions about both

---

19. Robert Lado, *Linguistics across Cultures* (Ann Arbor: University of Michigan Press, 1957); *Language Teaching: A Scientific Approach* (New York: McGraw-Hill Book Co., 1964).

20. *Non-Standard Speech and the Teaching of English*, ed. William A. Stewart ("Language Information Series," No. 2 [Washington: Center for Applied Linguistics, 1964]); *Social Dialects and Language Learning*, ed. Roger Shuy (Champaign, Ill.: National Council of Teachers of English, 1965); Ruth I. Golden, *Improving Patterns of Language Usage* (Detroit: Wayne State University Press, 1960).

21. Louise Lancaster, *Introducing English: An Oral Pre-Reading Program for Spanish-Speaking Primary Pupils* (New York: Houghton Mifflin Co., 1966); Jane Beasley Raph, "Language Development in Socially Disadvantaged Children," in *Education for Socially Disadvantaged Children*, entire issue of *Review of Educational Research*, XXXV (December, 1965), 389-400.

what children should be given to read and what social situations should be constructed in the classroom.[22]

In the last decade, a revolution has occurred in instructional materials, and part of that revolution has been a change in the conception of society and of the child's role in it. For many years in this country, the one unquestioned instructional material was the basal reader, the content of which represented the aspirations of "the society as a whole." It would be difficult to assess the influence of this one unifying element in our varied lives, one which stressed the values of cleanliness, harmony, family togetherness, home ownership, industriousness, and harmless fun.

It is not easy to recapture the frame of mind which accepted such a book, but essentially it included a belief that all members of society could approach this "good life" and benefit from having shed whatever made them different. Difference was a stigma that bore heavily upon immigrants and native minority groups alike. If, at the time the belief was widely accepted, there had been a publisher so bold as to issue an Ellis Island reader or a "lower class" primer, he could not have sold it. Parents wanted their children to have a book "as good as anybody's."

Television commercials have now taken the place of the basal reader as the great unifier, and the affluent society with vocal minorities now calls for and gets books created in their images. Psychologists and educators agree with sociologists that the first reading experiences of children should be about a life they understand and about characters with whom they can easily identify.[23] When the printed symbol becomes less strange, the learner is ready for content reflecting a multi-ethnic and multiclass society.

Unfortunately, such materials do not solve all problems. All

---

22. Martin Deutsch, "The Role of Social Class in Language Development and Cognition," *American Journal of Orthopsychiatry*, XXXV (January, 1965), 78-88; Monroe Rowland and Patricia Hill, "Race, Illustrations and Interest in Materials for Reading and Creative Writing," *Journal of Negro Education*, XXXIV (Winter, 1965), 84-87; W. Wesley Tennyson and Lawrence P. Monnens, "The World of Work through Elementary Readers," *Vocational Guidance Quarterly*, XII (Winter, 1963-64), 85-88.

23. Ruth G. Strickland, *The Language of Elementary School Children: Its Relationship to the Language of Reading Textbooks and the Quality of Reading of Selected Children* (Bulletin of the School of Education, Indiana University, XXXVIII, No. 4 [Bloomington: Indiana University, 1962]).

children of a given race, class, or socioeconomic position do not fit a set description. The lumberjack's child whose home is anchored in the river may not recognize the home in the preprimer for children of his own economic level. Do these and other differences require different instructional materials and special grouping for instruction?

There is evidence that children can be taught in a group selected for reading instruction and can still maintain their social status and social contacts with others in the class.[24] Balance probably consists of providing for other types of grouping. But it is clear that teachers and children who create some of their own first reading materials prior to or along with their use of commercial products provide the best answer to meeting the individual child on home ground.

Balance in the social experiences within the classroom involves provision for whole-class participation, small-group activities, and individual endeavor; development of leadership and followership; and participation in exchanging ideas and molding decisions with respect for the contributions of others.

Psychology.—Relatively new reading programs, scientifically developed in Sweden, are said to benefit by (*a*) the delay of school entrance until the age of seven, (*b*) the limitation of class size to twenty-five children, (*c*) the general phonetic regularity of the Swedish language, (*d*) the relative uniformity of language background of the children, and (*e*) the fact that teachers stay with a task until it is mastered instead of passing on hopefully to the next lesson.[25] In the United States, the situation is quite different, generally on all counts.

An American reading program needs not only to fit children's individual differences but also to strike some kind of balance in exposure to materials and to instruction, in timing of initial instruction, and in pace of progress through sequential learnings. The psy-

---

24. Francis R. Deitrich "Comparisons of Sociometric Patterns of Sixth Grade Pupils in Two School Systems: Ability Grouping Compared with Heterogeneous Grouping," *Journal of Educational Research*, LVII (July-August, 1964), 507-13.

25. Eve Malmquist, "Provisions Made for Children Who Have Difficulties in Reading: Sweden," in *Reading Instruction: An International Forum*, ed. Marion D. Jenkinson (Newark, Del.: International Reading Association, 1967), pp. 109-126.

chologist notes with assurance the uniqueness of the individual, but so far it has been left to the teacher to determine what may safely be taught to groups and what differences in level of reading achievement and learning rates can be tolerated within a group without harm to individuals. The amount of guidance the child needs is an individual matter. But, with all that needs to be learned and experienced in a modern reading program, every child will be obliged to learn more on his own and to demand less individual attention. The value of the individual conference is well established,[26] but it cannot carry the entire burden of instruction. Increasingly, the teacher must teach children how to learn, giving them the responsibility for applying the method in further learning. Children may work in teams to make new discoveries and report their discoveries to others.

Studies of individual and group differences suggest differential treatment of children fitting certain descriptions. Some culturally deprived children need experience in speaking and listening to compensate for relatively non-verbal environments; they need to learn to substitute words for actions.[27] Children whose mothers' speech reflects concrete rather than abstract ideas require experiences leading to verbal expression of abstract ideas.[28] Children whose satisfactions must be immediate and tangible cannot be motivated by remote rewards.

In beginning reading programs, a good many boys require a more active physical involvement and a greater variety of approaches than do most girls. Reading matter expressive of action and reading methods requiring immediate active responses and a high degree of attention are being developed for such children.[29]

---

26. Harry W. Sartain, "The Roseville Experiment with Individualized Reading," *Reading Teacher*, XIII (April, 1960), 277-81.

27. Jean Malmstrom and Annabel Ashley, *Dialects U.S.A.* (Champaign, Ill.: National Council of Teachers of English, 1963).

28. Ellis G. Olim, Robert D. Hess, and Virginia C. Shipman, "Relationship between Mothers' Language Styles and Cognitive Styles of Urban Pre-School Children," (paper presented to the Society for Research in Child Development, March 25, 1965 [mimeographed; Chicago: Urban Child Study Center, 1965].

29. For example, materials being developed for first graders by Jo Stanchfield of Occidental College.

The child who has difficulty fitting into the usual patterns of expected behavior may have difficulty in developing the measure of discrimination and association essential in learning to read.[30] It stands to reason that programs for such a child should be so ordered that what he is expected to learn will coincide with his moments of greatest attention. Balance, for him, may be more discovery (personal initiative) under guidance and less passive listening.

The bright child who finds it easier to lean upon his imagination than to perform the more analytical activities may resist the work of word-form analysis in favor of the use of clues from context. His teacher must be particularly careful not to accept a good hunch as a studied conclusion, but should stop to ask him how he knew.

Generalizations may be misleading. The bilingual child may or may not become a retarded reader.[31] He may, indeed, be the best reader in the class. The disturbed child may have his problem solved through successful reading instruction or have his woes compounded by the attempt to teach him. The passive child who lets the effects of education wash over him may have developed this passivity for various reasons. The child of mixed dominance may or may not be defeated in reading from left to right.[32] It is quite possible that a brain-damaged child may be handicapped more by being taught in the special way the teacher thinks he should be taught than by the damage to his brain. Careful observation of the way children respond and patient exploration of the possible reasons for the types of response made are the teacher's best tools.[33] This is not to say that the generalizations are groundless but rather that they should not be applied to every child.

Psychologists have made reading specialists aware of the gamut

---

30. Muriel Potter Langman, "The Reading Process: A Descriptive, Interdisciplinary Approach," *Genetic Psychology Monographs*, LXII (August, 1960), 3-40.

31. J. Vernon Jensen, "Effects of Childhood Bilingualism," *Elementary English*, XXXIX (April, 1962), 358-66.

32. Patrick Groff, "A Study of Handedness and Reading Achievement," *Reading Teacher*, XVI (September, 1962), 31-40.

33. Ruth Strang, *Diagnostic Teaching of Reading* (New York: McGraw-Hill Book Co., 1964).

of cognitive processes of which a human being is capable.[34] Consciously or unconsciously, the reader leans upon his knowledge of these processes. Comprehension is based partly upon familiarity with and recognition of the modes of thought employed by the author of the material read. Interpretation applies the reader's own modes of thought to what he believes the author means.[35] Furthermore, the reading program shares with other fields in the curriculum the responsibility for the encouragement of a variety of modes of thought.

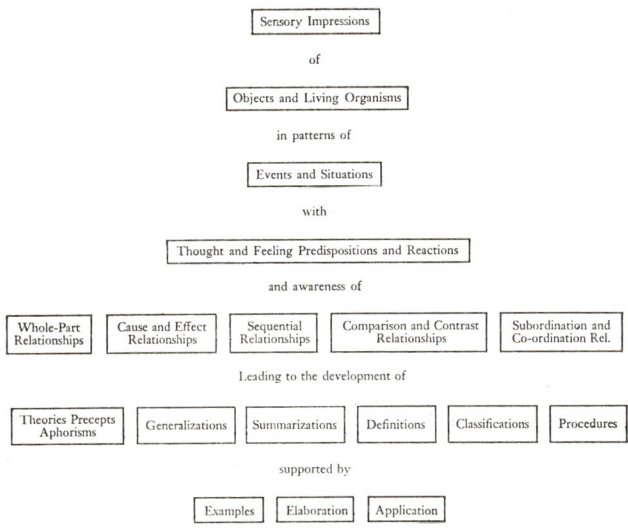

FIG. 1.—Thought patterns

Figure 1 charts the ingredients which an author uses in expressing his ideas and which a reader must use to gain and act upon those ideas.[36] Directions which thought may take in working out these relationships and products are inductive, deductive, con-

---

34. J. P. Guilford, "Human Abilities in Education," *California Journal for Instructional Improvement*, I (December, 1958), 3-6.

35. Russell G. Stauffer et al., *Language and the Higher Thought Processes* (Champaign, Ill.: National Council of Teachers of English, 1965).

36. See Constance M. McCullough, *Preparation of Textbooks in the Mother Tongue* (New Delhi, India: Department of Curriculum, Methods, and Textbooks, National Institute of Education, 1965).

vergent, divergent, and evaluative. The path an author takes from one point to another on this chart is highly individual; hence the importance of being able to follow his path. To give examples:

He ran. (cause)
His lungs were straining for air. (effect)

He ran. (effect)
The bear was after him. (cause)

As he ran, he seemed to favor his right foot.
 (event)   (detail of event)

Looking over his shoulder as he ran,
  (event)   +   (effect)
he could see that the bear was still after him.
       (event)   +   (cause)

Embedded in this last example is an implied sequence:

The bear came. He ran. The bear still came.

Children who do not know the English language well enough to benefit by its signals and structure will miss the direction of thought dependent upon them. More of the same comprehension exercise that they cannot understand is not the answer for them.

Culturally deprived children whose homes have not given them verbal experiences with related ideas may need readiness experiences in seeing, hearing, and expressing relationships before they are called upon to read material and express such relationships. Children untrained in shifting quickly from one relationship to another may fail tests which shift in this way, not because they do not recognize the words or comprehend language but because they are confused by the item-to-item shifts from one type of thought requirement to another. To give an example:

A dog can bark fly sew (observable function)
Milk turns sour sweet bitter (observable process)
The day before is today yesterday tomorrow (synonym or definition)

Vocabulary study which begins and ends with a definition or synonym withholds the richness of concept exploration possible through the other relationships and products indicated in Figure 1. Also, such **vocabulary study limits the child's versatility in in-**

stances in which he encounters a word used in an unusual way in a new context. Balanced vocabulary building and concept development may take the direction of exploring words related to a given word as well as that of the usual exploration of one relationship for many words (up-down, in-out, etc.) Note, for example, the dimensional word study of the word *monkey* which follows.[37]

whole-part: monkey—animal kingdom; leg—monkey
generalization or classification: monkey—mammal
coordination-subordination: monkey, camel=animals housed and controlled by keeper of zoo
cause-effect: hungry—eats; hears noise—frightened
comparison-contrast: with ape, with cat, with man
conditions: food, shelter, no department store bills
qualities: number, amount, texture, flavor, moisture, color, sweetness, solidity, size, shape, odor, sound (apply as suitable)
habits and actions: scratching, jumping, swinging, hanging, clinging, pushing, pulling, chewing, picking, screaming, chattering, lying, sitting, looking, smelling, leaping, running, traveling in herds
uses: entertainment (zoo, circus, organ grinder), experiments (medical, outer space)
time relationships: birth to adulthood changes, life span, evolution
place relationships: habitat (trees, jungle, etc.)
synonyms, antonyms, homonyms
multiple meanings: monkey wrench, monkey in tree, monkey around, make monkey of, monkey suit, grease monkey, monkey pod, you little monkey
derivation of word: from Turkish
definition: a man-like animal, etc.
word form: monkey, plural—monkeys (variant forms)

Balanced exercise in part-whole relationships would give children opportunities on different occasions to contribute parts or wholes, sometimes with choices given, sometimes with no suggestion:

A part of a monkey is a   leg   crank   fin.
A leg is a part of a   fish   monkey   car.
A leg is to a monkey as a fin is to a ———. (analogy = part-whole).
A monkey is to a leg as a fish is to a ———.
A leg is a part of a monkey or   fish   bird   wagon.

Psychologists have also helped the reading teacher to consider

---

37. *Ibid.*, paraphrasing pp. 94-97.

the balance of efforts, hers and the children's. The involved person will remember; the spectator or listener may not. The child who must do something with what he has learned learns it better because he knows he will have to use it, and he learns it better because he does use it. If the child who has discovered the sound represented by the letter *m* by means of the teacher's models, *milk* and *man*, then has to record his own induction with his own models (such as *mouse* and *match*, which he chooses), he will remember what he has learned better and will have a record from which to retrieve it if he forgets it. There is a balance between teacher guidance and pupil utilization of what he has learned, including his use of the learned method for discoveries of his own, that needs to be developed in the classroom.

Physiology.—Physiological studies of the reading process have contributed ideas concerning the essential conditions for physical comfort and efficient operation in the reading act: the proper fusion of eyes at reading distance, the establishment of left-to-right eye movements, proper lighting and contrast of print with paper, legibility, length and spacing of lines, size and style of type, paper without glare, and the like.[38] Neurologists propose that certain kinds of brain damage, dysfunction, or discrepant development require special approaches to reading.[39]

Studies reveal that the eye can see clearly only about an inch of print, though it can see more peripherally, whereas nerve impulses may travel at the rate of two hundred miles an hour.[40] These facts suggest that efforts to increase the eye span may not be so rewarding a part of a balanced program as efforts at developing a sight vocabulary. Furthermore, while the eye rests, the brain has

---

38. Miles A. Tinker, "Experimental Studies on the Legibility of Print: An Annotated Bibliography," *Reading Research Quarterly*, I (Summer, 1966), 67-118.

39. Carl H. Delacato, *The Treatment and Prevention of Reading Problems* (Springfield, Ill.: Charles C. Thomas, 1959); H. K. Goldberg, C. Marshall, and E. Sims, "The Role of Brain Damage in Congenital Dyslexia," *American Journal of Ophthalmology*, L (October, 1960), 586-90.

40. Lee C. Deighton "The Flow of Thought through an English Sentence" in *Vistas in Reading*, ed. J. Allen Figurel (Proceedings of the Eleventh Annual Convention of the International Reading Association [Newark, Del.: International Reading Association, 1966]), pp. 322-26.

time to mull over the relationships among words and their effect upon each other, thus clarifying cumulative meanings.

The little man in the big car turned out to let the truck pass.
The little man in the big car turned out to be a monkey advertising the coming circus.

With instruction in word relationships in a sentence, the reader can recreate the meaning less by trial and error and more by studied conclusion.

Evaluation.—The field of evaluation has expanded to involve more than attention to the easily measured aspects of reading achievement. Presently, evaluation requires the observation of behaviors and records of reading.[41] Thus, the reading teacher is aware of the fact that limited test results are not the only objective. The child who does not choose to use his reading skills for personal purposes has failed to achieve a major objective of the total program.

Diagnosis is viewed as continuous exploration rather than as something to be applied only at the initial encounter.[42] Diagnostic tests have revealed the unevenness of accomplishment in a variety of skills. Tests of subskills of visual and auditory discrimination have made it possible to identify individual needs.

Objective tests are increasingly useful in determining the level of difficulty at which a child can grasp a variety of dimensions of meaning and can engage in the study of the implications and applications of the ideas obtained. Cross-reference techniques used in designing tests enable the teacher to determine not only that a child missed a certain item but also, to an extent, the factors (other than chance) which possibly were or were not responsible for the failure.

Informal testing through open-ended questions can reveal the highly individual meanings which children of different backgrounds may gain from the same material. Children permitted to explain why they feel as they do about a selection frequently make more sense and reveal more of themselves than might have been made evident by the expected answer. The emotional meanings may be as important as the intellectual ones.

41. Mary Austin *et al., Reading Evaluation: Appraisal Techniques for School and Classroom* (New York: Ronald Press Co., 1961).

42. Strang, *op. cit.*

Viewing the contributions of the fields of linguistics, psychology, and evaluation, one can anticipate future developments in test construction. Perhaps tests will explore the dimensions of meanings of a few representative words as well as deal in the usual way with one dimension of many words. Perhaps the subskills of comprehension so far neglected in comprehension tests (linguistic elements and thought patterns) will reveal the needs in comprehension as subtests of word analysis now reveal the special needs in the solution of unknown words. Perhaps it will be realized that even teaching has been largely testing. Balance in evaluation will ultimately encompass more elements than we currently recognize or teach.

Available Materials for Balance

If a reading program is to offer balanced experience to every child, materials must be selected not only with reference to the many elements which must be balanced but also in view of the special needs of individuals. While the different types of materials available to the teacher may be used for more than one purpose, it is useful to consider the services for which each type is generically suitable and its role in balanced development.

The following criteria were used by the writer in constructing instructional materials in reading. They suggest some of the kinds of questions that teachers and administrators may wish to ask about prepared materials. Some questions may be altered to harmonize with different concepts of reading.

BASES FOR EVALUATION OF A READER AND RELATED MATERIALS [43]

Validity:

1. Is it a realistic expectation that children who have used the book and teaching materials as they were designed to be used will develop power in reading and a desire to read more?
2. Has research preceded or accompanied the development of the reading series to validate its content and methods?
3. Has the evaluation of this program been based either upon actual tryout with pupils or upon the judgment of teachers as to its feasibility?

---

43. Paraphrased and quoted from McCullough, *Preparation of Textbooks in the Mother Tongue, op. cit.,* pp. 115-18.

Content:

4. Does the reader present characters with whom the child can identify?
5. Does it reflect American life, leading from the present which the child knows to the past or remote?
6. Does it reflect the best in American and world literature?
7. Does the translation of world literature do justice to the quality of the original?
8. Does it reflect the ideals of the society without being unrealistic?
9. Is it interesting to children of the age group for which it is intended?
10. Does it inform as well as entertain, giving the child a greater self-knowledge and a greater understanding and appreciation of his environment?
11. Do succeeding volumes reflect the expanding world of the growing child?
12. Is there some direct attempt to correlate the readers of the series with the content and goals of the other subject areas of the curriculum?

Language:

13. Does the series utilize the basic vocabulary in the language, starting with forms which children hear and use?
14. Does it present the common sentence structures, grammatical structures, and word inflections, beginning with simple, common forms and proceeding to the complex?
15. Does it use the punctuation required by the contents?
16. Does it present words containing letters easy to write and then proceed to more difficult forms?
17. Are new words presented gradually and repeated often enough to assist learning?
18. Are words of multiple meanings presented, with only one meaning given at a time?
19. When one of two common words might have been appropriate in the text, has the choice clearly contributed either to repetition of something learned or to the development of a new learning?
20. Do sentences, paragraphs, and stories increase in length and complexity throughout the books in the series, presenting more and more challenge to established skills?
21. Has some attempt been made to gear this increased length and complexity to the language, interest, and reading ability of the majority of children of the different levels concerned?
22. Is the language in the early books informal and natural without being undesirable?

23. Have the authors avoided introducing easily confused word forms in the same lesson until each has been well established in previous lessons?

Physical Aspects:

24. Is the book suitably durable for the use it is to have?
25. Is its appearance inviting to the reader of the age for which it is intended?
26. Is the paper thick enough not to show print on the reverse side?
27. Is the paper off-white and dull in finish, without glare?
28. Is the print black enough to make a clear contrast with the paper?
29. Is the print large enough for the ocular accommodation of children learning to read?
30. Is the type highly legible, so that letters are not confused with one another?
31. Is the print placed clear of the illustrations?
32. Is the page artistically balanced?
33. Can the child hold the book without covering part of the print?
34. Does the book open flat, so that the child is reading a flat surface?
35. Is the teacher's manual easy to use in relation to the child's book?

Illustrations:

36. Is viewing the illustrations an aesthetic experience for the child?
37. Do the illustrations assist in the recognition of words?
38. Do the illustrations help the child determine the identity of the speaker whose words are found in the text?
39. Do the illustrations supplement the text without completely stealing the verbal content (i.e., without making the words superfluous)?
40. Are the illustrations expressive of mood as well as of thought and action?
41. Do the illustrations attract the child by use of color?
42. Do the illustrations emphasize common elements in the culture?

Teaching Materials:

43. Do the accompanying materials provide for the assessment of readiness for new learnings?
44. Do they provide exercises for the development of readiness?
45. Do they teach the use of the book (such as the reading of the table of contents)?
46. Do they put the burden of active learning on the child, by such means as: (*a*) asking for picture interpretation, (*b*) asking for generalization and induction, (*c*) asking comprehension questions which require thought rather than finding the place that gives the answer verbatim?
47. Do the teaching materials establish quick recognition of a word at

sight as well as the recognition of letters in new words?
48. Are there cards and charts which provide practice in word, phrase, and sentence recognition outside the book itself, so that sheer memorization of pages does not subvert the learning program?
49. Do the teaching materials provide for the assessment of the child's needs and achievement?
50. Do they provide for silent as well as oral reading?
51. Do they provide for skimming exercise ("Find the place that tells. . . .")?
52. Do they encourage children to think in many ways about the material they read (*a*) by setting a question before they read and (*b*) by setting questions and related activities after they read?
53. Are there suggestions for children who are slow to learn and for children who learn rapidly?
54. Do writing, speaking, and listening activities support the reading program?
55. Are discussions and other activities suggested for emphasis upon incidental learnings in the content fields?
56. Are the learnings carefully built, one upon another?
57. Is the skills-development program of the first-grade materials as broadly conceived as that for the higher levels (for growth in word form, word meaning, comprehension, interpretation, and study skills)?
58. Are skills taught rather than merely tested?
59. Is the child given opportunities for self-evaluation?
60. Is the teacher guided in how to observe individual child behavior as well as to test for growth?
61. Are the tests broadly conceived, not simply limited to letter pronunciation or word-calling?
62. Are directions to the pupil which he is to read to himself written in words he can understand, and are they expressed clearly?
63. Are directions to the teacher sufficiently simple, clear, detailed, and even, in some cases, illustrated by pictures or diagrams so that the novice can follow them?
64. Are additional teaching aids which are not provided but are suggested or required in connection with activities in the learning program easily and cheaply available wherever the books are likely to be used?

BASAL READERS

Basal readers are designed to allow teachers to develop many different skills on successive levels of difficulty through the use of a single selection. The plan is to provide efficiency and to initiate new skills.[44] In these readers, the vocabulary may be developed gradually, the difficulty being minimized so that skills may be developed unhampered. Exercises and teaching sequences are ordinarily indicated in the teacher's manual. These may be modifiable for special needs or used like one-a-day vitamins.

The assumption is that the exposure to topics, kinds of literature, styles of writing, skills, and so forth presented in the readers will be supplemented by other reading activities. The idea is not to put the child into the most difficult book possible but to keep him developing and practicing. Basal readers, then, can be used as part of a reading program, to orient children in a variety of interests, styles, and reading problems and to prevent the loss of skills through neglect. They are, without doubt, the most comprehensive program yet developed, if the manuals and other teaching aids are used as intended.

For some time, authors of basal readers assumed that the reading skills needed in the content fields would be dealt with in those fields, but, increasingly, the basal fare has included types of material encountered in the content fields—sometimes in the basal reader itself, sometimes in workbook exercises, and sometimes in co-basal texts devoted to the content fields.

Different ability levels are recognized in separate lesson plans, separate recommendations for gifted or slow students, or separate books for different "tracks."

The contents of basal readers have been altered in response to the accusations of "middle-class values." While some reader series are clearly aimed at suburbia, others are multi-ethnic or urban. Some affluent members of minority groups have yet to see themselves in multi-ethnic readers.

The notion of balance as represented in basal readers is a quite varied one. Some of the teaching programs lean heavily upon memorization, giving the child little need to think for himself. Some teach more phonics rules than are useful. Some are strongly phonetic in the initial stages, often using only regularly sounded words at first. Others are concerned with using the children's own language and a sentence approach. In some, the emphasis upon

---

44. *Ibid.*, pp. 58-67.

sound systems makes any attempt at comprehension seem artificial and strained. Some eliminate pictures in the text, fearing to detract from word analysis; others eliminate them in the workbook for the same reason, presenting pictures in the text as in children's books. The formats may differ; there may be one or more than one book for each grade; they may be bound in hard or soft covers; and they may be reusable or consumable books.

The educator who chooses a basal reader these days must be ready to meet challenges to his own concept of reading, for the selection is broad and each package is full of surprises.

The workbook and manual exercises from different levels of the series can be used for remedial purposes, as the readiness materials and the tests can be used for diagnosis.

EASY BOOKS OF GRADED DIFFICULTY

Today there are hundreds of easy books for children for which difficulty levels and interest appeal have been established. They have numerous uses in a balanced reading program: supplementary reading, research on a special topic, independent selection, a basis for individual conference, speed reading for a relatively undemanding purpose, creative reaction, and following directions (how-to-do-it type books).

The problem of selection involves four major considerations: (*a*) suitability of the topic to the interests of a class; (*b*) difficulty appropriate to the reading levels in a class (independent level, not struggle level); (*c*) worth in literary quality; and (*d*) worth in terms of the behaviors depicted. A number of educational associations and school systems have developed lists of recommended books to make the task of selection less formidable.

CHARTS

Charts made by the teacher with the help of the children can be used to record experiences or to remind children of rules learned, procedures to follow, word meanings, and so on.

Commercially produced charts come in a large variety, some providing pictures of environments (farm, store, city street, woodland) as bases for comparison, vocabulary development, classification, or developing sequential relationships. Illustrations based upon stories are useful for recall and for language expression.

Selection of commercial charts should be guided by the background of the children taught and by the concepts, abilities, and attitudes they bring to the study of the material. Phonics charts should be reviewed for their agreement with linguistic principles, the over-all program, and the newer findings on the relative usefulness of phonics rules.[45]

WORKBOOKS

While basal reader workbooks tend to be comprehensive in their purposes, some other types of exercise books stress one or a few special skills at successively higher levels of difficulty. Those which deal with the content fields can supplement a story-type reading emphasis. A child who needs special exercise in getting the main idea either can use an exercise book devoted to this one skill or can be directed to select the main-idea question from each lesson.

Workbooks accompanying basal readers are not programed for completely independent pupil progress, for they assume that the teacher has introduced certain skills in the basal lesson plans. In the main, their contents are designed to extend meanings or skills initiated in a group situation and to determine the child's ability to work by himself. A balanced program should include some independent work to provide opportunity for the child to identify the nature of his errors and to help plan his own program of improvement.

Some children do not need all the skills practice provided in a workbook of a given reader series. Others need more of one kind than another. Still others profit by using parts of a workbook exercise over a period of days, the culmination being the successful completion of the workbook page as a review or test. Balance for some children would be independent exploration beyond the page, such as finding examples in other materials to which the same skill may be applied. Teachers who do not use workbooks should still

---

45. Theodore Clymer, "The Utility of Phonic Generalizations in the Primary Grades," *Reading Teacher*, XVI (January, 1963), 252-58; Mildred Hart Bailey, "The Utility of Phonic Generalizations in Grades One through Six," *Reading Teacher*, XX (February, 1967), 413-18; Robert Emans, "The Usefulness of Phonic Generalizations above the Primary Grades," *Reading Teacher*, XX (February, 1967), 419-25.

insist upon independent skills follow-up, and they should not assume that any skill has been maximally explored by the able child who already knows what others are still learning.

PROGRAMED MATERIALS

Programed materials today come in three popular forms for use in a balanced program: material to be inserted into a mechanical device, material on separate cards, and material in the form of a workbook, booklet, or book.

The educator selecting these materials with an eye to balance must consider a number of differences in the content as well as in the form. Some programs are intended as developmental programs and must be compared with others for comprehensiveness in skills development as well as for the care with which the difficulty is increased from step to step. If the educator chooses a less comprehensive program, he must be prepared to offer the neglected learnings through another medium.

Some programs begin with a phonics approach, synthesizing elements until sentences of regularly formed words can be achieved. Some offer routine practice rather than develop insight and, therefore, require the guidance of the teacher to help the children develop the meanings of the processes through which they go.

The buyer must further decide for which children the material is suitable: whether it allows for skipping steps if the child comprehends quickly; whether it takes steps small enough for the child who grasps ideas slowly; whether it will hold a child's interest through its content, format, and gadget-appeal; whether written responses reinforce the learning; whether the careless child has immediate notification of his error and the reason for it.

Many of the programed materials are admirable for supplementary reading. Some introduce children to parts of stories which they might like to read in their entirety. Some provide thought-provoking and interesting questions requiring more than robot response and explanations of the worth of children's choices of answers. Some develop a particular area of skill to an extent that would not be possible in a teacher-led balanced program. The buyer must decide whether the material is to be used to introduce a skill, with further practice in it to be offered deliberately through other class activities, or whether the material is to be used in the follow-up and maintenance of skills previously developed with the teacher.

In a balanced program, the teacher is more than a custodian of boxes, machinery, and booklets; and the amount of time children spend in such activity is not uniform.

It would be unfortunate to reject such material because some children cheat themselves with the answer key or because some teachers use it as an opportunity for a needed rest. It would be equally unfortunate to value it as a score-centered, labor-saving device. What it demands of the child, what it contributes to the acquisition of skills and of ideas, the degree to which it commands the child's attention, the author's grasp of the reading and learning processes—these considerations should be paramount.

GAMES AND DEVICES

Numerous games and devices are available for independent or unsupervised group use. Granted that they are probably enticing and have a certain degree of durability and physical attractiveness, screening them for a balanced reading program requires analysis of the skills which they promote and the level of difficulty they represent. If the skills program already provides amply for the skill exercised, the buyer may turn to another type of purchase, If, however, this is not the case, he must still evaluate the material's suitability in terms of level and purpose.

Some material which might be rejected as a means to provide practice before a learning has been firmly established might be quite acceptable as reinforcement at a later stage of learning. A game played too long without substitution of new items in it can lead to overlearning of something known too well already. But, if children can add new items, the value of the game is extended. Likewise, some material might be rejected because it permits extensive practice of error without correction or might be accepted if a child who can make the corrections is teamed with a learner who cannot make them unaided.

One may ask how much of the child's time such practice deserves and what other parts of the reading program compensate for having limited the practice to a single facet of reading skill. Another good question is whether the time involved in the game is largely time devoted to actual reading or mainly to manipulation.

TAPES AND WORKSHEETS

The involvement of children with tape recorders and worksheets reminds one of Laocoön and the python. They could not be more captive, hearing and seeing and saying and writing, with no senses left to think about recess. Intensive learning experiences and concentrated reviews are well served by these media. The evidence on the worksheet is the child's demonstration of accomplishment and, in part, of his motivation. Groups can cluster in a corner of the room for taped work while the teacher instructs other children. For the child of foreign-language background, the tapes provide a model of the spoken English language. Special tapes contain spaced content, giving the child an opportunity to repeat or reply.

The possibilities for the use of the tape recorder are numerous. The only question is whether teachers are wise enough to make the tape experience a constructive part of a balanced program.

FILMS AND FILMSTRIPS

Films and filmstrips have a variety of roles in the balanced reading program. They may be used in (*a*) building background for a story or unit of stories; (*b*) reviewing a story already read, children commenting; (*c*) portraying a different story before it is read; (*d*) providing skill exercise or skill review; (*e*) identifying points of need in word analysis; or (*f*) controlling and speeding the reading.

The quality of these materials is so uneven and the purposes are so varied that choices must be made with care. Users concerned with balance should avoid having all children exposed to films or filmstrips a given number of minutes every week or day, regardless of the content and value of the exposure to them. The buyer needs to determine the level of difficulty and the kind of contribution he wants made to his reading program and then see whether these media are the answer. Even though another kind of material may be equally effective, he may consider using films or filmstrips as relief from the monotony of another type of presentation.

Films accompanied by booklets give the child background for his reading and indicate materials to be read. As this combination offers a visual and sometimes an auditory stimulus, they have some of the same advantages found in the tape-worksheet combination.

LITERATURE SERIES OR SETS

Some educators think of a balanced program as being partly "reading instruction" and partly "literature reading." To others, literature may be considered the heart of the reading program. Still others use anthologies as supplementary free reading or as a source of stories for special occasions.

A unit of study of historical figures, inventors, or explorers may draw upon a collection of biographies. Momentary preference of future occupation or heroic role can determine a child's choice of biography. The child who has not tied his ambition to anything but growing may be inspired by an example in such a book. Such books may be used for easy supplementary reading or challenging guided reading, as the need is seen.

TRADE BOOKS

The reading of trade books (children's literature) is one of the goals of the reading program. So is the acquisition of the ability to select books for oneself. Balanced development includes the investigation of topics, reading for pleasure, exploring varied types of literature, experiencing various styles of authorship with increasing awareness of literary quality and human values, observing human behavior, and interpreting and evaluating such behavior in varied circumstances.

If a child comes from a home in which book reading is a major pastime, balance for him may mean less book reading at school and more stress upon skills development and book selection. If a child has no time to read at home and little encouragement to be a reader, the school diet should desirably compensate for the deprivation, and some effort to ease home conditions for reading should be made.

While it is easy to talk about such adjustments of the school's program for each child, it is not easy to make them wisely or at all if a school policy on class organization or a teacher's preference for a currently popular program creates a barrier.

MAGAZINES

The habit of magazine reading can have its beginning in the

classroom if no beginning has been made in the home. Magazines can be used for casual exploration or for instruction. Children can learn to read the varieties of literary form in them and to find the way to favorite departments.

The achievement of balance is, to a certain extent, frustrated when only one magazine is available, for this provides examples of only one organization and content; but certainly one is better than none.

Individual differences are partly met by separate editions of the same magazine for readers at different levels or for retarded readers. Some magazines for children include questions on content, thus fostering some of the same comprehension skills which are being developed elsewhere in the school program.

NEWSPAPERS

Newspapers written especially for children prepare the child for adult newspaper reading in the same way that children's magazines prepare them for adult magazine reading. Through reading them a habit is formed. Different editions within the same classroom are suited to the children's different reading levels, and news can be shared, with genuine audience listening, because not all are reading exactly the same thing.

Desirably, as children are able to read them, adult newspapers should be introduced and compared for their different treatment of content.

ENVIRONMENTAL MATERIAL

Signs, ads, letters, and the like which the child sees around him and brings to or reports about at school can be employed as examples of usage, vocabulary, propaganda, and interpretation. A balanced program will include a child's own creative responses to such messages, in order to confirm his understanding of their purpose and character.

REFERENCE MATERIAL

Reference material, which starts with the kindergarten teacher's picture file, soon becomes a wealth of references, so frequently useful that duplicate copies are commonly present in classrooms that can afford them. Some of these references are accompanied by booklets on their use and even by exercises to give experience in kinds of investigation.

It is possible now to have encyclopedias or dictionaries for the child who leans mainly upon pictures, the child who reads well in his class, and the child who reads better than the teacher. Even an adult dictionary may be kept in a classroom for its special information on word origins.

DIAGNOSTIC AND EVALUATIVE MATERIAL

Achieving balanced reading development can be assisted now through the use of early and continuous information on the child's reading status. Diagnostic tests and inventories make it possible for the teacher to identify areas of weakness and strength at the beginning of a school year. This information, combined with that obtained from the previous teacher's records and from interviews with her, form the basis for planning a suitable program. Diagnosis now goes beyond the discovery of whether or not the child recognizes words, understands what he reads, and reads with typical speed and accuracy to the identification of some of the reasons why he may not do so. At one time, it was good enough for the teacher to know the right answer as found in the teacher's edition. Now she must know why it is right and help the child discover the reasons why it is right.

Current Innovations and the Concept of Balance

Current innovations in reading programs are difficult to evaluate for balance. There are many promotional studies to persuade the educator and fewer truly evaluative studies to help him make a judgment. Even the evaluative studies, however, have not yet met the teacher's need, for they tend to present mean differences instead of noting the success and reaction of types of individuals, and they also tend to test one program against another instead of determining the most effective combination of programs. At the present time, we know that many types of programs have value.[46]

46. Reports on the U.S. Office of Education's co-operative studies of twenty-seven programs are discussed in the *Reading Teacher*, XIX (May, 1966), 563-675, and XX (October, 1966), 6-42.

Programs tend to be composed of favorable and unfavorable elements. For example, positive values in "i.t.a." (initial teaching alphabet) are the immediate use of written expression and the rapid learning of a regular phonetic system. Possible negative features are (a) the dictation of the sounds associated with a letter instead of their discovery by the child; (b) representation of the language as regular; (c) the longer tolerance of the child's own pronunciation in the transition to "book English"; (d) the delay of experience with the true configuration of many words (larj for large); (e) the lack of support in the environment; and (f) the need finally to substitute the traditional orthography. Definitive studies which succeed in isolating the effect of the special feature, apart from all the features two programs may have in common, are still to be reported.

Certainly, if the future is to be at all like the past decade with respect to trials and resurrections, the future is uncertain. But, on the assumption that educators will appreciate the value of balance for the individual, this chapter will proceed to consider the probable results of current innovations for different types of individuals.

SPECIAL PHONICS PROGRAMS

Programs which begin with the sounds of letters have had a vigorous growth in recent years. They appeared as an answer to basal reader programs which did not yield immediate success in sounding out words. School systems either used them exclusively or added them to their established programs.

From the linguistic standpoint, these phonics programs, in assigning single letters a certain sound, misrepresent the nature of the language, because very few letters in English spelling consistently represent the same sound, and the consonants cannot be sounded without the addition of a vowel sound.

When used alone, a phonics program gives the child the impression that English is regularly spelled and that all words can be sounded out, that reading is sounding and that once the symbols are decoded into sound the reading is accomplished.

Some children may have difficulty learning to read by this one approach because of its heavy reliance upon auditory discrimination. The difficulty may be pronounced for a child of foreign-language background, a child with a hearing loss, a child who does not hear the differences among some English consonants and vowels (more often a boy than a girl and often a child of some special dialect of English).

The child who knows from home and school experiences that reading is a way of getting meanings, thinking about them, and using the resultant ideas and who has good auditory discrimination and a good speaking vocabulary in English may do well with this phonics beginning. Sooner or later, however, with loss in the establishment of sight words in the meantime, he must learn instant recognition of whole words which are exceptions to the rules of spelling and which are, unfortunately, numerous in the language of children. And here, again, is a snag: with concentration on phonics, it is some time before the child can read the language of children like himself.

The retarded reader who has good auditory discrimination and a store of sight words but has not learned to sound out words may also do well in a phonics program.

We shall never know, but we can wonder whether these phonics programs would ever have gained extensive use had basal reader authors (*a*) put their phonics programs into their books as well as their manuals, (*b*) let the sound program parallel the sight program from the very beginning, (*c*) introduced vowels and consonants in an order that produced the largest number of words, (*d*) given as much attention to using phonics as to teaching it, and (*e*) used a method of group instruction which demanded continuous response from every child. If basal reader authors do this in the future, however, we may see whether extrinsic phonics programs survive.

LANGUAGE-ARTS APPROACH

The language-arts approach, beginning with the child's own language, which he dictates, sees written by the teacher, and later writes and reads, rates high in motivation and in meaningfulness. The learning itself is impressive because the child is the initiator of the language, and his experience with the words is multisensory (in other words, demanding great attention).

If the child's language resembles "book English," the words he learns can be useful in the reading of commercial materials. However, the child who is fluent in English, who enunciates well and has good hand-eye co-ordination, may do well in a language-arts approach. The child with a behavior problem may do well if his great need is to be involved and to be the center of attention.

The child whose language does not resemble "book English" cannot get full value from this approach unless "book English" is added to his spoken vocabulary. The child of foreign background needs a speech-readiness program prior to this approach, for he must learn the meanings of the spoken words of English and the sentence patterns.

The child who wants to know why these words say what they do, who wants the answer to the phonics riddle and is ready for it, may be uneasy if the approach does not involve or is not paralleled by a phonics approach.

The task of comprehending the meaning that a strange author intends to convey receives less attention, and the child who does not easily grasp the ideas others express may fail to comprehend the author's meaning. The exclusive use of the language-arts approach in beginning reading has contributed useful ideas for the construction of a program which balances language-arts with other desirable activities.

INDIVIDUALIZED PROGRAMS

Individualized reading programs grew out of the wealth of children's literature, the abundance of materials for independent study, and the desire to serve the individual directly with respect to reading preferences, needs, and pace. Schools in which three instructional groups marked the upper limit of individualization gave impetus to the movement. In the new programs, the child was getting help in reading his choice of material, whereas, in the "three-group" organization, the teacher was too much occupied with instructional groups to help with independent reading activities. The individual conference, though rare as compared with daily group encounters, made the child know that the reading program was his and made the teacher know some of the child's strengths and needs. Special-needs grouping was efficient in that the teacher offered only what she knew was needed to the children who needed it.

The child who is well motivated and self-propelling, who can concentrate for extended periods without the teacher's help, may adjust well to an individualized program. It is tailor-made for the child whose personal problems the teacher knows and whom the teacher guides in the selection of content which will give him insight.

However, it can be frustrating to the child who is overly dependent or to the child who needs more rather than less of the teacher's time. The child who cannot sit still unless the scenery is changing or unless the teacher has given him a specific task and deadline may not stay with any material long enough to profit by it.

One of the views most distressing to this author is that which holds that only the top group or, at best, the top and intermediate groups of children should have experiences of the kind emphasized in these programs. If among the goals of reading are the development of independence and of the ability to make choices and the fostering of sharing the delights of reading with an interested audience, from whom should the apprenticeship be withheld? And, if there is, indeed, more rather than less for a child to learn as he becomes a more able reader, why should instruction be given less time as his ability to read increases? Promising developments in the direction of balance are to be noted in increased provisions for (*a*) independent reading (and help in it); (*b*) individual conferences; (*c*) selected and whole-class activities; and (*d*) types of grouping which recognize instructional levels, special needs, research tasks, special interests, and team organization for mutual help or tutoring.

LINGUISTIC APPROACHES

Those linguistic approaches which start with sounds and proceed to word, phrase, and sentence patterns may show some results that resemble those of the phonics programs. The regularity of words in some is extreme, requiring the rhyming of every word in a sentence, a characteristic which detracts from comprehension because it is both fascinating and unnatural.

Other linguistic approaches feature the repetition of basic sentence types with substitution of words within sentences. This is in the tradition of ear and speech training for foreign-language speakers, which may have its use for children in this country. To the extent that a basic sentence type is repeated without relief, the language lacks its natural variety. Thus, in the main, linguistic programs are chiefly interested in form; representations of meaning tend to be contrived. The child who has achieved good visual and auditory discrimination and who brings much experience to reading, who has heard stories in the natural langauge and who knows that all words are not regularly spelled and rhymed, may enjoy a linguistic approach without harm to his conception of reading or loss of a central desire for meaning.

"Words in Color" and "i.t.a.," two programs which provide associations which must later be withdrawn, may ultimately be seen as techniques to be used with children who reject the direct attack on the symbols of English.

Final Statement

The lesson of history (including the history of reading programs) seems clear. To accept one embodiment of an idea as the best expression of it may do the idea a disservice. To accept one embodiment of a "new" idea as a suitable substitute for all that other programs offer is probably to mistake a new part for the whole and to invite a harmful imbalance. Blind men who have felt a part of the elephant are certain of the value of their discoveries; but, if they are concerned with truth, they will have to admit the possible value of the discoveries of others. What if they tried to put this elephant together?

Perhaps it is possible to have a sequential program, based upon the natural language of children and proceeding into all types of material, and to have it supported throughout by language activities involving both creative expression and linguistic knowledge. Readiness could promote the building of concepts, the development of subskills of word analysis and form recognition, and the exploration of the possibilities in language and literature. Deliberate provision of exercise in different thought processes could be made. The story method, sentence method, word method, and letter method, all of which are appropriate to the language, could be used simultaneously.

The child could do some of the thinking. He might think about (*a*) what the shape of a letter means to *him*, (*b*) what two pictures show and what the print must "say" (bat, cat), and (*c*) what are the common elements that *he* sees and hears and what the letters must therefore "say." He might also think about the steps *he* has just taken to learn something and how *he* can record this learning and apply the technique to other unknowns. He could make firsthand discoveries of forms, patterns, meanings, interpretations, and uses. He could learn respect for the versatility in role and meaning of structure words and signal words.[47] Teachers themselves could learn.

They might avoid the logical pitfalls which endanger reading programs: the confusion in introducing words together that look alike, sound alike, or represent closely related things; the insistence upon sight before sound, consonants before vowels, phonics before meaning, reading before writing, and leaps from sentence meaning to paragraph meaning without consideration of sentence-to-sentence relationships.

Plans should be made first, with full cognizance of the kinds of individuals the programs must accommodate. The choice of materials should come second. And, throughout, the elephant should not be neglected. If "blind men" continue to explore, some day their hands may join.

47. McCullough, "Linguistics, Psychology, and the Teaching of Reading," *op. cit.*

CHAPTER X

Professional Training of Reading Personnel

MARY C. AUSTIN

Impetus for Change

The past decade has witnessed extensive inquiries into the education of teachers, including those in the field of reading. Along with these probings have come recommendations for important changes in teacher preparation. Nation-wide, there have been several conditions which have provided the impetus for re-evaluation and innovation in the professional training of reading personnel.

First among these is the increase in the number and in the range of abilities of children and youth. Reports reveal that school enrolment is larger not only because of general population expansion but also because students are remaining in school longer. This increase in enrolment is now found in colleges and universities as well as in elementary and secondary schools. In 1960, total registration for credit in institutions of higher learning was 3,610,000.[1] The United States Office of Education estimated that in the year 1966-67 the number of students matriculating in colleges and universities was 6,000,000.[2]

Compulsory school attendance laws, child labor statutes, civil rights legislation, and antipoverty programs are factors which have strengthened the holding power of the school and which also have resulted in greater heterogeneity of the school population. Accordingly, educators have recognized the need to adjust instruction to a wide variety of individual differences. A greater understanding of child growth and development, a more comprehensive definition

---

1. Earl V. Pullias, "Higher Education in Modern Society," *Improving College and University Teaching,* XII (Spring, 1964), 113-14.

2. "Education in 1966," *School and Society,* XCIV (December 24, 1966), 468-69.

of the reading process, and an interdisciplinary approach to reading instruction have contributed to improved techniques for helping each child mature in reading.

A second factor is the mobility of population of the United States, which has created special problems for schools. Within one metropolitan region may be found vast differences in educational needs, interests, values, and attributes of students. Readiness for reading in a first-grade classroom in an inner-city school is far different from that of first-graders in a suburban area. Nation-wide, the schools must be prepared to meet the needs of the American family on the move. Not only must common elements in the curriculum be defined so there can be continuity of school experiences as students move from one community to another but basic communication skills should be incorporated into the curriculum. Teacher-training institutions need to expand instruction beyond the concerns which confront one community or stratum. These institutions should take into account the multiple forces that influence the teaching-learning process.

Third, human knowledge has broadened so dramatically during the present decade that greater reading skill and efficiency are needed to cope with this information and to utilize it. No longer can the elementary school alone bear the responsibility for total reading instruction. Indeed, the trend for some time has been toward a continuation of reading instruction throughout secondary-school and adult levels, resulting in an extension and refinement of reading skills, attitudes, and habits. The complexity, vastness, and nature of the new knowledge have negated the possibility of grasping it merely as a collection of memorized basic facts. Literal comprehension is insufficient. Emphasis upon methods of inquiry and discovery, problematic approaches, and investigations of the fundamental structure of subject matter have underscored the importance of critical and creative reading as essential components of the reading program. In short, attention must be devoted to helping pupils learn to learn.

Fourth, studies in teacher education have been made by research teams and by college and university faculties, all of which have suggested changes. Notable among the reports of the sixties are those of Conant and the Harvard-Carnegie reading studies, which will be discussed later.

Fifth, funds have become increasingly available for studies of teacher education. Both the federal government and the foundations have increased their support for education. The Ford Foundation has supported experiments in teaching and learning with millions of dollars. The Carnegie Corporation has recognized reading as one of the most controversial areas in elementary and secondary education. Therefore, support has been given for conferences and training programs as well as for studies of the education of teachers of reading, of methods for teaching beginning reading, and of research in reading and its influence on practice.

Since 1964, the federal government has subsidized institutes during the summer for teachers of English and reading. The Higher Education Act of 1965 has provided university tuition for career teachers and teacher interns in programs stressing the sociology of poverty and investigating ways to improve instruction for culturally deprived students.

Sixth, state departments of education have continued to strengthen standards for certifying teachers, especially for higher-level or permanent certificates.[3] However, neither certification on a nationwide basis nor state reciprocity has been fully realized.

Seventh, research has been initiated to determine the beliefs and practices of reading teachers,[4] and a number of studies, to be discussed later, have explored the knowledge possessed about specific aspects of teaching reading.

Teacher Preparation

STUDIES RELATING TO TEACHER COMPETENCE

Preservice education.—Attention has been focused by national

---

3. Donald L. Barnes and Charles D. Shipman, "Changing Patterns in State Requirements for Teacher Certification," *Clearing House*, XXXVI (November, 1961), 158-60.

4. James Bryant Conant, *The Education of American Teachers* (New York: McGraw-Hill Book Co., 1963); Mary C. Austin, Coleman Morrison, et al., *The Torch Lighters: Tomorrow's Teachers of Reading* (Cambridge: Graduate School of Education, Harvard University, 1961); Mary C. Austin and Coleman Morrison, *The First R: The Harvard Report on Reading in Elementary Schools* (New York: Macmillan Co., 1963).

surveys on the depth of preparation of teachers in general and of reading teachers in particular. Conant, who conducted a two-year study of the education of elementary and secondary teachers, reported a diversity of opinion and practice in institutions of higher learning.[5] He found disagreement on many aspects of the programs for prospective teachers. He made twenty-seven recommendations calling for drastic changes in teacher preparation. In the teaching of reading, Conant suggested a minimum of three semester hours for all elementary-school teachers and twice that amount for teachers of kindergarten and the lower three grades. The additional hours for teachers of young children would deal primarily with the identification and correction of reading problems.

The first Harvard-Carnegie reading study explored the preservice education of prospective teachers of reading.[6] It was concerned primarily with a survey of current practices in undergraduate collegiate programs throughout the United States during the academic year 1959-60. Data were obtained from 371 four-year institutions of higher learning by questionnaires and from 74 colleges and universities visited in a field study. During the visits, an examination of curriculums and observations of college reading-methods classes and of student-teaching situations suggested that many teachers-to-be were not being prepared sufficiently well to teach children to read. One reason for this shortcoming was found in the actual content of the reading-methods courses, which focused upon the teaching of reading in the primary grades to the neglect of upper-grade instruction. Typically, too, the courses were conducted by traditional lecture approaches which required passive listening on the part of the students.

The report also drew attention to the discrepancy between theories encountered in college classes and practices in student-teaching centers. Whereas college instructors emphasized the need for diagnostic teaching which would lead to greater individualization of instruction according to pupil needs, students had little opportunity to do such teaching during their preservice classroom experiences.

5. Conant, *op. cit.*

6. Austin, Morrison, *et al.*, *The Torch Lighters, op. cit.*

Another weakness of teacher-preparation programs was attributed to the fact that, of the 371 responding institutions in the questionnaire study, only 100 indicated that a secondary reading-methods course was offered to undergraduates and, of these, only 28 made such a course a requirement.

The authors of *The Torch Lighters* proposed twenty-two recommendations, mainly concerned with the content of college reading courses, pertinent student-teaching practices, other curriculum offerings, and administrative policies. Regarding preservice education, it was recommended that class time devoted to reading instruction, whether reading was taught as a separate course or integrated with the language arts, be equivalent to at least three semester hours for all prospective elementary- and secondary-school teachers and that senior faculty members with special competence in the field of reading play a more active role in the instruction of undergraduates. A recommendation was made also that content and instructional procedures appropriate for upper grades receive more attention. At the administrative level, it was suggested that an in-service program or college course in reading instruction be designed specifically for principals, supervisors, and co-operating teachers.

Practices and opinions of educators.—The report on the initial preparation of teachers was followed by the second Harvard-Carnegie reading study, which surveyed the content, conduct, and practices in elementary-level reading programs in 1,023 school systems in the United States in 1961-62.[7] Data were gathered by means of questionnaires completed by administrators, supervisors, and teachers and from field visits in 65 school systems. Interviews and observations of two thousand teachers revealed that their college preparation in reading had been seriously deficient. Particularly, teachers were using word-recognition drills which contributed to the neglect of word meanings, comprehension questions which stressed literal meanings of passages rather than more advanced skills of interpretation, oral reading activities of little value for diagnostic purposes or for stimulating pupil interests in reading, and grouping practices and materials which ignored individual differences. In ad-

7. Austin and Morrison, *The First R, op. cit.*

dition, teachers were failing to identify gifted or disabled readers, to develop skills needed in reading the content areas, and to provide broad personal reading experiences for students.

Forty-five recommendations were made in *The First R* for strengthening elementary-school reading programs. The report called upon educators to implement a broader concept of the reading process by initiating sequential programs for the development of such higher-level abilities as those involved in critical and creative reading. Because reading should pervade the entire curriculum, the authors proposed that teachers place greater emphasis upon reading and study skills unique to the content areas. These recommendations were intended in no way to minimize the importance of the rudimentary skills of word analysis. Rather, it was suggested that continued attention be directed to helping children develop proficiency in using a number of avenues to word attack, as opposed to relying solely upon phonics. Moreover, word-study activities should include attention not only to word-recognition techniques but also to vocabulary enrichment.

The "barbershop" style of oral reading was especially condemned in the Harvard-Carnegie report. More valuable forms of reading aloud were noted for diagnostic teaching purposes and for developing an appreciation of spoken language.

Small-group instruction in reading was approved as a means of taking pupil differences into account, particularly in situations in which pupils were permitted to cross grade lines with all reading materials. Classification of children into three stereotyped reading groups was, however, more common at elementary levels than would seem desirable from existing data on wide ranges of achievement. Inflexible grouping plans were opposed, whether they pertained to the number of reading groups within a classroom or to the prevailing practice of assigning a pupil to the "turtles" for his entire school career. Regardless of the type of organization used, flexible groups which depend upon the nature and purpose of the on-going activity should be instituted. But, once the groups have been established, instruction should reflect an awareness of the constellation of abilities which was responsible for the original separation of students.

Now that administrators and teachers are paying more than "lip-service" to the consideration of individual differences, pupils whose reading abilities deviate markedly from the grade norm are receiving greater recognition. Unfortunately, they are not identified in many schools until they are in the upper grades. For this reason, *The First R* advocated that both superior and poor readers be identified early in the primary grades and that, thereafter, able readers should be given opportunities to participate in reading activities which challenge and stimulate them, while children with reading disabilities should receive diagnostic and corrective attention through readily accessible, well-staffed, and well-equipped reading centers.

A major goal of school reading programs is the motivation and expansion of reading interests. Educators usually stress the importance of recreational and independent reading as a means of accomplishing this goal and as a way to accommodate individual differences within a program of group instruction. In view of the fact that teachers generally have failed to promote lifelong reading habits, the second Harvard-Carnegie report made a strong plea for use in the reading program of selected aspects of the individualized reading approach, namely, self-selection of reading materials, pupil-teacher conferences, and written anecdotal records of each student's progress.

Similarly, other nation-wide and local studies of instructional skills of classroom reading teachers have disclosed the necessity for compensatory programs to overcome certain weaknesses. Adams analyzed the degree of need felt by 268 Florida elementary-school teachers for learning about given aspects of the teaching of reading.[8] At least 90 per cent of the respondents expressed a "great need" or "some need" to learn about remedial and corrective reading, diagnosis and treatment of reading problems, and ways of meeting individual differences. These findings confirm those of the Harvard-Carnegie studies. They also suggest lack of confidence as well as competence on the part of teachers. If lack of confidence fosters uneasiness, the teachers' insecurity may be transmitted to the children and may account for negative, random, or meaningless responses in both developmental and corrective reading sessions.

8. Mary Lourita Adams, "Teachers' Instructional Needs in Teaching Reading," *Reading Teacher*, XVII (January, 1964), 260-64.

A survey of 52 school systems by Komarek to learn how the deficiencies of retarded readers were met revealed that classroom teachers were responsible for all of the help given to poor readers in 70 per cent of those systems.[9] Most of the teachers had received no training in determining reading retardation and had had no formal course work in the diagnosis and treatment of reading disabilities. Clearly, a dilemma exists: many teachers are fully aware of their inadequacies as they try to discharge the responsibilities which schools impose upon them, but they have not taken the initiative to remedy the situation. Nor can the school administrators be absolved completely of blame. They frequently have permitted unqualified personnel to work with disabled readers rather than abandon special programs when trained personnel were not available.

Both Brekke[10] and Leahy[11] reported an overemphasis on technical skills at the expense of purposeful, functional, creative, and analytical reading. Yet the Harvard-Carnegie studies, Farinella's study,[12] and others have pointed out that teachers lack knowledge of the technical skills of structural and phonic analysis which were deemed so vital by their own admission.

Inadequacies of teacher preparation in reading at the secondary level have also been reported in a number of studies. McGinnis' survey of 570 Michigan secondary teachers (1961) led her to conclude that these teachers were not providing reading instruction, nor were they prepared to do so.[13] Seventy secondary teachers

---

9. Henrietta Komarek, "In-Service Training To Help Teachers Meet the Needs of the Retarded Reader," in *The Underachiever in Reading* (Proceedings of the Annual Conference on Reading at the University of Chicago, "Supplementary Educational Monographs," No. 92 [Chicago: University of Chicago Press, 1962]), 162-66.

10. Gerald W. Brekke, "Actual and Recommended Allotments of Time for Reading," *Reading Teacher*, XVI (January, 1963), 234-37.

11. Mildred King Leahy, "The Stated Practices and Beliefs Concerning the Teaching of Reading of One Hundred Elementary School Teachers" (Ed.D., Columbia University, 1962), *Dissertation Abstracts*, XXIII (May, 1963), 4262.

12. John Thomas Farinella, "An Appraisal of Teacher Knowledge of Phonetic Analysis and Structural Analysis" (Ph.D., University of Connecticut, 1960), *Dissertation Abstracts*, XXI (January, 1961), 1805-6.

13. Dorothy J. McGinnis, "The Preparation and Responsibility of Secondary Teachers in the Field of Reading," *Reading Teacher*, XV (November, 1961), 92-97.

representing nine curriculum areas responded to Braam and Roehm's questionnaire.[14] While some 28 per cent had received formal training in teaching reading, neither this training nor in-service education appeared to help them identify important reading skills in their areas.

The studies by McGinnis and by Braam and Roehm lend strong support to the position that specific reading training of secondary teachers at the preservice level and on the job is a necessity. In actual practice, a formal reading program may not be considered an essential part of the high-school curriculum. Furthermore, if there is a reading teacher, he may be placed in the English department as a matter of expedience.

Simmons[15] and Applebee[16] have demonstrated the limitations involved in assigning the reading program entirely to the English department. In fact, limiting reading instruction to any single content area appears to be ineffectual and incompatible with the tenet that reading is an integral part of any subject that uses printed media.

In elementary schools, in which reading usually receives high priority, administrators also have expressed dissatisfaction with the quality of instruction. Results of two surveys of 640 public school administrators in a two-year period indicated that approximately 44 per cent of them agreed that the most effective method of teaching reading was not being utilized in their schools. While acknowledging that some methods were shaky, administrators placed a large share of the blame on teachers' training in colleges and on teachers' methods.[17]

As expected, teachers, administrators, and reading experts ap-

14. Leonard S. Braam and Marilyn A. Roehm, "Subject-Area Teachers' Familiarity with Reading Skills," *Journal of Developmental Reading*, VII (Spring, 1964), 188-96.

15. John S. Simmons, "Who Is Responsible: The Need for Qualified Supervision of Reading Programs," *English Journal*, LII (February, 1963), 86-88.

16. Roger K. Applebee, "National Study of High School English Programs: A Record of English Teaching Today," *English Journal*, LV (March, 1966), 273-81.

17. "Large Minority Is Not Satisfied with Methods of Teaching Reading," *Nation's Schools*, LXIX (March, 1962), 94; "Reading Methods Are Shaky, Most Schoolmen Admit," *Nation's Schools*, LXXIV (September, 1964), 76, 87

praised teaching proficiencies from diverse frames of reference. Lack of preparation and teacher inadequacies were the chief problems cited by 42 per cent of the administrators who took part in the Western Michigan study.[18] This was in contrast to the teachers, 1.7 per cent of whom felt that these inadequacies were major deterrents to good teaching practices. Thirty-seven per cent of the 549 elementary teachers maintained that the major problem related to reading was the development of basic reading skills. Not one of 54 administrators who participated in the survey considered this a problem. In this investigation, both administrators and teachers seemed to be concerned about the inadequacy of instruction but held diametrically opposite views regarding its causes.

Barton and Wilder's data showed contradictions in the outlooks of administrators, reading experts, and teachers.[19] About 80 per cent of the teachers considered themselves professionals, although they preferred to rely on basal readers, manuals, workbooks, and other material prepared by experts. Only 37 per cent of the experts and about 60 per cent of the principals adjudged elementary-school teaching to be a full profession, yet they wanted teachers to use basal readers and workbooks less and to concentrate on individualized approaches. Approximately 85 per cent of the teachers felt they should be free to select methods they deemed best for their situations, despite the fact that the great majority considered standard teaching materials either essential or of great importance. Only 58 per cent of the reading experts were inclined to grant freedom to teachers in the choice of methods used. Regrettably, the chasm between optimum and actual practices cannot be bridged until professional roles are defined and professional preparation is in accord with what is expected or what will be accepted.

PROVISIONS FOR TEACHER EDUCATION IN READING

Education in reading admittedly has its limitations, and some

18. Research Committee, Western Michigan Chapter of the International Reading Association, "Instructional Problems in Reading as Viewed by Teachers and Administrators," *Reading Teacher*, XIV (November, 1960), 75-80.

19. Allen H. Barton and David E. Wilder, "Research and Practice in the Teaching of Reading: A Progress Report," in *Innovation in Education*, ed. Matthew B. Miles (New York: Teachers College, Columbia University, 1964), 361-97.

teacher-training institutions have taken giant steps in revising their programs. Indeed, the momentum for change has increased during the sixties, bringing an unprecedented receptivity for new ideas. Although some of the following programs were designed to improve teacher education generally, the implications for reading are evident.

Undergraduate education.—Various programs which gained popularity during the past decade were attempts to ease the beginning teacher into the instructional environment while also taking into account the affective aspects of teaching. The Oregon program, for example, was designed to upgrade the quality of teacher preparation by providing a teaching internship for a full year before state certification. Subjective judgments by principals and supervising teachers who evaluated the program disclosed that intern teachers recognized individual differences and attempted to give differentiated instruction earlier than did traditionally trained first-year personnel.[20]

The Teacher Education Program initiated by twenty-nine Michigan school systems in conjunction with Central Michigan University featured a five-year program in which prospective teachers spent a semester in full-time school experience in each of their third, fourth, and fifth years. By the last semester, the interns, who were paid a portion of the teachers' salaries, assumed full teaching functions, with a reduced workload and under extensive supervision. The partnership arrangement between school and university resulted in the accessibility to schools of current techniques, information, and consultant services. The university, on the other hand, received "feedback" as to those features of its instructional program which were feasible in practice and those which needed modification.[21]

Intern teams, which merge the salient features of an internship and a team approach, became vehicles for teacher education in this decade also. In this approach, one or two university student-interns were assigned as junior staff members to a competent senior teacher,

---

20. William T. Ward and Joy Hills Gubser, "Developing the Teaching Internship Concept in Oregon," *Journal of Teacher Education*, XV (September, 1964), 252-61.

21. Kenneth E. White, "A Plan for Student Interns in Teaching Positions," *American School Board Journal*, CXLVI (April, 1963), 9-10.

who served as team leader and supervising teacher in the school situation. It was a joint endeavor of the university and the school district to prepare the senior teacher of the team for his supervisory task. In performing this task, the team leader became an associate of the university staff engaged in teacher education.[22] It is the association which deserves comment, because the prestige a "master teacher" gains from his recognition by the university may foster even deeper commitment to his important work.

Another version of team teaching is one in which the professor and his students compose a research-laboratory team. Fresno State College adopted this approach in its undergraduate reading-methods course, which was conducted in a public school. Under the guidance of their professor, college students helped pupils who needed individual assistance in reading. Following the tutorial sessions, reading skills were stressed in a presentation by the instructor; then student teams of four members described and evaluated their problems, plans, materials, and procedures as they related to the children they had tutored.[23]

In-service education.—Attention to future and first-year teachers is highly desired, but the realities of the professional preparation of those persons teaching in today's classrooms must be faced also. Industries have long provided on-the-job training to equip employees with skills peculiar to specialized business needs. Similarly, schools must tailor the continuing education of teachers to meet the specific needs of their unique student populations. In-service programs should not be limited to beginning teachers; they are of value to experienced teachers who are not cognizant of innovations and current procedures. Former teachers who are returning to the classroom will benefit from in-service education, and the entire staff will be able to acquaint themselves with new materials and new methods.

Whatever form the program takes, everything planned for teachers should be based upon problems cited by them and common to many and should be continuous, operating from year to year.

---

22. Norman J. Boyan, "The Intern Team as a Vehicle for Teacher Education," *Journal of Teacher Education*, XVI (March, 1965), 17-24.

23. Donald D. Durrell, "Training Teachers for Today's Reading Program," in *Reading as an Intellectual Activity* (International Reading Association Conference Proceedings, Vol. 8, New York, 1963), pp. 87-90.

The planning of in-service activities should be a co-operative venture, with teachers as active participants. Moreover, teachers should be released from their teaching duties to attend sessions or possibly be given monetary compensation if the programs are held after school hours.

Title I of the Elementary and Secondary Education Act has provided funds which have enabled school systems to initiate new approaches in the training of reading teachers.[24] Albany, Georgia, has designed a program in which fourteen classroom teachers, selected from both the elementary and the secondary levels, are prepared in diagnostic and corrective procedures in reading each semester. These teachers have no regular classroom obligations and spend half of each day in a reading center and clinic. Under the supervision of a competent staff representing many disciplines, the teachers learn how to administer and interpret achievement, intelligence, interest, attitude, and reading tests of all kinds. The participants are instructed in the use and evaluation of devices, instruments, books, and materials. The participants work with seriously handicapped readers in groups of two or three. Case studies of problem readers are made and discussed, and corrective procedures are determined for these children. For the remainder of the day, the teachers return to their home buildings, where, for three ninety-minute sessions weekly, they conduct remedial classes for groups of ten students. Two ninety-minute sessions weekly are devoted to developmental reading instruction for twenty students. Supervision by the clinic staff is provided in the school buildings as well as in the reading center.

These reading-teachers-in-training have opportunities to share their knowledge and techniques with their colleagues in faculty meetings and informal situations. After the completion of their semester of training, these teachers will serve as resource personnel to provide in-service education and help for their co-workers. However, the staff of the central clinic will also be available as consultants. The goal of the project is to have two trained reading teachers in each building. Whether this goal will be realized is dependent upon further funding, but this school system is assured of twenty-eight

---

24. Western Reserve University, "ESEA, Title I, Reading Survey, 1967" (unpublished report of field visit).

resource teachers as a result of the functioning of this program for one year.

Another Georgia school system has made use of the newer technology in teacher education. Decatur, Georgia, uses closed-circuit television to demonstrate developmental and corrective reading techniques. As many as 500 teachers can be accommodated in an auditorium to view demonstrations conducted by the staff in the well-equipped reading laboratory. The lessons are followed by discussions of the procedures by the clinicians. Though the clinic is small, the use of closed-circuit television enables many teachers to learn.

A new dimension has been added to the use of speakers from outside the school district for in-service education. Kenmore, New York, embarked upon a continuous program of this nature for secondary and elementary administrators and teachers in public and private schools. Designed to deal with specific topics relating to classroom teachers' needs, the content for the series of meetings was provided by outstanding speakers, panel discussions, and demonstrations. Minutes of the sessions and materials supplied by speakers were compiled in a booklet for participants. As part of the evaluation of the program, a locally constructed pre- and post-survey instrument was administered. Data were gathered concerning preservice preparation for reading and concerning areas in which help was desired (pre-) and gained (post-). Suggestions for improving the meetings were also gathered. The project deserves mention because it took into account the importance of continuity, of evaluation, and of serving the needs of the staff.

A procedure to enable many teachers to evaluate their own and others' teaching performances is the use of video-tape recordings. This technique is being employed in the training of prospective teachers as well as of experienced ones in universities and schools. Although research on this procedure has not appeared in the literature, there were several reports presented at the AERA (American Educational Research Association) Convention in 1967 which indicated the various uses of video-tape recordings in teacher education. It was reported that, in one instance, video-taped recordings were made of college classrooms in which prospective teachers gave short lessons, of student teachers in actual teaching situations, and of master teachers. The ready availability and permanent nature of the record of visual and oral performance are invaluable in assessing teacher competence and provide valuable feedback to the university faculty member as to how his theories have been translated into practical action.

In-service education practices are multitudinous, limited only by one's imagination and definition of the reading process. Mere presence at workshop sessions does not yield changes in classroom instruction per se. Benefits accrue to the extent that teachers actively experiment with new procedures and materials in their own classrooms.

Post-baccalaureate training.—The federal government has recognized the need for in-service education of school personnel by its extension of the National Defense Education Act to include reading. Since the summer of 1965, a great variety of programs has been offered to elementary- and secondary-level classroom teachers, reading specialists, supervisors, and co-ordinators. A notable feature of NDEA Institutes is their attention to various degrees of competency and to the needs of participants. Free tuition, college credit, and a minimum weekly stipend (tax free) have enabled many professionals to pursue advanced studies in reading. In-depth study in specialized areas of reading has expanded the horizons of thousands. Upon return to their school systems, many graduates of NDEA Institutes have served as resource persons, in-service leaders, supportive personnel for reading programs, or as classroom teachers. While objective evaluations of the influence of the total program are not available, common information suggests that the influence of the institutes has been great.

In contrast to the short-term NDEA Institutes, the U.S. Office of Education Teacher Fellowship Program provides subsidized graduate study for experienced teaching personnel for an academic year. During 1967-68, seven universities are offering programs in reading. Hopefully, the training thus provided will result in an addition of well-qualified persons to the reading profession.

STATE CERTIFICATION OF READING PERSONNEL

Each state has at its disposal a strong weapon to bring pressure to bear upon teacher-education institutions to strengthen their programs. In the past decade, general education and subject-matter course requirements have been increased.[25] Regulations relating specifically to reading have been enacted, although by less than one-third of the states.

In reviewing the requirements for teacher certification in reading, the lack of agreement among states concerning operational definitions of "reading teachers," "remedial reading personnel," and "reading consultants" is evident. Until state departments and professional associations establish criteria for these levels of competence and define the roles and responsibilities of reading personnel, data cannot be collated in a meaningful manner. Therefore, this section will be limited to information documented by Donalson's study.[26] He examined current requirements for reading certification of the fifty states for the general elementary teacher, for the elementary teacher certified in reading, and for the reading specialist. He found that fifteen states require a separate reading course as part of the professional education of the general elementary teacher. However, only six states make provision for the certification of the elementary or secondary teacher as a specially trained reading teacher. Common requirements identified among these states for the additional certification to teach reading are (a) the holding of the baccalaureate degree and the completion of courses beyond that degree, (b) certification as a regular classroom teacher, and (c) at least three years of successful teaching experience.

The reading specialist was certified in twelve states. Donalson included only those states the requirements of which specifically mentioned "a person prepared to perform duties associated with the detection and correction of reading difficulties and/or supervision of a remedial reading clinic." These states also have adopted approved professional training programs that include courses in the diagnosis and correction of reading disabilities and supervised laboratory practice with problem readers.

Completion of a course in the teaching of reading as a pre-

---

25. Barnes and Shipman, *op. cit.*

26. William R. Donalson, *A Comparison of Certification Requirements in Reading for the Reading Specialist, for the Elementary Teacher Certified in Reading, and for the General Elementary Teacher* (unpublished Master of Science thesis, Florida State University, 1965).

requisite for secondary-school certification is virtually non-existent. Indiana requires that persons teaching at the junior-high-school level (but not elementary- or high-school levels) have a reading course as part of their preservice education. Since October 1, 1964, Pennsylvania has required a course in basic reading instruction for the issuance of a provisional college certificate which is necessary to teach academic subjects at the secondary level.

Though state regulations regarding reading are desirable, the certification requirements must be realistic. One state has made it mandatory for reading specialists to complete twenty-one credit hours of course work in reading for certification. However, at present no university in the state offers more than fifteen formal course hours in reading. The need for communication between state boards of education and colleges and universities is obvious.

FUTURE DIRECTIONS

The next few years must bring a realistic revolution in teacher preparation. Ideally, every prospective teacher should receive an excellent undergraduate education, including a broad background in the liberal arts and sciences. This period of undergraduate education should be followed by two years of intensive preparation in which the teacher-to-be gains a thorough understanding of psychological and pedagogical theories of teaching and learning and participates in a public school internship of sufficient quality and duration to insure his success on the job.

Four years of preparation beyond high school, however, will hardly lead to vast improvements in teaching. The A.B. or B.S. program does not provide sufficient time to prepare elementary and secondary teachers adequately. Therefore, it may be essential that future teachers possess a Master of Arts in Teaching degree or its equivalent before state certification.

Some states now require a five-year program, covering three years of general academic preparation and two years of professional education. Although plans may differ, the latter two years should include courses in curriculum content and methodology and two semesters of apprentice teaching at a minimal salary under the direction of challenging master teachers.

Collegiate preparation in reading has been notably weak in the past, according to teachers themselves and those who supervise them. Studies of teachers' needs have been numerous in this decade, each contributing to an evaluation of our past accomplishments and pointing out areas to be strengthened by our future endeavors.

To ameliorate preservice deficiencies, college faculties must continue to re-evaluate present reading-course content and conduct. Furthermore, college reading personnel should work more closely with public schools in establishing optimal conditions for apprentice teaching. It is especially important that interns be assigned to highly competent co-operating teachers and that college reading instructors visit schools frequently enough to assess an intern's individual strengths and weaknesses. Certainly, a harmoniously functioning team can and should accomplish more in the preparation of classroom teachers than any individual member alone.

In the sixties, there has been an increased recognition on the part of local school systems of the need to provide continuing education for all teachers, whether beginning or experienced. Earlier in-service attempts have been both meager and mediocre. Fortunately, many schools have undertaken appropriate steps to reduce the effect of factors responsible for earlier failures by offering programs which are designed to augment the knowledge and competence of teachers. Such programs are being planned on a continuous, year-to-year basis; teachers are being released from school, or paid to attend meetings; participants are taking active roles in planning content; projects are being funded more adequately; and a greater variety of media, procedures, and commercially prepared or locally developed devices and materials are being employed. In-service education should be conducted for the total faculty, including administrative officers who are responsible for the guidance of their reading teachers and of their school aides. With the involvement of the entire staff in a program of continuing professional education, all will reap the benefits—the most important beneficiaries being the children.

One of the serious problems of the present decade is the shortage of qualified teachers of reading at all levels. Various means have been used, as explained earlier, to secure and retain competent school personnel. The rapid teacher turnover in some schools leaves them with inexperienced personnel. Better ways must be found to train teachers and to retain them so that in-service education pays the promised dividends.

Administrators and Reading

LEADERSHIP ROLE

Along with the chronic need for skilled teachers to work directly with children and youth is the equally chronic need for skilled administrative officers. The administrator is instrumental in creating a climate in which effective teaching and maximum learning take place. He is responsible for the implementation of broad curriculum objectives, as set forth by the central office, in accordance with the educational requirements of students in his building. To fulfil this function, he must know the strengths and weaknesses of his teachers, the interests and abilities of his student population, and the aspiration levels of his community.

As a leader who works closely with his staff, the principal must possess skill in human relations. The task of guiding a mature and competent staff is not easy. The administrator who can give the entire staff a feeling of importance and of being valuable contributors to the educational program is an effective public-relations person. Certainly, the explosion of knowledge and the changing times have increased the school principal's dependency upon resource personnel, such as the curriculum director, instructional supervisors, and consultants, to keep him abreast of current research and thinking. If his school system is fortunate in having a reading consultant, the principal must of necessity rely heavily upon the consultant's evaluation of research, new materials, and new techniques as consideration is given to the adoption of new practices. The administrator's leadership role is extensive, but his preparation may have barely touched upon areas in which he is expected to be more knowledgeable than his teachers.

Because the school principal is often the individual most likely to influence teaching habits, the Harvard-Carnegie study staff sought to determine the role filled by the principal in matters relating to the reading program. The function most frequently reported by 776 elementary-school administrators dealt with the selection, distribution, and use of materials. Conferences with teachers rated next in importance, mention having been made of assistance given to teachers in grouping children for instruction, selecting children for special programs, and offering advice to those whose pupils had specific reading problems. Principals also reported that the evaluation of test results or the actual administration of tests to groups of children or to individuals comprised a main responsibility.[27]

Aside from the principal's professional preparation, which may or may not have been adequate, the Harvard-Carnegie study made it perfectly clear that his many other duties precluded his acceptance of the direction of reading in his school.

PREPARATION FOR LEADERSHIP

Recognizing the expanded role of the principal, the Department of Elementary School Principals of the National Educational Association formulated guidelines in 1961 for an effective preparatory program for these school officers. Two years of graduate training were recommended. The suggested program of preparation included work in administration, supervision, curriculum (with special emphasis on reading instruction), psychological and social foundations, and an internship in administration.[28]

Although reading was specifically mentioned in the NEA guidelines, a survey of requirements for initial and advanced certification for elementary principals in fifty states revealed that a formal course in reading was not mandatory.[29] How effective can the principal be as a resource person or director of a reading program if his preparation has been limited to his own experience?

IN-SERVICE GROWTH

For the administrator, in-service growth and in-service education are synonymous. These do not merely involve courses for credit, because his increasing responsibility and his need for still greater competence demand a continuing education beyond formal college courses. Local school systems might provide administrative seminars for their staff and perhaps institute local leadership-training pro-

27. Austin and Morrison, *The First R, op. cit.*

28. Donald L. Schilson, "The Elementary Principal: Selection and Training," *American School Board Journal*, CL (April, 1965), 65-67.

29. Bill Bryant, "Academic and Professional Education Requirements for Elementary Administrative Credentials," *Journal of Teacher Education*, XVI (March, 1965), 74-76.

grams for the orientation of beginning leaders. These may take the form of a one-year series of high-level, purposeful, monthly sessions with department chairmen, consultants, and specialists within the district. Newly appointed administrators and supervisors can meet in a forum to explore mutual problems and opportunities within the school system, in reading as well as in other areas.

Both new and experienced administrators may profit from participation in a human-relations seminar, developed, perhaps, in cooperation with the National Training Laboratories staff of NEA, to help them learn about themselves and their relationships with their co-workers.[30]

Beginning and experienced administrative officers alike should participate in on-the-job workshops in reading along with their teachers. The old adage, "Don't do as I do, but as I say," is difficult to accept in the contemporary school situation. The administrator who is involved as a scholar and a teacher not only widens his academic horizons but also enhances his leadership qualities.

Reading Consultants

SCOPE OF OPERATIONS

The broadened scope of reading instruction in the past decade has led to the sharing of responsibility for reading instruction among various members of the school organization and, in some schools, to the creation of the position of reading consultant. At present, there is no clear-cut description of what may be expected of this individual. Indeed, the variety of titles assigned to the reading specialist may be indicative of present-day confusion. The consultant's responsibilities are equally diverse, ranging from the co-ordination of the reading programs (K–XII) in a large city system to the instruction of groups of disabled readers in a small one.

Although activities of the reading consultant may differ, his main goal is the improvement of reading instruction. In working toward this goal, he may serve in several capacities. Robinson and Rauch have identified as his major roles those of resource person, adviser, in-service leader, investigator, diagnostician, instructor, and

---

30. Helen M. Johnson, "Fostering Growth: Preservice and In-Service," *Educational Leadership*, XX (November, 1962), 97-100.

evaluator.[31] In short, the consultant is an organizer of programs, personnel, and materials.

Umans reported on the relationship, in a large city school system, of the reading consultant to the board of education, the operational superintendent, the school principal, the classroom teacher, the special reading teacher, teacher preparation, and parents.[32] The reading consultant informed the board of education of the goals, needs, and rationale of the reading program. The operational superintendent received a semiannual or annual summary about the local program. The reading consultant was requested by school principals to supply information about textbook use, independent reading practices, and teacher and pupil progress and to suggest new instructional materials or certain program changes.

In few instances does the reading consultant work alone. He must be keenly aware of and sensitive to the human-relations aspect of his position. The attitudes and emotions of those people with whom he works must be considered along with their professional competencies.

The relationship of the consultant to the classroom teacher will vary according to the teacher's professional preparation in reading, his experience, the quality of his teaching, and his attitude toward receiving assistance. Both individual and group in-service activities must often be arranged for and given by the consultant. In working with a special reading teacher, the consultant is supportive in carrying out the former's program and in fostering positive staff relations. In some situations, the reading consultant assumes leadership in preservice education by teaching reading courses in local colleges. Finally, through workshops and conferences, the consultant informs parents about the reading program. His success in communication with parents will be reflected frequently by active community support of the program. All persons involved in the reading program should feel that their participation is essential for the program's success.

31. H. Alan Robinson and Sidney J. Rauch, *Guiding the Reading Program: A Reading Consultant's Handbook* (Chicago: Science Research Associates, 1965), pp. 1-3.

32. Shelley Umans, "The Responsibility of the Reading Consultant," *Reading Teacher*, XII (September, 1963), 16-24.

In addition to the foregoing, many reading consultants recently have assumed still another role: they have worked with an administrative group in planning, developing, and implementing projects (*a*) to improve reading skills of disadvantaged youth, (*b*) to establish instructional and reading centers, (*c*) to undertake new approaches for teaching bilingual children, (*d*) to organize extensive in-service work for teachers in private and public schools, and (*e*) to purchase great quantities of reading materials and equipment.

The following section illuminates selected phases of the work of the consultant.

ILLUSTRATIVE ACTIVITIES

Specific help for teachers.—The reading consultant or supervisor can serve as a "teacher's teacher" in providing direct technical aid. Such assistance may take place on an individual basis as the specialist helps teachers in on-the-job teaching and learning situations. In three schools of one urban system, an experiment was conducted in Grades IV, V, and VI to determine the effect upon student reading achievement of frequent supervisory visits. Following these visits, which occurred periodically from November to May, the supervisor and the teacher met to plan for student needs, to discuss and demonstrate reading techniques, and to evaluate lessons. Analysis of pre- and post-test data for the students revealed an average gain in comprehension and vocabulary of twice that which was expected under normal teaching conditions. It was concluded that adequate supervision can help teachers improve the reading achievement of intermediate students by increments that are practically and statistically significant.[33]

Team approach to in-service education.—In New York City, a reading-improvement project at the junior-high level involved teams of reading consultants who worked with teachers of English, social studies, mathematics, science, and industrial arts through a demonstration-teaching approach. Each reading-team consultant met with seven content-area teachers. The first week of a six-week period was spent in orientation by the reading team through individual and

---

33. Sister Josephina, C.S.J., "The Role of Supervision in Improving Reading," *Elementary School Journal*, LXV (April, 1965), 375-80.

group conferences, and in the study of the school population, school plant, instructional materials, and diagnostic procedures used in the school.

During the next five weeks, a basic plan was put into operation. The format included a demonstration reading lesson by the reading consultant in a participating teacher's class, followed by a conference between the teacher and the consultant. A jointly devised follow-up lesson was then taught by the participating teacher, again followed by a conference. The cycle of demonstration lesson, conference, classroom-teacher lesson, conference continued. Workshops and weekly meetings in which parents could participate were planned.[34]

Co-operation between consultants and colleges.—The reading consultant may play an important role in the preparation of teachers by working with schools of education in co-operative planning for a well-rounded program of reading instruction and, in some instances, in the capacity of a college instructor.

New York City has used collegiate talent by establishing the Reading Academy of the Elementary Division. A group of 125 college reading instructors and city school personnel confer regularly about the improvement of reading. They also arrange co-operative studies, report on research, try out new ideas, and help each other analyze problems.[35]

EDUCATION OF READING SPECIALISTS

Judging from the range of responsibilities previously indicated, present-day reading consultants face expectations of such magnitude and, in some cases, so unrealistic that it is remarkable that they perform as well as they do. In many instances, their preparation has been too meager to enable them to meet the demands placed upon them. In fact, the availability of those persons who possess the requisite skills is limited, and their training frequently is incomplete or impractical. Consequently, universities should design special pro-

---

34. Umans, *op. cit.*

35. Helene M. Lloyd, "Meeting the In-Service Needs of Elementary Teachers in Reading Instruction," in *Improvement of Reading through Classroom Practice* (International Reading Association Conference Proceedings, Vol. 9, New York, 1964), pp. 209-211.

grams for training teachers to become qualified, knowledgeable reading consultants. The lamentably limited supply to fill the large demand for reading specialists can perpetuate mediocrity if the supply is not significantly augmented in the immediate future.

I.R.A. standards.—The need for a close look at the preparation of reading consultants has been evident throughout the sixties. Standards proposed by the International Reading Association in 1959 have served as guidelines for colleges and state departments of education, but they were intended as minimal requirements for reading specialization.[36] At present, the following standards are in effect: (*a*) a minimum of three years of successful teaching and/or clinical experience and (*b*) a Master's degree or its equivalent of a Bachelor's degree plus 30 graduate hours in reading and related areas, including a minimum of 12 semester hours in graduate-level reading courses.

The responsibilities entailed in a reading consultant's position require formal course preparation and experience beyond the I.R.A. standards. However, these guidelines are worthy, if minimum, and it is hoped that universities will accept and implement programs based upon them.

Proposed sixth year.—Programs for the preparation of reading specialists are now offered by several universities. More graduate schools are encouraging prospective consultants to undertake a two-year program of specialization leading to a six-year certificate. Following a year of professional courses and directed observations in classrooms and reading centers at the master's degree level, a second year should be devoted to seminars and field experiences. Participation in the planning and conducting of school- or system-wide reading evaluations is an essential part of the second year. Through action research and teacher interviews, a beginning reading specialist can become more perceptive of the classroom teachers' strengths and weaknesses. Furthermore, field experiences of this nature should eliminate or at least decrease the frequent criticism that professional preparation is impractical and idealistic.

Field experiences.—Because the consultant is expected to assist

---

36. Professional Standards and Ethics Committee, International Reading Association, *Minimum Standards for the Professional Training of Reading Specialists,* Newark, Del., 1961.

inexperienced teachers as well as experienced ones, he should be required to complete a graduate practicum in a public school situation, in which he would work with a "master" reading consultant. In this way, he could combine theory with practice by obtaining firsthand knowledge of the problems encountered in the teaching of reading. He would be able to identify typical problems of new teachers, for example, and, through individual study and discussion with other "interns," become better equipped to solve them.

Practicum experiences in university and school reading centers are invaluable also. Diagnostic and corrective reading procedures can be mastered, skill in developing case studies can be acquired, and the importance of a professional multidiscipline team approach to learning problems can be demonstrated.

Interdisciplinary approach.—The reading specialist requires a background which includes more than a passing acquaintance with those disciplines related to reading development. This philosophy is reflected in the offering by the University of Vermont of a graduate course in the analysis of reading difficulties. Specialists from the fields of vision, speech and hearing, psychiatry, psychology, pediatrics, and neurology present recent research and opinion from their disciplines, emphasizing interdisciplinary approaches to the remediation of reading disabilities.[37]

NEED FOR ARTICULATION STUDIES

Actually, little is known about the articulation between preservice graduate education and the problems experienced by neophyte reading consultants. No follow-up studies of the products of specialized programs for these individuals have been reported. Today, research is needed to evaluate the quality of content and experiences afforded by a curriculum for the preparation of reading consultants and, subsequently, to form the basis for revisions of existing programs.

Two types of studies will be useful: (*a*) those which concentrate on the needs of both beginning and experienced reading specialists and (*b*) those which focus on the program of professional preparation. Studies of the first type should be conducted for the purpose

---

37. Stanley I. Mour, "A New Approach to an Old Course," *Journal of Reading*, VIII (November, 1964), 135-40.

of identifying and analyzing typical instructional problems. Results of such surveys may demonstrate the relationship of specific factors to the success or failure of reading personnel. Studies of the second type might concern themselves primarily with the effectiveness of the program in reading specialization and, by means of interview and questionnaire techniques, might attempt to identify the most viable approaches to the graduate education of reading consultants.

Education of future reading specialists could and should be assisted by substantial grants from foundations, the NDEA, and educational publishing houses and equipment manufacturers. If grants were made available to twenty-five or more universities, each to train twenty-five experienced teachers per year during the next decade, a great cadre of well-qualified consultants could be released to upgrade the quality of reading instruction in our schools.

College Teachers

QUALITY OF COLLEGE TEACHING

Public dissatisfaction with the teaching of reading has been aimed most consistently at the public school level. The colleges, however, are not entirely without blame. This is due, in part, to the shortage of college reading personnel, both in quantity and quality.

The first Harvard-Carnegie study (1960) found a preponderant emphasis on elementary education and general education in the backgrounds of college reading faculty members.[38] Of the 638 instructors who completed a study questionnaire, 96 per cent held master's degrees, but only 4 per cent of these were awarded in reading. Of the 38 per cent who held doctor's degrees, 11 per cent had majored in reading in their doctoral program. It appears, then, that undergraduate courses in reading instruction were being taught by those whose own preparation had been in education generally rather than in reading specifically.

Instructors in 74 colleges in the field study reported in *The Torch Lighters* were asked to name barriers which they believed were blocking the accomplishment of their course objectives. The most frequent response was lack of time to present even mini-

---

38. Austin, Morrison, *et al., The Torch Lighters, op. cit.*

mum content. Those who expressed greatest concern were teaching a general curriculum course in which reading was integrated with other language arts and with subject-matter areas. Instructors mentioned three additional obstacles: (*a*) lack of student observational facilities; (*b*) placement of the "reading methods" course early in the professional curriculum; and (*c*) a total educational environment in some co-operating schools which was not conducive to effective teacher preparation. It is interesting to note that not one faculty member admitted deficiencies in his own professional competence or in his personal relationships with students and local school personnel as deterrents to the realization of his instructional objectives.

The field study also made it clear that about half of the reading staff interviewed did not supervise their students during the apprentice-teaching period. Many, in fact, seldom visited local classrooms to observe reading lessons. Although instructors often preferred to evaluate students by observing their teaching performances, they were unable to do so because the course in "reading" was separated from the student-teaching experience by as much as two years in some instances. Consequently, the reading faculty relied upon college supervisors and public school personnel to make the evaluation of their own course instruction.

Theoretically, the college instructor is expected to exert considerable influence upon the future teaching practices of his students. In practice, college personnel, public school administrators, and students maintained that the co-operating teacher was the real influence in shaping student teachers' approaches to reading instruction.[39] Co-operating teachers, too, were convinced that their role was dominant in molding the habits of future teachers of reading. Granted that college reading faculties should exert more influence over the instructional practices of beginning teachers than they do, what specific recommendations may be offered?

PREPARATION OF COLLEGE READING INSTRUCTORS

Teaching and supervisory experiences.—To insure that the college reading instructor will be able to communicate with prospective teachers and public school personnel, a rich background of success-

---

39. *Ibid.*

ful teaching and supervision appears essential for him. Most of the participants in the first Harvard-Carnegie study had had five years or more of actual classroom experience, but criteria other than length of service should be taken into account in assessing a college faculty member's potential for effective communication. At least equal value should be placed upon breadth of experience (i.e., teaching and supervisory positions at different levels and work with both novice and full-fledged teachers). Such a well-rounded background should pave the way for wholesome, positive relationships with students and co-operating teachers in local school systems.

Wherever possible, college reading instructors should observe their students at work in classroom situations. As more teacher education institutions organize university instructional-supervisory teams composed of two or more members, reading professors will have opportunities, as part of their academic loads, to visit schools to which their student teachers have been assigned. On the basis of these visits and their professional *expertise*, they can provide help specifically related to the needs of students, through individual or small-group conferences or in a seminar which meets concurrently with student teaching. Periodically and systematically, they and the co-operating teachers can evaluate strengths and weaknesses of the student teachers. Ultimately, the university instructional-supervisory team should establish mutually advantageous relationships between "town" and "gown."

Field of study and degrees.—A college teacher of reading should be committed to reading as his major field of study. Many universities require from eighteen to twenty-four credit hours in reading to provide in-depth training. Such courses may acquaint graduate students with what is known about teaching and learning in reading at elementary, secondary, college, and adult levels. They pose the unanswered questions and point up areas in which logical deductions have had to be used in the absence of research. They may include critical analysis of reading curriculums and means for devising new ones. The understanding of reading retardation and of means to correct it is important. Courses may require critical analysis of past research dealing with the sociology, physiology, and psychology of reading as well as with its teaching. In addition to acquaintance with the research, familiarity with research techniques provides a basis for the production and consumption of future research.

A broad knowledge of interdisciplinary areas related to reading is increasingly important, as chapter vii of this yearbook reveals.

There has been a noticeable trend in the sixties toward obtaining a Ph.D. or Ed.D. degree as preparation for college teaching. While these degrees usually insure scholarly ability, they do not presume effective teaching of methods courses. An experimental course at the University of Chicago is providing potential Ph.D. students in reading with the opportunity to develop a curriculum, to prepare instruction, and to teach a class. Continuous feedback from colleagues and the instructor as well as from the teachers-in-training appears to improve instructional procedures.

Course content and conduct.—In addition to academic achievement, the college professor must be skilful in dealing with people and able to communicate his knowledge. Yet the typical college instructor of reading in the first Harvard-Carnegie study completely ignored the human element, citing instead the lack of time as *the* obstacle to successful attainment of his course goals.

The scope of reading is so broad that the professor must make use of projects, demonstrations, case studies, films, and professional literature to complement the usual lecture. Through their use, he should be able to provide an environment in which there is intellectual excitement and involvement on the part of the prospective teachers. Fortunately, the traditional lecture based upon required readings from a college textbook or two is being replaced by interaction among students and between students and teacher. Rather than a professor-dominated classroom, the academic setting should be one in which the professor serves as a catalyst.

Professional growth and publications.—In the area of professional growth for college reading instructors, the implications are clear. These teachers must possess the kind of intellectual and personal flexibility that will permit them to make full and effective use of feedback from students, observations of current procedures, personal study and research, and the background gained from participation in professional conferences over the years.

Although the "publish or perish" ultimatum has been of greater concern in the past ten years, reading professors generally are noted for their productivity. Quantity does not necessarily beget quality, of course, but, with a growing body of knowledge and a more critical reading public, it is hoped that college personnel themselves will take steps to improve the content of educational books and articles. Though the finished products will be dependent upon the authors' experience and skill, the amount of time allotted for the writing and the manner in which the time is used are contributing elements.

Since university teachers should strive constantly to extend their knowledge by purposeful and systematic research, they must be given opportunities to be part-time researchers if they are to retain their intellectual vigor and to share it with their students. Nothing could do more to augment the reading profession's efficiency, prestige, and morale. When research is considered, it should be thought of in its broadest context.

Researchers in Reading

STATUS OF RESEARCH

During the sixties, research in reading has been voluminous. In 1964, Barton and Wilder described the research as "of poor quality and non-cumulative." [40] They attributed the quality to inadequate training of researchers, relatively low regard for producing research, and isolation from related disciplines. In recent years, a definite trend toward higher quality is discernable. Undoubtedly, the quality of research will continue to improve as the profession seeks better experimental designs, methods of statistical inference, and interpretations of statistical inferences.

A clarification of the role of the educational researcher has been evident also. Tyler wrote, for example, that basic educational research should produce, construct, and test theories so that they can be implemented by practitioners.[41] Necessarily, research in reading must reflect informed attention to design, but it must also take into consideration the complexity of the reading process. In this Strang concurs, as she cites the need for studies which deal with

---

40. Barton and Wilder, *op. cit.*, p. 397.

41. Ralph W. Tyler, "Specific Contributions of Research to Education," *Theory into Practice,* I (April, 1962), 75-80.

the dynamic processes by which individuals of different ages and abilities and from diverse backgrounds actually comprehend and interpret what they read.[42] Introspective and retrospective accounts can furnish direct information of this kind, and she noted that research at the University of Chicago is probing the processes involved in comprehension and interpretation of material read by elementary, secondary, and college students.

PREPARATION AND GROWTH OF RESEARCHERS

The growing demand for educational research specialists, created primarily by new federally sponsored programs, cannot be met unless training is given the highest priority by those agencies which have drained the field. Legislation by Congress in 1965 recognized this need, and an appropriation of six million dollars was set aside for 1966-67. Assuming that larger and more stable financial support will be forthcoming eventually, what kinds of people should be recruited and what kind of program is deemed desirable for educational researchers?

Recruitment.—More able students must be recruited for educational research through a combination of devices, both tangible and intangible. Scholarships and fellowships might attract superior talent from behavioral sciences and education. But money will not remedy the situation completely. In university communities in which schools of education are held in low esteem, the best students in the behavioral sciences may avoid graduate work in education and remain uninformed of the possibilities for research in reading in their own specializations—psychology, sociology, anthropology, or linguistics. Obviously, an effective recruitment program must create awareness that in reading there are problems to challenge the most able researcher, whether he is most interested in "pure" research (i.e., components of reading), research on problems of application (i.e., synthetic vis-à-vis analytic approaches to reading), or in those that lie between these two extremes. Productive possibilities are limited only by an individual's own skills and creativity.

Differentiation in the degree program.—With regard to the program itself, a separation of the degree program into programs for

42. Ruth Strang, "Reactions to Research on Reading," *Educational Forum*, XXVI (January, 1962), 187-92.

research workers, for practitioners, and for college instructors has been proposed. Many universities have required prospective researchers to take the same courses as other students enrolled in graduate education, with only minor changes. Under the degree-separation plan, those persons preparing for research specialization would engage in formal study which emphasized research methodology, the scientific study of education, instruction in behavioral sciences, and the interaction of research and theory. A special residency in local school systems, encompassing classroom observations, presence at school board and administrative meetings to become acquainted with policy- and decision-making processes, and familiarity with the work of staff specialists, would provide current knowledge of public schools.[43]

Moreover, both doctoral and post-doctoral students should affiliate with a well-established research and development center for training in research. Because many such centers have evolved during this decade, opportunities now are available to prepare great numbers of persons systematically through on-the-job experiences. Some university centers provide research experience for potential researchers. Also, twenty national post-doctoral fellowships in educational research were provided by the USOE for 1967-68. Successful applicants pursued training at or in conjunction with any of the Research and Development Centers or Regional Educational Laboratories supported by the USOE or at any institution eligible to receive funds under the training program mentioned previously.

Research projects.—Three representative projects which have been in progress for some time and which could be useful in stimulating growth in research skills will be described briefly.

The USOE has established research and development centers to design, carry out, and evaluate basic and applied research. Their findings are translated into educational procedures, which are then evaluated before resulting information is disseminated to interested schools. Educational proving grounds have been organized at the University of Oregon, the University of Pittsburgh, the University of Wisconsin, and Howard University. The centers focus on any

---

43. Paul F. Lazarafeld and Sam D. Sieber, *Organizing Educational Research*, (Englewood Cliffs, N.J.: Prentice-Hall, Inc., 1964), 61-73.

area of significance in education and encourage co-operation among universities, schools of education, state departments, and local school systems.[44]

A basic research project in reading, "Project Literacy," is being conducted at Cornell University.[45] Sponsored by the USOE, the project uses an interdisciplinary approach which has brought together reseachers and educators to examine how individuals acquire reading skills. Investigations are carried on in such areas as learning psychology, visual perception, cognitive behavior, child development, linguistics, psycholinguists, the neuropsychology of vision, and the sociology of educational innovation.

The National Institute of Child Health and Development is supporting the Human Communications Program, directed toward research on the role of communication in human growth and development. Areas of study include the investigation of how a child learns to talk, when he should be taught to read, and the effect of language communication on these two processes. This research, basic to reading, involves individual investigations as well as multidisciplinary ones.[46]

Certainly the educational researcher has an obligation, both professionally and personally, to keep informed of current technology, methodology, and trends. Keeping informed involves his participation in conferences which map out interdisciplinary content areas of research, concepts of the behavioral sciences which are applicable to education, and current issues which are judged crucial by the profession. It also involves his own study of current literature, maintenance of an academic library, and membership and active participation in scholarly societies.

TEACHERS, SUPERVISORS, AND ADMINISTRATORS—PARTNERS IN RESEARCH

The USOE has made it possible for countless teachers, super-

---

44. Hendrik D. Gideonse, "Federal Support for Educational Research and Development," in *Action for Improvement of Teacher Education* (Eighteenth Yearbook, 1965, Annual Meeting of the American Association of Colleges for Teacher Education, Washington, 1965), 68-76.

45. Warren G. Cutts, "Sponsored Research in Reading: Projects and Prospects," *Journal of Reading*, VIII (May, 1965), 378-83.

46. *Ibid.*

visors, and administrators to be involved directly in research in reading. Twenty-seven studies on the first-grade level were conducted in the 1964-65 school year in different geographical regions. These studies represented the largest co-ordinated reading project in the history of education. Fourteen of these studies have been extended through the second and third grades. Bond and Dykstra noted that "teachers who participated in the cooperative study also gained much from the experience. The research program proved to be a valuable technique for the in-service training of teachers."[47]

However, the classroom teachers were not the only persons to reap the advantages from involvement in these research studies. Reading supervisors and administrators who participated in these co-operative ventures, in which their schools and classrooms were used as laboratories, also benefited from their direct association with research.

Technology has aided researchers in the classrooms of the past and will play a greater role in those of the future. Video-tape recordings, for instance, are of value as sources of data and in controlling experimental situations. It is possible to take portable video-tape systems into the classroom and to record visually and auditorily the specific techniques being examined. This permanent record of actual performances enables tests of reliability to be conducted, can help eliminate the bias of the researcher, and is accessible for other persons to use in replicating research. Needless to say, video-tape may be used in all classrooms from first grade through post-graduate seminars.

Public school personnel must become increasingly concerned about and familiar with reading research. Fortunately, several sources of information are readily available to them, two of which will be mentioned.

DISSEMINATION OF RESEARCH FINDINGS

The publication of the *Reading Research Quarterly* by the International Reading Association, beginning in the fall of 1965, marked a significant milestone in this decade. Since the establishment of

---

47. Guy L. Bond and Robert Dykstra, "The Role of the Coordinating Center in the Cooperative Research Program," *Reading Teacher,* XIX (May, 1966), 565-68.

this journal, reports of experimental, statistical, and technical articles have been presented in it in depth and detail for careful perusal by the profession.

A second milestone was achieved with the funding of ERIC (Educational Research Information Center). The center is a nationwide information system under the aegis of the USOE. It was established in 1966 to serve American education in the collection, analysis, and dissemination of information. Central ERIC is located in Washington, D.C., and there are twelve decentralized clearinghouses which serve as input arms. One, located at Indiana University, is concerned specifically with reading. Its purpose is stated as follows:

> The Clearinghouse on Reading is responsible for acquiring research reports, materials, and information related to all aspects of reading behavior with emphasis on physiology, psychology, sociology, and the teaching of reading. Included are reports on the development and evaluation of instructional materials, curricula, tests and measurements, preparation of reading teachers and specialists, and methodology at all levels; the role of libraries and other agencies in fostering and guiding reading; and diagnostic and remedial services in school and clinic settings.[48]

In addition to the input-output service, the reading clearinghouse proposes to (*a*) analyze information, (*b*) initiate publications to help educators cope with information problems in reading, (*c*) provide information on reading through a retrieval system, (*d*) develop a catalogue of available published instructional reading materials, (*e*) issue summary reports on topics in reading, and (*f*) conduct and co-ordinate research.

Clearly the federal government, universities, professional associations, and public schools have combined efforts to professionalize research and to initiate programs based upon research findings. This has resulted, in part, from the facts that (*a*) modern technology has made the fruits of research more accessible, (*b*) mass media have stretched their tentacles over a world-wide domain, (*c*) the public is demanding action, (*d*) the schools are in the throes of an instructional revolution, and (*e*) financial support is more readily available. Needed now are more skilled reseachers who can forge ahead in obtaining new insights and translate the knowledge gained from

---

48. *ERIC/CRIER Newsletter*, I (January, 1965), 4p.

basic and applied research into such form that practitioners can implement the findings. Hopefully, these co-operative ventures will lead to the ultimate goal—excellence of education for all.

Training for Paraprofessionals

DUTIES OF NON-TEACHING PERSONNEL

As teaching has become more specialized and professionalized, the position is being adopted that non-teaching responsibilities should be delegated to teacher assistants or aides. Counted among the various duties which aides might perform in the classroom are those of a clerical nature, the operation of audiovisual equipment, and actual work with groups or individual children. Aides may read aloud to children to stimulate their interest in books or to broaden their backgrounds in the content areas. They may read also to those children whose reading disabilities prevent them from completing required assignments. When aides have been prepared to do so, they can work with students on skills-development activities after classroom teachers have introduced new concepts. In addition, volunteers may prepare taped exercises for use at the listening center, show filmstrips to strengthen specific concepts and skills, present work on an overhead projector, do vocabulary work with pupils, encourage oral language usage, and help children develop reference skills.

Literally thousands of paraprofessionals have entered the nation's schools with the advent of new programs for disadvantaged youth. Some of these individuals are serving as paid workers who have received specific preparation for their new roles. Others continue to serve on a voluntary basis, with or without training. While success is dependent upon many factors, effective preparation is considered an essential ingredient. Three programs designed for teacher aides are described in the following section.

REPRESENTATIVE TRAINING PROGRAMS

Portland Community College.—A training program for instructional-materials aides was conducted at Portland Community College under the Manpower Development and Training Act, an act to provide training for people who are underemployed or unemployable. The college developed a course of approximately seven-and-one-half months, in which participants attended class for six hours a day to learn how to operate audiovisual equipment and to prepare audiovisual materials. The students learned how to make transparencies, record lectures, produce slides, plan bulletin board displays, and clean and operate duplicators and other equipment. The program stressed learning by doing and "over-the-shoulder" instruction. Students took field trips to schools and area instructional-materials centers to gain greater knowledge of the requirements of their jobs. After completion of the course, the aides were prepared to be an important part of an instructional team, taking over necessary tasks in the use of audiovisual materials and freeing the teacher to teach.[49]

VISTA Project.—By the end of 1965, approximately five thousand persons in the Volunteers in Service to America (VISTA) were involved in the war on poverty as tutors, counselors' aides, recreation leaders, tenant-education workers, youth-development leaders, and in other roles in communities which requested their help. Volunteers enrolled in a four- to six-week training period under the auspices of colleges and universities, where they learned about poverty and techniques for applying their skills in specific situations. This period was followed by supervised field experience. In a six-week pilot project at the University of Pennsylvania, twelve future VISTA participants taught remedial reading, current events, and mathematics to classes composed of young men from the streets of Philadelphia.[50]

Volunteer reading tutors.—Community-service organizations, with their corps of volunteer workers, have become increasingly active in the socialization of and in ministering to the needs of culturally disadvantaged youths and adults. Volunteers have been recruited to assist in literacy programs. However, they need specialized instruction in reading in order to be effective in reducing illiteracy among the educationally deprived.

The Center for Youth and Community Studies (CYCS) and the Community Service Projects (CSP), both activist community-

---

49. Amo De Barnardis, "The New Challenge for Community Colleges," *Educational Screen and Audiovisual Guide*, XLIV (December, 1965), 34-35.

50. Lois Muss, "VISTA'S War on Poverty: Junior Colleges Can Supply Volunteers," *Junior College Journal*, XXXV (February, 1965), 18-20.

service organizations in Washington, D.C., and both sponsored by Howard University, have devoted significant portions of their general programs to the development of literacy for some of their clients. A structured institute for the training of volunteer reading tutors was planned. A syllabus was designed to introduce the volunteer to a developmental-instructional approach in reading, and to familiarize the trainee with special problems of culturally deprived individuals. The training program consisted of a minimum of ten hours of class instruction within a two-week period, including lectures, demonstrations, and discussions. It made use of home assignments, and mimeographed bulletins were provided for reinforcement purposes.[51]

The type and extent of the preparation for paraprofessionals are determined by the nature of the tasks these individuals are to perform. All persons assisting in schools should attend orientation sessions for the purpose of becoming acquainted with school policies and regulations. Those assuming more technical duties will require training commensurate with their functions. Needless to say, however, aides should be permitted to work with children in reading only after receiving specific instruction in reading activities.

Looking Ahead

Looking ahead to reading in the next decade, one expects to find an inundation of books and reading materials. Students, of necessity, will need to be trained to be critical and discriminative in their choice of reading matter as well as to be more proficient in using reading as a basic tool for independent learning. Programed instruction, computer scheduling and teaching, and utilization of auto-instructional devices will free the teacher to devote more attention to individual instruction. Employment of teacher aides for non-professional duties will enable the teacher to become more highly specialized in teaching. The physical change in school buildings from separate classrooms to clusters of pods around central study or resource areas may also be a factor in changing the role of the teacher. The teacher will act as a guide and a poser of questions for which the students themselves will discover the answers.

51. Eunice Shaed Newton, "Training the Volunteer Reading Tutor," *Journal of Reading*, VIII (January, 1965), 169-74.

In preparing teachers for the demands of the 1970's, there will be greater selectivity in the admission of teacher applicants. As the functions of the reading teacher and consultant become more specialized, there will be stricter adherence to the standards set forth by such professional organizations as the International Reading Association. The recognition that learning to read is a lifelong process will continue to focus instruction in reading at all levels, from preschool to adulthood, and prospective teachers will be trained according to this philosophy. More field experiences, internships, and residencies may be expected in the preservice education of teachers. Continuous in-service work will provide teachers and administrators with information on new techniques and media, awareness of human-relations needs, and opportunities to plan, implement, and evaluate procedures. Data-processing equipment and more refined evaluative techniques will aid in the assessment of existing programs. Information retrieval centers will keep schools informed of research findings and innovations. The responsibility for teacher education will not be borne solely by the university but will be a co-operative venture of teacher-training institutions, researchers, state departments of education, and local schools. And who will be the beneficiaries of these intensive and extensive efforts to produce teachers of excellence? All society will, for it is today's children who will be the adult citizens of tomorrow.

CHAPTER XI

The Next Decade

HELEN M. ROBINSON

Introduction

The purposes of this chapter are, first, to sum up the trends described in previous chapters; second, to point out major problems, some of which are suggested or implied in earlier chapters; third, to clarify the roles of experimentation and research in schools; fourth, to show some of the reasons why problems have not yet been solved; and fifth, to identify recent trends and new developments which must be considered in the future.

SOME GENERALIZATIONS

Current knowledge about innovations and changes in the teaching of reading has been examined from various points of view in the preceding ten chapters. Some useful generalizations can be made, some of which are drawn from more than one chapter.

First, the greatest number of innovations and changes have been for children beginning to read. New methods, materials, classroom organizations, and models of reading have been devised primarily for younger children. The optimum age for beginning reading has been challenged. Reading research at the beginning levels has been voluminous, and the results have been controversial. It is apparent that the controversy bears a close relationship to wide criticism of reading instruction by public media. Another stimulating factor in producing innovations has been the entry of specialists in disciplines related to reading. Linguists have prepared instructional materials and proposed differing methods for teaching beginning reading. Furthermore, psychologists have explored selected aspects of learning and retention, an exploration which has resulted in a reexamination of various aspects of instruction. All of these factors have combined to raise questions about current practices in the minds of teachers which have helped them to be ready to experiment with innovations.

Second, it is apparent that few innovations or marked changes have occurred in reading instruction beyond the primary grades. Many of the basic assumptions about sequence, methods, and materials remain unchallenged. While scattered efforts are being made to group pupils for more effective instruction, only a few innovations in teaching reading beyond the word-recognition level have occurred. The "higher illiteracy" described by Chase, for example, has had little attention.[1] Furthermore, the reading of books by adults continues to be limited to a minority of the population. In addition, the uses of reading appear to be more closely related to practical demands than to the cultivation of social understanding and personal satisfaction as described by de Grasia.[2] Teachers and administrators appear to be satisfied if standardized test results meet some predetermined expectations and if pupils can move forward in school. The demands of a changing social order have not yet had a marked impact on the teaching of reading at the upper levels. For example, Rogers found in her study of high-school seniors that students read to remember facts and answer questions, with little awareness of evaluation of the materials.[3]

Third, it is obvious that myriad questions continue to be asked at all levels and that few answers are forthcoming. Although more studies of reading than of any other school activity have been conducted, uncertainty and difference of opinion still pervade practice. Scholars in the field suggest that the most productive questions have not been asked and that most experimentation continues to focus on problems of minor import.

Fourth, although unanswered questions persist, some evidence

---

1. Francis S. Chase, "Demands on the Reader in the Next Decade," in *Controversial Issues in Reading and Promising Solutions*, ed. Helen M. Robinson ("Supplementary Educational Monographs," No. 91 [Chicago: University of Chicago Press, 1961]), pp. 7-78.

2. Sebastian de Grasia, *Of Time and Leisure* (New York: Twentieth Century Fund, 1962), p. 413.

3. Bernice Rogers, "Directed and Undirected Critical Reading Responses of High School Students" (unpublished Doctor's dissertation, University of Chicago, 1960).

has been accumulated to guide decisions about sound practices in reading. Although children do learn to read through many procedures, the evidence is clear that their rate of progress may be increased through added knowledge of more effective procedures. Insightful experiences combined with logical deductions have gradually produced curriculums and methods that permit a large proportion of children to learn to read. Research evidence is increasingly coming to direct changes in parts of the program.

Fifth, the basal reader materials have a strong influence on procedures adopted in schools. Even though teachers express some dissatisfaction with these materials, they continue to rely on them. For this reason, most experimentation with innovations has come only after instructional materials have been published. Obviously, a grave responsibility for improving reading instruction falls on the publishers of materials which children use in learning to read.

Sixth, the teacher continues to be the most significant influence on reading progress. The major comparative studies of methods and materials reveal marked differences in the effectiveness of their use, with the teacher making the significant difference. At the present time, investigators are attempting to identify the characteristics of teachers which are most conducive to pupils' learning in order that these characteristics may be cultivated in the neophyte teacher. Furthermore, both preservice and in-service programs of teacher training may be made more effective as more is learned about teacher effectiveness. The shortage of teachers entering the profession and the rapid turnover of teachers in many schools suggest that innovations in both preservice and in-service training are urgently needed.

Finally, research in reading is being given a new impetus by funds from the government, foundations, and private enterprise. Public concern about the teaching of reading has created a favorable atmosphere in which research should thrive. The diverse techniques of research and the knowledge of allied professions are available to add to the repertoire of the reading specialist. Past research is being assembled and disseminated so that the researcher may profit from what has already been learned. There is an urgent need for a greater number of scholarly investigators who can find the solutions to the problems not yet solved.

Unsolved Problems

The literature of the twentieth century is filled with problems in reading which require research. Not only does almost every research report make note of newly identified problems but specialists also produce organized lists of them. Representative lists from earlier decades reveal the persistence of similar problems.[4] Furthermore, each of the foregoing chapters of this yearbook suggests needed research. The problems, instead of being specifically enumerated, are grouped and identified by general topics in this summary.

THE READING PROCESS

Major effort in the past has been given to methods and procedures for teaching reading, with considerably less attention being given to how children learn or to the process of learning to read. While fragments of information are emerging, not enough is yet known to develop a descriptive model of the reading process.

The major deterrent to research on the reading process is the inefficiency of techniques for investigating the problem. The techniques employed so far have been indirect and yield evidence largely by implication. Perhaps indirect approaches are the only means by which the reading process can be studied, but it is anticipated that new approaches will be devised which will be capable of extending understandings.

Just as eye-movement photography produced a large number of investigations in the early part of this century, so would other research procedures lead to significant investigations. Eye-movement photography yielded indirect evidence which resulted in numerous changes in reading instruction.

It may be that sufficient use has not been made of systematic observation with periodic testing. At the beginning levels, Clay's "Emergent Reading Behavior" provides an example of a beginning

---

4. D. D. Durrell, "Research Problems in Reading in the Elementary Schools," *Elementary English Review*, XIII (April, 1936), 149-56, and (May, 1936), 184-92; William S. Gray, "Needed Research in Reading," *Elementary English*, XXIX (February, 1952), 100-109.

attempt to describe some of the process involved in learning.[5] She observed one hundred children regularly and made analyses of their errors in oral reading as a means of supplying clues to the ways in which pupils processed print. She interpreted the behavior in terms of the kinds of cue reductions among those who learned to read most rapidly. This study suggests that a wealth of information about processes could be secured from carefully planned continuous or periodic examination of children's reading behavior. As unexplained characteristics become apparent, new devices will be needed to explore aspects other than those already identified. While these techniques may be most productive at the beginning stages of reading, their usefulness at later levels needs to be explored.

Similar to observation is the structured interview, in which children reply to common questions. The investigation by Weintraub and Denny illustrates judicious use of questions to elicit young children's concepts of what reading is and how and why they expect to learn or not to learn.[6] It also provides leads as to the sources of their ideas about reading. Of special interest is the finding of these investigators that many pupils learning to read had no clearer concepts of reading at the end of the first year than when they began school.

Introspection and retrospection have been revived as techniques to elicit information about differences between good and poor readers in comprehension, in reading for different purposes, and in reading in different content areas. For example, Piekarz discovered that sixth-grade pupils with difficulty in interpreting print often engaged in free association about the content, so that they were unable to distinguish between the author's message and their own thoughts.[7] Smith learned that high-school students had little notion

---

5. Marie M. Clay, "Emergent Reading Behavior" (unpublished Doctor's thesis, University of Auckland, New Zealand, 1966).

6. Samuel Weintraub and Terry P. Denny, "What Do Beginning First-Graders Say about Reading?" *Childhood Education*, XLI (February, 1965), 326-27.

7. Josephine A. Piekarz, "Individual Differences in Interpretive Responses in Reading" (unpublished Doctor's dissertation, University of Chicago, 1954).

of the purposes for which they read.[8] H. Alan Robinson identified the skills which pupils used in reading social studies.[9]

The forementioned indirect techniques have two major limitations. First, they depend heavily on each child's awareness of his thoughts and his willingness or ability to verbalize them. Second, the results are subject to the inferences made by the investigator and therefore may be interpreted in different ways. Nevertheless, the insights gained from such studies lead to new hypotheses which are capable of rigorous testing.

During the 1960's, psychologists have increasingly studied aspects of reading, not because of their concern with reading per se but primarily because it is a task which lends itself to experimental procedures. Many have used direct techniques for the study of visual perception, learning paired associates, and similar tasks. In so doing, the reading act is so fractionized that it is necessary to collate the data before meaningful interpretations are possible. Yet such intensive studies may offer important leads to understanding the reading process. Levin has reported a number of such studies in his "Project Literacy" reports.[10] A number of others are summarized by Robinson, Weintraub, and Smith.[11]

A renewed interest in the reading process on the part of neurologists and psychoneurologists focuses primarily on minimal brain dysfunction and its effects on learning to read.[12] Likewise, the concern of those in other allied professions portends more productive research by interdisciplinary teams.

---

8. Helen K. Smith, "The Responses of Good and Poor Readers When Asked To Read for Different Purposes" (unpublished Doctor's dissertation, University of Chicago, 1965).

9. H. Alan Robinson, "Reading Skills Employed in Solving Social Studies Problems," *Reading Teacher*, XVIII (January, 1965), 263-69.

10. Harry Levin, *Project Literacy Reports*, Numbers 1-8 (Ithaca, N.Y.: Cornell University, 1964-67).

11. Helen M. Robinson, Samuel Weintraub, and Helen K. Smith, "Summary of Investigations Relating to Reading, July 1, 1964, to June 30, 1965," *Reading Research Quarterly*, I (Winter, 1965), 5-126; "Summary of Investigations Relating to Reading, July 1, 1965, to June 30, 1966," *Reading Research Quarterly*, II (Winter, 1966-67), 7-141.

12. A. A. Silver and Rosa A. Hagin, "Maturation of Perceptual Functions in Children with Specific Reading Disability," *Reading Teacher*, XIX (January, 1966), 253-59.

HIGHER LEVEL READING ABILITIES

Innovations have been more numerous at the beginning levels, where emphasis is primarily on learning to recognize words. While children beyond the primary grades need to increase their mastery of words, both in recognition and in meaning, fewer research reports have been made and fewer ideas for instruction have been proposed at the advanced levels.

Some writers propose and models suggest that, beyond the recognition of words, reading is synonymous with thinking. Perhaps reading and thinking are very similar, although neither process is fully understood. In models of communication, especially those involving language and thought processes, few distinctions are made.

Reading requires an active search for the ideas and thoughts of the writer. Some ideas of writers are clearly set forth, while others are implied by the choice of their words and the ways in which words and sentences are combined. The nuances of the apprehension and processing of written language are not fully understood. Research designed to determine the reciprocal effects of instruction in higher-level reading skills on similar types of thinking should be profitable.

The urgent need to identify and to better understand the continuance of the primary skills at higher reading levels has not been a deterrent to the continuance of instruction using the old methods, which has achieved some measure of success. The major issue is whether more effective means may be devised to produce greater competence on the part of a larger number of students.

For the most part, instruction is based (*a*) on establishing in the child a mental set that prompts the securing of particular kinds of information from printed text, (*b*) on demonstrating the clues one may use to gain such information, (*c*) on permitting pupils to read, and (*d*) on asking the right kinds of questions to elicit maximal understanding of or reaction to the ideas gleaned. Obviously, these procedures depend, to a greater extent, on the competence of the teacher in his own reading and in his understanding of or probing for the causes of students' errors.

The quality and types of questions asked by teachers and their ability to accept diverse answers also appears to be significant in producing higher-level skills. Answers are usually not wholly right or wrong but have necessary qualifications. Using models of thinking, such as those by Bloom [13] and Guilford,[14] some ingenious teachers have been stimulated to devise questions about selections which may usher in a new era of the development of higher-level reading skills.

Guilford's model, with sample items developed by Spache, has been explained in chapter i.

Bloom suggests six major classes of objectives, each at increasing levels of complexity: (*a*) knowledge, (*b*) comprehension, (*c*) application, (*d*) analysis, (*e*) synthesis, and (*f*) evaluation. Questions to elicit knowledge and comprehension are used most frequently in the classroom. Questions involving application might ask that the student who reads a principle show how it applies to his life, his problems, or the classroom situation. The situation should be a new one, real rather than fictitious. Questions dealing with analysis might require the student to differentiate between a conclusion and the statements that support it or to analyze the relations of statements supporting or refuting an argument. In contrast, questions to elicit synthesis should call for putting together the elements of a passage into a pattern or generalization not stated by the author. Finally, evaluation questions require judgments of accuracy, value, or worth based on criteria supplied by the student or by the teacher. At this level, questions would be very similar to those calling for critical reading.

Investigations such as that by King *et al.* also illustrated attempts to improve teachers' questions and to develop critical reading skills.[15] It is encouraging that scattered studies are preceding public pressure to improve the most crucial of the reading abilities.

---

13. Benjamin S. Bloom (ed.), *Taxonomy of Educational Objectives. Handbook I: Cognitive Domain* (New York: Longmans, Green & Co., 1956).

14. Joy P. Guilford, "Frontiers in Thinking That Teachers Should Know About," *Reading Teacher*, XIII (February, 1960), 176-82.

15. Martha King *et al.*, "Observations of Teacher-Pupil Verbal Behavior during Critical Reading Lessons" ("Occasional Papers Series" [Columbus, Ohio: Division for the Study of Education, Ohio State University, 1967]).

SEQUENCES IN READING INSTRUCTION

Assumptions about the order of introduction and mastery of various reading skills have been sharply challenged in new approaches to programing the content of reading for instruction. Many programs have adopted the sequence recommended by some linguists and psychologists, who suggest teaching the code (word identifications) first and then teaching an understanding of the patterns of printed language. Such innovations have sharpened the questions many people have posed but not answered about the most effective sequences for reading instruction.

Questions are raised not only about the sequences of teaching the major aspects of reading, such as those first mentioned, but also about the sequences within each aspect. For example, should instruction in consonant sounds precede that of vowels? Is it more effective to teach children to understand details before main ideas? Can pupils learn to get sensory images without first developing other skills?

Almost all curriculums and basal reading programs are built on logical steps believed to progress from the simple to the complex. But studies have demonstrated that adult appraisals of the simplicity of tasks are not equivalent to those of children. A great deal of experimentation and research is needed to solve these problems so that, as simpler skills are mastered, they may be integrated and used as a part of more complex skills.

Some research suggests that children differ with respect to the sequences by which they learn best. Perhaps some pupils learn more easily by synthetic than by analytic approaches. Differences among pupils may be found in the ease of convergent and divergent thinking. Consequently, it is urgent that studies be made of effective learning sequences for pupils with strengths in differing modalities and with different types of intellectual abilities and personalities.

As a recent summary points out, millions of dollars are being spent by industry and government for hardware, while the major problem is "software," or what to teach and how to teach it.[16]

16. "Computers Find School Is Tough," *Business Week* (July 1, 1967), pp. 106-8.

Experimentation with sequences of instruction is essential for the development of materials for such programs. Within the next ten years, a large amount of additional information on effective sequences should be available.

In the meantime, most teachers will continue to follow the most logical sequences that can be set up by school curriculums and by published reading materials. Innovative teachers may make a marked contribution through experimentation with various published sequences and through observation of children who appear to learn in different ways or who seem to master skills considered more difficult while exhibiting problems in learning skills believed to be easier. Such observations may suggest ways to approach the problems of developing differential sequences for instruction.

THE ROLE OF THE TEACHER

Intuitively, administrators have always known that the key factor in reading instruction is the teacher. Confirmation of this conclusion is appearing with increasing frequency in research reports. The most convincing of these reports comes from the analysis of data supplied by the "First-Grade Reading Studies." Bond observed, "As would be expected, there was greater variation between the teachers within the methods than there was between the methods. This again points up the importance of the teacher's role in learning situations." [17] Likewise, studies at later levels reveal that reading success is dependent upon teachers rather than upon methods or materials per se.

Various aspects of teacher efficiency have been studied in the last decade. Ratings based on verbal behavior, classroom atmosphere, and social interaction among pupils and teacher have taken precedence over judgments based on subjective rating scales. Rippey has begun to contrast instruction using programed materials without the teacher with the same instruction given by the teacher to determine the over-all contribution of the teacher.[18] Moreover, he is

---

17. Guy L. Bond, "First Grade Reading Studies: An Overview," *Elementary English*, XLIII (May, 1966), 469.

18. Robert M. Rippey, "Fitting Research on Instruction into the Conceptual Model" (mimeographed; paper delivered at the American Psychological Association, September 5, 1965).

testing differences in learning which require higher and lower levels of mental processes, while sequence and materials are held constant. His early studies showed that the teacher was more effective than the program alone in both higher- and lower-process items. Although the teacher made no more adjustments to the students than did the programed materials, the presentation by the teacher had a positive effect on learning and retention on the part of the students. The question yet unanswered is why the teacher was more effective. Did the presence of the teacher provide external motivation? Or did the students achieve better because they were accustomed to teacher expectations? Many questions must be answered before it is possible to determine both the essential characteristics of the teacher and ways to translate these characteristics into effective programs to teach reading. Research will surely continue to search for objective characteristics until knowledge is sufficient either to identify future teachers who possess personal characteristics predictive of success or to indicate how these characteristics may be developed.

The attack on the problems of (*a*) understanding the reading process, (*b*) learning how to teach higher-level reading skills, (*c*) developing effective teaching and learning sequences, and (*d*) determining the various roles of the teacher is a large order for the next decade.

Experiment and Research

Teachers and administrators are often bombarded with the magic statement, "But research says . . ." They become disillusioned when they learn that there are published reports to support and refute claims for the values of most innovations and changes currenty advocated. Thus, they are unable to reach conclusions based on what is described as research. Without considerable experience and guidance, teachers find it difficult to distinguish among carefully controlled and loosely controlled research and uncontrolled experiments. It is important to distinguish among them because the dependability of the generalizations that can be made is determined by the nature of the investigation.

CHARACTERISTICS OF EXPERIMENTS

An experiment is defined as a test or trial in order to find out something about a tentative procedure. Throughout this yearbook, suggestions have been made that schools experiment with promising innovations in order to produce desired changes.

Experiments of this type provide many insights and are extremely useful but should not be confused with research. For example, sensitive teachers may be selected to use new instructional materials and to keep a careful evaluative record of strengths and weaknesses of the materials. If teachers of similar kinds of learners agree in their assessments, school personnel have a basis for choice. A second example deals with an innovation in methods of instruction. One or several perceptive teachers may wish to try the innovation, keeping careful diary records of problems they encounter, of types of pupils who learn well and of those who experience difficulty, of points in the program at which the sequence causes confusion and supplementary instruction is required, and the like. Moreover, such classes may serve as observation centers for others in the school or school system to determine whether the innovation in methods or materials should be subjected to further study.

Teachers who engage in experiments often benefit markedly by gaining new insights into how they teach. Furthermore, with guidance, they may become increasingly aware of individual differences among learners and may devise means for meeting diverse needs. Often teachers who experiment develop new enthusiasm for teaching and may find the new method better adapted to their teaching styles and to their pupils. Obviously, such enthusiasm may be the real source of success. Therefore, caution is offered about expectations of the new method if it is used by less enthusiastic teachers.

NEEDED EXPERIMENTS

Experimentation in schools is needed because each school differs from others. Experimental results from other schools should be evaluated and even the findings from research should be tried before being accepted completely. A few important areas for experimentation are suggested in the following sections.

Methods and materials for teachers.—Reports have shown that individual teachers are more successful in teaching reading if their convictions about their favorite methods and materials are respected. Teachers with strong preferences may become far less effective if they are forced to conform by changing completely, even with in-service training. New teachers may need structured guidance to develop competence in using different methods, but experienced and successful teachers often evolve their own plans. Experimentation in schools may help to determine the best combination of methods, materials, and types of pupils for different teachers.

Methods and materials for learners.—Individual differences in learning have long been recognized, but children and youth are still expected to conform to fairly uniform reading programs. Experimentation may enable schools to identify those learners who profit more from highly structured than from loosely structured programs, those who learn at different ages or by different sequences, and those who profit from particular types of materials.

Ideally, if learners' preferences for methods and materials could be matched with teachers' preferences, the rate of learning to read should be increased. Intuitively, some administrators assign particular children to certain teachers. Experimentation may suggest some evidence to enhance intuition.

Contributions of parents.—Increasingly, schools are involving parents in school activities as well as in supportive roles. Furthermore, parents make direct as well as indirect contributions to their children's learning to read.

A few experiments have been reported in which help has been provided for parents so that home and school can work harmoniously.[19] However, only small segments of the total range of possibilities have been examined to date. Innovations in determining the contribution of parents to the reading of their children are urgently needed. Experimentation is needed in all types of schools and with pupils of different ages and levels of achievement.

---

19. Margaret Lipchik, "A Saturday School for Mothers and Pre-Schoolers," *National Elementary Principal*, XLIV (November, 1964), 29-31; Helen M. Lloyd, "New York City's Program for Developing the Role of Parents in Reading Progress," *Reading Teacher*, XVIII (May, 1965), 629-33; Joseph E. Brzeinski, "Beginning Reading in Denver," *Reading Teacher*, XVIII (October, 1964), 16-21.

Other areas for experimentation have been suggested in previous chapters. Schools will surely continue to experiment in many ways other than those suggested throughout this yearbook. Experimentation often identifies and refines urgent problems which can be investigated more carefully through planned research.

CHARACTERISTICS OF RESEARCH

Research is careful, unbiased investigation of a problem in reading in which the results are based on demonstrable data. In this respect, research should be a more rigorous test of the values and limitations of innovations in reading than is possible with experimentation (as described in the previous section).

Research dealing with innovations and changes in reading instruction must be carried on in schools. Since schools are autonomous, administrators are accustomed to making their own decisions, and teachers habitually devise variations in their use of methods and materials, research in schools is often hazardous. Problems arise because administrators decide to reorganize their schools. Without being aware of their adjustments, teachers may fail to follow the procedures of the experimental design and may thus contaminate the evidence. Extreme care must be taken to secure dependable evidence, especially in longitudinal studies in which pupil attrition adds to the chances of errors.

Larger schools often have a research division staffed by competent persons to plan and execute carefully controlled research. Also, many researchers in colleges and universities use the schools as their laboratories to test the effectiveness of innovations. However, many schools and some researchers carry on comparative studies with minimal controls. Such research has value if the limitations are recognized and the results are not generalized beyond the limitations imposed by the design of the study.

First-level research.—A number of reports attempt to evaluate an innovation in reading instruction by comparing it with the instruction already being given in the school. Frequently the study is loosely controlled, with wide variation in teachers and pupils, without careful checks on the time allotted to instruction, and with considerable Hawthorne effect. Some studies appear to have been conceived after the treatment was administered, so that the use of pretests or other matching devices has been omitted. Post-test scores are then compared and the differences attributed to the innovation.

As an example, a school system may wish to experiment with a new method of instruction. Teachers and children may be matched as well as possible, but many other factors may vary. It is possible that different materials will accompany the new method. Perhaps the principals or supervisors will need to give more time and assistance to the teachers who must learn to use the new method. In convincing parents that their children's progress will not be retarded, undue enthusiasm necessarily may be generated. Teachers from other schools in the system and visitors may make the teachers and children feel very special. If, by the end of one, two, or three years, the experimental pupils read better than the control pupils, can the difference be attributed to the new method? Obviously not, because methods, materials, supervision, and enthusiasm, as well as other unrecognized differences may have accounted for this superiority. In other words, for the method to succeed equally well in another school in the system, even with the same kinds of teachers and pupils, all of the factors noted in the preceding statements may need to be present.

Studies which are subject to some of the forementioned limitations are numerous; they may lead to what Campbell and Stanley described as "disillusionment with experimentation in education." [20] Wittick pointed out the seriousness of this problem in chapter iii as she attempted to evaluate the innovations in primary-grade reading instruction.

Second-level research.—Innovations should receive a fair but rigorous trial by submitting them to carefully controlled investigation. Otherwise, as Gates stated, the new method of the 1960's will soon become the dull old program, easily defeated by the next new one.[21]

In examining a research report, therefore, the reader should be alert for signs of obvious bias. For example, reports which state

20. Donald T. Campbell and Julian C. Stanley, "Experimental and Quasi-Experimental Designs for Research on Teaching," in *Handbook of Research on Teaching*, ed. N. L. Gage (Chicago: Rand McNally & Co., 1963), p. 172.

21. Arthur I. Gates, "The Future of Research in Reading," *Education*, LXXXII (May, 1962), 549.

that the purpose is to "prove" the superiority of one method over another reflect this bias and cue the reader to anticipate that the results will support the favored method. Other investigators may not express their biases so clearly; hence, critical examination of the details of the report is necessary. A few important aspects to consider are suggested in the next paragraphs.

A research report should demonstrate the investigator's familiarity with previous research dealing with related topics. The demonstration of such familiarity is important because it shows that the investigator is aware of relevant facts established by earlier studies. Moreover, the reader has an opportunity to note whether the findings of the current study agree with or refute previous conclusions. A second function of the review of research is to place the particular study in a broader setting, particularly to reveal the segment of reading which is under investigation.

A research report should have hypotheses, clearly stated and in such form that they can be tested. Because some reports have no stated hypotheses, the reader can only surmise from the findings and conclusions what was being tested.

The design of an investigation should be appropriate to the problem and as rigorous as circumstances permit.[22] Comparative studies of methods of teaching, for example, should specify the goals sought by each method and the major differences between the two approaches. The inclusion in the design of means for determining the stages of change rather than just final meaures of progress is especially useful. Such information provides data for identifying strengths and weaknesses of each method so that school personnel may be fully aware of the problems which might be encountered should they adopt the innovation.

Unfortunately, many research reports omit a description of the components of methods or materials. An extreme example is the report which states that a new method was compared with a basal reader method, without even specifying the basal reader. Even more vague is the statement that the new method was compared with that in use in the school. In this instance the reader is at a total loss to know what is being compared. The reader should be able

---

22. Campbell and Stanley, *op. cit.*, p. 204.

to identify the variables being studied and to have some assurance that others were considered and equated as well as possible.

The selection of subjects for study is a significant item to consider. Since it is almost impossible to match subjects on more than one or two characteristics, many other characteristics are not considered. Random assignment of subjects to two treatments helps to equate factors which may distort the results, since each pupil has an equal opportunity to be a part of either treatment. In some research reports, experimental subjects appear to be brighter, to be more mature, or to have other favorable advantages.

The method of selection of teachers for comparative studies should also be reported. In some investigations highly motivated volunteers are assigned to the new procedures while teachers who do not volunteer are used as controls. The matching of such factors as age, education, and years of experience may be less important than the eagerness of a volunteer teacher to try a different procedure. Matching volunteer with non-volunteer teachers may contribute to the "halo" or Hawthorne effect revealed by the findings.

The "halo" or Hawthorne effect is often difficult to control, but a research report should reveal the steps taken to do so or, if none were taken, it should reveal this fact in interpreting the results.

Many factors known to influence reading progress should be accounted for in a research report. For example, time given to reading instruction may differ in two programs. In that case, one may not know whether the extra time or the new method or a combination of the two was responsible for differences in the progress of two groups. Reading gains may be due to increased instructional time, thus decreasing the time available for other aspects of the curriculum.

Measures of progress of two groups in a study should be chosen to include the goals of each method. If one method emphasizes word recognition while the other emphasizes comprehension, evaluation of both should be made. Such evaluation allows the reader to judge the relative progress in each area in terms of what he wishes pupils to achieve.

Careful scrutiny of the statistical treatment of the data should be made. Some reports of comparative studies merely include differences in scores, per cents of gains, or mean differences. Today, statistical methods have been designed to offer more rigorous tests of the confidence to be placed in differences; computers can supply such data readily. Few researchers and even fewer teachers are competent statisticians, so it is often necessary to consult a specialist in evaluating the statistical treatments of data. One of the common errors in interpreting data is to assign a cause-and-effect relationship to the association established between two variables by one of several statistical procedures. Correlation does not mean causation.

Conclusions should be based on the findings rather than on the hopes of the investigator. In one comparative study at the first-grade level, the findings showed no significant difference between the results of the two treatments, yet the conclusions favored the new procedure. For many years the conclusions were quoted again and again, without reference to the fact that they were unsupported.

Most comparative studies should be carried on long enough to determine the impact of the new method or approach. Furthermore, longitudinal studies are needed to assess the later effects of early gains attributed to an innovation. Nearly a half century ago, Buswell noted that children progress toward maturity in reading by different routes and that only repeated assessment of progress will determine the ultimate effects of different methods resulting in various routes.[23] Yet few investigators have charted the routes. To do so requires frequent assessment of aspects of reading which have been learned as well as of those that have not been mastered. This record of attainment can be assessed using the principles set forth in chapter ix by McCullough. This procedure must continue long enough to determine the outcomes that are needed for competence in reading a wide variety of materials.

The foregoing examples of types of weaknesses which appear in comparative research reports were aimed to alert the reader to be critical in accepting published research. It is clear that some of these defects in research have prevented the authors of earlier

---

23. Guy Thomas Buswell, *Fundamental Reading Habits: A Study of Their Development* ("Supplementary Educational Monographs," No. 21 [Chicago: University of Chicago Press, 1922]), p. 86.

chapters from reaching conclusions about innovations that they have noted or described.

In the future, rigorous criticism of published research will be more available to practitioners. One of the stated functions of the Educational Resources Information Center (ERIC) established by the U.S. Office of Education is to sort out dependable from undependable investigations.[24] When time permits expert critics to analyze the mass of research reports, the confusion about methods and materials should be reduced. At the least, teachers who are told that "research says" a certain method is superior to others will more readily be able to check the validity of the statement.

NEEDED CO-OPERATIVE EFFORTS

Whether the researcher is a part of a school system, a university, or a special research center, he needs the schools for his laboratory if he is to begin to solve some of the crucial problems in reading. The interaction of teachers, pupils, methods, materials, and school organization is indeed complex. In order to determine the most important elements to improve teaching and learning, administrators, teachers, and parents should become aware of the essential control imposed by careful research. In return, the investigator owes the schools an honest and readable report of his research to help the school improve instruction. Furthermore, it is usually necessary for the researcher and teacher to keep careful records of instruction and of learners' progress and problems if maximal insights into the sequences and the routes to reading competence are to be gained.

As Campbell and Stanley pointed out, even the best co-operation between school personnel and a researcher provides quasi-experimental evidence because numerous unaccountable factors enter into the school setting.[25] Hence, replication in the same schools

---

24. Other information retrieval centers are being established. Phi Delta Kappa has just announced the establishment of an education reference library, School Research Information Service (SRIS), designed to gather and disseminate descriptions of innovative practices. A working relationship with ERIC will avoid duplication of efforts.

25. Campbell and Stanley, *op. cit.*, p. 204.

and in different schools provides more dependable evidence of the values of innovations than does one study, no matter how well it it controlled.

Experimentation by schools is equally essential. Frequently school experimentation suggests and defines urgent problems for the researcher. Research time can be saved if some of the needed pilot or preliminary study has already been completed by the school.

Co-operative efforts not only help to solve problems but, in most instances, also improve school achievement. With a larger number of trained investigators and increasingly competent school personnel, the lists of problems needing investigation may be subsequently reduced in the next decade.

Future Experimentation and Research

The explosion in the production of new types of instructional materials will, of necessity, increase the amount of experimentation in schools. Therefore, as Austin suggests in chapter x, teachers and administrators should be prepared to adjust to innovations and changes. However, experiments should be planned with the whole school program in focus, as Congreve states in chapter viii.

Furthermore, larger schools will wish to plan and carry out their own research. Thus, the present trend toward the demand for reading researchers in school systems is likely to increase.

Already the dearth of researchers in reading and the language arts is acute, and competition for their services is extremely keen. Schools must continue to compete with universities and now with industry. While the USOE and private foundations are supporting the education of a greater number of potential scholars, additional steps will be needed before the supply begins to meet the demand.

If reading research is to be taken seriously in the next decade, concerted efforts must be made to improve the quality of research. This need should be accepted as a challenge to every university offering a doctoral program. For those whose training in research has been inadequate, post-doctoral fellowships and even intensive summer programs may be useful. Professional associations such as the American Educational Research Association and the International Reading Association are already sponsoring preconference workshops to keep researchers informed of new techniques and procedures.

What will be the effect of more and better-trained research persons? First, it should be possible to reduce some of the confusion in the field of reading. Short-term studies with inadequate designs which state sweeping but unjustified conclusions will surely be so severely criticized that professional journals may become increasingly discriminating about the quality of reports they publish. Scientists outside the field have noted with surprise the dearth of criticism of published research in reading. More rigorous criticism of research should be of great value to practitioners who are bombarded with claims of scientific support for conflicting views.

Second, the next generation of reading researchers should be able to exchange information on promising exploratory investigations without being compelled to draw final conclusions. Hence, replication of potentially useful studies will become reputable and will permit a large accumulation of data before conclusions are reached. In this case, unsupported generalizations for total populations may be largely eliminated, and differential recommendations will be made for specific populations. Whereas the researcher of the midsixties is now pressed for immediate results both by practitioners who need answers and by universities that demand quantity of publication, tomorrow's researcher may have more time for careful, substantial studies. In exploratory research, especially, the researcher will gain respect by testing new theories and procedures, some of which will prove to be inadequate. Furthermore, the profession will surely tolerate and profit from reports of research the hypotheses of which were *not* supported.

Third, with a central source like ERIC for collecting and disseminating information on completed research, there will be no reason for the repetition of studies that have proved to be of minimal value. Each major library can afford to acquire and store all significant reports of research. Reports of insignificant research can be acquired when a complete bibliography is requested. Even poorly designed investigations may inspire new attacks on old problems.

The foregoing implies a new attitude toward research in reading which must develop to spawn significant insights.

Fourth, the new technology rapidly becoming available to the creative researcher will extend the range and increase the number of types of problems that he may investigate. Moreover, it will continue to reduce the lag between the time of data collection and interpretation. Data-processing machines now provide complicated statistical analyses in minutes. Scanning devices that score tests, programs that count and analyze words and phrases, and automatic recording devices that keep permanent records of behavior are only a few of the aids becoming available. Videotapes and other types of records of behavior may eliminate the need for observers in classrooms in which research is in progress. Such records can be analyzed at leisure to determine exactly what occurred in the classroom. They should be especially useful in studying teacher-pupil interaction, types of questions used, and similar problems.

In addition to the foregoing functions of technology, computerized instruction in reading will surely continue to develop. In the production of programs for the computer, the sequences of skills and abilities for effective learning will necessarily be investigated in minute detail. Lange suggests that preschool programs as well as those for an entire school curriculum are envisaged.[26] Before such programs can be effective, it will be necessary to gain increased knowledge of learner characteristics basic to reading success. As Durkin points out in chapter ii, it will also be essential to devise appropriate means for teaching younger children, since the procedures in current use may be quite inappropriate.

The ability of the computer to store, sort, and reproduce isolated pieces of information makes possible promising studies of the relationship among factors which may be combined to insure pupils' learning to read. In the process of program development, new kinds of diagnostic reading tests will emerge. The values of such tests in studying retarded readers should be great. As the writer stated

---

26. Phil C. Lange, "Future Developments," in *Programed Instruction*, ed. Phil C. Lange (Sixty-sixth Yearbook of the National Society for the Study of Education, Part II [Chicago: Distributed by University of Chicago Press, 1967]), p. 296.

earlier, self-diagnosis and prescription may ultimately be possible.[27] While the next decade may not realize all of the envisaged possibilities, great progress is anticipated.

Accompanied by reorganization of the schools to provide for individual progress, such as Sartain described in chapter vi, patterns of pupils' learning successes and failures will offer new leads to research in reading.

The new technology for capturing, recording, and retrieving fugitive stimuli and resulting behavior suggests unprecedented research opportunities. It appears that the range of problems to be investigated will soon be limited only by the kinds of questions researchers are ready to pose.

Finally, the impact of an increased number of able reading researchers should reduce the waste in time and effort on the part of school personnel, who are exposed to continuous public criticism and who lack research support for many of their practices. Concurrently, respect for reading research should be elevated to the point that it really makes a difference in the beliefs and practices of teachers and administrators.

What possible effects may be anticipated from increased support for research? If the support for research includes both finances and professional recognition, many able people may be engaged in full-time research rather than spread their energies over a wide area of activities. A sufficient number of persons so engaged should provide continuity in exploring a problem until all of its aspects have been taken into account. In this way, the new problems arising from a particular investigation may be explored by the person who already possesses interest and insight into the ways to solve them.

Will the competent reading researcher work alone? A few creative scholars will continue to spark new ideas, but in all probability many more research centers will be developed. A community of scholars with a central focus can be rewarding. Concurrently,

---

27. Helen M. Robinson, "Looking Ahead in Reading," in *Recent Developments in Reading*, ed. H. Alan Robinson (Proceedings of the Annual Conference on Reading held at the University of Chicago, 1965; "Supplementary Educational Monographs," No. 95 [Chicago: University of Chicago Press, 1965]), pp. 217-27.

able researchers can inspire and supervise those who are less mature. Furthermore, technology moves so rapidly that specialists in this area will be essential.

Many scholars with other types of orientation are using reading as an area of application for their studies of learning. Consequently, both accumulated information and techniques for reading research can be enriched by providing centers for interdisciplinary research. A few university reading centers already have members of other disciplines on their research staffs. In addition, agencies or groups, such as the Center for Applied Linguistics, have sponsored meetings to explore fruitful relationships among linguists, psychologists, and reading specialists. An impetus to co-ordinated research and practice is the national Interdisciplinary Committee on Reading Problems, formed in September, 1966. At the time this chapter is being prepared, five task forces are at work. They plan to prepare authoritative documents to serve as a guide for action at the national level. The five reports on reading planned are: (*a*) definition, etiology, and diagnosis; (*b*) incidence and implications; (*c*) treatment and prevention; (*d*) application to schools and schools of education; and (*e*) research. Such authoritative documents may be the beginning of mutual understanding which will guide research into increasingly productive areas.

The foregoing discussion suggests that research in reading can be more productive in the next decade than it has been in any previous one.

New Materials and Services

Changes in instructional materials, especially basal readers and related materials, have been gradual, with few dramatic innovations prior to 1960. Both Wittick and Huus have noted the changes and have described some of the new materials. These include basal readers, supplementary readers, programed books, workbooks, kits, filmstrips, and various machines.

Just on the horizon at this time are corporate giants which are entering the educational materials field. Reports of recent purchases by large corporations of publishing companies and agencies engaged in producing reading materials include the following: IBM has purchased Science Research Associates; Raytheon, D. C. Heath;

Xerox, Wesleyan University Press; Radio Corporation of America, Random House; Columbia Broadcasting System, Holt, Rinehart and Winston. In addition, General Electric and Time, Inc., have formed a partnership, calling their new subsidiary General Learning Corporation. Other unions are reported to be in progress.

The effects of the entry of big business into the publishing industry are speculative. Some educators fear that there will be a spate of materials which are narrowly conceived and prepared under the direction of persons who are oriented toward sales of machines. At the opposite extreme are those who expect a revolution in materials for instruction because the most creative talent can be purchased to design materials. In all probability, the products will vary greatly in quality. One can speculate that various systems and programs to accompany machines will be made available. Whatever the plan may be, it is safe to conclude that books will accompany the other materials.

The new materials will undoubtedly be promoted by advertising similar to that used by business today. If claims for the success of each program should resemble claims for commercial products, parents may be expected to place great pressure on schools to "use the best." One effect will surely be to expect school personnel to become well informed about all types of instructional materials. Indirectly, the necessity to evaluate different types of materials may lead schools to specify their goals in reading and the steps to be taken to achieve those goals. When these steps are described, appropriate instructional materials may then be chosen to facilitate progress toward the specified goals.

Many smaller schools will have neither the money nor the talent to keep abreast of new products. This need may be met by a new organization, Educational Products Information Exchange (EPIE), 52 Vanderbilt Avenue, New York 10017, which was established in the mid-sixties as a non-profit agency. The purposes stated in the prospectus are: "to improve the educator's ability to select wisely among the increasingly numerous and complex products of the education industry; increase the exchange of information between users and producers of instructional materials, equipment, and systems with the object of improving their design, development, and use; encourage educational innovation by calling attention to new products and to innovative uses of familiar products; and contribute to the humanistic use of technology in education." This interchange should stimulate continuous improvement of materials as well as help school personnel. Products will not be rated but rather described and, as empirical data are gathered, reports will be available to schools showing the results in different instructional settings and with different types of learners.

Even with the best of service from different sources, school personnel will experience increased difficulty in choosing the best of new materials.

Programs for Illiterates and Poor Readers

Traditionally, reading instruction has been allocated almost entirely to the schools. In the mid-sixties, a great many supplementary programs have developed. Most are of such recent origin that no satisfactory evaluations have been made. The impact of such programs remains to be determined, as Huus pointed out in chapter iv, in which she described some television programs for illiterates.

Schools are making many efforts to reduce adult illiteracy through the use of remedial reading classes and, more recently, by after-school tutoring. However, so few adults have been tutored to date that the impact of such tutoring is negligible.

After-school tutoring.—To increase the rate of progress in reading, a wide variety of programs have been designed. In most instances, their purpose is to accelerate reading progress of the culturally deprived students. Many studies, such as that of Cooper, show that, as these children progress through the elementary grades, their retardation in reading becomes more acute.[28] To reverse this trend, the federal government and some local schools have supplied funds for tutoring such children after school.

Many classroom teachers and some remedial teachers have participated. Programs reportedly vary from basic instruction for developing reading competency to direct assistance with daily class assignments, most of which cannot be read by the children who

---

28. Bernice Cooper, "An Analysis of the Reading Achievement of White and Negro Pupils in Certain Public Schools in Georgia," *School Review*, LXXII (Winter, 1964), 462-71.

are tutored. Preliminary unpublished reports vary markedly as to the effects of the tutoring. Undoubtedly, the success of these programs will be related to the competency of the teachers, the motivation of the pupils, the availability of appropriate instructional materials, and the supervision provided.

Another type of tutoring is being provided by volunteers, most often by high-school and college students and by housewives. Some college tutoring programs are reporting better school achievement on the part of the children being tutored, while others appear to be less successful and are being abandoned. At the time this is written, neither an evaluation of what has been accomplished nor a prediction for the future is possible.

Perhaps some intensive training for volunteers, such as that described by Austin in chapter x, may make a difference in the results achieved. Structured programs for untrained teachers are being produced, but their use may be varied and less than satisfactory. The potential of volunteer tutors needs exploration using innovative plans.

Job Corps.—The adolescents and young adults who are school dropouts and have joined the Job Corps need help with reading. One of the major problems is lack of instructional materials and adequate techniques for teaching these students. A Job Corps center in Iowa is assembling professionally trained reading consultants and writers to develop a program tailored to the specific needs of youth rather than of children. This program is still being prepared and has not been tried. However, one report from another center reveals a marked increase in achievement accompanying additional experimentation. For example, 26 per cent of the youth leaving the Corps in the last half of fiscal year 1966 had advanced the equivalent of more than four years in reading and mathematics.[29]

Tests for children are quite inappropriate when used for adults, both in vocabulary and illustrations. The new *Adult Basic Learning Examination* (Harcourt, Brace and World, 1967), called ABLE, has just been released. Level I is for those achieving at about Grades II-V; Level II is for those reading at Grades V-VII. The examination includes tests of vocabulary (listening), reading comprehension,

---

29. *Education Recaps*, VI (March, 1967), 7 (a publication of the Educational Testing Service, Princeton, New Jersey, ed. Ann Z. Smith).

spelling, arithmetic computation, and problem solving. Scores are equated to children's grade norms, but percentiles are suggested for use with the students.

As appropriate procedures and materials are tried and more is learned about instruction, these experiments may provide leads for teaching younger children as well as for raising the literacy level of those who enlist in the Job Corps.

Illiteracy programs.—In the last decade, various estimates of illiteracy and functional illiteracy have been formulated. In a manpower survey, the number of persons over eighteen years of age with less than eight grades of schooling was reported to be more than 19 million, of which 816,000 were unemployed. Moveover, the Selective Service estimates that one in every six registrants fails his pre-induction educational achievement tests.[30]

Increasingly, surveys of the unemployed show the low levels of literacy of all but a small per cent. It is not surprising, therefore, to find reports from the USOE dealing with programs involving literacy training related to vocational rehabilitation. In one study, thirty-six questionnaires were sent out to selected centers; fourteen were returned, and seven centers were chosen for study in depth.[31] The programs surveyed were planned around local job opportunities. Reading and writing instruction was oriented to the occupational vocabulary—thus overcoming one of the most serious problems, motivation within foreseeable goals. The instructional materials were prepared by the staff until the students could handle the *Reader's Digest Skill Builders*, newspapers, and materials from industry. Based on the survey, a number of pertinent recommendations were made. For example, it was suggested that comprehensive programs lead the trainee from zero literacy and job skills to at least eighth-grade literacy and competence for semiskilled jobs.

The USOE has recently published a curriculum guide for *Adult Basic Education* including twenty units, each planned for a five-day

---

30. *Educationally Deficient Adults: Their Education and Needs* (U.S. Department of Health, Education, and Welfare Report, Office of Education 13029 [Washington: Government Printing Office, 1965]), pp. 7-8.

31. *Ibid.*

week of eight hours per day.[32] The suggestions to teachers are relatively specific, including preparation, teaching aids, and methodology. A second part of the guide suggests types of additional exercises and correlated subject matter and presents advice for testing.

In short, boards of education, universities, churches, welfare departments, private foundations, and the federal government are among the agencies engaged in training adult illiterates. In 1966, for example, over two hundred thousand people above eighteen years of age are reported to have participated in state programs for impoverished adults whose educational levels are below the eighth grade. Another $26 million has been alloted for fiscal year 1967.[33]

One study, supported by the Office of Economic Opportunity, field-tested four basic adult reading systems, using 540 functional illiterates (below fifth grade) in each of three states. Teachers varied from high-school graduates to professionals, some of whom were retired. The criteria used to judge the systems included efficiency of learning on the part of adult illiterates, the use of retrained teachers, flexibility as to time of entry, level of interest, operation feasibility (cost and reuse), and the like. The report states that, in terms of reading gains, the four systems yielded similar results but that differences were noted when each of the eight specific criteria were applied. The conclusion was reached that "all need improvement, but all are effective in teaching the functionally illiterate adult to read and improve his social understanding."[34] In this study, as in those with children, there was wide variation in teacher efficiency. The personal qualities of "warmth," "understanding," "flexibility," "humor," and "the ability to accept persons of the lower socio-economic group" were judged to be more important than educational qualifications.

The evaluation of the four reading systems is expected to improve them. In addition, it points to a multitude of questions which educational researchers and practitioners may explore.

32. *Curriculum Guide to Adult Basic Education, Intermediate Level*, ed. Jennie-Clyde Hollis (Washington: Government Printing Office, 1966).

33. *Education Recaps*, VI (February, 1967), 12.

34. *Field Test and Evaluation of Selected Adult Basic Education Systems* (New York: Greenleigh Associates, Inc., September, 1966), p. 106.

Programs for industry.—As chapter iv points out, industry has had a long history of providing reading instruction. For the most part, instruction has been offered to management to improve speed of reading. Other programs have been offered, however, for workers at all levels.

A more recent development in reading instruction is a part of labor-education programs for union leaders. Portman described one program sponsored by the United Automobile Workers.[35] She began with rate training to "sell" the program, accompanied by programed materials to teach vocabulary and comprehension of the main points.

With the comparatively recent changeover to automated equipment, some industries are offering in-service courses to displaced workers to help them meet new demands. Increased literacy may be needed for workers to master the content and to succeed in moving to more complicated jobs.

In the mid-sixties, the labor shortage has resulted in scattered attempts by industry to develop literacy training programs. An example is Eastman Kodak Company's program, which combines literacy training with that for specific jobs. Although no job promises are made, those who complete the course and are judged to fit the needs of the company are employed. If the present trends continue, this pattern of literacy training may be expanded to other areas where labor is needed.

The national government is stimulating a wide range of programs for illiterates and functional illiterates. Local communities are partners in this effort, through school systems and many other agencies. Industry is supporting and sometimes operating programs which offer promise.

The next decade undoubtedly will yield new instructional procedures and materials, new tests, and a wealth of supporting reading materials written at different levels. In addition to books will come newspapers and industrial bulletins and pamphlets directed toward the neo-literate.

---

35. Lisa Portman, "A Reading Course for Labor Unions," *Journal of Reading*, X (October, 1966), 29-32.

While isolated reports of the progress in reading made by illiterates are available, the ultimate effects of the scattered programs must be awaited. Whatever the preliminary results may be, the total activities in this area undoubtedly will be sharply increased by both business and government.

National and International Assessment

The Project on Assessing the Progress of Education planned for American schools will provide essential information about the status of achievement in school and adult life. One of the areas to be assessed is reading and language arts. Of special interest, first, is the statement of objectives endorsed by scholars, teachers, and lay citizens. The objectives may influence the curriculum in reading. A second noteworthy development is that paper-and-pencil tests are supplemented by such procedures as interviews, questionnaires, and observations, which may provide information about interests, habits, skills, and practices as they relate to different age levels.[36] These procedures may foster a broader type of evaluation of reading progress. Third, the assessment is planned for four age groups: nine, thirteen, seventeen, and adult. Information about adult reading, which has been difficult to obtain, will be especially suggestive for the school curriculum, because at present little is known about many aspects or areas of adult reading. Finally, the plan for repeated assessment, perhaps each decade, should provide objective evidence of the future effects of innovation and change in reading instruction over a period of time.

Work on the second phase of the program of the International Project for the Evaluation of Educational Achievement is underway and will provide comparative data on reading comprehension among a number of countries. The first report, which dealt with mathematics, suggested the importance of determining why certain national groups excel in mathematics. It is anticipated that comparative data on reading achievement may suggest advantages or disadvantages of the alphabets with consistent phoneme-grapheme correspondence,

---

36. Ralph W. Tyler, "The Current Status of the Project on Assessing the Progress of Education," *Educational Horizons*, XLV (Summer, 1967), 184-90.

of various instructional procedures, and, perhaps, of the cultural values placed on literacy. It is anticipated that, within a few years, the results may suggest basic issues for further research.

Needs and Expectations

Today's society demands literacy from every segment of its people. Concerted efforts are being made in schools to meet the needs of those children who come from cultures which in the past have had little or no appreciation for literacy. National, state, and local money is being appropriated for massive attacks on the problem. So far, no adequate solutions have been found; indeed, it is uncertain whether they will be found soon. In the next decade there will be many ineffective programs as well as some that produce sharp improvements in reading and related language skills.

In the meantime, it is obvious that equal or greater efforts will be exerted to reduce adult illiteracy, which will persist long after solutions are found to the problem of effective reading instruction for the culturally deprived.

There is real danger that schools will neglect the children who have progressed satisfactorily and the superior readers. This neglect may occur if history repeats itself—if schools become so absorbed with solving the problems of one social level that innovating practices at other levels are not attempted. At present, it is difficult to anticipate that equal attention will be given to improving the reading of all students.

Undoubtedly, curriculum, methods, and materials will be altered to meet the needs of our rapidly changing society. It seems likely that greater emphasis will be placed on motivation for independent activities, on teaching children and youth how to learn on their own. This premise implies increased use of developing techniques, such as programed and computerized instruction, in appropriate situations. Moreover, the concept of reading must include more than word recognition and must aim for critical response to print. If students are to learn independently, they must be able to judge veracity and worth. In the process, some students may become active participators, carrying on a dialogue with the author and accepting and using only ideas supported by data or logic.

In order to meet society's increased demands for literacy, innovation and change in reading instruction will probably increase in the next decade. Undoubtedly, different patterns of organizing the schools are just over the horizon. As the age of school entrance is lowered, greater differentiation can be made, permitting children to begin to read when they are competent and when interest becomes keen. Continuous individual progress rather than that stipulated for a year must be provided by some plans that alter the so-called grade lock-step. Such plans would change the design of graded instructional materials. Continuous progress calls for instructional units of less duration than a year or a semester, frequent diagnostic testing, and remedial materials designed to correct specific problems.

In addition to changes in schools, curriculums, and materials, an increase in exposure to books, magazines, newspapers, and pamphlets will undoubtedly enrich the reading program. If pupils become accustomed to using these types of printed messages independently while in school, perhaps adults of the future will use reading to a greater extent than they do today. Furthermore, it may be possible for an increasing number of adults to be more readily retrained for jobs as well as to become better informed citizens and to make better use of leisure time for self-improvement.

Today's society is searching for new methods of teaching reading and different materials for instruction. Important as these methods may be, research has demonstrated that the way they are used is the key to success in teaching reading. Thus, the teacher becomes the central figure in tomorrow's reading instruction. Preservice education must prepare teachers for change. The number of courses in teaching reading will become less significant than the kinds of learning involved. Rather than employing recipes for reading instruction, teachers need to understand *how* and *why* certain procedures are more successful than others. Teachers must be encouraged to adapt to differences in pupils. Simulation offers some hope of reducing the time needed to acquire some of the basic procedures. Understanding of children and of how they learn should enable neophytes to be more flexible. Since schools will differ markedly in the changes they make in the next decade, in-service training will be required to induct the new teacher into the particular school program. Because of the mobility of teachers, more efficient programs of in-service training are sorely needed. Closed-circuit and educational television, kinescopes, and other devices need to be exploited.

Greater insights into the characteristics of effective teachers are being reported today. Undoubtedly, this research dealing with teaching and learning can be of first importance in both pre- and in-service programs.

Finally, if segments of or all of society expect excellence in reading instruction, society's members need to accept their responsibilities for providing support for teachers—not just financial support but the support of all correlated agencies of the society.

Research in the next decade may increase in scope and improve in quality and may thus better assist in providing some of the basic understandings of the reading process so important for teaching and learning. While basic research is in progress, the logic of various specialists and innovators will point to the continuous need for schools to make choices among procedures and materials. Wise choices based on known principles of learning, on the recognition of individual differences among learners, and on knowledge of the competence of teachers will continue to be most essential in the future.

Index

Abrams, Alfred L., 168
Achievement in reading, variables having influence on, 279-81
Adams, Mary L., 363
Adams, Phyllis S., 106, 179
Administrator(s): criteria of, for selecting innovations, 5; in-service growth of, 376-77; leadership role of, in reading, 375-76; preparation of, for leadership, 376
Adults, literacy training for, 140-43
After-school tutoring, programs of, 422-23
Allen, R. Van, quoted, 105
American Educational Research Association (AERA), 370, 416
American Library Association, Adult Services Division of, 142
Ames, Wilbur, 132
Anastasiow, Nicholas J., 80
Anderson, A. W., 134
Anderson, Robert H., quoted, 221
Applebee, Robert K., 365
Arbuckle, Dugald S., 280
Arthur, Grace, 36
Artley, A. Sterl, 6
Ashton-Warner, Sylvia, 89
Association for Childhood Education International (ACEI), 46
Austin, Mary C., 6, 301; quoted 76; quoted (with C. Morrison), 219
Ausubel, David P., quoted, 49

Balance in reading development, 320-56; concept of, 323-25; definition of, 320-21; problem of, 321-23
Balancing the reading program, materials available for, 338-55
Balow, Irving H., 173, 193, 206, 207, 219, 287
Ballard, Grady L., 133
Barnhart, Clarence L., 79, 189
Barrett, Thomas C., 17, 18, 19, 28, 85, 119, 174

Barton, Allen N., 115, 366, 387; quoted, 166-67
Barwick, Janice M., 280
Basal readers, use of, in balancing programs, 341-43
Basic skills, improvement of, 129-43
Bateman, Barbara, 265, 285
Beery, Keith F., 174, 175
Behavior-analysis research in relation to reading, 274-76
Belmont, Lillian, 289
Bender, Lauretta, 168, 285
Berg, Paul, 139
Berman, Phyllis W., 288
Betts, Emmett A., 11, 163, 214
Birch, Herbert G., 289
Blau, Harold, 187
Bliesmer, Emery P., 106
Bloom, Benjamin S., 18, 43, 404
Bloomer, Richard H., 131, 189, 264, 270
Bloomfield, Leonard, 10, 79
Bond, Guy L., 100, 101, 105, 179, 391; quoted, 101, 406; quoted (with R. Dykstra), 100; quoted (with E. B. Wagner), 211
Bonhorst, Ben A., 106
Borg, Walter R., 204, 205, 206
Bormuth, John R., 130, 131, 271
Braam, Leonard, 135, 365
Braidford, Margaret, 106
Brekke, Gerald W., 364
Bruner, Jerome S., 41
Bryant, N. Dale, 285
Budoff, Melton, 275
Bunger, Marianne, 140
Burns, John L., 96
Burr, Marvin A., 204
Burton, Dwight L., 248
Buswell, Guy T., 279, 414

Calvert, James J., 172
Cambria, Richard, 282
Campbell, Donald T., 411, 415

Carbone, Robert F., 229
Carnegie Corporation, 359
Carner, R. L., 143, 144
Carrigan, Patricia M., 13, 170, 191, 277, 285
Carroll, John B., 143, 266; quoted, 65-66
Certification of reading personnel by the state, 371-73
Chall, Jeanne, 73, 76, 112, 123; quoted, 73, 86, 97, 98
Chansky, Norman M., 179
Charts, use of, in balancing program, 343-44
Chase, Francis S., 398
Child development, contributions of field of, to reading, 250
Childhood education, goals of, 250-55
Clark, Christine H., 107
Clark, Philip, 278
Class structure, teacher in relation to, 243-46
Clay, Marie M., 400
Cleland, Donald L., 17, 99, 178
Clements, Sam D., 171; quoted, 168
Clinical psychology, interaction of field of, with reading, 284-88
Cloward, Robert D., 192
Cloze exercises and procedures, 131-32; use of, 269-70
Clymer, Theodore, 3, 6; quoted (with W. W. Cook), 203
Coghill, G. E., 30, 31
Cognitive development, reading in relation to research in, 255-58
Cohn, Robert, 286
Coleman, E. B., 131
College reading instructors, preparation of, 384-87
Comparing Reading Approaches in First-Grade Teaching (CRAFT), 109, 110
Comprehension, improvement of, 130-34
Comprehension models, 14-23
Comprehension questions, sequence for presentation of, 132-33
Comprehensive Skills Model, 23-27
Conant, James B., 359, 360
Congreve, Willard, 5, 416
Concepts, development of, 143-45
Consultant in reading, involvement of, in teachers' concerns, 301-2
Consultants and Colleges, co-operation between, 380

Consultants in reading, scope of operations of, 377-79
Continuous Progress Plan, 230-32
Cook, Walter W.: quoted, 208; quoted (with T. Clymer), 203
Cooper, Bernice, 422
Co-operative teaching, discussion of, 221-23
Corrective instruction, organization of, 182-84
Cox, Brian J., 283
Critchley, Macdonald, 162, 167, 169; quoted, 168
Critical reading: definitions of, 146-47; development of, 146-49
Crome, George F., 172
Cruikshank, W. M., 171, 287

Dale, Edgar, 90, 145; quoted, 211
Daniels, J. C., 74, 189
Davis, Frederick B., 117, 259
Dawe, Helen C., 251, 252
Decoding program, stronger types of, 77-87
Deficiency (reading), definition of, 160
De Grasia, Sebastian, 398
De Hirsch, Katrina, 117, 181
Deighton, Lee C., 17
Delacato, Carl H., 114, 115, 170, 185
Denny, Terry P., 114, 401
Departmentalization, studies relating to, 217-19
Deutsch, Cynthia P., 175
Deutsch, Martin, 176
Dewey, John, 31, 73
Diack, Hunter, 74, 189
Diacritical Marking System (DMS), 82, 84, 104; see also, Modified alphabets
Diagnosis, determining necessary level of, 180-81
Diagnostic and evaluative material, use of, in balancing programs, 350
Diagnostic reading tests, discussion of, 120-21
Differentiated vs. uniform instruction, 209-11
Directed vs. independent study, 211-13
Disabled reader, identification of, 178-80
Donalson, William R., 372
Downing, John A., 83, 103
Dual Progress Plan, 221-22

Duncan, Robert L., 98
Durkin, Dolores, 3, 120, 418; quoted, 77
Durrell, Donald D., 85, 227
Dykstra, Robert, 101, 105, 113, 175, 289, 391; quoted (with G. L. Bond), 100
Dyrud, Jarl E., 189; quoted (with I. Goldiamond), 190
Dyslexia, 182; definition of, 160; discussion of, 167-71

Eames, Thomas H., 282
Early, Margaret, 6
Edmiston, R. W., 205
Educational Products Information Exchange (EPIE), 421
Educational Policies Commission, 41
Educational programs, need for better evaluation of, 307-8
Educational psychology, contributions of, to reading, 272-81
Educational Resources Information Service (ERIC), 415, 417
Edwards, Thomas J., 189
Ekstrom, Ruth, 204
Elementary and Secondary Education Act, 74, 107, 166, 167, 183, 369
Elkind, David, 288
Eller, William, 137
Ellinger, Bernice D., 146, 148
Ellson, Douglas G., 190, 273
Ennis, Robert H., 146
Ernhart, Clair B., 288
Evaluation, studies in field of, bearing on balancing of reading program, 337-38
Experimentation: need for, in schools, 408; types of, needed, 409-10
Experiments in reading, characteristics of, 408

Fader, Daniel N., 152
Falk School, the continuous-progress plan in, 230-32
Farinella, John T., 364
Feldmann, Shirley C., 112, 121, 123, 249
Fernald, Grace M., 87, 162, 186
Field experience, need for, in preparation of reading specialists, 381-82
Films and filmstrips, use of, in balancing program, 347-48

First R, The, 363; recommendations of, for reading programs, 362
Flesch, Rudolph, 63; see also, *Why Johnny Can't Read*
Ford Foundation Project, 93, 359
Foundation for World Literacy, 128
Francis, W. N., 259
Friedman, Mildred, 270
Fries, Charles C., 79, 189, 266; quoted, 10
Frost, Barry P., 179
Frostig, Marianne, 114, 174, 186, 187
Fry, Edward B., 81, 104
Future developments in reading instruction: generalizations with respect to, 397-99; unsolved problems relating to, 400-7

Gallegher, James J., 287
Games and devices, use of, in balancing program, 346-47
Gates, Arthur I., 69, 162, 165, 279, 411; quoted, 38-39, 39, 65
Gattegno, Caleb, 84
Gesell, Arnold, 33, 34, 35, 39, 46, 251, 253
Getzels, Jacob W., 256
Giammatteo, Michael C., 241
Gibb, E. Glenadine, quoted (with D. C. Matala), 233
Gibson, Eleanor, J., 11, 288
Gillingham, Anna, 189
Goals, assessment of, in reading, 5-6
Gold, Lawrence, quoted (with others), 110
Goldberg, Lynn, 265
Goldberg, Miriam L., 204; quoted (with others), 205, 208-9; quoted (with A. H. Passow), 206-7
Goldiamond, Israel, 189; quoted (with J. E. Dyrud), 190
Goodlad, John I., 293; quoted, 197
Gordon, Ira J., 107
Graham, Frances K., 288
Grattan, Paul E., 282
Gray, Clarence T., 162
Gray, William S., 23, 24, 25, 26, 28, 121, 128, 162; quoted, 129
Gray-Robinson model, 23-27
Greene, John D., quoted, 209
Great Cities School Improvement Project, 92
Griffin, William J., 261
Groff, Patrick, 89, 105; quoted, 107
Guilford, Joy P., 14, 15, 278, 404

Gurren, Louise, 99
Guzak, James, 18

Hafner, Lawrence E., 270, 271
Hagin, Rosa A., 186, 287
Hallgren, Bertil, 164, 169
Hanna, Jean S., 264
Hanna, Paul R., 264
Hansen, Duncan, 80
Harrell, Lester E., Jr., 262
Harris, Albert J., 117, 233; quoted, 118; quoted (with others), 110
Hartill, R. W., 205
Harvard-Carnegie Reading Studies, 127, 359, 360, 361, 363, 364, 375, 376, 383, 386
Havighurst, Robert J., 40
Hawthorne effect, 111, 115, 122, 189, 248, 310, 311, 413-14
Hay, Julie, 78
Hayes, Robert B., 108
Head Start, 43, 167
Healy, Ann K., 239
Heathers, Glen, 221; quoted, 222-23
Herber, Harold L., 138
Hermann, Knud, 164, 169
Hersch, Marilyn F., 186
Hetrogeneous *vs.* homogeneous sectioning, 202-9
Higher Education Act, 359
Higher-level reading abilities, innovations in procedures for development of, 403-4
Hill, Edwin H., 241
Hillson, Maurie, 229
Hilson, Helen H., 106
Hinshelwood, James, 162, 164
Hirsch, Monroe J., 283
Holmes, Jack A., 12, 13, 276, 277, 285
Hopkins, Kenneth D., 229
Howards, Melvin, 148
Huey, Edmund B., 31
Hughes, Ann, 99
Hull, Clark L., 204
Hull, Lorene, quoted, 258-59
Hunt, J. McVicker, 42, 43; quoted, 34
Hunt, Kellogg W., 260
Huus, Helen, 4, 420, 422; quoted, 146

Illiterates, problems for, 412-17
Illiteracy programs, 424-25
Illustrations, innovations in, 92

Independent *vs.* directed study, 211-13
Individualized programs, approach to balance through, 353-54
Individualized reading, discussion of, 223-25
Individually Prescribed Instruction, discussion of program of, 225-27
Industry, literacy programs of, 426-27
Ingram, Vivien, 229
Initial Teaching Alphabet (i.t.a.), 77, 82, 83, 103, 187, 277, 355; *see also,* ITA, i.t.a., Modified Alphabets
Innovations: case study of, in reading, 299-307; designing the evaluation component of, 309-11; evaluation of, 307-17; evaluation of, in terms of concept of balance, 350-55; involving parents and community in, 299; methods designed to facilitate introduction of, in reading, 303; need of rationale for, 294; practical view of, 311-14
Innovative approaches to reading, list of, 305-6
Innovative reading programs, evaluation of, 314-17
In-service education of teachers, 368-71; team approach to, 379-80
Institute of Applied Linguistics, 166
Instructional changes, causes of, 2
Interclass grouping within self-contained classrooms, 213-17
International Project for the Evaluation of Educational Achievement, 427
International Reading Association, 45, 46, 184, 391, 416; standards of, proposed for certification of reading specialists, 381
Irwin, Ruth, 259
ITA, 103, 109; *see also,* Initial Teaching Alphabet, i.t.a., Modified Alphabets
i.t.a., 77, 82, 83, 103, 187, 277, 355; *see also,* Initial Teaching Alphabet, ITA, Modified Alphabets
Izzo, Ruth K., 106

Jackson, Joseph, 218
Jansky, Jeannette J., 117, 181
Jenkins, Frances, quoted, 37
Job Corps, work of, 423-24
Johnson, Marjorie S., 186
Jones, Daisy M., 210

INDEX 435

Joos, Loyal W., 189
Joplin Interclass Grouping Plan, 219-20
Justman, Joseph, 204; quoted (with others), 205; 208-9

Kanzer, Paul, 275
Karlsen, Bjorn, 265
Katz, Phyllis A., 176
Keliher, Alice, 204
Keller, Helen, 162
Kephart, Newell C., 171, 172, 185
King, Martha, 133, 404
Kingston, Albert J., 12, 17, 85
Kirk, Samuel A., 287
Kohlberg, Lawrence, quoted, 67
Komarek, Henrietta, 364
Krippner, Stanley, 190

Laboratory programs, example of, 156-57
Lancaster, Louise, 328
Lange, Phil C., 418; quoted, 91
Langford, William S., 117, 181
Language-arts approach in relation to balanced programs, 352-53
La Pay, Margaret H., 265
Larson, Margaret, 288
Lashinger, Donald R., 111
Leahy, Mary K., 364
Learning theory, research on, relation to reading, 276-78
Learning to read, time for beginning of, 55-68
Leavell, Ullin W., 185
Lerner, Janet W., 318
Letson, Charles, 136
Letton, Mildred C., 18; see also, Wittick, Mildred L.
Levin, Harry, 10, 11, 265, 275, 402
Library books, importance of, in reading, 150-53
Liddle, William, 137
Linguistic approach in relation to balance, 354-55
Linguistic offering, balance in, for development of child as a reader, 327-28
Linguistics: reading in relation to developments in, 258-66; research in, in relation to balanced reading instruction, 326-28
Literacy for Adults and Related Knowledge (LARK), 142

Literacy Instruction for Texas (LIFT), 142
Literary training for adults, 140-43
Literature, problems of balance in reading development posed by contributions of field of, 325-26
Llorens, Lela A., 288
Loban, Walter D., 122, 259, 260
Lockard, John, 275

McCallister, James M., 324
McCarthy, Dorothea, 259
McCarthy, James J., 287
McCarthy, W., 187
McCord, Hallack, 191
McCracken, Glenn, 40
McCullough, Constance, 5, 9, 15, 16, 147, 414
McDonald, Arthur, 135, 136
McGinnis, Dorothy J., 364, 365
McGraw, Myrtle B., 34, 35
McLeod, John, 182
McMenemy, Richard A., 179
Magazines, use of, in balancing programs, 348-49
Malmquist, Eve, 165, 170, 181
Malone, John R., 83
Mann, Horace, 195
Manpower Development and Training Act, 393
Marburger, Carl L., 92
Marchbanks, Gabrielle, 275
Marquardt, William F., 262, 263
Martinson, Ruth A., 205
Mass media, contributions of, to reading, 239-40
Matala, Dorothy C., quoted (with E. G. Gibb), 233
Mathews, Mitford M., 72
Matin, Milton B., 287
Maxwell, Martha J., 135
Mazurkiewicz, Albert J., 103, 279
Meshover, Leonard, 120
Methods and materials: changes in, in reading, 420-22; major current innovations in, 74-96
Miller, George A., 264
Miller, Harry B., 99
Milner, Esther, 253
Mitzel, Harold E., 13, 277
Models for reading, 11-23
Modified Alphabets: list and discussion of, 82-85; use of, 187-88; see also, Diacritical Marking System,

Initial Teaching Alphabet, ITA, i.t.a., Unifon Sound Alphabet
Monroe, Marion, 163, 165, 179
Moore, O. K., 44, 86, 94
Montessori education, 44
Montessori, Maria, 44, 87, 250
Montessori Method, The, 87
Moray, Kenneth, 282
Morgan, W. Pringle, 162
Morphett, Mabel V., 36
Morrison, Coleman, 301; quoted (with M. C. Austin), 219
Morrone, Victor E., quoted, 98
Morrow, William R., 280
Motor and perceptual training in remediation, 185-86
Muehl, Siegmar, 275
Multisensory approaches in remediation, 186-87

National Academy of Sciences, 41
National assessment of education, program of, 417-18
National Defense Education Act, 74, 166, 383; institutes of, 371
National Education Association, 43; Department of Elementary School Principals of, 376; National Training Laboratories of, 377
National Institute of Child Health and Development, 390
National Society for the Study of Education, 35, 36, 55; yearbooks on reading of, 1
Neurological patterning procedures in remediation, 185
Newspapers, use of in balancing programs, 349
Nichols, Nancy J., 111
Noall, Mabel S., 153
Non-graded classes, discussion of reading in, 228-29
Non-professional help, use of in remediation, 191
Non-teaching accessory procedures, use of, in remediation, 190-91
Norris, Raymond C., 261
"Numbers in Color", 84

O'Donnell, Roy C., 261
Office of Economic Opportunity, 167, 425
Ofman, William, 187, 275
Oliver, J., 187
Olson, Arthur V., 114, 174, 186, 255

Olson, Willard C., 39, 188
One-teacher *vs.* multiple-teacher instruction, 200-2
Ong, Jin, 282
Optometry and Ophthalmology, contributions of specialists in, to reading, 281-84
Organization (classroom), patterns of, for reading instruction, 5
Organizational innovations, recommendations for planning of, 235-36
Organizational patterns: changing of, 232-36; criteria for evaluation of, 199-200; evaluation of general patterns of, 200-213
Organizational procedures, establishment of multiple standards for, 196-200
Orton, June L., 188
Orton, Samuel T., 163, 164, 188
Orton Society, 161, 164
O'Shea, M. V., 79
Otto, Wayne, 179, 218, 276

Paraprofessionals: duties of, 393; training of, 393-95
Parents and community, involvement of, in innovations, 299
Passow, A. Harry, 204; (with M. L. Goldberg), 206-7; quoted (with others), 205, 208-9
Peil, Margaret, 242
Perception: influence of clinical studies of, on reading, 288-89; tests of, for predicting reading, 174-76
Personality maladjustment, effects of, on reading, 177-78
Phonics systems, discussion of, 77-79
Physiology, studies in, contributing to balance in reading programs, 336-37
Piaget, Jean, 250, 251, 253, 255, 288
Piekarz, Josephine A., 401
Pitman, James, 82, 187-88
Portman, Lisa, 426
Post-baccalaureate training of teachers, 371
Powell, Marvin, 279
Practitioner and researcher: co-operative roles of, 292-94; disjunction between, 291-92
Preparation of teachers, 359-75
Preschool reading: claims in support of, 63-68; traditional objections to, 58-63

INDEX

Preservice education of teachers, 359-61
Pressey, S. L., 154, 155
Preston, Ralph C., 279, 285
Primary reading disability, 167-71
Programed instruction, 90-92, 154-55
Programed materials, use of, in balancing programs, 345-46
Progressive Education movement, 35, 37
Project on Assessing the Progress of Education, 427
Psycholinguistics, bearing of research in, on reading, 266-72
Psychology, research in, contributing to development of balance in reading programs, 330-36
Pupil-team study, program of, urged by Durrell, 227-28

Quinlan, Donald, 275

Rabinovitch, Ralph D., 161, 168, 171, 285; quoted, 167, 169
Rankin, Earl F., Jr., 269, 278
Ramsey, Wallace, quoted, 220
Rasmussen, Donald, 265
Rate of reading, improvement of, 134-37
Rauch, Sidney J., 377
Raygor, Alton L., 274
Razik, Taher, 145
Readers and related materials, bases for evaluation of, 338-41
Reading: definitions of, 7-11; linguistic approaches to, 79-82; models of, 11; see also, Reading instruction, Reading process, Reading readiness, etc.
Reading: Chaos and Cure, 63, 74
Reading consultant(s): role of, 379; scope of operations of, 377-79
Reading disability: definition of, 160; prediction of, 181-82
Reading instruction: contributions of psychology, etc. to, 4; future experimentation and research in, 416-20; materials and methods for, 4; time for beginning of, 31-35
Reading process, future innovations in improvement of, 400-402
Reading readiness, 4; assessment of, 49; changing views relating to, 44; concept of, 35-37; current scene with respect to, 49; meaning of, 49; recapitulation of, 49-53
Reading readiness tests, discussion of, 118-20
Readiness and beginning readers, 53-54
Reading specialists, education of, 380-83
Recruitment of researchers in reading, 388
Reed, David W., 9, 262
Reference material, use of, in balancing program, 349
Regional Educational Laboratories, 389
Remedial instruction, organization of, 182-84
Rentel, Victor H., 139
Research characteristics of, 410-15; dissemination of findings of, 391-93; needed co-operative efforts in, 415
Research and Development Centers, 389
Research in reading: characteristics of, 408; comments on, 115-17; nature of, 97-98; sources of, 98-115; status of, 387-88
Research specialists in reading, 387-93; preparation and growth of, 388-90
Researcher and practitioner, disjunction between, 291-92
Responsive Environment, 94; Moore's development of, 86
Retardation (reading), definition of, 159-60
Rippey, Robert M., 406
Robbins, Melvyn P., 114, 170
Robinson, H. Alan, 377, 402
Robinson, Helen M., 11, 12, 14, 23, 25, 26, 27, 28, 75, 165, 171, 224, 285, 402; quoted (with others), 100
Roehm, Marilyn A., 365
Rogers, Bernice, 398
Rojas, Pauline M., 93
Roman, Melvin, 191
Roosinck, P. L., 270
Rosborough, Pearl M., 171, 172
Roston, Sylvia W., 106
Rouse, Margaret, 218
Ruddell, Robert B., 111, 130
Rudisill, Mabel, 98
Russell, David H., 324

Sanders, Norris M., 18

Sartain, Harry W., 5, 419
Schmitt, Clara, 162
Schneider, Kenneth, 282
Schneyer, J. Wesley, 110, 132; quoted, 110-11
School practices, effects of, on reading, 176
Schramm, Wilbur, 239, 272
Secondary reading disability, 171-73
Sellers, Sophia, 106
Sequences in reading instruction, assumptions relating to, 405-6
Services in reading, new types of, available, 420-22
Serwer, Blanche L., 233; quoted (with others), 110
Severson, Eileen E., 138
Sheldon, William D., 111, 144; quoted (with R. L. Carner), 143
Sherbourne, Julia F., 153
Shoevitz, Morton, 187, 275
Silvaroli, Nicholas J., 119
Silver, Archie A., 186, 287
Simmons, John S., 365
Simpson, R. E., 205
Singer, Harry, 276, 277, 285
Sinks, Naomi B., 279
Sister M. Marita, 108
Sister Theophemia, 135
Six-year programs, proposed for, for reading specialists, 381
Skapski, Mary, 229
Skinner, B. F., 90, 154
Skolnick, Sidney, 107
Slingerland, Beth H., 118
Smith, Donald E. P., 13, 170, 191, 274, 277, 278, 285
Smith, Helen K., 134, 401, 402; quoted (with others), 100
Smith, Henry L., Jr., 79
Smith, Karl U., 282
Smith, Nila B., 72, 79, 88, 323; quoted, 146
Social psychology, contributions of, to reading, 246-50
Sociocultural disadvantage, effects of, on reading, 176-77
Socioeconomic forces militating against universal education, 240-42
Sociology: contributions of, to reading, 238-46; suggestions from, for developing balanced reading programs, 328-30

Spache, George D., 5, 8, 14, 120, 137, 212, 282; quoted (with others), 113
Sparks, Jack A., 13, 277
Special mental abilities, tests of, for predicting reading, 173-74
Special phonics programs, approach through, to balance in reading program, 351-52
Specialists in reading, education of, 380-83
Sperry, Florence, 106
Spivak, Monroe L., 218
Staiger, Ralph C., 191
Standardized reading achievement tests, use of, 120-21
Stanley, Julian C., 411, 415
State certification of reading personnel, 371-73
Stauffer, Russell G., 90; quoted, 214, 233
Steffan, James, 282
Stewart, Colin, 283
Strang, Ruth, 14, 147, 316
Strauss, A. A., 171
Strickland, Ruth G., 79, 259, 260
Studholme, Janice M., 191
Study skills, improvement of, 137-38
Sullivan, M. W., 190
Summers, Edward G., 139

Tapes and worksheets, use of in balancing programs, 347
Taylor, Earl A., 171, 172
Taylor, Stanford E., 137
Taxonomy of Cognitive and Affective Dimensions of Reading Comprehension (Barrett), 19-23
Teacher, problems relating to the role of, 406-7
Teacher behavior in relation to innovation, 317
Teacher competence, studies relating to, 359-66
Teacher education in reading, provisions for, 366-71; see also, Preparation of teachers, Teacher, Teacher preparation
Teacher-made materials, use of, 153
Teacher preparation, future directions in, 373-74; see also, Preparation of teachers
Teaching machines, 154-55
Team-teaching, discussion of, 221-23
Technology, innovations in, 94-96
Templin, Mildred C., 259

INDEX 439

Terms descriptive of readers, definitions of, 159-62
Thalberg, Stanton P., 137
Theoretical models, research on, in relation to reading, 276-78; *see also,* Models for reading
Theories of reading, summary of, 3
Thinking, developing higher levels of, 143-49
Thomas, Glenn G., 106
Thorndike, E. L., 33
Tillman, Chester E., 282
Tinker, Miles A., 9, 179
T O, definition of, 103; *see also,* Traditional orthography
Torch Lighters, 383; recommendations of, on college reading courses, 361
Torgerson, Theodore L., 179
Torrance, E. Paul, 256
Toussaint, Isabelle, 178
Trade books, use of, in balancing program, 348
Traditional orthography, 83; *see also,* TO
Training of reading personnel, 6
Training programs for paraprofessionals, description of, 393; VISTA project as example of, 394
Traxler, Robert E., 147
Trump, J. Lloyd, 293
Tyler, Fred T., quoted, 207
Tyler, Ralph W., 387; quoted, 75-76

Uhl, W. L., 162
Umans, Shelley, 378; quoted, 96
Underachiever in reading, characteristics of, 160
Undergraduate education of teachers, 367-68
Unifon Sound Alphabet, 77, 82, 83, 104, 188; *see also,* Modified alphabets
U.S. Armed Forces Institute (USAFI), 149

U.S. Office of Education, 45, 99, 102, 103, 115, 166, 166, 176, 224, 233, 357, 389, 390, 392, 415, 416; Teacher Fellowship Program of, 371

Van Doorninck, William, 288
Veatch, Jeanette, 223
Vernon, M. D., 165
Vinache, W. Edgar, 143, 144
Vocabulary development, 145-46

Wagner, Eva Bond, quoted (with G. L. Bond), 211
Walcutt, Charles C., 9
Walker, Frederick R., 210
Walton, Howard N., 280
Washburne, Carleton, 36, 72
Watson, John B., 34
Weaver, Wendell W., 266, 267, 268, 269, 270, 271, 278
Weintraub, Samuel, 114, 120, 121, 401, 402; quoted, 124; quoted (with others), 100
Wetherell, Janis, 265
Whipple, Gertrude, 92
Why Johnny Can't Read, 63, 74, 126, 296
Wick, Ralph E., 283
Wilder, David E., 115, 366, 387
Wilson, Robert C., 280
Wilt, Miriam E., quoted, 215-16
Wingo, Charles F., 78
Wittick, Mildred L., 4, 420
Witty, Paul A., 239
Wolf, William, 147
Woodbury, Charles A., 179
Woolman, Myron, 189
"Words in Color," 82, 85, 355
Workbooks, use of, in balancing program, 344
Wuest, Richard C., 109
Wyatt, Nita M., 123; quoted, 112

Yarborough, Betty H., 106, 185

Zangwill, O. L., quoted, 172-73
Zigler, Edward, 275

CONSTITUTION AND BY-LAWS
OF
THE NATIONAL SOCIETY FOR THE STUDY OF EDUCATION

(As adopted May, 1944, and amended June, 1945, February, 1949, and September, 1962)

ARTICLE I

NAME

The name of this corporation shall be "The National Society for the Study of Education," an Illinois corporation not for profit.

ARTICLE II

PURPOSES

Its purposes are to carry on the investigation of educational problems, to publish the results of same, and to promote their discussion.

The corporation also has such powers as are now, or may hereafter be, granted by the General Not For Profit Corporation Act of the State of Illinois.

ARTICLE III

OFFICES

The corporation shall have and continuously maintain in this state a registered office and a registered agent whose office is identical with such registered office, and may have other offices within or without the State of Illinois as the Board of Directors may from time to time determine.

ARTICLE IV

MEMBERSHIP

Section 1. *Classes*. There shall be two classes of members—active and honorary. The qualifications and rights of the members of such classes shall be as follows:

(*a*) Any person who is desirous of promoting the purposes of this corporation is eligible to active membership and shall become such on payment of dues as prescribed.

(*b*) Active members shall be entitled to vote, to participate in discussion, and, subject to the conditions set forth in Article V, to hold office.

(*c*) Honorary members shall be entitled to all the privileges of active members, with the exception of voting and holding office, and shall be exempt from the payment of dues. A person may be elected to honorary membership by vote of the active members of the corporation on nomination by the Board of Directors.

(*d*) Any active member of the Society may, at any time after reaching the age of sixty, become a life member on payment of the aggregate amount of the regular annual dues for the period of life expectancy, as determined by standard actuarial tables, such membership to entitle the member to receive all yearbooks and to enjoy all other privileges of active membership in the Society for the lifetime of the member.

Section 2. *Termination of Membership.*

(*a*) The Board of Directors by affirmative vote of two-thirds of the members of the Board may suspend or expel a member for cause after appropriate hearing.

(*b*) Termination of membership for nonpayment of dues shall become effective as provided in Article XIV.

Section 3. *Reinstatement.* The Board of Directors may by the affirmation vote of two-thirds of the members of the Board reinstate a former member whose membership was previously terminated for cause other than nonpayment of dues.

Section 4. *Transfer of Membership.* Membership in this corporation is not transferable or assignable.

Article V

BOARD OF DIRECTORS

Section 1. *General Powers.* The business and affairs of the corporation shall be managed by its Board of Directors. It shall appoint the Chairman and Vice-Chairman of the Board of Directors, the Secretary-Treasurer, and Members of the Council. It may appoint a member to fill any vacancy on the Board until such vacancy shall have been filled by election as provided in Section 3 of this Article.

Section 2. *Number, Tenure, and Qualifications.* The Board of Directors shall consist of seven members, namely, six to be elected by the members of the corporation, and the Secretary-Treasurer to be the seventh member. Only active members who have contributed to the Yearbook shall be eligible for election to serve as directors. A member who has been elected for a full term of three years as director and has not attended at least two-thirds of the meetings duly called and held during that term shall not be eligible for election again before the fifth annual election after the expiration of the term for which he was first elected. No member who has been elected for two full terms as director in immediate succession shall be elected a director for a term next succeeding. This provision shall not apply to the Secretary-Treasurer who is appointed by the Board of Directors. Each director shall hold office for the term for which he is elected or appointed and until his successor shall have been selected and qualified. Directors need not be residents of Illinois.

Section 3. *Election.*

(*a*) The directors named in the Articles of Incorporation shall hold office until their successors shall have been duly selected and shall have qualified. Thereafter, two directors shall be elected annually to serve three years, beginning March first after their election. If, at the time of any annual election, a vacancy exists in the Board of Directors, a director shall be elected at such election to fill such vacancy.

(*b*) Elections of directors shall be held by ballots sent by United States mail as follows: A nominating ballot together with a list of members eligible to be directors shall be mailed by the Secretary-Treasurer to all active members of the corporation in October. From such list, the active members shall nominate on such ballot one eligible member for each of the two regular terms and for any vacancy to be filled and return such ballots to the office of the Secretary-Treasurer within twenty-one days after said date of mailing by the Secretary-Treasurer. The Secretary-Treasurer shall prepare an election ballot and place thereon in alphabetical order the names of persons equal to three times the number of offices to be filled, these persons to be those who received the highest number of votes on the nominating ballot, provided, however, that not more than one person connected with a given institution or agency shall be named on such final ballot, the person so named to be the one receiving the highest vote on the nominating ballot. Such election ballot shall be mailed by the Secretary-Treasurer to all active members in November next succeeding. The active members shall vote thereon for one member for each such office. Election ballots must be in the office of the Secretary-Treasurer within twenty-one days after the said date of mailing by the Secretary-Treasurer. The ballots shall be counted by the Secretary-Treasurer, or by an election committee, if any, appointed by the Board. The two members receiving the highest number of votes shall be declared elected for the regular term and the member or members receiving the next highest number of votes shall be declared elected for any vacancy or vacancies to be filled.

Section 4. *Regular Meetings.* A regular annual meeting of the Board of Directors shall be held, without other notice than this by-law, at the same place and as nearly as possible on the same date as the annual meeting of the corporation. The Board of Directors may provide the time and place, either within or without the State of Illinois, for the holding of additional regular meetings of the Board.

Section 5. *Special Meetings.* Special meetings of the Board of Directors may be called by or at the request of the Chairman or a majority of the directors. Such special meetings shall be held at the office of the corporation unless a majority of the directors agree upon a different place for such meetings.

Section 6. *Notice.* Notice of any special meeting of the Board of Directors shall be given at least fifteen days previously thereto by written notice delivered personally or mailed to each director at his business address, or by telegram. If mailed, such notice shall be deemed to be delivered when deposited in the United States mail in a sealed envelope so addressed, with postage thereon prepaid. If notice be given by telegram, such notice shall be deemed to be delivered when the telegram is delivered to the telegraph company. Any director may waive notice of any meeting. The attendance of a director at any meeting shall constitute a waiver of notice of such meeting, except where a director attends a meeting for the express purpose of objecting to the transaction of any business because the meeting is not lawfully called or convened. Neither the business to be transacted at, nor the purpose of, any regular or special meeting of the Board need be specified in the notice or waiver of notice of such meeting.

Section 7. *Quorum.* A majority of the Board of Directors shall constitute a quorum for the transaction of business at any meeting of the Board, provided, that if less than a majority of the directors are present at said meeting, a majority of the directors present may adjourn the meeting from time to time without further notice.

Section 8. *Manner of Acting.* The act of the majority of the directors present at a meeting at which a quorum is present shall be the act of the Board of Directors, except where otherwise provided by law or by these by-laws.

Article VI

THE COUNCIL

Section 1. *Appointment.* The Council shall consist of the Board of Directors, the Chairmen of the corporation's Yearbook and Research Committees, and such other active members of the corporation as the Board of Directors may appoint.

Section 2. *Duties.* The duties of the Council shall be to further the objects of the corporation by assisting the Board of Directors in planning and carrying forward the educational undertakings of the corporation.

Article VII

OFFICERS

Section 1. *Officers.* The officers of the corporation shall be a Chairman of the Board of Directors, a Vice-Chairman of the Board of Directors, and a Secretary-Treasurer. The Board of Directors, by resolution, may create additional offices. Any two or more offices may be held by the same person, except the offices of Chairman and Secretary-Treasurer.

Section 2. *Election and Term of Office.* The officers of the corporation shall be elected annually by the Board of Directors at the annual regular meeting of the Board of Directors, provided, however, that the Secretary-Treasurer may be elected for a term longer than one year. If the election of officers shall not be held at such meeting, such election shall be held as soon thereafter as conveniently may be. Vacancies may be filled or new offices created and filled at any meeting of the Board of Directors. Each officer shall hold office until his successor shall have been duly elected and shall have qualified or until his death or until he shall resign or shall have been removed in the manner hereinafter provided.

Section 3. *Removal.* Any officer or agent elected or appointed by the Board of Directors may be removed by the Board of Directors whenever in its judgment the best interests of the corporation would be served thereby, but such removal shall be without prejudice to the contract rights, if any, of the person so removed.

Section 4. *Chairman of the Board of Directors.* The Chairman of the Board of Directors shall be the principal officer of the corporation. He shall preside at all meetings of the members of the Board of Directors, shall perform all duties incident to the office of chairman of the Board of Directors and such other duties as may be prescribed by the Board of Directors from time to time.

Section 5. *Vice-Chairman of the Board of Directors.* In the absence of the Chairman of the Board of Directors or in the event of his inability or refusal to act, the Vice-Chairman of the Board of Directors shall perform the duties of the Chairman of the Board of Directors, and when so acting, shall have all the powers of and be subject to all the restrictions upon the Chairman of the Board of Directors. Any Vice-Chairman of the Board of Directors shall perform such other duties as from time to time may be assigned to him by the Board of Directors.

Section 6. *Secretary-Treasurer.* The Secretary-Treasurer shall be the managing executive officer of the corporation. He shall: (*a*) keep the minutes of the meetings of the members and of the Board of Directors in one or more books provided for that purpose; (*b*) see that all notices are duly given in accordance with the provisions of these by-laws or as required by law; (*c*) be custodian of the corporate records and of the seal of the corporation and see that the seal of the corporation is affixed to all documents, the execution of which on behalf of the corporation under its seal is duly authorized in accordance with the provisions of these by-laws; (*d*) keep a register of the postoffice address of each member as furnished to the secretary-treasurer by such member; (*e*) in general perform all duties incident to the office of secretary and such other duties as from time to time may be assigned to him by the Chairman of the Board of Directors or by the Board of Directors. He shall also: (1) have charge and custody of and be responsible for all funds and securities of the corporation; receive and give receipts for moneys due and payable to the corporation from any source whatsoever, and deposit all such moneys in the name of the corporation in such banks, trust companies or other depositories as shall be selected in accordance with the provisions of Article XI of these by-laws; (2) in general perform all the duties incident to the office of Treasurer and such other duties as from time to time may be assigned to him by the Chairman of the Board of Directors or by the Board of Directors. The Secretary-Treasurer shall give a bond for the faithful discharge of his duties in such sum and with such surety or sureties as the Board of Directors shall determine, said bond to be placed in the custody of the Chairman of the Board of Directors.

Article VIII

COMMITTEES

The Board of Directors, by appropriate resolution duly passed, may create and appoint such committees for such purposes and periods of time as it may deem advisable.

Article IX

PUBLICATIONS

Section 1. The corporation shall publish *The Yearbook of the National Society for the Study of Education*, such supplements thereto, and such other materials as the Board of Directors may provide for.

Section 2. *Names of Members.* The names of the active and honorary members shall be printed in the Yearbook or, at the direction of the Board of Directors, may be published in a special list.

Article X

ANNUAL MEETINGS

The corporation shall hold its annual meetings at the time and place of the Annual Meeting of the American Association of School Administrators of the National Education Association. Other meetings may be held when authorized by the corporation or by the Board of Directors.

Article XI

CONTRACTS, CHECKS, DEPOSITS, AND GIFTS

Section 1. *Contracts.* The Board of Directors may authorize any officer or officers, agent or agents of the corporation, in addition to the officers so authorized by these by-laws to enter into any contract or execute and deliver any instrument in the name of and on behalf of the corporation and such authority may be general or confined to specific instances.

Section 2. *Checks, drafts, etc.* All checks, drafts, or other orders for the payment of money, notes, or other evidences of indebtedness issued in the name of the corporation, shall be signed by such officer or officers, agent or agents of the corporation and in such manner as shall from time to time be determined by resolution of the Board of Directors. In the absence of such determination of the Board of Directors, such instruments shall be signed by the Secretary-Treasurer.

Section 3. *Deposits.* All funds of the corporation shall be deposited from time to time to the credit of the corporation in such banks, trust companies, or other depositories as the Board of Directors may select.

Section 4. *Gifts.* The Board of Directors may accept on behalf of the corporation any contribution, gift, bequest, or device for the general purposes or for any special purpose of the corporation.

Article XII

BOOKS AND RECORDS

The corporation shall keep correct and complete books and records of account and shall also keep minutes of the proceedings of its members, Board of Directors, and committees having any of the authority of the Board of Directors, and shall keep at the registered or principal office a record giving the names and addresses of the members entitled to vote. All books and records of the corporation may be inspected by any member or his agent or attorney for any proper purpose at any reasonable time.

Article XIII

FISCAL YEAR

The fiscal year of the corporation shall begin on the first day of July in each year and end on the last day of June of the following year.

Article XIV

DUES

Section 1. *Annual Dues.* The annual dues for active members of the Society shall be determined by vote of the Board of Directors at a regular meeting duly called and held.

Section 2. *Election Fee.* An election fee of $1.00 shall be paid in advance by each applicant for active membership.

Section 3. *Payment of Dues.* Dues for each calendar year shall be payable in advance on or before the first day of January of that year. Notice of dues for the ensuing year shall be mailed to members at the time set for mailing the primary ballots.

Section 4. *Default and Termination of Membership.* Annual membership shall terminate automatically for those members whose dues remain unpaid after the first day of January of each year. Members so in default will be reinstated on payment of the annual dues plus a reinstatement fee of fifty cents.

Article XV

SEAL

The Board of Directors shall provide a corporate seal which shall be in the form of a circle and shall have inscribed thereon the name of the corporation and the words "Corporate Seal, Illinois."

Article XVI

WAIVER OF NOTICE

Whenever any notice whatever is required to be given under the provision of the General Not For Profit Corporation Act of Illinois or under the provisions of the Articles of Incorporation or the by-laws of the corporation, a waiver thereof in writing signed by the person or persons entitled to such notice, whether before or after the time stated therein, shall be deemed equivalent to the giving of such notice.

Article XVII

AMENDMENTS

Section 1. *Amendments by Directors.* The constitution and by-laws may be altered or amended at any meeting of the Board of Directors duly called and held, provided that an affirmative vote of at least five directors shall be required for such action.

Section 2. *Amendments by Members.* By petition of twenty-five or more active members duly filed with the Secretary-Treasurer, a proposal to amend the constitution and by-laws shall be submitted to all active members by United States mail together with ballots on which the members shall vote for or against the proposal. Such ballots shall be returned by United States mail to the office of the Secretary-Treasurer within twenty-one days after date of mailing of the proposal and ballots by the Secretary-Treasurer. The Secretary-Treasurer or a committee appointed by the Board of Directors for that purpose shall count the ballots and advise the members of the result. A vote in favor of such proposal by two-thirds of the members voting thereon shall be required for adoption of such amendment.

MINUTES OF THE ANNUAL MEETING OF THE SOCIETY

The 1967 meeting of the Society was held in the American Room of the Traymore Hotel in Atlantic City at 3:00 P.M., Sunday, February 12, with Harold G. Shane presiding and with some three hundred members and friends present.

The annual meeting has been most often devoted to presentations of Parts I and II of the yearbook. However, since Part II, *Programed Instruction*, had been scheduled for presentation in New York and Dallas, only Part I, *The Educationally Retarded and Disadvantaged*, was presented. The programs of the three meetings follow:

PROGRAM OF THE ATLANTIC CITY MEETING

Joint Meeting of the National Society for the Study of Education and the American Association of School Administrators

Sunday, February 12, 3:00 P.M.
American Room, Traymore Hotel

Presiding: Harold G. Shane, Professor of Education, Indiana University; Vice-Chairman of the Board of Directors of the National Society for the Study of Education

Presentation of

The Educationally Retarded and Disadvantaged

(Part I of the Society's Sixty-sixth Yearbook)

Introducing the Yearbook

Paul A. Witty, Professor Emeritus of Education, Northwestern University; Chairman of the Board of Directors; and Editor of the Yearbook

Critique of the Yearbook

John H. Fischer, President of Teachers College, Columbia University, New York City

Informal Discussion

Mr. Shane, Mr. Witty, Mr. Fischer, and Audience

PROGRAM OF THE NEW YORK MEETING

Joint Meeting of the American Educational Research Association and the National Society for the Study of Education

MINUTES OF THE ANNUAL MEETING

Friday, February 17, 10:00 A.M.
West Room, Statler Hilton Hotel

Presiding: Paul A. Witty, Professor Emeritus of Education, Northwestern University; Chairman of the Board of Directors of the National Society

Presentation of

Programed Instruction

(Part II of the Society's Sixty-sixth Yearbook)

Presentation of the Yearbook

Phil C. Lange, Professor of Education, Teachers College, Columbia University; Editor of the Yearbook

Critique of the Yearbook

N. L. Gage, Professor of Education and Psychology, Stanford University

Audience Participation

PROGRAM OF THE DALLAS MEETING

Joint Meeting of the Association for Supervision and Curriculum Development
and the National Society for the Study of Education

Saturday, March 11, 7:00 P.M.
Grand Ballroom, Adolphus Hotel

Presiding and Introducing the Yearbook: Harold G. Shane, Professor of Education, Indiana University; Chairman of the Board of Directors of the National Society

Critique of the Yearbook

James D. Finn, Director, National Special Media Institutes, School of Education, University of Southern California

Audience Participation

SYNOPSIS OF THE PROCEEDINGS OF THE BOARD OF DIRECTORS OF THE SOCIETY FOR 1967

I. Meeting of February 12, 1967

The Board of Directors met on February 12 in the Traymore Hotel (Atlantic City) with the following members present: Messrs. Edgar Dale, Robert J. Havighurst, Harold G. Shane, Paul A. Witty (presiding), and Herman G. Richey (Secretary).

1. The Secretary reported that the election of members of the Board of Directors held in November and December of 1966 had resulted in the election of Ralph W. Tyler and William C. Kvaraceus, each for a term of three years beginning March 1, 1967.

2. Officers of the Board of Directors for the year beginning March 1, 1967, were elected as follows: Harold G. Shane, Chairman; Edgar Dale, Vice-Chairman; and Herman G. Richey, Secretary.

3. The Secretary-Treasurer reported on finances, membership, and sales for the fiscal year ending June 30, 1966, and for the following six months.

4. The Board expressed its thanks to the American Association of School Administrators, the American Educational Research Association, and the Association for Supervision and Curriculum Development for the assistance given to the Society in the presentations of its yearbooks.

5. Progress reports were presented for the following authorized yearbooks: *Metropolitanism: Its Challenge to Education* (Robert J. Havighurst), *Innovation and Change in Reading Instruction* (Helen M. Robinson), *International Education* (Harold G. Shane), *Evaluation* (Ralph W. Tyler), and *Linguistics* (Albert H. Marckwardt).

6. The Secretary presented a statement from Mr. E. G. Begle and an outline of a proposed yearbook on mathematics education that he had prepared at the request of the Board. The Board agreed that the proposed yearbook should be published and asked that Mr. Begle present a formal proposal at the next meeting of the Board.

7. Mr. Dale presented a proposal by Dr. Taher A. Razik for a yearbook on creativity. The Board voted to postpone discussion of the proposed yearbook until after its members had studied the proposal at greater length and had examined more carefully the supporting documents which accompanied it.

8. Other proposals and suggestions for yearbooks were discussed. Among these were plans for yearbooks on social studies (John Palmer), philosophy (Laurence G. Thomas), industrial education (Joseph F. Luetkemeyer), and curriculum (Harold G. Shane).

9. The Board voted to finance a meeting of a committee to continue the work outlined in Mr. Havighurst's memorandum, "The Project on Biographies of Leaders in Education."

II. Meeting of July 21-22, 1967

The Board of Directors met on July 21 and 22 in the Conrad Hilton Hotel (Chicago) with the following members present: Messrs. Edgar Dale, William C. Kvaraceus, Harold G. Shane (presiding), Ralph W. Tyler, and Herman G. Richey (Secretary).

1. The Secretary reported briefly on finances, membership, and sales. The report of the Treasurer for 1966-67 follows these minutes.

2. It was reported that plans were being completed to present *Metropolitanism: Its Challenge to Education*, Part I of the Sixty-seventh Yearbook, at the Atlantic City meeting (A.A.S.A. Convention) on February 18, 1968. It was also reported that Part II, *Innovation and Change in Reading Instruction*, is to be presented on April 25 at the annual meeting of the International Reading Association in Boston.

3. Progress reports on scheduled and tentatively scheduled yearbooks were presented. Titles or working titles of these projected yearbooks are as follows: *Metropolitanism: Its Challenge to Education* (1968); *Innovation and Change in Reading Instruction* (1968); *International Education* (1969); *Evaluation* (1969); and *Linguistics* (1970).

4. The proposal for a yearbook on mathematics education submitted by Mr. E. G. Begle was approved, and publication of this yearbook was scheduled for January, 1970.

5. The proposal for a yearbook on the curriculum submitted by Mr. Shane for the committee on curriculum was approved. Publication was scheduled for 1971.

6. Mr. Havighurst (chairman) and other members of the committee on the autobiographical studies of educational leaders (Paul Woodring, Robert L. McCaul, and Jonathan Messerl) met with the Board and presented a proposal for a yearbook to be published in 1971. Mr. Havighurst reported on the progress made on the study. The Board approved the proposal.

7. Suggestions and proposals for yearbooks on creativity, childhood education, industrial education, educational philosophy, social studies, and others were discussed. Further discussion was deferred until the next meeting.

REPORT OF THE TREASURER OF THE SOCIETY

1966-67

Receipts and Disbursements

Receipts:

Membership Dues	$ 39,469.67
Sale of yearbooks	53,724.85
Interest and dividends	2,246.69
Miscellaneous	723.28
Total	$ 96,164.49

Disbursements:

Yearbooks:

Manufacturing	$ 33,791.54
Reprinting	35,227.30
Preparation	4,738.85
Meetings of Board and Society	2,013.80

Secretary's Office:

Editorial, secretarial, and clerical	22,203.15
Supplies	3,868.62
Equipment	875.70
Telephone and telegraph	289.90

Miscellaneous:

Bank charges	78.40
Refunds and transfer of commercial orders	75.95
Safe deposit box	4.00
Fidelity bond	31.00
Filing fee	1.00
Permit mailing fee	30.00
Chapter reprints (reclaimable from authors)	444.75
Total	$103,673.96

Cash in bank June 30, 1966	$ 29,477.22
Excess disbursements over receipts	(7,509.47)
Resulting cash balance, June 30, 1967	$ 21,967.75
Transferred to savings, 1966-67	$ 25,000.00
Deficit in checking account, June 30, 1967	$ 3,032.25

STATEMENT OF CASH AND SECURITIES

As of June 30, 1967

Cash:

University National Bank, Chicago, Illinois—
Checking account ....($ 3,032.25)	
Savings account	$ 8,115.65
Hyde Park Savings and Loan Assn....................	15,000.00
Chicago Federal Savings and Loan Assn...............	10,000.00
Home Federal Savings and Loan Assn.................	10,000.00
Telegraph Savings and Loan Assn....................	10,000.00

Securities: (Cost)

38 shares, First National Bank of Boston, capital stock...	1,063.97
U.S. Government "H" Bonds, dated March 1, 1967.....	15,000.00

Total assets $66,147.37

MEMBERS OF THE NATIONAL SOCIETY FOR THE STUDY OF EDUCATION

[This list includes all persons enrolled November 1, 1967, whether for 1967 or 1968. An asterisk (*) indicates Life Members of the Society.]

Aarestad, Amanda B., 1887 Gilmore Ave., Winona, Minn.
Aaron, Ira Edward, Col. of Educ., University of Georgia, Athens, Ga.
Abate, Harry, Board of Education, 607 Walnut Ave., Niagara Falls, N.Y.
Abbott, Frank C., Colorado Comm. on Higher Education, Denver, Colo.
Abbott, Samuel Lee, Jr., Plymouth State College, Plymouth, N.H.
Abbott, Whitt K., Alice Robertson Junior High School, Muskogee, Okla.
Abel, Frederick P., Western Illinois University, Macomb, Ill.
Abel, Harold, Sch. of Educ., University of Oregon, Eugene, Ore.
Abelson, Harold H., Sch. of Educ., City University, New York, N.Y.
Ables, Jack B., East Aurora Jr. High School, East Aurora, N.Y.
Abraham, Willard, Arizona State University, Tempe, Ariz.
Abrahamson, Stephen, Sch. of Med., Univ. of So. Calif., Los Angeles, Calif.
Abramowitz, Mortimer J., 345 Lakeville Rd., Great Neck, N.Y.
Achilles, Charles M., Box 317 B, Rt. # 1, Geneva, N.Y.
Ackerlund, George C., Southern Illinois Univ., Edwardsville, Ill.
Ackerman, Thomas J., Educ. Spec., 400 Maryland Ave., S.W., Washington, D.C.
Adams, Mrs. Daisy Trice, 2637 Park Ave., Kansas City, Mo.
Adams, Donald K., Sch. of Educ., Syracuse Univ., Syracuse, N.Y.
Adams, Fern B., Office of Co. Supt. of Schls., Los Angeles, Calif.
Adams, James A., 1106 S. State St., Tahlequah, Okla.
Adams, Mrs. Ruth R., Sch. of Educ., New York City College, New York, N.Y.
Adatto, Albert, 228—165th Ave., N.E., Bellevue, Wash.
Adcock, William, 24661 Lahser Rd., Southfield, Mich.
Adelberg, Arthur J., Supt., Schl. Dist. #3, Elmhurst, Ill.
* Adell, James C., 16723 Fernway Rd., Shaker Heights, Ohio
Aden, Robert C., Middle Tennessee St. Univ., Murfreesboro, Tenn.
Adkisson, D. F., City Public Schools, Bristol, Tenn.
Adler, Mrs. Leona K., 101 Central Park W., New York, N.Y.
Adler, Manfred, John Carroll University, Cleveland, Ohio
Adler, Norman A., 51 West 52nd St., New York, N.Y.
Adolphsen, Louis J., Hinsdale Senior High School, Hinsdale, Ill.
Ahrendt, Kenneth M., 130 W. Keith Rd., North Vancouver, B.C., Canada
Ahrnsbrak, Henry C., 425 Berwyn Dr., Madison, Wis.
Airasian, Peter W., 206 Krotiak, Park Forest, Ill.
Akins, Harold S., 1300 High St., Wichita, Kan.
Alagna, Agostino A., 478 W. 26th St., Chicago, Ill.
Alberg, Gary L., 1990 Lakeaires Blvd., White Bear Lake, Minn.
Albohm, John C., Supt. of Schools, Alexandria, Va.
Albrecht, Milton C., State Univ. of New York, Buffalo, N.Y.
Albright, Frank S., 37 Yale Terrace, West Orange, N.J.
Alcock, Wayne T., Dillond Univ., New Orleans, La.
Alexander, Burton F., Petersburg High School, Petersburg, Va.
Alexander, Elenora, Rm. 234, 1300 Capitol Ave., Houston, Texas
Alexander, William M., Col. of Educ., Univ. of Florida, Gainesville, Fla.
Alkin, Marvin C., University of California, Los Angeles, Calif.

Allen, Beatrice Ona, 5347 N. Wayne Ave., Chicago, Ill.
Allen, David, 8437 Truxton Ave., Los Angeles, Calif.
Allen, Dwight W., Sch. of Educ., Stanford University, Stanford, Calif.
Allen, Edward E., Akron Central Schools, Akron, N.Y.
Allen, Graham, Coburg Teachers College, Coburg, Melbourne, Australia
Allen, James Robert, 1249 Lake Ave., Fort Wayne, Ind.
Allen, John E., 306 Arbour Dr., Newark, Dela.
Allen, Ross L., State Univ. College, Cortland, N.Y.
Allen, Warren G., State Teachers College, Minot, N.D.
Allison, Preston B., 1225 N. Gen. Pershing St., Hammond, La.
Allman, Reva White, Alabama State College, Montgomery, Ala.
Alm, Richard S., Dept. of Educ., University of Hawaii, Honolulu, Hawaii
Almcrantz, Mrs. Georgia, 402 Brown Circle, Knox, Ind.
Almroth, Frank S., 20 Hilltop Ter., Wayne, N.J.
Alper, Arthur E., University of Florida, Gainesville, Fla.
Alpert, Harvey, 20 Woodland Dr., Old Bethpage, N.Y.
Alprin, Stanley I., Fisk University, Nashville, Tenn.
Al-Rubaiy, Abdul Amir, L-10 Pine Grove, Ypsilanti, Mich.
Alt, Pauline M., Central Connecticut State College, New Britain, Conn.
Altman, Harold, 12006 Stanwood Dr., Los Angeles, Calif.
Altman, Herbert H., 832 Ocean Ave., Brooklyn, N.Y.
Amacher, Mrs. Walter, 7471 Mudbrook St., N.W., Massillon, Ohio
Amar, Wesley F., Waller High School, Chicago, Ill.
Ambrose, Edna V., 2124 N.E. 7th Ter., Gainesville, Fla.
Amershek, Kathleen, Col. of Educ., Univ. of Maryland, College Park, Md.
Ames, John L., Queens College, Kissena Blvd., Flushing, N.Y.
Amidon, Edna P., 65—30th Ave., W., Eugene, Ore.
Amioka, Shiro, University of Hawaii, Honolulu, Hawaii
Amsden, Robert L., 17 Parker Ave., Maplewood, N.J.
Anders, Mrs. Elizabeth M., 3601 Palm Dr., Riviera Beach, Fla.
Anderson, Alice J., 5757 College Ave., San Diego, Calif.
Anderson, Bernard, John Spry Elementary School, Chicago, Ill.
Anderson, Donald G., Oakland Public Schls., 1025 Second Ave., Oakland, Calif.
Anderson, Ernest M., Kansas State Col., Pittsburg, Kansas
Anderson, Earnest V., University of Detroit, Detroit, Mich.
Anderson, Edmond C., Sequoyah Junior High School, Dallas, Tex.
Anderson, Floydelh, West Virginia State College, Institute, W.Va.
Anderson, G. Lester, University of New York, Buffalo, N.Y.
Anderson, Harold, 925 Fulton St., Aurora, Colo.
Anderson, Harold, Wausau Public Schools, Wausau, Wis.
Anderson, Harold A., Dept. of Educ., University of Chicago, Chicago, Ill.
Anderson, Howard R., Houghton Mifflin Co., Boston, Mass.
Anderson, Isabel C., Sch. of Educ., Temple University, Philadelphia, Pa.
Anderson, J. Paul, Col. of Educ., Univ. of Maryland, College Park, Md.
Anderson, James W., 742 Ashland Ave., St. Paul Park, Minn.
Anderson, Kenneth E., Sch. of Educ., Univ. of Kansas, Lawrence, Kan.
Anderson, Lester W., Sch. of Educ., Univ. of Michigan, Ann Arbor, Mich.
Anderson, Linnea M., Dir. of Spec. Educ., State Col. of Iowa, Cedar Falls, Iowa
Anderson, Mrs. Marcile, Fort Wayne State School, Fort Wayne, Ind.
Anderson, Marion A., Ginn & Co., Statler Office Bldg., Boston, Mass.
Anderson, Morris L., Wayne State College, Wayne, Neb.
Anderson, Oliver M., 2315 Greenwood Ave., Cedar Falls, Iowa
Anderson, Patricia S. B., 25 Lascelles Blvd., Toronto, Ont., Canada
Anderson, Philip S., Wisconsin State University, River Falls, Wis.
Anderson, Robert A., University of Washington, Seattle, Wash.
Anderson, Robert Henry, Grad. Sch. of Educ., Harvard Univ., Cambridge, Mass.
Anderson, Roger C., St. Cloud State Col., St. Cloud, Minn.
Anderson, Ruth, 372 Central Park West, New York, N.Y.
Anderson, Stuart A., Riverside-Brookfield Twp. High School, Riverside, Ill.
Anderson, Vernon E., Col. of Educ., University of Maryland, College Park, Md.
Anderson, William J., P.O. Box 288, Georgetown, Texas

Andree, R. G., Southern Illinois University, Edwardsville, Ill.
Andregg, Neal B., 2553 Richmond Hill Rd., Augusta, Ga.
Andrews, Clay S., Dept. of Educ., San Jose State College, San Jose, Calif.
Andrews, Richard L., 11372 Cherry Hill Rd., Beltsville, Md.
Andrews, Sam D., Bowling Green State University, Bowling Green, Ohio
Andrews, Stella F., 83 Alexander Ave., Yonkers, N.Y.
Andrews, Wendell B., Public Schools, 108 Union St., Schenectady, N.Y.
Andrisek, John R., 119 Meadow Dr., Berea, Ohio
Angelini, Arrigo L., University of Sao Paulo, Sao Paulo, Brazil
Angell, George W., State University College, Plattsburgh, N.Y.
Angelo, Rev. Mark V., St. Bonaventure Univ., St. Bonaventure, N.Y.
*Annis, Helen W., 6711 Conway Ave., Takoma Park, Md.
Annis, Mrs. Jane B., 421 Marywood Dr., Alpena, Mich.
Ansel, James O., Western Michigan University, Kalamazoo, Mich.
Anselm, Karl R., Ventura Hall, Stanford University, Stanford, Calif.
Anthony, Sally M., San Diego State Col., San Diego, Calif.
Antoine, Tamlin C., P.O. Box 1647, Taipei, Taiwan, Rep. of China
Antonelli, Luiz K., Queens College, Flushing, N.Y.
Apel, J. Dale, Kansas State Univ., Manhattan, Kansas
Apple, Joe A., San Diego State College, San Diego, Calif.
Appleton, David, Supt. of Schools, Pine St., North Conway, N.H.
Apt, Madeline H., Div. of Educ., Wright State Univ., Dayton, Ohio
Arcarese, Lawrence C., State Univ. Col. of Arts & Sci., Plattsburgh, N.Y.
Archer, Marguerite P., 137 Highbrook Ave., Pelham, N.Y.
Archer, N. Sidney, East. Reg. Inst. for Educ., Inc., Syracuse, N.Y.
Arends, Wade B., 439 Wildwood, Park Forest, Ill.
Armistead, Roy B., 9234 Queenston Dr., St. Louis, Mo.
Armogida, Harry, Dept. of Educ., Miami University, Oxford, Ohio
Armstrong, Betty W., 2231 Diana Pl., Covington, Ky.
Armstrong, Mrs. Carmen L., Tulip Tree Apt. 701, Bloomington, Ind.
Armstrong, Mrs. Jenny R., Univ. of Wisconsin, Madison, Wis.
Armstrong, J. Niel, Sch. of Educ., Agric. & Tech. College, Greensboro, N.C.
Arnaud, E. E., Our Lady of the Lake College, San Antonio, Tex.
*Arnesen, Arthur E., 440 East First South St., Salt Lake City, Utah
Arnoff, Melvin, 4325 Groveland Rd., University Heights, Ohio
Arnold, Gala, 740 "J" Ave., Coronado, Calif.
Arnold, J. E., Box 8540, University Station, Knoxville, Tenn.
Arnold, Marshall, 301 S. Water St., Henderson, Ky.
Arnold, Phyllis D., 628 Patterson Ave., San Antonio, Tex.
Arnsdorf, Val E., Sch. of Educ., Univ. of Delaware, Newark, Del.
Arnstein, George E., ACCESS, NEA, 1201—16th St., N.W., Washington, D.C.
Aromi, Eugene J., Univ. of So. Alabama, Mobile, Ala.
Arthur, Douglas C., Petaluma City Schools, Petaluma, Calif.
Arveson, Raymond G., 38060 Logan Dr., Fremont, Calif.
Ash, Dorothy, 1800 Grand Ave., Des Moines, Iowa
Ashe, Robert W., Dept. of Educ., Arizona State University, Tempe, Ariz.
Ashmore, Myron L., Broward County Schools, Fort Lauderdale, Fla.
Askins, Billy E., Box 4234, Tex. Tech. Stn., Lubbock, Texas
Atkins, Thurston A., Teachers Col., Columbia Univ., New York, N.Y.
Atkinson, Francis D., Jr., 1100 E. Lemon St., Tempe, Ariz.
Atkinson, William N., Jackson Junior College, Jackson, Mich.
Aubin, Albert E., 3258 Sawtelle Blvd., Los Angeles, Calif.
Auble, Donavon, Western Col. for Women, Oxford, Ohio
Aubry, A. J., L. B. Landry School, New Orleans, La.
Auer, B. F., Sycamore High School, Cincinnati, Ohio
Aurand, Wayne O., 904 Columbia Dr., Cedar Falls, Iowa
Austin, David B., Tchrs. Col., Columbia University, New York, N.Y.
Austin, Mary C., 2263 Demington Dr., Cleveland, Ohio
Austin, Martha Lou, Univ. of South Florida, Tampa, Fla.
Austin, Roy S., State University College, Potsdam, N.Y.
Ausubel, David P., 102 Bloor St., W., Toronto, Ont., Canada

Avegno, T. Sylvia, Sch. of Educ., Fordham University, New York, N.Y.
Ayer, Joseph C., 3108 Grand Ave., Middleton, Ohio
Azzarelli, Joseph J., New York University, Washington Sq., New York, N.Y.

Babcock, Chester D., Dept. of Public Instruction, Olympia, Wash.
Babcock, William E., 131 W. Nittany Ave., State College, Pa.
Bach, Jacob O., Southern Illinois University, Carbondale, Ill.
Bachar, James R., 586 East End Ave., Pittsburgh, Pa.
Bachman, Ralph V., South High School, Salt Lake City, Utah
Backus, Thomas A., 570—115th Ave., Treasure Island, Fla.
Bacon, William P., Sch. of Educ., Univ. of the Pacific, Stockton, Calif.
Bacsalmasi, Stephen, York Cent. Dist. H. S. Brd., Richmond Hill, Ont., Canada
Baer, Campion, Capuchin Sem. of St. Mary, Crown Point, Ind.
Bagott, Nancy, 835 N. Sixth Ave., Tucson, Ariz.
Bahn, Lorene A., 2843 Lomita Circle, Springfield, Mo.
Bahner, John M., 1410 N.E. Second Ave., Miami, Fla.
Bahrenburg, Erma M., 27 Ninth St., Carle Place, L.I., N.Y.
Baich, Henry, University of Portland, Portland, Ore.
Bailer, Joseph R., Dept. of Educ., Western Maryland College, Westminster, Md.
Bailey, Lucile, 119 E. University Dr., Tempe, Arizona
Baird, Forrest J., San Jose State College, San Jose, Calif.
Bajek, Robert S., 3830 S. Scoville, Berwyn, Ill.
Bajwa, Ranjit Singh, 2235 Georgetown Blvd., Ann Arbor, Mich.
Baker, Arthur F., 10 Ditson Place, Methuen, Mass.
Baker, Charles, Gladwin High School, Gladwin, Mich.
Baker, Charles R., P.O. Box 367, San Andreas, Calif.
Baker, Mrs. Earlene P., 43 Barnes St., Providence, R.I.
Baker, Eugene H., 6950 N.E. Prairie Rd., Lincolnwood, Ill.
Baker, Harry J., 19050 Wiltshire, Lathrup Village, Mich.
Baker, I. D., Greenville College, Greenville, Ill.
Baker, John E., Col. of Educ. & Nurs., Univ. of Vermont, Burlington, Vt.
Baker, Rebecca, Southern Illinois University, Carbondale, Ill.
Baker, Robert C., Bemidji State College, Bemidji, Minn.
Baker, Robert E., Sch. of Educ., George Washington Univ., Washington, D.C.
Baker, William E., 11247 Dempsey Ave., Granada Hills, Calif.
Baldauf, R., 122 Forest Ave., Oak Park, Ill.
Baldwin, Alan L., Redwood City Sch. Dist., Redwood City, Calif.
Baldwin, Rollin, 924 West End Ave., New York, N.Y.
Balian, Arthur, 6804 W. Dickinson St., Milwaukee, Wis.
Ball, George G., State College of Iowa, Cedar Falls, Iowa
Ballantine, Francis A., San Diego State College, San Diego, Calif.
Ballantyne, Robert H., 2510 Wrightwood Ave., Durham, N.C.
Ballmann, Donald L., St. Joseph's College, Rensselaer, Ind.
Ballou, Stephen V., Div. of Educ., Fresno State College, Fresno, Calif.
Balser, Paul, Forest Hills H.S., 67-01—110th St., Forest Hills, N.Y.
Balzer, David M., Pennsylvania State University, University Park, Pa.
Bandy, George R., Northern Montana College, Havre, Mont.
Banks, Marie, State University College, Plattsburgh, N.Y.
Banner, Carolyn, 409 Lafayette, Jefferson City, Mo.
Bany, Mary, 411 N. Third St., Alhambra, Calif.
Baratta, Anthony N., Sch. of Educ., Fordham University, New York, N.Y.
Barbaree, Frank, P.O. Box 547, Jackson, Ala.
Barbe, Richard H., Sch. of Educ., University of Delaware, Newark, Del.
Barbe, Walter B., 803 Church St., Honesdale, Pa.
Barber, Anson B., 4415 Main St., Apt. 18, Snyder, N.Y.
Barber, Grant W., 1251 Shipman St., Birmingham, Mich.
Barber, Richard L., Col. of Arts & Sci., Univ. of Louisville, Louisville, Ky.
Barclay, Doris, 5151 State College Dr., Los Angeles, Calif.
Barcliffe, Irving R., P.O. Box 127, Gatesville, N.C.
Bardellini, Justin M., 337 Menlo Court, Walnut Creek, Calif.
Barkhurst, W. Ted, 1100—4th St., S., Great Falls, Mont.

Barkley, Margaret V., Arizona State University, Tempe, Ariz.
Barlow, Melvin L., Sch. of Educ., Univ. of California, Los Angeles, Calif.
Barnard, J. Darrell, 16 Links Drive, Great Neck, N.Y.
Barnard, W. Robert, Evans Chem. Lab., 88 W. 18th Ave., Columbus, Ohio
Barnes, Cyrus W., Beachlake, Pa.
Barnes, Fred P., Col. of Educ., University of Illinois, Urbana, Ill.
Barney, Angelo T., 818 Black Rd., Joliet, Ill.
Barr, Charlotte A., Chicago Teachers College, Chicago, Ill.
Barr, Dixon A., Sch. of Educ., East. Kentucky State Col., Richmond, Ky.
Barratt, Thomas K., Supt., Warren County Sch. Dist., Warren, Pa.
Barrett, George M., 121 Third St., Wyoming, Del.
Barron, Donald, 240 W. 22nd St., Deer Park, N.Y.
Barron, William E., University of Texas, Austin, Tex.
Barros, Raymond, Catholic University of Valparaiso, Valparaiso, Chile
Barry, Florence G., 5956 Race Ave., Chicago, Ill.
Bartel, Fred C., 2921 Richland Ave., Louisville, Ky.
Barter, Alice K., 4675 Booth Rd., Oxford, Ohio
Bartlett, Robert C., 6850 Crandon Ave., Chicago, Ill.
Bartley, Imon R., S.W. Missouri State Col., Springfield, Mo.
Barton, Carl L., Superintendent, Community Cons. Sch. Dist. 70, Freeburg, Ill.
Barton, George E., Jr., 1010 Short St., New Orleans, La.
Batha, Robert, Chester Junior-Senior High School, Chester, Calif.
Batinich, Mary Ellen, 9215 S. Troy Ave., Chicago, Ill.
Batten, James W., Box 2455, East. Carolina College, Greenville, N.C.
Battle, J. A., University of South Florida, Tampa, Fla.
Battle, John A., 11 Jones St., New Hyde Park, N.Y.
Battles, John J., 2811 Avenue "D," Brooklyn, N.Y.
Bauer, Edith B., Brigham Young University, Provo, Utah
Bauer, Norman J., 1522 Doemel St., Oshkosh, Wis.
Baugher, James K., R.D. # 2, Littlestown, Pa.
Bauman, Frank O., Minot State College, Minot, N.D.
Baumann, Max, 3800 Washington Ave., Baltimore, Md.
Baumann, Reemt R., Col. of Educ., Univ. of Toledo, Toledo, Ohio
Baumgartner, Reuben A., Senior High School, Freeport, Ill.
Baumgartner, Rolla W., 607 Ohio St., Walkerton, Ind.
Baxter, Marlin B., Moline Public Schools, 1619 Eleventh Ave., Moline, Ill.
Beach, Lowell W., 3606 Univ. H.S., Univ. of Michigan, Ann Arbor, Mich.
Beamer, George C., North Texas State College, Denton, Tex.
Beamer, Rufus W., Virginia Polytechnic Inst., Blacksburg, Va.
Bear, David E., 12 Ramona Pl., Godfrey, Ill.
Beard, Richard L., 1812 Meadowbrook Hgts. Rd., Charlottesville, Va.
Beaton, Daniel W., 425 S. Catalina Ave., Redondo Beach, Calif.
Beattie, George W., P.O. Box 100, Aptos, Calif.
Beatty, Charles J., 9304 Piney Branch Rd., Silver Spring, Md.
Beatty, Walcott H., 209 Kensington Way, San Francisco, Calif.
Beaty, Edgar, Middle Tennessee State College, Murfreesboro, Tenn.
Beaubier, Edward W., 19692 Lexington Lane, Huntington Beach, Calif.
Beauchamp, George A., Sch. of Educ., Northwestern University, Evanston, Ill.
Beaumont, Urville J., Tenney High School, Methuen, Mass.
Beaver, Eugene H., Chicago Vocational High School, Chicago, Ill.
Bebb, Randall R., State College of Iowa, Cedar Falls, Iowa
Bebell, Clifford S., Southern Colorado State Col., Pueblo, Colo.
Beck, Hubert Park, Sch. of Educ., City College, 523 W. 121st St., New York, N.Y.
Beck, John M., 5832 Stony Island Ave., Chicago, Ill.
Beck, Norman W., Supt., Monroe County Schls., Waterloo, Ill.
Beck, Robert H., 233 Burton Hall, University of Minnesota, Minneapolis, Minn.
Becken, Elliot D., Supt. of Schools, Medford, Ore.
Becker, Harry A., Superintendent of Schools, Norwalk, Conn.
Becker, Millie A., 7637 S. Loomis Blvd., Chicago, Ill.
Bedell, Ralph, 701 Lewis Hall, Univ. of Missouri, Columbia, Mo.
Beebe, Nelson, Jr., Pennsville Memorial High School, Pennsville, N.J.

Beery, Cleo C., La Verne College, La Verne, Calif.
Beery, John R., Sch. of Educ., University of Miami, Coral Gables, Fla.
Beggs, David W., Sch. of Educ., Indiana Univ., Bloomington, Ind.
Behal, Rose, 9812 Broadview Rd., Brecksville, Ohio
Behrens, Herman D., 811 S. Johnson St., Ada, Ohio
* Behrens, Minnie S., Pomeroy, Iowa
Beighley, Archie F., Dept. of Educ., Winona State Col., Winona, Minn.
Beitler, Roger T., 2676 Walnut Blvd., Ashtabula, Ohio
Belcastro, Frank P., Merrimack College, North Andover, Mass.
Belcher, Eddie W., Louisville Public Schls., 506 W. Hill St., Louisville, Ky.
Belgum, Loretta E., San Francisco State College, San Francisco, Calif.
Bell, Dorothy M., Bradford Junior College, Bradford, Mass.
Bell, Jack, Superintendent of Schools, Overland Park, Kan.
Bell, Keith A., 22906—72 Pl., W., Mountlake Terrace, Wash.
Bell, Mildred, Harding College, Searcy, Ark.
Bell, Robert M., 2819 W. Sherwin Ave., Chicago, Ill.
Bell, Wilmer V., 702 Kingston Rd., Baltimore, Md.
Bellack, Arno A., Tchrs. Col., Columbia University, New York, N.Y.
Bemis, James R., 19041 Tango Ave., Yorba Linda, Calif.
Benben, John S., 7 Victoria Rd., Ardsley, N. Y.
Benda, Harold, Educ. Dept., West Chester State College, West Chester, Pa.
Bender, Kenneth R., University of Mississippi, University, Miss.
Bender, Martin L., 384 Prospect Ave., Hackensack, N.J.
Bender, Ralph E., Ohio State University, Columbus, Ohio
Benner, Robert D., Dept. of Elem. Educ., Colorado State Col., Greeley, Colo.
Bennett, Dale E., Col. of Educ., Univ. of Ill., Urbana, Ill.
Bennett, Doris, Jacksonville State College, Jacksonville, Ala.
Bennett, Lloyd M., Texas Woman's University, Denton, Tex.
Bennett, Robert N., Greene Central School, Greene, N.Y.
Bennett, William R., 335 N. Ashley, Bourbonnais, Ill.
Bennie, William A., Univ. of Texas, Austin, Texas
Bentley, Caryl B., Rt. 1, Co. T, Sun Prairie, Wis.
Bentley, Harold, Northern Essex Community Col., Haverhill, Mass.
Bentley, Mrs. Harriett P., 2985 Wooster Rd., Rocky River, Ohio
Bentley, Ralph R., Educ. Bldg., Purdue University, West Lafayette, Ind.
Bentley, Robert, 1535 Walton Ave., Bronx, N.Y.
Benvenuto, Arthur, 158 Garden Pkwy., Henrietta, N.Y.
Beran, D. L., University of Missouri, Columbia, Mo.
Berg, Arthur D., Music Consult., Dearborn Pub. Schools, Dearborn, Mich.
Berg, Dorothy D., 5924 N. Forest Glen Ave., Chicago, Ill.
Berg, Pauline G., Odebolt, Iowa
Berg, Selmer H., 1216 Running Springs Rd., Walnut Creek, Calif.
Berger, Allen, Southern Illinois University, Carbondale, Ill.
Bergeson, Clarence O., State University College, Geneseo, N.Y.
Bergeson, John B., 2415 Skyline St., Kalamazoo, Mich.
Berghoefer, Clara, 5433 S. Dorchester Ave., Chicago, Ill.
Berkihiser, Frances, Evangel College, Springfield, Mo.
Berkowitz, Edward, 2 Loretta Dr., Syosset, L.I., N.Y.
Berkowitz, Howard, State University College, Oneonta, N.Y.
Berlin, Pearl, 1945 Orleans, Detroit, Mich.
Berlin, Robert S., 383 Grand St., New York, N.Y.
Bernard, Donald H., 2035 Maury, St. Louis, Mo.
Bernard, Harold W., 1985 S.W. Warwick Ave., Portland, Ore.
Bernd, John M., 824 Ellis St., Stevens Point, Wis.
Bernert, Roman A., S.J., Marquette Univ., Milwaukee, Wis.
Bernhoft, Otto L., 1840 15th Ave., Fargo, N.D.
Berning, Norbert J., 204 W. Sunset Pl., DeKalb, Ill.
Bernstein, Abbot A., 104 Edwards Rd., Clifton, N.J.
Bernstein, Abraham, Dept. of Educ., Brooklyn College, Brooklyn, N.Y.
Bernstein, Mrs. Jean C., 310 Illinois St., Park Forest, Ill.
Berry, Daryl, Millikin University, Decatur, Ill.

Berry, Henry W., P.O. Box 266, Normal, Ala.
Berson, Mrs. Minnie, 1909 Locust Grove Rd., Silver Spring, Md.
Bertness, Henry J., 2909 N. 29th St., Tacoma, Wash.
Bertolli, Robert L., Massachusetts Col. of Art, Boston, Mass.
Bertrand, John R., Berry College, Mt. Berry, Ga.
Best, Mrs. Drusilla, 1148—8th Ave., S.W., Faribault, Minn.
Bettelheim, Bruno, 1365 E. 60th St., Chicago, Ill.
Bettina, Al, Eastern New Mexico University, Portales, N.M.
Betts, Emmett A., Sch. of Educ., University of Miami, Coral Gables, Fla.
Beyer, Fred C., Superintendent of County Schools, Modesto, Calif.
Beyerl, Merrill C., Ball State University, Muncie, Ind.
Beynon, Robert P., Devel. & Resch., Bowling Green Univ., Bowling Green, Ohio
Bhola, H. S., Literacy House, Lucknow, India
Bickert, Roderick N., Supt. of Schools, Mason City, Iowa
Bidwell, Mrs. Wilma W., 1223 Western Ave., Albany, N.Y.
Bieber, Mrs. Ida P., 7357 Cornell Ave., University City, Mo.
Biersdorf, John E., 475 Riverside Dr., New York, N.Y.
* Bigelow, M. A., Litchfield, Conn.
Bigelow, Roy G., 404 S. 37th Ave., Hattiesburg, Miss.
Biggs, Sarah Dorothy, 804 Court, Fulton, Mo.
Biggy, M. Virginia, 10 Alcott St., Acton, Mass.
Bilhorn, J. Chester, 3846 N. Kedvale Ave., Chicago, Ill.
Bills, Mark W., Superintendent of Schools, Peoria, Ill.
Billups, Mrs. Clairene B., 2409 Tidewater Dr., Norfolk, Va.
Binford, George H., Central High School, Charlotte Courthouse, Va.
Binford, Linwood T., J. Andrew Bowler School, Richmond, Va.
Bingham, William C., Rutgers University, New Brunswick, N.J.
Binkley, Marvin Edward, 1000 Noelton Ln., Nashville, Tenn.
Bird, Barbara R., 541 Sligh Blvd., N.E., Grand Rapids, Mich.
Bird, Charles A., 23 Fraser Pl., Hastings on Hudson, N.Y.
Birdsell, Don F., Supt. of Schools, Wheaton, Ill.
Bishop, Clifford L., State College of Iowa, Cedar Falls, Iowa
Bishop, Martha D., Dept. of Educ., Winthrop College, Rock Hill, S.C.
Bishop, W. E., Superintendent of Schools, Englewood, Colo.
Bjork, Alton J., Dept. of Educ., Univ. of North Dakota, Grand Forks, N.D.
Black, Hubert P., Lee College, Cleveland, Tenn.
Black, Hugh C., Dept. of Educ., Univ. of California, Davis, Calif.
Black, Leo P., State Dept. of Educ., State Office Bldg., Denver, Colo.
Black, Mrs. Marian W., Sch. of Educ., Florida State Univ., Tallahassee, Fla.
Black, Millard H., 10031 Vecino Lane, La Habra, Calif.
Blackburn, Clifford S., 420 West "D" St., North Little Rock, Ark.
Blackledge, Mrs. Helen V., Southern Heights Sch., Fort Wayne, Ind.
Blackman, Charles A., Michigan State Univ., East Lansing, Mich.
Blackshear, John S., 3066 Bethune Ave., Macon, Ga.
Blackwell, Leslie, 5618 20th St., N.E., Seattle, Wash.
Blackwell, Lewis F., Jr., Box 1026, University, Ala.
Blackwell, Sara, N.Y. State Col. of H.E., Cornell Univ., Ithaca, N.Y.
Blaine, Russell K., 1816 Park Ave., S.E., Cedar Rapids, Iowa
Blake, Duane L., Colorado State Univ., Fort Collins, Colo.
Blakely, Edward J., Univ. of California, Los Angeles, Calif.
Blakely, Richard F., Iona College, New Rochelle, N.Y.
Blanchard, Robert W., 22 Valley Rd., Montclair, N.J.
Blanchard, Walter J., Rhode Island Col., Warwick, R.I.
Blaney, Mrs. Rose Marie, Manhasset Public Schools, Manhasset, N.Y.
Blank, Stanley S., Univ. of Calgary, Calgary, Alba., Canada
Blankenship, A. H., Educational Research Council, Cleveland, Ohio
Blanton, Roy R., Jr., Appalachian State Tchrs. College, Boone, N.C.
Blaser, John W., Wahtonka High School, The Dalles, Ore.
Blessington, John P., Whitby School, Greenwich, Conn.
Blezien, Stephen S., 2630 N. Fairfield Ave., Chicago, Ill.
Bliesmer, Emery P., Read. Ctr., Pennsylvania State Univ., University Park, Pa.

Bligh, Harold F., 81 Lincoln Ave., Ardsley, N.Y.
Blocher, R. Banks, So. Shore Academy & Day Sch., South Hanover, Mass.
Block, Elaine C., Hunter College, New York, N.Y.
Blomenberg, Gilbert, 345 North 2nd St., Seward, Neb.
Blomgren, Glen H., Fresno State College, Fresno, Calif.
Blommers, Paul, East Hall, State University of Iowa, Iowa City, Iowa
Blum, Mrs. Joanne L., Point Park Junior College, Pittsburgh, Pa.
Blythe, L. Ross, 65 Lori Lee Dr., Lafayette, Ind.
Boario, Dora A., 422 Third St., Leechburg, Pa.
Bock, R. Darrell, Dept. of Educ., Univ. of Chicago, Chicago, Ill.
Bodkin, Lee D., 24 Mariposa Lane, Orinda, Calif.
Bodkin, Raymond C., Page County High School, Shenandoah, Va.
Boeck, Clarence H., 5101 Ewing Ave., So., Minneapolis, Minn.
Boeck, Robert W., 939 K. Cherry Ln., East Lansing, Mich.
Boenig, Robert W., State Univ. Col., Fredonia, N.Y.
Boger, D. L., Morehouse College, Atlanta, Ga.
Boggess, Violet F., 2445 New Milford Rd., Atwater, Ohio
Bogle, Frank P., Superintendent of Schools, Millville, N.J.
Boisclair, Cecile, University of Montreal, Montreal, Que., Canada
Bolton, Mrs. Anne S., 1907 Dauphin St., Mobile, Ala.
Bolton, Dale L., Dept. of Educ., Univ. of Washington, Seattle, Wash.
Boltuck, Charles J., St. Cloud State Col., St. Cloud, Minn.
Bonar, Hugh S., Lewis College, Joliet, Ill.
Bond, George W., 3 Julia Ave., New Paltz, N.Y.
Bond, Horace M., Sch. of Educ., Atlanta University, Atlanta, Ga.
Bongiovanni, Lawrence M., 182 Tremont St., Boston, Mass.
Bonk, Edward C., North Texas University, Denton, Tex.
Booker, Ann, 849 E. 215th St., Bronx, N.Y.
*Booker, Ivan A., N.E.A. Mem. Div., 1201 Sixteenth St., N.W., Washington, D.C.
Bookwalter, Karl W., Indiana University, Bloomington, Ind.
Boord, Robert O., Nevada Southern University, Las Vegas, Nev.
Booth, Delores C., 6604 Tremont St., Oakland, Calif.
Borden, Miles B., Amityville Pub. Schools, Amityville, N.Y.
Borders, Frances R., 3617 Raymond St., Chevy Chase, Md.
Borg, Robert L., Scott Hall, University of Minnesota, Minneapolis, Minn.
Borg, Walter R., 1 Garden Cir., Hotel Claremont, Berkeley, Calif.
Borga, Victor D., First Natl. Bank Bldg., Iron Mountain, Mich.
Bortz, A. G., Bridgewater Col., Bridgewater, Va.
Bosch, Gerald, 228 Ellen Ave., State College, Pa.
Bosco, James, Western Michigan University, Kalamazoo, Mich.
Bossard, Grace, Route 3, Box 6, Seaford, Del.
Bossier, Antonia M., 1661 No. Roman St., New Orleans, La.
Bossing, Nelson L., Col. of Educ., Southern Ill. Univ., Carbondale, Ill.
Bothell, John E., Colorado State College, Greeley, Colo.
Bouchard, John B., State Univ. Col., Fredonia, N.Y.
Boula, James A., 316 S. 2nd St., Springfield, Ill.
Boulac, Brian Michael, University of Notre Dame, Notre Dame, Ind.
Bouseman, John W., Cent. Y.M.C.A. Comm. Col., Chicago, Ill.
Bowen, Alton O., Bryan City Public Schools, Bryan, Tex.
Bower, Robert K., 1905 E. Loma Alta Dr., Altadena, Calif.
Bowers, A. Eugene, Fayette County Schools, Fayetteville, Ga.
Bowers, Norman D., Sch. of Educ., Northwestern Univ., Evanston, Ill.
Bowers, Victor L., Southwest Texas State College, San Marcos, Tex.
Bowman, Howard A., Box 3307, Terminal Annex, Los Angeles, Calif.
Box, Russell C., Univ. of the Americas, Mexico City, Mexico
Boyajy, Robert J., 154 Park Ave., West Caldwell, N.J.
Boyce, Floyd A., 3316 Pecos St., Austin, Texas
Boyd, Laurence E., Sch. of Educ., Atlanta University, Atlanta, Ga.
Boyd, Robert D., Dept. of Educ., Univ. of Wisconsin, Madison, Wis.
Boyd, Robert M., Col. of Educ., Ohio University, Athens, Ohio
Boyer, Francis J., Northern Illinois University, DeKalb, Ill.

Boyer, Roscoe A., Sch. of Educ., Univ. of Mississippi, University, Miss.
Boykin, Leander L., Florida A. & M. University, Tallahassee, Fla.
Boyle, Patrick J., Campion College High School, Regina, Sask., Canada
Boyle, William J., State Supv., Voc.-Tech. Educ., Madison, Wis.
Boyles, Mrs. Beatrice C., 704 Wilson Rd., Wilmington, Del.
Boynton, Paul M., Connecticut State Dept. of Educ., Hartford, Conn.
Braam, L. S., Read. Ctr., Syracuse University, Syracuse, N.Y.
Bracewell, George, Southern Illinois University, Carbondale, Ill.
Brackbill, A. L., Jr., Millersville State College, Millersville, Pa.
Bradford, James L., 1692 Northwest Blvd., Columbus, Ohio
Bradley, Mrs. Eunice, 2031 Poyntz Ave., Manhattan, Kansas
Bradley, Mrs. George W., East Tenn. State Univ., Johnson City, Tenn.
Bradley, Juanita, Peru State College, Peru, Neb.
Bradtmueller, Weldon G., State Dept. of Educ., Tallahassee, Fla.
Brady, Florence A., 186 Oakland Rd., Maplewood, N.J.
Brady, Francis X., Elmira College, Elmira, N.Y.
Brady, John C., Bemidji State College, Bemidji, Minn.
Brain, George B., Col. of Educ., Washington State Univ., Pullman, Wash.
Brainard, Lois, San Jose State College, San Jose, Calif.
Bramwell, John R., Univ. of Oregon, Eugene, Ore.
Brandt, Willard J., University of Wisconsin-Milwaukee, Milwaukee, Wis.
Branom, Wayne T., Superintendent of Schools, Hillside, N.J.
Brantley, Mabel, 623 N. First St., DeKalb, Ill.
Brantley, Mrs. Sybil, 108 Lomaland Dr., West Monroe, La.
Brauer, Walter L., Washington H.S., Milwaukee, Wis.
Braun, Frank, Burton Hall, University of Minnesota, Minneapolis, Minn.
Braun, Gertrude E., West Conn. State Col., Danbury, Conn.
Braun, Irma D., 228 Ocean Blvd., Atlantic Highlands, N.J.
Braun, Ray H., 101 N. McCullough St., Urbana, Ill.
Bravo, Anna, 32 Beach Hill St., Ft. Salonga, N.Y.
Bredesen, Dorothy A., 644 "D" St., N.E., Washington, D.C.
Breeding, Clifford C., 2708 Bridal Wreath Ln., Dallas, Texas
Bregman, Sydell, 17 Bodnarik Dr., Edison, N.J.
Breihan, Edna, 1512 Briggs St., Lockport, Ill.
Brenner, Anton, Merrill-Palmer School, 71 Ferry E., Detroit, Mich.
Brereton, Matthew J., 22 Oakland Ter., Newark, N.J.
Bresina, Bertha M., 8308 E. Highland Ave., Scottsdale, Arizona
Breslin, Frederick D., Glassboro State College, Glassboro, N.J.
Bretsch, Howard S., Sch. of Educ., University of Michigan, Ann Arbor, Mich.
Bretz, Frank H., 1999 Arlington Ave., Columbus, Ohio
Brewer, Jack W., 3024 Galena St., Simi, Calif.
Brewster, Maurice A., Jr., Memorial Univ., St. John's, Newfoundland
Brewton, Raymond E., Supt. of County Schools, Palo Pinto, Texas
Brick, Michael, Tchrs. Col., Columbia University, New York, N.Y.
Brickman, Benjamin, Dept. of Educ., Brooklyn College, Brooklyn, N.Y.
Brickman, William W., University of Pennsylvania, Philadelphia, Pa.
Bridges, C. M., Col. of Educ., University of Oklahoma, Norman, Okla.
Bridges, Lonnie H., Box 10194, Southern University, Baton Rouge, La.
Bridges, Raymond H., Box 10194, Southern University, Baton Rouge, La.
Briggs, Albert A., Dunbar Vocational High School, Chicago, Ill.
Bright, John H., 628 Cuesta Ave., San Mateo, Calif.
* Bright, Orville T., 516½ Prospect Ave., Lake Bluff, Ill.
Brill, Donald M., 5420 Maher Ave., Madison, Wis.
Brim, Burl, West Texas State University, Canyon, Tex.
Brimhall, Mrs. Alice, 111 Monticello Ave., Piedmont, Calif.
Briner, Conrad, 1221 Cambridge Ave., Claremont, Calif.
Brink, William G., Sch. of Educ., Northwestern University, Evanston, Ill.
Brinkman, A. John, 5529 S. Blackstone Ave., Chicago, Ill.
Brinkman, J. Warren, Kansas State Tchrs. College, Emporia, Kan.
Brinkmann, E. H., So. Illinois Univ., Edwardsville, Ill.
Brinkmeier, Oria A., 2203 Carter Ave., St. Paul, Minn.

Briscoe, Laurel A., 2019 Marine St., Santa Monica, Calif.
Brish, William M., Supt., Washington Co. Schools, Hagerstown, Md.
Brislawn, J., 28th & Lilac St., Longview, Wash.
Bristol, Stanley T., Joseph Sears School, Kenilworth, Ill.
Bristow, William H., Bur. of Cur. Devel., City Schools, New York, N.Y.
Britt, Laurence V., S.J., John Carroll Univ., Cleveland, Ohio
Brittain, Clay V., 1810 Panda Ln., McLean, Va.
Britton, Edward C., Sacramento State Col., Sacramento, Calif.
Britton, Ernest R., Superintendent of Schools, Midland, Mich.
Broadbent, Frank W., 6401 Allison Ave., Des Moines, Iowa
Broderick, Catherine M., City Sch. Dist., South Rochester, N.Y.
Brody, Erness B., Rutgers University, New Brunswick, N.J.
Broening, Angela M., Baltimore Public Schls., 3 East 25th St., Baltimore, Md.
Bromwich, Rose M., 13507 Hart St., Van Nuys, Calif.
Bronars, Joseph C., DePaul University, Chicago, Ill.
Bronson, Clement A., 1920 Patterson St., Tuskegee Inst., Ala.
Bronson, Homer D., Chico State College, Chico, Calif.
Bronson, Moses L., 290 Ninth Ave., New York, N.Y.
Brookins, Jack E., 1323 Bayview, North Bend, Ore.
Brooks, B. Marian, City College, 135th and Convent, New York, N.Y.
Brophy, John M., Col. of Business, Univ. of Rochester, Rochester, N.Y.
Brostoff, Theodore M., 10474 Santa Monica Blvd., Los Angeles, Calif.
Brother Adelbert James, Manhattan College, New York, N.Y.
Brother Alfred, St. Mary's College, Winona, Minn.
Brother Cosmas Herlihy, St. Francis College, Brooklyn, N.Y.
Brother Francis Wray, St. Mary's Col., Winona, Minn.
Brother Joseph Brusnahan, 5900 Walnut Grove, Memphis, Tenn.
Brother Stephen Walsh, St. Edward's University, Austin, Tex.
Brother U. Cassian, St. Mary's Col., St. Mary's, Calif.
Brottman, Marvin A., 8926 Bellefort, Morton Grove, Ill.
Brougher, John F., Shippensburg State College, Shippensburg, Pa.
Brousseau, Sandy E., 43 Carlos Ct., Walnut Creek, Calif.
Brown, Aaron, 1468 President St., Brooklyn, N.Y.
Brown, Mrs. Anne A., 7834 S. Clyde, Chicago, Ill.
Brown, Camille, University of California, Los Angeles, Calif.
Brown, Charles I., Fayetteville State College, Fayetteville, N.C.
Brown, Chester J., 7002 Arrowhead Dr., Tucson, Ariz.
Brown, Clark, Mt. Diablo Unified Sch. Dist., Concord, Calif.
Brown, Cynthiana Ellen, 6644 Wildlife Rd., Malibu, Calif.
Brown, Douglas H., Pine Wood Dr., Contoocook, N.H.
Brown, Douglas M., Superintendent of Schools, Shorewood, Wis.
Brown, Mrs. Edith F., 2821 N. 2nd St., Harrisburg, Pa.
Brown, Francis A., 2821 N. 2nd St., Harrisburg, Pa.
Brown, George W., Superintendent of Schools, Webster Groves, Mo.
Brown, Gerald W., California State College, Hayward, Calif.
Brown, Gertrude E., 2835 Milan St., New Orleans, La.
Brown, Howard L., Schl. Admin. Center, 49 E. College Ave., Springfield, Ohio
Brown, Jeremy, Castleton State Col., Castleton, Vt.
Brown, Kenneth B., University of Missouri, Columbia, Mo.
Brown, Kenneth R., California Tchrs. Assn., 1705 Murchison Dr., Burlingame, Calif.
Brown, Lawrence D., Sch. of Educ., Indiana University, Bloomington, Ind.
Brown, Marion R., 404 Riverside Dr., New York, N.Y.
Brown, Mrs. Marjorie D., 4455 West 64th St., Los Angeles, Calif.
Brown, Marjorie M., University of Minnesota, St. Paul, Minn.
Brown, Perry, Lock Haven State College, Lock Haven, Pa.
Brown, Robert S., 218 Argyle, San Antonio, Texas
Brown, Roy A., Dept. of Pub. Instr., Harrisburg, Pa.
Brown, Sara M., So. Connecticut State Col., New Haven, Conn.
Brown, Susan C., Box 155, Fall River Mills, Calif.
Brown, Rev. Syl, St. Mary's Col., Winona, Minn.

Brown, Thomas J., Hofstra Univ., Hempstead, N.Y.
Brown, Virginia H., 1 Lafayette Plaisance, Detroit, Mich.
Brown, Warren M., Supt. of Schools, Ferguson, Mo.
Brown, Woodrow W., Superintendent of Schools, York, Pa.
Brownell, Samuel M., Yale Univ. & Univ. of Conn., New Haven, Conn.
Brownell, William A., 701 Spruce St., Berkeley, Calif.
Browning, Roy W., Ottawa University, Ottawa, Kan.
Brownstein, Jewell, Dept. of Educ., Univ. of Louisville, Louisville, Ky.
Browy, Marjorie J., California State College, Los Angeles, Calif.
Brubaker, Leonard A., 409 Marian Ave., Normal, Ill.
Bruce, William C., Bruce Publishing Co., Milwaukee, Wis.
Brueckner, Leo J., 10790 Clarmon Pl., Culver City, Calif.
Brumbaugh, W. Donald, University of Utah, Salt Lake City, Utah
Brunelle, Paul E., 31 Herring Ave., Biddeford, Me.
Bruning, Charles R., University of Minnesota-Morris, Morris, Minn.
Brunner, Edward F., Murray State College, Murray, Ky.
Bruno, Gordon A., Darien H.S., Darien, Conn.
Brunson, Mrs. Dewitt, P.O. Box 484, Orangeburg, S.C.
Brunsvold, P. O., Supt. of Schools, Mason City, Iowa
Bryan, Ray J., 220 Curtiss Hall, Iowa State Univ., Ames, Iowa
Bryant, B. Carleton, 810 Clear Lake Ave., West Palm Beach, Fla.
Bryant, Ira B., Kashmere Gardens High Sch., Houston, Tex.
Bryant, Merle L., University of Minnesota, Duluth, Minn.
Bryant, R. A., Box 268, Cedartown, Ga.
Bryner, James R., 185 Salisbury Dr., Saskatoon, Sask., Canada
Bryson, Ronald, 608 E. McMillan St., Cincinnati, Ohio
Buchanan, Alfred K., 80 Grove St., Plantsville, Conn.
Buchanan, Paul G., 19 Elmdale St., Dorchester, Mass.
Buckley, J. L., Superintendent of Schools, Lockhart, Tex.
Buckley, Richard Dale, Univ. of Pennsylvania, Philadelphia, Pa.
Buckner, John D., 4246 W. North Market St., St. Louis, Mo.
Buckner, William N., 2643—15th St., N.W., Washington, D.C.
Budd, Mrs. Edith M., 3227 Parker Ave., West Palm Beach, Fla.
Bueker, Armin H., Superintendent of Schools, Marshall, Mo.
Buelke, John A., Western Michigan University, Kalamazoo, Mich.
Bullock, James E., 41 Westbrook Rd., West Hartford, Conn.
Bullock, Portia C., 408 Tea St., N.W., Washington, D.C.
Bullock, William J., Superintendent of Schools, Kannapolis, N.C.
Bunger, Marianne, Wesleyan College, Macon, Ga.
Bunker, James G., Supt., Novato Unified Sch. Dist., Novato, Calif.
Bunnell, Mrs. Constance O., Mamaroneck High School, Mamaroneck, N.Y.
Bunnell, Robert A., Ford Foundation, 477 Madison Ave., New York, N.Y.
Buntrock, Richard M., West Bend Pub. Schools, West Bend, Wis.
Buol, Mary Steudler, 91 Ten Acre Rd., New Britain, Conn.
Burch, Charles H., 1602 S. Anderson St., Urbana, Ill.
Burdett, C. Fred., Burdett College, 160 Beacon St., Boston, Mass.
Burdick, A. E., Arkansas State Teachers College, Conway, Ark.
Burdick, Richard L., Educ. Dept., Carroll College, Waukesha, Wis.
Burg, Mrs. Mary, 2259 Wolfangle Rd., Cincinnati, Ohio
Burgdorf, Otto P., 36-12—210th St., Bayside, N.Y.
Burgess, Van, 1112-E San Pablo Ave., Albany, Calif.
Burke, Arvid J., N.Y. State Tchrs. Assn., Albany, N.Y.
Burke, Carolyn L., 52 Portage, Highland Park, Mich.
Burke, Doyle K., Newport Spec. Sch. Dist., Newport, Ark.
Burke, Eileen M., 48 Bayberry Rd., Trenton, N.J.
* Burke, Gladys, 244 Outlook, Youngstown, Ohio
Burke, Henry R., 197 Ridgewood Ave., Glen Ridge, N.J.
Burke, Paul J., 1 Lookout Pl., Ardsley, N.Y.
Burke, Thomas O., 424 Bayberry Dr., Plantation, Fla.
Burke, Thomas S., 6926 S. Wolcott Ave., Chicago, Ill.
Burkett, Lowell A., 1025 15th St., N.W., Washington, D.C.

Burks, Herbert M., Jr., 134 Mimosa Dr., Charlottesville, Va.
Burks, John B., Jersey City State College, Jersey City, N.J.
Burnett, Clinton E., P.O. Box 773, San Marcos, Tex.
Burnett, Joe R., University of Illinois, Urbana, Ill.
Burns, Constance M., University of Bridgeport, Bridgeport, Conn.
Burns, Cranford H., Box 1549, Mobile, Ala.
Burns, Hobert W., San Jose State Col., San Jose, Calif.
Burns, James W., 447 Hillcrest Ave., State College, Pa.
Burr, Elbert W., Monsanto Chemical Co., Lindbergh and Olive, St. Louis, Mo.
Burrell, E. William, Salve Regina Col., Newport, R.I.
Burrough, Rudolph V., S.W. Ark. Diag. & Remed. Cent., Magnolia, Ark.
Burrows, Alvina Treut, 117 Nassau Ave., Manhasset, N.Y.
Burt, Lucile, Lincoln School, 338 Forest Ave., Fond du Lac, Wis.
Bushnell, Allan C., 2324 Loma Prieta Lane, Menlo Park, Calif.
Buswell, Guy T., 1836 Thousand Oaks Blvd., Berkeley, Calif.
Butler, Mrs. B. LaConyea, Spelman College, Atlanta, Ga.
Butler, E. Frank, Contra Costa College, San Pablo, Calif.
Butler, Laurence, 630 Leonard St., Ashland, Ore.
Butler, Paul W., 721 Australian Ave., West Palm Beach, Fla.
Butler, Thomas M., 1166 W. North St., Decatur, Ill.
Butts, David P., University of Texas, Austin, Tex.
Butts, Franklin A., 54 N. Hamilton St., Poughkeepsie, N.Y.
Butts, Gordon K., Southern Illinois University, Carbondale, Ill.
Butts, R. Freeman, Tchrs. Col., Columbia University, New York, N.Y.
Buyse, R., Sch. of Educ., University of Louvain, Tournai, Belgium
Buzash, G. A., 65 Colonial Ave., Pitman, N.J.
Byerly, Carl L., 5057 Woodward Ave., Detroit, Mich.
Byers, Joe L., Michigan State Univ., East Lansing, Mich.
Bynum, James H., University of Missouri, Kansas City, Mo.
Byram, Harold M., Sch. of Educ., Michigan State Univ., East Lansing, Mich.
Byrne, Richard Hill, Col. of Educ., Univ. of Maryland, College Park, Md.

Caccavo, Emil. 123 Willow St., Roslyn Heights, N.Y.
Cadd, Ayrles W., Box 17, Shandon, Calif.
Cadwell, Herbert M., 265 N. San Rafael Ave., Pasadena, Calif.
Cady, Henry L., Ohio State University, Columbus, Ohio
Cafiero, Albert J., Supt., Oradell Pub. Schools, Oradell, N.J.
Cafone, Harold C., Dept. of Educ., Oakland Univ., Rochester, Mich.
Cahan, Mrs. Ruth, 1916 Overland Ave., Los Angeles, Calif.
Cahn, Meyer M., San Francisco State Col., San Francisco, Calif.
Cain, E. J., University of Nevada, Reno, Nev.
Cain, Lee C., Georgia Southern Branch, Statesboro, Ga.
Cain, Ralph W., Sutton Hall, University of Texas, Austin, Tex.
Caird, Florence B., Joyce Kilmer School, Chicago, Ill.
Caldwell, Cleon C., 2917 Noble Ave., Bakersfield, Calif.
Caldwell, O. K., Fostoria High School, Fostoria, Ohio
Califf, Stanley N., Chapman College, Orange, Calif.
Calip, Rev. Osmundo A., St. John's University, Jamaica, N.Y.
Call, Mrs. Ardell, Utah Education Association, Salt Lake City, Utah
Callahan, William T., Education Council, 131 Mineola Blvd., Mineola, N.Y.
Callan, John H., Bayley Hall, Seton Hall University, South Orange, N.J.
Callas, Eliza E., 7080 Oregon Ave., N.W., Washington, D.C.
Callaway, A. Byron, Col. of Educ., Univ. of Georgia, Athens, Ga.
Calmes, Robert E., 5216 Mission Hill Dr., Tucson, Ariz.
Calvert, Lloyd, Supt. of Schools, Windsor, Conn.
Camhi, Paul S., 6121 S. Norwalk Blvd., Whittier, Calif.
Campbell, A. Leedy, Dir., Urban Educ., Brd. of Educ., Kansas City, Mo.
Campbell, Clyde M., Michigan State University, East Lansing, Mich.
Campbell, E. G., Col. of Educ., Univ. of Maryland, College Park, Md.
Campbell, L. L., 5107 Woodmoor Dr., Austin, Tex.
Campbell, R. Lee, Campbellsville College, Campbellsville, Ky.

Campbell, Roald F., Sch. of Educ., University of Chicago, Chicago, Ill.
Campin, Reginald W., P.O. Box 26, Blaine, Wash.
Campos, Mrs. M. A. Pourchet, Caixa Postal 30.F86, Sao Paulo, S. P., Brazil
Canar, Donald A., Central YMCA Schls., 211 W. Wacker Dr., Chicago, Ill.
Candoli, Italo C., 1452 B Spartan Village, East Lansing, Mich.
Canfield, John M., Superintendent of Schools, West Plains, Mo.
Cannici, Peter, 189 Columbia Ave., Passaic, N.J.
Cannon, Frances O., Alabama College, Montevallo, Ala.
Cannon, Wendell, Univ. of So. California, Los Angeles, Calif.
Cantlon, R. Jerry, Illinois State University, Normal, Ill.
Capehart, Bertis E., 120 Squire Hill Rd., Upper Montclair, N.J.
Capocy, John S., 4628 Seeley St., Downers Grove, Ill.
Cappa, Dan, California State Col., Los Angeles, Calif.
Cappelluzzo, Emma M., University of Massachusetts, Amherst, Mass.
Capps, Lelon R., Bailey Hall, University of Kansas, Lawrence, Kan.
Capps, Mrs. Marian P., Virginia State College, Norfolk, Va.
Carder, W. Ray, Hillsboro High School, Hillsboro, Ore.
Cardina, Philip J., Box 269, R.D. 2, Farmingdale, N.J.
Cardinale, Anthony, Dir., Dependents Educ., Dept. of Defense, Washington, D.C.
Cardwell, Robert H., Tyson Junior High School, Knoxville, Tenn.
Carey, Clarence B., Dir., Jones Commercial H.S., Chicago, Ill.
Carey, Jess Wendell, Park College, Parkville, Mo.
Carey, Justin P., 105 Lyncroft Rd., New Rochelle, N.Y.
Carle, Richard F., Div. of Gen. Educ., Boston University, Boston, Mass.
Carlin, James B., Supv. of Read., City Schools, Meridian, Miss.
Carline, Donald E., 2513 Stanford Rd., Fort Collins, Colo.
Carlisle, John C., Col. of Educ., Utah State Univ., Logan, Utah
Carlson, Mrs. Evelyn F., 6899 N. Wildwood, Chicago, Ill.
Carlson, F. Roy, Mt. Ida Junior College, Newton Centre, Mass.
Carlson, Robert A., 601-H Eagle Hgts., Madison, Wis.
Carlson, Mrs. Ruth K., 1718 LeRoy Ave., Berkeley, Calif.
Carlson, Thorston R., 415 Monte Vista Lane, Santa Rosa, Calif.
Carlson, Waymann, Southern California College, Costa Mesa, Calif.
Carlson, Wesley H., 4th St. & Bayard Ave., Wilmington, Del.
Carmichael, John H., 913 Cherry Ln., East Lansing, Mich.
Carnahan, Eleanor, 11 Forest Rd., Oakmont, Wheeling, W.Va.
Carne, Vernon E., 1383 Dorothy Dr., Decatur, Ga.
Carnochan, John L., Jr., Route 5, Frederick, Md.
Carpenter, Aaron C., P.O. Box 387, Grambling, La.
Carpenter, N. H., Superintendent, City Schools, Elkin, N.C.
Carr, Carolyn Jane, 227 Whitemarsh Rd., Ardmore, Pa.
Carr, Julian W., 705 Kinderkamack Rd., River Edge, N.J.
Carriere, Robert H., 57 Theroux Dr., Fairview, Mass.
Carroll, Clifford, Gonzaga University, Spokane, Wash.
Carroll, John B., Educational Testing Service, Princeton, N.J.
Carroll, Margaret L., 208 Fairmont Rd., DeKalb, Ill.
Carruth, Edwin Ronald, University of Southern Mississippi, McComb, Miss.
Carsello, Carmen J., University of Illinois Circle Campus, Chicago, Ill.
Carstater, Eugene D., Bur. of Naval Personnel, Washington, D.C.
Carter, Harold D., Sch. of Educ., University of California, Berkeley, Calif.
Carter, James S., North High School, Phoenix, Ariz.
Carter, Dr. Lamore J., Grambling Col., Grambling, La.
Carter, Richard C., Supt. of Schools, Palmer, Alaska
Carter, Sims, 214 Spalding Dr., Beverly Hills, Calif.
Carter, Thomas D., Alamo Hgts. Indep. Sch. Dist., San Antonio, Texas
Carter, Vincent, San Jose City College, San Jose, Calif.
Cartwright, William H., Duke University, Durham, N.C.
Caselli, Robert E., 1614 S. Phillips Ave., Sioux Falls, S.D.
Casey, Barbara A., 2817 38th St., N.W., Washington, D.C.
Casey, J. E., Box 546, Bryn Mawr, Pa.
Casey, John J., 674 Academy St., New York, N.Y.

Casey, Neal, 71-B Escondido Village, Stanford, Calif.
Cash, Christine B., Jarvis Christian College, Marshall, Tex.
Cashen, Carol J., 61 Lattimore Rd., Rochester, N.Y.
Caskey, Helen C., Tchrs. Col., University of Cincinnati, Cincinnati, Ohio
Cassidy, Rosalind, University of California, 405 Hilgard Ave., Los Angeles, Calif.
Castelli, Albert, 2933 Shawnee Lane, Drayton Plains, Mich.
Castrale, Remo, Supt. of Schools, Johnston City, Ill.
Catrambone, A. R., Superintendent of Schools, Camden, N.J.
Caughran, Alex M., 93 N. Main St., Orono, Me.
Caulfield, Patrick J., Dept. of Educ., St. Peter's College, Jersey City, N.J.
Cawein, Paul E., 2032 Belmont Rd., N.W., Apt. 600, Washington, D.C.
Cawrse, Robert C., 26927 Osborn Rd., Bayvillage, Ohio
Cayco, Florentino, President, Arellano University, Manila, Philippines
Cecco, Mrs. Josephine L., Springfield College, Springfield, Mass.
Center, William R., Col. of Educ., C.E.B., Knoxville, Tenn.
Chadderdon, Hester, Home Econ. Div., Iowa State University, Ames, Iowa
Chall, Jeanne, Grad. Sch. of Educ., Harvard University, Cambridge, Mass.
Chambers, William M., 205 Maple, S.E., Albuquerque, N.M.
Champagne, R. P., Holy Savior Central High School, Lockport, La.
Champlin, Ardath I., Seattle Pacific College, Seattle, Wash.
Champoux, Mrs. Elen M., 301 Mendenhall St., Greensboro, N.C.
Chandler, H. E., 1320 Haskell Ave., Lawrence, Kan.
Chang, Alvin K., 3642 S. Court St., Palo Alto, Calif.
* Chang, Jen-chi, Florida Normal and Ind. Mem. College, St. Augustine, Fla.
Chang, Mrs. Lynette Y. C., Univ. of Minnesota, Minneapolis, Minn.
Channell, W. R., Argentine High School, Kansas City, Kan.
Chansky, Norman M., Temple University, Philadelphia, Pa.
Chao, Sankey C., 154 Redwood Ave., Wayne, N.J.
Chapline, Elaine Burns, Queens Col., Flushing, N.Y.
Chapman, Catherine, Weatherford College, Weatherford, Tex.
Chappell, Bartlett E. S., The Anderson School, Staatsburg, N.Y.
Charles, Ramon L., 327 Nickell Rd., Topeka, Kan.
Charlton, Huey E., 3785 Wisteria Lane, S.W., Atlanta, Ga.
Chase, Francis S., Dept. of Educ., Univ. of Chicago, Chicago, Ill.
Chase, Naomi C., University of Minnesota, Minneapolis, Minn.
Chasnoff, Robert. Newark State College, Union, N.J.
Chatwin, Jerry M., P. O. Box 276, Borrego Springs, Calif.
Chay, Josephine S., 2534 W. Charleston Ave., Chicago, Ill.
Cheeks, L. E., 213 McFarland St., Kerrville, Tex.
Cheers, Arlynne Lake, Grambling College, Grambling, La.
Cheever, William R., 646 N. Indiana St., Griffith, Ind.
Cherlin, Dennis L., 295 Crown St, New Haven, Conn.
Chern, Mrs. Nona E., 492 Concord Rd., Broomall, Pa.
Chiavaro, John, Newfane Cent. Sch., Newfane, N.Y.
Chidekel, Samuel J., Prin., James Madison Sch., Skokie, Ill.
Chidester, Charles B., 8646 Linden St., Munster, Ind.
Chievitz, Gene L., Bldg. 12, University of New Mexico, Albuquerque, N.M.
Childs, John W., 17101 Edwards, Southfield, Mich.
Childs, Vernon C., 1514 South 14th St., Manitowoc, Wis.
Christenson, Bernice M., 5045 Alta Canyada Rd., La Canada, Calif.
Christine, Ray O., Arizona State University, Tempe, Ariz.
Chuck, Harry C., 265 Kanoelani Dr., Hilo, Hawaii
Chudler, Albert A., 3540 Summerfield Dr., Sherman Oaks, Calif.
Churchill, Donald W., Bemidji State College, Bemidji, Minn.
Cianciolo, Patricia J., Michigan State University, East Lansing, Mich.
Ciccoricco, Edward A., 48 Clark St., Brockport, N.Y.
Ciklamini, Joseph, 921 Carnegie Ave., Plainfield, N.J.
Cioffi, Joseph M., 652 Doriskill Ct., River Vale, N.J.
Clabaugh, R. E., Superintendent of Schools, Arlington Heights, Ill.
Clanin, Edgar E., 309 Highland Dr., West Lafayette, Ind.
Clague, W. Donald, La Verne Col., La Verne, Calif.

Clare, Mrs. Elizabeth Rae, 949 N. Alfred St., Los Angeles, Calif.
Clark, Daniel, 1025 Woodrow St., Beaumont, Texas
Clark, David L., 3105 Brown Cliff Rd., Bloomington, Ind.
Clark, Elmer J., Col. of Educ., Southern Illinois Univ., Carbondale, Ill.
Clark, Francis E., Dept. of Educ. Psych., Univ. of Hawaii, Honolulu, Hawaii
Clark, Franklin B., Dist. Supt. of Schools, Athens, N.Y.
Clark, John F., 507 Marview Lane, Solana Beach, Calif.
Clark, Leonard H., 240 Van Nostrand Ave., Jersey City, N.J.
Clark, Lewis E., Supt., Coquille Sch. Dist. # 8, Coquille, Ore.
Clark, Lois M., National Education Assn., 1201—16th St., N.W., Washington, D.C.
Clark, Maurice P., Supt. of Schools, Western Springs, Ill.
Clark, Max R., Supt. of Schools, 142 Main St., Calmar, Iowa
Clark, Moses, Alabama State College, Montgomery, Ala.
Clark, Raymond M., Michigan State University, East Lansing, Mich.
Clark, Richard M., State University of N.Y., Albany, N.Y.
Clark, Sidney L., 855 Bronson Rd., Fairfield, Conn.
Clark, Stephen C., U.S. Office of Education, Washington, D.C.
Clark, Thomas H., 525 Plymouth St., Missoula, Mont.
Clark, Woodrow Wilson, 101 W. Leake St., Clinton, Miss.
Clarke, Stanley C. T., 11615—78th Ave., Edmonton, Alba., Canada
Clarkston, Emmerine A., 8216 Eberhart Ave., Chicago, Ill.
Classon, Miss Marion E., 19 Nantes Rd., Parsippany, N.J.
Clayton, Joseph E., Dept. of Educ., Trenton, N.J.
Clayton, Thomas E., 7 Kelly Dr., Manlius, N.Y.
Clegg, Ambrose A., Sch. of Educ., Univ. of Massachusetts, Amherst, Mass.
Cleland, Donald L., Sch. of Educ., Univ. of Pittsburgh, Pittsburgh, Pa.
Clifford, Dennis J., Tchrs. Col., Columbia University, New York, N.Y.
Clifford, Mrs. Miriam, 920 Monmouth Ave., Durham, N.C.
Clifford, Paul I., Sch. of Educ., Atlanta University, Atlanta, Ga.
Clift, Virgil A., Sch. of Educ., New York University, New York, N.Y.
Cline, Marion, Jr., Univ. of Texas, El Paso, Texas
Clinton, Robert, Jr., 3002 McElroy, Austin, Texas
Clouser, John J., 901 Graceland St., Des Plaines, Ill.
Clouthier, Raymond P., St. Norbert College, West DePere, Wis.
Clymer, Theodore W., Col. of Educ., University of Minnesota, Minneapolis, Minn.
Cobb, Beatrice M., Cambell Shore Rd., Gray, Me.
Cobb, Jacob E., Indiana State Univ., Terre Haute, Ind.
Cobban, Margaret R., 9 William St., Stamford, Conn.
Coblentz, Dwight, 930 Pleasant Lane, Glenview, Ill.
Cobley, Herbert F., Superintendent of Schools, Nazareth, Pa.
Cobun, Frank E., State University College, New Paltz, N.Y.
Cochi, Oscar R., 471 Manse Ln., Rochester, N.Y.
Cochran, Alton W., Supt. of Schools, Charlestown, Ind.
Cochran, John R., Kalamazoo Public Schools, 1220 Howard St., Kalamazoo, Mich.
Cochran, Russell T., Woodrow Wilson Jr. H.S., Hanford, Calif.
Code, Allen L., 208 S. Third St., Seneca, S.C.
Coen, Alban Wasson, II, Central Michigan University, Mt. Pleasant, Mich.
Cofell, William L., St. John's University, Collegeville, Minn.
Coffee, James M., Clark University, 950 Main St., Worcester, Mass.
Coffey, Thomas F., 5900 N. Glenwood Ave., Chicago, Ill.
Coffey, Warren C., 7416 East Parkway, Sacramento, Calif.
Cogger, Robert V., 50A S. Main St., Spring Valley, N.Y.
Cogswell, Mark E., Northern State College, Aberdeen, S.D.
Cohen, George, 8 Etheride Pl., Park Ridge, N.J.
Cohen, Hyman Z., 744 Henry Rd., Far Rockaway, N.Y.
Cohen, Jerome, Miami-Dade Jr. Col., Miami, Fla.
Cohen, Robert I., Roosevelt University, Chicago, Ill.
Cohen, Samuel, 60 Everit Ave., Hewlett, N.Y.
Cohen, Samuel J., 9 Coventry Rd., Syosset, N.Y.
Cohler, Milton J., 330 Diversey Pkwy., Chicago, Ill.
Cohodes, Aaron, 1050 Merchandise Mart, Chicago, Ill.

MEMBERS OF THE NATIONAL SOCIETY

Colbath, Edwin H., 97-16 118th St., Richmond Hill, N.Y.
Colburn, A. B., Cascade Senior High School, Everett, Wash.
Cole, Glenn A., University of Arkansas, Fayetteville, Ark.
Cole, James C., 1946 Mira Flores, Turlock, Calif.
Cole, James E., University of Utah, Salt Lake City, Utah
Cole, Mary I., Western Kentucky State College, Bowling Green, Ky.
Coleman, Alwin B., Sch. of Educ., West. Mich. Univ., Kalamazoo, Mich.
Coleman, Mary Elisabeth, University of Pennsylvania, Philadelphia, Pa.
Colestock, Hazelmae, 1517 S. Theresa, St. Louis, Mo.
Colla, Frances S., 49 Regina St., Trumbull, Conn.
Collier, Mrs. Anna K., 903 Fourth St., Liverpool, N.Y.
Collier, Calhoun C., Michigan State University, East Lansing, Mich.
Collier, Richard E., 4822 Eades St., Rockville, Md.
Collings, Miller R., 9201 W. Outer Dr., Detroit, Mich.
Collins, F. Ethel, Box 138, R.D. 2, Altamont, N.Y.
Collins, Helen C., 1203 Gilpin Ave., Wilmington, Del.
Collins, Kathleen M., Catholic University of America, Washington, D.C.
Collins, Mary Lucille, Beaubien Sch., 5025 N. Laramie Ave., Chicago, Ill.
Collins, Paul W., R. #5, Box 221C, Ocala, Fla.
Collins, Robert E., State Dept. of Education, St. Paul, Minn.
Colman, John E., C.M., Sch. of Educ., St. John's University, Jamaica, N.Y.
Combs, W. E., Florida A. & M. University, Tallahassee, Fla.
Comer, J. M., Box 820, Rt. 2, Collinsville, Ill.
Conan, Mrs. Beatrice, 2063—74th St., Brooklyn, N.Y.
Conaway, John O., 431 S. Brown, Terre Haute, Ind.
Condra, James B., Birmingham-Southern College, Birmingham, Ala.
Congreve, Willard J., Lab. Schls., University of Chicago, Chicago, Ill.
Conley, William H., Sacred Heart University, Bridgeport, Conn.
Connelly, John C., San Francisco State College, San Francisco, Calif.
Conner, John W., Col. of Educ., Univ. of Hawaii, Honolulu, Hawaii
Connolly, Joyce, 342 Beeler Dr., Berea, Ohio
Connor, E. Faye, Huntington College Library, Huntington, Ind.
Connor, William H., Washington Univ. Grad. Inst. of Education, St. Louis, Mo.
Conry, Rev. Thomas P., S.J., John Carroll Univ., Cleveland, Ohio
Converse, David T., State Univ. Col., Buffalo, N.Y.
Conway, Marie M., Jefferson Court No. 31, 4925 Saul St., Philadelphia, Pa.
Cook, Frances Colwell, Lincoln Cons. Lab. School, Ypsilanti, Mich.
Cooke, Dorothy E., 11 S. Lake Ave., Albany, N.Y.
Cooley, Robert L., Champaign Comm. Schls., 703 S. New St., Champaign, Ill.
Cooling, Elizabeth, 600 Mt. Pleasant Ave., Providence, R.I.
Coon, Herbert L., Sch. of Educ., Ohio State University, Columbus, Ohio
Cooper, Bernice L., Baldwin Hall, Univ. of Georgia, Athens, Ga.
Cooper, Dian Annise, 500 E. 33rd St., Chicago, Ill.
Cooper, George H., 2913 Washington Blvd., Chicago, Ill.
Cooper, J. David, 1610 Dorchester Dr., Bloomington, Ind.
Cooper, John H., 63 Lucero St., Thousand Oaks, Calif.
Cooper, Joyce, University of Florida, Gainesville, Fla.
Copeland, Harlan G., U.S. Dept. of Agriculture, Washington, D.C.
Coppolino, Ida S., California State College, Fullerton, Calif.
Corbally, John E., University of Washington, Seattle, Wash.
Corbin, Joseph W., 6253 Templeton Dr., Carmichael, Calif.
Cordasco, Frank M., Montclair State Col., Upper Montclair, N.J.
Corey, Stephen M., University of Miami, Coral Gables, Fla.
Corley, Clifford L., Oregon College of Education, Monmouth, Ore.
Corman, Bernard R., 705-11025—82nd Ave., Edmonton, Alba., Canada
Cornell, Francis G., 7 Holland Ave., White Plains, N.Y.
Cornish, Robert L., Sch. of Educ., Kansas University, Lawrence, Kan.
Corona, Bert C., P.O. Box 390, San Rafael, Calif.
Cortage, Cecelia, 2053 Illinois Ave., Santa Rosa, Calif.
Cortner, Frederick D., Pembroke State College, Pembroke, N.C.
Corwin, Betty Jane, Dept. of Psych., Ohio Univ., Athens, Ohio

Cory, N. Durward, 908 W. North St., Muncie, Ind.
Cosby, Joseph H., Hargrave Military Academy, Chatham, Va.
Cosentino, Bruno, 6 Glenside Dr., New City, N.Y.
Cosper, Cecil, Western Carolina College, Culowhee, N.C.
Coster, John K., North Carolina State University, Raleigh, N.C.
Cotner, Janet, Scott, Foresman & Co., Collingswood, N.J.
Cotter, Katharine C., Boston Col., Chestnut Hill, Mass.
Cotton, Henry F., Lynnfield High School, Lynnfield, Mass.
Cottone, Sebastian C., 2534 S. Colorado St., Philadelphia, Pa.
Couch, Paul E., Arkansas State College, State College, Ark.
Couche, Martha E., Rust College, Holly Springs, Miss.
Coughlan, Robert J., Sch. of Educ., Northwestern Univ., Evanston, Ill.
Coulson, Roger W., Col. of Educ., Butler University, Indianapolis, Ind.
Coulter, Myron L., Sch. of Educ., West. Michigan Univ., Kalamazoo, Mich.
Council, Mrs. Juanita, 2290 Potts St., Beaumont, Texas
Coupland, Joe, Morgan County High School, Hartselle, Ala.
* Courtis, S. A., 22445 Cupertino Rd., Cupertino, Calif.
Courtney, Robert W., Box 198, Middlebush, N.J.
Covert, Warren O., Western Illinois University, Macomb, Ill.
Cowan, Persis H., 1612 Fair Oaks Ave., South Pasadena, Calif.
Coward, Gertrude O., Charlotte-Mecklenburg Bd. of Educ., Charlotte, N.C.
Cowles, Clifton V., Jr., Arkansas State College, State College, Ark.
Cowles, James D., T-112-A Northington, Tuscaloosa, Ala.
Cowles, Milly, Sch. of Educ., Univ. of South Carolina, Columbia, S.C.
Cox, Edwin A., Superintendent of Schools, North Parade, Stratford, Conn.
Cox, Hugh F., Rt. 1, Box 478, Gridley, Calif.
Cox, John A., 735 N. Allen St., State College, Pa.
Cozine, June E., Oklahoma State University, Stillwater, Okla.
* Craig, Gerald S., Tchrs. Col., Columbia University, New York, N.Y.
Craig, James C., 9403 Crosby Rd., Silver Spring, Md.
Craig, Robert C., Michigan State University, East Lansing, Mich.
Cramer, Beatrice E., 1365 Weaver St., Scarsdale, N.Y.
Crarey, Hugh W., 751 E. 84th Pl., 3E, Chicago, Ill.
Craton, Edward J., 1777 Glenwood Ct., Bakersfield, Calif.
Crawford, A. Wylie, 726 Xenia Ave., Yellow Springs, Ohio
Crawford, Dorothy M., 212 W. Washington St., Ottawa, Ill.
Crawford, T. James, Sch. of Business, Indiana University, Bloomington, Ind.
Crawley, Harold B., 710 Giblin Dr., Iowa City, Iowa
Crawshaw, Stanley M., Roseland, Neb.
Creason, Frank, 200 Research Dr., Manhattan, Kan.
Cresci, Gerald D., 1171 Los Molinos Way, Sacramento, Calif.
Crescimbeni, Joseph, Jacksonville University, Jacksonville, Fla.
Crespy, H. Victor, 94 Broad St., Freehold, N.J.
Creswell, Mrs. Rowena C., 305 Montclair Ave., So., College Station, Tex.
Crews, Alton C., Superintendent of Schools, Huntsville, Ala.
Crews, Roy L., Aurora College, Aurora, Ill.
Criscuolo, Nicholas P., Read. Spec., Pub. Schools, New Haven, Conn.
Crocker, Richard F., Jr., Superintendent of Schools, Caribou, Me.
Cromartie, Sue W., Col. of Educ., University of Georgia, Athens, Ga.
Crombe, William A., 1087 Webster Rd., Webster, N.Y.
Cron, Celeste Maia, 801 Gull Ave., San Mateo, Calif.
Cronin, Rev. Robert E., Rio St., Apt. 811, Falls Church, Va.
Crook, Robert B., Queens Col., Flushing, N.Y.
Cross, Donald A., Bathurst Tchrs. Col., Bathurst, N.S.W., Australia
Cross, William C., New Mexico State University, University Park, N.M.
Crossland, Mrs. Kathryn M., 3600 Tremont Dr., Durham, N.C.
Crosson, Robert Henry, 2747 West 35th Ave., Denver, Colo.
Crow, A. L., Superintendent of Schools, Kirkwood, Mo.
* Crow, Lester D., 5701 Jackson St., Hollywood, Fla.
Crowell, R. A., Col. of Educ., University of Arizona, Tucson, Ariz.
Crowley, Mary C., 7 Boone Lane, Dearborn, Mich.

Crowley, Robert J., 545 S. Fifth Ave., Ann Arbor, Mich.
Crull, Garry Lloyd, No. Illinois Univ., DeKalb, Ill.
Crum, Clyde E., Div. of Educ., San Diego State College, San Diego, Calif.
Culbertson, Jack A., Ohio State University, 65 S. Oval Dr., Columbus, Ohio
Cumbee, Carroll F., Col. of Educ., University of Florida, Gainesville, Fla.
Cummings, C. Thomas, Canajoharie Central Schools, Canajoharie, N.Y.
Cummings, Mabel Anna, 6044 Linden St., Brooklyn, N.Y.
Cummings, Reta Gines, 190 S. Prospect St., Orange, Calif.
Cummings, Susan N., Arizona State University, Tempe, Ariz.
Cummins, L. Ross, Dept. of Educ. & Psych., Bates Col., Lewiston, Me.
Cummins, Lester L., 3512 S. 263rd St., Kent, Wash.
Cummins, Terry, Pendleton High School, Falmouth, Ky.
Cunningham, George S., 4 Glenwood St., Orono, Me.
Cunningham, Luvern L., Dean of Educ., Ohio State Univ., Columbus, Ohio
Cunningham, Myron, Col. of Educ., University of Florida, Gainesville, Fla.
Cunningham, Mrs. Shirley, Florida Atlantic Univ., Hollywood, Fla.
Cunningham, William, 15600 Parkland Dr., Cleveland, Ohio
Cupp, Gene R., 1704 N. Park Ave., Canton, Ohio
Currey, Ralph B., State Dept. of Education, Charleston, W.Va.
Currier, Mrs. Lynor O., 713 Giddings Ave., Annapolis, Md.
Curry, John F., Box 6765, North Texas State College, Denton, Tex.
Curtin, James R., Col. of Educ., University of Minnesota, Minneapolis, Minn.
Curtin, James T., 4140 Lindell Blvd., St. Louis, Mo.
Curtin, John T., Wayne State University, Detroit, Mich.
Curtis, Delores M., University of Hawaii, Honolulu, Hawaii
Curtis, E. Louise, Macalester College, St. Paul, Minn.
Curtis, Francis H., Univ. of Scranton, Scranton, Pa.
Curtis, James E., 325 Conifer Ln., Santa Cruz, Calif.
Cusick, Ralph J., 6443 N. Wayne Ave., Chicago, Ill.
Cyr, Rev. Rene, O.S.B., Marmion Military Academy, Aurora, Ill.

Daddazio, Arthur H., 41 Brady Ave., Newburgh, N.Y.
Daeufer, Carl J., Trust Ter. of Pacific Islands, Marianas Isls.
D'Agostino, Nicholas E., Wolcott High School, Wolcott, Conn.
Dahl, John A., California State College, Los Angeles, Calif.
Daines, Mrs. Delva, 615 E. 700 North, Provo, Utah
Dale, Arbie Myron, Sch. of Commerce, New York University, New York, N.Y.
Dale, Edgar, Sch. of Educ., Ohio State University, Columbus, Ohio
Dale, Edwin L., 1601 Clifford, Pullman, Wash.
Dal Santo, John, 1634 Greenwood Ave., Glenview, Ill.
Daly, Edmund B., 1839 N. Richmond St., Chicago, Ill.
Daly, Francis M., Jr., Eastern Michigan University, Ypsilanti, Mich.
Dandoy, Maxine A., Fresno State College, Fresno, Calif.
Daniel, George T., N. 319 Locust Rd., Spokane, Wash.
Daniel, Dr. Kathryn B., 83 Nob Hill, Columbia, S.C.
Daniel, Sheldon C., 4073 Ardmore Lane, Sarasota, Fla.
Daniels, Paul R., 4300 N. Charles St., Baltimore, Md.
Danielson, Paul J., Col. of Educ., University of Arizona, Tucson, Ariz.
Danowski, Charles E., Tchrs. Col., Columbia University, New York, N.Y.
Darcy, Natalie T., Dept. of Educ., Brooklyn College, Brooklyn, N.Y.
Darling, Dennis E., 125 Kenberry Dr., East Lansing, Mich.
Darnielle, Max, 2701 N. Dunn St., Bloomington, Ind.
Darr, George F., 155 Rodeo Rd., Glendora, Calif.
Darroch, Frank W., 27 Princeton Rd., Toronto, Ont., Canada
D'Ascoli, Louis N., 5 Hughes Ter., Yonkers, N.Y.
Daubek, Gerald G., Univ. of Kentucky Ext., Fort Knox, Ky.
Dave, Vidya Deodatta, Ranchhod Bhuvan, Ambawadi, Ahmedabad, India
Davenport, William R., University of Michigan at Flint, Flint, Mich.
Davey, Mrs. Elizabeth P., 5748 Harper Ave., Chicago, Ill.
Davidson, Mrs. Evelyn K., Dept. of Educ., Kent State University, Kent, Ohio
Davidson, Jack L., Superintendent of Schools, Oak Ridge, Tenn.

Davies, Daniel R., Croft Consult. Serv., Tucson, Ariz.
Davies, Don, NCTEPS (NEA), 1201—16th St., N.W., Washington, D.C.
Davies, J. Leonard, Bur. of Educ. Resch., Univ. of Iowa, Iowa City, Iowa
Davies, Joseph J., Jr., Superintendent of Schools, Chalmette, La.
Davies, Lillian S., Illinois State University, Normal, Ill.
Davis, A. L., 3525 Linecrest Rd., Ellenwood, Ga.
Davis, Alice Taylor, 3800 Williams Ln., Chevy Chase, Md.
Davis, Benjamin F., 10 Lahey St., New Hyde Park, L.I., N.Y.
Davis, David Carson, 902 Cornell Ct., Madison, Wis.
Davis, Donald E., University of Minnesota, Minneapolis, Minn.
Davis, Donald Jack, Texas Technological College, Lubbock, Tex.
Davis, Dwight E., 6726 S. Washington Ave., Lansing, Mich.
Davis, Dwight M., 505 Glenview Dr., Des Moines, Iowa
Davis, Mrs. Eldred D., Knoxville College, Knoxville, Tenn.
Davis, Frederick B., 3700 Walnut St., Philadelphia, Pa.
Davis, Guy C., Trinidad State Junior College, Trinidad, Colo.
Davis, H. Curtis, 1605 Park Ave., San Jose, Calif.
Davis, Harold S., Educ. Res. Council, Rockefeller Bldg., Cleveland, Ohio
Davis, Hazel Grubbs, Queens Col., City Univ. of N.Y., Flushing, N.Y.
Davis, Howard, 1142 Medway Rd., Philadelphia, Pa.
Davis, J. Clark, Col. of Educ., University of Nevada, Reno, Nev.
Davis, J. Sanford, Box 646, Madison, Conn.
Davis, Joseph H., 8300 Jackson St., St. Louis, Mo.
Davis, Marianna W., Claflin College, Orangeburg, S.C.
Davis, Milton J., 725 West 18th St., North Chicago, Ill.
Davis, O. L., Jr., Col. of Educ., Univ. of Texas, Austin, Tex.
Davis, Paul Ford, Morehead State Univ., Morehead, Ky.
Davis, Ron W., 223 Hillcrest Cir., Chapel Hill, N.C.
Davis, Warren C., 65 S. Plymouth Ave., Rochester, N.Y.
Davison, David D., 457 E. Naples Dr., Las Vegas, Nev.
Davoren, David, Superintendent of Schools, Milford, Mass.
Dawkins, M. B., 1110 Izard St., Little Rock, Ark.
Dawson, Kenneth E., Sch. of Educ., Morehead State Univ., Morehead, Ky.
Dawson, W. Read, Baylor University, Waco, Tex.
Day, James F., Dept. of Educ., Univ. of Texas, El Paso, Texas
Deady, John E., Supt. of Schools, Springfield, Mass.
Deam, Calvin W., Sch. of Educ., Boston University, Boston, Mass.
Dease, E. Richard, 413 Lorraine Rd., Wheaton, Ill.
DeBates, James R., R.R. 1, McNabb, Ill.
DeBernardis, Amo, 6049 S. W. Luradel, Portland, Ore.
Debin, Louis, 83-37—247th St., Bellerose, N.Y.
DeBoer, Dorothy L., 3930 W. Southport Ave., Chicago, Ill.
DeBoer, John J., Col. of Educ., University of Illinois, Urbana, Ill.
DeBus, Raymond L., 666 Malabar Rd., Maroubra, N.S.W., Australia
Deever, Merwin, Col. of Educ., Arizona State University, Tempe, Ariz.
DeGrow, Gerald S., 509 Stanton St., Port Huron, Mich.
Dejnozka, Edward L., 11 Marion Rd., Upper Montclair, N.J.
DeKock, Henry C., Col. of Educ., State Univ. of Iowa, Iowa City, Iowa
Delaney, Eleanor C., Sch. of Educ., Rutgers Univ., New Brunswick, N.J.
Della Penta, A. H., Superintendent of Schools, Lodi, N.J.
Deller, W. McGregor, Superintendent of Schools, Fairport, N.Y.
Delmonaco, Thomas M., 44 Lanewood Ave., Framingham Centre, Mass.
Delon, Floyd G., 302 Natl. Old Line Bldg., Little Rock, Ark.
DeLong, Arthur R., Grand Valley State College, Allendale, Mich.
Demming, John A., Bldg. S-502, 6th St., N., West Palm Beach, Fla.
DeMoraes, Maria P. Tito, WHO Reg. Off., 8 Scherfigsvej, Copenhagen, Denmark
Denemark, George W., University of Wisconsin-Milwaukee, Milwaukee, Wis.
Denning, Mrs. Bernadine, 5057 Woodward, Rm. 1338, Detroit, Mich.
Dennis, Donald A., 756 Bonita Dr., South Pasadena, Calif.
Dennis, Ronald T., Northwestern State College, Natchitoches, La.
Deno, Stanley L., Col. of Educ., Univ. of Delaware, Newark, Del.

Denny, Earl W., California State College, Los Angeles, Calif.
Denova, Charles C., Hughes Tool Co., Culver City, Calif.
Denson, Lucille D., Braemar House, Hollywood Pk., Liverpool, N.Y.
De Ortega, Eneida Santizo, Calle Real 6101, Betania-Panama, Rep. of Panama
DePaul, Frank J., 2727 North Long Ave., Chicago, Ill.
Derby, Orlo Lee, State Univ. Col., Brockport, N.Y.
DeRidder, Lawrence M., Col. of Educ., Univ. of Tennessee, Knoxville, Tenn.
DeRoche, Edward F., Marquette Univ., Milwaukee, Wis.
Dershimer, Richard A., American Educ. Research Assn., Washington, D.C.
DeSantis, Joseph P., 430 Buffalo Ave., Niagara Falls, N.Y.
Desjarlais, Lionel, 20801 Saunderson Dr., Ottawa, Canada
Desoe, Hollis L., Board of Educ., 51 Route 100, Briarcliff Manor, N.Y.
DeStefano, Anthony J., 48 Lenox Ave., Hicksville, N.Y.
Detrick, Frederick M., 10 Sheldon Rd., Pemberton, N.J.
Deutschman, Mrs. Marilyn L., 201 St. Pauls Ave., Jersey City, N.J.
DeVault, M. Vere, University of Wisconsin, Madison, Wis.
Devine, Florence E., 4822 Central Ave., Western Springs, Ill.
Devine, Joseph P., Superintendent of Schools, Newport, R.I.
Devine, Thomas G., Sch. of Educ., Boston University, Boston, Mass.
Devor, J. W., 6309 E. Holbert Rd., Bethesda, Md.
DeWaal, Ronald, Colorado State Univ., Ft. Collins, Colo.
DeWalt, Homer C., Supt. of Schools, Diocese of Erie, Erie, Pa.
Deyell, J. Douglas, Provincial Teachers College, North Bay, Ont., Canada
Dickerson, James L., 180 South View Dr., Athens, Ga.
Dickey, Otis M., Superintendent of Schools, Oak Park, Mich.
Dickmeyer, Mrs. K. H., 200 8th Ave., S.E., Fairfax, Minn.
Dickson, Paul, Sch. of Educ., Florida State Univ., Tallahassee, Fla.
* Diederich, A. F., St. Norbert College, West DePere, Wis.
Diedrich, Richard C., 155 Knox Dr., West Lafayette, Ind.
Diefenderfer, Omie T., 828 Third St., Fullerton, Pa.
Diehl, Mary Jane, Monmouth Col., Pennington, N.J.
Diehl, T. Handley, Miami University, Oxford, Ohio
Diener, Russell E., 1034 Novara St., San Diego, Calif.
Dierzen, Mrs. Verda, Comm. Consol. Sch. Dist., Woodstock, Ill.
Dieterle, Louise E., 10700 S. Avenue F, Chicago, Ill.
Dietz, Elisabeth H., 1093 Northern Blvd., Baldwin, N.Y.
Diffley, Jerome, St. Bernard College, St. Bernard, Ala.
Diggs, Eugene A., Supt., Sch. Dist. # 110, Overland Park, Kansas
DiGiacento, Mrs. Rose, 68 Pilgrim Ave., Yonkers, N.Y.
DiLeonarde, Joseph H., 6309 N. Cicero Ave., Chicago, Ill.
DiLieto, Ray Marie, 4 Bayberry Lane, Westport, Conn.
Dillman, Duane H., 2613 Henderson Ave., Wheaton, Md.
Dillon, Frances H., Moorhead State Col., Moorhead, Minn.
Dillon, Jesse D., Jr., David W. Harlan School, Wilmington, Del.
DiLuglio, Domenic R., 1849 Warwick Ave., Warwick, R.I.
Dimitroff, Lillian, 1525 Brummel St., Evanston, Ill.
Dimond, Ray A., Jr., 4034 E. Cambridge, Phoenix, Ariz.
Dimond, Stanley E., 2012 Shadford Rd., Ann Arbor, Mich.
DiNardo, V. James, Massachusetts State College, Bridgewater, Mass.
DiPasquale, Vincent C., Moorhead State Col., Moorhead, Minn.
Dirienzo, Angelo E., 650 Hawthorne Ave., Derby, Conn.
Disberger, Jay, Box 188, Pomona, Kansas
Disko, Michael, 16 Briarwood Dr., Athens, Ohio
Distin, Mr. Leslie, Connetquot High School, Bohemia, N.Y.
Dittmer, Daniel G., 1647 Francis Hammond Pkwy., Alexandria, Va.
Dittmer, Jane E., Kouts High School, Kouts, Ind.
Dix, M. S., North Shore School, 1217 Chase Ave., Chicago, Ill.
Dixon, Glendora, Talmadge Jr. H.S., Independence, Ore.
Dixon, James T., 13 Lake Rd., Huntington Station, L.I., N.Y.
Dixon, W. Robert, University of Michigan, Ann Arbor, Mich.
Dobbs, Edith, Fort Hays Kansas State College, Hays, Kan.

Dodd, John M., State Univ. Col., Buffalo, N.Y.
Dodds, A. Gordon, Superintendent of Schools, Edwardsville, Ill.
Dodge, Norman B., 523 S. Oneida Way, Denver, Colo.
Dodson, Dan W., New York University, Washington Sq., New York, N.Y.
Dohemann, H. Warren, IDEA, 1100 Glendon Ave., Los Angeles, Calif.
Dohmann, C. William, 640 Main St., El Segundo, Calif.
Dolan, Francis, LaSalle-Peru Twp. High School, LaSalle, Ill.
Doll, Ronald C., 17 Rossmore Ter., Livingston, N.J.
Domian, E. O., 1595 Northrop, St. Paul, Minn.
Dommer, Carolyn, Michigan State Univ., East Lansing, Mich.
Donahoe, Thomas J., 74 Fallston St., Springfield, Mass.
Donatelli, Rosemary V., Loyola University, Chicago, Ill.
Donner, Arvin N., Col. of Educ., University of Houston, Houston, Tex.
Donoghue, Mildred R., California State College, Fullerton, Calif.
Donovan, Charles F., Sch. of Educ., Boston College, Chestnut Hill, Mass.
Donovan, Daniel E., C.M., St. John's Prep. Sch., Brooklyn, N.Y.
Donovan, David, 119 S. Highland, Ossining, N.Y.
Doody, Louise E., 191 Dedham St., Newton Highlands, Mass.
Doremus, Albert F., 600 S. Maple Ave., Glen Rock, N.J.
Dorricott, H. J., Western State College, Gunnison, Colo.
Doss, Jesse Paul, 12631 Fletcher Dr., Garden Grove, Calif.
Dotson, John M., 154 Jones Dr., Pocatello, Idaho
Douglass, Harl R., Col. of Educ., University of Colorado, Boulder, Colo.
Douglass, Malcolm P., Claremont Grad. Sch., Claremont, Calif.
Dow, John A., 2597 W. Calimyrna, Fresno, Calif.
Dowling, Thomas I., Superintendent, Dist. No. 50, Greenwood, S.C.
Downing, Carl, Central State Col., Edmond, Okla.
Downing, Mrs. Gertrude L., 87 Huron Rd., Bellerose Village, N.Y.
Doyle, Andrew McCormick, 1106 Bellerive Blvd., St. Louis, Mo.
Doyle, Rev. E. A., 255 N. Eighth St., Ponchatoula, La.
Doyle, James F., 2930 Forrest Hills Dr., S.W., Atlanta, Ga.
Doyle, Jean, 511 E. High St., Lexington, Ky.
Doyle, Walter, University of Notre Dame, Notre Dame, Ind.
Drag, Francis L., California Western Univ., San Diego, Calif.
Dragositz, Anna, Educational Testing Service, Princeton, N.J.
Drake, Thelbert L., Univ. of Connecticut, Storrs, Conn.
Draves, David D., University of New Hampshire, Durham, N.H.
Drechsel, Lionel C., 2009 Fillmore, Ogden, Utah
* Dreikurs, Rudolph, 6 N. Michigan Ave., Chicago, Ill.
Dreisbach, Dodson E., Gibraltar, Pa.
Dressel, Paul L., Michigan State University, East Lansing, Mich.
Drew, Alfred S., Purdue University, Lafayette, Ind.
Drew, Robert E., Community Unit School Dist. 303, St. Charles, Ill.
Driver, Cecil E., Vandenberg Elem. School, APO, New York, N.Y.
Dropkin, Stanley, Queens College, Flushing, N.Y.
Drucker, Howard, 1423 Galleon Way, San Luis Obispo, Calif.
Drummond, Harold D., Univ. of New Mexico, Albuquerque, N.M.
Drummond, William H., 623 S. Decatur, Olympia, Wash.
DuBois, Helen, Glen Cove Junior High School, Glen Cove, N.Y.
Ducanis, Alex J., State University of New York, Binghamton, N.Y.
Duckers, Ronald L., 320 Jon Court, Des Plaines, Ill.
Duckworth, Alice, 100 Reef Rd., Fairfield, Conn.
Dudley, James, Col. of Educ., Univ. of Maryland, College Park, Md.
Duff, Franklin L., Bur. of Instr. Res., Univ. of Illinois, Urbana, Ill.
Duffett, John W., 341 Bellefield Ave., Pittsburgh, Pa.
Duffey, Robert V., 9225 Limestone Pl., College Park, Md.
Dufford, William E., 1020 S.W. 3rd Ave., Gainesville, Fla.
DuFour, Stuart, Hartnell College, Salinas, Calif.
Duggan, John M., College Entrance Examination Board, New York, N.Y.
Duke, Ralph L., Sch. of Educ., University of Delaware, Newark, Del.
Duke, Reese D., Dept. of Educ., Rice Univ., Houston, Texas

Dumler, Marvin J., Concordia Teachers College, River Forest, Ill.
Duncan, Ernest R., Sch. of Educ., Rutgers Univ., New Brunswick, N.J.
Duncan, J. A., Agric. Hall, University of Wisconsin, Madison, Wis.
Duncan, William B., Miami Edison Senior High School, Miami, Fla.
Dungan, Earl W., Southwestern College, Winfield, Kan.
Dunham, Ralph E., 2117 Popkins Ln., Alexandria, Va.
Dunkel, Harold B., Dept. of Educ., University of Chicago, Chicago, Ill.
Dunkeld, Colin G., 414 W. Ells, Champaign, Ill.
Dunkle, Maurice Albert, Superintendent, Calver Co. Schls., Prince Frederick, Md.
Dunnell, John P., 1004 Wenonah, Oak Park, Ill.
Dunning, Frances E., 125 Owre Hall, Univ. of Minnesota, Minneapolis, Minn.
Durant, Adrian J., Jr., 1115 Holiday Park Dr., Champaign, Ill.
Durante, Spencer E., 1615 Van Buren Ave., Charlotte, N.C.
Durflinger, Glenn W., 5665 Cielo Ave., Goleta, Calif.
Durkee, Frank M., Box 911, Harrisburg, Pa.
Durost, Walter N., RFD #2, Box 120, Dover, N.H.
Durr, William K., Col. of Educ., Michigan State Univ., East Lansing, Mich.
Durrell, Donald D., Boston University, 332 Bay State Rd., Boston, Mass.
Dutton, Wilbur H., 1913 Greenfield Ave., Los Angeles, Calif.
DuVall, Lloyd A., 583 Harley Dr., Apt. 6, Columbus, Ohio
Dwyer, John E., Superintendent of Schools, Elizabeth, N.J.
Dwyer, Roy E., 610 Lakewood Rd., Pensacola, Fla.
Dyer, Frank E., 1331 Cecil Ave., Delano, Calif.
Dyke, Elwood E., Southport Elem. Sch., 723—76th St., Kenosha, Wis.
Dykes, Mrs. Alma, 9755 Cincinnati-Columbus Rd., Cincinnati, Ohio
Dykes, Mrs. Eunice P., 119 West Woodbine, Kirkwood, Mo.
Dyson, R. E., 202 Northlawn Ave., East Lansing, Mich.
Dziak, Suzanne S., 527 S. 36th St., Apt. 4, Omaha, Neb.
Dziuban, Charles D., 3460 Buford Hgwy., Atlanta, Ga.

Eaddy, Edward Allen, Superintendent of Schools, Georgetown, S.C.
Earles, Lucius C., Jr., 123 Peabody St., N.W., Washington, D.C.
Early, Margaret J., Read. Lab., Syracuse Univ., Syracuse, N.Y.
Eash, Maurice J., Hunter College, 695 Park Ave., New York, N.Y.
Easterly, Ambrose, Murray State Univ., Murray, Ky.
Eaton, Edward J., Rt. 4, Hattiesburg, Miss.
Ebel, Robert L., Michigan State University, East Lansing, Mich.
Eberle, August William, Indiana Univ., Bloomington, Ind.
Eberman, Paul W., 1801 John F. Kennedy Blvd., Philadelphia, Pa.
Ebersole, Benjamin P., 1337 Brook Rd., Baltimore, Md.
Eboch, Sidney C., Dept. of Educ., Ohio State Univ., Columbus, Ohio
Eckert, Ruth E., Col. of Educ., University of Minnesota, Minneapolis, Minn.
Eckhardt, John W., 13 Panorama Gardens, Bakersfield, Calif.
Eddins, William N., P.O. Box 9036, Crestline Heights Br., Birmingham, Ala.
Edelmann, Anne M., 7614 Garden Rd., Cheltenham, Pa.
Eden, Donald F., Adams State College, Alamosa, Colo.
Edick, Helen M., 125 Terry Rd., Hartford, Conn.
Edinger, Lois V., University of North Carolina, Greensboro, N.C.
Edmundson, W. Dean, Detroit Public Schls., 12021 Evanston, Detroit, Mich.
Edson, William H., 206 Burton Hall, Univ. of Minnesota, Minneapolis, Minn.
Edstrom, A. E., Senior High School, 1001 State Hwy., Hopkins, Minn.
Edwards, Andrew S., Georgia Southern College, Statesboro, Ga.
Edwards, Arthur U., Eastern Illinois University, Charleston, Ill.
Edwards, Charles W., Jr., Superintendent of Schools, Woodstock, Ill.
Edwards, Derwin W., Miami University, Oxford, Ohio
Edwards, Gerald F., Rt. 2, Box 406, Edgerton, Wis.
Edwards, Marcia, Burton Hall, University of Minnesota, Minneapolis, Minn.
Edwards, T. Bentley, Sch. of Educ., Univ. of California, Berkeley, Calif.
Egan, Gerard V., 79 Ward Pl., South Orange, N.J.
Egan, Roger, Silver Burdett Co., Morristown, N.J.
Egelston, Elwood, Jr., Illinois State University, Normal, Ill.

MEMBERS OF THE NATIONAL SOCIETY xxxvii

Egge, Donald E., 325 N.E. 10th St., Newport, Ore.
Eherenman, William C., Wisconsin State University, Platteville, Wis.
Ehlers, Henry J., Duluth Branch, University of Minnesota, Duluth, Minn.
Ehrenreich, Mrs. Betty, Miami-Dade Jr. Col., Miami, Fla.
Ehrhart, Mrs. Marion D., Box 388, Trumansburg, N.Y.
Ehrlich, Emanuel, 92 Joyce Rd., East Chester, N.Y.
Eibler, Herbert J., University of Michigan, Ann Arbor, Mich.
Eidell, Terry L., CAESA, Univ. of Oregon, Eugene, Ore.
Eikaas, Alf T., Kjolsdalen, Nordfjord, Norway
Einolf, W. L., Birchrunville, Pa.
Eisenstein, Herbert S., State University of N.Y., Buffalo, N.Y.
Eiserer, Paul E., Tchrs. Col., Columbia University, New York, N.Y.
Eisner, Elliot W., Stanford University, Stanford, Calif.
Eke, Verne M., 954 S. Carondelet St., Los Angeles, Calif.
Ekman, Lincoln G., Macalester College, St. Paul, Minn.
Elder, Richard D., Child Study Cent., Kent State Univ., Kent, Ohio
Elequin, Dr. Eleanor T., State Univ. of New York, Oneonta, N.Y.
Elkins, Keith E., Dept. of Educ., Univ. of Chicago, Chicago, Ill.
Elland, A. H., Hutchinson Junior College, 1300 Plum, Hutchinson, Kan.
Elle, Martin J., Southern Oregon College, Ashland, Ore.
Ellenburg, Fred C., Rt. # 1, Grove Lakes, Statesboro, Ga.
Ellerbrook, Louis William, Box 4628, S.F.A. Sta., Nacogdoches, Tex.
Ellery, Marilynne, Ohio Northern University, Ada, Ohio
Ellingson, Mark, Rochester Institute of Technology, Rochester, N.Y.
Elliott, A. R., 520 Campbell Ave., Geneva, Ill.
Elliott, David L., Sch. of Educ., Univ. of California, Berkeley, Calif.
Ellis, Mrs. Celia Diamond, 1125 S. LaJolla Ave., Los Angeles, Calif.
Ellis, G. W., Drew Jr. H.S., 1801 N.W. 60th St., Miami, Fla.
Ellis, Frederick E., Western Washington State Col., Bellingham, Wash.
Ellis, John F., Simon Fraser University, Burnaby, B.C., Canada
Ellis, Joseph R., Northern Illinois University, DeKalb, Ill.
Ellis, Robert L., 1125 S. LaJolla Ave., Los Angeles, Calif.
Ellison, Alfred, New York University, Washington Sq., New York, N.Y.
Ellison, F. Robert, 1354 Laurel St., Casper, Wyo.
Ellison, Jack L., Francis W. Parker Sch., Chicago, Ill.
Ellwein, Mrs. Ileane, 2905 S. Jefferson St., Sioux Falls, S.D.
Emeson, David L., 411 N. Dubuque St., Iowa City, Iowa
Emmet, Thomas A., 5440 Cass Ave., Suite 412, Detroit, Mich.
Ende, Russell S., Northern Illinois University, DeKalb, Ill.
Endres, Mary P., 55 Walnut St., S.W., Atlanta, Ga.
Endres, Richard J., 707 Salisbury Rd., Columbus, Ohio
Engel, Barney M., Dept. of Educ., Dalhousie Univ., Halifax, N.S., Canada
Engelhardt, Jack E., 1500 Maywood Ave., Ann Arbor, Mich.
Engelhardt, Nickolaus L., Jr., Purdy Station, N.Y.
Engle, Shirley H., Sch. of Educ., Indiana University, Bloomington, Ind.
English, John W., Superintendent of Schools, Southfield, Mich.
English, Marvin D., National College of Education, Evanston, Ill.
Enoch, June E., Manchester College, North Manchester, Ind.
Entwisle, Doris, Johns Hopkins University, Baltimore, Md.
Entwistle, Charles C., 93 Laurel St., Fairhaven, Mass.
Eraut, Michael R., Office of Instr. Resources, Chicago, Ill.
Erbe, Wesley A., Col. of Educ., Univ. of Iowa, Iowa City, Iowa
Erdman, Robert L., Univ. of Utah, Salt Lake City, Utah
Erickson, Harley E., State College of Iowa, Cedar Falls, Iowa
Erickson, L. W., Sch. of Educ., Univ. of California, Los Angeles, Calif.
Erickson, Ralph J., Virginia Union University, Richmond, Va.
Erickson, Ralph W., 105 Third Ave., Columbus, Miss.
Ermlick, William F., 120 Alexander Ave., Monongahela, Pa.
Ersted, Ruth, State Department of Education, St. Paul, Minn.
Ervin, John B., 5933 Enright St., St. Louis, Mo.
Ervin, William B., 1 Midland Pl., Newark, N.J.

Erxleben, Arnold C., 157 Bemis Dr., Seward, Neb.
Erzen, Richard, Bradley Univ., Peoria, Ill.
Eson, Morris E., State University of New York, Albany, N.Y.
Essig, Lester Clay, Jr., Utah State University, Logan, Utah
Estes, Kenneth A., Superintendent of Schools, Owensboro, Ky.
Estle, Glen L., 1000 Pfingsten Rd., Northbrook, Ill.
Estvan, Frank J., Col. of Educ., Wayne State Univ., Detroit, Mich.
Ether, John A., State Univ. of New York, Albany, N.Y.
Etheridge, Robert F., Miami University, Oxford, Ohio
Etscovitz, Lionel, 5 Shaw Pl., Lexington, Mass.
Ettinger, Mrs. Bernadette C., 474 Brooklyn Blvd., Brightwaters, L.I., N.Y.
Eurich, Alvin C., P.O. Box 219, Aspen, Colo.
Evans, Edgar Ernest, Alabama State College, Montgomery, Ala.
Evans, Harley, Jr., 35952 Matoma Dr., Eastlake, Ohio
Evans, J. Bernard, 3163 Warrington Rd., Shaker Heights, Ohio
Evans, John C., Jr., 6325 South, 550 East, Bountiful, Utah
Evans, Mary Beth, Dir., Tchr. Educ., Graceland Col., Lamoni, Iowa
Evans, Ralph F., Fresno State College, Fresno, Calif.
Evans, Rupert N., Col. of Educ., Univ. of Illinois, Urbana, Ill.
Evans, Warren D., 27 Anchor Dr., Washington, Pa.
Eve, Arthur W., 99 Virginia Ave., Centerville, Ohio
Evenson, Warren L., 1528 S. Douglas St., Springfield, Ill.
Evertts, Eldonna L., N.C.T.E., 508 S. Sixth St., Champaign, Ill.
Ewart, Mrs. Annie G., Shorewood Public Schools, Shorewood, Wis.
* Ewigleben, Mrs. Muriel, 3727 Weisser Park Ave., Ft. Wayne, Ind.
Ewing, Parmer L., Dept. of Educ. Admin., So. Ill. Univ., Carbondale, Ill.
Eyster, Elvin S., Dept. of Bus. Educ., Indiana Univ., Bloomington, Ind.

Fadden, Joseph A., Marywood College, Scranton, Pa.
Faddis, Mrs. Gabrielle J., Col. of Educ., Temple University, Philadelphia, Pa.
Faerber, Louis J., 4301 Roland Ave., Baltimore, Md.
Failor, Harvey A., 13800 Ford Road, Dearborn, Mich.
Fair, Jean E., Wayne State University, Detroit, Mich.
Fairbanks, Gar, Supt. of Schools, Rocky Hill, Conn.
Fairfield, Ethel D., 502 S. Post Oak Lane, Houston, Tex.
Falk, Alma M., 1330 New Hampshire Ave., N.W., Washington, D.C.
Falk, Philip H., 3721 Council Crest, Madison, Wis.
Fallon, Berlie J., Dept. of Educ., Texas Technological Col., Lubbock, Tex.
Fanslow, W. V., 1203 Los Trancos Rd., Portola Valley, Calif.
Fargen, J. Jerome, Catherine Spalding College, Louisville, Ky.
Farley, Gilbert J., Belmont Abbey Col., Belmont, N.C.
Farmer, Geraldine, University of Alberta, Edmonton, Alba., Canada
Farrell, Joseph I., 109 Cornell Ave., Hawthorne, N.J.
Farris, William M., Superintendent of Schools, Groton, Conn.
Fasan, Walter R., 3401 West 65th Pl., Chicago, Ill.
Faulkner, Richard, 7550 Mackenzie Rd., St. Louis, Mo.
Faunce, Roland C., Wayne State University, Detroit, Mich.
Faust, Claire Edward, 206 Floral Ave., Mankato, Minn.
Fawcett, Claude W., Sch. of Educ., Univ. of California, Los Angeles, Calif.
Fawley, Paul C., Dept. of Educ., University of Utah, Salt Lake City, Utah
Fay, Leo C., Sch. of Educ., Indiana University, Bloomington, Ind.
Fea, Henry Robert, University of Washington, Seattle, Wash.
Fee, Edward M., Bok Technical High School, Philadelphia, Pa.
Feelhaver, Carl T., Supt. of Schools, 5 North 16th St., Fort Dodge, Iowa
Feely, Robert W., 10117 Albany Ave., Evergreen Park, Ill.
Feingold, S. Norman, 1640 Rhode Island Ave., N.W., Washington, D.C.
Feiock, Vernon L., Escondido Village, Stanford, Calif.
Feley, Ruth A., North Main St., East Granby, Conn.
Feller, Dan, 9951-B Robbins Dr., Beverly Hills, Calif.
Feltner, Bill D., Inst. of Higher Educ., Univ. of Georgia, Athens, Ga.
Fenderson, Julia K., Culver City Unified Schools, Culver City, Calif.

Fennema, Elizabeth H., 121 N. Allen, Madison, Wis.
Fenollosa, George M., Houghton Mifflin Co., 110 Tremont St., Boston, Mass.
Fenske, Arthur S., 106 Highland Ave., Hartland, Wis.
Ferguson, Arthur L., # 2 White's Place, Bloomington, Ill.
Feringer, F. R., Western Washington State College, Bellingham, Wash.
Ferris, Donald, 1316 N. Salisbury St., West Lafayette, Ind.
Fesperman, Mrs. Kathleen C., Newberry College, Newberry, S.C.
Feuerbach, F. Kenneth, Hammond High School, Hammond, Ind.
Feuers, Mrs. Stelle, Pierce College, Woodland Hills, Calif.
Ficek, Daniel E., 413 Girard, S.E., # 1, Albuquerque, N.M.
Fiedler, E. L., Superintendent of Schools, Abilene, Kan.
Field, Robert L., 1506 Jackson St., Oshkosh, Wis.
Fields, Ralph R., Tchrs. Col., Columbia University, New York, N.Y.
Fielstra, Clarence, Sch. of Educ., Univ. of California, Los Angeles, Calif.
Fielstra, Helen, San Fernando Valley State College, Northridge, Calif.
Fieman, Marvin E., 307 S. Arnaz Dr., Los Angeles, Calif.
Figurel, J. Allen, 8542 Inkster Rd., Dearborn Heights, Mich.
Filbeck, Orval, Abilene Christian College, Abilene, Tex.
Filbeck, Robert W., Lincoln Job Corps Center, Lincoln, Neb.
Filosa, Mary G., 32 Ross Hall Blvd., No., Piscataway, N.J.
Fina, Robert P., 522 Fourth St., Catasauqua, Pa.
Finch, F. H., Col. of Educ., Univ. of Illinois, Urbana, Ill.
Finder, Morris, State University of N.Y., Albany, N.Y.
Findlay, Stephen W., Delbarton School, Morristown, N.J.
Findley, Warren G., Col. of Educ., University of Georgia, Athens, Ga.
Findley, William H., Jr., 111 Curtiss Pkwy., Miami Springs, Fla.
Fink, Abel K., State University College, 1300 Elmwood Ave., Buffalo, N.Y.
Fink, Herbert J., Tuley High School, 1313 N. Claremont Ave., Chicago, Ill.
Fink, Martin B., 3713 Merridan Dr., Concord, Calif.
Fink, Paul J., 31 S. Penn St., Allentown, Pa.
Fink, Stuart D., Northern Illinois University, DeKalb, Ill.
Finster, Mrs. Virginia, P.O. Box 714, Raceland, La.
Finucan, J. Thomas, Assumption High School, Wisconsin Rapids, Wis.
Firth, Gerald R., University of Minnesota, Minneapolis, Minn.
Fischer, John H., Tchrs. Col., Columbia University, New York, N.Y.
Fischer, Louis, San Fernando Valley State College, Northridge, Calif.
Fischler, Abraham S., 5000 Taylor St., Ft. Lauderdale, Fla.
Fischoff, Ephraim, 15 Riverview Pl., Lynchburg, Va.
Fish, Lawrence D., NWREL, 710 S.W. 2nd Ave., Portland, Ore.
Fishback, Woodson W., 718 William St., River Forest, Ill.
Fishell, Kenneth N., Syracuse University, Syracuse, N.Y.
Fisher, Carol M., R.R. #2, 5747 Detrick-Jordan Rd., Springfield, Ohio
Fisher, Ijourie Stocks, Miami-Dade Junior College, Miami, Fla.
Fisher, James A., Boston University, 688 Boylston, Boston, Mass.
Fisher, Joseph T., University of South Dakota, Vermillion, S.D.
Fisher, Lawrence A., Col. of Medicine, Univ. of Illinois, Chicago, Ill.
Fisher, Wayne D., Dept. of Educ., Univ. of Chicago, Chicago, Ill.
* Fisher, Mrs. Welthy H., Literacy Village, P.O. Singar Nagar, Lucknow, U.P., India
Fishler, Edward, 216-23—73rd Ave., Bayside, N.Y.
Fisk, Robert S., State University of New York, Buffalo, N.Y.
Fitz, John Allen, 2923 West 235th St., Torrance, Calif.
Fitzgerald, William F., 5835 Kimbark Ave., Chicago, Ill.
Fitzpatrick, E. D., Illinois State University, Normal, Ill.
Fitzpatrick, Evelyn, Radford College, Radford, Va.
Fitzsimons, Frank P., 2467 Ocean Ave., Brooklyn, N.Y.
Flagg, E. Alma, 44 Stengel Ave., Newark, N.J.
Flaherty, Joseph E., Mt. St. Mary's College, Emmitsburg, Md.
Flamand, Ruth K., 72 Goldenridge Dr., Levittown, Pa.
Flanagan, John C., P.O. Box 1113, Palo Alto, Calif.
Flanagan, William F., 100 Tanner Ave., Warwick, R.I.

Flanders, Ned A., Sch. of Educ., Univ. of Mich., Ann Arbor, Mich.
Fleck, Henrietta, H.E. Dept., New York Univ., Washington Sq., New York, N.Y.
Fleming, Elyse S., Western Reserve University, Cleveland, Ohio
Fleming, Harold D., 2020 Birchmont Dr., Bemidji, Minn.
Fleming, Robert S., State Dept. of Educ., 175 W. State St., Trenton, N.J.
Fletcher, Ruby J., University of Utah, Salt Lake City, Utah
Fliegel, Norris E., 98 Riverside Dr., New York, N.Y.
Fliegler, Louis A., Dept. of Spec. Educ., Kent State Univ., Kent, Ohio
Fligor, R. J., Southern Illinois University, Carbondale, Ill.
Flint, Jack M., Kansas City Community Junior College, Kansas City, Kan.
Flores, Vetal, Drawer M, Bronte, Tex.
Flower, George E., Ontario Inst. for Studies in Educ., Toronto, Ont., Canada
Flowers, Anne, Dept. of Educ., Columbia Col., Columbia, S.C.
Flug, Eugene R. F., Stout State University, Menomonie, Wis.
Fluitt, John L., Col. of Educ., Louisiana State Univ., New Orleans, La.
Flusche, Ernest A., P.O. Box 506, Oklahoma City, Okla.
Fochs, John S., 1732 Wauwatosa Ave., Wauwatosa, Wis.
Focht, James R., Educ. Dept., Salisbury State Col., Salisbury, Md.
Fogg, William E., Long Beach State College, Long Beach, Calif.
Foley, Robert, Waterloo Comm. Schls., Waterloo, Iowa
Foley, Robert L., 7252 S. Maplewood Ave., Chicago, Ill.
Fonacier, Andres M., Laoag, Ilocos Norte, Philippines
Foord, James, Wolverhampton Tchrs. Col., Wolverhampton, England
Foran, Joseph A., Superintendent of Schools, Milford, Conn.
Foran, Mary Ellen, 6301 N. Sheridan Rd., Chicago, Ill.
Force, Dewey G., Jr., Pattee Hall, Univ. of Minnesota, Minneapolis, Minn.
Force, William R., 704 Duchess Rd., Milford, Mich.
Ford, Fraughton G., 38 Radford Village, Radford, Va.
Ford, Gervais W., San Jose State College, San Jose, Calif.
Ford, Roxana R., Sch. of Home Econ., Univ. of Minnesota, St. Paul, Minn.
Fordell, Pat, Dearborn Board of Educ., Dearborn, Mich.
Forrester, Carl M., Lake Park H.S., 6 N. 600 Medina Rd., Roselle, Ill.
Fortess, Lillian, 96 Bay State Rd., Boston, Mass.
Fortin, John E., Dunwoody Inst., 818 Wayzata Blvd., Minneapolis, Minn.
Fosback, Alta B., P.O. Box 443, Carlton, Ore.
Foshay, Arthur W., Tchrs. Col., Columbia University, New York, N.Y.
Fossieck, Theodore H., The Milne Sch., State Univ. of New York, Albany, N.Y.
Foster, E. M., Fresno State Col., 4021 Mt. Vernon Ave., Bakersfield, Calif.
Foster, Gordon, Merrick Hall, Univ. of Miami, Coral Gables, Fla.
Foster, Mrs. Mardis, 2368—16th Ave., San Francisco, Calif.
Foster, Richard S., 324 Grace Ave., Newark, N.Y.
Fournier, Rev. Edmond A., 241 Pearson Ave., Ferndale, Mich.
Fowler, William, Ontario Inst. for Stud. in Educ., Toronto, Ont., Canada
Fowlkes, John Guy, 204 Educ. Bldg., Univ. of Wisconsin, Madison, Wis.
Fox, Claire E., 2135 Jenkintown Rd., Glenside, Pa.
Fox, David J., 609 W. 114th St., New York, N.Y.
Fox, Esther, Ferrum Junior College, Ferrum, Va.
Fox, Marion W., 3200 Atlantic Ave., Atlantic City, N.J.
Fox, Robert S., 102 Univ. Sch., University of Michigan, Ann Arbor, Mich.
Frain, Thomas J., 1931 Brunswick Ave., Trenton, N.J.
Francis, Ida L., P.O., Box 243, Somerville, N.J.
Frandsen, Arden N., Utah State University, Logan, Utah
Frankland, Elizabeth M., 512 Algoma Blvd., Oshkosh, Wis.
Franklin, Arthur J., Univ. of So. Louisiana, Lafayette, La.
Franklin, David L., 5742 S. Laurel, LaGrange, Ill.
Franklin, Ruby Holden, Roosevelt University, 430 S. Michigan Ave., Chicago, Ill.
Franson, Arthur H., 50 N. Spring, LaGrange, Ill.
Franz, Evelyn B., Dept. of Educ., Trenton State College, Trenton, N.J.
Franzen, William L., Col. of Educ., Univ. of Toledo, Toledo, Ohio
Frase, H. Weldon, 1635 Hutchinson, S.E., Grand Rapids, Mich.
Fraser, Dorothy McClure, Hunter College, New York, N.Y.

MEMBERS OF THE NATIONAL SOCIETY

Fraser, Hugh W., 32 Beckwith Ter., Rochester, N.Y.
Frasier, Vance C., 1921 Harrison Ave., Evanston, Ill.
Frazier, Andrew J., 303 Biddle Ave., Harrison, Ohio
Fred, Bernhart G., 108 McCormick Dr., DeKalb, Ill.
Frederick, William C., Shoreline School District, Seattle, Wash.
Fredrick, James R., Arizona State College, Flagstaff, Ariz.
Freeberg, Howard, 207 Sixth Ave. East, West Fargo, N.D.
Freedman, Albert M., Pacific Univ., Forest Grove, Ore.
Freeman, Donald, 831 Crown Blvd., East Lansing, Mich.
Freeman, Kenneth H., RFD 1, Peru, Ill.
Freeman, Robert P., 406 Hollywood Ave., Hampton, Va.
Freeman, Ruges Richmond, Jr., 8027 Bennett Ave., St. Louis, Mo.
Fremont, Herbert, Queens College, Flushing, N.Y.
French, Henry P., 2 Bedford Way, Pittsford, N.Y.
French, William M., Muhlenberg College, Allentown, Pa.
Frerichs, Allen H., Northern Illinois University, DeKalb, Ill.
Fretwell, Elbert K., Jr., Pres., State Univ. Col., Buffalo, N.Y.
Freund, Evelyn, 5954 Guilford, Detroit, Mich.
Frick, Herman L., Florida State University, Talahassee, Fla.
Fridlund, John V., 414 N. Elm St., Itasca, Ill.
Frieberg, Carter N., Loyola University, 820 N. Michigan Ave., Chicago, Ill.
Friedhoff, Walter H., Illinois State University, Normal, Ill.
Friedrich, Kurt, San Diego State College, San Diego, Calif.
Frisbie, Mrs. Babette, Gloversville Public Schools, Gloversville, N.Y.
Frisk, Jack L., Superintendent of Schools, Port Angeles, Wash.
Froehlich, Gustave J., Bur. of Inst. Res., Univ. of Illinois, Urbana, Ill.
Frohnhoefer, Joseph J., Jr., 2644 Grand Ave., Baldwin, N.Y.
Froling, Raymond S., Nether Providence Sch. Dist., Wallingford, Pa.
Frost, Ralph J., Jr., Maine Twp. High School East, Park Ridge, Ill.
Frost, S. E., Jr., Brooklyn Col., Bedford and Ave. H., Brooklyn, N.Y.
Frutchey, Fred P., U.S. Department of Agriculture, Washington, D.C.
Fulchino, Albert R., Revere High School, Revere, Mass.
Full, Harold, 870 United Nations Plaza, New York, N.Y.
Fullagar, William A., Col. of Educ., Univ. of Rochester, Rochester, N.Y.
Fuller, John J., Winona State College, Winona, Minn.
Fuller, R. Buckminster, Southern Illinois University, Carbondale, Ill.
Fullerton, Craig K., 2712 North 52nd St., Omaha, Neb.
Fulton, Helen L., 955 Campbell Rd., Houston, Texas
Fultz, Mrs. Jane N., Col. of Educ., Univ. of Hawaii, Honolulu, Hawaii
Funderburk, Earl C., Fairfax County Schools, Fairfax, Va.
Furey, Mary Z., 4513 19th Rd., N., Arlington, Va.
Furlow, Mrs. Florine D., 2968 Collier Dr., N.W., Atlanta, Ga.
Furst, Philip W., 790 Riverside Dr., New York, N.Y.
Futch, Olivia, Woman's College, Furman University, Greenville, S.C.

Gabler, June, Mt. Clemens Sch. Dist., 167 Cass Ave., Mt. Clemens, Mich.
Gadbury, Mrs. Nada M., 2401 New York Ave., Muncie, Ind.
Gage, N. L., Sch. of Educ., Stanford University, Stanford, Calif.
Gaines, Berthera E., 3418 S. Claiborne Ave., New Orleans, La.
Gaines, John C., State of Tennessee, Nashville, Tenn.
Gaiter, Worrell G., Florida A. & M. University, Tallahassee, Fla.
Galbreath, Dorothy J., 3001 South Parkway, Chicago, Ill.
Gale, Ann V., 403 Jackson Ave., Glencoe, Ill.
Gallagher, Erwin A., Superintendent of Schools, Westwood, Mass.
Gallicchio, Francis A., 325 College Ave., Mt. Pleasant, Pa.
Gallington, Ralph O., Southern Illinois University, Carbondale, Ill.
Galloway, Geraldine, 111 Northwest Tenth St., Fairfield, Ill.
Gambert, Charles A., 606 Sixth St., Niagara Falls, N.Y.
Gamelin, Francis C., 231 Madison Ave., New York, N.Y.
Gammill, James R., Educ. Dept., Texas Tech. Col., Lubbock, Texas
Gandy, Frances C., 2597 Avery Ave., Memphis, Tenn.

MEMBERS OF THE NATIONAL SOCIETY

Gannon, John T., Supt. of Schools, Eagle Grove, Iowa
Gans, Leo, 4300 West 62nd St., Indianapolis, Ind.
Gansberg, Lucille, 2255-C Goodrich St., Sacramento, Calif.
Gantz, Ralph M., Superintendent of Schools, New Britain, Conn.
Garbe, Lester, 2110 W. Marne Ave., Milwaukee, Wis.
Garbee, Frederick E., State Dept. of Educ., Los Angeles, Calif.
Garbel, Marianne, 6732 Crandon Ave., Chicago, Ill.
Garber, M. Delott, Central Connecticut State College, New Britain, Conn.
Gardner, Harrison, 1007 Ravinia, West Lafayette, Ind.
Gardner, James E., 24450 Hatteras St., Woodland Hills, Calif.
Garinger, Elmer H., 2625 Briarcliff Pl., Charlotte, N.C.
Garland, Colden B., 61 Lechase Dr., Brockport, N.Y.
Garlich, Marvin O., 8901 McVicker Ave., Morton Grove, Ill.
Garoutte, Bill Charles, Univ. of California Medical Center, San Francisco, Calif.
Garrett, Charles G., 837 N. Cline St., Griffith, Ind.
Garrett, John L., Jr., Louisiana State University, Baton Rouge, La.
Garrison, C. B., Supt. of Schools, Pine Bluff, Ark.
Garrison, Harry L., 4802 E. Mercer Way, Mercer Island, Wash.
Garrison, Martin B., 640 Harvard Ave., University City, Mo.
Garrity, William J., Jr., 45 Gaynos Dr., Bridgeport, Conn.
Garvey, Reba, Allegheny College, Meadville, Pa.
Gaston, Don, 1273 North Ave., New Rochelle, N.Y.
* Gates, Arthur I., Tchrs. Col., Columbia University, New York, N.Y.
Gates, James O., Jr., East Cent. State Col., Ada, Okla.
Gathercole, F. J., Superintendent of Schools, Saskatoon, Sask., Canada
Gatti, Ora J., 20 Irving St., Worcester, Mass.
Gauerke, Warren E., 316 Merriweather Rd., Grosse Pointe Farms, Mich.
Gaunt, W. F., Sch. Dist. of Affton, 8309 Mackenzie Rd., Affton, Mo.
Gauvey, Ralph E., Roger Williams Jr. Col., Providence, R.I.
Gavin, Ann M., State College of Boston, Boston, Mass.
Gaynor, Alan K., 220 Sullivan St., Apt. 3-F, New York, N.Y.
Gazelle, Hazel N., 60 N. Auburn Ave., Sierra Madre, Calif.
Geer, Owen C., Sch. of Educ., University of Bridgeport, Bridgeport, Conn.
Geer, William D., Newton South High School, Newton Centre, Mass.
Geeslin, Robert H., Florida State Univ., Tallahassee, Fla.
Geigle, Ralph C., Superintendent of Schools, Reading, Pa.
Geis, H. Jon, 175 West 13th St., New York, N.Y.
Geiss, Doris T., 32-59—47th St., Astoria, L.I., N.Y.
Gelerinter, Alfred, 82 Meigs St., Rochester, N.Y.
Gellman, William, Jewish Vocational Service Library, Chicago, Ill.
Geng, George, Glassboro State College, Glassboro, N.J.
Gentry, George H., P.O. Box 30, Baytown, Tex.
George, Howard A., Northwest Missouri State College, Maryville, Mo.
George, John E., Sch. of Educ., Univ. of South Carolina, Columbia, S.C.
Georgiades, William, Univ. of Southern California, Los Angeles, Calif.
Georgiady, Nicholas P., 110 W. Bull Run Dr., Oxford, Ohio
Gephart, Woodrow W., Supt. of Schools, Jefferson, Ohio
Geraty, T. S., 7422 Hancock Ave., Takoma Park, Md.
Gerber, Wayne J., Bethel College, Mishawaka, Ind.
Gerhardt, Frank, 2355 S. Overlook Rd., Cleveland Heights, Ohio
Gerheim, Mearl F., Supt., Kiski Area Schools, Vandergriff, Pa.
Gerlach, Vernon S., Arizona State University, Tempe, Ariz.
Gerletti, John D., 1901 Mission St., South Pasadena, Calif.
Gerlock, D. E., Dept. of Educ., Valdosta State College, Valdosta, Ga.
Gernert, H. F., Jr., 2175 Hudson Terr., Ft. Lee, N.J.
Gesler, Harriet L., 70 Agnes Dr., Manchester, Conn.
Gest, Mrs. Viola S., P.O. Box 254, Seguin, Tex.
Getzels, J. W., Dept. of Educ., University of Chicago, Chicago, Ill.
Geyer, John J., Sch. of Educ., Rutgers Univ., New Brunswick, N.J.
Ghalib, Hanna, P. O. Box 4638, Beirut, Lebanon
Gholson, G. James, Fairmont Heights High School, Washington, D.C.

Gialas, George J., 1150 Wayland Ave., Cornwells Heights, Pa.
Gibbons, Constance M., 74 Franklin Ave., Oakville, Conn.
Gibbony, Hazel L., Ohio State University, Columbus, Ohio
Gibbs, Edward Delmar, Univ. of Puget Sound, Tacoma, Wash.
Gibbs, Edward, III, 1145 Clinton Ter., South Plainfield, N.J.
Gibbs, John Donald, 1147 S. Ash St., Moses Lake, Wash.
Gibbs, Wesley, Superintendent, Dist. No. 68, 9300 N. Kenton, Skokie, Ill.
Gibert, James M., Randolph-Macon Woman's College, Lynchburg, Va.
Gibson, Mrs. Kathryn Snell, Prairie View A & M College, Prairie View, Tex.
Gibson, R. Oliver, State University of New York, Buffalo, N.Y.
Giesecke, G. Ernst, Provost, University of Toledo, Toledo, Ohio
Giesy, John P., 1017 Blanchard, Flint, Mich.
Gilbert, Mrs. Doris Wilcox, 1044 Euclid Ave., Berkeley, Calif.
Gilbert, Floyd O., Minnesota State College, St. Cloud, Minn.
Gilbert, Jerome H., 815 Ashbury, El Cerrito, Calif.
Gilbert, John H., Dept. of Educ., Monmouth College, West Long Branch, N.J.
Gilbert, William B., Onondaga Central School, Nedrow, N.Y.
Giles, LeRoy H., University of Dubuque, Dubuque, Iowa
Gili, Joe D., West Washington High School, Campbellsburg, Ind.
Gilk, Edwin John, P.O. Box 642, Columbia Falls, Mont.
Gilkey, Richard W., 5516 S.W. Seymour St., Portland, Ore.
Gill, Bernard I., Moorhead State Col., Moorhead, Minn.
Gill, Margaret, Mills College, Oakland, Calif.
Gilland, Thomas M., 504 S. Washington St., Greencastle, Pa.
Gillespie, Paul R., Miami-Dade Junior College, Miami, Fla.
Gillette, B. Frank, Superintendent of Schools, Los Gatos, Calif.
Gillham, Mrs. Millie G., 3814 W. Rovey Ave., Phoenix, Arizona
Gilligan, Michael B., Jersey City State College, Jersey City, N.J.
Gilmore, Douglas M., 1255 Ethel St., Okemos, Mich.
Gilson, Harry V., Superintendent of Schools, Winchester, Mass.
Gingerich, Julia B., 1815 W. 40th St., Davenport, Iowa
Gits, Gerald B., 6363 Keokuk, Indian Head Park, La Grange, Ill.
Gjerstad, Olive, 653 Park Ave. W., Highland Park, Ill.
Glaser, Robert, Res. & Dev. Cent., Univ. of Pittsburgh, Pittsburgh, Pa.
Glaess, Herman L., Concordia Teachers College, Seward, Neb.
Glasow, Ogden L., P.O. Box 143, Macomb, Ill.
Glass, Olive Jewell, 3910 Latimer St., Dallas, Tex.
Glassman, Milton R., Kent State University, Kent, Ohio
Glatt, Charles A., Sch. of Educ., Ohio State Univ., Columbus, Ohio
Glaza, Stephen M., Superintendent of Schools, Marshall, Mich.
Glenn, J. Curtis, 1531 West 103rd St., Chicago, Ill.
Glicken, Irwin J., 2135 W. Walters, Northbrook, Ill.
Glock, Marvin D., Stone Hall, Cornell University, Ithaca, N.Y.
Glogau, Arthur H., Oregon College of Education, Monmouth, Ore.
Glover, Mrs. Benjamin H., 3706 Spring Trail, Madison, Wis.
Gobetz, Wallace, 540 East 22nd St., Brooklyn, N.Y.
Goble, Robert I., McGuffey No. 360, Miami University, Oxford, Ohio
Godfrey, Mary E., Pennsylvania State University, University Park, Pa.
Goebel, E. J., Supt., Archdiocese of Milwaukee, Milwaukee, Wis.
Goff, Howard J., P.O. Box 174, Moline, Ill.
Goff, Robert J., Univ. of Massachusetts, Amherst, Mass.
Gold, Louis L., 1030 Washington St., Indiana, Pa.
Gold, Milton J., Hunter College, 695 Park Ave., New York, N.Y.
Goldberg, Miriam L., Tchrs. Col., Columbia University, New York, N.Y.
Goldberg, Nathan, 75-47—196 St., Flushing, N.Y.
Goldhammer, Keith, 2929 Highland Way, Corvallis, Ore.
Goldman, Bert A., Sch. of Educ., Univ. of North Carolina, Greensboro, N.C.
Goldman, Harvey, University of Wisconsin, Milwaukee, Wis.
Goldman, Samuel, Sch. of Educ., Syracuse University, Syracuse, N.Y.
Goldner, Ralph H., Sch. of Educ., New York University, New York, N.Y.
Goldstein, Allan, 925 Ensenada Ave., Berkeley, Calif.

MEMBERS OF THE NATIONAL SOCIETY

Goldstein, Herbert, Yeshiva University, 110 W. 57th St., New York, N.Y.
Goldstein, Sanford G., 115 Woodgate Terr., Rochester, N.Y.
Goleman, Clarence E., Southern Louisiana College, Hammond, La.
Goltry, Keith, Dept. of Educ., Parsons College, Fairfield, Iowa
Gomberg, Adeline W., Beaver College, Glenside, Pa.
Gomes, Lawrence A., Jr., 4 Vincent Ave., Belmont, Mass.
Gonzalez, Alice M., University of Puerto Rico, Rio Piedras, Puerto Rico
Goo, Frederick J. K., c/o Bur. of Indian Affairs Sch., Barrow, Alaska
Good, Carter V., Tchrs. Col., University of Cincinnati, Cincinnati, Ohio
Good, Richard M., 12521 Eastbourne Dr., Silver Spring, Md.
Good, Warren R., 1604 Stony Run Dr., Northwood, Wilmington, Del.
Goodlad, John I., Sch. of Educ., Univ. of California, Los Angeles, Calif.
Goodman, John O., University of Connecticut, Storrs, Conn.
Goodman, Kenneth S., Wayne State Univ., Detroit, Mich.
Goodpaster, Robert L., University of Kentucky-Ashland Center, Ashland, Ky
Goodside, Samuel, 504 Beach 139th St., Belle Harbor, L.I., N.Y.
Goodwin, William L., 136 Pine St., Lewisburg, Pa.
Googins, Duane G., 2964—116th Ave., N.W., Coon Rapids, Minn.
Goolsby, Thomas M., Florida State Univ., Tallahassee, Fla.
Goossen, Carl V., 108 Burton Hall, Univ. of Minnesota, Minneapolis, Minn.
Gordon, Alice S., 6532 N. Newgard Ave., Chicago, Ill.
Gordon, Mrs. Catherine J., 326 Wellesley Rd., Philadelphia, Pa.
Gordon, Irving, 5859 Beacon St., Pittsburgh, Pa.
Gordon, Ted E., 317 N. Lucerne, Los Angeles, Calif.
Gordon, William M., 520 South Park, Bloomington, Ind.
Gorham, Marion, 10 Alcott St., Acton, Mass.
Gorman, Anna M., Col. of Educ., University of Kentucky, Lexington, Ky.
Gorman, Frank H., Col. of Educ., University of Omaha, Omaha, Neb.
Gorman, William J., 219-40—93rd Ave., Queens Village, N.Y.
Gormley, Charles L., Dept. of Educ., Alabama College, Montevallo, Ala.
Gorn, Mrs. Janice L., New York University, Washington Sq., New York, N.Y.
Gorton, Harry B., L57 Alexander Dr., R.D. 2, Irwin, Pa.
Gotsch, Richard E., 8701 Mackenzie Rd., St. Louis, Mo.
Gottenid, Allan J., Comm. on Educ., ELCT, P.O. Box 412, Arusha, Tanzania
Gough, Jessie P., LaGrange College, LaGrange, Ga.
Gould, George, Cathedral of Learn., Univ. of Pittsburgh, Pittsburgh, Pa.
Gould, Norman M., Supt., Madera County Schools, Madera, Calif.
Gow, J. Steele, Jr., College Park, R.D. 1, Lewisburg, Pa.
Gowan, John Curtis, San Fernando Valley State Col., Northridge, Calif.
Gowin, D. Bob, Stone Hall, Cornell University, Ithaca, N.Y.
Graber, Eldon W., Dept. of Educ., Bluffton College, Bluffton, Ohio
Grabowski, A. A., 2512 Southport Ave., Chicago, Ill.
Grady, Joseph E., St. Bernard's Seminary, 2260 Lake Ave., Rochester, N.Y.
Graff, Orin B., Col. of Educ., University of Tennessee, Knoxville, Tenn.
Grahm, Milton L., Cambridge School of Business, Boston, Mass.
Grant, Eugene B., Northern Illinois University, DeKalb, Ill.
Grant, Wayman R. F., Booker T. Washington Junior High School, Mobile, Ala.
Grau, R. T., Clinton Public Schls., Box 110, Clinton, Iowa
Graven, John P., 7337-B South Shore Dr., Chicago, Ill.
Graves, Jack A., 922 Riley Dr., Albany, Calif.
Graves, Linwood D., 115 Leathers Circle, N.W., Atlanta, Ga.
Gray, Ashley C., 41 Liberty St., New Britain, Conn.
Gray, Dorothy, Dept. of Educ., Queens College, Flushing, N.Y.
Gray, Ronald F., Canadian Nazarene Col., Winnipeg, Manitoba, Canada
Graybeal, William S., 1330 Massachusetts Ave., N.W., Washington, D.C.
Graye, Mytrolene L., 25 W. 132nd St., New York, N.Y.
Grayson, William H., Jr., 21-71—34th Ave., Long Island City, N.Y.
Green, C. M., 310 Hunting Hill Ave., Middletown, Conn.
Green, Donald Ross, 1419 Cornell Rd., N.E., Atlanta, Ga.
Green, Gertrude B., 100 W. Hickory Grove Rd., Bloomfield Hills, Mich.
Green, John A., Col. of Educ., Univ. of Idaho, Moscow, Idaho

Greenberg, Gilda M., Fisk University, Nashville, Tenn.
Greenberg, Mrs. Judith W., Sch. of Educ., City College, New York, N.Y.
Greenblatt, Edward L., 211 Calle de Arboles, Redondo Beach, Calif.
Greene, Bert I., 1111 Grant St., Ypsilanti, Mich.
Greene, Charles E., P.O. Box 185, East Side Sta., Santa Cruz, Calif.
Greene, Frank P., 707 Sumner Ave., Syracuse, N.Y.
Greene, John G., 142 Chestnut St., Boston, Mass.
Greene, Mrs. Maxine, 1080—5th Ave., New York, N.Y.
Greene, Mrs. Minnie S., 1121 Chestnut St., San Marcos, Tex.
Greenfield, Curtis O., 345 W. Windsor Ave., Phoenix, Ariz.
Greenman, Mrs. Floy, Job Corps Center for Women, Excelsior Springs, Mo.
Greenman, Mrs. Margaret H., Country Fair, Champaign, Ill.
Greenwood, Edward D., Menninger Clinic, Box 829, Topeka, Kan.
Greer, Evelyn, Fayette County Schls., 400 Lafayette Dr., Lexington, Ky.
Greer, Mrs. Shirley J., 8441 E. Hubbell St., Scottsdale, Arizona
Gregg, Russell T., Sch. of Educ., University of Wisconsin, Madison, Wis.
Gregory, Herbert W., P.O. Box 669, College Station, Hammond, La.
Greif, Ivo P., Illinois State University, Normal, Ill.
Greivell, Richard, Waukesha Public Schls., South Campus, Waukesha, Wis.
Grenda, Ted T., Box 189, Stone Ridge, N.Y.
Grennell, Robert L., State University College, Fredonia, N.Y.
Griffin, Gary A., 1255 New Hampshire Ave., N.W., Washington, D.C.
Griffin, Michael T., Superintendent of Schools, Poughkeepsie, N.Y.
Griffing, Barry L., State Office Bldg., 217 W. First St., Los Angeles, Calif.
Griffith, Maurice F., Superintendent of Schools, Casper, Wyo.
Griffith, William J., Ohio State University, Columbus, Ohio
Griffith, William S., Dept. of Educ., Univ. of Chicago, Chicago, Ill.
Griffiths, Daniel E., 54 Clarendon Rd., Scarsdale, N.Y.
Griffiths, John A., Superintendent of Schools, Monongahela, Pa.
Griffiths, Ruth, 184 Middlesex St., North Andover, Mass.
Grimes, Wellington V., 4 Liberty Sq., Boston, Mass.
Grimsley, Mrs. Edith E., Danville, Ga.
* Grizzell, E. Duncan, 640 Maxwelton Ct., Lexington, Ky.
Groff, Frank E., New Hope-Solebury Joint School Dist., New Hope, Pa.
Groff, Warren H., 721 Highland Ave., Jenkintown, Pa.
Gromacki, Chester P., 1000 N. Lemon St., Fullerton, Calif.
Gronlund, Norman E., Col. of Educ., University of Illinois, Urbana, Ill.
Grose, Robert F., Amherst College, Amherst, Mass.
Gross, Lydia E., State College, Lock Haven, Pa.
Gross, Neal, 8 Prescott St., Cambridge, Mass.
Gross, Robert Dean, 3800 Yellowstone Court, Dorado Hills, Calif.
Grossman, Ruth H., Sch. of Educ., City College of N.Y., New York, N.Y.
Grossnickle, Foster E., 1116 Melbourne Ave., Melbourne, Fla.
Grotberg, Edith H., Dept. of Educ., American University, Washington, D.C.
Grover, Burton L., 706 N. 8th St., Manitowoc, Wis.
Groves, Vernon T., Olivet Nazarene College, Kankakee, Ill.
Gruber, Frederick C., Grad. Sch. of Educ., Univ. of Pa., Philadelphia, Pa.
Grudell, Regina C., 45 Chadwick Rd., Teaneck, N.J.
Guba, Egon G., NISEC, Indiana Univ., Bloomington, Ind.
Guckenheimer, S. N., Heath Area Vocational School, Heath, Ohio
Guditus, C. W., Dept. of Educ., Lehigh University, Bethlehem, Pa.
Guilford, Jerome O., 705 Searles Rd., Toledo, Ohio
Guillaume, Harry G., Dept. of Art, State College of Iowa, Cedar Falls, Iowa
Gulutsan, Metro, University of Alberta, Edmonton, Alba., Canada
Gunn, Jack G., 2828 Fifth Ave., Laurel, Miss.
Gurr, Rev. John E., 1032 Eighth Ave., Fairbanks, Alaska
Guss, Carolyn, R.R. 2, Box 139, Bloomington, Ind.
Gussner, William S., Superintendent of Schools, Jamestown, N.D.
Gustafson, A. M., Alice Vail Junior High Sch., 5350 E. 16th St., Tucson, Ariz.
Gustafson, Alma L., 1211 North 5th St., East Grand Forks, Minn.
Guttchen, Robert S., 137-16 231st St., Jamaica, N.Y.

Guyler, Mrs. Hazel M., Beech St., Topsham, Me.
Gwynn, J. Minor, 514 North St., Chapel Hill, N.C.

Haage, Catherine M., College of New Rochelle, New Rochelle, N.Y.
Haas, Richard J., Jr., 119 Stubbs Dr., Trotwood, Ohio
Haberman, Martin, University of Wisconsin-Milwaukee, Milwaukee, Wis.
Hack, Walter G., Ohio State University, Columbus, Ohio
Hackmann, Jane, 38 Signal Hill Blvd., East St. Louis, Ill.
Hackney, Ben H., Jr., 4618 Walker Rd., Charlotte, N.C.
Hadden, John F., 61 Rochester St., Bergen, N.Y.
Haddock, Thomas T., 7232 N. 12th Ave., Phoenix, Ariz.
Haffner, Hyman, 6229 Nicholson St., Pittsburgh, Pa.
Hagen, Donald E., 13028 Root Rd., Columbia Station, Ohio
Hagen, Elizabeth, Tchrs. Col., Columbia University, New York, N.Y.
Hager, Walter E., 4625 S. Chelsea Ln., Bethesda, Md.
Haggerson, Nelson L., 132 W. Balboa Dr., Tempe, Ariz.
Hagglund, Oliver C., Gustavus Adolphus College, St. Peter, Minn.
Hagstrom, Ellis A., 1330 Christmas Lane, N.E., Atlanta, Ga.
Hahn, Albert R., Veterans' Administration Hospital, Phoenix, Ariz.
Haight, Wilbur T., 314 S. DuPont Blvd., Milford, Del.
Haimowitz, Clement, Mental Measurements Yrbk., Highland Park, N.J.
Halbert, Bernice, 204 Whaley, Marshall, Texas
Hale, Gifford G., Sch. of Educ., Florida State University, Tallahassee, Fla.
Hale, R. Nelson, State Teachers College, Slippery Rock, Pa.
Haley, Charles F., Col. of Educ., Northeastern University, Boston, Mass.
Haley, Elizabeth, 1938 Channing Ave., Palo Alto, Calif.
Haley, Gerald J., 5625 N. Natoma Ave., Chicago, Ill.
Haley, Mrs. Margaret T., 2100 Nineteenth St., N.W., Washington, D.C.
Halfter, Mrs. Irma Theobald, 222 N. Grove Ave., Oak Park, Ill.
Hall, Barbara C., 2 Knollcrest Court, Normal, Ill.
Hall, Clarence L., Pacific Grove Unified Schl. Dist., Pacific Grove, Calif.
Hall, J. Floyd, 301 S. Harvey, Oak Park, Ill.
Hall, James A., Superintendent of Schools, Port Washington, N.Y.
Hall, John E., Jackson State College, Jackson, Miss.
Hall, Joseph I., Holt, Rinehart & Winston, Inc., New York, N.Y.
Hall, Keith A., Pennsylvania State Univ., University Park, Pa.
Hall, Leon P., Bd. of Educ., 1200 N. Telegraph Rd., Pontiac, Mich.
Hall, Morris E., Stephen F. Austin State Col., Nacogdoches, Texas
Hall, Robert H., Gulf Coast Junior College, Panama City, Fla.
Hall, Walter J., Jr., Haverford Senior High School, Havertown, Pa.
Hall, William Frank, 125 E. Lincoln St., Phoenix, Ariz.
Hall, William H., 509 W. 121st St., New York, N.Y.
Hall, William P., Gaithersburg Senior High School, Gaithersburg, Md.
Hallenbeck, Edwin F., Roger Williams Junior College, Providence, R.I.
Hallgren, Ragnar F., Box 297, R.D. 1, Mount Joy, Pa.
Halligan, W. W., Jr., Converse College, Spartanburg, S.C.
Halliwell, Joseph W., State Univ. Col., Cortland, N.Y.
Halpern, Aaron, Clifton Senior High School, Clifton, N.J.
Hamada, Kiyoshi, Gakuin Univ., Chofu, Tokyo, Japan
Hamalainen, Arthur E., 306 Third Ave., East Northport, N.Y.
Hamblen, Charles P., The Norwich Free Academy, Norwich, Conn.
Hamilton, DeForest S., Supt., Sonoma County Schools, Santa Rosa, Calif.
Hamilton, Gene E., Edgewood Elementary School, Minneapolis, Minn.
Hamilton, Herbert M., Sch. of Bus. Adm., Miami Univ., Oxford, Ohio
Hamilton, Lester L., Box 5285, North Charleston, S.C.
Hammel, John A., 1275 Cook Rd., Grosse Pointe Woods, Mich.
Hammer, Eugene L., Dept. of Educ., Wilkes College, Wilkes-Barre, Pa.
Hammer, Viola, Redwood City Schools, Redwood City, Calif.
Hammock, Robert C., Grad. Sch. of Educ., Univ. of Penn., Philadelphia, Pa.
Hammond, Granville S., 8321 Ashwood Dr., Alexandria, Va.
Hancock, Emily, Florida Southern College, Lakeland, Fla.

Handley, W. Harold, Olympus High School, Salt Lake City, Utah
Hanigan, Levin B., Superintendent, Echobrook School, Mountainside, N.J.
Hanisits, Richard M., 8623 S. Kilpatrick Ave., Chicago, Ill.
Hanitchak, John J., Sch. of Educ., Indiana Univ., Bloomington, Ind.
Hankerson, M. R., Superintendent of Schools, Thief River Falls, Minn.
Hanna, Alvis N., John Tyler High Schools, 331 S. College St., Tyler, Tex.
Hanna, Ben M., Baylor University, Waco, Tex.
Hanna, Paul R., Stanford University, Stanford, Calif.
Hannemann, Charles E., 931 E. 5th Ave., Lancaster, Ohio
Hannifin, Mrs. Blanche B., 5259 Strohm Ave., North Hollywood, Calif.
Hannon, Elizabeth F., 1432 S. Crescent Ave., Park Ridge, Ill.
Hansen, Dorothy Gregg, 722 Ivanhoe Rd., Tallahassee, Fla.
Hansen, G. G., Superintendent of County Schools, Aurora, Neb.
Hansen, Helge E., 15735 Andover Dr., Dearborn, Mich.
Hansen, Henry R., Sacramento State College, Sacramento, Calif.
Hansen, Maxine Mann, Northwest Comm. Col., Powell, Wyo.
Hansen, R. G., 2075 St. Johns Ave., Highland Park, Ill.
Hansen, Robert E., Cherry Hill High School, Cherry Hill, N.J.
Hansen, Stewart R., St. John's University, Collegeville, Minn.
Hanson, Donald L., 1709 Cherry Lane, Cedar Falls, Iowa
Hanson, Earl H., 3243 Ninth Ave., Rock Island, Ill.
Hanson, Eddie, Jr., Rt. # 1, Box 1432, Auburn, Calif.
Hanson, Frances F., Sch. of Educ., Portland State Col., Portland, Ore.
Hanson, Gordon C., Wichita State Univ., Wichita, Kansas
Hanson, Ralph A., 5835 Kimbark Ave., Chicago, Ill.
Hanson, Wesley L., 3021 Washburn Pl., Bloominton, Minn.
Hanuska, Julius P., 550 Edith Ave., Johnstown, Pa.
Happy, Kenneth F., State University College, Plattsburgh, N.Y.
Hardee, Melvene D., Florida State University, Tallahassee, Fla.
Hardesty, Cecil D., 6401 Linda Vista Rd., San Diego, Calif.
Harding, Lowry W., Arps Hall, Ohio State University, Columbus, Ohio
Harding, Merle D., 421 Irving St., Beatrice, Neb.
Hardy, J. Garrick, Alabama State College, Montgomery, Ala.
Hargett, Earl F., Brunswick Junior College, Brunswick, Ga.
Hargrave, Ruth T., Central State College, Wilberforce, Ohio
Harkness, Harvey F., Jr., State Dept. of Educ., Concord, N.H.
Harlow, James G., Pres., West Virginia Univ., Morgantown, W.Va.
Harmon, Ruth E., 1720 Commonwealth Ave., West Newton, Mass.
Harnack, Robert S., Sch. of Educ., State Univ. Col., Buffalo, N.Y.
Harney, Paul J., University of San Francisco, San Francisco, Calif.
Harootunian, Berj, Sch. of Educ., Syracuse Univ., Syracuse, N.Y.
Harper, Aaron W., Univ. of Kansas State Col., Pittsburg, Kansas
Harper, Ray G., Michigan State Univ., East Lansing, Mich.
Harrach, Russell, W., 7550 Starr, Lincoln, Neb.
Harrington, Edmund Ross, 309 Ave. E., Redondo Beach, Calif.
Harrington, Johns H., 7615 McGroarty St., Tujunga, Calif.
Harrington, Shirley L., 54 Kehr St., Buffalo, N.Y.
Harris, Albert J., 345 E. Grand St., Mt. Vernon, N.Y.
Harris, Ben M., 325 Sutton Hall, University of Texas, Austin, Texas
Harris, C. W., P.O. Box 1510, Deland, Fla.
Harris, Charles R., Box 4163, Midland, Texas
Harris, Claude C., 501 S. 30th St., Muskogee, Okla.
Harris, Dale B., Burrowes Bldg., Pennsylvania State Univ., University Park, Pa.
Harris, Eugene, Capitol Area Vocational School, Baton Rouge, La.
Harris, Fred E., Baldwin-Wallace College, Berea, Ohio
Harris, Janet D., 130 Boylston St., Chestnut Hill, Mass.
Harris, John W., Niles Township Comm. High School, Skokie, Ill.
Harris, Kenneth F., 2596 Baird Rd., Penfield, N.Y.
Harris, Lewis E., 3752 N. Hight St., Columbus, Ohio
Harris, Mary Jo, Educ. Dept., Univ. of South. Alabama, Mobile, Ala.
Harris, Nelson H., Fayetteville College, Fayetteville, N.C.

Harris, Raymond P., Mt. Vernon Public Schools, Mt. Vernon, N.Y.
Harris, Robert B., Bryan Adams High School, Dallas, Tex.
Harris, Ruby Dean, Univ. Hall, University of California, Berkeley, Calif.
Harris, Theodore L., Sch. of Educ., University of Wisconsin, Madison, Wis.
Harrison, C. Barker, 6143 Haddington St., Memphis, Tenn.
Harrison, Edward N., Park Terrace Apts., Jefferson City, Tenn.
Harry, David P., Jr., 1659 Compton Rd., Cleveland Heights, Ohio
Harsanyi, Mrs. Audrey, Pennsylvania State University, University Park, Pa.
Harshbarger, Lawrence H., Educ. Dept., Ball State Univ., Muncie, Ind.
Hart, Mrs. Lawrence W., P.O. Box 14, Rock Falls, Ill.
Hart, Mary A., 10 Windmill Rd., Pittsford, N.Y.
Hart, Richard H., 452 N. Third Ave., Hillsboro, Ore.
Hart, Ruth M. R., 1100 Douglas Ave., Minneapolis, Minn.
Harting, Roger A., 4711 Orchard Ln., Columbia, Mo.
Hartley, Harold V., Jr., Clarion State Col., Clarion, Pa.
Hartley, James R., Univ. Extn., University of California, Riverside, Calif.
Hartsell, Horace C., Univ. of Texas, Dental Branch, Houston, Texas
Hartsig, Barbara A., California State College, Fullerton, Calif.
Hartstein, Jacob I., Kingsborough Community College, Brooklyn, N.Y.
Hartung, Maurice L., Dept. of Educ., University of Chicago, Chicago, Ill.
Hartwell, Mrs. Lois, Northern State Col., Aberdeen, S.D.
Harvey, Jasper, University of Alabama, University, Ala.
Harvey, Valerien, Univ. Laval, Quebec, Canada
Harwell, John Earl, Nicholls State Col., Thibodaux, La.
Hasanen, Kenneth L. C., Box 2118, Duncan, B.C., Canada
Hasenpflug, Thomas R., 600 Hunt Rd., Jamestown, N.Y.
Hash, Mrs. Virginia, State College of Iowa, Cedar Falls, Iowa
Haskell, Charlotte L., 89 Royal Rd., Bangor, Me.
Haskew, Laurence D., Col. of Educ., University of Texas, Austin, Tex.
Hasman, Richard H., 61 Oakwood Ave., Farmingdale, N.Y.
Hastie, Reid, University of Minnesota, Minneapolis, Minn.
Hastings, Glen R., Dept. of Educ., State Col. of Iowa, Cedar Falls, Iowa
Hastings, Howard H., 255 W. Vermont, Villa Park, Ill.
Hastings, J. Thomas, Educ. Bldg., University of Illinois, Urbana, Ill.
Hatalsan, John W., 4184 Palisades Rd., San Diego, Calif.
Hatashita, Elizabeth S., 3556 San Marino St., Los Angeles, Calif.
Hatch, J. Cordell, Univ. of Wisconsin, Madison, Wis.
Hatch, Terrance E., Col. of Educ., Utah State University, Logan, Utah
Hatfield, Donald M., Dept. of Educ., University of California, Berkeley, Calif.
Haubrich, Vernon F., Sch. of Educ., Univ. of Wisconsin, Madison, Wis.
Hauer, Nelson A., Louisiana State University, Baton Rouge, La.
Haupt, Leonard R., 2801 Glenview Rd., Glenview, Ill.
Hauschild, Mrs. J. R., 20528 Rhoda St., Woodland Hills, Calif.
* Havighurst, Robert J., Dept. of Educ., University of Chicago, Chicago, Ill.
Haweeli, Norman, Glenbrook H.S., 2300 Sherman, Northbrook, Ill.
Hawk, Travis L., University of Tennessee, Knoxville, Tenn.
Hawkins, Edwin L., Horace Mann High School, Little Rock, Ark.
Hawkins, Valerie T., Long Island Univ., C.W. Post Col., Brookville, N.Y.
Hawley, Leslie R., 94 Walden Dr., RFD No. 1, Lakeview, Erie Co., N.Y.
Hawley, Ray C., Superintendent of County Schools, Ottawa, Ill.
Hayden, Alice H., MRCDC, Univ. of Washington, Seattle, Wash.
Hayden, Alice H., Miller Hall, University of Washington, Seattle, Wash.
Hayden, James R., 166 William St., New Bedford, Mass.
Hayes, Allen P., 757 McKinley Ave., Auburn, Ala.
Hayes, Larry K., Col. of Educ., Oklahoma State Univ., Stillwater, Okla.
Hayes, Paul C., 3761 Mayfair Dr., Grove City, Ohio
Hayes, Robert K., Dept. of Pub. Instr., Harrisburg, Pa.
Haynes, Hubert Ray, 108 E. Tilden Dr., Brownsburg, Ind.
Hays, Albert Z., Abilene Christian College, Abilene, Tex.
Hays, Harry N., 407 Jesse St., Philipsburg, Pa.
Hays, Warren S., 3218 N. Reno Ave., Tucson, Ariz.

Hayward, W. George, 27 Grant Ave., East Orange, N.J.
Hazell, Joseph W., 1106-C San Pablo Ave., Albany, Calif.
Hazleton, Edward W., Bogan High School, Chicago, Ill.
Headd, Pearl Walker, Box 362, Tuskegee Institute, Ala.
Headley, Ross A., 3 Sandy Dr., Smithtown, N.Y.
Heagney, Genevieve, Towson State Col., Baltimore, Md.
Heald, James E., 4277 Tacoma Blvd., Okemos, Mich.
Heathers, Glen, New York University, New York, N.Y.
Heavenridge, Glen G., 5844 Gilman St., Garden City, Mich.
Hebeler, Jean R., University of Maryland, College Park, Md.
Hecht, Irvin Sulo, 1282 E. 29th St., Brooklyn, N.Y.
Heck, Theodore, St. Meinrad Seminary, St. Meinrad, Ind.
Hedden, Gerald W., 23422 Happy Valley Dr., Newhall, Calif.
Hedges, William D., 529 Purdue, St. Louis, Mo.
Heding, Howard W., Col. of Educ., Univ. of Missouri, Columbia, Mo.
Heemstra, Mrs. Jean M., Indian Comm. Action Proj., Yankton, S.D.
Heffernan, Helen, 3416 Land Park Dr., Sacramento, Calif.
Heger, Herbert K., 3020 Oaklawn St., Columbus, Ohio
Hegman, M. Marian, 332 South Ave., Medina, N.Y.
Hein, William J., Lane Community Col., Eugene, Ore.
Heine, Margaret, 3126 W. Kilbourn, Milwaukee, Wis.
Heinz, John A., California State Polytechnic College, San Luis Obispo, Calif.
Heisler, Florence, Dept. of Educ., Brooklyn College, Brooklyn, N.Y.
Heisner, H. Fred, Redlands Unified Sch. Dist., Redlands, Calif.
Heist, Paul H., 4606 Tolman Hall, Univ. of California, Berkeley, Calif.
Held, John T., 426 College Ave., Gettysburg, Pa.
Helge, Erich E., 1118 Sunrise Dr., Seward, Neb.
Heller, Melvin P., Dept. of Educ., Loyola University, Chicago, Ill.
Hellerich, Mahlon H., Wartburg College, Waverly, Iowa
Helmer, Robert D., Superintendent of Schools, Canandaigua, N.Y.
* Helms, W. T., 1109 Roosevelt Ave., Richmond, Calif.
Heltibridle, Mary E., 39 Sullivan St., Mansfield, Pa.
Heming, Hilton P., 12 Leonard Ave., Plattsburgh, N.Y.
Hemingway, William C., Western Apts., Billings, Mont.
Hemink, Lyle H., 4134 Trailing Dr., Williamsville, N.Y.
Hencley, Stephen P., 1505 Indian Hills Dr., Salt Lake City, Utah
Henderson, Edward, New York University, Washington Sq., New York, N.Y.
Henderson, Robert A., Col. of Educ., University of Illinois, Urbana, Ill.
Hendrick, Irving G., University of California, Riverside, Calif.
Hendrickson, Gordon, University of Cincinnati, Cincinnati, Ohio
Hendrix, Holbert H., Nevada Southern Univ., Las Vegas, Nev.
Hengesbach, Robert W., 7886 Munson Rd., Mentor, Ohio
Hengoed, James, Boston University, Boston, Mass.
Henion, Ethel S., 435 N. Central Ave., Ramsey, N.J.
Henjum, Arnold, University of Minnesota, Minneapolis, Minn.
Henle, R. J., 221 N. Grand Blvd., St. Louis, Mo.
Henry, Bailey Ray, Supt. of Schools, Farmington, Mo.
Henry, George H., Alison Hall, Univ. of Delaware, Newark, Del.
* Henry, Nelson B., 2665 Alta Glen Dr., Birmingham, Ala.
Henry, William G., Jr., Stout State Univ., Menomonie, Wis.
Hensarling, Paul R., Texas A. & M., University, College Station, Tex.
Herbst, Leonard A., 3550 Crestmoor Dr., San Bruno, Calif.
Herge, Henry C., USAID/Jamaica, Dept. of State, Washington, D.C.
Herget, George H., 2619 N.W. 11th Ave., Gainesville, Fla.
Herman, James A., 4325 Virgusell Circle, Carmichael, Calif.
Herman, Wayne L., Jr., Col. of Educ., Univ. of Maryland, College Park, Md.
Hermanowicz, Henry J., Illinois State University, Normal, Ill.
Herr, Ross, 3452 W. Drummond Pl., Chicago, Ill.
Herr, William A., 536 W. Maple St., Hazleton, Pa.
Herrington, Mrs. Evelyn F., Texas A. & I. Univ., Kingsville, Texas
Herrmann, D. J., College of William and Mary, Williamsburg, Va.

MEMBERS OF THE NATIONAL SOCIETY

Hershberger, James K., Spring Grove Area Sch. Dist., Spring Grove, Pa.
* Hertzler, Silas, 1618 So. 8th St., Goshen, Ind.
Herz, Mort, 1864 Pattiz Ave., Long Beach, Calif.
Hesla, Arden E., Mankato State College, Mankato, Minn.
Heslep, Thomas R., Superintendent of Schools, Altoona, Pa.
Hess, Clarke F., Marshall College, Huntington, W.Va.
Hess, Glenn C., 44 W. Wheeling St., Washington, Pa.
Hesse, Alexander N., 90 Salisbury Ave., Garden City, L.I., N.Y.
Hetrick, Dr. J. B., Dept. of Educ., Edinboro State Col., Edinboro, Pa.
Hetzel, Walter L., Superintendent of Schools, Ames, Iowa
Heuer, Josephine C., 8444 Edna St., St. Louis, Mo.
Heusner, William W., Michigan State University, East Lansing, Mich.
Heussman, John W., Concordia Seminary, Springfield, Ill.
Hickey, Bernard, 7 Digren Rd., Natick, Mass.
Hickner, Marybelle R., 1515½ Main St., Menomonie, Wis.
Hicks, Mrs. Aline Black, 812 Lexington St., Norfolk, Va.
Hicks, Samuel I., Inst. of Educ., Ahmadu Bello Univ., Zaria, Nigeria
Hicks, William R., Southern University, Baton Rouge, La.
Hidy, Mrs. Elizabeth Willson, Box 287, Gila Bend, Ariz.
Hiebert, Noble C., 504 Madison Ave., Plainfield, N.J.
Hieronymus, Albert N., East Hall, State Univ. of Iowa, Iowa City, Iowa
Hiers, Mrs. Turner M., 5661 S.W. Second Court, Fort Lauderdale, Fla.
Higdon, Claude J., 1106 S. Harvard Blvd., Los Angeles, Calif.
Higgins, Mrs. Ardis, 1527 E. Mountain Dr., Santa Barbara, Calif.
Higgins, F. Edward, 9524 S. Keeler Ave., Oak Lawn, Ill.
Hightower, Emory A., 14 W. 64th St., New York, N.Y.
Hilgard, Ernest R., Dept. of Psych., Stanford University, Stanford, Calif.
Hill, Alberta D., Dept. of H. Econ., Iowa State University, Ames, Iowa
Hill, Charles E., 529 Fifth St., S.W., Rochester, Minn.
Hill, George E., Dept. of Educ., Ohio University, Athens, Ohio
Hill, Ione A., State Department of Education, Baton Rouge, La.
Hill, Joseph K., Downstate Medical Center, Brooklyn, N.Y.
Hill, Katherine E., Press 23, New York Univ., Washington Sq., New York, N.Y.
Hill, Robert A., 5609 Ruth Rd., Camp Springs, Md.
Hill, Suzanne D., Louisiana State University, New Orleans, La.
Hillerich, Robert L., 950 Huber Lane, Glenview, Ill.
Hillesheim, Rev. Francis E., 1130 W. Bridge St., Wausau, Wis.
Hillson, Maurie, 1208 Emerson Ave., Teaneck, N.J.
Himelrick, John B., Sr., State Dept. of Educ., Charleston, W. Va.
Himler, Leonard E., 1225 Fair Oaks Pkwy., Ann Arbor, Mich.
Hinds, Jean, 1541 Campus Rd., Los Angeles, Calif.
Hinds, Lillian Ruth, 13855 Superior Rd., Cleveland, Ohio
Hindsman, Edwin, S.W. Educ. Dev. Corp., Commodore Perry Hotel, Austin, Tex.
Hines, Vynce A., 1220 S.W. Ninth Rd., Gainesville, Fla.
Hintz, Edward R., Westwood Heights Schools, Flint, Mich.
Hipkins, Wendell C., 1311 Delaware Ave., S.W., Washington, D.C.
Hirst, Wilma E., 3458 Green Valley Rd., Cheyenne, Wyo.
Hitchcock, Catharine, 1837 E. Erie Ave., Lorain, Ohio
Hites, Christopher, 302 Portola Rd., Portola Valley, Calif.
Hitt, Harold H., 802 Lawson St., Midland, Tex.
Hittinger, Martha S., 12345 E. Beverly Dr., Whittier, Calif.
Ho, Thomas C. K., 72 Distler Ave., West Caldwell, N.J.
Hoagland, Robert M., 627 Houseman, La Canada, Calif.
Hoak, Duane C., 1031 Newbury St., Toledo, Ohio
Hobbie, Katherine E., State University College, Oneonta, N.Y.
Hobbs, Billy S., White House High School, White House, Tenn.
Hobbs, Earl W., Renton Sch. Dist., 1525 Fourth Ave., N., Renton, Wash.
Hochstetler, Ruth, 225 S. Nichols, Muncie, Ind.
Hock, Louise E., Sch. of Educ., New York Univ., New York, N.Y.
Hodge, Harry F., P.O. Box 940, State University, Ark.
Hodge, William Carey, 306 S. Forest, Carbondale, Ill.

MEMBERS OF THE NATIONAL SOCIETY   li

Hodges, Lawrence W., University of Montana, Missoula, Mont.
Hodges, Richard E., Grad. Sch. of Educ., Univ. of Chicago, Chicago, Ill.
Hodges, Ruth Hall, Morris Brown College, Atlanta, Ga.
Hodgins, George W., Paramus High School, Paramus, N.J.
Hodnett, Ruth Germann, Scott, Foresman & Co., Chicago, Ill.
Hoekstra, S. Robert, 2215 Sylvan Ave., S.E., Grand Rapids, Mich.
Hoerauf, William E., 19990 Beaufait, Harper Woods, Mich.
Hoerger, Mrs. Lois S., 9001 S. Laflin St., Chicago, Ill.
Hoerning, Duane L., R.R. # 1, Brussells, Wis.
Hoffman, Carl B., Tenafly Public Schls., 27 W. Clinton Ave., Tenafly, N.J.
Hoffman, Matthew R., 180 Ridgeway Ave., Rochester, N.Y.
Hofstrand, John M., USAID/HR, Santo Domingo, Dominican Rep.
Hohl, George W., Superintendent of Schools, Waterloo, Iowa
Holda, Frederick W., 26 Hampden Rd., Monson, Mass.
Holden, A. John, Jr., 19-A Charlesbank Rd., Newton, Mass.
Holden, Marion S., 1026 E. Washington St., Iowa City, Iowa
Holland, Benjamin F., Sutton Hall, University of Texas, Austin, Tex.
Holland, Donald F., 7251 N. Bell Ave., Chicago, Ill.
Holliday, Jay Newton, R. 1, Box 405, Ontario, Ore.
Holloway, George E., Jr., State Univ. of New York, Buffalo, N.Y.
Holm, Joy A., 104 Eisenhower Dr., Bloomington, Ill.
Holman, W. Earl, Jackson High School, 544 Wildwood Ave., Jackson, Mich
Holmes, Daniel L., Willett School, Attleboro, Mass.
Holmes, Emma E., California State Col., Fullerton, Calif.
Holmes, Robert W., Windham College, Putney, Vt.
Holmquist, Emily, Indiana Univ. School of Nursing, Indianapolis, Ind.
Holt, Charles C., 228 S. St. Joseph St., South Bend, Ind.
Holton, Samuel M., University of North Carolina, Chapel Hill, N.C.
Homer, Francis R., 4800 Conshohocken Ave., Philadelphia, Pa.
Honeychuck, Joseph M., 2808 Parker Ave., Silver Spring, Md.
Hood, Edwin M., 19 Seneca Ave., White Plains, N.Y.
Hood, Evans C., Superintendent of Schools, Palestine, Tex.
Hood, W. R., 2627—29th St., S.W., Calgary, Alba., Canada
Hooker, Clifford P., University of Minnesota, Minneapolis, Minn.
Hooper, George J., 3631 S. Yorktown, Tulsa, Okla.
Hoops, Robert C., 76 Branch Ave., Red Bank, N.J.
Hoover, Erna B., Tennessee A. & I. State Univ., Nashville, Tenn.
Hoover, Louis H., 2304 Tenth Ave. So., Broadview, Ill.
Hopkins, Everett H., 2016 Campus Dr., Durham, N.C.
Hopkins, Monroe, Hannibal-LaGrange College, Hannibal, Mo.
Hopmann, Robert P., 210 N. Broadway, St. Louis, Mo.
Hoppock, Anne, State Department of Education, Trenton, N.J.
Horn, Ernest, East Hall, State University of Iowa, Iowa City, Iowa
Horn, Ernest W., Indiana University, Bloomington, Ind.
Horn, Margaret, Concordia College, St. Paul, Minn.
Horn, Thomas D., Sutton Hall, University of Texas, Austin, Texas
Hornback, Mrs. May, Rt. 1, Old Sauk Rd., Middleton, Wis.
Hornburg, Mabel C., 118 Champlain Ave., Ticonderoga, N.Y.
Horning, Leora N., University of Nebraska, Lincoln, Neb.
Horrocks, John E., Ohio State University, Columbus, Ohio
Horsman, Ralph D., Supt., Mt. Lebanon Public Schools, Pittsburgh, Pa.
Horvat, John J., 825 East 8th Ave., Bloomington, Ind.
Horwich, Frances R., 400 E. Randolph St., Chicago, Ill.
Hosford, Marian H., St. John's Univ., New York, N.Y.
Hoskins, Charles W., 822 Gilman St., Wichita, Kan.
Hoskins, Glen C., Dept. of Educ., Southern Methodist Univ., Dallas, Texas
Hotaling, Mrs. Muriel P., 140 Jensen Rd. So., Vestal, N.Y.
Hough, John M., Jr., Mars Hill College, Mars Hill, N.C.
Hough, Robert E., Arthur L. Johnson Regional High School, Clark, N.J.
Houghton, Charles J., 7401 S.W. 72nd Court, Miami, Fla.
Houghton, John J., Superintendent of Schools, Ferndale, Mich.

Houlahan, F. J., Catholic University of America, Washington, D.C.
Houle, Cyril O., Dept. of Educ., University of Chicago, Chicago, Ill.
Householder, Daniel L., Sch. of Tech., Purdue University, Lafayette, Ind.
Houston, James J., Jr., Patterson State Col., Wayne, N.J.
Houston, John, Superintendent of Schools, Medford, Mass.
Houston, W. Robert, Col. of Educ., Mich. State University, East Lansing, Mich.
Houts, Earl, Westminster College, New Wilmington, Pa.
Hovet, Kenneth O., University of Maryland, College Park, Md.
Howard, Alexander H., Jr., Central Washington State Col., Ellensburg, Wash.
Howard, Daniel D., Pestalozzi-Froebel Tchrs. College, Chicago, Ill.
Howard, Elizabeth Z., Col. of Educ., Univ. of Rochester, Rochester, N.Y.
Howard, Glenn W., Queens College, Flushing, N.Y.
Howard, Harry, Box 765, Hillsborough, N.C.
Howd, M. Curtis, 200 Winthrop Rd., Muncie, Ind.
Howe, Walter A., 6840 Eastern Ave., N.W., Washington, D.C.
Howell, Mrs. Mary N., Home Ec. Dept., Mars Hill College, Mars Hill, N.C.
Howell, Wallace J., Penfield Senior High School, Penfield, N.Y.
Howlett, Dorn, R.D. 1, Edinboro, Pa.
Howsam, Robert B., University of Houston, Houston, Tex.
Hoyle, Dorothy, Temple University, Philadelphia, Pa.
Hoyt, Cyril J., Burton Hall, Univ. of Minnesota, Minneapolis, Minn.
Hoyt, Donald P., Box 168, Iowa City, Iowa
Hubbard, Ben, Illinois State University, Normal, Ill.
Huber, H. Ronald, 723 Portland Ave., Huntingdon, Pa.
Hubert, Frank W. R., Texas A. & M. Univ., College Station, Texas
Hudson, Bruce M., 11020 Cranston Ave., Livonia, Mich.
Hudson, Douglas, 392 Dohner Dr., Wadsworth, Ohio
Hudson, L. P., 1225 Oakwood St., Bedford, Va.
Hudson, Robert I., University of Manitoba, Winnipeg, Manitoba, Canada
Hudson, Wilburn, Cordova High School, Cordova, Ala.
Hudspeth, DeLayne, Syracuse University, Syracuse, N.Y.
Huebner, Dwayne E., Tchrs. Col., Columbia University, New York, N.Y.
Huebner, Mildred H., So. Connecticut State Col., New Haven, Conn.
Huebner, Ralph R., 10012 S. Morgan St., Chicago, Ill.
Huehn, Kermith S., Superintendent of County Schools, Eldora, Iowa
Huelsman, Charles B., Jr., 203 Selby Blvd., West, Worthington, Ohio
Huff, Jack F., 9030 Glorieta Ct., Elk Grove, Calif.
Hufford, G. N., Dept. of Educ., Lewis College, Lockport, Ill.
Hug, John W., 2090 Frank Rd., Columbus, Ohio
Hughes, Larry W., Superintendent of Schools, Crestline, Ohio
Hughes, McDonald, 1732–32nd Ave., Tuscaloosa, Ala.
Hughes, Thomas G., Ventura College, Ventura, Calif.
Hughes, Thomas M., 990 Brower Rd., Memphis, Tenn.
Hughes, Vergil H., San Jose State College, San Jose, Calif.
Hughes, Msgr. William A., Supt., Diocese of Youngstown, Youngstown, Ohio
Hughson, Arthur, 131 East 21st St., Brooklyn, N.Y.
Hulbert, Dolores S., 16301 Lassen St., Sepulveda, Calif.
Hull, J. H., Superintendent of Schools, Torrance, Calif.
Hull, John W., Supt., Hernando County Schools, Brooksville, Fla.
Hulteen, Curtis D., # 39 Hilltop Park, R.R. # 2, Bloomington, Ill.
Hultgren, Robert B., 708 Tana Lane, Joliet, Ill.
Hult, Esther, State College of Iowa, Cedar Falls, Iowa
Humelsine, Martha, Roberts Wesleyan College, North Chili, N.Y.
Hummel, Mrs. Leonore B., Paterson State College, Wayne, N.J.
Humphrey, Charles F., 6001 Berkeley Dr., Berkeley, Mo.
Humphrey, G. C., 316 Fraser Dr. East, Mesa, Ariz.
Hunkins, Francis P., University of Washington, Seattle, Wash.
Hunsicker, C. L., Mansfield State College, Mansfield, Pa.
Hunt, Dorothy D., 2000 East 46th St., N., Kansas City, Mo.
Hunt, Herold C., Grad. Sch. of Educ., Harvard University, Cambridge, Mass.
Hunt, William A., Dept. of Psych., Northwestern University, Evanston, Ill.

Hunter, Eugenia, Woman's Col., Univ. of North Carolina, Greensboro, N.C.
Hunter, James J., Jr., San Diego State College, San Diego, Calif.
Hunter, Robert W., Grambling College, Grambling, La.
* Huntington, Albert H., 736 Fairview Ave., Webster Groves, Mo.
Huntington, John F., Miami Univ., Oxford, Ohio
Hurd, Blair E., 4900 Heatherdale Lane, Carmichael, Calif.
Hurd, Paul DeH., Sch. of Educ., Stanford University, Stanford, Calif.
Hurlburt, Lydia Delpha, 311 Richmond, S.E., Salem, Ore.
Hurt, E. L., Jr., Gragg Junior High School, Memphis, Tenn.
Hurt, Mary Lee, Office of Education, Dept. of H.E.W., Washington, D.C.
Husk, William L., Dept. of Educ., Univ. of Louisville, Louisville, Ky.
Husmann, John L., 256 Ash St., Crystal Lake, Ill.
Huss, Francis C., 4655 Parker Rd., Florissant, Mo.
Husson, Chesley H., Husson College, 157 Park St., Bangor, Me.
Husted, Inez M., P.O. Box 1165, Kingston, Pa.
Husted, Vernon L., Supt., Armstrong Twp. High School, Armstrong, Ill.
Huston, Michael Lynn, 824 Bethany Rd., Burbank, Calif.
Hutchison, James M., 26904 Grayslake Rd., Palos Verdes Peninsula, Calif.
Hutson, Percival W., University of Pittsburgh, Pittsburgh, Pa.
Hutto, Jerome A., Los Angeles State College, Los Angeles, Calif.
Hutton, Harry K., Pennsylvania State University, University Park, Pa.
Hyatt, Aaron, 680 Ashtabula Court, Columbus, Ohio
Hyer, Anna L., 7613 Wiley Dr., Lorton, Va.
Hyman, Ronald, Rutgers University, New Brunswick, N.J.
Hyram, George H., 4092 Fieldstone Dr., Florissant, Mo.

Iannacone, George, Supt. of Schools, Palisades Park, N.J.
Iannaccone, Laurence, 10 Donnybrook Dr., Demarest, N.J.
Iglesias-Borges, Ramon, P.O. Box 226, San Lorenzo, Puerto Rico
Ihrman, Donald L., Superintendent of Schools, Holland, Mich.
Ikenberry, Stanley O., West Virginia University, Morgantown, W.Va.
Ilowit, Roy, C. W. Post College, Greenvale, L.I., N.Y.
Imbriano, Louis A., Revere Public Schools, Revere, Mass.
Imes, Orley B., 3985 La Cresenta Rd., El Sobrante, Calif.
Imhoff, Myrtle M., California State College, Fullerton, Calif.
Inabnit, Darrell J., Sacramento State College, Sacramento, Calif.
Incardona, Joseph S., 325 Busti Ave., Buffalo, N.Y.
Ingebritson, Kasper I., 2790 Sunny Grove Ave., Arcata, Calif.
Ingle, Robert, 5321 N. Hollywood, Whitefish Bay, Wis.
Ingram, Margaret H., East Carolina College, Greenville, N.C.
Ingrelli, Anthony V., University of Wisconsin-Milwaukee, Milwaukee, Wis.
Inlow, Gail M., Sch. of Educ., Northwestern University, Evanston, Ill.
Inman, Mary Frances, 47 Warner St., Chico, Calif.
Inskeep, James E., Jr., San Diego State College, San Diego, Calif.
Ireland, Robert S., Superintendent of Schools, Monument St., Concord, Mass.
Irish, Elizabeth, University of California, Santa Barbara, Goleta, Calif.
Irizarry, Casandra Rivera de, 1628 Ave. Central, Caparra Terrace, Puerto Rico
Irsfeld, H. L., Superintendent of Schools, Mineral Wells, Tex.
Irving, James Lee, 5713 Ogontz Ave., Philadelphia, Pa.
Irwin, Alice M., Dept. of Spec. Classes, Public Schls., New Bedford, Mass.
Isaacs, Ann F., Natl. Assn. Gifted Children, Cincinnati, Ohio
Isacksen, Roy O., 783 E. Nevada, St. Paul, Minn.
Isenberg, Robert M., 3117 Helsel Dr., Silver Spring, Md.
Ishimatsu, Tomiye, Col. of Nursing, Univ. of Utah, Salt Lake City, Utah
Israel, Benjamin L., 711 Shore Rd., Long Beach, N.Y.
Ives, Josephine Piekarz, New York University, New York, N.Y.
Ivie, Claude M., Div. of Curric., State Dept. of Educ., Atlanta, Ga.
Ivins, George H., Roosevelt Univ., 430 S. Michigan Ave., Chicago, Ill.
Ivins, Wilson H., Col. of Educ., Univ. of New Mexico, Albuquerque, N.M.
Izzo, Raymond J., 12 Girard Rd., Winchester, Mass.

Jacklin, William, 411 E. 17th St., Lombard, Ill.
Jackson, Bryant H., Illinois State University, Normal, Ill.
Jackson, Franklin J., P.O. Box 132, Eau Claire, Mich.
Jackson, Philip W., Dept. of Educ., Univ. of Chicago, Chicago, Ill.
Jackson, Ronald, Frankfurt International Sch., Oberursel, Germany
Jackson, Thomas A., Florida A. & M. Univ., Tallahassee, Fla.
Jacobi, Mrs. Eileen M., Adelphi Univ., Garden City, L.I., N.Y.
Jacobs, J., 26141 Schoolcraft Rd., Detroit, Mich.
Jacobs, John F., 12299 Univ. Stat., Gainesville, Fla.
Jacobs, Robert, American Embassy, APO San Francisco, Calif.
Jaeckel, Solomon, 13701 Bracken St., Pacoima, Calif.
Jaeger, Alan Warren, 10220 Dale Dr., San Jose, Calif.
Jaeger, Eloise M., 158 Morris Gym, Univ. of Minnesota, Minneapolis, Minn.
Jaeger, Herman F., Box 10, Grandview, Wash.
Jaffarian, Sara, 251 Waltham St., Lexington, Mass.
Jahns, Irwin R., Florida State Univ., Tallahassee, Fla.
James, Mrs. Bernice O., 822 Avenue L., Galveston, Tex.
James, C. Rodney, 1687 Guilford Rd., Columbus, Ohio
James, Carl A., Superintendent of Schools, Emporia, Kan.
James, Herbert C., 330 E. Torrence Rd., Columbus, Ohio
James, Mrs. Jo Nell, William Carey Col., Hattiesburg, Miss.
James, Louise, 4015 Lemon St., Riverside, Calif.
* James, Preston E., Dept. of Geog., Syracuse University, Syracuse, N.Y.
James, Viola, Administration Library, 1800 Grand Ave., Des Moines, Iowa
James, W. Raymond, 9 Bugbee Rd., Oneonta, N.Y.
Jameson, Sanford C., Reg. Dir., Col. Entr. Exam. Brd., Evanston, Ill.
Jansen, Udo H., Tchrs. Col., Univ. of Nebraska, Lincoln, Neb.
* Jansen, William, 900 Palmer Rd., Bronxville, N.Y.
Jansic, Anthony F., Educ. Clinic, City College of New York, New York, N.Y.
Jardine, Alex, 2105—19th Ave., Greeley, Colo.
Jarvie, Lawrence L., Pres., Fashion Inst. of Tech., New York, N.Y.
Jarvis, Galen M., 9040 Kostner Rd., Skokie, Ill.
Jason, Hilliard, Col. of Med., Michigan State Univ., East Lansing, Mich.
Jaspen, Nathan, New York University, New York, N.Y.
Jeffers, Jay W., 931 Franklin Ave., Las Vegas, Nev.
Jefferson, James L., 866 Lincoln St., S.W., Birmingham, Ala.
Jeffries, Thomas S., P.O. Box 26, Lebanon Junction, Ky.
Jelinek, James J., Col. of Educ., Arizona State University, Tempe, Ariz.
Jellins, Miriam H., 2849 Dale Creek Dr., N.W., Atlanta, Ga.
Jenkins, Clara Barnes, St. Paul's College, Lawrenceville, Va.
Jenkins, David S., Supt., Anne Arundel County Schools, Annapolis, Md.
Jenkins, Ernest W., Box 70, Fullerton, Neb.
Jenkins, James J., University of Minnesota, Minneapolis, Minn.
Jenkins, Jerry Allen, Sch. of Educ., Indiana State Univ., Terre Haute, Ind.
Jenkins, Offa Lou, Marshall University, Huntington, W.Va.
Jenkins, Walter D., 712 Cactus Lane, Las Vegas, Nev.
Jenks, William F., Holy Redeemer College, Washington, D.C.
Jenness, L. S., Forest View High School, Arlington Heights, Ill.
Jensen, Arthur M., Tuttle School, 1042—18th Ave., Minneapolis, Minn.
Jensen, Arthur R., University of California, Berkeley, Calif.
Jensen, Esther M., University of Wisconsin, Milwaukee, Wis.
Jensen, Gale E., 3055 Lakewood Dr., Ann Arbor, Mich.
Jensen, Grant W., South High School, 1101 Planz Rd., Bakersfield, Calif.
Jensen, John A., Col. of Educ., Univ. of Rochester, Rochester, N.Y.
Jenson, Dean, Bowling Green State University, Bowling Green, Ohio
Jenson, T. J., 1024 Lyn Rd., Bowling Green, Ohio
Jeremiah, James T., Pres., Cedarville Col., Cedarville, Ohio
Jess, C. Donald, Superintendent of Schools, Bergenfield, N.J.
Jetton, Clyde T., 720 Amherst, Abilene, Tex.
Jewell, R. Ewart, Superintendent of Schools, 547 Wall St., Bend, Ore.
Jex, Frank B., Dept. of Educ. Psych., Univ. of Utah, Salt Lake City, Utah

Jinks, Elsie H., 1597 Lochmoor Blvd., Grosse Pointe Woods, Mich.
Jobe, Mrs. Mildred, Moffat County High School, Craig, Colo.
John, Martha A., Sch. of Educ., Boston Univ., Boston, Mass.
Johns, Edward B., Dept. of P.E., University of California, Los Angeles, Calif.
Johns, O. D., Col. of Educ., Univ. of Oklahoma, Norman, Okla.
Johns, Mrs. Thomas L., 9000 Breezewood Ter., Greenbelt, Md.
Johnsen, E. Peter, Col. of Educ., Univ. of Rochester, Rochester, N.Y.
Johnson, B. Lamar, Sch. of Educ., Univ. of California, Los Angeles, Calif.
Johnson, Calvin T., Mt. Baker Junior-Senior High School, Deming, Wash.
Johnson, Claudine, 112-39—175th St., Jamaica, N.Y.
Johnson, Dale L., Dept. of Psych., University of Houston, Houston, Tex.
Johnson, Mrs. Dorothea N., 317 Whitman Blvd., Elyria, Ohio
Johnson, Mrs. Dorothy K., 7 Dalston Circle, Lynbrook, N.Y.
Johnson, Douglas A., 3750 Esperanzo Dr., Sacramento, Calif.
Johnson, Eleanor M., Box 360, Middletown, Conn.
Johnson, G. Orville, 805 S. Crouse Ave., Syracuse, N.Y.
Johnson, George L., Lincoln University of Missouri, Jefferson City, Mo.
Johnson, Gladys V., 3229—4th Ave., South, Great Falls, Mont.
Johnson, Harry C., Duluth Branch, Univ. of Minnesota, Duluth, Minn.
Johnson, Homer M., Dept. of Educ. Admin., Utah State Univ., Logan, Utah
Johnson, Irwin T., Col. of Educ., Univ. of Wyoming, Laramie, Wyo.
Johnson, J. O., Central Jr. H.S., Rochester, Minn.
Johnson, Jasper H., Whitworth College, Spokane, Wash.
Johnson, John L., 805 S. Crouse Ave., Syracuse, N.Y.
Johnson, Leonard E., Prin., Bugbee Sch., West Hartford, Conn.
Johnson, Mrs. Lois S., 4454 Hillcrest Dr., Madison, Wis.
Johnson, Lois V., California State Col., Los Angeles, Calif.
Johnson, Loren W., 37 Eglantine, Pennington, N.C.
Johnson, Margaret E., Alpine School District, American Fork, Utah
Johnson, Mrs. Marjorie Seddon, 61 Grove Ave., Flourtown, Pa.
Johnson, Mrs. Mary Jane, 275 Clinton Ave., Brooklyn, N.Y.
Johnson, Olive Lucille, 1925 Thornwood Ave., Wilmette, Ill.
Johnson, Paul E., Livonia Public Schools, Livonia, Mich.
Johnson, Paul O., Salem H.S., Geremonty Dr., Salem, N.H.
Johnson, Philip E., Coffin School, Brunswick, Me.
Johnson, Robert Leonard, 2500 South 118th St., West Allis, Wis.
Johnson, Robert S., 111 Richland Dr., Pullman, Wash.
Johnson, Roger E., 218 Park Ridge Ave., Temple Terrace, Fla.
* Johnson, Roy Ivan, 2333 Southwest Eighth Dr., Gainesville, Fla.
Johnson, Theodore D., 5236 N. Bernard St., Chicago, Ill.
Johnson, Valdimar K., University of Victoria, Victoria, B.C., Canada
Johnson, Walter F., Col. of Educ., Michigan State Univ., East Lansing, Mich.
Johnson, Walter R., Libertyville High School, Libertyville, Ill.
Johnson, Wilma L., University of Arizona, Tucson, Ariz.
Johnston, Aaron M., Col. of Educ., Univ. of Tennessee, Knoxville, Tenn.
Johnston, Edgar G., 2301 Vinewood Ave., Ann Arbor, Mich.
Johnston, Lillian B., 538 W. Vernon Ave., Phoenix, Ariz.
Johnston, William R., 1222 Salisbury Ln., Whitewater, Wis.
Joll, Leonard W., 144 Mulberry St., Plantsville, Conn.
Jonas, Russell E., Black Hills Teachers College, Spearfish, S.D.
Jones, Clyde A., University of Connecticut, Storrs, Conn.
Jones, Daisy M., Sch. of Educ., Arizona State University, Tempe, Ariz.
Jones, Dilys M., 316 S. Fayette St., Shippensburg, Pa.
Jones, Donald W., 508 W. North St., Muncie, Ind.
Jones, Elvet Glyn, Western Washington State Col., Bellingham, Wash.
Jones, Henry W., Western Washington State College, Bellingham, Wash.
Jones, Hildred B., Ohio Northern University, Ada, Ohio
Jones, Howard Robert, State University of Iowa, Iowa City, Iowa
Jones, Kenneth G., State University College, Oswego, N.Y.
Jones, Lloyd Meredith, State University of New York, Farmingdale, N.Y.
Jones, Lowell B., Anaheim Union High School, Curric. Lab., Anaheim, Calif.

Jones, Mary Elliott, 18 Engle St., Tenafly, N.J.
Jones, Mildred L., 43-B Escondido Village, Stanford, Calif.
Jones, Nevin, Box 121, Shannon, Ga.
Jones, Olwen M., Fox Run Lane, Greenwich, Conn.
Jones, Richard N., Carroll Rd., Monkton, Md.
Jones, Richard V., Jr., Stanislaus State College, Turlock, Calif.
Jones, Robert W., 9400 Biddulph Rd., Cleveland, Ohio
Jones, Robert William, Lincoln Community High School, Lincoln, Ill.
Jones, Ronald D., Urbana College, College Way, Urbana, Ohio
Jones, Tudor M., 309 Taurus Ave., Oakland, Calif.
Jones, Vyron Lloyd, R. 7, Box 346, Terre Haute, Ind.
Jones, Wendell P., Sch. of Educ., Univ. of California, Los Angeles, Calif.
Jones, William E., California State College, Hayward, Calif.
Joneson, Della, 1040 State St., Ottawa, Ill.
Jonsson, Harold, Div. of Educ., San Francisco State Col., San Francisco, Calif.
Jordan, A. B., 5811 Riverview Blvd., St. Louis, Mo.
Jordan, Benjamin W., Educ. Bldg., Wayne State Univ., Detroit, Mich.
Jordan, Beth C., Virginia Polytechnic Institute, Blacksburg, Va.
Jordan, Lawrence V., West Virginia State College, Institute, W.Va.
Jordan, Ralph, State University College, Brockport, N.Y.
Joselyn, Edwin G., 4068 Hampshire Ave., N., Minneapolis, Minn.
Joy, Donald M., Light & Life Press, Winona, Ind.
Joyce, Bruce R., 27 Wood Hill Rd., Wilton, Conn.
Joyce, James M., Roncalli High School, Aberdeen, S.D.
Joyner, Judith R., University of South Carolina, Columbia, S.C.
Juan, K. C., Fisk University, Nashville, Tenn.
Judenfriend, Harold, 363 Beech Spring Rd., South Orange, N.J.
Julstrom, Eva, 7647 Colfax Ave., Chicago, Ill.
June, Elmer D., 619 Bamford Rd., Cherry Hill, N.J.
Jung, Christian W., Sch. of Educ., Indiana University, Bloomington, Ind.
Junge, Charlotte W., Col. of Educ., Wayne University, Detroit, Mich.
Junker, Margaret, 9138 S. Claremont Ave., Chicago, Ill.
Jurjevich, J. C., Jr., 1844 74th Ave., Elmwood Park, Ill.
Justman, Joseph, Sch. of Educ., Fordham Univ., New York, N.Y.
Justman, Joseph, Dept. of Educ., Brooklyn College, Brooklyn, N.Y.
Juvancic, William A., Eli Whitney Elem. Sch., Chicago, Ill.

Kaar, Mrs. Galeta M., 7050 Ridge Ave., Chicago, Ill.
* Kaback, Goldie Ruth, 375 Riverside Dr., New York, N.Y.
Kabrud, Margaret J., Univ. of North Dakota, Ellendale Cent., Ellendale, N.D.
Kaffer, Roger L., St. Charles Borromeo Seminary, Lockport, Ill.
Kahler, Carol, St. Louis University, St. Louis, Mo.
Kahn, Albert S., Sch. of Educ., Boston University, Boston, Mass.
Kahnk, Donald L., 720 East Ninth St., Fremont, Neb.
Kahrs, Mary V., Mankato State College, Mankato, Minn.
Kairies, Eugene B., Jr., 1263 Fifield Pl., St. Paul, Minn.
Kaiser, Louis H., Arizona State University, Tempe, Ariz.
Kalina, David L., 288 Bay 38 St., Brooklyn, N.Y.
Kalish, Thomas F., Marshall Public Schools, Marshall, Wis.
Kallenbach, W. Warren, San Jose State College, San Jose, Calif.
Kalme, Albert P., West Virginia State Col., Institute, W.Va.
Kandyba, Bernard S., 9403 N. Parkside Dr., Des Plaines, Ill.
Kane, Elmer R., 7530 Maryland Ave., Clayton, Mo.
Kane, James L., Stratford School, Garden City, L.I., N.Y.
Kantor, Bernard R., 117 S. Poinsettia Pl., Los Angeles, Calif.
Kaplan, Lawrence, 65 Clover Ln., Lido Beach, N.Y.
Kaplan, Louis, 111 Via Monte de Oro, Redondo Beach, Calif.
Karabinus, Robert A., Col. of Educ., Univ. of Arizona, Tucson, Arizona
Karaginanis, Leslie D., Dalhousie Univ., Halifax, N.S., Canada
Karlin, Robert, Dept. of Educ., Queens College, Flushing, N.Y.
Karlsen, Bjorn, Sonoma State Col., Rohnert Park, Calif.

Karr, Johnston T., Dept. of Pub. Instr., State House, Indianapolis, Ind.
Kasdon, Lawrence M., 13 W. 13th St., New York, N.Y.
Kass, Corrine E., S608—429 N. St., S.W., Washington, D.C.
Kata, Joseph J., Redbank Valley Joint Schools, New Bethlehem, Pa.
Katenkamp, Theodore W., Jr., 9128 Bengal Rd., Randallstown, Md.
Katz, Mrs. Florine, Educ. Clinic, City College, New York, N.Y.
Katz, Joseph, University of British Columbia, Vancouver, B.C., Canada
Kauffman, Merle M., Col. of Educ., Bradley University, Peoria, Ill.
Kaufman, Jennie M., 21 N. Fourth St., Grand Haven, Mich.
Kaulfers, Walter V., University of Illinois, Urbana, Ill.
Kavanaugh, Anne, 2521 E. Second St., Bloomington, Ind.
Kavanaugh, J. Keith, 1639 So. Maple Ave., Berwyn, Ill.
Kawalek, Thaddens P., 700 N. LaGrande Rd., La Grange Park, Ill.
Kaya, Esin, New York University, Washington Sq., New York, N.Y.
Kean, John M., Sch. of Educ., Univ. of Wisconsin, Madison, Wis.
Kearl, Jennie W., State Department of Education, Salt Lake City, Utah
Kearney, George G., Rt. No. 1, Box 1108, Morgan Hill, Calif.
Keck, Winston B., Westfield State College, Westfield, Mass.
Keefer, Daryle E., Southern Illinois University, Carbondale, Ill.
Kehas, Chris D., Claremont Graduate School, Claremont, Calif.
Keilty, Joseph, 128 Scott Ave., Watertown, Conn.
Keislar, Evan R., University of California, Los Angeles, Calif.
Keleher, Gregory C., Dept. of Educ., St. Anselm's College, Manchester, N.H.
* Keliher, Alice V., Wheelock College, Boston, Mass.
Kelleher, William J., Hirsch High School, Chicago, Ill.
Keller, Carol, 994 S.W. 16th Ave., Gainesville, Fla.
* Keller, Franklin J., 333 E. Mosholu Pkwy., New York, N.Y.
Keller, Horace T., Glassboro State College, Glassboro, N.J.
Keller, Robert J., Col. of Educ., Univ. of Minnesota, Minneapolis, Minn.
Kelley, Claude, Col. of Educ., University of Oklahoma, Norman, Okla.
Kelley, H. Paul, University of Texas, Austin, Tex.
Kelley, William F., S.J., Creighton Univ., Omaha, Neb.
Kellogg, E. G., Superintendent of Schools, West Allis, Wis.
Kelly, Dean, 175 Tamarack Dr., Berea, Ohio
Kelly, Edward J., 2109 Buena Vista Dr., Greeley, Colo.
Kelly, James A., 101 Borromeo Ave., Placentia, Calif.
Kelly, John W., 27 Earle Pl., New Rochelle, N.Y.
Kelly, Preston W., Holt, Rinehart & Winston, Inc., New York, N.Y.
Kelly, Shaun, Jr., 333 E. 55th St., New York, N.Y.
Kelner, Bernard G., 1804 Ashurst Rd., Philadelphia, Pa.
Kelsey, Roger R., Educ. Annex, University of Maryland, College Park, Md.
Kemp, Edward L., Sch. of Educ., New York Univ., New York, N.Y.
Kennedy, Anna Helen, 101 N. Grand Ave., Pasadena, Calif.
Kennedy, Clephane A., Benjamin Franklin University, Washington, D.C.
Kennedy, D. L., Caddo Parish Schools, Shreveport, La.
Kennedy, K. M., Southern Missionary Col., Collegedale, Tenn.
Kentner, Harold M., Rochester Institute of Technology, Rochester, N.Y.
Keohane, Robert E., Shimer College, Mt. Carroll, Ill.
Keough, William F., Jr., Superintendent of Schools, Burlington, Vt.
Kephart, N. C., Dept. of Educ., Purdue University, Lafayette, Ind.
Kephart, Ruby G., 562 W. Spring Ave., Lima, Ohio
Keppers, George L., University of New Mexico, Albuquerque, N.M.
Kerelejza, Joan D., Farmington Public Schools, Farmington, Conn.
Kerns, LeRoy, Lab. Sch., Colorado State College, Greeley, Colo.
Kerr, Everett F., Superintendent of Schools, Blue Island, Ill.
Kerr, Margaret, 7558 Drexel Dr., University City, Mo.
Kerr, R. D., 113 Hill Hall, Univ. of Missouri, Columbia, Mo.
Kerst, Marjorie, Wisconsin State University, Stevens Point, Wis.
Keske, Eldora E., 2329 Chalet Gardens Rd., Madison, Wis.
Kessler, Clifton L., 1909 Buffalo Rd., West Des Moines, Iowa
Kester, Scott W., Oklahoma Baptist Univ., Shawnee, Okla.

MEMBERS OF THE NATIONAL SOCIETY

Ketcherside, William J., Central Missouri State Col., Warrensburg, Mo.
Keuscher, Robert E., 1100 Glendon Ave., Los Angeles, Calif.
Khouri, John W., Superintendent of Schools, Bethlehem, Pa.
Kiah, Calvin L., Savannah State College, Savannah, Ga.
Kicklighter, Ray S., Resch. Physicist, Eastman Kodak, Rochester, N.Y.
Kidder, William W., 216 Walton Ave., South Orange, N.J.
Kilbourn, Mrs. Robert W., 4902 Argyle St., Dearborn, Mich.
Kilburn, H. Parley, Evening Div., Bakersfield College, Bakersfield, Calif.
Kilpatrick, Arnold R., Pres., Northwestern State Col., Natchitoches, La.
Kilpatrick, Joel Fred, Western Carolina College, Cullowhee, N.C.
Kincaid, Marylou, 2029 N. Farwell Ave., Milwaukee, Wis.
Kincheloe, James B., University of Kentucky, Lexington, Ky.
Kind, Dan E., Ginn & Co., Statler Bldg., Boston, Mass.
Kindred, Leslie W., Temple University, Philadelphia, Pa.
Kindy, Harold G., 110 Bleecker St., New York, N.Y.
King, Charles T., 374 Millburn Ave., Millburn, N.J.
King, Fred M., 76 Branch Ave., Red Bank, N.J.
King, George G., Montclair State Col., Montclair, N.J.
King, Mrs. June, Box 39, Prince Frederick, Md.
King, Kent H., 103 Thayer Ave., Mankato, Minn.
King, Lloyd H., Sch. of Educ., Univ. of the Pacific, Stockton, Calif.
King, Robert N., 15 Quade St., Glens Falls, N.Y.
King, Thomas C., Col. of Educ., Univ. of Vermont, Burlington, Vt.
Kingdon, Frederick H., Western State College, Gunnison, Colo.
Kingsley, Iva Marie, Box 157, Bellmont Rur. Sta., Flagstaff, Arizona
Kinlin, J. F., 44 Eglinton Ave., W., Toronto, Ont., Canada
Kinsellar, Frances M., Rye St., Broad Brook, Conn.
* Kinsman, Kephas Albert, 2009 Appleton St., Long Beach, Calif.
Kintzer, Frederick C., University of California, Los Angeles, Calif.
Kinyon, Charles W., Prin., Rush-Henrietta Central H.S., Henrietta, N.Y.
Kinzer, John R., 5756 East 6th St., Tucson, Arizona
Kirby, Inabell T., 2002 E. Main St., Decatur, Ill.
Kirchhaefer, Esther, Illinois State University, Normal, Ill.
Kirk, Samuel A., Col. of Educ., Univ. of Arizona, Tucson, Arizona
Kirk, W. E., P. O. Box 28295, Dallas, Texas
Kirk, William G., 204 S. Roosevelt, Bloomington, Ill.
Kirkland, J. Bryant, North Carolina State College, Raleigh, N.C.
Kirkman, Ralph E., Middle Tennessee State University, Murfreesboro, Tenn.
Kirkpatrick, James E., Black Hills State College, Spearfish, S.D.
Kirsch, Paul E., 125 Kent Blvd., Salamanca, N.Y.
Kise, Leonard, Northern Illinois Univ., DeKalb, Ill.
Kissinger, Doris C., 34 Roosevelt St., Glen Head, L.I., N.Y.
* Kitch, Donald E., State Dept. of Educ., 721 Capitol Mall, Sacramento, Calif.
Kittell, Jack E., Col. of Educ., University of Washington, Seattle, Wash.
Kitts, Harry W., Dept. of Agric. Educ., Univ. of Minn., St. Paul, Minn.
Kizer, George A., Iowa State Univ., Ames, Iowa
Kjarsgaard, Donald R., Western Washington State Col., Bellingham, Wash.
Klahn, Richard P., Des Moines Indep. Comm. Sch. Dist., Des Moines, Iowa
Klaus, Catherine R., Box 337, Clermont, Iowa
Klausmeier, Herbert J., Sch. of Educ., University of Wisconsin, Madison, Wis.
Klein, Philip, 1520 Spruce St., Philadelphia, Pa.
Klein, Richard K., Department of Public Instruction, Bismarck, N.D.
Kleinpell, E. H., Wisconsin State College, River Falls, Wis.
Kleis, Russell J., Michigan State University, East Lansing, Mich.
Klevan, Albert, Educ. Div., USAID, c/o American Embassy, Lagos, Nigeria
Kleyensteuber, Carl J., Northland College, Ashland, Wis.
Klinckmann, Evelyn, San Francisco Col. for Women, San Francisco, Calif.
Kline, Charles E., Purdue University, Lafayette, Ind.
Kline, Frances F., 232A West Irving Ave., Oshkosh, Wis.
Kling, Martin, Grad. Sch. of Educ., Rutgers State Univ., New Brunswick, N.J.
Klohr, Paul R., 420 Walhalla Rd., Columbus, Ohio

Klopf, Gordon J., Bank Street Col. of Educ., New York, N.Y.
Klopfer, Leopold E., Grad. Sch. of Educ., Univ. of Chicago, Chicago, Ill.
Kluwe, Mary Jean, Lang. Educ. Dept., Public Schools, Detroit, Mich.
Knape, Clifford S., 1024 North 18-A St., Waco, Tex.
Knapp, Frederick C., 272 Rochelle Park, Tonawanda, N.Y.
Knapp, William D., 6800 Schodway, Greendale, Wis.
Kneller, George F., Sch. of Educ., Univ. of California, Los Angeles, Calif.
Knight, Octavia B., North Carolina College, Durham, N.C.
Knight, Reginald R., 4338 Heather Rd., Long Beach, Calif.
Knirk, Frederick G., 161 Brookside Lane, Fayetteville, N.Y.
Knolle, Lawrence M., Chatham College, Pittsburgh, Pa.
Knorr, Amy Jean, University of Arizona, Tucson, Ariz.
Knowlden, Gayle E., 3003 Laurel Ave., Manhattan Beach, Calif.
Knox, Carl S., 2017 Louisiana St., Lawrence, Kan.
Knox, Stanley C., St. Cloud State College, St. Cloud, Minn.
Knuti, Leo Leonard, Montana State College, Bozeman, Mont.
Koch, Mrs. Sylvia L., 539 N. Highland Ave., Los Angeles, Calif.
Koehler, Everette E., The King's College, Briarcliff Manor, N.Y.
Koehring, Dorothy, State College of Iowa, Cedar Falls, Iowa
Koenig, Adolph J., 7916 Maryknoll Ave., Bethesda, Md.
Koenig, Juanita, 303 S.W. Erickson St., Beaverton, Ore.
Koenig, Vernon H., 11878 Ridgecrest Dr., Riverside, Calif.
Koerber, Walter F., Scarborough Board of Education, Scarborough, Ont., Canada
Koerner, Warren A., 4608 West 106th St., Oak Lawn, Ill.
Koester, George A., San Diego State College, San Diego, Calif.
Koff, Robert H., 652 Glenbrook Dr., Palo Alto, Calif.
Kohler, Lewis T., 11600 Eldridge Ave., Suite 211, Pacoima, Calif.
Kohlmann, Eleanor L., 169 MacKay Hall, Iowa State University, Ames, Iowa
Kohn, Martin, 35 West 92nd St., New York, N.Y.
Kohrs, E. V., 189 Columbia Ave., Passaic, N.J.
Kokras, Nocolaos, 713 Graduate House, Lafayette, Ind.
Kolesnik, Walter B., Dept. of Educ., Univ. of Detroit, Detroit, Mich.
Kollar, Theodore H., Paterson Cath. Reg. H.S., Paterson, N.J.
Konecny, Frank J., 101 S. Rita St., Waco, Tex.
Konishi, Walter K., San Jose State College, San Jose, Calif.
Konrad, Abram G., Tabor College, Hillsboro, Kan.
Konsh, Adeline, 7 East 14th St., New York, N.Y.
Konstantinos, K. K., Lenape Regional High School, Medford, N.J.
Kontos, George, Jr., 351 N.E. Chambers Ct., Newport, Ore.
Koos, Leonard V., Route 2, Newago, Mich.
Kopan, Andrew T., 5401 S. Hyde Park Blvd., Chicago, Ill.
Kopfstein, Kurt A., 6230 N. Avers, Chicago, Ill.
Korey, Harold, 5026 Jarlath, Skokie, Ill.
Korntheuer, Gerhard A., St. Johns College, Winfield, Kan.
Kovach, Gaza, Pocahontas High School, Pocahontas, Va.
Kozelka, Robert F., 110 W. Lawrence Ave., Springfield, Ill.
Kozma, Ernest J., 8081 Worthington Park Dr., Strongsville, Ohio
Krafft, Larry J., 811C Cherry Lane, East Lansing, Mich.
Kraft, Milton Edward, Earlham College, Richmond, Ind.
Kramer, William A., 3558 S. Jefferson Ave., St. Louis, Mo.
Kratz, Gerald B., Huron Valley Schools, Milford, Mich.
Kraus, Howard F., 512 Alameda de las Pulgas, Belmont, Calif.
Kraus, Philip E., Hunter College, New York, N.Y.
Krause, Victor C., Concord Teachers College, River Forest, Ill.
Kravetz, Nathan, 555 Kappock St., Riverdale, N.Y.
Kravetz, Sol, 11545 Duque Dr., Studio City, Calif.
Krawitz, Harris, 431 Oakdale Ave., Chicago, Ill.
Kreismer, Clifford R., Clara E. Coleman Sch., 100 Pinelynn Rd., Glen Rock, N.J.
Kreitlow, Burton W., Dept. of Educ., University of Wisconsin, Madison, Wis.
Kress, Roy A., 800 Moredon Rd., Meadowbrook, Pa.
Krich, Percy, Dept. of Educ., Queens College, Flushing, N.Y.

Krippner, Stanley C., Dept. of Psychiatry, Maimonides Hosp., Brooklyn, N.Y.
Krolikowski, W. P., Loyola University, Chicago, Ill.
Kroman, Nathan, Col. of Educ., Michigan State Univ., East Lansing, Mich.
Kropp, John P., 12455 Russell Ave., Chino, Calif.
Kropp, Russell P., Florida State University, Tallahassee, Fla.
Krueger, Louise W., 1520 Laburnum Ave., Chico, Calif.
Krug, Edward, Dept. of Educ., University of Wisconsin, Madison, Wis.
Krumboltz, John D., Sch. of Educ., Stanford University, Stanford, Calif.
Kruszynski, Eugene S., San Francisco State College, San Francisco, Calif.
Krzesinski, Daniel J., R.D. 1, Attica, N.Y.
Kubalek, Josef, Karlinske nam. 6, Praha 8 Karlin, CSSR, Czech.
Kubik, Edmund J., 9741 S. Leavitt St., Chicago, Ill.
Kugler, William B., 5535 Carlton Way, Los Angeles, Calif.
Kuhn, Donald K., 8520 Mackenzie Rd., St. Louis, Mo.
Kuhn, Joseph A., 99 Buffalo Ave., Long Beach, N.Y.
Kuhnen, Mrs. Mildred, 2106 Park Ave., Chico, Calif.
Kulberg, Janet M., 24 Peters St., Orono, Me.
Kullman, N. E., Jr., 153 Murray Ave., Delmar, N.Y.
Kumpf, Carl H., Superintendent of Schools, Clark, N.J.
Kunimoto, Mrs. Tadako, 734—16th Ave., Honolulu, Hawaii
Kuntz, Allen H., 72 Lombardy St., Lancaster, N.Y.
Kunzler, William J., 1413 Sycamore St., Iowa City, Iowa
Kurtz, John J., Inst. for Child Study, Univ. of Maryland, College Park, Md.
Kusmik, Cornell J., 7400 Augusta St., River Forest, Ill.
Kutz, Frederick B., Newark High School, Newark, Del.
Kvaraceus, W. C., Tufts University, Medford, Mass.
Kyle, Helen F., Rhode Island College, Providence, R.I.
Kynard, Alfred T., Prairie View A. & M. College, Prairie View, Tex.

Labatte, Henry, 40 College St., Toronto, Ontario, Canada
Lacey, Archie L., Hunter Col., City University of N.Y., New York, N.Y.
Lache, Sheldon, 43 Mansfield Apts., Storrs, Conn.
Lackey, Kenneth E., 1412 Highway 63 N., Columbia, Mo.
Lacy, David W., 210 W. Water St., Converse, Ind.
Ladd, Edward T., Emory University, Atlanta, Ga.
Ladd, Eleanor M., Box 719, Clearwater, Fla.
Ladd, Paul, Wooster High School, Wooster, Ohio
LaDue, Donald C., Elem. Educ. Dept., Temple University, Philadelphia, Pa.
LaFauci, Horatio M., 871 Commonwealth Ave., Boston, Mass.
Lafferty, Henry M., East Texas State Univ., Commerce, Texas
Lafferty, H. M., East Texas State Teachers College, Commerce, Tex.
LaForce, Charles L., 426 Malden Ave., LaGrange Park, Ill.
Lafranchi, W. E., Stabley Library, State College, Indiana, Pa.
LaGrone, Herbert F., Sch. of Educ., Texas Christian Univ., Fort Worth, Tex.
Lahaderne, Henrietta M., IDEA, 1100 Glendon Ave., Los Angeles, Calif.
Laird, A. W., Western Kentucky State College, Bowling Green, Ky.
Lake, Doris S., State Univ. Col., Oneonta, N.Y.
Lamb, Howard E., Sch. of Educ., University of Delaware, Newark, Del.
Lambert, Philip, Educ. Psych. Dept., Univ. of Wisconsin, Madison, Wis.
Lambert, Pierre D., Sch. of Educ., Boston College, Chestnut Hill, Mass.
Lambert, Ronald T., University of Minnesota, Minneapolis, Minn.
Lambert, Sam M., N.E.A., 1201 Sixteenth St., N.W., Washington, D.C.
Lampard, Dorothy M., University of Alberta, Edmonton, Alba., Canada
Lampshire, Richard H., Drake University, Des Moines, Iowa
Landskov, Norvin L., Univ. of Southern Mississippi, Hattiesburg, Miss.
Lane, Frank T., USAID, Rio de Janiero/SUN, APO New York, NY.
Lane, Mrs. Mary B., 10 Lundy's Lane, San Mateo, Calif.
Lang, Mrs. Pauline N., Southern Connecticut State Col., New Haven, Conn.
Lange, Lorraine, State Univ. of New York, Buffalo, N.Y.
Lange, Paul W., 2304 Linden Dr., Valparaiso, Ind.
Lange, Phil C., Tchrs. Col., Columbia University, New York, N.Y.

Langeveld, M. J., Prins Hendriklaan 6, Bilthoven, Holland
Langland, Lois E., 4021 Olive Hill Dr., Claremont, Calif.
Langley, Elizabeth M., 4937 W. Wellington Ave., Chicago, Ill.
Langman, Muriel Potter, 913 Congress St., Ypsilanti, Mich.
Langston, Genevieve R., Eureka College, Eureka, Ill.
Langston, Roderick G., 1451 S. Loma Verde St., Monterey Park, Calif.
Lanham, Frank W., 3212 Charing Cross, Ann Arbor, Mich.
Lanier, Ruby, Route #2, Box 619, Hickory, N.C.
Lanning, Frank W., Northern Illinois University, DeKalb, Ill.
Lano, Richard L., University of California, Los Angeles, Calif.
Lansing, Marvin G., 122 Mappa St., Eau Claire, Wis.
Lansu, Walter J., 6036 Metropolitan Plaza, Los Angeles, Calif.
Lantz, James S., 330 Washington St., Tekonsha, Mich.
Lantz, Ralph G., Pennsylvania State University, University Park, Pa.
Laramy, William J., Haverford Junior High School, Havertown, Pa.
Larkin, Lewis B., 15818 Westbrook, Detroit, Mich.
Larmee, Roy A., Cntr. for Educ. Admn., Ohio State Univ., Columbus, Ohio
Larsen, Arthur Hoff, Illinois State University, Normal, Ill.
Larson, Eleanore E., Col. of Educ., Univ. of Rochester, Rochester, N.Y.
Larson, L. C., Audio-Visual Center, Indiana University, Bloomington, Ind.
Larson, Raymond O., Whitewater State Tchrs. Col., Whitewater, Wis.
Larson, Vera M., 13601 N.E. Fremont St., Portland, Ore.
Lashinger, Donald R., State University of New York, Albany, N.Y.
Laska, John, Sutton Hall, Univ. of Texas, Austin, Texas
Laska, John J., 300 Oakland Ave., Terre Haute, Ind.
Lassanske, Paul A., 4389 Hodgson Rd., St. Paul, Minn.
Lathrop, Irvin T., California State College, Long Beach, Calif.
Lattimer, Everett C., Magee Rd., Glenmont, N.Y.
Laudico, Minerva G., Centro Escolar University, Manila, Philippines
Lauren, Paul M., 111-15—62nd Dr., Forest Hills, N.Y.
Lauria, Joseph L., 6401 Shoup Ave., Canoga Park, Calif.
Laurier, Blaise V., Les Clercs de Saint-Viateur, Montreal, Quebec, Canada
Lautenschlager, Harley, Lab. School, Indiana State University, Terre Haute, Ind.
Lavenburg, F. M., Public Schls., 155 Broad St., Bloomfield, N.J.
Laverty, John A., 5944 S. Washtenaw Ave., Chicago, Ill.
Lawhead, Victor B., Ball State University, Muncie, Ind.
Lawler, Marcella R., Tchrs. Col., Columbia University, New York, N.Y.
Lawrence, Mrs. Bessie F., LeMoyne School, 851 Waveland Ave., Chicago, Ill.
Lawrence, Clayton G., Marion College, Marion, Ind.
Lawrence, Richard E., AACTE, 1201 Sixteenth St., N.W., Washington, D.C.
Lawrence, Ruth E., 627 Grove St., Denton, Tex.
Lawrie, Jack D., Superintendent of Schools, Washington, N.C.
Lawski, A. J., Edsel Ford High School, 20601 Rotunda Dr., Dearborn, Mich.
Lazar, Alfred L., 1010 Esplanade #5, Redondo Beach, Calif.
Lazow, Alfred, Thayer Towers, 575 Thayer Ave., Silver Spring, Md.
Leavitt, Jerome E., Col. of Educ., Univ. of Arizona, Tucson, Arizona
Lebofsky, Arthur, 485 E. Lincoln Ave., Mt. Vernon, N.Y.
Lechiara, Francis J., 1400 Miller Rd., Coral Gables, Fla.
Lee, Annabel, Univ. of Puget Sound, Tacoma, Wash.
Lee, Ernest C., High School, Drouin, Victoria, Australia
Lee, Harold Fletcher, Box 38, Lincoln University, Jefferson City, Mo.
Lee, Howard D., Atwater School, Shorewood, Wis.
Lee, J. Murray, Southern Illinois University, Carbondale, Ill.
Lee, James Michael, University of Notre Dame, Notre Dame, Ind.
Lee, John J., Col. of Educ., Wayne State University, Detroit, Mich.
Lee, William B., U.S.D.E.S.E.A., APO New York, N.Y.
Lee, William C., Col. of Educ., Fairleigh Dickinson Univ., Teaneck, N.J.
Leeds, Donald S., 50 Lionel Ave., Waltham, Mass.
Leeds, Willard L., Ford Foundation, Caracas, Venezuela, S.A.
Leese, Joseph, State Univ. Col., Albany, N.Y.
Leeseberg, Norbert H., 663 Manor Rd., Staten Island, N.Y.

MEMBERS OF THE NATIONAL SOCIETY

Lefcourt, Ann, Anthony Apartments, Muncie, Ind.
Lefever, David Welty, Sch. of Educ., Univ. of California, Los Angeles, Calif.
* Lefforge, Roxy, 1945 Fruit St., Huntington, Ind.
Lehman, Lloyd W., 435 N. Michigan Ave., Chicago, Ill.
Lehmann, Irvin J., Michigan State University, East Lansing, Mich.
Lehmkuhl, Carlton B., 4 Wilogreen Rd., Natick, Mass.
Lehsten, Nelson G., Sch. of Educ., Univ. of Michigan, Ann Arbor, Mich.
Leib, Joseph A., 240 Sinclair Pl., Westfield, N.J.
Leibert, Robert E., 1005 W. Gregory Ave., Kansas City, Mo.
Leibik, Leon J., 204 Dodge Ave., Evanston, Ill.
Leigh, Robert K., 2925 Ladoga Ave., Long Beach, Calif.
Leitch, John J., Jr., Admin. Off., Wheeler Rd., Central Islip, N.Y.
Lemin, Paul C., Superintendent of Schools, Cheboygan, Mich.
Lennon, Joseph L., Providence College, Providence, R.I.
Lennon, Lawrence J., 310 N. Webster Ave., Scranton, Pa.
Leonard, Lloyd L., Dept. of Educ., Northern Illinois Univ., DeKalb, Ill.
Leonard, William P., Univ. of Pittsburgh, Pittsburgh, Pa.
Lepera, Alfred G., 254 Franklin St., Newton, Mass.
LePere, Jean M., Michigan State University, East Lansing, Mich.
Lepore, Albert R., 2614 Lancaster Rd., Hayward, Calif.
Lester, J. William, Superintendent, Diocesan Schls., Fort Wayne, Ind.
Leverson, Leonard O., 201 W. Newhall Ave., Waukesha, Wis.
Levin, Alvin I., 12336 Addison St., North Hollywood, Calif.
Levin, J. Joseph, 221 N. Cuyler Ave., Oak Park, Ill.
Levine, Daniel U., Sch. of Educ., Univ. of Missouri, Kansas City, Mo.
LeVine, James, Jr., 1106 Koko Head Ave., Honolulu, Hawaii
Levine, Murray, Dept. of Psych., Yale University, New Haven, Conn.
Levine, Stanley L., 1627 Anita Ln., Newport Beach, Calif.
Levinson, Leo, Clarkston Sch. Dist. # 1, New City, N.Y.
Levit, Martin, Dept. of Educ., Univ. of California, Davis, Calif.
Levy, Nathalie, 506 Mississippi Ave., Bogalusa, La.
Lewin, Lee Mabel, 211 East 53rd St., New York, N.Y.
Lewis, Arthur J., Tchrs. Col., Columbia University, New York, N.Y.
Lewis, Edward R., 5293 Greenridge Rd., Castro Valley, Calif.
Lewis, Elizabeth V., P.O. Box 1833, University, Ala.
Lewis, Mrs. J. R., Blue Mountain College, Blue Mountain, Miss.
Lewis, Maurice S., Col. of Educ., Arizona State University, Tempe, Ariz.
Lewis, Philip, 6900 S. Crandon Ave., Chicago, Ill.
Lewis, Robert, 915 N. Union St., Natchez, Miss.
Lewis, Roland B., Eastern Washington State College, Cheney, Wash.
Lewis, William, Millikin Univ. Library, Decatur, Ill.
Leyton-Soto, Mario, Univ. de Chile, Castro 441, Santiago, Chile
Liberman, Norman J., 390 West End Ave., New York, N.Y.
Licata, William, State Univ. Col., Buffalo, N.Y.
Lichtey, E. A., Illinois State University, Normal, Ill.
Lidberg, Richard G., University of Minnesota, Duluth, Minn.
Lieberman, Ann, 13040 Hartland St., North Hollywood, Calif.
Lieberman, Marcus, 5835 Kimbark Ave., Chicago, Ill.
Lien, Ronald L., Mankato State College, Mankato, Minn.
Lifton, Eli, Winthrop Junior High School, Brooklyn, N.Y.
Liggitt, William A., 703 St. Marks Ave., Westfield, N.J.
Light, Alfred B., 93 Bailey Ave., Plattsburgh, N.Y.
Lighthall, Frederick, Dept. of Educ., Univ. of Chicago, Chicago, Ill.
Ligon, Mary Gilbert, Hofstra College, Hempstead, N.Y.
Liljeblad, Maynard T., P.O. Box 1067, Hanford, Calif.
Lilley, Leonard D., Jr., Pinetops, N.C.
* Lincoln, Edward A., Thompson St., Halifax, Mass.
Lind, Arthur E., 1422 Johnston Ave., Richland, Wash.
Lindberg, Lucile, Queens College, Flushing, N.Y.
Lindeman, Richard H., Tchrs. Col., Columbia University, New York, N.Y.
Lindemer, George Charles, Seton Hall University, South Orange, N.J.

MEMBERS OF THE NATIONAL SOCIETY   lxiii

Lindgren, Henry Clay, 1975—15th Ave., San Francisco, Calif.
Lindvall, C. Mauritz, Sch. of Educ., University of Pittsburgh, Pittsburgh, Pa.
Linehan, Mrs. Louise W., 4 Bolton Pl., Fair Lawn, N.J.
Linnemann, Calvin C., Superintendent, Alamance County Schls., Graham, N.C.
Linson, Marvin G., 933 Fulton St., Aurora, Colo.
Lipham, James M., Dept. of Educ., University of Wisconsin, Madison, Wis.
Lipscomb, William A., 107 Yellowstone Dr., Jerome, Idaho
Liske, Wilfred W., Andrews Univ., Berrien Springs, Mich.
Lissovoy, Vladimir de, Pennsylvania State Univ., University Park, Pa.
Litherland, Bennett H., 541—21st St., Rock Island, Ill.
Litin, Mrs. Annette, 5302 N. Granite Reef Rd., Scottsdale, Ariz.
Litsinger, Dolores A., San Fernando Valley State College, Northridge, Calif.
Little, J. Kenneth, Bascom Hall, University of Wisconsin, Madison, Wis.
Little, Lawrence C., 1 Ridge View Dr., Westminster, Md.
Little, Sara, Presbyterian Sch. of Christian Education, Richmond, Va.
Littlefield, Roy S., Superintendent of Schools, Dell, Ark.
Littlejohn, Mary T., Winthrop College, Rock Hill, S.C.
Litzky, Leo, 11 Pomona Ave., Newark, N.J.
Livingston, Thomas B., Box 4060, Texas Tech. Station, Lubbock, Tex.
Livo, Norma J., 465 E. Seventh Ave., Tarentum, Pa.
Llewellyn, Ardelle A., San Francisco State College, San Francisco, Calif.
Lloyd, Francis V., Jr., 5834 Stony Island Ave., Chicago, Ill.
Lloyd-Jones, Esther M., 430 West 116th St., New York, N.Y.
Lobdell, Lawrence O., Union Free School Dist. 30, Valley Stream, N.Y.
Lockett, B. T., 1848 Tiger Flowers Dr., N.W., Atlanta, Ga.
Lockwood, William L., 215 Harbor St., Glencoe, Ill.
Loew, Climmont C., 1733 North 76th Ct., Elmwood Park, Ill.
Lofgren, Marie Luise S., 5068 Cocoa Palm Way, Fair Oaks, Calif.
Logan, Lillian May, Brandon Univ., Brandon, Manitoba, Canada
Logan, William B., Sch. of Educ., Ohio State University, Columbus, Ohio
Logdeser, Mrs. Thomas, 11616 Woodview Blvd., Parma Heights, Ohio
Lohman, Maurice A., Tchrs. Col., Columbia University, New York, N.Y.
Lohmann, Victor L., State Teachers College, St. Cloud, Minn.
Lomax, James L., Lomax Junior High School, Valdosta, Ga.
London, Jack, 2328 Derby St., Berkeley, Calif.
Long, Isabelle, 4343 Harriet Ave., S., Minneapolis, Minn.
Longsdorf, Homer H., 703 E. 48th St., Kansas City, Mo.
Lonsdale, Mrs. Maxine deLappe, 1405 Campbell Lane, Sacramento, Calif.
Lonsdale, Richard C., 220 Palmer Ave., North Tarrytown, N.Y.
Lonsway, Rev. Francis A., O.F.M., Bellarmine Col., Louisville, Ky.
Looby, Thomas F., 241 S. Ocean Ave., Patchogue, N.Y.
Loomis, Arthur K., 917 W. Bonita Ave., Claremont, Calif.
Loomis, William G., 684 Illinois Ave., N.E., Salem, Ore.
Looney, William F., Pres., State Col. at Boston, Boston, Mass.
Loop, Alfred B., 2619 Franklin St., Bellingham, Wash.
Loree, M. Ray, Box 742, University of Alabama, University, Ala.
Lorenz, Donald W., Lutheran High School East, Harper Woods, Mich.
Lorenzen, R. W., Div. of Voc. Educ., Univ. of California, Los Angeles, Calif.
Loudon, Mrs. Mary Lou, 1408 Stephens Ave., Baton Rouge, La.
Loughlin, Leo J., 257 Rolfe Rd., DeKalb, Ill.
Loughrea, Mildred K., 659 City Hall, St. Paul, Minn.
Love, Virginia H., 700 N. Grand Ave., Sherman, Tex.
Lovette, Joanne P., 88 Rt. 119 South, Indiana, Pa.
Lowe, A. J., University of South Florida, Tampa, Fla.
Lowe, Alberta L., Col. of Educ., University of Tennessee, Knoxville, Tenn.
Lowe, Mary G., Dept. of H.E., University of Utah, Salt Lake City, Utah
Lowe, Viola C., 1512 S. Gamon Rd., Wheaton, Ill.
Lowe, R. N., Sch. of Educ., University of Oregon, Eugene, Ore.
Lowe, William T., Stone Hall, Cornell University, Ithaca, N.Y.
Lowenstein, Frederick H., 613 Dartmouth St., Westbury, N.Y.
Lowery, Zeb A., Rutherford County Schools, Rutherford, N.C.

MEMBERS OF THE NATIONAL SOCIETY

Lowes, Ruth, 2004 Seventh Ave., Canyon, Tex.
Lowey, Warren G., Box 64, Setauket, L.I., N.Y.
Lowther, Malcolm A., Sch. of Educ., Univ. of Michigan, Ann Arbor, Mich.
Lowther, William L., Supt. of Schools, Boonton, N.J.
Lubell, Richard M., 2 Stoddard Pl., Brooklyn, N.Y.
Lubin, Harry, Supt. of Schools, Bellmawr, N.J.
Lucas, Ann F., Fairleigh Dickinson Univ., Teaneck, N.J.
Lucas, J. H., 2006 Fayetteville St., Durham, N.C.
Lucas, R. E., 709 E. Riverview, Fort Morgan, Colo.
Lucash, Benjamin, 9801 Montour St., Philadelphia, Pa.
Lucietto, Lena, 5835 Kimbark Ave., Chicago, Ill.
Lucio, William H., Sch. of Educ., University of California, Los Angeles, Calif.
Lucito, Leonard J., University of South Florida, Tampa, Fla.
Ludwig, Adela E., 2453 N. Grant Blvd., Milwaukee, Wis.
Luebke, Martin F., 1704 W. Jackson St., Springfield, Ill.
Luetkemeyer, Joseph F., 7002 St. Annes Ave., Lanham, Md.
Luhmann, Philip R., 1451 E. 55th St., Chicago, Ill.
Lukens, Mrs. Eunice T., 12421 South 69th Ave., Palos Heights, Ill.
Luker, Arno Henry, Colorado State College, Greeley, Colo.
Lund, S. E. Torsten, 45-B Tolman Hall, Univ. of California, Berkeley, Calif.
Lunde, Mrs. Josephine, 505 Oxford, Grand Forks, N.D.
Lunney, Gerald H., University of Massachusetts, Amherst, Mass.
Lunt, Robert B., Supt. of Schools, Town Hall, Cape Elizabeth, Me.
LuPone, O. J., 4520 Culbertson, LaMesa, Calif.
Lutz, Frank W., New York University, New York, N.Y.
Lutz, Jack, Plymouth-Whitemarsh Jt. High School, Plymouth Meeting, Pa.
Luvaas, Clarence B., 1112—32nd St., S.E., Cedar Rapids, Iowa
Lyman, Howard B., University of Cincinnati, Cincinnati, Ohio
Lynch, James M., Superintendent of Schools, Rt. No. 9, East Brunswick, N.J.
Lynch, James T., Canandaigua Academy, Canandaigua, N.Y.
Lynch, John C., DePaul University, Chicago, Ill.
Lynch, Patrick D., Col. of Educ., Univ. of New Mexico, Albuquerque, N.M.
Lyon, Bruce W., Wright State Univ., Dayton, Ohio
Lyons, Mrs. Cora E., P.O. Box 133, Amboy, Ill.
Lyons, John H., 17 Colton Rd., Somers, Conn.

Maag, Raymond E., 122 W. Franklin Ave., Minneapolis, Minn.
Maccia, George S., Dept. of Educ., Ohio State University, Columbus, Ohio
MacConnell, John C., Muhlenberg College, Allentown, Pa.
MacDonald, Donald V., University of Scranton, Scranton, Pa.
Macdonald, Leland S., 5609—19th St., N., Arlington, Va.
MacDonald, M. Gertrude, 78 Sheffield Rd., Melrose, Mass.
MacDonald, Robert L., P. O. Box 2005, Van Nuys, Calif.
MacGown, Paul C., 3128 N. Ash St., Spokane, Wash.
MacInnes, Thane E., Xerox Educ. Div., New York, N.Y.
Mack, Esther, San Jose State College, San Jose, Calif.
* MacKay, James L., 3737 Fredericksburg Rd., San Antonio, Tex.
MacKay, Vera A., Col. of Educ., Univ. of British Columbia, Vancouver, B.C.
MacKay, William R., 124 Underhill Rd., Bellingham, Wash.
Mackenzie, Donald M., White House, Park College, Parkville, Mo.
MacKenzie, Elbridge G., Anderson College, Anderson, Ind.
Mackenzie, Gordon N., Tchrs. Col., Columbia University, New York, N.Y.
Mackintosh, Helen K., 215 Wolfe St., Alexandria, Va.
MacLean, Effie, Saskatoon Pub. Sch. Brd., Saskatoon, Sask., Canada
MacLeay, Ian A., P.O. Box 560, Lennoxville, Quebec, Canada
MacLeod, James J., 6300 Grand River, Detroit, Mich.
MacNaughton, Elizabeth A., 2990 Richmond Ave., Houston, Texas
MacNicoll, David A., Bernards High School, Bernardsville, N.J.
MacRae, Douglas G., Fulton County Board of Educ., Atlanta, Ga.
Maddox, Mrs. Clifford R., 525 Enid Ave., Dayton, Ohio
Madeja, Stanley S., Northern Illinois Univ., DeKalb, Ill.

Madonna, Mrs. Shirley M., 47-27—215th St., Bayside, N.Y.
Madore, Normand William, Illinois State University, Normal, Ill.
Maehara, Oei, 3535 Pinao St., Honolulu, Hawaii
Magary, James F., Sch. of Educ., Univ. of So. California, Los Angeles, Calif.
Maginnis, Maria, 20522 Parthenia St., Canoga Park, Calif.
Magoon, Thomas M., 1316 Canyon Rd., Silver Spring, Md.
Magram, P. Theodore, 34 Park Drive E., Syosset, N.Y.
Mahaffey, James P., State Dept. of Educ., Columbia, S.C.
Mahar, Robert J., Emory University, Atlanta, Ga.
Maher, Alan E., Unqua School, Massapequa, N.Y.
Maher, Trafford P., St. Louis University, 15 N. Grand Blvd., St. Louis, Mo.
Mailey, James H., University of Southern Mississippi, Hattiesburg, Miss.
Mailliard, Mrs. Margaret E., 221 E. 49th St., Chicago, Ill.
Mains, Mrs. Susie T., 29 West St., Barre, Vt.
Malan, Russell, Superintendent of Schools, Harrisburg, Ill.
Mallett, Jerry J., 3912 Garrison, Toledo, Ohio
Mallick, Patricia, 531 Deming Pl., Chicago, Ill.
Mallory, Berenice, Office of Education, Dept. of H.E.W., Washington, D.C.
Maloof, Mitchell, 63 Main St., Williamstown, Mass.
Manchester, Frank S., Radnor School Dist., Wayne, Pa.
Mandel, E. Jules, 20918 Calimali Rd., Woodland Hills, Calif.
Mangan, John C., Marshall University, Huntington, W.Va.
Mangum, G. C., P.O. Box 494, Darlington, S.C.
Manker, Charles C., Jr., University of South Florida, Tampa, Fla.
Manley, Francis J., Frontier Central Sch., Bay View Rd., Hamburg, N.Y.
Mann, James W., Roosevelt University, Chicago, Ill.
Mann, Jesse A., Georgetown Univ., Washington, D.C.
Mann, Mrs. Thelma T., 949 Hunakai St., Honolulu, Hawaii
Mann, Vernal S., Box 266, State College, Miss.
Mannos, Nicholas T., Niles Twp. High School West, Skokie, Ill.
Manoil, Adolph, Sch. of Educ., Boston University, Boston, Mass.
Manolakes, Theodore, Col. of Educ., University of Illinois, Urbana, Ill.
Manone, Carl, 34 Kirkline Ave., Hellertown, Pa.
Manuel, Herschel T., University of Texas, Austin, Tex.
Mapel, Seldon B., Jr., 1919 Mercedes Rd., Denton, Tex.
Mapes, Cecil S., 29 Payne Ave., Chatham, N.Y.
Marburger, Carl L., Dept. of Educ., 225 W. State St., Trenton, N.J.
Marc-Aurele, Paul, 162 Marois Blvd., Laval-des-Rapids, Montreal, Quebec
Marchie, Howard E., 26 Norman St., Springfield, Mass.
Marcus, Marie, Louisiana State University, New Orleans, La.
Margarones, John J., 210 College St., Lewiston, Me.
Margolin, Mrs. Edythe, 12013 Rose Ave., Los Angeles, Calif.
Margolis, Henry, 2030 S. Taylor Rd., Cleveland Heights, Ohio
Mark, Arthur, 6 Cross Brook Ln., Westport, Conn.
Markarian, Robert E., Springfield College, Springfield, Mass.
Marker, Robert W., State University of Iowa, Iowa City, Iowa
Markle, David H., Ohio Northern University, Ada, Ohio
Marks, Merle B., University of So. California, Los Angeles, Calif.
Marksberry, Mary Lee, Sch. of Educ., Univ. of Missouri, Kansas City, Mo.
Marksheffel, Ned D., Oregon State University, Corvallis, Ore.
Markus, Frank N., 4110 Prairie Lane, Prairie Village, Kansas
Marquard, Richard L., Besser Technical School, Alpena, Mich.
Marquardt, Robert L., Thiokol Chemical Corp., Ogden, Utah
Marquis, Francis N., Wright State Campus, Dayton, Ohio
Marquis, R. L., Jr., Box 5282, North Texas Sta., Denton, Tex.
Marsden, W. Ware, 2217 West 5th St., Stillwater, Okla.
Marsh, Mrs. Augusta B., 252 Bronner St., Prichard, Ala.
Marshall, B. F., Pleasantville Jt. Schools, Pleasantville, Pa.
Marshall, Beth, 1325 S. Orange, Fullerton, Calif.
Marshall, Charles R., 1827 Lakehurst Dr., Olympia, Wash.
Marshall, Daniel W., Filene Center, Tufts University, Medford, Mass.

Marshall, H. H., 400 Banknight Rd., Saluda, S.C.
Marshall, Thomas O., 17 Mill Rd., Durham, N.H.
Marshall, Wayne P., 704 East 36th St., Kearney, Neb.
Marston, Mrs. Marjorie, 860 Lake Shore Dr., Chicago, Ill.
Martin, C. Keith, 400 S. Swain Ave., Bloomington, Ind.
Martin, Mrs. Clayton, College of Emporia, Emporia, Kan.
Martin, Edwin D., 2341 Quenby, Houston, Tex.
Martin, F. Gerald, Sacred Heart Seminary, Detroit, Mich.
Martin, Frieda, 2428½ Wabash, Terre Haute, Ind.
Martin, Ignatius A., Supt., Diocese of Lafayette, Drawer E., Lafayette, La.
Martin, Jackson J., 661 Grace St., Livermore, Calif.
Martin, Kathryn J., 2208 Fairhill Ave., Glenside, Pa.
Martin, Mavis D., SWCEL, 117 Richmond, N.E., Albuquerque, N.M.
Martin, R. Lee, State Univ. Col., Oswego, N.Y.
Martin, Robert M., University of Hawaii, Honolulu, Hawaii
Martin, William R., 320 N.W. 19th Ave., Fort Lauderdale, Fla.
Martini, Angiolina A., 2524 Benvenue Ave., Berkeley, Calif.
Martinson, John S., 801 Wetmore Rd., Everett, Wash.
Martire, Harriette A., St. Joseph College, West Hartford, Conn.
Martorana, Sabastian V., State University of New York, Albany, N.Y.
Marvin, John H., 34 Green St., Augusta, Me.
Marx, George L., Col. of Educ., University of Maryland, College Park, Md.
Marzolf, Stanley S., Illinois State University, Normal, Ill.
Marzullo, Santo P., Manpower Training Center, Rochester, N.Y.
Masia, Bertram B., Dept. of Educ., Western Reserve Univ., Cleveland, Ohio
Masiko, Peter, Miami-Dade Junior College, Miami, Fla.
Mason, Dr. Barbara, Job Corps Center, Clinton, Iowa
Mason, George E., 235 Pine Forest Dr., Athens, Ga.
Mason, John M., Michigan State University, East Lansing, Mich.
Masoner, Paul H., University of Pittsburgh, Pittsburgh, Pa.
Massey, William J., 4906 Roland Ave., Baltimore, Md.
Massialas, Byron G., University of Michigan, Ann Arbor, Mich.
Massingill, Richard A., 15905 Harrison, Livonia, Mich.
Masterson, John A., 3128 Searcy Dr., Huntsville, Ala.
Mateja, Philip J., Whiting High School, Whiting, Ind.
Mathias, C. Wilbur, State Teachers College, Kutztown, Pa.
Mathiott, James E., 3165 Ramona, Palo Alto, Calif.
Mathis, Claude, Sch. of Educ., Northwestern University, Evanston, Ill.
Matthew, Eunice Sophia, 340 Riverside Dr., New York, N.Y.
Matthews, James W., 5009 Tomahawk Trail, Madison, Wis.
Matthews, William P., 1114 N. Centennial, High Point, N.C.
Mattila, Ruth Hughes, P.O. Box 872, Las Vegas, N.M.
Mattison, Robert J., Plymouth State Col., Plymouth, N.H.
Mattox, Daniel V., Jr., Pennsylvania State Univ., State College, Pa.
Matwijcow, Peter, Roger Williams Jr. Col., Providence, R.I.
Matzner, G. C., Eastern Illinois University, Charleston, Ill.
Maucker, James William, State College of Iowa, Cedar Falls, Iowa
Mauk, Gertrude, 14220 Dale St., Detroit, Mich.
Maurer, Marion V., 148 Ann St., Apt. 23, Clarendon Hills, Ill.
Maurer, Robert L., California State Polytechnic College, Pomona, Calif.
Mauth, Leslie J., Ball State University, Muncie, Ind.
Maw, Wallace H., Sch. of Educ., University of Delaware, Newark, Del.
Maxwell, Ida E., 9 Chester Creek Rd., Cheyney, Pa.
May, Charles R., 653 Stark Ct., Columbus, Ohio
May, John B., State Teachers College, Salisbury, Md.
May, Robert E., Emerson Vocational High School, Buffalo, N.Y.
Mayer, Lewis F., 4275 W. 196th St., Fairview Park, Ohio
Mayer, Ronald W., 275 Vernon St., San Francisco, Calif.
Mayhew, Lewis B., 945 Valdez Pl., Stanford, Calif.
Mayhew, Thomas H., Superintendent of Schools, Maywood, N.J.
Maynard, Glenn, Kent State University, Kent, Ohio

MEMBERS OF THE NATIONAL SOCIETY   lxvii

Mayo, Samuel T., Sch. of Educ., Loyola University, Chicago, Ill.
Mayor, John R., AAAS, 1515 Massachusetts Ave., N.W., Washington, D.C.
Mays, Dewey W., Jr., Harden-Simmons University, Abilene, Tex.
Mazyck, Harold E., Jr., 2007 Chelsea Lane, Greensboro, N.C.
McAllister, David, USAID Education, APO 09254, New York, N.Y.
McArthur, L. C., Jr., Drawer 1180, Sumter, S.C.
McAuliffe, M. Eileen, 5649 N. Kolmar Ave., Chicago, Ill.
McBirney, Ruth, Boise Junior College, Boise, Idaho
McBride, James H., 1031 Hayes Ave., Sandusky, Ohio
McBride, Ralph, Supt., Buckley-Loda Unit #8, Loda, Ill.
McBride, William B., Ohio State University, Columbus, Ohio
McBrine, Joseph, Superintendent of Schools, Lincoln, Me.
McBurney, Mrs. Doris, 1641 West 105th St., Chicago, Ill.
McCaffrey, Austin J., Amer. Textbook Pub. Inst., 432 Park Ave., New York, N.Y.
McCahon, David M., 2307 Tilbury Ave., Pittsburgh, Pa.
McCaig, Thomas E., 3447 W. Pierce Ave., Chicago, Ill.
McCain, Paul M., Arkansas College, Batesville, Ark.
McCall, Miss Martha M., 6929 Town North, Dallas, Texas
McCann, Lewis E., 18637 San Fernando Mission Blvd., Northridge, Calif.
McCann, Thomas W., 19 Jeffery Pl., Trumbull, Conn.
McCarthy, Joseph F. X., 641 Forest Ave., Larchmont, N.Y.
McCartney, Hilda, 2916 Redwood Ave., Costa Mesa, Calif.
McCarty, Henry R., San Diego County Bd. of Educ., San Diego, Calif.
McClain, Warren J., Superintendent of Schools, Woodbury, N.J.
McClanahan, L. D., 5820 Woolman Ct., Parma, Ohio
McCleary, Lloyd E., University of Illinois, Urbana, Ill.
McClellan, James E., 70 Greentree Dr., Doylestown, Pa.
McClendon, LeRoy, P.O. Box 6161 SFA Station, Nacogdoches, Tex.
McClendon, Patricia R., Winthrop College, Rock Hill, S.C.
McClendon, Paul E., Jacksonville University, Jacksonville, Fla.
McClintock, Eugene, Centralia Twp. H.S. and Jr. Col., Centralia, Ill.
McClintock, James A., Drew University, Madison, N.J.
McClure, Donald E., Eureka College, Eureka, Ill.
McClure, L. Morris, Col. of Educ., Univ. of Maryland, College Park, Md.
McClure, Nancy, Col. of Educ., Univ. of Kentucky, Lexington, Ky.
McClure, Robert M., 3360 Runnymede Pl., N.W., Washington, D.C.
McClurkin, W. D., Peabody College, Nashville, Tenn.
McClusky, Howard Yale, Elem. Sch., University of Michigan, Ann Arbor, Mich.
McCollum, Elinor C., 619 Ridge Ave., Evanston, Ill.
McConnell, Emma, Vassar College, Poughkeepsie, N.Y.
McConnell, Gaither, Cen. for Tchr. Educ., Tulane Univ., New Orleans, La.
McConnell, John C., Windward School, Inc., White Plains, N.Y.
McConnell, Thomas R., Center for Study of Higher Educ., Berkeley, Calif.
McCook, T. Joseph, Supt., Brevard County Schools, Titusville, Fla.
McCormick, Ethel M., Lehigh Univ., Bethlehem, Pa.
McCormick, Felix J., Tchrs. Col., Columbia University, New York, N.Y.
McCormick, Jerome C., Southwest High School, Green Bay, Wis.
McCracken, Oliver, Jr., Superintendent of Schools, Skokie, Ill.
McCuaig, Susannah, 222 Babcock St., Brookline, Mass.
McCue, L. H., Jr., E. C. Glass High School, Lynchburg, Va.
McCue, Robert E., 2308 N. Hazelwood Ave., Davenport, Iowa
McCuen, John T., 1340 Loretta Dr., Glendale, Calif.
McCullough, Betty, Biola College, La Mirada, Calif.
McCullough, Constance M., 80 Vincente Rd., Berkeley, Calif.
McCully, Clyde C., Antelope Valley College, Lancaster, Calif.
McCuskey, Dorothy, Western Michigan University, Kalamazoo, Mich.
McCutcheon, Nancy Sue, Sch. of Educ., Univ. of South Carolina, Columbia, S.C.
McDaniel, Ernest D., Educ. Resch. Cent., Purdue Univ., Lafayette, Ind.
McDaniel, Marjorie C., Indiana State University, Terre Haute, Ind.
McDaniels, Garry L., 1310 Harbrooke, Ann Arbor, Mich.
McDavit, H. W., South Orange-Maplewood Public Schools, South Orange, N.J.

McDiarmid, Garnet Leo, 102 Bloor St. West, Toronto, Ont., Canada
McDonald, Donald, Texas Technological College, Lubbock, Tex.
McDonald, John J., S.J., Xavier High School, 30 W. 16th St., New York, N.Y.
McDonald, L. R., Woodruff Senior High School, Peoria, Ill.
McDowell, John B., 111 Blvd. of Allies, Pittsburgh, Pa.
McElhinney, James, 3816 Brook Dr., Muncie, Ind.
McElroy, Louis A., 620 East 10th Pl., Gary, Ind.
McElroy, Marguerite E., 8150 Terrace Dr., El Cerrito, Calif.
McEwen, Gordon B., 13602 E. Walnut, Whittier, Calif.
McFadden, Edward C., 990 Capistrano Ave., Laguna Beach, Calif.
McFarland, Donald F., Jr., State University College, Fredonia, N.Y.
McFarland, John W., Sch. of Educ., Univ. of Texas, El Paso, Texas
McFarren, G. Allen, 11 Willow Lane Ct., Tonawanda, N.Y.
McFeaters, Margaret M., 608 Brown's Lane, Pittsburgh, Pa.
McGary, Carroll R., 125 Stroudwater St., Westbrook, Me.
McGavern, John H., University of Hartford, Hartford, Conn.
McGee, R. T., Los Alamos Schools, P.O. Box 90, Los Alamos, N.M.
McGee, Ralph G., 1526 Washington Ave., Wilmette, Ill.
McGee, Robert T., Yardley Ave., Pennsbury, Pa.
McGeoch, Dorothy M., Tchrs. Col., Columbia University, New York, N.Y.
McGinnis, Frederick A., Wilberforce University, P.O. Box 22, Wilberforce, Ohio
McGinnis, James H., Knoxville College, Knoxville, Tenn.
McGlasson, Maurice A., Sch. of Educ., Indiana University, Bloomington, Ind.
McGrath, Earl J., 525 West 120th St., New York, N.Y.
McGrath, G. D., Col. of Educ., Arizona State University, Tempe, Ariz.
McGrath, J. H., Dept. of Ed. Adm., University of Utah, Salt Lake City, Utah
McGrath, John W., Superintendent of Schools, Belmont, Mass.
McGuire, George K., 7211 Merrill Ave., Chicago, Ill.
McGuire, J. Carson, Col. of Educ., University of Texas, Austin, Tex.
McHugh, Walter J., California State College, Hayward, Calif.
McInerney, George K., 88-42—210th St., Jamaica, N.Y.
McIntyre, Margaret, George Washington Univ., Washington, D.C.
McIntyre, Richmond E., 422 Richmond Ave., Burlington, N.C.
McIsaac, John S., 2829 Fourth Ave., Beaver Falls, Pa.
McKay, Jean W., Board of Education, Manassas, Va.
McKean, Robert C., Col. of Educ., University of Colorado, Boulder, Colo.
McKee, Frances, Div. of Educ., Bemidji State College, Bemidji, Minn.
McKelpin, Joseph P., North Carolina College, Durham, N.C.
McKenna, Charles D., 9703 Conway Rd., St. Louis, Mo.
McKenna, John J., Jr., Brd. of Educ., Greenvillage Rd., Madison, N.J.
McKenney, James L., Grad. Sch. of Business, Harvard Univ., Boston, Mass.
McKenzie, Francis W., Brd. of Educ., Box 1167, Darien, Conn.
McKercher, Mrs. Berneth N., 1600 Dryden Rd., Metamora, Mich.
McKinley, S. Justus, Emerson College, 130 Beacon St., Boston, Mass.
* McKinney, James, 505 Aragon Blvd., San Mateo, Calif.
McKinney, Lorella A., State Univ. Col., New Paltz, N.Y.
McKnight, Eloise, Rt. 208, Box 258, New Paltz, N.Y.
McKown, George W., 2603 S. Forest Ave., Palatine, Ill.
McKune, Esther J., State Univ. Col., Oneonta, N.Y.
McLaren, Dallas C., 3240 Manoa Rd., Honolulu, Hawaii
McLaughlin, Edward R., Superintendent of Schools, Lead, S.D.
McLaughlin, Eleanor T., Albion College, Albion, Mich.
McLaughlin, Kenneth F., 871 N. Madison, Arlington, Va.
McLaughlin, Richard C., Col. of Educ., Univ. of Rochester, Rochester, N.Y.
McLaughlin, Rita E., 242 Marlborough St., Boston, Mass.
McLendon, Jonathan C., Col. of Educ., Univ. of Georgia, Athens, Ga.
McLennan, John A., Farmingdale Senior High School, Farmingdale, L.I., N.Y.
McMahan, F. J., St. Ambrose College, 518 W. Locust St., Davenport, Iowa
McMahan, John Julia, State Univ. of A. E. & S., University Park, N.M.
McMahon, Charles W., 22218 Gregory, Dearborn, Mich.
McManamon, James, O.F.M., Supt., P.O. Box 644, Columbus, Neb.

MEMBERS OF THE NATIONAL SOCIETY   lxix

McManus, William E., Supt. Catholic Schls, 430 N. Michigan, Chicago, Ill.
McMaster, Blanche E., 102 Hull St., Bristol, Conn.
McMillan, Ann, Box 356, Blue Mountain Col., Blue Mountain, Miss.
McMillan, Marian, Wayne State University, Detroit, Mich.
McMillian, Nathaniel B., 859 E. Colonial Circle, Holly Hill, Fla.
McMurray, Foster, Col. of Educ., Univ. of Illinois, Urbana, Ill.
McMurtrey, Violet, 3365 S.W. 103rd, Beaverton, Ore.
McNally, Harold J., 7132 N. Crossway Rd., Fox Point, Wis.
McNutt, C. R., 116 Ridge Rd., Woodbridge, Va.
McPhee, Roderick F., Superintendent of Schools, Glencoe, Ill.
McPherson, Virgil L., Adams State College, Alamosa, Colo.
* McPherson, W. N., Darke County Superintendent of Schools, Greenville, Ohio
McSwain, E. T., University of North Carolina, Greensboro, N.C.
McTeer, Blanche R., 803 Lafayette St., Beaufort, S.C.
McWilliams, Earl M., Winchester-Thurston School, Pittsburgh, Pa.
McWilliams, Elma A., William Carey College, Hattiesburg, Miss.
* Mead, Arthur R., 1719 N.W. 6th Ave., Gainesville, Fla.
Meade, David W., Red Wing High School, Red Wing, Minn.
Meaders, O. Donald, Col. of Educ., Michigan State Univ., East Lansing, Mich.
Mease, Clyde D., Superintendent of Schools, Humboldt, Iowa
Medeiros, Edward J., State Dept. of Education, Providence, R.I.
Medeiros, Joseph V., Superintendent of Schools, New London, Conn.
Medler, Byron W., Ball State Univ., Muncie, Ind.
Mednick, Martha T., 523 Sunset Rd., Ann Arbor, Mich.
Medsker, Leland L., Ctr., Study of Higher Educ., Univ. of Calif., Berkeley, Calif.
Medved, A. A., Cherry Lawn School, Darien, Conn.
Meeks, Heber J., Box 252, Borrego Springs, Calif.
Meer, Samuel J., 631 Lafayette Ave., Mt. Vernon, N.Y.
Megiveron, Gene Erwin, 3170 Angelus Dr., Pontiac, Mich.
Megonegal, E. Russell, 464 Granite Ter., Springfield, Pa.
Mehrens, William, Michigan State Univ., East Lansing, Mich.
Meier, Frederick A., State Col. at Salem, Salem, Mass.
Meier, Mrs. Paralee B., 13 Woodside Ln., Chico, Calif.
Meier, Willard H., Dept. of Educ., La Sierra Col., Riverside, Calif.
Meinberg, Shirley, McGraw-Hill Book Co., Manchester, Mo.
Meinke, Dean L., Indiana State University, Terre Haute, Ind.
Meissner, Harley W., 13 Devonshire, Pleasant Ridge, Mich.
Melberg, Merritt E., 1222 W. 22nd St., Cedar Falls, Iowa
Melbo, Irving R., University of Southern California, Los Angeles, Calif.
Melby, Ernest O., Michigan State University, East Lansing, Mich.
Mellott, Malcolm E., Col. of Educ., Temple University, Philadelphia, Pa.
Melnick, Curtis C., Supt., Dist. 14, Chicago Public Schls., Chicago, Ill.
Melnik, Amelia, Col. of Educ., University of Arizona, Tucson, Ariz.
Melnyk, Maria, 4432 S. Christiana Ave., Chicago, Ill.
Melrose, Ezra, Weaver High School, Hartford, Conn.
Melton, Arthur W., Dept. of Psychol., Univ. of Michigan, Ann Arbor, Mich.
Melvin, Keith L., Peru State College, Peru, Neb.
Mendel, Mrs. Dolores M., Paterson State College, Wayne, N.J.
Mendenhall, Alan D., 5205 Sunny Point Pl., Palos Verdes, Calif.
* Mendoza, Romulo Y., 17 Iba, Sta. Mesa Heights, Quezon City, Philippines
Menge, Carleton P., University of New Hampshire, Durham, N.H.
Menge, Joseph W., Wayne University, Detroit, Mich.
Merchant, Vasant V., 308 W. Forest Ave., Flagstaff, Ariz.
Meredith, Cameron W., Southern Illinois Univ., Edwardsville, Ill.
Meredith, Thomas R., Prentice-Hall, Inc., Englewood Cliffs, N.J.
Merenda, Peter F., 258 Negansett Ave., Warwick, R.I.
Merideth, Howard V., Central Sch. Dist. No. 2, Syosset, L.I., N.Y.
Merigis, Harry, Eastern Illinois University, Charleston, Ill.
Merkhofer, Beatrice E., Chicago State College, Chicago, Ill.
Merritt, C. B., Col. of Educ., Univ. of Arizona, Tucson, Ariz.
Merryman, John E., Geneva College, Beaver Falls, Pa.

MEMBERS OF THE NATIONAL SOCIETY

Mersand, Joseph, Jamaica High Sch., 168th St. and Gothic Dr., Jamaica, N.Y.
Merwin, Jack C., 1896 Dellwood Ave., St. Paul, Minn.
Mesa, Sergio Lopez, Allen University, Columbia, S.C.
Mestdagh, William A., 1840 Vernier Rd., Grosse Pointe Woods, Mich.
Metcalfe, William W., 68 Blue Hills Rd., Amherst, Mass.
Metfessel, Newton S., Univ. of Southern California, Los Angeles, Calif.
Metzner, William, 1121 Welsh Rd., Philadelphia, Pa.
Meyer, Ammon B., Route 1, Fredericksburg, Pa.
Meyer, George A., University of Hawaii, Honolulu, Hawaii
Meyer, Lorraine V., 4501 N. 41st St., Milwaukee, Wis.
Meyer, Mrs. Marie, Douglass Col., Rutgers Univ., New Brunswick, N.J.
Meyer, Richard C., East. Texas State University, Commerce, Tex.
Meyer, Warren G., 5829 Portland Ave., So., Minneapolis, Minn.
Meyer, William T., Adams State College, Alamosa, Colo.
Meyers, Howard E., Peru State Col., Peru, Neb.
Meyers, Max B., 324 E. 59th St., Brooklyn, N.Y.
Meyers, Robert E., Middlebury High School, Middlebury, Ind.
Michael, Calvin B., Col. of Educ., East. Mich. Univ., Ypsilanti, Mich.
Michael, Lloyd S., Evanston Township High School, Evanston, Ill.
Michael, Lois M., 2037 S. Beverly Glen, Los Angeles, Calif.
Michael, William B., Sch. of Educ., Univ. of So. California, Los Angeles, Calif.
Michaelis, John U., Sch. of Educ., Univ. of California, Berkeley, Calif.
Michaels, Melvin L., Highland Park High School, Highland Park, N.J.
Michalak, Daniel A., 13941 Minock Ave., Detroit, Mich.
Micheels, William J., Stout State University, Menomonie, Wis.
Michie, James K., Superintendent of Schools, St. Cloud, Minn.
Mickelsen, John K., 106 Jackson Dr., Liverpool, N.Y.
Mickelson, John M., Sch. of Educ., Temple University, Philadelphia, Pa.
Middledorf, Carl W., St. Peter's Lutheran School, East Detroit, Mich.
Middleton, C. A., State College of Iowa, Cedar Falls, Iowa
Mikulak, Michael N., 620 Sunset St., Iowa City, Iowa
Milchus, Norman J., 20504 Williamsburg Rd., Dearborn Heights, Mich.
Milheim, Robert P., Wright State Univ., Dayton, Ohio
Milhollan, Frank E., 6003—85th Pl., Hyattsville, Md.
Millar, Allen R., Southern State Tchrs. College, Springfield, S.D.
Miller, Arthur L., 5625 Rosa Ave., St. Louis, Mo.
Miller, Benjamin, 251 Ft. Washington Ave., New York, N.Y.
Miller, C. Earl, Jr., 157 Eldridge Ave., Mill Valley, Calif.
Miller, Carroll H., Dept. of Educ., Northern Illinois Univ., DeKalb, Ill.
Miller, Carroll L., Howard University, Washington, D.C.
Miller, Eliza Beth, Catskill High School, Catskill, N.Y.
Miller, Ethel B., 133 Joanne Ln., DeKalb, Ill.
Miller, G. Dean, State Dept. of Educ., St. Paul, Minn.
Miller, G. Harold, Gastonia City Schools, Gastonia, N.C.
Miller, George E., Univ. of Illinois Col. of Medicine, Chicago, Ill.
Miller, Mrs. Helen H., 1471 Westhaven Rd., San Marino, Calif.
Miller, Henry, Sch. of Educ., City College of New York, New York, N.Y.
Miller, Herbert R., 159 Coolidge Rd., Rochester, N.Y.
Miller, Ingrid O., Edina-Morningside Senior High School, Edina, Minn.
Miller, Ira E., Eastern Mennonite College, Harrisonburg, Va.
Miller, Jack W., Box 35, Peabody College, Nashville, Tenn.
Miller, Jacob W., Brooke Rd., Saybrooke Park, Pottstown, Pa.
Miller, John L., Supt. of Schools, Great Neck, N.Y.
Miller, Leon F., Northwest Missouri State College, Maryville, Mo.
Miller, Lyle L., Col. of Educ., University of Wyoming, Laramie, Wyo.
Miller, Mrs. Marian B., Dept. of Pub. Instr., Dover, Del.
Miller, Mrs. Mildred T., Box 215, Mooresville, N.C.
Miller, N. A., Jr., Watauga High School, Boone, N.C.
Miller, Norman N., Superintendent of Schools, Tyrone, Pa.
Miller, Paul A., 608 E. McMillan St., Cincinnati, Ohio
Miller, Ralph, Superintendent of Schools, Georgetown, Ill.

MEMBERS OF THE NATIONAL SOCIETY   lxxi

Miller, Richard I., Col. of Educ., University of Kentucky, Lexington, Ky.
Miller, Ross, West Georgia College, Carrollton, Ga.
Miller, Texton R., North Carolina State University, Raleigh, N.C.
Milling, Euleas, 231 Spring St., N.W., Concord, N.C.
Mills, Boyd C., Eastern Washington State Col., Cheney, Wash.
Mills, Donna M., 530 Taft Place, Gary, Ind.
Mills, Forrest L., Racine Public Library, Racine, Wis.
Mills, Henry C., Provost, St. John's Univ., Jamaica, N.Y.
Mills, Ruth I., Concord College, Athens, W.Va.
Mills, William H., Sch. of Educ., Univ. of Michigan, Ann Arbor, Mich.
Milner, Ernest J., Sch. of Educ., Syracuse University, Syracuse, N.Y.
Mims, Samuel, Bethany Bible College, Santa Cruz, Calif.
Mincy, Homer F., Superintendent of Schools, Greeneville, Tenn.
Miniclier, Gordon E., 1965 Laurel Ave., St. Paul, Minn.
Mininberg, Elliot I., 4 Washington Square Village, New York, N.Y.
Minkler, F. W., 15 Oakburn Crest, Willowdale, Ont., Canada
Minkoff, Sol., 601 N. Eastwood, Mt. Prospect, Ill.
Minnis, Roy B., 7889 E. Kenyon Ave., Denver, Colo.
Minock, Mrs. Daniel F., 5520 Donna Ave, Tarzana, Calif.
Minogue, Mildred M., 612 Ridge Ave., Evanston, Ill.
Minor, Pearle Estelle, 1716 Allison St., N.W., Washington, D.C.
Misner, Paul J., Western Michigan Univ., Kalamazoo, Mich.
Mitby, Norman P., 211 N. Carroll St., Madison, Wis.
Mitchell, Donald P., 5166 Tilden St., N.W., Washington, D.C.
Mitchell, Guy Clifford, Sch. of Educ., Baylor University, Waco, Tex.
Mitchell, Mrs. Marian A., 1331 Bernard St., N.W., Atlanta, Ga.
Mitra, Gopal C., Dept. of Art Educ., Univ. of Minnesota, Minneapolis, Minn.
Mitzel, Harold E., 928 S. Sparks St., State College, Pa.
Mobley, Frank, Northwestern State College, Natchitoches, La.
Modica, Frank, John Spry Elem. School, Chicago, Ill.
Moffatt, Maurice P., 210 Valencia Blvd., Largo, Fla.
Mohr, Raymond E., 2050 S. 108th St., Milwaukee, Wis.
Molenkamp, Alice, 5 Homeside Lane, White Plains, N.Y.
Moll, Boniface E., St. Benedict's College, Atchison, Kan.
Molloy, Eugene J., Superintendent, Catholic Schools, Brooklyn, N.Y.
Monell, Ira H., 2714 Augusta Blvd., Chicago, Ill.
Monfort, Jay B., 3150 Maranja Dr., Walnut Creek, Calif.
Monnin, Lloyd N., R.R. #1, Yellow Springs, Ohio
Monroe, Bruce Perry, 640 Sea Breeze Dr., Seal Beach, Calif.
Monroe, Charles R., Wilson Junior College, 7047 S. Stewart Ave., Chicago, Ill.
Monroe, Helen V., 521 Hawkeye, Iowa City, Iowa
Monsanto, David, P.O. Box 672, Charlotte Amalie, Virgin Islands
Montgomery, John F., Greenbrier College, Lewisburg, W.Va.
Monts, Elizabeth A., Home Ec. Dept., Univ. of Wisconsin, Madison, Wis.
Moody, Lamar, 1140 S.W. Peppridge Tr., Boca Raton, Fla.
Moore, Alexander M., Crispus Attucks High School, Indianapolis, Ind.
Moore, Arnold J., Dept. of Educ., Creighton University, Omaha, Neb.
Moore, Barry E., 103 William Dr., Normal, Ill.
Moore, C. Fletcher, Box 186, Elon College, N.C.
Moore, Harold E., Col. of Educ., Arizona State University, Tempe, Ariz.
Moore, Robert Ezra, 20 Tapia Dr., San Francisco, Calif.
Moore, Wilhelmina E., C. D. Hine Library, State Office Bldg., Hartford, Conn.
Moore, William J., 372 High St., Richmond, Ky.
Moorefield, Thomas E., 1211 McGee St., Kansas City, Mo.
Moorhead, Sylvester A., Sch. of Educ., Univ. of Mississippi, University, Miss.
Moray, Joseph, San Francisco State College, San Francisco, Calif.
Morehouse, Charles O., 601 S. Howard St., Kimball, Neb.
Moreland, Kenneth O., 107 William Dr., Normal, Ill.
Moretz, Elmo E., Grad. Sch. of Educ., Eastern Kentucky Univ., Richmond, Ky.
Morford, John A., John Carroll University, Cleveland, Ohio
Morgan, Donald L., 1314 Pine St., Iowa City, Iowa

MEMBERS OF THE NATIONAL SOCIETY

Morgan, J. Stanley, Jr., Summer Hill School, Cartersville, Ga.
Morgan, Lorraine Lee, 6909 Meade St., Pittsburgh, Pa.
Morgan, Muriel, Newark State College, Union, N.J.
Morgan, Roland R., Superintendent, Mooresville City Schls., Mooresville, N.C.
Morgenroth, Edwin C., 714 W. California Blvd., Pasadena, Calif.
Morgenstern, Anne, 2037 Oliver Way, Merrick, L.I., N.Y.
Moriarty, Thomas E., 112 Independence, Kingston, R.I.
Moriconi, R. J., 400 N.W. 21st Ln., # 45, Gainesville, Fla.
Morley, Franklin P., 101 Arthur Ave., Webster Groves, Mo.
Morris, Earl W., Rt. 5, East Lake Drive, Edwardsville, Ill.
Morris, George L., Kearney State Col., Kearney, Neb.
Morris, James D., Col. of Educ., Univ. of Hawaii, Honolulu,, Hawaii
Morris, James L., 675 Omar Circle, Yellow Springs, Ohio
Morris, James Vaughn, 131 Warren Ave., Oxford, N.C.
Morris, Rev. John E., Diocesean Schls., Paterson, N.J.
Morris, M. B., 1133 Westridge, Abilene, Tex.
Morris, Mrs. Marjorie S., 16225 Moorpark, Encino, Calif.
Morrison, D. A., East York Bd. of Educ., 670 Cosburn Ave., Toronto, Ont.
* Morrison, J. Cayce, 580 North Bank Ln., Lake Forest, Ill.
Morrison, Leger R., 16 Brown St., Warren, R.I.
Morrissey, Madeline M., 110 Livingston St., Brooklyn, N.Y.
Morrow, Richard G., 502 State St., Madison, Wis.
Morrow, Robert O., Col. of Educ., Univ. of Tennessee, Knoxville, Tenn.
Morse, Richard N., 2109 Lemmon Way, Hanford, Calif.
Morse, William C., 2010 Penncraft Ct., Ann Arbor, Mich.
Morton, R. Clark, 210 Drummond St., Warrensburg, Mo.
Mosbo, Alvin O., Colorado State College, Greeley, Colo.
Moseley, S. Meredith, 424 N.W. 15th Way, Fort Lauderdale, Fla.
Moser, Robert P., 310 Educ. Bldg., Univ. of Wisconsin, Madison, Wis.
Moser, William G., 95 Concord Rd., Chester, Pa.
Moses, Elizabeth, 22 Bucareli Dr., San Francisco, Calif.
Mosher, Frank K., Utica Col. of Syracuse University, Utica, N.Y.
Mosier, Earl E., 28 Woodhampton Dr., Trenton, N.J.
Moss, Theodore C., 88 Sixth Ave., Oswego, N.Y.
Mother A. Husson, Convent of the Sacred Heart, Portsmouth, R.I.
Mother C. Welch, San Francisco College for Women, San Francisco, Calif.
Mother Margaret Burke, Barat Col. of the Sacred Heart, Lake Forest, Ill.
Mother Mary Aimee Rossi, San Diego Col. for Women, San Diego, Calif.
Mother Mary Dennis, Rosemont College, Rosemont, Pa.
Mother M. Gonzaga, Blessed Sacrament College, Cornwells Heights, Pa.
Mother Miriam Regina, Sacred Heart School, Vineland, N.J.
Mother Rose Alice, 2675 Larpenteur Ave. East, St. Paul, Minn.
Mott, Edward B., R.F.D., Richmondville, N.Y.
Motyka, Agnes L., 6311 Utah Ave., N.W., Washington, D.C.
Moulton, Gerald L., Rt. 3, Box 19A-3, Ellensburg, Wash.
Mour, Stanley I., University of Louisville, Louisville, Ky.
Mouritsen, Roger, 3229 Melbourne, Salt Lake City, Utah
Muck, Mrs. Ruth E. S., 1091 Stony Point Rd., Grand Island, N.Y.
Muck, Webster C., Bethel Col., St. Paul, Minn.
Muellen, T. K., 3606 Spruell Dr., Silver Spring, Md.
Mueller, Richard J., Northern Illinois University, DeKalb, Ill.
Mueller, Siegfried G., 202½ Friedline Dr., Carbondale, Ill.
Mulligan, Glenn, 11109 Trails North Drive, Fort Wayne, Ind.
Mulhern, Joseph C., Spring Hill College, Mobile, Ala.
Mullen, Norman, Superintendent of Schools, Woodsville, N.H.
Muller, Philippe H., University of Neuchatel, Neuchatel, Switzerland
Mulliner, John H., 1509 Topp Lane, Glenview, Ill.
Mulrooney, Thomas W., Board of Public Education, Wilmington, Del.
Mumford, Kennedy A., 14845 Robinson St., Miami, Fla.
Muns, Arthur C., Northern Illinois Univ., DeKalb, Ill.
Munshaw, Carroll, 555 Byron St., Plymouth, Mich.

MEMBERS OF THE NATIONAL SOCIETY lxxiii

Muntyan, Milosh, Michigan State University, East Lansing, Mich.
Munves, Elizabeth D., New York University, 37 Washington Sq., New York, N.Y.
Murdick, Olin J., Superintendent, Diocesan Schools, Saginaw, Mich.
Murdock, Mrs. Ruth, Andrews University, Berrien Springs, Mich.
Murphy, Anne P., 480 S. Jersey St., Denver, Colo.
Murphy, Daniel A., Seton Hall University, South Orange, N.J.
Murphy, Dennis K., Grinnell College, Grinnell, Iowa
Murphy, Forrest W., Florida Atlantic University, Boca Raton, Fla.
Murphy, Kenneth B., Jersey City State Col., Jersey City, N.J.
Murphy, Loretta, 303 Lime St., Joliet, Ill.
Murray, Joseph A., Jr., Cranston School Dept., Cranston, R.I.
Murray, Walter I., Brooklyn College, Brooklyn, N.Y.
Murray, William J., 1 Bay View Pl., South Boston, Mass.
Musgrave, Ray S., Univ. of Southern Mississippi, Hattiesburg, Miss.
Muskal, Fred, 1517 East 54th St., Chicago, Ill.
Myer, Marshall E., Jr., University of South Carolina, Columbia, S.C.
Myers, Donald A., 1100 Glendon Ave., Los Angeles, Calif.
Myers, G. T., Superintendent of Schools, Lancaster, S.C.
Myers, Garry Cleveland, 968 Main St., Honesdale, Pa.

Nafziger, Mary K., Goshen College, Goshen, Ind.
Nagel, Wilma I., 1849 Warwick Ave., Warwick, R.I.
Nagle, Robert J., Superintendent of Schools, Fall River, Mass.
Nagy, Richard, North Junior High School, Bloomfield, N.J.
Nahm, Helen, Dean, Sch. of Nurs., Univ. of California, San Francisco, Calif.
Nahshon, Samuel, Bureau of Jewish Educ., 2030 S. Taylor Rd., Cleveland, Ohio
Nair, Ralph K., University of California, Santa Barbara, Calif.
Nakashima, Mitsugi, 1412 I Spartan Village, East Lansing, Mich.
Nally, Thomas P., University of Rhode Island, Kingston, R.I.
Nance, Mrs. Afton Dill, State Educ. Bldg., 721 Capitol Ave., Sacramento, Calif.
Nance, Helen M., Illinois State University, Normal, Ill.
Narkis, William F., 4921 W. Ferdinand St., Chicago, Ill.
Nash, Philip C., Rt. 1, 21 Sycamore Pl., Carmel, Calif.
Naslund, Robert A., Sch. of Educ., Univ. of So. California, Los Angeles, Calif.
Nason, Doris E., University of Connecticut, Storrs, Conn.
Nasser, Sheffield, 2576 Hillview St., Sarasota, Fla.
Nasstrom, Roy R., Jr., 6212 Antioch St., Oakland, Calif.
Nault, William H., Field Enterprises Educational Corp., Chicago, Ill.
Naus, Grant H., 374 "D" Ave., Coronado, Calif.
Naylor, Marilyn, 233 W. Cascade, River Falls, Wis.
Neal, Ellis H., Superintendent of Schools, Pendleton, Ore.
Neale, Daniel C., Col. of Educ., University of Minnesota, Minneapolis, Minn.
Nearhoff, Orrin, 2745 Bennett Ave., Des Moines, Iowa
Nebel, Dale, Colorado State College, Greeley, Colo.
Nelson, Carl B., New York State University College, Cortland, N.Y.
Nelson, Clifford L., Dept. of Ag. Ed., Univ. of Minnesota, St. Paul, Minn.
Nelson, Edith I., 380 Claremont Ave., Montclair, N.J.
Nelson, Ethel C., 692 Des Plaines Ave., Des Plaines, Ill.
Nelson, Florence A., Univ. of South Carolina, 825 Sumter St., Columbia, S.C.
Nelson, Frank G., R. 2, Box 169-0, Pullman, Wash.
Nelson, Jack L., State Univ. Col., Buffalo, N.Y.
Nelson, John M., Dept. of Educ., Purdue University, Lafayette, Ind.
Nelson, Kenneth G., 2312 Glasgow Rd., Alexandria, Va.
Nelson, L. Warren, Miami University, Oxford, Ohio
Nelson, Lois Ney, 7 Lakeview Dr., Daly City, Calif.
Nelson, Margaret B., State College of Iowa, Cedar Falls, Iowa
Nelson, Norbert J., 2103 Indiana Trail Dr., West Lafayette, Ind.
Nelson, Orville W., Stout State College, Menomonie, Wis.
Nelson, Pearl Astrid, Boston University, 332 Bay State Rd., Boston, Mass.
Nelson, Quentin D., Univ. Libre du Congo, Kisangani, Rep. of Congo
Nelson, Sylvia, 415 W. 8th St., Topeka, Kans.

Nelson, Torlef, University of Hawaii, Honolulu, Hawaii
Nelum, J. Nathaniel, Div. of Educ., Bishop College, Dallas, Tex.
Nemzek, Claude L., Educ. Dept., Univ. of Detroit, Detroit, Mich.
Nerbovig, Marcella, Northern Illinois University, DeKalb, Ill.
Nesbitt, Hyacinth P., Box 712, Frederiksted, St. Croix, U.S. Virgin Is.
Nesbitt, William O., University of Houston, Houston, Tex.
Nesi, Carmella, 906 Peace St., Pelham Manor, N.Y.
Netsky, Martin G., Dept. of Path., University of Virginia, Charlottesville, Va.
Neuner, Elsie Flint, 2 Atlas Place, Mt. Vernon, N.Y.
Neville, Donald, Child Study Center, Peabody College, Nashville, Tenn.
Neville, Richard F., Col. of Educ., University of Maryland, College Park, Md.
Newburn, H. K., Col. of Educ., Arizona State University, Tempe, Ariz.
Newbury, David N., 22929 John Rd., Hazel Park, Mich.
Newcomer, Charles A., Lock Haven State Col., Lock Haven, Pa.
Newman, Herbert M., Educ. Dept., Brooklyn College, Brooklyn, N.Y.
Newman, Wilfred, West High School, Rochester, N.Y.
Newsom, Herman A., P.O. Box 5243, North Texas Station, Denton, Tex.
Newton, Eunice S., Howard University, Washington, D.C.
Newton, W. L., Florida State University, Tallahassee, Fla.
Nicholas, William T., 1019 Caldwell Ave., Modesto, Calif.
Nichols, David L., University of Maine, Orono, Me.
Nichols, Richard H., 1703 S.W. 16th Ct., Gainesville, Fla.
Nichols, Richard J., Troy Village, Troy Dr., Springfield, N.J.
Nicholson, Jon M., Carleton College, Northfield, Minn.
Nicholson, Lawrence E., Psych. Dept., Harris Tchrs. Col., St. Louis, Mo.
Nicholson, Omega, Texas Wesleyan Col., Ft. Worth, Texas
Nicholson, Sarah Alice, 1009 E. Hatton St., Pensacola, Fla.
Nickerson, Donald R., Beaver Country Day School, Chestnut Hill, Mass.
Niehaus, Philip C., Sch. of Educ., Duquesne University, Pittsburgh, Pa.
Niemeyer, John H., Bank Street College of Education, New York, N.Y.
Nigg, William J., Superintendent of Schools, Mankato, Minn.
Niland, William P., 417 Candleberry Rd., Walnut Creek, Calif.
Nilsen, Robert A., 15 Graves St., Staten Island, N.Y.
Nimroth, William T., 1011 Wood Bridge, Ann Arbor, Mich.
Nix, J. Gordon, Jr., Harlingen Senior High School, Harlingen, Tex.
Nixon, Clifford L., East Carolina College, Greenville, N.C.
Nixon, John Erskine, Sch. of Educ., Stanford University, Stanford, Calif.
Noar, Gertrude, 500 E. 77th St., New York, N.Y.
Noe, Samuel V., 506 West Hill St., Louisville, Ky.
Nolan, William J., Superintendent of Schools, Falls Village, Conn.
Nolde, Randall L., 2146 Sherman Ave., Evanston, Ill.
Noll, Frances E., 1810 Taylor St., N.W., Washington, D.C.
Noll, Victor H., Col. of Educ., Michigan State Univ., East Lansing, Mich.
Noon, Elizabeth F., F. A. Owen Publishing Co., Dansville, N.Y.
Norberg, Kenneth D., Sacramento State College, Sacramento, Calif.
Norcross, Claude E., 301 E. Lucard, Taft, Calif.
Nord, Larry R., Supt., Southington Local Schools, Southington, Ohio
Nordberg, H. Orville, Sacramento State College, Sacramento, Calif.
Norem, Grant M., Minot State College, Minot, N.D.
Norman, Ralph Paul, 18395 Clemison Ave., Saratoga, Calif.
Norman, Robert H., 315—4th Ave., N.W., Faribault, Minn.
Norris, Mrs. Dorothy G., 1907 Dumaine St., New Orleans, La.
Norris, Ralph C., 112-116—11th St., Des Moines, Iowa
North, Stewart D., 502 State St., Madison, Wis.
Northey, Ethel May, 224 Iowa Ave., Muscatine, Iowa
Northrup, Sunbeam Ann, 1816 Queens Lane, Arlington, Va.
Norton, Frank Edgar, Jr., 225 Fairway Dr., Wharton, Texas
Nosek, Walter K., Superintendent of Schools, Wheaton, Minn.
Novak, Benjamin J., Frankford High School, Philadelphia, Pa.
Novotney, Jerrold M., 1100 Glendon Ave., Los Angeles, Calif.
Now, Herbert O., State Dept. of Educ., Findlay, Ohio

MEMBERS OF THE NATIONAL SOCIETY   lxxv

Nowak, Arlene T., Educ. Dept., Univ. of Detroit, Detroit, Mich.
Nowicki, Ervin E., 2967 N. Prospect Ave., Milwaukee, Wis.
Noyes, M. Elliot, Great Neck No. Senior High School, Great Neck, N.Y.
Nunnally, Nancy, 5016 Monticello Ave., Cincinnati, Ohio
Nussel, Edward J., Col. of Educ., Univ. of Toledo, Toledo, Ohio
Nutter, H. E., Norman Hall, University of Florida, Gainesville, Fla.
* Nutterville, Catherine, 1701—16th St., N.W., Washington, D.C.
Nutting, William C., 4653 Fortuna Way, Salt Lake City, Utah
Nuzum, Lawrence H., Marshall University, Huntington, W.Va.
Nye, Robert E., Sch. of Music, University of Oregon, Eugene, Ore.
Nygaard, Joseph M., Butler University, Indianapolis, Ind.
Nystrand, Raphael O., Ohio State Univ., Columbus, Ohio

Oakland, Thomas, 305 E. Vermilya, Bloomington, Ind.
Oaks, Ruth E., B-104 Haverford Villa, Haverford, Pa.
Ober, Richard L., 4048 N.W. 13th Ave., Gainesville, Fla.
Oberholtzer, Kenneth E., Superintendent of Schools, Denver, Colo.
Obourn, L. C., Superintendent of Schools, East Rochester, N.Y.
O'Brien, Cyril C., P.O. Box 666, Edmonton, Alba., Canada
O'Connor, Clarence D., Supt., Lexington School for Deaf, New York, N.Y.
O'Connor, John D., Maple Park, Ill.
O'Connor, Mrs. Marguerite O., Maple Park, Ill.
O'Donnell, Beatrice, Michigan State University, East Lansing, Mich.
Oehring, Esther A., Southern Oregon College, Ashland, Ore.
Oen, Urban T., Michigan State Univ., East Lansing, Mich.
O'Fallon, O. K., Sch. of Educ., Kansas State University, Manhattan, Kan.
O'Farrell, John J., Loyola University, 7101 W. 80th St., Los Angeles, Calif.
O'Hare, Mary Rita, 212 Hollywood Ave., Tuckahoe, N.Y.
O'Hearn, George T., 576 Park Lane, Madison, Wis.
Ohlsen, Merle M., Col. of Educ., University of Illinois, Urbana, Ill.
Ohm, Robert E., Col. of Educ., University of Oklahoma, Norman, Okla.
Ohnmacht, Fred W., University of Georgia, Athens, Ga.
Ojeman, Ralph H., Educ. Research Council, Rockefeller Bldg., Cleveland, Ohio
O'Kane, Robert M., Rutgers State University, New Brunswick, N.J.
O'Keefe, Kathleen, University of Pittsburgh, Pittsburgh, Pa.
Okula, Frederick S., 90 Mattatuck Rd., Bristol, Conn.
Olander, Herbert T., University of Pittsburgh, Pittsburgh, Pa.
Oldendorf, Dorothy, Wilmette Bd. of Educ., Dist. #39, Wilmette, Ill.
* Oldham, Mrs. Birdie V., 621 W. 2nd St., Lakeland, Fla.
Olds, Victoria M., CSWE, 345 E. 46th St., New York, N.Y.
O'Leary, Francis V., 67 Sterling Rd., Westwood, Mass.
Olicker, Isidore I., 85-17—143rd St., Jamaica, N.Y.
Olivas, Romeo A., Univ. of the Philippines, Diliman, Rizal, Philippines
Oliver, George J., Richmond Professional Institute, Richmond, Va.
Olmsted, M. D., State University College, Oneonta, N.Y.
Olphert, Warwick B., Univ. of New England, Armidale, N.S.W., Australia
Olsen, Eugene A., Purdue University, Lafayette, Ind.
Olsen, Hans C., Jr., Col. of Educ., Wayne State University, Detroit, Mich.
Olson, Boyd E., P.O. Box 226, Singapore, Rep. of Singapore
Olson, Gerald Victor, 8610 W. 19th St., Phoenix, Ariz.
Olson, Manley E., Col. of Educ., Univ. of Minnesota, Minneapolis, Minn.
Olson, R. A., Ball State University, Muncie, Ind.
* Olson, Willard C., Sch. of Educ., University of Michigan, Ann Arbor, Mich.
Olson, William L., 1945 Sharondale Ave., St. Paul, Minn.
O'Malley, Mrs. Martha R., 44 Glenview Dr., Belleville, Ill.
O'Mara, J. Francis, 29 Snowling Rd., Uxbridge, Mass.
Omark, Donald R., 5704 S. Harper, Chicago, Ill.
Omark, Donald R., West Leyden High School, Northlake, Ill.
O'Neill, John H., 1039 W. Vine St., Springfield, Ill.
O'Neill, John J., State College of Boston, 625 Huntington Ave., Boston, Mass.
O'Neill, Leo W., Jr., Col. of Educ., University of Maryland, College Park, Md.

O'Neill, Patrick J., Superintendent, Diocesan Schools, Fall River, Mass.
Onkle, Paul, 8309 Mackenzie Rd., St. Louis, Mo.
Oole, Eugenia M., 6012 Drew Ave. So., Minneapolis, Minn.
O'Piela, Joan M., Res. & Dev., Detroit Pub. Schools, Detroit, Mich.
Oppenheim, Alan, 5200 Blackstone Ave., Chicago, Ill.
Oppenheimer, J. J., Belknap Campus, University of Louisville, Louisville, Ky.
Oppleman, Dan L., P.O. Box 182, Cedar Falls, Iowa
Ore, Malvern L., 903 East 52nd St., Chicago, Ill.
Ore, Stanley H., Jr., 2221 Emmers Dr., Appleton, Wis.
O'Reilly, Robert C., Municipal University of Omaha, Omaha, Neb.
Orlich, Donald C., Idaho State University, Pocatello, Idaho
Orlovich, Joseph, Jr., 416 Keepataw Dr., Lemont, Ill.
O'Rourke, Joseph, 3197 Gerbert Rd., Columbus, Ohio
Orr, Beryl, 609 Gladys Dr., Middletown, Ohio
Orr, Charles W., 137 Oakmont Circle, Durham, N.C.
Orr, Louise, 925 Crockett St., Amarillo, Tex.
Orton, Don A., Lesley College, Cambridge, Mass.
Orton, Kenneth D., Tchrs. Col., University of Nebraska, Lincoln, Neb.
Osborn, Wayland W., 2701 Hickman Rd., Des Moines, Iowa
O'Shea, John T., 767 Ridge Rd., Lackawana, N.Y.
O'Shields, Eva W., 6600 Arcadia Woods Rd., Columbia, S.C.
Osibov, Henry, University of Oregon, Eugene, Ore.
Ostler, Ruth-Ellen, 318 State St., Albany, N.Y.
Ostrander, Raymond H., 15 Winter St., Weston, Mass.
Ostrom, Gerald, 291 Wagner Rd., Northfield, Ill.
Ostwalt, Jay H., P.O. Box 387, Davidson, N.C.
Osuch, A. E., 6636 N. Odell, Chicago, Ill.
Osuna, Pedro, Sch. of Educ., Univ. of the Pacific, Stockton, Calif.
Oswalt, Howard C., 1518 N. McAllister Ave., Tempe, Ariz.
Oswalt, William W., Jr., 9 Berger St., Emmaus, Pa.
Otomo, Aiko, 3085 Felix St., Honolulu, Hawaii
O'Toole, James J., Valley Central Jr. H.S., Middletown, N.Y.
Ott, Francis M., 723 E. Pittsburgh St., Greensburg, Pa.
Otto, Arleen, Tchrs. Col., Columbia University, New York, N.Y.
Otto, Henry J., University of Texas, Austin, Tex.
Otts, John, University of South Carolina, Columbia, S.C.
Overfield, Ruth, State Educ. Bldg., 721 Capitol Ave., Sacramento, Calif.
*Overstreet, George Thomas, 811 S. Frances St., Terrell, Tex.
Owen, John M., Psych. Dept., State University College, Potsdam, N.Y.
Owens, Robert M., 524 Woodland Hills Dr., Athens, Ga.
Owings, Ralph S., Univ. of Southern Mississippi, Hattiesburg, Miss.

Pace, C. Robert, Sch. of Educ., University of California, Los Angeles, Calif.
Packer, C. Kyle, 629 Deerfield Dr., North Tonawanda, N.Y.
Page, Ellis B., Bur. of Educ. Res., Univ. of Connecticut, Storrs, Conn.
Pagel, Betty Lou, 304 E. 5th Ave., Cheyenne, Wyo.
Painter, Fred B., Superintendent, Brighton School Dist. No. 1, Rochester, N.Y.
Palisi, Anthony T., Seton Hall Univ., 181 Stanton, Rahway, N.J.
Palisi, Marino A., 300 Woodland Ave., Point Pleasant Beach, N.J.
Palladino, Joseph R., State College, Framingham, Mass.
Pallesen, Lorraine Sysel, 2727 Royal Ct., Lincoln, Neb.
Palliser, Guy C., C.P.O. Box 1525, Wellington, New Zealand
Palmer, Albert, Stockton College, Stockton, Calif.
Palmer, Anne M. H., 22277 Cass Ave., Woodland Hills, Calif.
Palmer, Dale H., Univ. of Washington, Seattle, Wash.
Palmer, Frank J., 208 Church St., North Syracuse, N.Y.
Palmer, John C., Tufts University, Medford, Mass.
Palmer, Lulu, State Department of Education, Montgomery, Ala.
Paltridge, James G., 2632 Tamalipas Ave., El Cerrito, Calif.
Panos, Robert J., 12903 Crookston Lane, Rockville, Md.
Papanek, Ernst, 1 West 64th St., New York, N.Y.

MEMBERS OF THE NATIONAL SOCIETY   lxxvii

Papke, Ross R., Wisconsin State Univ., Richland Center, Wis.
Paquin, Laurence G., 3 East 25th St., Baltimore, Md.
Parisho, Eugenia G., International House, 1414 E. 59th St., Chicago, Ill.
Park, Mary Frances, Educ. Dept., Sam Houston State Col., Huntsville, Texas
Park, Maxwell G., 44 Clayton Ave., Cortland, N.Y.
Parker, Don H., Emlimar, Big Sur, Calif.
Parker, Glenn C., 653 Sandra Ave., Harrisburg, Pa.
Parker, James R., 210 Thornbrook Rd., DeKalb, Ill.
Parker, Mrs. Lilla C., Box 464-A, Donnan Road, Macon, Ga.
Parker, Virjean, 765 Commonwealth Ave., Boston, Mass.
Parker, Wilfred G., 322 Eagle Dr., Placentia, Calif.
Parkinson, Daniel S., 409 W. Vine St., Oxford, Ohio
Parkyn, George W., 178-182 Willis St., Wellington, New Zealand
Parr, Kenneth E., Box 1348, c/o Tapline, Beirut, Lebanon
Parrett, Betty J., Marion County Interm. Educ. Dist., Salem, Ore.
Parry, O. Meredith, William Penn Senior High School, York, Pa.
Parsey, John M., 305 Droste Circle, East Lansing, Mich.
Parsley, Kenneth M., Briarcliff-on-Severn, Arnold, Md.
Parsons, Brooks A., Superintendent of Schools, Norwood, Ohio
Parsons, David R., Alexander Mackie Col., Paddington, N.S.W., Australia
Pascoe, David D., LaMesa Spring Valley Sch. Dist., LaMesa, Calif.
Passow, Aaron Harry, Teachers College, Columbia University, New York, N.Y.
Paster, G. Nicholas, 117 W. Center College St., Yellow Springs, Ohio
Paster, Julius, 867 Barbara Dr., Teaneck, N.J.
Patch, Robert B., 4 Carleton Dr., Glens Falls, N.Y.
Pate, Mildred, 1806 East 6th St., Greenville, N.C.
Paterson, John J., 377 Lawnview Dr., Morgantown, W.Va.
Paton, James M., Univ. of Toronto, Toronto, Ont., Canada
Paton, Maurice, 936 N. Ashland Ave., Chicago, Ill.
Paton, William, Superintendent of Schools, Oconomowoc, Wis.
Patrick, Edward M., Jr., 77 Belchertown Rd., Amherst, Mass.
Patrick, Ernest W., Henderson State Col., Arkadelphia, Ark.
Patrick, Robert B., 433 W. Park Ave., State College, Pa.
Patt, Jack M., Soc. Sci. Div., San Jose State College, San Jose, Calif.
Patterson, Gordon E., New Mexico Highlands Univ., Las Vegas, N.M.
Patterson, Harold D., 3736 Crestbrook Rd., Birmingham, Ala.
* Patterson, Herbert, 406 S. Stallard Ave., Stillwater, Okla.
Patterson, Walter G., 1330 Highland Ave., Needham, Mass.
Patton, Earl D., Superintendent of Schools, Culver City, Calif.
Patty, Delbert L., 9103 Lincolnshire W., DeKalb, Ill.
Paul, Marvin S., 4750 W. Glenlake Ave., Chicago, Ill.
Paulsen, Gaige B., 36 Fairview Ave., Athens, Ohio
Paulson, Alice T., 113½ N. Main St., Blue Earth, Minn.
Paulson, Casper F., Jr., Oregon College of Education, Monmouth, Ore.
Paulston, Rolland G., Tchrs. Col., Columbia Univ., USAID, Lima, Peru
Pautz, Wilmer A., Wisconsin State University, Eau Claire, Wis.
Paxson, Robert C., Troy State College, Troy, Ala.
Paxton, Mrs. J. Hall, 1405 Pine St., Apt. 606, St. Louis, Mo.
Payne, David L., Box 310, MSCW, Columbus, Miss.
Payne, LaVeta M., P.O. Box 591, Pierson and Suhrie Dr., Collegedale, Tenn.
Payne, M. Arlene, University of Chicago, Chicago, Ill.
Paynovich, Nicholas, Rt. 4, Box 840, Tucson, Ariz.
Payzant, Thomas W., 2011 Shalett St., New Orleans, La.
Pearce, Dale N., Grove City Area School Dist., Grove City, Pa.
Pearson, Frank, Col. of Educ., University of Oklahoma, Norman, Okla.
Pearson, Lois, State University College, Buffalo, N.Y.
Pebley, Wilson A., 310 Lincoln Way East, McConnellsburg, Pa.
Peccolo, Charles M., 2840 Nevada St., Manhattan, Kan.
Peckenpaugh, Donald H., Rt. 1, West Bend, Wis.
Pederson, Arne K., Pacific Lutheran University, Tacoma, Wash.
Pederson, Clara A., Dept. of Educ., Univ. of North Dakota, Grand Forks, N.D.

Peiffer, Paul D., 5902 Jonestown Rd., Harrisburg, Pa.
Pella, Milton O., Wisconsin High School, Univ. of Wisconsin, Madison, Wis.
Pellegrin, Lionel, 945 E. River Oaks Dr., Baton Rouge, La.
Pellett, Vernon L., 1103 Catalpa Cir., Madison, Wis.
Pelton, Frank M., Dept. of Educ., Univ. of Rhode Island, Kingston, R.I.
Peltz, Seamen, 6650 S. Ellis Ave., Chicago, Ill.
Pendarvis, S. T., McNeese State College, Lake Charles, La.
Penn, Floy L., Mt. Lebanon Public Schls., Bower Hill Rd., Pittsburgh, Pa.
Penniman, Blanche L., Bergenfield High School, Bergenfield, N.J.
Pentecost, Percy M., 540 Coconut St., Satellite Beach, Fla.
Perdew, Philip W., Sch. of Educ., University of Denver, Denver, Colo.
Peregoy, C. G., Woodrow Wilson High School, Beckley, W.Va.
Perkins, Frederick D., Alto High School, Alto, La.
Perry, Arthur V., Superintendent of Schools, Batavia, Ill.
Perry, Harold J., 1040 Park Ave., West Highland Park, Ill.
Perry, James Olden, 3602 S. MacGregor Way, Houston, Tex.
Perry, T. Edward, Chagrin River Rd., Gates Mills, Ohio
Perryman, Lucile C., 330 Third Ave., New York, N.Y.
Pescosolido, John R., Central Connecticut State College, New Britain, Conn.
Peters, J. L., Sr., Atlanta Univ., Atlanta, Ga.
Peters, Jon S., California State College, Hillary Rd., Hayward, Calif.
Peters, Mary Magdalene, 1366 Lafayette Rd., Claremont, Calif.
Petersen, Clarence E., 19 Fulton St., Redwood City, Calif.
Petersen, Dorothy G., Trenton State College, Trenton, N.J.
Petersen, Dwain F., 323 Emerson Ln., Mankato, Minn.
Peterson, Bernadine H., University of Wisconsin, Madison, Wis.
Peterson, Donald G., St. Cloud State College, St. Cloud, Minn.
Peterson, Donald W., 4708—25th Ave., Rock Island, Ill.
Peterson, Donovan, 600 Cararra Dr., Allison Park, Ill.
Peterson, Douglas W., Dept. of Educ., Kalamazoo College, Kalamazoo, Mich.
Peterson, Mrs. Leona, 341 Poplar Ave., Elmhurst, Ill.
Peterson, Miriam E., 5422 Wayne Ave., Chicago, Ill.
Peterson, Vianna, 300 Humphrey St., Logansport, Ind.
Pethick, Wayne M., 6136 Northwest Hwy., Chicago, Ill.
Petor, Andrew P., 661 Catalpa St., New Kensington, Pa.
Petrequin, Gaynor, 3905 S.E. 91st Ave., Portland, Ore.
Petrich, Paul, Norwich Free Academy, Norwich, Conn.
Pettersch, Carl A., 200 Southern Blvd., Danbury, Conn.
Petterson, Mrs. Muriel, County Schls. Serv. Center, San Luis Obispo, Calif.
Pettigrew, Julia R., 14622 N.W. 13th Rd., Miami, Fla.
Pettiss, J. O., Dept. of Educ., Louisiana State University, Baton Rouge, La.
Petty, Mary Clare, Col. of Educ., University of Oklahoma, Norman, Okla.
Petty, Rev. Michael, S.J., 1314 E. 54th St., Chicago, Ill.
Petty, Olan L., Box 6906, Col. Sta., Duke University, Durham, N.C.
Petty, Walter T., Sch. of Educ., State Univ. of New York, Buffalo, N.Y.
Pewitt, Edith M., North Texas State Univ., Denton, Texas
Pezzullo, Thomas J., 268 Greenville Ave., Johnston, R.I.
Phay, John E., Bur. of Educ. Res., University of Mississippi, University, Miss.
Phelan, William F., 201 Sunrise Hwy., Patchogue, N.Y.
Phelps, H. Vaughn, 8727 Shamrock Rd., Omaha, Neb.
Phelps, Harold R., Illinois State University, Normal, Ill.
Phelps, Roger P., 718 Barnes Ave., Baldwin, L.I., N.Y.
Philippi, Harlan A., Dept. of Sec. Educ., Boston University, Boston, Mass.
Phillips, Cecil K., State College of Iowa, Cedar Falls, Iowa
Phillips, Don O., 1158 S. Harris Ave., Columbus, Ohio
Phillips, James A., Jr., Col. of Educ., Kent State University, Kent, Ohio
Phillips, James E., 1446 E. Maryland Ave., St. Paul, Minn.
Phillips, Leonard W., Nevada Southern Univ., Las Vegas, Nev.
Phillips, Paul, Supt. of Schools, 520 W. Palmer St., Morrisville, Pa.
Phillips, Richard C., Univ. of North Carolina, Chapel Hill, N.C.
Phillips, Thomas Arthur, 1536 S. Sixth St., Terre Haute, Ind.

Phillips, Thomas P., 7814 Elba Rd., Alexandria, Va.
Philp, William A., 440 Williams Ave., Natchitoches, La.
Phleger, John V., Superintendent of Schools, Geneseo, Ill.
Phoenix, William D., 8561 Holmes Rd., Kansas City, Mo.
Piche, Gene L., Univ. of Minnesota, Minneapolis, Minn.
Pickard, Joseph A., P.O. Box F, Selma, Ala.
Pickett, Louis L., County Supt. of Schools, Court House, Davenport, Iowa
Pickett, Paul C., Upper Iowa University, Fayette, Iowa
Pickett, Vernon R., Area 10 Comm. Col., Cedar Rapids, Iowa
Pickett, Wilda D., Troy State College, Troy, Ala.
Pickrel, Glenn E., Supt. of Schools, Dists. 58 and 99, Downers Grove, Ill.
Pierce, Arthur N., Scotch Plains-Fanwood Public Schls., Scotch Plains, N.J.
Pierce, Raymond K., 81 Thimbleberry Lane, Levittown, Pa.
Pierce, Truman M., Sch. of Educ., Auburn University, Auburn, Ala.
Pierleoni, Robert G., 21 Nova Ln., Rochester, N.Y.
Pietrini, Dan H., 2737 N. Sayre, Chicago, Ill.
Piggush, Kenneth J., 324 Sauganash, Park Forest, Ill.
Pikunas, Justin, Psych. Dept., University of Detroit, Detroit, Mich.
Piland, Joseph C., 1117 W. Market St., Normal, Ill.
Pilch, Mrs. Mary M., State Dept. of Education, Centennial Bldg., St. Paul, Minn.
Ping, Charles J., Tusculum College, Greeneville, Tenn.
Pinkham, Mrs. Rossalie G., Southern Connecticut State College, New Haven, Conn.
Pino, Charles E., 74 Eastern Ave., Revere, Mass.
Pins, Arnulf M., 345 E. 46th St., New York, N.Y.
Pirtle, Mrs. Ivyl, Palm Beach Curric. Lab., West Palm Beach, Fla.
Pitkin, Royce, Goddard College, Plainfield, Vt.
Pitman, John C., 88 Chestnut St., Camden, Me.
Pitt, F. N., Catholic School Board, 435 S. Fifth St., Louisville, Ky.
Pittman, Dewitt Kennieth, 6700 Monroe Rd., Charlotte, N.C.
Piucci, Virginio, Rhode Island Col., Providence, R.I.
Pledger, Maud M., 1406 Moore St., Commerce, Texas
Pletcher, James D., Niagara County Community College, Niagara Falls, N.Y.
Pletcher, Paul R., Jr., 3001 Floravista Ct., Riverside, Calif.
Pletsch, Douglas H., 676 Harley Dr., Columbus, Ohio
Plimpton, Blair, Superintendent of Schools, 400 S. Western Ave., Park Ridge, Ill.
Pliska, Stanley Robert, 1041 S. Lexan Cr., Norfolk, Va.
Plumb, Valworth R., University of Minnesota, Duluth Branch, Duluth, Minn.
Pockat, Delmar B., 6614 Arcadia Woods Rd., Columbia, S.C.
Podlich, William F., Jr., 1630 College Ave., Tempe, Ariz.
Poehler, W. A., Concordia College, St. Paul, Minn.
Poelker, Msgr. Gerard L., Supt., Diocesan Schls., Jefferson City, Mo.
Pogue, E. Graham, Ball State University, Muncie, Ind.
Pohek, Marguerite V., 13 Coolidge Ave., Glen Head, N.Y.
Pohlmann, Neil A., Bowling Green State University, Bowling Green, Ohio
Pole, E. John, Ball State University, Muncie, Ind.
Polglase, Robert J., 10 Amy Dr., Westfield, N.J.
Pollach, Samuel, California State College, Long Beach, Calif.
Pollack, Alan, 3010 Duncan St., Apt. 1, Columbia, S.C.
Polley, Warren P., Antioch Community High School, Antioch, Ill.
Polmantier, Paul C., University of Missouri, Columbia, Mo.
Pond, Millard Z., Superintendent of Schools, Dist. No. 4, Eugene, Ore.
Poole, Albert E., 214 N. Washington Cir., Lake Forest, Ill.
Pooley, Robert C., University of Wisconsin, Madison, Wis.
Popper, Samuel H., Burton Hall, University of Minnesota, Minneapolis, Minn.
Portee, Richard C., 4939 Dorchester Ave., Chicago, Ill.
Porter, Donald A., 10733—101st St., Edmonton, Alba., Canada
Porter, LeRoy E., 770 E. Meadow Dr., Palo Alto, Calif.
Porter, M. Roseamonde, University of Hawaii, Honolulu, Hawaii
Porter, R. H., The Steck Co., P.O. Box 2028, Austin, Tex.
Porter, William E., Pulaski High School, Pulaski, Va.
Porter, Willis P., Sch. of Educ., Indiana University, Bloomington, Ind.

Potell, Herbert, 1719—48th St., Brooklyn, N.Y.
Potter, Conrad H., 852 Ames Ave., Palo Alto, Calif.
Potts, Alfred M., ERIC, New Mexico State Univ., University Park, N.M.
Potts, John F., Voorhees Junior College, Denmark, S.C.
Poulos, Thomas H., Michigan School for the Deaf, Flint, Mich.
Poulter, James R., Superintendent of Schools, Anamosa, Iowa
Pound, Miss G., 1911 Kenwood St., Prince George, B.C., Canada
Pounds, Ralph L., Tchrs. Col., University of Cincinnati, Cincinnati, Ohio
Powell, O. Bert, Winthrop College, Rock Hill, S.C.
Powell, Mrs. Ruth Marie, 1601 Lock Rd., Nashville, Tenn.
Powers, Francis P., State College, Fitchburg, Mass.
Powers, Fred R., 619 Cleveland Ave., Amherst, Ohio
Powers, Philander, Ventura College, 4667 Telegraph Rd., Ventura, Calif.
Prasch, John, 4805 Dunberry Lane, Edina, Minn.
Pratt, Mrs. Anne M., 2018 King's Lane, San Mateo, Calif.
Preseren, Herman J., Wake Forest College, Winston-Salem, N.C.
Pressman, Florence, 3080 Broadway, New York, N.Y.
Preston, Ralph C., Sch. of Educ., University of Pennsylvania, Philadelphia, Pa.
Prestwood, Elwood L., 426 Righters Mill Rd., Gladwyne, Pa.
Pricco, Ernest, Melrose Park School, Melrose Park, Ill.
Price, John, Lyman Hall High School, Wellingford, Conn.
Price, Louis E., University of New Mexico, Albuquerque, N.M.
Price, Rebecca W., Norristown Public Schls., Norristown, Pa.
Price, Robert Diddams, 7819 Pinemeadow Lane, Cincinnati, Ohio
Price, Robert R., Agric. Hall, Oklahoma State Univ., Stillwater, Okla.
Price, Uberto, Appalachian State College, Boone, N.C.
Prichard, Neal W., Stout State University, Menomonie, Wis.
Pridgen, Mrs. Ennie Mae, 1507 Russell St., Charlotte, N.C.
Prince, Mrs. Virginia Faye, P.O. Box 4015, St. Louis, Mo.
Pringle, Glenn L., Wheaton College, Wheaton, Ill.
Pritchett, John P., Trenton Junior College, 101 W. State St., Trenton, N.J.
Pritchett, Karen, Educ. Res. Counc. of Amer., Cleveland, Ohio
Procunier, Robert W., 999 Kedzie Ave., Flossmoor, Ill.
Propeck, G. E., California State College, Long Beach, Calif.
Propsting, Mrs. M., 44 Henrietta St., Waverley, N.S.W., Australia
Protheroe, Donald W., 154 Chambers Bldg., University Park, Pa.
Pruitt, Robert E., Superintendent of Schools, Quincy, Mass.
Prutzman, Stuart E., 135 Alum St., Lehighton, Pa.
Pryor, Guy C., Our Lady of the Lake Col., San Antonio, Texas
Puffer, Richard J., 4401—6th St., S.W., P.O. Box 1689, Cedar Rapids, Iowa
Pugh, James B., Superintendent of Schools, Midland Park, N.J.
Pugmire, Dorothy Jean, 468 E. Fourth St. No., Logan, Utah
Purdy, Ralph D., Century House, Lincoln, Neb.
Puryear, Royal W., Florida Normal and Ind. Mem. College, St. Augustine, Fla.
Putnam, John F., Office of Education, Dept. of H.E.W., Washington, D.C.

Quall, Alvin B., Whitworth College, Spokane, Wash.
Quanbeck, Martin, Augsburg College, Minneapolis, Minn.
Quaranta, Joseph L., 3534 Maxwell Rd., Toledo, Ohio
Queen, Bernard, Marshall University, Huntington, W.Va.
Quick, Henry E., 293 Main St., Box 279, Oswego, Tioga County, N.Y.
Quick, Otho J., Northern Illinos University, DeKalb, Ill.
Quilling, Joan I., Owen Hall, Michigan State Univ., East Lansing, Mich.
Quinn, Villa H., State Department of Education, Augusta, Me.
Quintero, Angel G., Secretary of Education, Rio Piedras, Puerto Rico
Quish, Bernard A., 4343 W. Wrightwood Ave., Chicago, Ill.

Raack, Mrs. Marilyn L., San Francisco State College, San Francisco, Calif.
Rabin, Bernard, Bowling Green State University, Bowling Green, Ohio
Rabinowitz, Irene G., 420 West End Ave., New York, N.Y.
Rachford, George R., Col. of Grad. Studies, Univ. of Omaha, Omaha, Neb.

Rackauskas, John A., 6558 S. Rockwell St., Chicago, Ill.
Racky, Donald J., Lane Technical High School, Chicago, Ill.
Radcliffe, David H., 516 N. Jackson St., Danville, Ill.
Rademaker, Dean B., Superintendent of Schools, Virginia, Ill.
Raffone, Alexander M., Woodbridge Public Schools, Woodbridge, Conn.
Ragan, William Burk, University of Oklahoma, Norman, Okla.
Ragouzis, Perry, 401 Scott Ave., Fort Collins, Colo.
Ragsdale, Ted R., 301 W. College St., Carbondale, Ill.
Railton, Esther P., California State Col., Hayward, Calif.
Rains, S. L., 1827 Swan Dr., Dallas, Texas
Ramer, Earl M., University of Tennessee, Knoxville, Tenn.
Ramey, Mrs. Beatrix B., Dept. of Educ., Appalachian State Univ., Boone, N.C.
Ramig, Clifford L., 516 Kendall Lane, DeKalb, Ill.
Ramos, John P., Jr., 117 Green Ave., Madison, N.J.
Ramos, Rafael E., 164 A Hook Rd., APO New York, N.Y. 09845
Ramsey, J. W., Anawalt Junior High School, Northfork, W.Va.
Ramseyer, John A., Ohio State University, Columbus, Ohio
Ramseyer, Lloyd L., Blufften College, Blufften, Ohio
Rand, E. W., Texas Southern University, Houston, Tex.
Randall, Edwin H., Western State College, Gunnison, Colo.
Randall, William M., Wilmington College, 1220 Market St., Wilmington, N.C.
Randolph, Helen, Fresno State College, Fresno, Calif.
Rankin, Earl F., Jr., 3921 Lynncrest Dr., Fort Worth, Tex.
Rankin, Paul T., 16823 Plainview Rd., Detroit, Mich.
Rankine, Fred C., 5573 Toronto Rd., Vancouver, B.C., Canada
Rappaport, David, 2747 Coyle Ave., Chicago, Ill.
Rappaport, Mary B., 64 Delaware Ave., Delmar, N.Y.
Rasmussen, Elmer M., Dana College, Blair, Neb.
Rasmussen, H. L., 427 S.W. Bade Ave., College Place, Wash.
Rasmussen, L. V., Superintendent of Schools, Duluth, Minn.
Rasmussen, Robert T., 30 Falmouth Rd., Cranston, R.I.
Rath, Patricia M., 1423 Tower Rd., Winnetka, Ill.
Rausch, Richard G., "Rescue," 120 Main St., Danbury, Conn.
Rawson, Kenneth O., Superintendent of Schools, Clintonville, Wis.
Ray, Rolland, State University of Iowa, Iowa City, Iowa
Razik, Taher A., State University of New York, Buffalo, N.Y.
Rea, Robert E., 8001 National Bridge St., St. Louis, Mo.
Rea, Thelma M., Fresno State College, Fresno, Calif.
Read, Edward M., St. Paul Academy, 1712 Randolph Ave., St. Paul, Minn.
Reavis, Peyton, 125 E. Prince Rd., Tucson, Ariz.
Red, S. B., University of Houston, 3801 Cullen Blvd., Houston, Tex.
Reddin, Estoy, Dept. of Educ., Lehigh University, Bethlehem, Pa.
* Reddy, Anne L., P.O. Box 64, Runnymede, Bluffton, S.C.
Rediger, Milo A., Taylor University, Upland, Ind.
Reed, Harold J., Office of Educ., Dept. of HEW, Washington, D.C.
Reed, John L., 122 White St., Saratoga Springs, N.Y.
Reed, Zollie C., 3636 Kingshill Rd., Birmingham, Ala.
Reeves, Emily D., Centre College of Kentucky, Danville, Ky.
Reeves, Glenn D., Saginaw Public Schools, Saginaw, Tex.
Reeves, Louis H., Box 864, R.R. 4, Ottawa, Ont., Canada
Reeves, Wilfred, Washington Junior High School, Olympia, Wash.
Regier, Margaret, Roosevelt Univ., 430 S. Michigan Ave., Chicago, Ill.
Regner, Olga W., 116 South 4th St., Darby, Pa.
Rehage, Kenneth J., Dept. of Educ., University of Chicago, Chicago, Ill.
Reid, Clarence E., Jr., 8740 Skyview, Beaumont, Texas
Reid, L. Leon, Gr. Pitts. Guild for the Blind, 5231 Center Ave., Pittsburgh, Pa.
Reilley, Albert G., 28 Long Ave., Framingham, Mass.
Reiner, Kenneth, 3191 S. Evelyn Way, Denver, Colo.
Reiner, William B., Hunter College, 695 Park Ave., New York, N.Y.
* Reinhardt, Emma, Pittsfield, Ill.
Reinstein, Barry J., Univ. of South Carolina, Columbia, S.C.

Reisin, Seymour, 365 West 28th St., New York, N.Y.
Reisman, Diana J., 223 N. Highland Ave., Merion Station, Pa.
Reisman, Morton, Anshe Emet Day Sch., 3760 N. Pine Grove Ave., Chicago, Ill.
Reiter, Anne, 155 West 68th St., New York, N.Y.
Reitz, Donald J., Loyola College, 4501 N. Charles St., Baltimore, Md.
Reitz, Louis M., St. Thomas Seminary, 7101 Brownsboro Rd., Louisville, Ky.
Reller, Theodore L., Sch. of Educ., Univ. of California, Berkeley, Calif.
Rempel, P. J., 495 Mariposa Dr., Ventura, Calif.
Renard, John N., Oxnard Evening High School, Oxnard, Calif.
Renfrow, O. W., Thornton Township High School, Harvey, Ill.
Rennels, Max R., 4032 W. Grand Ave., Bloomington, Ind.
Renouf, Edna M., 116 Yale Square, Swarthmore, Pa.
Replogle, V. L., Metcalf School, Normal, Ill.
Reuter, George S., Jr., Sioux Empire College, Hawarden, Iowa
Reuwsaat, Emily A., Bloomsburg State College, Bloomsburg, Pa.
Revie, Virgil A., California State Col., Long Beach, Calif.
Rex, Ronald G., Michigan State University, East Lansing, Mich.
Reyna, L. J., 227 Beacon St., Boston, Mass.
Reynolds, Mrs. Dorothy S., 640 Hudson St., Denver, Colo.
Reynolds, James Walton, Box 7998, University of Texas, Austin, Tex.
Reynolds, James W., Box 7307 Univ. Sta., Austin, Texas
Reynolds, Lee, 113 Woodland Dr., Boone, N.C.
Reynolds, M. C., University of Minnesota, Minneapolis, Minn.
Rhea, Buford, Boston College, Chestnut Hill, Mass.
Rhoads, Philip A., 4709 Meise Dr., Baltimore, Md.
Rhodes, Gladys L., State University College, Geneseo, N.Y.
Rhodes, Patricia Hertert, 805 Tully Rd., Modesto, Calif.
Ricciardi, Richard S., Dept. of Education, 100 Reef Rd., Fairfield, Conn.
Rice, Arthur H., R.R. 3, 3705 Cameron, Bloomington, Ind.
Rice, David, Ball State University, Muncie, Ind.
Rice, Dick C., 120 Houck Ave., Centerbury, Ohio
Rice, John E., Jenkintown High School, Jenkintown, Pa.
Rice, Robert K., 4820 Campanile Dr., San Diego, Calif.
Rice, Roy C., Arizona State University, Tempe, Ariz.
Rice, Theodore D., 33963 N. Hampshire, Livonia, Mich.
Richards, Eugene, Sol R. Crown Elem. School, 2123 S. St. Louis, Chicago, Ill.
Richards, H. L., P.O. Box 326, Grambling, La.
Richardson, Canute M., Paine College, Augusta, Ga.
Richardson, John S., Sch. of Educ., Ohio State Univ., Columbus, Ohio
Richardson, Orvin T., Ball State University, Muncie, Ind.
Richardson, Thomas H., 852 Valley Rd., Upper Montclair, N.J.
Richardson, William R., R. 1, Box 362, Chapel Hill, N.C.
Richey, Herman G., Dept. of Educ., University of Chicago, Chicago, Ill.
Richey, Robert W., Sch. of Educ., Indiana University, Bloomington, Ind.
Richey, Ruth, P.O. Box 41, Alpena, Mich.
Richmond, George S., 507½ E. Locust, Normal, Ill.
Richter, Charles O., Public Schools, 7 Whiting Lane, West Hartford, Conn.
Ridge, Thomas A., Litchfield High School, Litchfield, Conn.
Riedel, Mark T., 210 S. Edgewood, LaGrange, Ill.
Riederer, L. A., 2160 Cameron St., Regina, Sask., Canada
Riehm, Carl L., 1300 Fisherman Dr., Norfolk, Va.
Riese, Harlan C., 511 North Ave., East, Missoula, Mont.
Riethmiller, Gorton, Olivet College, Olivet, Mich.
Riggle, Earl L., 180 Highland Dr., New Concord, Ohio
Riggs, William J., 716 Clover Ct., Cheney, Wash
Rigney, Mrs. Margaret G., Hunter College, Park Ave. and 68th St., New York, N.Y.
Rigney, Raymond P., 31 East 50th St., New York, N.Y.
Rikkola, V. John, Dept. of Educ., Massachusetts State Col., Salem, Mass.
Riley, Edward F., St. Mary's Seminary, Perryville, Mo.
Riley, Garland G., 910 Colby Ct., DeKalb, Ill.
Rimestad, Sig K., Superintendent of Schools, Winnebago, Ill.

MEMBERS OF THE NATIONAL SOCIETY lxxxiii

Rimmel, Erma L., 2980 S. Steele St., Denver, Colo.
Rinehart, John, Oakfield Rd., St. James, L.I., N.Y.
Ringler, Leonore, New York Univ., New York, N.Y.
Ringler, Mrs. Norma, 3721 Lytle Rd., Shaker Heights, Ohio
Rinsland, Roland Del, 100 W. 73rd St., New York, N.Y.
Riordan, Eugene, Queen of Apostles College, Dedham, Mass.
Ripper, Eleanor S., Geneva College, Beaver Falls, Pa.
Rippey, Andrew D., Fresno State College, Fresno, Calif.
Rippey, Robert M., 18845 Hood Ave., Homewood, Ill.
Ripple, Richard E., Stone Hall, Cornell University, Ithaca, N.Y.
Risinger, Robert G., Col. of Educ., University of Maryland, College Park, Md.
Risinger, Mrs. Rosalie C., Essex County Voc. & Tech. H.S., Newark, N.J.
Risk, Thomas M., 319 Elm St., Vermillion, S.D.
Ritchie, Harold L., Superintendent of Schools, West Paterson, N.J.
Ritscher, Richard C., General Beadle State Col., Madison, S.D.
Ritter, William E., 2910 E. State St., Sharon, Pa.
Rivard, Thomas L., Superintendent of Schools, Chelmsford, Mass.
Rivlin, Harry N., 302 Broadway, New York, N.Y.
Roaden, Arliss, Dept. of Education, Ohio State University, Columbus, Ohio
Roark, Bill, 1209 Ash St., Buckeye, Ariz.
Robarts, James R., University of Connecticut, Storrs, Conn.
Robbins, Edward T., 235 East Oakview Pl., San Antonio, Texas
Robbins, Jerry H., Sch. of Educ., Univ. of Miss., Oxford, Miss.
Robbins, Melvyn P., Ontario Inst. for Stud. in Educ., Toronto, Ont., Canada
Robeck, Mildred C., 452 Venado Dr., Santa Barbara, Calif.
Roberson, James A., 816 Apricot St., Mt. Vernon, Ill.
Roberts, Dodd Edward, University of Maine, Orono, Me.
Roberts, Jack D., Dept. of Educ., Queens College, Flushing, N.Y.
Roberts, James B., Dept. of Educ., West Texas State Col., Canyon, Tex.
Roberts, James P., 19201 Schoolcraft St., Reseda, Calif.
Roberts, R. Ray, 3309 Rocky Mount Rd., Fairfax, Va.
Robertson, Anne McK., Tchrs. Col., Columbia University, New York, N.Y.
Robertson, Robert L., 315 East Main St., Springfield, Ky.
Robinson, Alice, Board of Educ., 115 E. Church St., Frederick, Md.
Robinson, Cliff, Chico State College, Chico, Calif.
Robinson, H. Alan, Hofstra Univ., Hempstead, L.I., N.Y.
Robinson, Herbert B., California State Col., Long Beach, Calif.
Robinson, Mrs. Helen M., Dept. of Educ., University of Chicago, Chicago, Ill.
Robinson, Phil C., 1367 Joliet Pl., Detroit, Mich.
Robinson, Robert S., Jr., Eastern Michigan Univ., Ypsilanti, Mich.
Robinson, Russell D., 2457 N. Lefeber Ave., Milwaukee, Wis.
Robinson, Thomas L., Alabama State Col., Montgomery, Ala.
Robinson, Walter J., Northwestern State College, Natchitoches, La.
Robinson, Walter K., New England College, Henniker, N.H.
Robison, W. L., Norfolk City Schools, Norfolk, Va.
Roche, Lawrence A., Duquesne University, Pittsburgh, Pa.
Rockwell, Perry J., Jr., Wisconsin State Univ., Platteville, Wis.
Roden, Aubrey H., State Univ. of New York, Buffalo, N.Y.
Rodgers, John O., 4115 Honeycomb Cir., Austin, Texas
Rodgers, Margaret, Lamar State College of Technology, Beaumont, Tex.
Rodgers, Paul R., 255 W. Vermont St., Villa Park, Ill.
Rodriguez-Dias, Manolo, Alfred Univ., Alfred, N.Y.
Roe, Anne, 5151 E. Holmes St., Tucson, Arizona
Roenigk, Elsie Mae, R.D. No. 1, Box 311, Cabot, Pa.
Roeper, George A., City and Country School, Bloomfield Hills, Mich.
Roff, Mrs. Rosella Zuber, 4410 S. 148th St., Seattle, Wash.
Rogers, Dolan, Scott County Central High School, Morley, Mo.
Rogers, Martha E., Div. of Nurse Educ., N.Y.U., New York, N.Y.
Rogers, Ralph V., 3315—19th St., Boulder, Colo.
Rogers, Virgil M., 3810 Birchwood Rd., Falls Church, Va.
Rohan, William, E. G. Foreman High School, Chicago, Ill.

MEMBERS OF THE NATIONAL SOCIETY

Rolfe, Howard C., 5160 Atherton, Long Beach, Calif.
Roller, Lawrence W., King George County Public Schls., King George, Va.
Rolleta, Vincent M., Pres. Vill., 71 West Ave., Brockport, N.Y.
Rollins, William B., Jr., 7772 Otto St., Downey, Calif.
Rolloff, John A., University of Arkansas, Fayetteville, Ark.
Romano, Louis, Michigan State University, East Lansing, Mich.
Romano, Louis A., 227—65th St., West New York, N.J.
Rome, Samuel, 9852 Cerritos Ave., Anaheim, Calif.
Romer, Robert D., 23864 Berdon St., Woodland Hills, Calif.
Romoser, D. Richard C., 176 Greenville Ave., Clarion, Pa.
Rondinella, Orestes R., 48 Sheridan Ave., West Orange, N.J.
Rosamilia, M. T., 183 Union Ave., Belleville, N.J.
Roschy, Bertha B., 204 Greenwell Dr., Hampton, Va.
Rose, Gale W., Dept. of Educ., Western Reserve Univ., Cleveland, Ohio
Rose, Mrs. Ruth R., 908 S.W. 18th Ct., Fort Lauderdale, Fla.
Rosebrock, Allan F., State Dept. of Educ., 175 W. State St., Trenton, N.J.
Rosecrance, Francis C., Florida Atlantic University, Boca Raton, Fla.
Roseman, Ruth V., City College, New York, N.Y.
Rosen, Carl L., 175 Wood Valley Lane, Athens, Ga.
Rosen, Sidney, Col. of Educ., University of Illinois, Urbana, Ill.
Rosenbaum, Wyatt I., 2645 Chesapeake Lane, Northbrook, Ill.
Rosenberg, Marguerite G., 216 Conroy Ave., Scranton, Pa.
Rosenberg, Max, 5057 Woodward Ave., Detroit, Mich.
Rosenberger, Russell S., Dept. of Educ., Gettysburg Col., Gettysburg, Pa.
Rosenbluh, Benjamin J., Central High School, Bridgeport, Conn.
Rosenblum, Beth W., 45 East 40th St., Paterson, N.J.
Rosenstein, Pearl, 5 Tanglewood Circle, Cheshire, Conn.
Rosenthal, Alan G., 18 Homeside Lane, White Plains, N.Y.
Rosenthal, Lester, 94 Stirling Ave., Freeport, N.Y.
Rosenthal, Samuel, 5213 N. Moody Ave., Chicago, Ill.
Rosenzweig, Celia, 6239 N. Leavitt St., Chicago, Ill.
Rosewell, Paul T., Hanover College, Hanover, Ind.
Rosin, Bill, Box 2096, Eastern New Mexico Univ., Portales, N.M.
Ross, Mrs. Alice M., 1446 Wilbraham Rd., Springfield, Mass.
Ross, John G., Haviland Hall, University of California, Berkeley, Calif.
Ross, Richard H., P.O. Box 197, Menomonie, Mich.
Rossien, Saul, Mercer County Comm. Col., Trenton, N.J.
Rossmiller, Richard, Sch. of Educ., University of Wisconsin, Madison, Wis.
Roth, Mrs. Frances, 21598 Ellacott Pkwy., Cleveland, Ohio
Roth, Lois H., State Dept. of Education, Denver, Colo.
Rothenberger, Otis J., 1517 Pennsylvania St., Allentown, Pa.
Rothstein, Jerome H., San Francisco State College, San Francisco, Calif.
Rothwell, Angus B., State Superintendent of Public Instruction, Madison, Wis.
Rouse, Mary J., Sch. of Educ., Indiana Univ., Bloomington, Ind.
Roush, Donald C., New Mexico State University, University Park, N.M.
Rousseve, Numa Joseph, Xavier University, New Orleans, La.
Row, Howard E., State Dept. of Pub. Instr., Dover, Del.
Rowley, Judge Kernan, Morris Brown College, Atlanta, Ga.
Rozran, Andrea Rice, 1255 N. Sandberg Terrace, Chicago, Ill.
Rubadeau, Duane O., State University College, Geneseo, N.Y.
Ruch, Mary A. R., R.F.D. No. 1, Tower City, Pa.
Rucinski, Philip R., Wisconsin State Univ., Oshkosh, Wis.
Rucker, Chauncy N., Rockridge Apt., Baxter Rd., Storrs, Conn.
Rucker, W. Ray, U.S. International Univ., San Diego, Calif.
Ruddell, Arden K., Sch. of Educ., Univ. of California, Berkeley, Calif.
Rudman, Herbert C., Col. of Educ., Michigan State Univ., East Lansing, Mich.
Rudolf, Kathleen Brady, 53 Cook St., Rochester, N.Y.
Rueff, Charles M., Jr., 626 S. Sixth St., McComb, Miss.
Rugen, Mabel E., Sch. of Pub. Health, Univ. of Michigan, Ann Arbor, Mich.
Rugen, Myrtle L., 2240 Pfingsten Rd., Northbrook, Ill.
Ruggles, Stanford D., 3095 Kellner Pl., Columbus, Ohio

MEMBERS OF THE NATIONAL SOCIETY   lxxxv

Rule, Philip, East Otero School Dist., Rt. 1, LaJunta, Colo.
Rummel, J. Francis, Sch. of Educ., Univ. of Montana, Missoula, Mont.
Rumpf, Edwin L., 1805 Rupert St., McLean, Va.
Runbeck, Junet E., Bethel College, St. Paul, Minn.
Runyan, Charles S., Marshall University, Huntington, W.Va.
Rusch, Reuben R., State University of New York, Albany, N.Y.
Rushall, Brent S., 402 N. Park Ave., Bloomington, Ind.
Russel, John H., Col. of Educ., Univ. of Toledo, Toledo, Ohio
Russell, Mrs. Audrey B., Admin. Bldg., 228 W. Franklin St., Elkhart, Ind.
Russell, David L., Dept. of Psych., Ohio University, Athens, Ohio
Russell, Earle Stone, Superintendent of Schools, Windsor, Conn.
Russell, Irene, Lock Haven State College, Lock Haven, Pa.
* Russell, John Dale, R.R. 10, Russell Rd., Bloomington, Ind.
Russell, William J., Pelham Memorial High School, Pelham, N.Y.
Russo, Anthony J., Dept. of Public Schools, 211 Veazie St., Providence, R.I.
Rutledge, James A., Univ. High School, Univ. of Nebraska, Lincoln, Neb.
Ruud, Josephine B., North Dakota State Univ., Fargo, N.D.
Ryan, Bernice, Jersey City State College, Jersey City, N.J.
Ryan, Carl J., 220 W. Liberty St., Cincinnati, Ohio
Ryan, W. Carson, 1303 Mason Farm Rd., Chapel Hill, N.C.
Rye, Howard H., 6 Kent Dr., Normal, Ill.
Rzepka, Louis, DePaul University, Chicago, Ill.

Saadeh, Ibrahim Q., San Fernando Valley State College, Northridge, Calif.
Sabo, B. G., Chugiak High School, Eagle River, Alaska
Sachs, Moses B., 3115 Ottawa Ave., Minneapolis, Minn.
Sack, Saul, Grad. Sch. of Educ., Univ. of Pennsylvania, Philadelphia, Pa.
Saettler, Paul, Sacramento State Col., Sacramento, Calif.
Safford, George R., 6444 Leonard Dr., Redding, Calif.
Sage, Daniel D., Syracuse University, Syracuse, N.Y.
Sager, Kenneth, Lawrence University, Appleton, Wis.
Sahlin, Clarence J., North Park College, Chicago, Ill.
Salatino, A. P., State University of New York, Geneseo, N.Y.
Salinger, Herbert E., 26036 Adamor Rd., Calabasas, Calif.
Salisbury, Arnold W., Superintendent of Schools, Cedar Rapids, Iowa
Salisbury, C. Jackson, 410 Conshohocken St. Rd., Narberth, Pa.
Sallee, Mrs. Mozelle T., 4401 North Ave., Richmond, Va.
Salmon, Hanford A., 310 Stratford St., Syracuse, N.Y.
Salmons, George B., State College, Plymouth, N.H.
Salsbury, Carl C., Millburn Senior High School, Millburn, N.J.
* Salser, G. Alden, 516 E. Estelle, Wichita, Kan.
Salten, David G., 41 Park Ave., New York, N.Y.
Saltz, Martin, Keene State College, Keene, N.H.
Saltzman, Irving J., Dept. of Psych., Indiana Univ., Bloomington, Ind.
Salyer, Rufus C., Col. of Educ., University of Washington, Seattle, Wash.
Sam, Norman H., Lehigh University, Bethlehem, Pa.
Samlin, John R., Illinois Valley Comm. Col., LaSalle, Ill.
Sample, William J., 33 Chestnut Ave., Vineland, N.J.
Samson, Gordon E., Cleveland State University, Cleveland, Ohio
Sand, Ole, Natl. Educ. Assn., 1201 Sixteenth St., N.W., Washington, D.C.
Sander, Paul J., 3139 E. Monterosa, Phoenix, Ariz.
Sanders, Leslie A., Superintendent, Coweta County Schls., Turin, Ga.
Sanders, Richard H., 10639 Drew St., Chicago, Ill.
Sanders, Mrs. Ruby, P.O. Box 1956, Waco, Tex.
Sandilos, James C., United Township High School, East Moline, Ill.
Sandilos, Peter C., Superintendent of Schools, West Long Branch, N.J.
Sands, Miss Billie L., Michigan State Univ., East Lansing, Mich.
Sangster, Cecil Henry, 1248 Cross Cres. S.W., Calgary, Alba., Canada
Santigian, M. Marty, 4596 E. Fredora, Fresno, Calif.
Sapir, Selma, 60 Bretmore Ave., Yonkers, N.Y.
Saprid, Solomon, Univ. of the East, Claro M. Recto Ave., Manila, Philippines

MEMBERS OF THE NATIONAL SOCIETY

Sartain, Harry W., Falk Lab. Schls., Univ. of Pittsburgh, Pittsburgh, Pa.
Sarver, Cyril C., Hillsdale Jr. H.S., Box 49, Hillsdale, Ill.
Satterlee, O. Ward, State University College, Potsdam, N.Y.
Saunders, Margaret C., 2201 South 14th St., Lincoln, Neb.
Sauter, Joyce C., 1355 N. Sandburg Ter., Chicago, Ill.
Sauvain, Walter H., Dept. of Educ., Bucknell Univ., Lewisburg, Pa.
Savage, Kent B., Fairview Senior High School, Berkeley, Mo.
Saville, Anthony, Sch. of Educ., Nevada Southern Univ., Las Vegas, Nev.
Sax, Gilbert, University of Washington, Seattle, Wash.
Saxe, Richard W., Univ. of Toledo, Toledo, Ohio
Saylor, Charles F., 535 Kathryn St., New Wilmington, Pa.
Saylor, Galen, Tchrs. Col., University of Nebraska, Lincoln, Neb.
Scales, Eldridge E., 795 Peachtree St., Atlanta, Ga.
Scanlan, William J., Highland Park Sr. High School, St. Paul, Minn.
Scanlon, Kathryn I., Sch. of Educ., Fordham University, New York, N.Y.
Scarborough, C. C., North Carolina State University, Raleigh, N.C.
Scarbrough, Paul, Univ. of Texas at El Paso, Texas
Scarnato, Samuel, 263 Prairie Ave., Morgantown, W.Va.
Schaadt, Mrs. Lucy G., Cedar Crest College, Allentown, Pa.
Schaefer, Wilbert S., 194 Hillside Ave., Mineola, L.I., N.Y.
Schaeffer, Norma C., 10700 S. Hamlin, Chicago, Ill.
Schaibly, Colon L., Waukegan Township High School, Waukegan, Ill.
Schantz, Betty B., R.D. #2, Willow Street, Pa.
Scharf, Louis, 350 Sterling St., Brooklyn, N.Y.
Schasteen, Joyce W., 2500 Spruce St., Bakersfield, Calif.
Schectman, Aaron H., Monmouth College, Monmouth, N.J.
Schell, Leo M., Col. of Educ., Kansas State Univ., Manhattan, Kansas
Schenke, Lahron H., 301 Chamberlin Dr., Charleston, Ill.
Schenkman, Jerome G., 255 E. Houston St., New York, N.Y.
Scherer, Frank H., 32 Beverly Rd., Piscataway, N.J.
Schifreen, Edward B., 314 Iris Rd., Cherry Hill, N.J.
Schiller, Clarke E., 73F, Escondido Village, Stanford, Calif.
Schilling, Paul M., Superintendent of Schools, LaGrange Park, Ill.
Schlegel, Miriam A., 355 Marburg/Lahn, An der Schäfferbucke 11, W. Germany
Schleif, Mabel, 1908 Hennepin Ave., Minneapolis, Minn.
Schlenker, Alma H., 1450 Westgate Dr., Bethlehem, Pa.
Schlessinger, Fred R., 1399 LaRochelle Dr., Columbus, Ohio
Schmidt, Florence, 785 Temple St., Long Beach, Calif.
Schmidt, L. G. H., J. J. Cahill Mem. Sch., Mascot, N.S.W., Australia
Schmidt, Mary M., Southeastern Louisiana College, Hammond, La.
Schmidt, Ralph L. W., 568 Magnolia Wood Dr., Baton Rouge, La.
Schmidt, William S., County Superintendent of Schools, Upper Marlboro, Md.
Schminke, Clarence W., Sch. of Educ., Univ. of Oregon, Eugene, Ore.
Schnabel, Robert V., 6902 S. Calhoun St., Fort Wayne, Ind.
Schneider, Albert A., Superintendent of Schools, Albuquerque, N.M.
Schneider, Bernhard W., 166 Laurel Rd., Northport, N.Y.
Schneider, Erwin H., Sch. of Music, Ohio State University, Columbus, Ohio
Schneider, Raymond C., University of Washington, Seattle, Wash.
Schneider, Samuel, 315 West 70th St., New York, N.Y.
Schnell, Fred, 2724 Highland Terrace, Sheboygan, Wis.
Schnell, Rodolph L., Univ. of Calgary, Calgary, Alba., Canada
Schnepf, Virginia, 1009½ Main St., Cedar Falls, Iowa
Schneyer, J. Wesley, 7454 Ruskin Rd., Philadelphia, Pa.
Schnitzen, Joseph P., University of Houston, Houston, Tex.
Schoch, Norman J., Newark Sr. H.S., East Delaware Ave., Newark, Del.
Schoeller, Arthur W., 8626 W. Lawrence Ave., Milwaukee, Wis.
Schoeppe, Aileen, Sch. of Educ., New York University, New York, N.Y.
Schoer, Lowell, Col. of Educ., State Univ. of Iowa, Iowa City, Iowa
Scholl, Margaret, 1206 Marshall Lane, Austin, Tex.
Scholl, Paul A., Univ. of Connecticut, Storrs, Conn.
Schomer, John T., Jr., 45 Pleasant St., Natick, Mass.

Schooler, Virgil E., 209 S. Hillsdale Dr., Bloomington, Ind.
Schooling, Herbert W., Col. of Educ., Univ. of Missouri, Columbia, Mo.
Schor, Theodore, 149 N. Fifth Ave., Highland Park, N.J.
Schorow, Mitchell, 806 Milburn, Evanston, Ill.
Schott, Marion S., Central Missouri State College, Warrensburg, Mo.
Schowe, Ben M., Jr., 500 Morse Rd., Columbus, Ohio
Schreiber, Daniel, 205 West End Ave., New York, N.Y.
Schreiber, Herman, 80 Clarkson Ave., Brooklyn, N.Y.
Schroeder, Carl N., 39 Othoridge Rd., Lutherville, Md.
Schroeder, Marie L., 3125 N. Spangler St., Philadelphia, Pa.
Schroeder, W. P., State Polytechnic College, San Luis Obispo, Calif.
Schuller, Charles F., Michigan State University, East Lansing, Mich.
Schulman, Milton, 660 Locust St., Mt. Vernon, N.Y.
Schulte, Emerita S., Ball State University, Muncie, Ind.
Schultz, Kenneth M., 466 West 41st Pl., Hialeah, Fla.
Schumann, Victor, 1537 Cedar Lane, Waukesha, Wis.
Schumer, Harry, Dept. of Psych., Univ. of Massachusetts, Amherst, Mass.
Schuster, Rev. James F., Supt., Altoona-Johnstown Cath. Schools, Altoona, Pa.
Schwanholt, Dana B., Valparaiso University, Valparaiso, Ind.
Schwartz, Alfred, Drake University, Des Moines, Iowa
Schwartz, Fred R., Michigan State Univ., East Lansing, Mich.
Schwartz, William P., 273 Ave. P., Brooklyn, N.Y.
Schwebel, Milton, Sch. of Educ., New York University, New York, N.Y.
Schwertfeger, Mary Jane, 6 Parkview Pl., Ann Arbor, Mich.
Sciranka, Paul G., 323 Monte Vista Ave., Oakland, Calif.
Scobey, Mary-Margaret, San Francisco State College, San Francisco, Calif.
Scofield, Alice Gill, San Jose State College, San Jose, Calif.
Scofield, J. Woodleigh, 17169 Hawthorne Ave., Fontana, Calif.
Scott, Guy, 1521 N. Webster, Liberal, Kan.
Scott, Loren L., Oregon College of Education, Monmouth, Ore.
Scott, Thomas B., University of Tennessee, Knoxville, Tenn.
Scott, Waldo I., Soundview Gardens, Port Washington, N.Y.
Scritchfield, Floyd C., Nevada Southern Univ., Las Vegas, Nev.
Seagoe, May V., Sch. of Educ., University of California, Los Angeles, Calif.
Searles, Warren B., Queens Col., Flushing, N.Y.
Sears, Jesse B., 40 Tevis Pl., Palo Alto, Calif.
Seaton, Donald F., Superintendent of Schools, Boone, Iowa
* Seay, Maurice F., Michigan State University, East Lansing, Mich.
Sechler, Hazel B., Western New Mexico Univ., Silver City, N.M.
See, Harold W., Col. of Educ., Univ. of Bridgeport, Bridgeport, Conn.
Seedor, Marie M., 820 Meredith Dr., Wesley Manor, Media, Pa.
Sehmann, Henry R., 1171 Bryant Rd., Long Beach, Calif.
Seidman, Eric, University of Maryland, College Park, Md.
Seifert, George G., Bowling Green State Univ., Bowling Green, Ohio
Seifert, Leland B., Haverstraw-Stony Point School Dist., Stony Point, N.Y.
Seitz, Robert, 1603 N. Denver Dr., Marion, Ind.
Seitzer, Robert H., Superintendent of Schools, East Orange, N.J.
Sekerak, Martha M., Box G-1067, Hanford, Calif.
Selden, Edward H., Dept. of Psych., Wisconsin State Univ., River Falls, Wis.
Self, David W., Univ. of Alabama, University, Alabama
Sellers, Beulah E., Dept. of H.E. Educ., Ohio University, Athens, Ohio
Sellery, Austin R., 344 Sunset Way, Palm Springs, Calif.
Seltzer, Richard W., 639 Redlion Rd., Huntingdon Valley, Pa.
Seltzer, Ronald, University Apts. W314, Bloomington, Ind.
Selzer, Edwin, 168-06 Jewel Ave., Flushing, N.Y.
Semmel, Melvyn I., University of Michigan, Ann Arbor, Mich.
Sentman, Everett E., United Educators, Inc., Lake Bluff, Ill.
Servey, Richard E., San Diego State College, San Diego, Calif.
Serviss, Trevor K., L. W. Singer Co., 249 W. Erie Blvd., Syracuse, N.Y.
Severino, D. Alexander, Alisal H.S., Salinas, Calif.
Severson, John E., 11 Chalon Cir., Salinas, Calif.

MEMBERS OF THE NATIONAL SOCIETY

Seyfert, Warren C., 5607 Gloster Rd., Washington, D.C.
Shack, Jacob H., 127 Remsen St., Brooklyn, N.Y.
Shaddick, Bryan A., 1023 Lincoln St., Hobart, Ind.
Shafer, Robert E., 4826 N. 76th Pl., Scottsdale, Ariz.
Shafer, William C., 25 Bar Beach Rd., Port Washington, N.Y.
Shafran, Lillian, 1870 Schieffelin Ave., Bronx, N.Y.
Shallcross, Mrs. Margaret, 4803 Oakridge, Toledo, Ohio
Shane, Harold G., Sch. of Educ., Indiana University, Bloomington, Ind.
Shank, Lloyd L., Superintendent of Schools, Arkansas City, Kan.
Shankman, Mrs. Florence, 20 Garner St., South Norwalk, Conn.
Shapiro, Benjamin, Grad. Sch. of Educ., Rutgers Univ., New Brunswick, N.J.
Shapiro, Lillian L., 82-30—210th St., Hollis Hills, N.Y.
Shaplin, Judson T., Washington University, St. Louis, Mo.
Sharp, George M., Lakewood Terr., New Milford, Conn.
Shaw, Frances, 4717 Central Ave., Indianapolis, Ind.
Shaw, M. Luelle, 1126 N.W. Eighth Ave., Miami, Fla.
Shaw, Robert C., Superintendent of Schools, Columbia, Mo.
Shea, James, 59 Old Farm Road, Levittown, N.Y.
Shea, Warren D., New Mexico Inst. of Mining and Tech., Socorro, N.M.
Shear, Twyla M., Michigan State Univ., East Lansing, Mich.
Shedd, Mark R., Superintendent of Schools, Englewood, N.J.
Sheeley, Vernon, Box 3585, University Sta., Laramie, Wyo.
Sheerin, James S., Eliz. Carter Brooks School, New Bedford, Mass.
Sheldon, John M., San Diego State College, San Diego, Calif.
Sheldon, Muriel Inez, Los Angeles City Board of Educ., Los Angeles, Calif.
Sheldon, William Denley, 508 University Pl., Syracuse, N.Y.
Shelton, Nollie W., 328 Blowing Rock Rd., Boone, N.C.
Shepard, Loraine V., Antioch Col., Yellow Springs, Ohio
Shepard, Samuel, Jr., 4633 Moffitt Ave., St. Louis, Mo.
Sheppard, Lawrence E., 737—46th Ave., San Francisco, Calif.
Sherer, Harry, 5284 Bardwell Ave., Riverside, Calif.
Sherer, Lorraine, 1109 Magnolia Ave., Los Angeles, Calif.
Sheridan, Alton, NEA, 1201 Sixteenth St., N.W., Washington, D.C.
Sheridan, T. J., Kendall, Wis.
Sheridan, William C., 333 Washington St., Brookline, Mass.
Sherk, John K., Jr., 6112 Summit St., Kansas City, Mo.
Sherman, Mrs. Helene, 350 Central Park West, New York, N.Y.
Sherman, Mrs. Twyla, Col. of Educ., Wichita State Univ., Wichita, Kansas
Shermis, S. Samuel, R. 1, West Lafayette, Ind.
Sherwood, Virgil, 1123 Grove Ave., Radford, Va.
Sherwyn, Fred, 110 Kiely Blvd., Santa Clara, Calif.
Shier, John B., 200 Elm High Dr., Edgerton, Wis.
Shinol, Julian W., Edinboro State College, Edinboro, Pa.
Shive, Mrs. Mae L., 600 Michael Rd., Newton, Kan.
Shnayer, Sidney W., Chico State College, Chico, Calif.
Shohen, Samuel S., 229 Friends Lane, Westbury, L.I., N.Y.
Sholund, Milford, Gospel Light Press, 725 E. Colorado, Glendale, Calif.
Shope, Nathaniel H., Appalachian State Univ., Boone, N.C.
Shores, J. Harlan, University of Illinois, Urbana, Ill.
Short, Edmund C., University of Toledo, Toledo, Ohio
Short, Robert Allen, 17059 Fifth N.E. St., Seattle, Wash.
Short, William T., 2368 Walnut Grove Ave., San Jose, Calif.
Showalter, Miriam R., Roosevelt University, Chicago, Ill.
Showkeir, James R., 1909 Penbrook Lane, Flint, Mich.
Shroff, Piroja, California Col. of Arts & Crafts, Oakland, Calif.
Shulman, Lee S., Col. of Educ., Michigan State Univ., East Lansing, Mich.
* Shuman, Elsie, 805 S. Florence St., Kirksville, Mo.
* Sias, A. B., Route 3, Box 459B, Orlando, Fla.
Sidden, Curtis A., 357 Lake Forest Dr., Spartanburg, S.C.
Siders, Stanford K., R.D. #2, West Salem, Ohio
Siegel, Martin, 1472 Dalton Dr., Schenectady, N.Y.

MEMBERS OF THE NATIONAL SOCIETY lxxxix

Siegner, C. Vernon, Peru State College, Box 75, Peru, Neb.
Siemons, Alice E., San Francisco State College, San Francisco, Calif.
Sieving, Eldor C., Concordia Teachers College, River Forest, Ill.
Siewers, Karl, 2301 Estes Ave., Chicago, Ill.
Sigwalt, J. Q., Box 351, Republic, Pa.
Silberman, Charles E., 342 Madison Ave., New York, N.Y.
Silva, J. Winston, California State Dept. of Educ., Sacramento, Calif.
Silvaroli, Nicholas J., Arizona State University, Tempe, Ariz.
Silver, Albert W., 1341 Nicolet Pl., Detroit, Mich.
Silvern, Leonard Charles, 979 Teakwood Rd., Los Angeles, Calif.
Sim, William E., 153 Pardee Manor Rd., Orange, Conn.
Simmons, I. F., Samford University, Birmingham, Ala.
Simmons, Muriel H., 304—22nd Ave. North, Nashville, Tenn.
Simmons, Virginia Lee, 1001 Essex House, Indianapolis, Ind.
Simms, Naomi, 333 College Ct., Kent, Ohio
Simon, Dan, Superintendent of Schools, East Chicago, Ind.
Simon, Herman, 3410 Palisades Ave., Union City, N.J.
Simons, Herbert D., 46 Shepard St., Cambridge, Mass.
Simpkins, Katherine W., P.O. Box 88, Chesapeake, Ohio
Simpson, Mrs. Anne E., Bethel Park Senior High School, Bethel Park, Pa.
Simpson, Mrs. Elizabeth A., 5627 Blackstone Ave., Chicago, Ill.
Simpson, Frederick W., University of Tulsa, Tulsa, Okla.
Simpson, Mrs. Hazel D., Col. of Educ., University of Georgia, Athens, Ga.
Simpson, Ray H., Col. of Educ., University of Illinois, Urbana, Ill.
Simpson, Raymond J., San Francisco State College, San Francisco, Calif.
Sims, Harold W., 9423 Harvard Ave., Chicago, Ill.
Sims, Stephen B., Leonia Public Schools, Leonia, N.J.
Sincock, William R., Allegheny College, Meadville, Pa.
Sinderson, Louise, Chicago State Col., Chicago, Ill.
Singer, H. Halleck, University of Pennsylvania, Philadelphia, Pa.
Singer, Harry, Div. of Soc. Sci., Univ. of California, Riverside, Calif.
Singletary, James Daniel, USAID/Education, APO San Francisco, Calif. 96243
Singleton, Edward M., 2804 Wilmot Ave., Columbia, S.C.
Singleton, Stanton J., Col. of Educ., University of Georgia, Athens, Ga.
Sipay, Edward R., State University of New York, Albany, N.Y.
Sipe, H. Craig, State Univ. of New York, Albany, N.Y.
Sires, Ely, 5018 LaCrosse Lane, Madison, Wis.
Sister Angelita, O.S.F., St. John Grade Sch., Bancroft, Iowa
Sister Ann Augusta, 400 The Fenway, Boston, Mass.
Sister Anna Clare, College of St. Rose, Albany, N.Y.
Sister Anna Marie (Weinreis), Presentation College, Aberdeen, S.D.
Sister Anne Martina (Ganser), St. Joseph's Col., Crookston, Minn.
Sister Charles Marie, Col. of St. Francis, Joliet, Ill.
Sister Dorothy Marie Riordan, College of St. Elizabeth, Convent Station, N.J.
Sister Fides Huber, College of St. Catherine, St. Paul, Minn.
Sister Irene Elizabeth, 1 Main St., Groton, Mass.
Sister Irene Rita Fontaine, Holy Union Convent, 1 Main St., Groton, Mass.
Sister James, S.Sp.S., St. Rose de Lima H.S., Bay St. Louis, Miss.
Sister James Claudia, Siena Heights College, Adrian, Mich.
Sister James Edward, Brescia College, Owensboro, Ky.
Sister John Vianney Coyle, St. Francis Convent, Graymoor, Garrison, N.Y.
Sister Josephina Concannon, 71 Walnut Park, Newton, Mass.
Sister Margaret Mary, R.S.M., Gwynedd-Mercy College, Gwynedd Valley, Pa.
Sister Margaret Mary, Monsignor O'Brien High School, Kalamazoo, Mich.
Sister Margaret Mary O'Connell, College of Notre Dame of Md., Baltimore, Md.
Sister Marie Claudia, Barry College, Miami Shores, Fla.
Sister Marie Gabrielle, Diocesan Sisters College, Woodstock, Conn.
Sister Marietta Marlock, M. Celine Hse. of Studies, Port Chester, N.Y.
Sister Mary Agnello, Regis College, Framingham Campus, Framingham, Mass.
Sister Mary Agnes Hennessey, Mount Mercy College, Cedar Rapids, Iowa
Sister Mary Albertus, Mt. St. Vincent College, Halifax, Nova Scotia, Canada

Sister Mary Alma, St. Mary's College, Notre Dame, Ind.
Sister M. Anacleta Schuette, Sacred Heart College, Wichita, Kan.
Sister M. Angela Betke, Cantalician Ctr. for Child., 3233 Main St., Buffalo, N.Y.
Sister Mary Antonius, Mt. St. Mary Col., Hooksett, N.H.
Sister Mary Basil, Good Counsel College, White Plains, N.Y.
Sister Mary Basil, Notre Dame of the Lake, Nequon, Wis.
Sister Mary Benedict Phelan, Clarke College, Dubuque, Iowa
Sister Mary Bernice, Our Lady of the Elms, Akron, Ohio
Sister Mary Bonnita, Felician College, Chicago, Ill.
Sister M. Brideen Long, Holy Family College, Manitowoc, Wis.
Sister Mary Camilla, St. Francis Convent, Jerseyville, Ill.
Sister M. Camille Kliebhan, Cardinal Stritch College, Milwaukee, Wis.
Sister Mary Charles, Molloy Catholic College for Women, Rockville Centre, N.Y.
Sister Mary Chrysostom, College of Our Lady of the Elms, Chicopee, Mass.
Sister Mary Clarissa, Dominican College of Blauvelt, Blauvelt, N.Y.
Sister Mary Conleth McCarthy, Mt. Alvernia College, Newton, Mass.
Sister Mary David, College of St. Benedict, St. Joseph, Minn.
Sister Mary de Lourdes, Saint Joseph College, West Hartford, Conn.
Sister Mary Dolores, College of St. Francis, Joliet, Ill.
Sister Mary Dorothy, Queen of Apostles Col. Library, Harrimon, N.Y.
Sister Mary Edward, 1229 Mt. Loretto Ave., Dubuque, Iowa
Sister Mary Edwina, 5286 South Park Ave., Hamburg, N.Y.
Sister Mary Elaine, College of St. Mary, Omaha, Neb.
Sister Mary Fidelia, Immaculata College, Bartlett, Ill.
Sister Mary Fidelma, Marylhurst College, Marylhurst, Ore.
Sister M. Fleurette, St. Willibrord Convent, Chicago, Ill.
Sister M. Francis Regis, 444 Centre St., Milton, Mass.
Sister Mary Fridian, Dept. of Educ., St. Francis College, Fort Wayne, Ind.
Sister Mary Gabrieline, Marygrove College, Detroit, Mich.
Sister Mary Gabrielle, Nazareth College, Nazareth, Mich.
Sister Mary Giles, Mariam College, Indianapolis, Ind.
Sister M. Gregory, Marymount Col., Palo Verdes Estates, Calif.
Sister M. Harriet Sanborn, Aquinas College, Grand Rapids, Mich.
Sister Mary Helen, Dominican Col., Racine, Wis.
Sister Mary Hugh, Fontbonne College, St. Louis, Mo.
Sister Mary Hyacinth, Mount Senario College, Ladysmith, Wis.
Sister Mary Irmina Saelinger, Villa Madonna College, Covington, Ky.
Sister M. Jeanne, St. Mary's Academy, South Bend, Ind.
Sister Mary Joanice, St. Mary's College, Notre Dame, Ind.
Sister Mary Joanne, Marycrest College, Davenport, Iowa
Sister Mary John Francis, Mount Mercy Col., Milwaukee, Wis.
Sister M. Judith, Villa Madonna Academy, Covington, Ky.
Sister Mary Judith, Dept. of Educ., Briar Cliff College, Sioux City, Iowa
Sister Mary Kathleen, Mt. St. Agnes College, Mt. Washington, Baltimore, Md.
Sister M. Laurina, Mount Mary College, Yankton, S.D.
Sister Mary Lawrence, Mary Manse College, Toledo, Ohio
Sister Mary Lawrence Huber, Mt. St. Joseph Teachers College, Buffalo, N.Y.
Sister Mary Leo, Immaculata College, Immaculata, Pa.
Sister M. Leonella, 262 Gaffey Rd., Watsonville, Calif.
Sister Mary Liguori, Mercyhurst College, Erie, Pa.
Sister M. Louis, 144 W. Wood St., Youngstown, Ohio
Sister Mary Madeleine, Col. of Our Lady of Mercy, Burlingame, Calif.
Sister M. Margaret Michael, Mt. St. Mary, Newburgh, N.Y.
Sister M. Margarita, Rosary College, River Forest, Ill.
Sister M. Matthew, Sacred Heart Dominican College, Houston, Tex.
Sister Mary Mercita, St. Mary College, Xavier, Kan.
Sister M. Merici, Educ. Dept., Ursuline College, Louisville, Ky.
Sister M. Merle, St. Matthia School, Chicago, Ill.
Sister Mary Nila, Cardinal Cushing Education Clinic, Boston, Mass.
Sister M. Olivia Frietsch, Marian Scholasticate, Oldenburg, Ind.
Sister Mary Paul, Mt. Mercy College, Pittsburgh, Pa.

Sister M. Petrine, S.S.N.D., S. Cent. Provincial House, Irving, Texas
Sister M. Pierre, Marian College of Fond du Lac, Fond du Lac, Wis.
Sister Mary Priscilla, Notre Dame College, Cleveland, Ohio
Sister Mary Rachel, 345 Belden Hill Rd., Wilton, Conn.
Sister Mary Raymial, 10216 South Vernon Ave., Chicago, Ill.
Sister Mary Rosalia, Salve Regina College, Newport, R.I.
Sister Mary Rose Agnes, Our Lady of Cincinnati College, Cincinnati, Ohio
Sister M. Rosine, Dunbarton College, Washington, D.C.
Sister Mary St. George, Mundelein College, Chicago, Ill.
Sister Mary of St. Michael, College of the Holy Names, Oakland, Calif.
Sister Mary Theodine, Viterbo College, LaCrosse, Wis.
Sister M. Veronice Engelhardt, Maria Regina College, Syracuse, N.Y.
Sister Mary Vianney, St. Xavier College, 103rd and Central Park, Chicago, Ill.
Sister Mary Vincent Therese Tuohy, 245 Clinton Ave., Brooklyn, N.Y.
Sister Mary Zeno, Notre Dame College, 320 E. Ripa Ave., St. Louis, Mo.
Sister Mildred Clare, Nazareth College, Nazareth, Ky.
Sister Miriam Richard, Holy Cross Convent, Philadelphia, Pa.
Sister Muriel Hogan, Ottumwa Heights College, Ottumwa, Iowa
Sister Patrick Mary, 501 E. 163rd St., Calumet City, Ill.
Sister Regina Clare, Mt. St. Mary's College, Los Angeles, Calif.
Sister Rita Donahue, Notre Dame College, Staten Island, N.Y.
Sister Rose Matthew, Marygrove College, Detroit, Mich.
Sister Rosemarie Julie, Educ. Dept., College of Notre Dame, Belmont, Calif.
Sister Saint Catherine, Nazareth College of Rochester, Rochester, N.Y.
Skaggs, Darcy A., 3699 N. Holly Ave., Baldwin Park, Calif.
Skalski, John M., Sch. of Educ., Fordham University, New York, N.Y.
Skard, Mrs. Aase Gruda, Fjellvn 2, Lysaker, Norway
Skatzes, D. H., Box 125, Old Washington, Ohio
Skinner, Halver M., Montana State College, Bozeman, Montana
Skinner, Ray, Jr., Col. of Educ., Ohio Univ., Athens, Ohio
Skinner, Richard C., Clarion State College, Clarion, Pa.
Skipper, Mrs. Dora Sikes, Florida State University, Tallahassee, Fla.
Skogsberg, Alfred H., Bloomfield Junior High School, Bloomfield, N.J.
Skonberg, Mrs. Madelon, 2601 Sunnyside Ave., Chicago, Ill.
Slater, J. Marlowe, Dept. of Educ. Psych., Univ. of Illinois, Urbana, Ill.
Sletten, Vernon, Sch. of Educ., Univ. of Montana, Missoula, Mont.
Sliepcevich, Elena M., 1425 "N" St., N. W., Washington, D.C.
Sligo, Joseph R., 102 N. Lancaster St., Athens, Ohio
Slobetz, Frank, St. Cloud State College, St. Cloud, Minn.
Slocum, Helen M., Norris Gym, Univ. of Minnesota, Minneapolis, Minn.
Slocum, Thomas J., 11 S. Cagwin, Joliet, Ill.
Smallenburg, Harry W., Supt. of Schools, Los Angeles Co., Los Angeles, Calif.
Smedstad, Alton O., Superintendent, Elem. Schools, Hillsboro, Ore.
Smelser, Rex H., 501 Broad St., Lake Charles, La.
Smerling, William H., Ohio Northern University, Ada, Ohio
Smiley, Marjorie B., Hunter College, 695 Park Ave., New York, N.Y.
Smith, Mrs. Adean M., 2519 North 41st St., Milwaukee, Wis.
Smith, Alvin H., St. Andrews Presbyterian College, Laurinburg, N.C.
Smith, Ara K., 609 Lafayette St., Michigan City, Ind.
Smith, B. Othanel, Col. of Educ., University of Illinois, Urbana, Ill.
Smith, Cleovis C., 4801 Tremont St., Dallas, Tex.
Smith, Clodus R., 9203 St. Andrews Pl., College Park, Md.
Smith, David C., Michigan State University, East Lansing, Mich.
Smith, E. Brooks, Wayne State University, Detroit, Mich.
Smith, Emmitt D., Box 745, West Texas Station, Canyon, Tex.
Smith, Frank A., 531-A West Ninth Pl., Mesa, Arizona
Smith, Garmon B., Austin College, Sherman, Tex.
Smith, Gary F., 400 E. Market St., Salem, Ind.
Smith, Gary R., 14520 Asbury Park, Detroit, Mich.
Smith, Gerald R., 407 Hillsboro Pkwy., Syracuse, N.Y.
Smith, Harry E., 608 S. Dearborn St., Chicago, Ill.

Smith, Hannis S., State Office Annex, 117 University Ave., St. Paul, Minn.
Smith, Henry P., Sch. of Educ., University of Kansas, Lawrence, Kan.
Smith, Herbert A., Colorado State University, Fort Collins, Colo.
Smith, Hilda C., Dept. of Educ., Loyola University, New Orleans, La.
Smith, Jack D., 4 Vine Court, Kent, Ohio
Smith, James B., 221 S. Missouri, Belleville, Ill.
Smith, James O., 504 Roosevelt Dr., Shelbyville, Ind.
Smith, John W., 10001 Princeton Ave., Chicago, Ill.
Smith, Joseph M., 172 Charter Rd., Wethersfield, Conn.
Smith, Kenneth E., Grad. Sch. of Educ., Univ. of Chicago, Chicago, Ill.
Smith, Lawrence J., Central Michigan University, Mt. Pleasant, Mich.
Smith, Leslie F., 705 N. Killingsworth, Portland, Ore.
Smith, Lloyd N., Dept. of Educ., Indiana State University, Terre Haute, Ind.
Smith, Mary Alice, State College, Lock Haven, Pa.
Smith, Mrs. Maxine, 172 W. Third St., San Bernardino, Calif.
Smith, Menrie M., Rte. 4, Hamilton, Ala.
Smith, Nila Banton, 1111 S. Broadway, Pitman, N.J.
Smith, Paul E., Board of Education, Wilmington, Del.
Smith, Paul M., 7271 East Ave., U-3, Littlerock, Calif.
Smith, Philip John, Box 13, P.O. Cottesloe, Western Australia
Smith, Priscilla R., Western State Col., Gunnison, Colo.
Smith, Robert M., Pennsylvania State Univ., University Park, Pa.
Smith, Russell F. W., 9 Bursley Pl., White Plains, N.Y.
Smith, Sara E., Western Maryland College, Westminster, Md.
Smith, Sisera, 115 South 54th St., Philadelphia, Pa.
* Smith, Stephen E., East Texas Baptist College, Marshall, Tex.
Smith, W. Holmes, El Camino Col., Torrance, Calif.
Snapper, Marion, Calvin College, Grand Rapids, Mich.
Snead, William E., 3106 Carlisle Dr., Austin, Texas
Snearline, Paul A., 815 Market St., Lewisburg, Pa.
Snider, Glenn R., Col. of Educ., University of Oklahoma, Norman, Okla.
Snider, Hervon Leroy, Sch. of Educ., University of Idaho, Moscow, Idaho
Sniderman, S. M., Highland Park Pub. Schools, Highland Park, Mich.
Snodgrass, Mr. Glyndol L., 1201 Guthrie, Waco, Texas
Snowden, Terrence J., Campus Sch., Wisconsin State Col., Stevens Point, Wis.
Snyder, Agnes, 50 Central Ter., Clifton Park, Wilmington, Del.
Snyder, Darl E., 424 S. Sixth Ave., La Grange, Ill.
Snyder, Harvey B., Pasadena College, 1539 E. Howard St., Pasadena, Calif.
Snyder, Helen I., 1020 W. Beaver Ave., State College, Pa.
Snyder, Jack, Encyclopaedia Britannica Educ. Corp., Chicago, Ill.
Snyder, Jerome R., 1114 Mogford St., Midland, Tex.
Snyder, Marjorie Sims, Child Study Cntr., Kent State Univ., Kent, Ohio
Snyder, Robert D., Superintendent of Schools, Wayzata, Minn.
Snyder, Ruth C., 110 Laurelton Rd., Rochester, N.Y.
Soares, Anthony T., 290 Lawrence Rd., Trumbull, Conn.
Sobel, Morton J., 1712 New Hampshire Ave., N.W., Washington, D.C.
Sobel, Stuart W., 135 Hawthorne St., Brooklyn, N.Y.
Sobin, Gloria A., 370 Seymour Ave., Derby, Conn.
Soeberg, Mrs. Dorothy, 106 Ridge Rd., Whittier, Calif.
Sokol, John, Tchrs. Col., Columbia University, New York, N.Y.
Soles, Stanley, San Francisco State College, San Francisco, Calif.
Solomon, Benjamin, Indust. Rela. Cntr., Univ. of Chicago, Chicago, Ill.
Solomon, Ruth H., 91 N. Allen St., Albany, N.Y.
Somers, Mary Louise, Sch. of SSA, Univ. of Chicago, Chicago, Ill.
Sommer, Maynard E., 1737 Country Club Dr., Bakersfield, Calif.
Sommers, Mildred, Board of Educ., 290 W. Michigan Ave., Jackson, Mich.
Sommers, Wesley S., 820 Sixth St., Menomonie, Wis.
Sonntag, Ida May, 5101 Norwich Rd., Toledo, Ohio
Sonstegard, Manford A., Southern Illinois Univ., Edwardsville, Ill.
Sorbo, Paul J., Jr., Board of Education, Windsor, Conn.
Sorensen, Edwin, P.O. Box 210, Northport, N.Y.

MEMBERS OF THE NATIONAL SOCIETY   xciii

Sorenson, A. Garth, Moore Hall, University of California, Los Angeles, Calif.
Sorenson, Helmer E., Oklahoma A. & M. Univ., Stilwater, Okla.
Sorenson, Mrs. Virginia, 105 N. Division Ave., Grand Rapids, Mich.
Sorenson, Wayne L., Hayward Unified Sch. Dist., Hayward, Calif.
Sosulski, Michael C., Dutchess Comm. Col., Poughkeepsie, N.Y.
Soucy, Leo A., Dist. Supt. of Schools, Auburn, N.Y.
Southall, Maycie K., Box 867, Peabody Col., Nashville, Tenn.
Sowards, G. Wesley, Sch. of Educ., Stanford University, Stanford, Calif.
Spalke, E. Pauline, P.O. Box 405, Salem Depot, N.H.
Sparling, Joseph J., 507 Church St., Ann Arbor, Mich.
Spaulding, Mrs. Clara G., 1356 E. Hyde Park Blvd., Chicago, Ill.
Spaulding, Robert L., Duke University, Durham, N.C.
Spaulding, Seth, Sch. of Educ., Univ. of Pittsburgh, Pittsburgh, Pa.
Spear, William G., 7233 W. Lunt Ave., Chicago, Ill.
Spears, Sol, El Marino School, Culver City, Calif.
Speciale, Anna G., 83 Rockledge Ave., White Plains, N.Y.
Speer, Hugh W., University of Missouri, Kansas City, Mo.
Speicher, A. Dean, 8008 Kennedy Ave., Highland, Ind.
Speights, Mrs. R. M., Limestone College, Gaffney, S.C.
Spence, Joseph R., Clarion State College, Clarion, Pa.
Spence, Ralph B., 355 Beechwood Dr., Athens, Ga.
Spencer, Doris U., Johnson State College, Johnson, Vt.
Spencer, Edward M., Fresno State College, Fresno, Calif.
Spencer, Elizabeth F., Ball State University, Muncie, Ind.
Spencer, James E., P.O. Box 813, Danville, Calif.
Sperber, Robert I., 21 Lowell Rd., Brookline, Mass.
Sperger, Zelma M., Board of Education, Salt Lake City, Utah
Spielman, Lester, 2970 Sheridan Rd., Chicago, Ill.
Spigle, Irving S., Park Forest Pub. Schools, Park Forest, Ill.
Spinks, Sam, Superintendent of Schools, Hattiesburg, Miss.
Spinner, Arnold, 926 Bloomfield Ave., Glen Ridge, N.J.
Spinola, A. R., Superintendent, Denville School Dist. No. 1, Denville, N.J.
Spitzer, Herbert F., Col. of Educ., State University of Iowa, Iowa City, Iowa
Sporing, W. Dwight, High School, 8th and Walnut Sts., Dayton, Ky.
Springman, John H., 1215 Waukegan Rd., Glenview, Ill.
Spruill, Betty Anne, 241 Langdon St., Madison, Wis.
Squire, James R., 805 W. Indiana Ave., Urbana, Ill.
Srisa-an, Wichit, 913 Weeks Ave., S.E., Minneapolis, Minn.
Stabler, Ernest, Wesleyan University, Middletown, Conn.
Stafford, H. D., P.O. Box 21, Murrayville, B.C., Canada
Staggs, Jack, Sam Houston State Col., Huntsville, Texas
Stahl, Albert F., Syracuse Univ., Syracuse, N.Y.
Stahlecker, Lotar V., Kent State University, Kent, Ohio
Stahly, Harold L., 8343 Manchester Dr., Grand Blanc, Mich.
Staidl, Doris J., 1 East Gilman, Madison, Wis.
Staiger, Ralph C., 701 Dallam Rd., Newark, Del.
Staiger, Roger P., Dept. of Chem., Ursinus College, Collegeville, Pa.
Stalnaker, John M., 569 Briar Lane, Northfield, Ill.
Stanard, David C., Cubberly H.S., 4000 Middlefield Rd., Palo Alto, Calif.
Stang, Genevieve E., 730 First St., Apt. H, Bowling Green, Ohio
Stanley, Calvin, Texas Southern University, Houston, Tex.
Stanley, Curtis E., 2952 Vandy Dr., Montgomery, Ala.
Stanton, William A., 2230 Riverview Way, Eureka, Calif.
Stark, Mrs. Shirley Alger, 5240 The Toledo, Long Beach, Calif.
Starner, Norman Dean, Wyalusing Valley Joint High School, Wyalusing, Pa.
Stathopulos, Peter H., 320 Second Ave., Phoenixville, Pa.
Statler, Charles R., Univ. of South Carolina, Columbia, S.C.
Stauffer, Arthur L., Jr., State Univ. Col., Fredonia, N.Y.
Stauffer, Richard F., Horton Watkins High School, St. Louis, Mo.
Stauffer, Russell G., University of Delaware, Newark, Del.
Staven, LaVier L., 1304 MacArthur Rd., Hays, Kan.

Steadman, E. R., 277 Columbia, Elmhurst, Ill.
Stedje, Raynard L., 3146 Minnehaha Ave., So., Minneapolis, Minn.
Steele, Joe Milan, 19 Dunnellen Dr., Urbana, Ill.
Steele, Lysle H., P.O. Box 66, Beloit, Wis.
Steen, Mrs. Peggy, 133 Mission St., Santa Cruz, Calif.
Steeves, Frank L., University of Vermont, Burlington, Vt.
Steg, Doreen E., 1616 Hepburn Dr., Villanova, Pa.
Stegall, Alma Lirline, Virginia State College, Petersburg, Va.
Steger, Robert I., 530 S. Tenth Ave., LaGrange, Ill.
Steider, Alma T., 207 S. Walnut St., Eureka, Ill.
Steigelman, Mrs. Vivian R., 7617 Potrero Ave., El Cerrito, Calif.
Stein, Jay W., Higher Educ. Facilities Comm., Des Moines, Iowa
Stein, Michael W., Western Jr. H.S., Greenwich, Conn.
Steinberg, Paul M., Hebrew Union Col., New York, N.Y.
Steinberg, Warren L., 2737 Dunleer Pl., Los Angeles, Calif.
Steiner, Harry, 5 Belaire Dr., Roseland, N.J.
Steinhagen, Margaret J., 107 McKendree Ave., Annapolis, Md.
Steininger, Earl W., 535 West 5th St., Dubuque, Iowa
Steinkellner, Robert H., Southern Illinois University, Edwardsville, Ill.
Stell, Samuel C., Robeson County Bd. of Educ., Lumberton, N.C.
Stephens, Bertha L., 121 E. Evans Ave., Pueblo, Colo.
Stephens, E. R., Univ. of Iowa, Iowa City, Iowa
Stephens, John M., University of British Columbia, Vancouver, B.C., Canada
Stephens, Kenton E., 276 Nuttall, Riverside, Ill.
Stephenson, Alan R., 11227 Plymouth Ave., Cleveland, Ohio
Sterling, A. M., 1017 Garner Ave., Schenectady, N.Y.
Sternberg, William N., Public Sch. 114, 1155 Cromwell Ave., New York, N.Y.
Sterner, William S., Rutgers Univ., Newark, N.J.
Stetson, Ethel A., 47 Westchester Ave., North Babylon, N.Y.
Stevens, J. H., 1819 Upper Wetumpka Rd., Montgomery, Ala.
Stevens, Paul C., Rapid City Public Schools, Rapid City, S.D.
Stewart, Frederick H., 3390 Bristol Rd., Chalfont R.D., Pa.
Stewart, James T., Delgado Institute, New Orleans, La.
Stewart, Lawrence H., University of California, Berkeley, Calif.
Stickler, W. Hugh, Florida State University, Tallahassee, Fla.
Stickley, William T., 2107 Adelbert Rd., Cleveland, Ohio
Stickney, Judith A., 3425 Maize Rd., Columbus, Ohio
Stiemke, Eugenia A., Valparaiso University, Valparaiso, Ind.
Stier, Lealand D., P.O. Box 247, Saratoga, Calif.
Stiles, Grace Ellen, 10 Fortin Rd., Kingston, R.I.
Stinebaugh, Demas J., Box 2242, A. & I., Station, Kingsville, Tex.
Stirzaker, Norbert A., 322 South 32nd St., Terre Haute, Ind.
Stitt, J. Howard, Sch. of Educ., Univ. of California, Los Angeles, Calif.
Stitt, Sam C., Superintendent of Schools, Ellinwood, Kan.
Stivers, Stephen N., Idaho State University, Pocatello, Idaho
Stockdale, Mrs. J. B., 547 "A" Ave., Coronado, Calif.
Stockman, Verne, Eastern Illinois University, Charleston, Ill.
Stockton, William S., Univ. of Minnesota, Minneapolis, Minn.
Stoddard, George D., 200 East End Ave., New York, N.Y.
Stofega, Michael E., 271 State St., Perth Amboy, N.J.
Stoia, George, 234 Conover Rd., Pittsburgh, Pa.
Stokes, Maurice S., Savannah State College, Savannah, Ga.
Stolee, Michael J., 6618 San Vincente Ave., Coral Gables, Fla.
Stolurow, Lawrence M., 110 Pleasant St., Lexington, Mass.
Stone, Franklin D., Univ. of Iowa, Iowa City, Iowa
Stone, George P., Union College, Lincoln, Neb.
Stone, Howard L., 1732 Wauwatosa Ave., Wauwatosa, Wis.
Stone, James C., University of California, Berkeley, Calif.
Stone, Paul T., Huntingdon College, Montgomery, Ala.
Stonehocker, D. Doyle, 1515 Oakdale St., Burlington, Iowa
Stoneking, Lewis W., Parsons College, Fairfield, Iowa

Stoner, Lee H., Sch. of Educ., Indiana Univ., Bloomington, Ind.
Stoops, John A., Dept. of Educ., Lehigh University, Bethlehem, Pa.
Stordahl, Kalmer E., Northern Michigan Univ., Marquette, Mich.
Storen, Helen F., 114 Morningside Dr., New York, N.Y.
Storlie, Theodore R., 1400 W. Maple Ave., Downers Grove, Ill.
Storm, Jerome F., Dept. of Educ., Pacific University, Forest Grove, Ore.
Stormer, Donald L., Rt. #1, Waunakee, Wis.
Stottler, Richard H., University of Maryland, College Park, Md.
Stoughton, Robert W., State Department of Education, Hartford, Conn.
Stoumbis, George C., Col. of Educ., Univ. of Utah, Salt Lake City, Utah
Strahler, Violet R., 5340 Brendonwood Ln., Dayton, Ohio
Strain, John Paul, Dept. of Educ., Tufts University, Medford, Mass.
Strain, Mrs. Sibyl M., 2236 Los Lunas St., Pasadena, Calif.
Strand, William H., Sch. of Educ., Stanford University, Stanford, Calif.
* Strang, Ruth, Col. of Educ., University of Arizona, Tucson, Ariz.
Strathairn, Pamela L., Women's Phy. Ed. Dept., Stanford Univ., Stanford, Calif.
Straub, Raymond R., Jr., 1120 S. Gay St., Phoenixville, Pa.
Strauss, John F., Jr. College of St. Thomas, St. Paul, Minn.
Strawn, Aimee W., Chicago State Col., South, Chicago, Ill.
Strayer, George D., Jr. Col. of Educ., University of Washington, Seattle, Wash.
Strebel, Jane D., Bd. of Educ., 807 N.E. Broadway, Minneapolis, Minn.
Street, William Paul, Univ. of Kentucky, Lexington, Ky.
Streich, William H., Farmington Pub. Schools, Farmington, Conn.
Streitmatter, Kenneth D., Rocky River High School, Rocky River, Ohio
Strem, Bruce E., 222 W. Gardner St., Long Beach, Calif.
Streng, Alice, University of Wisconsin-Milwaukee, Milwaukee, Wis.
Strickland, C. G., Sch. of Educ., Baylor University, Waco, Tex.
Strickland, Mrs. Helen B., Arlington High School, Arlington, Tex.
Stringfellow, Mrs. Jackie R., 1833 Second St., S.E., Moultrie, Ga.
Strohbehn, Earl F., 12151 Mellowood Dr., Saratoga, Calif.
Strole, Lois E., R.R. No. 2, West Terre Haute, Ind.
Stromberg, Frances, Sch. of H.E., University of Arizona, Tucson, Ariz.
Stroud, Sarah Jane, Western Michigan University, Kalamazoo, Mich.
Strowbridge, Edwin D., Oregon State University, Corvallis, Ore.
Stuardi, J. Edwin, 550 Dauphin St., Mobile, Ala.
Stuart, Alden T., St. Andrews Rd., Southampton, N.Y.
Stuart, Chester J., Canisius Hall, Fairfield University, Fairfield, Conn.
Stuber, George, Clayton School Dist., 7530 Maryland Ave., Clayton, Mo.
Stuenkel, Walter W., Concordia College, Milwaukee, Wis.
Stutzman, Carl R., 2130 Aaron Way, Sacramento, Calif.
Sudyk, James Edward, 830 Williams Way, Mountain View, Calif.
Suehr, John H., Michigan State University, East Lansing, Mich.
Suess, Alan R., M. Golden Labs., Purdue Univ., Lafayette, Ind.
Sugarman, Alan, Spring Valley Senior High School, Spring Valley, N.Y.
Sugden, W. E., Superintendent of Schools, 7776 Lake St., River Forest, Ill.
Suhd, Melvin, 8501 Tampa, Northridge, Calif.
Suhr, Virtus W., Northern Illinois University, DeKalb, Ill.
Suiter, Phil E., Chesapeake High School, Chesapeake, Ohio
Sullivan, Dorothy D., University of Maryland, College Park, Md.
Sullivan, Floyd W., 1015 Lena St., N.W., Atlanta, Ga.
Sullivan, John J., Roosevelt Sch. Dist., Phoenix, Arizona
Sullivan, Mona Lee R., Univ. of Chattanooga, Chattanooga, Tenn.
Sullivan, Robert E., Notre Dame Col., Cotabato City, Philippines
Sullivan, Ruth E., 306 Bayswater, Salem Harbour, Andalusia, Pa.
Sullivan, Stephen P., 3532 Herschel View, Cincinnati, Ohio
Sulzer, Edward Stanton, Southern Illinois University, Carbondale, Ill.
Summerer, Kenneth, Michigan State Univ., East Lansing, Mich.
Summerton, Rev. O., S.J., P.O. Sitagarha, DT. Hazaribagh, Bihar, India
Sun, Huai Chin, Johnson C. Smith University, Charlotte, N.C.
Sundquist, Ralph R., Jr., Hartford Seminary Foundation, Hartford, Conn.
Sunzeri, Adeline V., 6142 Afton Pl., Hollywood, Calif.

Supworth, Flora D., Miami-Dade Jr. Col., Coral Gables, Fla.
Suskowitz, Min, 81-31—188th St., Jamaica, N.Y.
Susskind, Edwin C., 405 Fountain St., New Haven, Conn.
Sutherland, Jack W., San Jose State College, San Jose, Calif.
Sutherland, Margaret, Col. of Educ., University of California, Davis, Calif.
Sutton, Elizabeth W., 800 Fourth St., S.W., Washington, D.C.
Swadley, Ellis C., Jr., Washington State College, Machias, Me.
Swann, Mrs. A. Ruth, 2713 Mapleton Ave., Norfolk, Va.
Swanson, Gordon I., Dept. of Agric. Educ., Univ. of Minnesota, St. Paul, Minn.
Swanson, Herbert L., El Camino Col., Torrance, Calif.
Swanson, J. Chester, Sch. of Educ., University of California, Berkeley, Calif.
Swanson, Reynold A., Board of Education, 100 N. Jefferson, Green Bay, Wis.
Swartout, Sherwin G., State Univ. Col., Brockport, N.Y.
Swartzmiller, Jean, 90 Ridge Ave., North Plainfield, N.J.
Sweany, H. Paul, Michigan State University, East Lansing, Mich.
Sweeney, Christine M., Emmanuel Col., Boston, Mass.
Swenson, Esther J., Box 1942, University, Ala.
Swertfeger, Floyd F., Route 3, Box 16, Farmville, Va.
Swindall, Wellington, Palmdale School, 3000 E. Wier Ave., Phoenix, Ariz.
Swindel, Mrs. Mabel A., Three Rivers Jr. Col., Poplar Bluff, Mo.
Syvinski, Henry B., Villanova University, Villanova, Pa.

Tadena, Tomas P., Univ. of the Philippines, Quezon City, Philippines
Tag, Herbert G., University of Connecticut, Storrs, Conn.
Tajima, Yuri, 1918 N. Bissell, Chicago, Ill.
* Tallman, Russell W., 2024 Avalon Rd., Des Moines, Iowa
Tamashunas, Edward, 2220 Park Ave., Bridgeport, Conn.
Tambe, Naren, P.O. Box 153, Normal, Ala.
Tanner, B. William, 650 S. Detroit Ave., Toledo, Ohio
Tanner, Daniel, University of Wisconsin-Milwaukee, Milwaukee, Wis.
Tanner, Wilbur H., Northwestern State University, Alva, Okla.
Tanruther, Edgar M., Indiana State Univ., Terre Haute, Ind.
Tant, Norman, Morehead State College, Morehead, Ky.
Tardif, Fernand R., La Salette Seminary, Enfield, N.H.
Tarver, K. E., John P. Odom School, 3445 Fannett Rd., Beaumont, Tex.
Tate, Virginia, 2228 Eighth St. Cr., Charleston, Ill.
Taylor, Mrs. Emily C., Mayo Elementary School, Edgewater, Md.
Taylor, Faith, 10427 Montrose Ave., Bethesda, Md.
Taylor, George E., Gateway Sch. Dist., Monroeville, Pa.
Taylor, James I., Miami-Dade Jr. Col., Coral Gables, Fla.
Taylor, Kenneth I., Madison Public Schools, Madison, Wis.
Taylor, M. Ruth, Hillcrest School, Drexel Hill, Pa.
Taylor, Marvin, Div. of Educ., Queens College, Flushing, N.Y.
Taylor, Marvin J., St. Paul School of Theology, Kansas City, Mo.
Taylor, Mrs. Mary C., Box 164, Rt. No. 1, New Lenox, Ill.
Taylor, Peter A., Grad. Sch. of Educ., Rutgers Univ., New Brunswick, N.J.
Taylor, Robert E., 1835 Riverhill Rd., Columbus, Ohio
Taylor, Wayne, 160 Kenberry, East Lansing, Mich.
Teague, Carroll, Pasadena Ind. School District, Pasadena, Tex.
Tcare, Benjamin R., Jr., Carnegie-Mellon Univ., Schenley Park, Pa.
Telfer, Richard G., Shorewood Public Schools, Shorewood, Wis.
Telford, Charles W., San Jose State College, San Jose, Calif.
Temp, George E., Educational Testing Service, Princeton, N.J.
Tempero, Howard E., Teachers Col., University of Nebraska, Lincoln, Neb.
Temple, F. L., Box 2185, University, Ala.
Templin, Mildred C., Inst. of Child Welfare, Univ. of Minnesota, Minneapolis, Minn.
TenEyck, Adelaide L. C., Tchrs. Col., Columbia Univ., New York, N.Y.
Tenny, John W., 630 Merrick Ave., Detroit, Mich.
Terlaje, Shirley A., P.O. Box 1719, Agana, Guam
Terrill, Maymie I., 2477 Overlook Rd., Cleveland Heights, Ohio

Tetz, Henry E., Oregon College of Education, Monmouth, Ore.
Thatcher, Alfred W., State Univ. Col., Potsdam, N.Y.
Thelen, L. J., University of Massachusetts, Amherst, Mass.
Theus, Robert, Southern Illinois University, Carbondale, Ill.
Thevaos, Deno G., 575 Westview Ave., State College, Pa.
Thomann, Don F., Dept. of Educ., Ripon College, Ripon, Wis.
Thomas, Cleveland A., Francis Parker School, 330 Webster Ave., Chicago, Ill.
Thomas, David C., University of Victoria, Victoria, B.C., Canada
Thomas, Granville S., Superintendent of Schools, Salem, N.J.
Thomas, James E., Supt. of Schools, Bristol, Tenn.
Thomas, John, 2250 Missouri, Las Cruces, N.M.
Thomas, Virginia F., Iowa State Univ., Ames, Iowa
Thomas, Wade F., Santa Monica City College, Santa Monica, Calif.
Thompson, Mrs. Alberta S., Dept. of H.E., Kent State Univ., Kent, Ohio
Thompson, Anton, Long Beach Public Schls., 715 Locust Ave., Long Beach, Calif.
Thompson, Barry B., Waco Independent School Dist., Waco, Tex.
Thompson, Bertha Boya, Western Col. for Women, Oxford, Ohio
Thompson, Charles H., Grad. Sch., Howard University, Washington, D.C.
Thompson, Franklin J., South Pasadena High School, South Pasadena, Calif.
Thompson, Fred R., Col. of Educ., Univ. of Maryland, College Park, Md.
Thompson, Helen M., Chapman College, Orange, Calif.
Thompson, Herbert W., Livingstone College, Salisbury, N.C.
Thompson, James H., 1011 Lanreco Blvd., Lancaster, Ohio
Thompson, John D., P.O. Drawer 877, Seminole Public Schools, Seminole, Tex.
Thompson, John F., 1483 Carver St., Madison, Wis.
Thompson, O. E., University of California, Davis, Calif.
Thompson, Olive L., 1541 Iroquois Ave., Long Beach, Calif.
Thompson, Ralph H., Western Washington State Col., Bellingham, Wash.
Thompson, Ray, North Carolina College, Durham, N.C.
Thompson, Mrs. Sheilah, 930 Whitchurch St., North Vancouver, B.C., Canada
Thoms, Denis, Campus View # 124, Bloomington, Ind.
Thomsen, Ronald W., Box 361, Sidney, Iowa
Thomson, Procter, Pitzer Hall, Claremont Men's College, Claremont, Calif.
Thorndike, Robert L., Tchrs. Col., Columbia University, New York, N.Y.
Thornsley, Jerome R., 764 Laurel Ave., Pomona, Calif.
Thornton, James W., Jr., San Jose State College, San Jose, Calif.
Threlkeld, A. L., Jamaica, Vt.
Throne, Elsie M., 306 Lincoln Ave., Avon-by-the-Sea, N.J.
Thursby, Marilyn P., Box 7237, Col. Sta., Durham, N.C.
Thursby, Mrs. Ruth E., 3628 Taft St., Riverside, Calif.
Thyberg, Clifford S., 1717 W. Merced Ave., West Covina, Calif.
Tidrow, Joe, Dept. of Educ. and Phil., Texas Tech. College, Lubbock, Tex.
Tidwell, Robert E., 1602 Alaca Pl., Tuscaloosa, Ala.
Tiedeman, Herman R., Illinois State University, Normal, Ill.
Tillan, Lynn, 417 Hillsboro Pkwy., Syracuse, N.Y.
Tillman, Charles M., Rayville High School, Rayville, La.
Tillman, Rodney, Sch. of Educ., Memphis State Univ., Memphis, Tenn.
Timmons, F. Alan, 1700 Octavia St., San Francisco, Calif.
Tinari, Charles, Shackamaxon School, Scotch Plains, N.J.
Tingle, Mary J., Col. of Educ., University of Georgia, Athens, Ga.
Tink, Albert K., 18 Wendall Pl., DeKalb, Ill.
Tinker, Miles A., P.O. Box 3193, Santa Barbara, Calif.
Tinney, James J., Superintendent of Schools, Pitman, N.J.
Tipton, Elis M., Box 502, Mariposa, Calif.
Tisdall, William J., University of Kentucky, Lexington, Ky.
Tittle, Carol Kehr, 3524 Osceola, Denver, Colo.
Todd, G. Raymond, R.D. No. 3, Bethlehem, Pa.
Todd, Neal F., 128 Main St., Ware, Mass.
Toepfer, Conrad F., Jr., State Univ. Col., Buffalo, N.Y.
Toles, Caesar F., Bishop Junior College, 4527 Crozier St., Dallas, Tex.

Tolleson, Sherwell K., Box 182A, Tenn. Polytech. Inst., Cookeville, Tenn.
Tollinger, William P., Superintendent, Wilson Borough Schls., Easton, Pa.
Tom, Chow Loy, 47 W. Brighton Rd., Columbus, Ohio
Tomaszewski, Raymond J., 333 Richard Ter., S.E., Grand Rapids, Mich.
Tomecek, Carolyn L., 2518 W. 59th St., Chicago, Ill.
Toops, Herbert A., 1430 Cambridge Blvd., Columbus, Ohio
Toporowski, Theodore T., Danbury State College, Danbury, Conn.
Topp, Robert F., Col. of Educ., Northern Illinois University, DeKalb, Ill.
Torchia, Joseph, Millersville State Col., Millersville, Pa.
Torgunrud, E. A., 3301 Sepuvelda Blvd., Los Angeles, Calif.
Torkelson, Gerald M., 408 Miller, Univ. of Washington, Seattle, Wash.
Torrance, E. Paul, University of Georgia, Athens, Ga.
Tothill, Herbert, Eastern Michigan University, Ypsilanti, Mich.
Totten, W. Fred, Mott Sci. Bldg., 1401 E. Court St., Flint, Mich.
Toussaint, Isabella H., 1670 River Rd., Beaver, Pa.
Towers, Richard L., Sch. of Educ., Univ. of South Carolina, Columbia, S.C.
Trachtman, Gilbert M., Sch. of Educ., New York Univ., New York, N.Y.
Tracy, Edward, Easton-Forks and Easton Area Joint Sch. System, Easton, Pa.
Tracy, Elaine M., St. Olaf College, Northfield, Minn.
Tracy, Neal H., University of North Carolina, Chapel Hill, N.C.
Traeger, Carl, 375 N. Eagle St., Oshkosh, Wis.
Traiber, Frank, USAID Mission, Guatemala, State Dept., Washington, D.C.
Trail, Orval L., Superintendent of Schools, Galesburg, Ill.
Trauger, Ruth, Dearborn Campus, Univ. of Michigan, Dearborn, Mich.
Travelstead, Chester C., Col. of Educ., Univ. of New Mexico, Albuquerque, N.M.
Travers, John F., Boston College, Chestnut Hill, Mass.
Travis, Vaud A., Dept. of Educ., Northeastern State College, Tahlequa, Okla.
Traxler, Arthur E., 6825 S.W. 59th St., Miami, Fla.
Treece, Marion B., Southern Illinois University, Carbondale, Ill.
Treffiner, Donald J., Elem. Sch., Cornell Univ., Ithaca, N.Y.
Tremont, Joseph J., 22 Fletcher St., Ayer, Mass.
Trice, J. A., Superintendent of Schools, Pine Bluff, Ark.
Trigg, Harold L., Dept. of Educ., Livingstone Col., Salisbury, N.C.
Triggs, Frances, Mountain Home, N.C.
Trippe, Matthew J., University of Michigan, Ann Arbor, Mich.
Tronsgard, David T., 200 W. Chisum, Roswell, N.M.
Trout, Douglas G., Tusculum College, Greenville, Tenn.
Trow, William Clark, Sch. of Educ., University of Michigan, Ann Arbor, Mich.
Truher, Helen Burke, 245 Hillside Rd., South Pasadena, Calif.
Trumble, Verna J., 42 West St., Johnson City, N.Y.
Trump, J. Lloyd, National Educ. Assn., 1201 Sixteenth St., N.W., Washington, D.C.
Trump, Paul L., American Col. Test. Program, Box 168, Iowa City, Iowa
Truncellito, Louis, Georgetown Univ., Washington, D.C.
Trusty, Francis M., University of Rochester, Rochester, N.Y.
Tucker, Jan L., 407 N. Roosevelt, Bloomington, Ind.
Tucker, Mrs. Sylvia B., 900 Spruce St., Riverside, Calif.
Tudyman, Al, 4470 Hillsborough Dr., Castro Valley, Calif.
Tully, Glover E., Board of Regents, Tallahassee, Fla.
Tupper, Frank B., 389 Congress St., Portland, Me.
Turansky, Isadore, Western Michigan University, Kalamazoo, Mich.
Turchan, Donald G., 1026 White Dr., New Castle, Ind.
Turck, Merton J., Jr., Tennessee Polytechnic Inst., Cookeville, Tenn.
Turner, Delia F., 3310 Edgemont, Tucson, Ariz.
Turner, Howard, Col. of Educ., Univ. of S.W. Louisiana, Lafayette, La.
Turner, Mrs. Nell B., 3431 Sangamon Ave., Dayton, Ohio
Turney, David T., Sch. of Educ., Indiana State Univ., Terre Haute, Ind.
Turnquist, Carl H., Detroit Pub. Schls., 5057 Woodward Ave., Detroit, Mich.
Tuseth, Alice A., 6410—37th Ave. No., Minneapolis, Minn.
Tuttle, Edwin A., Jr., State Univ. Col., New Paltz, N.Y.
Twombly, John J., Sch. of Educ., State Univ. of N.Y., Albany, N.Y.

MEMBERS OF THE NATIONAL SOCIETY xcix

Tydings, R. N., Hobbs Municipal Schools, Hobbs, N.M.
Tyler, Fred T., University of Victoria, Victoria, B.C., Canada
Tyler, I. Keith, Ohio State University, Columbus, Ohio
Tyler, Louise L., University of California, Los Angeles, Calif.
Tyler, Priscilla, Univ. of Missouri, Kansas City, Mo.
Tyler, Ralph W., 5825 Dorchester Ave., Chicago, Ill.
Tyler, Robert, Educ. Dept., Southwestern State College, Weatherford, Okla.
Tyree, Marshall J., New York University, New York, N.Y.
Tyrrell, Francis M., Immaculate Conception Seminary, Huntington, N.Y.
Tyson, Ivernia M., Arizona State College, Flagstaff, Ariz.
Tystad, Edna, Thoreau Public Schools, Thoreau, N.M.

Uhl, Norman P., 1106 Lullwater Rd., N.E., Atlanta, Ga.
Uhlir, Richard F., 800½ W. White St., Champaign, Ill.
Umansky, Harlan L., Emerson High School, Union City, N.J.
Umbarger, Helen D., East Chicago Public Schools, East Chicago, Ind.
Umholtz, Mrs. Anne K., 292 N. Fifth Ave., Highland Park, N.J.
Umstattd, James G., Sutton Hall, University of Texas, Austin, Tex.
Underwood, Mrs. Anna, Box 72, Southard, Okla.
Underwood, Mrs. Frances A., 5900 Hilltop Rd., Pensacola, Fla.
Underwood, Frederic, St. Paul's Schools, Garden City, N.Y.
Underwood, Helen B., 1920 Madrona, Napa, Calif.
Underwood, Mary Hope, R. 2, Chapel Dr., Whitewater, Wis.
Underwood, William J., 304 Lakeview, Lee's Summit, Mo.
Unger, Mrs. Dorothy Holberg, 99 Lawton Rd., Riverside, Ill.
Unruh, Adolph, Univ. of Missouri, 8001 Natural Bridge Rd., St. Louis, Mo.
Urbach, Floyd, Univ. of Nebraska, Waverly, Neb.
Urdang, Miriam E., Queens College, Flushing, N.Y.
Usery, Mary Lou, Ohio State University, Columbus, Ohio
Usitalo, Richard J., 2015 Clairemont Cir., Olympia, Wash.
Utley, Quentin, 136 E.S. Temple, Salt Lake City, Utah

* Vakil, K. S., 119, Marzbanabad, Andheri, Bombay, India
Valentine, Mrs. M., 138 Highland, Highland Park, Mich.
Valone, Katherine G., 6638 S. Marshfield, Chicago, Ill.
Van Auken, Robert A., Superintendent of Schools, North Olmsted, Ohio
Van Bruggen, John A., 1590 Innes St., N.E., Grand Rapids, Mich.
Vanderhoof, C. David, Superintendent of Schools, Little Silver, N.J.
Vander Horck, Karl J., 1892 N. Pascal, St. Paul, Minn.
Vander Linde, Louis F., 3344 Pall Dr., Warren, Mich.
Vander Meer, A. W., 627 W. Hamilton, State College, Pa.
Van de Roovaart, Elizabeth G., 203 East 113th St., Chicago, Ill.
Vanderpool, J. Alden, 1736 Escalante Way, Burlingame, Calif.
Vander Werf, Lester S., Long Island Univ., Brookville, N.Y.
Van Fleet, Ella Maye, Univ. of Tennessee, Knoxville, Tenn.
Van Horn, Paul J., University of Southern Louisiana, Lafayette, La.
Van Loo, Eleanor, South Macomb Com. College, Detroit, Mich.
Van Pelt, Jacob J., 721 N. Juanita St., LaHabra, Calif.
Van Wagenen, Marvin J., 1729 Irving Ave., South, Minneapolis, Minn.
Van Zanten, Mrs. Hazel, 4754 Curwood, S.E., Grand Rapids, Mich.
Van Zwoll, James A., Col. of Educ., University of Maryland, College Park, Md.
Varn, Guy L., Supt. of Schools, 1616 Richland St., Columbia, S.C.
Varner, Leo P., Bakersfield Cntr., Fresno State Col., Bakersfield, Calif.
Varty, Jonathan W., 149 Brixton Rd., Garden City, N.Y.
Vasey, Hamilton G., 346 Second Ave., S.W., Cedar Rapids, Iowa
Vaughan, W. Donald, R. D., Pipersville, Pa.
Vaughn, C. A., Jr., Howey Academy, Howey-in-the-Hills, Fla.
Vaught, Maxine H., 1415 Crestwood Dr., Fayetteville, Ark.
Vayhinger, Harold P., Ohio Northern Univ., Ada, Ohio
Veltman, Peter, 600 College Ave., Wheaton, Ill.
Venatta, Janet R., Ball State Univ., Muncie, Ind.

Verill, John E., University of Minnesota, Duluth, Minn.
Verseput, Robert Frank, 8 South St., Dover, N.J.
Versteegh, Madge, 3407 Grand Ave., Des Moines, Iowa
Vial, Lynda W., 6522 Pennsylvania Ave., Kansas City, Mo.
Vigilante, Nicholas J., 2046 N.W. 18th Lane, Gainesville, Fla.
Vikner, Carl F., Gustavus Adolphus College, St. Peter, Minn.
Vinicombe, Harry W., Jr., 2445 Lyttonsville Rd., Silver Spring, Md.
Vint, Virginia H., 7 Brookwood Dr., Normal, Ill.
Vislay, Patricia Jean, 1937 Greenfield Ave., Los Angeles, Calif.
Vlahakos, Irene J., Cent. Connecticut State Col., New Britain, Conn.
Vlcek, Charles, Central Washington State College, Ellensburg, Wash.
Voelker, Paul Henry, 552 N. Neville St., Pittsburgh, Pa.
Vogel, Francis X., Col. of Educ., Florida State Univ., Tallahassee, Fla.
Voigt, Harry R., St. Paul's College, Concordia, Mo.
Voigt, Virginia E., 9 East Clark Pl., South Orange, N.J.
Volante, William, 220 W. Jersey St., Elizabeth, N.J.
Vonk, Paul K., 35 Blithewood Dr., River Gardens, Pensacola, Fla.
Voris, George A., R.D. # 1, Goodyear Lake, Oneonta, N.Y.
Voss, Burton E., Univ. High Sch., University of Michigan, Ann Arbor, Mich.
Votaw, Daniel Charles, 1140 Alexandria Dr., San Diego, Calif.
Vroon, John W., 937 Woodland Ave., Knoxville, Tenn.

Waara, Bruno W., Arlington High School, Arlington Heights, Ill.
Wade, D. E., Col. of Educ., Univ. of Houston, Houston, Texas
Wade, Frances Joan, 3815 Monona Dr., Madison, Wis.
Wagner, Robert W., Ohio State University, Columbus, Ohio
Wagstaff, Lonnie H., 2601 Meadowbrook Dr., Norman, Okla.
Wagstaff, Robert F., Box 541, LeClaire, Iowa
Waimon, Morton D., Illinois State University, Normal, Ill.
Waine, Sidney I., 34 Thomas Dr., Hauppauge, N.Y.
Wainscott, Carlton O., 3607 Fleetwood, Austin, Tex.
Waldron, Margaret L., Ayrshire, Iowa
Walker, Charles Lynn, San Jose State College, San Jose, Calif.
Walker, John S., 308 N. Tillotson, Muncie, Ind.
Walker, K. P., Superintendent of Schools, Jackson, Miss.
Walker, Mary Louise, 502 Rio Vista Dr., Daytona Beach, Fla.
Walker, Robert N., 2629 Pocomoke St., North, Arlington, Va.
Walker, W. Del, Superintendent Jefferson County Schls., Lakewood, Colo.
Wall, G. S., Stout State University, Menomonie, Wis.
Wall, Harry V., 17013 Alwood St., West Covina, Calif.
Wall, Jessie S., Box 194, Univ. of So. Mississippi, Hattiesburg, Miss.
Wall, Paul L., 1451 E. 55th St., Chicago, Ill.
Wallace, Donald G., Col. of Educ., Drake University, Des Moines, Iowa
Wallace, James O., 1300 San Pedro Ave., San Antonio, Tex.
Wallace, Morris S., Dept. of Educ., Texas Tech. College, Lubbock, Tex.
Wallen, Norman E., San Francisco State Col., San Francisco, Calif.
Waller, Virginia P., Henderson City Schools, Henderson, N.C.
Walley, Bertha, McNeese College, Lake Charles, La.
Wallin, William H., 1765 Santa Anita, Las Vegas, Nev.
Walsh, J. Hartt, Col. of Educ., Butler University, Indianapolis, Ind.
Walsh, John E., International Textbook Co., Scranton, Pa.
Walter, Raymond L., Box 265, Millbrook, Ala.
Walter, Robert B., 434 N. DelMar Ave., San Gabriel, Calif.
Walz, Edgar, Concordia Senior College, Fort Wayne, Ind.
Walz, Garry R., 1718 Arbordale, Ann Arbor, Mich.
Wampler, W. Norman, Superintendent of Schools, Bellflower, Calif.
Wann, Kenneth D., Tchrs. Col., Columbia University, New York, N.Y.
Wantoch, Mrs. Ardell H., McNeal Hall, University of Minnesota, St. Paul, Minn.
Ward, Cecil M., 112 Williams Court, Mobile, Ala.
Ward, Ted, Michigan State University, East Lansing, Mich.
Ward, Virgil S., Sch. of Educ., University of Virginia, Charlottesville, Va.

Wardeberg, Helen L., Stone Hall, Cornell University, Ithaca, N.Y.
Ware, Mrs. Dorothy, 109 Touraine Rd., Grosse Pointe Farms, Mich.
Warren, Alex M., 101 Eddy St., Ithaca, N.Y.
Warren, John H., Carlton Manor, 1053 Beacon St., Brookline, Mass.
Warren, Mary Lou, 1334 Division St., Port Huron, Mich.
Warshavsky, Mrs. Belle, 35 Cooper Dr., Great Neck, N.Y.
Warshavsky, Bernard, 910 West End Ave., New York, N.Y.
Warwick, Raymond, Box 73, Delmont, N.J.
Washington, B. T., Williston School, 401 South 10th St., Wilmington, N.C.
Washington, Mrs. Justine W., 1228 Kent St., Augusta, Ga.
Washington, Walter, Utica Junior College, Utica, Miss.
Washton, Nathan S., Queens College, Flushing, N.Y.
Wasserman, Mrs. Lillian, 1684 Meadow Lane, East Meadow, N.Y.
Wasserstrom, Arthur H., 26 S. Hampton, Apt. D, Columbus, Ohio
Wasson, Margaret, 3705 University Blvd., Dallas, Tex.
Waterman, David C., Indiana State University, Terre Haute, Ind.
Waterman, Floyd T., University of Omaha, Omaha, Neb.
Waters, E. Worthington, Delaware State College, Dover, Del.
Waters, Mrs. Emma B., 228 E. Valley Ave., Holly Springs, Miss.
Watkins, Ralph K., 702 Ingleside Dr., Columbia, Mo.
Watkins, Ray H., Dallas Baptist College, Dallas, Tex.
Watkins, Thomas W., Supt., Wissahickon Sch. Dist., Ambler, Pa.
Watkins, W. O., Eastern New Mexico University, Portales, N.M.
Watson, Carlos M., Indiana State College, Terre Haute, Ind.
Watson, D. Gene, 5835 Kimbark Ave., Chicago, Ill.
Watson, David Roland, 6315 Mound Dr., Middleton, Wis.
Watson, Mrs. Marie, 22 Burlington St., Bordentown, N.J.
Watson, Norman E., Orange Coast College, Costa Mesa, Calif.
Watson, Paul E., Univ. of Pittsburgh, Pittsburgh, Pa.
Watson, William Crawford, 29 Woodstock Rd., Mt. Waverly, Victoria, Australia
Watt, Ralph W., 1206 Parker Ave., Hyattsville, Md.
Wattenberg, William W., 20220 Murray Hill, Detroit, Mich.
Watters, Velma V., 1365 Mozley Pl., S.W., Atlanta, Ga.
Watts, Mrs. Helen S., University of Dubuque, Dubuque, Iowa
Watts, Morrison L., Dept. of Educ., Province of Alberta, Edmonton, Alberta
Wawrzyniak, Alex S., 2329 Desmond Dr., Decatur, Ga.
Waxwood, Howard B., Jr., Witherspoon School, Princeton, N.J.
Way, Gail W., 1232 Henderson St., Chicago, Ill.
Wayson, William W., 832 Westmoreland Ave., Syracuse, N.Y.
Weakley, Mrs. Mary L., 1426 Center St., Geneva, Ill.
Weaver, Annie Belle, West Georgia College, Carrollton, Ga.
Weaver, Gladys C., 4708 Tecumseh St., College Park, Md.
Webb, E. Sue, 216 West 5th St., Shawano, Wis.
Webb, Holmes, Dept. of Educ., Texas Tech. College, Lubbock, Tex.
Webber, Warren L., Music Dept., Cedarville College, Cedarville, Ohio
Weber, Clarence A., N. Eagleville Rd., Storrs, Conn.
Weber, Martha Gesling, Bowling Green State University, Bowling Green, Ohio
Webster, Jerome O., Superintendent of Schools, Windom, Minn.
Weddington, Rachel T., Queens College, 65-30 Kissena Blvd., Flushing, N.Y.
Weeks, Shirley S., North Dakota State University, Fargo, N.D.
Weele, Jan C. Ter, Hanover Supv. Union # 22, Hanover, N.H.
Wees, W. R., 1500 Birchmount Rd., Scarborough, Ont., Canada
Weesner, Gary L., 619 Hendricks Court, Marion, Ind.
Wegrzyn, Helen A., 5240 W. Newport Ave., Chicago, Ill.
Wehner, Freda, Wisconsin State College, Oshkosh, Wis.
Wehrer, Charles S., Jr., Sioux Empire Col., Hawarden, Iowa
Weicker, Jack E., South Side High School, Ft. Wayne, Ind.
Weigert, Barbara, Mercyhurst College, Erie, Pa.
Weilbaker, Charles R., Tchrs. Col., University of Cincinnati, Cincinnati, Ohio
Weiner, Samuel G., Douglass College, New Brunswick, N.J.
Weinheimer, Norman P., Superintendent of Schools, Highland Park, Mich.

Weinhold, John D., 439 N. Taylor Ave., Oak Park, Ill.
Weinrich, Ernest F., Deer Park Rd., Dix Hills, Huntington, N.Y.
Weintraub, Sam, Dept. of Educ., University of Chicago, Chicago, Ill.
Weis, Harold P., 437—23rd Ave., Moline, Ill.
Weisbender, Leo F., 12792 Topaz St., Garden Grove, Calif.
Weisberg, Patricia H., 9411 S. Pleasant Ave., Chicago, Ill.
Weisiger, Louise P., 2722 Hillcrest Rd., Richmond, Va.
Weiss, George D., Kutztown State College, Kutztown, Pa.
Weiss, Joel, 4833½ S. Woodlawn Ave., Chicago, Ill.
Weiss, M. Jerry, Jersey City State College, Jersey City, N.J.
Weissleder, Claudette P., 135 Belmont Ave., Jersey City, N.J.
Welcenbach, Frank J., Trombly School, Grosse Pointe, Mich.
Welch, Rev. Cornelius A., Siena Col., Loudonville, N.Y.
Welch, Ronald C., Sch. of Educ., Indiana University, Bloomington, Ind.
Welker, Latney C., Jr., Univ. of So. Mississippi, Hattiesburg, Miss.
Welling, Helen F., 64 E. Arndt St., Fond du Lac, Wis.
Welliver, Paul W., 715 Lenox Dr., Jackson, Miss.
Wells, Carl S., Box 485, Col. Sta., Hammond, La.
Wells, Robert S., Superintendent of Schools, Reading, Mass.
Welsh, Walter C., 239 Pennsylvania Ave., Yonkers, N.Y.
Weltner, William H., 500 Riley Rd., Muncie, Ind.
Welton, William B., Prospect Public Schools, Prospect, Conn.
Wendt, Paul R., Southern Illinois University, Carbondale, Ill.
Wenger, Roy E., Kent State University, Kent, Ohio
Wenner, Harry W., 40 Mills St., Morristown, N.J.
Wenrich, Ralph C., Sch. of Educ., University of Michigan, Ann Arbor, Mich.
Werley, Harriet H., University of Utah, Salt Lake City, Utah
Wernick, Leo J., 3500 W. Douglas Blvd., Chicago, Ill.
Werstler, Richard E., Adrian College, Adrian, Mich.
Werth, Trostel G., 18549 S.E. Tibbetts Ct., Gresham, Ore.
Wesley, Emory J., Henderson State Tchrs. Col., Arkadelphia, Ark.
Wesner, Max E., Batavia High School, Batavia, Ill.
West, Mrs. B. Bradley, 4563 Nakoma Dr., Okemos, Mich.
West, Charles K., 1005 S. Mattis Ave., Champaign, Ill.
West, Edna, 648 Sunset Blvd., Baton Rouge, La.
West, Helene, Beverly Hills H.S., 310 S. Altmont Dr., Los Angeles, Calif.
West, Lorraine W., 3910 Bryn Mawr, Bakersfield, Calif.
West, William H., Supt., County Union Schls., Elizabeth, N.J.
Westbrook, Charles Hart, 17 Towana Rd., Richmond, Va.
Westbrooks, Sadye Wylena, 1433 Sharon St., N.W., Atlanta, Ga.
Westby-Gibson, Dorothy, San Francisco State College, San Francisco, Calif.
Westlund, Hildur L., 920 North 22nd St., Superior, Wis.
Westlund, Ruth E., Northern Illinois University, DeKalb, Ill.
Wetmore, Joseph N., Dept. of Educ., Ohio Wesleyan Univ., Delaware, Ohio
Wetzel, Rev. Chester M., 55 Elizabeth St., Hartford, Conn.
Wewer, William P., 638 Buttonwood St., Anaheim, Calif.
Weyer, F. E., Dept. of Educ., Campbell College, Buies Creek, N.C.
Whalen, Thomas J., 232 Pearl St., Stoughton, Mass.
Whaley, Charles, Kentucky Educ. Assn., 101 W. Walnut St., Louisville, Ky.
Whang, H. Henry, 2936 W. Highland Blvd., Milwaukee, Wis.
Wharton, William P., Allegheny College, Meadville, Pa.
Whayland, Charles W., Glen Burnie High School, Glen Burnie, Md.
Wheat, Leonard B., Southern Illinois University, Edwardsville, Ill.
Wheeler, Elizabeth, University of Wisconsin-Milwaukee, Milwaukee, Wis.
Wheeler, Helen, Indiana State University, Terre Haute, Ind.
Wheelock, Warren H., Reading Clinic, Univ. of Missouri, Kansas City, Mo.
Whelan, William J., Andersen EVGC, 1359 Harding Ave., Des Plaines, Ill.
Whetton, Mrs. Betty B., 1810 N. Mitchell St., Phoenix, Ariz.
Whilt, Selma E., 37-A E. 14th St., Huntington, N.Y.
Whitaker, Prevo L., Indiana University, Bloomington, Ind.
White, Andrew W., Col. of Santa Fe, Cerrillos Rd., Santa Fe, N.M.

White, George L., Harcourt, Brace & World, Inc., New York, N.Y.
White, John C., Edison School, Mesa, Ariz.
White, Joseph Benton, Col. of Educ., Univ. of Florida, Gainesville, Fla.
White, Kenneth B., Paterson State College, Wayne, N.J.
White, Kenneth E., Dept. of Educ., Hamline Univ., St. Paul, Minn.
White, Verna, California Test Bureau, Los Angeles, Calif.
Whiteford, Emma B., 740 River Dr., St. Paul, Minn.
Whitehead, Willis A., 23351 Chagrin Blvd., Beachwood, Ohio
Whitmer, Dana P., Superintendent of Schools, Pontiac, Mich.
Whitney, Charles S., County Superintendent of Schools, Garner, Iowa
Whitt, Robert L., Drake Univ., Des Moines, Iowa
Whittier, C. Taylor, APA Bldg., 1200—17th St., N.W., Washington, D.C.
Whybrew, William E., Northern Illinois University, DeKalb, Ill.
Wicke, Robert, William Jewell College, Liberty, Mo.
Wickes, Mrs. Una Southard, 141 N. Bonnie, Pasadena, Calif.
Wiebe, Elias H., Pacific College, Fresno, Calif.
Wiebe, Joel A., 315 S. Wilson Ave., Hillsboro, Kan.
*Wieden, Clifford O., 181 Main St., Presque Isle, Me.
Wiegand, Regis B., 182 Shenandoah Dr., Pittsburgh, Pa.
Wiggin, Gladys A., Col. of Educ., Univ. of Maryland, College Park, Md.
Wiggin, Richard G., 4151 North 25th St., Arlington, Va.
Wiggins, Thomas W., 706 N. Indian Hill, Claremont, Calif.
Wilburn, D. Banks, Glenville State College, Glenville, W.Va.
Wilcox, John, State University College, Oneonta, N.Y.
Wilde, Sim O., Jr., Wesleyan College, Rocky Mountain, N.C.
Wildebush, Sarah W., Dept. of Educ., Christiansted, St. Croix, V.I.
Wildey, Carl A., R.R. 5, North Vernon, Ind.
Wiley, Mrs. R. C., 2156 Sierra Way, San Luis Obispo, Calif.
Wiley, Walter E., 620 E. Tenth Pl., Gary, Ind.
Wilhelm, Chester E., Hawthorne High School, Hawthorne, N.J.
Wilkerson, Doxey A., Yeshiva Univ., New York, N.Y.
Wilkinson, H. A., Station ACC, Box 565, Abilene, Tex.
Willard, Robert L., Utica College, Utica, N.Y.
Willey, Lawrence V., Jr., 259 E. Erie St., Chicago, Ill.
Williams, Alfred H., 9712 Nova St., Pico Rivera, Calif.
Williams, Arloff L., St. John's Military Academy, Delafield, Wis.
Williams, Arthur E., Dillard Comprehensive High School, Fort Lauderdale, Fla.
Williams, Mrs. B. E., Spelman College, Atlanta, Ga.
Williams, Buford W., Southwest Texas State College, San Marcos, Tex.
Williams, Byron B., University of Rochester, Rochester, N.Y.
Williams, Catharine M., Ohio State University, Columbus, Ohio
Williams, Charles C., North Texas State College, Denton, Tex.
Williams, Chester Spring, Indiana State University, Terre Haute, Ind.
Williams, Clarence M., Col. of Educ., Univ. of Rochester, Rochester, N.Y.
Williams, Donald Foster, Berkeley Baptist Divinity Sch., Berkeley, Calif.
*Williams, Fannie C., 3108 Tours St., New Orleans, La.
Williams, Fountie N., 505 Pennsylvania Ave., Clarksburg, W.Va.
Williams, Frances I., Lab. Sch., Indiana State Univ., Terre Haute, Ind.
Williams, Gloria M., Univ. of Minnesota, St. Paul, Minn.
Williams, Harold A., Flat Top, W.Va.
Williams, Herman, 40 Elmwood St., Tiffin, Ohio
Williams, Howard Y., Jr., 3464 Siems Ct., St. Paul, Minn.
Williams, Jacob T., Carver High School, Gadsden, Ala.
Williams, Mrs. Lois, 200 North 18th St., Montebello, Calif.
Williams, Malcolm, Sch. of Educ., Tennessee A. & I. University, Nashville, Tenn.
Williams, Nat, Superintendent of Schools, Lubbock, Tex.
Williams, Paul E., Danbury State College, Danbury, Conn.
Williams, Richard H., 380 Moseley Rd., Hillsborough, Calif.
Williams, Robert Alan, San Jose State Col., San Jose, Calif.
Williams, W. Morris, USAID, Philippines, APO 96528, San Francisco, Calif.
Williams, Wilbur A., Eastern Michigan University, Ypsilanti, Mich.

Williams, William K., 2342 S. Glen Ave., Decatur, Ill.
Williamson, James L., Arlington Public Schools, Arlington, Tex.
Williamson, Jane, Pacific Lutheran University, Tacoma, Wash.
Wills, Benjamin G., 1550 Bellamy St., Santa Clara, Calif.
Wilson, Alan B., Sch. of Educ., Univ. of California, Berkeley, Calif.
Wilson, Alan S., Hillyer Col., University of Hartford, Hartford, Conn.
Wilson, Alan T., Faircrest Sch., St. Francis, Wis.
Wilson, David A., 2428 West 183rd St., Homewood, Ill.
Wilson, David H., Seneca St., Interlaken, N.Y.
Wilson, Dustin W., Jr., 945 Forrest St., Dover, Del.
Wilson, Frederick R., 336 S. Division, Ann Arbor, Mich.
Wilson, Harold M., 3006 N. Trinidad St., Arlington, Va.
Wilson, Herbert B., University of Arizona, Tucson, Ariz.
Wilson, James W., Rochester Institute of Technology, Rochester, N.Y.
Wilson, Jean Alice, 715 Tidball Ave., Grove City, Pa.
Wilson, John A. R., 2519 Chapala St., Santa Barbara, Calif.
Wilson, John Leod, Florida Mem. Col., St. Augustine, Fla.
Wilson, Merle A., 2800—62nd St., Des Moines, Iowa
Wilson, Robert D., Univ. of California, Los Angeles, Calif.
Wilson, Roy K., N.E.A., 1201—16th St., N.W., Washington, D.C.
Wilson, S. Roy, Stanislaus State College, Turlock, Calif.
Wilson, Yolande M., Sch. of Educ., Univ. of Chicago, Chicago, Ill.
Wilstach, Mrs. Ilah M., 2127 N. Eastern Ave., Los Angeles, Calif.
Wiltse, Earl W., Northern Illinois Univ., DeKalb, Ill.
Winchell, L. R., Jr., Granville Ave. School, Margate City, N.J.
Windoes, Frederic C., Indiana State University, Terre Haute, Ind.
Windsor, John G., 4354 West 9th Ave., Vancouver, B.C., Canada
Winfield, Kenneth, East Stroudsburg State Col., Stroudsburg, Pa.
Wing, Richard L., 845 Fox Meadow Rd., Yorktown Heights, N.Y.
Wing, Sherman W., Superintendent of Schools, Provo, Utah
Wingerd, Harold H., Superintendent of Schools, West Chester, Pa.
Winkley, Carol K., 125 Forsythe Ln., DeKalb, Ill.
Winsor, George E., Wilmington College, Wilmington, Ohio
Winston, Bertha H., 5942 South Parkway, Chicago, Ill.
Winter, Nathan B., 2015 Hawthorne Ave., Rockford, Ill.
Wise, Harold L., 7 Delisio Lane, Woodstock, N.Y.
Wishart, James S., 1638 Ridge Rd., West, Rochester, N.Y.
Wisniewski, Richard, Wayne State University, Detroit, Mich.
Wisniewski, Virginia, 4623 Ostrom, Lakewood, Calif.
Witchel, Barbara, 110 Ridge Ave., Passaic, N.J.
Witherspoon, W. H., P.O. Box 527, Rockhill, S.C.
Witt, Marquis G., 195-A Wing Rd., APO New York 09845
Witt, Paul W. F., Tchrs. Col., Columbia University, New York, N.Y.
Witte, Cyril M., R. 2, Box 264, Mt. Airy, Md.
Witten, Charles H., University of South Carolina, Columbia, S.C.
Witter, Sanford C., Superintendent of Schools, Dist. 202, Kansas City, Kan.
Wittick, Mildred Letton, 300 Pompton Rd., Wayne, N.J.
Wittmer, Arthur E., 315 Park Ave. S., Rm. 1920, New York, N.Y.
Witty, Paul A., Sch. of Educ., Northwestern University, Evanston, Ill.
Wixon, John L., 29080 Oxford Ave., The Knolls, Richmond, Calif.
Wixted, William G., Marymount College, Boca Raton, Fla.
Wochner, Raymond E., Arizona State University, Tempe, Ariz.
Woerdehoff, Frank J., Dept. of Educ., Purdue University, Lafayette, Ind.
Woestehoff, Orville W., Oak Park Elementary Schls., 122 Forest Ave., Oak Park, Ill.
Wohlers, A. E., Ohio State University, Columbus, Ohio
Wolbrecht, Walter F., 316 Parkwood, Kirkwood, Mo.
Wold, Stanley G., 703 Jersey Ave., Bloomington, Ill.
Wolf, Dan B., Indiana Univ., Indianapolis, Ind.
Wolf, Lloyd L., Mt. Pulaski, Ill.
Wolf, Mrs. Vivian C., 1400 E. 55th Pl., Rm. 413-S, Chicago, Ill.

Wolf, Ray O., Div. of Educ., Portland State College, Portland, Ore.
Wolf, William C., Jr., University of Massachusetts, Amherst, Mass.
Wolfe, Deborah P., Queens College, Flushing, N.Y.
Wolfe, Josephine B., Beaver Hill Apts., Jenkintown, Pa.
Wolfe, William G., Sutton Hall, University of Texas, Austin, Tex.
Wolfson, Bernice J., Schl. of Educ., Univ. of Chicago, Chicago, Ill.
Wolinsky, Gloria F., 69-52 Groton St., Forest Hills, N.Y.
Wong, William T. S., 1640 Paula Dr., Honolulu, Hawaii
Wood, Dan, Center for Urban Educ., 33 W. 42nd St., New York, N.Y.
Wood, Donald I., Dept. of Educ., Rice University, Houston, Tex.
Wood, Harrell E., Washington Co. H.S., Springfield, Ky.
Wood, Joseph E., 18 Duryea Rd., Upper Montclair, N.J.
Wood, Marion C., Hanson RFD, 725 Crescent St., East Bridgewater, Mass.
Wood, Mary Margaret Andrews, University of Georgia, Athens, Ga.
Wood, Roi S., Superintendent of Schools, Joplin, Mo.
Wood, W. Clement, Fort Hays Kansas State College, Hays, Kan.
Wood, Mrs. Wilma W., 608 Quincy St., N.W., Washington, D.C.
Woodard, Prince B., 10407 Walbrook Dr., Richmond, Va.
Woodburn, A. C., Alamogordo Public Schools, Alamogordo, N.M.
Woodburn, John H., Charles E. Woodward H.S., Rockville, Md.
Woodbury, Tom, Livonia Pub. Schools, Livonia, Mich.
Wooden, Maurice L., West Covina High School, West Covina, Calif.
Woodring, Wiley F., Southwest Missouri State College, Springfield, Mo.
Woods, Robert K., 125 N. Hickory St., Platteville, Wis.
Woodson, C. C., 435 S. Liberty St., Spartanburg, S.C.
Woodworth, Denny, Col. of Educ., Drake University, Des Moines, Iowa
Woodworth, William O., 999 Kedzie Ave., Flossmoor, Ill.
Woofter, James Andrew, 530 N. Simon St., Ada, Ohio
Woolson, Edith L., Box 203, Imperial, Calif.
Wooton, John W., Glen Rock Public Schools, Glen Rock, N.J.
Workman, Stanley, 149-07 Sanford Ave., Flushing, N.Y.
Wozencraft, Marian, State Univ. Col., Geneseo, N.Y.
Wray, Mabel Elizabeth, 224 Mower St., Worcester, Mass.
Wrenn, Michael P., 6544 Greenview Ave., Chicago, Ill.
Wright, Floyd K., 1432 Price Dr., Cape Girardeau, Mo.
Wright, John R., San Jose State College, San Jose, Calif.
Wright, Samuel Lee, 1907 Third St., N.W., Washington, D.C.
Wright, William H., Jr., 13542 E. Starbuck St., Whittier, Calif.
Wrightstone, J. Wayne, 21 Hickory Rd., Summit, N.J.
Wronski, Stanley P., Col. of Educ., Michigan State Univ., East Lansing, Mich.
Wu, Julia Tu, Hunter Col., New York, N.Y.
Wuerthner, Robert H., 353 Warren Rd., Ithaca, N.Y.
Wuolle, Mrs. Ethel, P.O. Box 173, Pine City, Minn.
Wyckoff, D. Campbell, Princeton Theological Seminary, Princeton, N.J.
Wyeth, E. R., 18111 Nordhoff St., Northridge, Calif.
Wyllie, Eugene D., Sch. of Bus., Indiana University, Bloomington, Ind.
Wynn, Dale R., Cathedral of Lrng., Univ. of Pittsburgh, Pittsburgh, Pa.
Wynn, Willa T., 1122 N. St. Clair St., Pittsburgh, Pa.

Yamamoto, Kaoru, State University of Iowa, Iowa City, Iowa
Yamashiro, Margaret H., 1720 Ala Moana Blvd., Honolulu, Hawaii
Yanis, Martin, 3524 September Dr., Camp Hill, Pa.
Yaple, Graydon W., 664 Timber Lane, Wilmington, Ohio
Yates, J. W., 223 Wham, Southern Illinois University, Carbondale, Ill.
Yauch, Wilbur A., Northern Illinois University, DeKalb, Ill.
Yeager, Paul M., Sheridan School, Second and Liberty Sts., Allentown, Pa.
Yee, Albert H., Univ. of Wisconsin, Madison, Wis.
Yelon, Stephen, Col. of Educ., Michigan State Univ., East Lansing, Mich.
Yelvington, James A., University of California, Los Angeles, Calif.
Yengo, Carmine A., Trenton State College, Trenton, N.J.
Yff, Joost, Sch. of Educ., Morehead St. Univ., Morehead, Ky.

Ylisto, Ingrid P., Eastern Michigan University, Ypsilanti, Mich.
Yochim, Louise Dunn, 9545 Drake, Evanston, Ill.
Young, Doris Kuhn, Col. of Educ., Univ. of Hawaii, Honolulu, Hawaii
Young, Harold L., Central Missouri State College, Warrensburg, Mo.
Young, Horace A., Jr., Texas Southern University, Houston, Tex.
Young, J. E. M., Macdonald College Post Office, Quebec
Young, Jean A., Sonoma State College, Rohnert Park, Calif.
Young, John A., 315 Ave. "C," New York, N.Y.
Young, John J., 63951 Miami Rd., South Bend, Ind.
Young, Paul A., Judson College, Elgin, Ill.
Young, Robert W., 1 Dellwood Dr., RD 2, Long Valley, N.J.
* Young, William E., State Education Department, Albany, N.Y.
Young, William Howard, 1460 Tampa Ave., Dayton, Ohio
Youngblood, Chester E., P.O. Box 413, College, Alaska
Younie, William J., Tchrs. Col., Columbia University, New York, N.Y.
Yourd, John L., Bemidji State Col., Bemidji, Minn.
Yuhas, Theodore Frank, Educ. Dept., Ball State University, Muncie, Ind.
Yunghans, Ernest E., Wartburg College, Waverly, Iowa

Zahm, Bernice S., 2610 Overland Ave., Los Angeles, Calif.
Zahn, D. Willard, 7118 McCallum St., Philadelphia, Pa.
Zahorsky, Mrs. Metta, San Francisco State College, San Francisco, Calif.
Zakrzewski, Aurelia R., 4806 Chovin St., Dearborn, Mich.
Zambito, Stephen Charles, Eastern Michigan University, Ypsilanti, Mich.
Zari, Rosalie V., Sch. of Educ., Univ. of California, Berkeley, Calif.
Zavarella, Victor, 806 N. Willis Ave., Champaign, Ill.
Zbornik, Joseph J., 3219 Clarence Ave., Berwyn, Ill.
Zdanowicz, Paul John, Supt. of Schools, Lee, Mass.
Zebrowski, Kenneth M., Bell School, New Glenview Rd., Wilmette, Ill.
Zeiler, Edward J., 5340 N. Santa Monica Blvd., Milwaukee, Wis.
Zeldin, David, Oriel Cottage, St. Mary's Rd., Mortimer, Berkshire, England
Zeller, William D., Dept. of Educ., Illinois State Univ., Normal, Ill.
Zelmer, A. C. Lynn, Rideau Park Jr. H.S., Calgary, Alba., Canada
Zepper, John T., Educ. Bldg., University of New Mexico, Albuquerque, N.M.
Ziebold, Edna B., 6401 Linda Vista Rd., San Diego, Calif.
Zieman, Orlyn A., Appleton Public Schools, Appleton, Wis.
Ziemba, Walter J., St. Mary's College, Orchard Lake, Mich.
Zierman, Raymond T., 606 Virginia St., Joliet, Ill.
Zim, Herbert Spencer, Box 34, Tavernier, Fla.
Zimmerman, Gary E., State University College, Buffalo, N.Y.
Zimmerman, Herbert M., Roosevelt High School, Chicago, Ill.
Zimmerman, William G., Jr., Hanover Public Schools, Hanover, N.H.
Zimnoch, W. Tresper Clarke H.S., Edgewood Dr., Westbury, L.I., N.Y.
Zinn, Charles F., 1414 Culhane St., Chester, Pa.
Zintz, Miles V., 3028 Marble Ave., N.E., Albuquerque, N.M.
Ziobrowski, Stasia M., Dept. of Educ., Queens College, Flushing, N.Y.
Zipper, Joseph H., 1569 West 41st St., Erie, Pa.
Zumsteg, Frederick C., 109 Michigan Dr., Terrace Park, Ohio
Zunigha, Bennie Jean, Box 354, Ft. Wingate, N.M.
Zweig, Richard L., 12859 Palm St., Garden Grove, Calif.

INFORMATION CONCERNING THE NATIONAL SOCIETY FOR THE STUDY OF EDUCATION

1. PURPOSE. The purpose of the National Society is to promote the investigation and discussion of educational questions. To this end it holds an annual meeting and publishes a series of yearbooks.

2. ELIGIBILITY TO MEMBERSHIP. Any person who is interested in receiving its publications may become a member by sending to the Secretary-Treasurer information concerning name, title, and address, and a check for $8.00 (see Item 5), except that graduate students, on the recommendation of a faculty member, may become members by paying $6.00 for the first year of their membership. Dues for all subsequent years are the same as for other members (see Item 4).

Membership is not transferable; it is limited to individuals, and may not be held by libraries, schools, or other institutions, either directly or indirectly.

3. PERIOD OF MEMBERSHIP. Applicants for membership may not date their entrance back of the current calendar year, and all memberships terminate automatically on December 31, unless the dues for the ensuing year are paid as indicated in Item 6.

4. DUTIES AND PRIVILEGES OF MEMBERS. Members pay dues of $7.00 annually, receive a cloth-bound copy of each publication, are entitled to vote, to participate in discussion, and (under certain conditions) to hold office. The names of members are printed in the yearbooks.

Persons who are sixty years of age or above may become life members on payment of fee based on average life-expectancy of their age group. For information, apply to Secretary-Treasurer.

5. ENTRANCE FEE. New members are required the first year to pay, in addition to the dues, an entrance fee of one dollar.

6. PAYMENT OF DUES. Statements of dues are rendered in October for the following calendar year. Any member so notified whose dues remain unpaid on January 1, thereby loses his membership and can be reinstated only by paying a reinstatement fee of fifty cents.

School warrants and vouchers from institutions must be accompanied by definite information concerning the name and address of the person for whom membership fee is being paid. Statements of dues are rendered on our own form only. The Secretary's office cannot undertake to fill out special invoice forms of any sort or to affix notary's affidavit to statements or receipts.

Cancelled checks serve as receipts. Members desiring an additional receipt must enclose a stamped and addressed envelope therefor.

7. DISTRIBUTION OF YEARBOOKS TO MEMBERS. The yearbooks, ready prior to each February meeting, will be mailed from the office of the distributors, only to members whose dues for that year have been paid. Members who desire yearbooks prior to the current year must purchase them directly from the distributors (see Item 8).

8. COMMERCIAL SALES. The distribution of all yearbooks prior to the current year, and also of those of the current year not regularly mailed to members in exchange for their dues, is in the hands of the distributor, not of the Secretary. For such commercial sales, communicate directly with the University of Chicago Press, Chicago, Illinois 60637, which will gladly send a price list covering all the publications of this Society. This list is also printed in the yearbook.

9. YEARBOOKS. The yearbooks are issued about one month before the February meeting. They comprise from 600 to 800 pages annually. Unusual effort has been made to make them, on the one hand, of immediate practical value, and, on the other hand, representative of sound scholarship and scientific investigation.

10. MEETINGS. The annual meeting, at which the yearbooks are discussed, is held in February at the same time and place as the meeting of the American Association of School Administrators.

Applications for membership will be handled promptly at any time on receipt of name and address, together with check for $8.00 (or $7.50 for reinstatement). Applications entitle the new members to the yearbook slated for discussion during the calendar year the application is made.

5835 Kimbark Ave.   HERMAN G. RICHEY, *Secretary-Treasurer*
Chicago, Illinois 60637

PUBLICATIONS OF THE NATIONAL SOCIETY FOR THE STUDY OF EDUCATION

NOTICE: Many of the early Yearbooks of this series are now out of print. In the following list, those titles to which an asterisk is prefixed are not available for purchase.

POSTPAID PRICE

*First Yearbook, 1902, Part I—*Some Principles in the Teaching of History*. Lucy M. Salmon ....

*First Yearbook, 1902, Part II—*The Progress of Geography in the Schools*. W. M. Davis and H. M. Wilson ....

*Second Yearbook, 1903, Part I—*The Course of Study in History in the Common School*. Isabel Lawrence, C. A. McMurry, Frank McMurry, E. C. Page, and E. J. Rice ....

*Second Yearbook, 1903, Part II—*The Relation of Theory to Practice in Education*. M. J. Holmes, J. A. Keith, and Levi Seeley ....

*Third Yearbook, 1904, Part I—*The Relation of Theory to Practice in the Education of Teachers*. John Dewey, Sarah C. Brooks, F. M. McMurry, et al. ....

*Third Yearbook, 1904, Part II—*Nature Study*. W. S. Jackman .....

*Fourth Yearbook, 1905, Part I—*The Education and Training of Secondary Teachers*. E. C. Elliott, E. G. Dexter, M. J. Holmes, et al. ....

*Fourth Yearbook, 1905, Part II—*The Place of Vocational Subjects in the High-School Curriculum*. J. S. Brown, G. B. Morrison, and Ellen Richards ....

*Fifth Yearbook, 1906, Part I—*On the Teaching of English in Elementary and High Schools*. G. P. Brown and Emerson Davis ....

*Fifth Yearbook, 1906, Part II—*The Certification of Teachers*. E. P. Cubberley ......

*Sixth Yearbook, 1907, Part I—*Vocational Studies for College Entrance*. C. A. Herrick, H. W. Holmes, T. deLaguna, V. Prettyman, and W. J. S. Bryan ....

*Sixth Yearbook, 1907, Part II—*The Kindergarten and Its Relation to Elementary Education*. Ada Van Stone Harris, E. A. Kirkpatrick, Marie Kraus-Boelté, Patty S. Hill, Harriette M. Mills, and Nina Vandewalker ....

*Seventh Yearbook, 1908, Part I—*The Relation of Superintendents and Principals to the Training and Professional Improvement of Their Teachers*. Charles D. Lowry

*Seventh Yearbook, 1908, Part II—*The Co-ordination of the Kindergarten and the Elementary School*. B. J. Gregory, Jennie B. Merrill, Bertha Payne, and Margaret Giddings ....

*Eighth Yearbook, 1909, Part I—*Education with Reference to Sex: Pathological, Economic, and Social Aspects*. C. R. Henderson ....

*Eighth Yearbook, 1909, Part II—*Education with Reference to Sex: Agencies and Methods*. C. R. Henderson and Helen C. Putnam ....

*Ninth Yearbook, 1910, Part I—*Health and Education*. T. D. Wood ....

*Ninth Yearbook, 1910, Part II—*The Nurse in Education*. T. D. Wood, et al. .....

*Tenth Yearbook, 1911, Part I—*The City School as a Community Center*. H. C. Leipziger, Sarah E. Hyre, R. D. Warden, C. Ward Crampton, E. W. Stitt, E. J. Ward, Mrs. E. C. Grice, and C. A. Perry ....

*Tenth Yearbook, 1911, Part II—*The Rural School as a Community Center*. B. H. Crocheron, Jessie Field, F. W. Howe, E. C. Bishop, A. B. Graham, O. J. Kern, M. T. Scudder, and B. M. Davis ....

*Eleventh Yearbook, 1912, Part I—*Industrial Education: Typical Experiments Described and Interpreted*. J. F. Barker, M. Bloomfield, B. W. Johnson, P. Johnson, L. M. Leavitt, G. A. Mirick, M. W. Murray, C. F. Perry, A. L. Safford, and H. B. Wilson ....

*Eleventh Yearbook, 1912, Part II—*Agricultural Education in Secondary Schools*. A. C. Monahan, R. W. Stimson, D. J. Crosby, W. H. French, H. F. Button, F. R. Crane, W. R. Hart, and G. F. Warren ....

*Twelfth Yearbook, 1913, Part I—*The Supervision of City Schools*. Franklin Bobbitt, J. W. Hall, and J. D. Wolcott ....

*Twelfth Yearbook, 1913, Part II—*The Supervision of Rural Schools*. A. C. Monahan, L. J. Hanifan, J. E. Warren, Wallace Lund, U. J. Hoffman, A. S. Cook, E. M. Rapp, Jackson Davis, and J. D. Wolcott ....

*Thirteenth Yearbook, 1914, Part I—*Some Aspects of High-School Instruction and Administration*. H. C. Morrison, E. R. Breslich, W. A. Jessup, and L. D. Coffman ..

*Thirteenth Yearbook, 1914, Part II—*Plans for Organizing School Surveys, with a Summary of Typical School Surveys*. Charles H. Judd and Henry L. Smith .....

*Fourteenth Yearbook, 1915, Part I—*Minimum Essentials in Elementary School Subjects—Standards and Current Practices*. H. B. Wilson, H. W. Holmes, F. E. Thompson, R. G. Jones, S. A. Courtis, W. S. Gray, F. N. Freeman, H. C. Pryor, J. F. Hosic, W. A. Jessup, and W. C. Bagley ....

*Fourteenth Yearbook, 1915, Part II—*Methods for Measuring Teachers' Efficiency*. Arthur C. Boyce ....

*Fifteenth Yearbook, 1916, Part I—*Standards and Tests for the Measurement of the Efficiency of Schools and School Systems*. G. D. Strayer, Bird T. Baldwin, B. R. Buckingham, F. W. Ballou, D. C. Bliss, H. G. Childs, S. A. Courtis, E. P. Cubberley, C. H. Judd, George Melcher, E. E. Oberholtzer, J. B. Sears, Daniel Starch, M. R. Trabue, and G. M. Whipple ....

cix

PUBLICATIONS

POSTPAID
PRICE

*Fifteenth Yearbook, 1916, Part II—*The Relationship between Persistence in School and Home Conditions.* Charles E. Holley..............................
*Fifteenth Yearbook, 1916, Part III—*The Junior High School.* Aubrey A. Douglass..
*Sixteenth Yearbook, 1917, Part I—*Second Report of the Committee on Minimum Essentials in Elementary-School Subjects.* W. C. Bagley, W. W. Charters, F. N. Freeman, W. S. Gray, Ernest Horn, J. H. Hoskinson, W. S. Monroe, C. F. Munson, H. C. Pryor, L. W. Rapeer, G. M. Wilson, and H. B. Wilson.............
*Sixteenth Yearbook, 1917, Part II—*The Efficiency of College Students as Conditioned by Age at Entrance and Size of High School.* B. F. Pittenger................
*Seventeenth Yearbook, 1918, Part I—*Third Report of the Committee on Economy of Time in Education.* W. C. Bagley, B. B. Bassett, M. E. Branom, Alice Camerer, J. E. Dealey, C. A. Ellwood, E. B. Greene, A. B. Hart, J. F. Hosic, E. T. Housh, W. H. Mace, L. R. Marston, H. C. McKown, H. E. Mitchell, W. C. Reavis, D. Snedden, and H. B. Wilson...
*Seventeenth Yearbook, 1918, Part II—*The Measurement of Educational Products.* E. J. Ashbaugh, W. A. Averill, L. P. Ayers, F. W. Ballou, Edna Bryner, B. R. Buckingham, S. A. Courtis, M. E. Haggerty, C. H. Judd, George Melcher, W. S. Monroe, E. A. Nifenecker, and E. L. Thorndike............................
*Eighteenth Yearbook, 1919, Part I—*The Professional Preparation of High-School Teachers.* G. N. Cade, S. S. Colvin, Charles Fordyce, H. H. Foster, T. S. Gosling, W. S. Gray, L. V. Koos, A. R. Mead, H. L. Miller, W. C. Whitcomb, and Clifford Woody..
*Eighteenth Yearbook, 1919, Part II—*Fourth Report of Committee on Economy of Time in Education.* F. C. Ayer, F. N. Freeman, W. S. Gray, Ernest Horn, W. S. Monroe, and C. E. Seashore...
*Nineteenth Yearbook, 1920, Part I—*New Materials of Instruction.* Prepared by the Society's Committee on Materials of Instruction............................
*Nineteenth Yearbook, 1920, Part II—*Classroom Problems in the Education of Gifted Children.* T. S. Henry...
*Twentieth Yearbook, 1921, Part I—*New Materials of Instruction.* Second Report by Society's Committee...
*Twentieth Yearbook, 1921, Part II—*Report of the Society's Committee on Silent Reading.* M. A. Burgess, S. A. Courtis, C. E. Germane, W. S. Gray, H. A. Greene, Regina R. Heller, J. H. Hoover, J. A. O'Brien, J. L. Packer, Daniel Starch, W. W. Theisen, G. A. Yoakam, and representatives of other school systems..........
*Twenty-first Yearbook, 1922, Parts I and II—*Intelligence Tests and Their Use,* Part I—*The Nature, History, and General Principles of Intelligence Testing.* E. L. Thorndike, S. S. Colvin, Harold Rugg, G. M. Whipple. Part II—*The Administrative Use of Intelligence Tests.* H. W. Holmes, W. K. Layton, Helen Davis, Agnes L. Rogers, Rudolf Pintner, M. R. Trabue, W. S. Miller, Bessie L. Gambrill, and others. The two parts are bound together.................................
*Twenty-second Yearbook, 1923, Part I—*English Composition: Its Aims, Methods and Measurements.* Earl Hudelson ....
*Twenty-second Yearbook, 1923, Part II—*The Social Studies in the Elementary and Secondary School.* A. S. Barr, J. J. Coss, Henry Harap, R. W. Hatch, H. C. Hill, Ernest Horn, C. H. Judd, L. C. Marshall, F. M. McMurry, Earle Rugg, H. O. Rugg, Emma Schweppe, Mabel Snedaker, and C. W. Washburne.............
*Twenty-third Yearbook, 1924, Part I—*The Education of Gifted Children.* Report of the Society's Committee. Guy M. Whipple, Chairman....................
*Twenty-third Yearbook, 1924, Part II—*Vocational Guidance and Vocational Education for Industries.* A. H. Edgerton and Others.............................
*Twenty-fourth Yearbook, 1925, Part I—*Report of the National Committee on Reading.* W. S. Gray, Chairman, F. W. Ballou, Rose L. Hardy, Ernest Horn, Francis Jenkins, S. A. Leonard, Estaline Wilson, and Laura Zirbes......................
*Twenty-fourth Yearbook, 1925, Part II—*Adapting the Schools to Individual Differences.* Report of the Society's Committee. Carleton W. Washburn, Chairman...
*Twenty-fifth Yearbook, 1926, Part I—*The Present Status of Safety Education.* Report of the Society's Committee. Guy M. Whipple, Chairman....................
*Twenty-fifth Yearbook, 1926, Part II—*Extra-Curricular Activities.* Report of the Society's Committee. Leonard V. Koos, Chairman.............................
*Twenty-sixth Yearbook, 1927, Part I—*Curriculum-making: Past and Present.* Report of the Society's Committee. Harold O. Rugg, Chairman....................
*Twenty-sixth Yearbook, 1927, Part II—*The Foundations of Curriculum-making.* Prepared by individual members of the Society's Committee. Harold O. Rugg, Chairman
*Twenty-seventh Yearbook, 1928, Part I—*Nature and Nurture: Their Influence upon Intelligence.* Prepared by the Society's Committee. Lewis M. Terman, Chairman...
*Twenty-seventh Yearbook, 1928, Part II—*Nature and Nurture: Their Influence upon Achievement.* Prepared by the Society's Committee. Lewis M. Terman, Chairman.
Twenty-eighth Yearbook, 1929, Parts I and II—*Preschool and Parental Education.* Part I—*Organization and Development.* Part II—*Research and Method.* Prepared by the Society's Committee. Lois H. Meek, Chairman. Bound in one volume. Cloth $5.00

PUBLICATIONS   cxi

POSTPAID
PRICE

Twenty-ninth Yearbook, 1930, Parts I and II—*Report of the Society's Committee on Arithmetic.* Part I—*Some Aspects of Modern Thought on Arithmetic.* Part II—*Research in Arithmetic.* Prepared by the Society's Committee. F. B. Knight, Chairman. Bound in one volume. Cloth.................................... $5.00

Thirtieth Yearbook, 1931, Part I—*The Status of Rural Education.* First Report of the Society's Committee on Rural Education. Orville G. Brim, Chairman. Cloth..   2.50

Thirtieth Yearbook, 1931, Part II—*The Textbook in American Education.* Report of the Society's Committee on the Textbook. J. B. Edmonson, Chairman. Cloth......   2.50
Paper..   1.75

*Thirty-first Yearbook, 1932, Part I—*A Program for Teaching Science.* Prepared by the Society's Committee on the Teaching of Science. S. Ralph Powers, Chairman. Paper

Thirty-first Yearbook, 1932, Part II—*Changes and Experiments in Liberal-Arts Education.* Prepared by Kathryn McHale, with numerous collaborators. Cloth........   3.00

Thirty-second Yearbook, 1933—*The Teaching of Geography.* Prepared by the Society's Committee on the Teaching of Geography. A. E. Parkins, Chairman. Cloth.......   5.00
Paper..   3.75

Thirty-third Yearbook, 1934, Part I—*The Planning and Construction of School Buildings.* Prepared by the Society's Committee on School Buildings. N. L. Engelhardt, Chairman. Cloth...   2.50

Thirty-third Yearbook, 1934, Part II—*The Activity Movement.* Prepared by the Society's Committee on the Activity Movement. Lois Coffey Mossman, Chairman. Cloth..   3.00
Paper..   2.25

Thirty-fourth Yearbook, 1935—*Educational Diagnosis.* Prepared by the Society's Committee on Educational Diagnosis. L. J. Brueckner, Chairman. Cloth............   5.00
Paper..   3.75

*Thirty-fifth Yearbook, 1936, Part I—*The Grouping of Pupils.* Prepared by the Society's Committee. W. W. Coxe, Chairman. Cloth....................................

*Thirty-fifth Yearbook, 1936, Part II—*Music Education.* Prepared by the Society's Committee. W. L. Uhl, Chairman. Cloth...

*Thirty-sixth Yearbook, 1937, Part I—*The Teaching of Reading.* Prepared by the Society's Committee. W. S. Gray, Chairman. Cloth....................................

*Thirty-sixth Yearbook, 1937, Part II—*International Understanding through the Public-School Curriculum.* Prepared by the Society's Committee. I. L. Kandel, Chairman. Paper

*Thirty-seventh Yearbook, 1938, Part I—*Guidance in Educational Institutions.* Prepared by the Society's Committee. G. N. Kefauver, Chairman. Cloth............

*Thirty-seventh Yearbook, 1938, Part II—*The Scientific Movement in Education.* Prepared by the Society's Committee. F. N. Freeman, Chairman. Paper.............

*Thirty-eighth Yearbook, 1939, Part I—*Child Development and the Curriculum.* Prepared by the Society's Committee. Carleton Washburne, Chairman. Paper........

Thirty-eighth Yearbook, 1939, Part II—*General Education in the American College.* Prepared by the Society's Committee. Alvin Eurich, Chairman. Paper..........   2.75

Thirty-ninth Yearbook, 1940, Part I—*Intelligence: Its Nature and Nurture. Comparative and Critical Exposition.* Prepared by the Society's Committee. G. D. Stoddard, Chairman. Cloth..   3.00

Thirty-ninth Yearbook, 1940, Part II—*Intelligence: Its Nature and Nurture. Original Studies and Experiments.* Prepared by the Society's Committee. G. D. Stoddard, Chairman. Cloth...   3.00

Fortieth Yearbook, 1941—*Art in American Life and Education.* Prepared by the Society's Committee. Thomas Munro, Chairman. Paper.........................   3.75

Forty-first Yearbook, 1942, Part I—*Philosophies of Education.* Prepared by the Society's Committee. John S. Brubacher, Chairman. Cloth......................   4.00
Paper..   3.25

Forty-first Yearbook, 1942, Part II—*The Psychology of Learning.* Prepared by the Society's Committee. T. R. McConnell, Chairman. Cloth.....................   4.50
Paper..   3.75

Forty-second Yearbook, 1943, Part I—*Vocational Education.* Prepared by the Society's Committee. F. J. Keller, Chairman. Cloth..............................   3.25
Paper..   2.50

Forty-second Yearbook, 1943, Part II—*The Library in General Education.* Prepared by the Society's Committee. L. R. Wilson, Chairman. Cloth..................   4.00

Forty-third Yearbook, 1944, Part I—*Adolescence.* Prepared by the Society's Committee. Harold E. Jones, Chairman. Cloth.................................   4.00
Paper..   3.25

cxii   PUBLICATIONS

                                                                                POSTPAID
                                                                                 PRICE
Forty-third Yearbook, 1944, Part II—*Teaching Language in the Elementary School.*
    Prepared by the Society's Committee. M. R. Trabue, Chairman. Cloth.......... $3.00
    Paper 2.25
Forty-fourth Yearbook, 1945, Part I—*American Education in the Postwar Period:
    Curriculum Reconstruction.* Prepared by the Society's Committee. Ralph W. Tyler,
    Chairman. Paper 2.25
*Forty-fourth Yearbook, 1945, Part II—*American Education in the Postwar Period:
    Structural Reorganization.* Prepared by the Society's Committee. Bess Goodykoontz,
    Chairman. Paper ....
*Forty-fifth Yearbook, 1946, Part I—*The Measurement of Understanding.* Prepared by
    the Society's Committee. William A. Brownell, Chairman. Paper................
Forty-fifth Yearbook, 1946, Part II—*Changing Conceptions in Educational Adminis-
    tration.* Prepared by the Society's Committee. Alonzo G. Grace, Chairman. Cloth.   3.00
    Paper 2.25
*Forty-sixth Yearbook, 1947, Part I—*Science Education in American Schools.* Pre-
    pared by the Society's Committee. Victor H. Noll, Chairman. Paper.............
Forty-sixth Yearbook, 1947, Part II—*Early Childhood Education.* Prepared by the
    Society's Committee. N. Searle Light, Chairman. Cloth.......................   4.50
    Paper 3.75
Forty-seventh Yearbook, 1948, Part I—*Juvenile Delinquency and the Schools.* Pre-
    pared by the Society's Committee. Ruth Strang, Chairman. Cloth..............   4.50
Forty-seventh Yearbook, 1948, Part II—*Reading in the High School and College.*
    Prepared by the Society's Committee. William S. Gray, Chairman. Cloth.......   4.50
    Paper 3.75
Forty-eighth Yearbook, 1949, Part I—*Audio-visual Materials of Instruction.* Prepared
    by the Society's Committee. Stephen M. Corey, Chairman. Cloth..............   4.50
Forty-eighth Yearbook, 1949, Part II—*Reading in the Elementary School.* Prepared
    by the Society's Committee. Arthur I. Gates, Chairman. Cloth................   4.50
    Paper 3.75
Forty-ninth Yearbook, 1950, Part I—*Learning and Instruction.* Prepared by the So-
    ciety's Committee. G. Lester Anderson, Chairman. Cloth.....................   4.50
    Paper 3.75
Forty-ninth Yearbook, 1950, Part II—*The Education of Exceptional Children.* Pre-
    pared by the Society's Committee. Samuel A. Kirk, Chairman. Cloth............   4.50
    Paper 3.75
Fiftieth Yearbook, 1951, Part I—*Graduate Study in Education.* Prepared by the
    Society's Board of Directors. Ralph W. Tyler, Chairman. Cloth................   4.50
    Paper 3.75
Fiftieth Yearbook, 1951, Part II—*The Teaching of Arithmetic.* Prepared by the So-
    ciety's Committee. G. T. Buswell, Chairman. Cloth.........................   4.50
    Paper 3.75
Fifty-first Yearbook, 1952, Part I—*General Education.* Prepared by the Society's
    Committee. T. R. McConnell, Chairman. Cloth..............................   4.50
    Paper 3.75
Fifty-first Yearbook, 1952, Part II—*Education in Rural Communities.* Prepared by
    the Society's Committee. Ruth Strang, Chairman. Cloth.....................   4.50
    Paper 3.75
Fifty-second Yearbook, 1953, Part I—*Adapting the Secondary-School Program to the
    Needs of Youth.* Prepared by the Society's Committee. William G. Brink, Chair-
    man. Cloth 4.50
    Paper 3.75
Fifty-second Yearbook, 1953, Part II—*The Community School.* Prepared by the So-
    ciety's Committee. Maurice F. Seay, Chairman. Cloth.......................   4.50
    Paper 3.75
Fifty-third Yearbook, 1954, Part I—*Citizen Co-operation for Better Public Schools.*
    Prepared by the Society's Committee. Edgar L. Morphet, Chairman. Cloth......   4.50
    Paper 3.75
Fifty-third Yearbook, 1954, Part II—*Mass Media and Education.* Prepared by the
    Society's Committee. Edgar Dale, Chairman. Cloth.........................   4.50
    Paper 3.75
Fifty-fourth Yearbook, 1955, Part I—*Modern Philosophies and Education.* Prepared
    by the Society's Committee. John S. Brubacher, Chairman. Cloth.............   4.50
    Paper 3.75
Fifty-fourth Yearbook, 1955, Part II—*Mental Health in Modern Education.* Prepared
    by the Society's Committee. Paul A. Witty, Chairman. Cloth.................   4.50
    Paper 3.75
Fifty-fifth Yearbook, 1956, Part I—*The Public Junior College.* Prepared by the So-
    ciety's Committee. B. Lamar Johnson, Chairman. Cloth......................   4.50

PUBLICATIONS cxiii

POSTPAID
PRICE

Fifty-fifth Yearbook, 1956, Part II—*Adult Reading*. Prepared by the Society's Committee. David H. Clift, Chairman. Cloth.................................. $4.50
    Paper 3.75
Fifty-sixth Yearbook, 1957, Part I—*In-service Education of Teachers, Supervisors, and Administrators*. Prepared by the Society's Committee. Stephen M. Corey, Chairman. Cloth.. 4.50
    Paper 3.75
Fifty-sixth Yearbook, 1957, Part II—*Social Studies in the Elementary School*. Prepared by the Society's Committee. Ralph C. Preston, Chairman. Cloth......... 4.50
    Paper 3.75
Fifty-seventh Yearbook, 1958, Part I—*Basic Concepts in Music Education*. Prepared by the Society's Committee. Thurber H. Madison, Chairman. Cloth............. 4.50
    Paper 3.75
Fifty-seventh Yearbook, 1958, Part II—*Education for the Gifted*. Prepared by the Society's Committee. Robert J. Havighurst, Chairman. Cloth................... 4.50
    Paper 3.75
Fifty-seventh Yearbook, 1958, Part III—*The Integration of Educational Experiences*. Prepared by the Society's Committee. Paul L. Dressel, Chairman. Cloth....... 4.50
    Paper 3.75
Fifty-eighth Yearbook, 1959, Part I—*Community Education: Principles and Practices from World-wide Experience*. Prepared by the Society's Committee. C. O. Arndt, Chairman. Cloth 4.50
    Paper 3.75
Fifty-eighth Yearbook, 1959, Part II—*Personnel Services in Education*. Prepared by the Society's Committee. Melvene D. Hardee, Chairman. Cloth................ 4.50
    Paper 3.75
Fifty-ninth Yearbook, 1960, Part I—*Rethinking Science Education*. Prepared by the Society's Committee. J. Darrell Barnard, Chairman. Cloth................... 4.50
Fifty-ninth Yearbook, 1960, Part II—*The Dynamics of Instructional Groups*. Prepared by the Society's Committee. Gale E. Jensen, Chairman. Cloth................ 4.50
    Paper 3.75
Sixtieth Yearbook, 1961, Part I—*Development in and through Reading*. Prepared by the Society's Committee. Paul A. Witty, Chairman. Cloth................... 5.00
    Paper 4.25
Sixtieth Yearbook, 1961, Part II—*Social Forces Influencing American Education*. Prepared by the Society's Committee. Ralph W. Tyler, Chairman. Cloth......... 4.50
Sixty-first Yearbook, 1962, Part I—*Individualizing Instruction*. Prepared by the Society's Committee. Fred T. Tyler, Chairman. Cloth........................ 4.50
Sixty-first Yearbook, 1962, Part II—*Education for the Professions*. Prepared by the Society's Committee. G. Lester Anderson, Chairman. Cloth.................... 4.50
Sixty-second Yearbook, 1963, Part I—*Child Psychology*. Prepared by the Society's Committee. Harold W. Stevenson, Editor. Cloth............................. 6.50
Sixty-second Yearbook, 1963, Part II—*The Impact and Improvement of School Testing Programs*. Prepared by the Society's Committee. Warren G. Findley, Editor. Cloth 4.50
Sixty-third Yearbook, 1964, Part I—*Theories of Learning and Instruction*. Prepared by the Society's Committee. Ernest R. Hilgard, Editor. Cloth................ 5.50
Sixty-third Yearbook, 1964, Part II—*Behavioral Science and Educational Administration*. Prepared by the Society's Committee. Daniel E. Griffiths, Cloth....... 4.50
Sixty-fourth Yearbook, 1965, Part I—*Vocational Education*. Prepared by the Society's Committee. Melvin L. Barlow, Editor. Cloth.......................... 5.00
Sixty-fourth Yearbook, 1965, Part II—*Art Education*. Prepared by the Society's Committee. W. Reid Hastie, Editor. Cloth.................................. 5.00
Sixty-fifth Yearbook, 1966, Part I—*Social Deviancy among Youth*. Prepared by the Society's Committee. William W. Wattenberg, Editor. Cloth................. 5.50
Sixty-fifth Yearbook, 1966, Part II—*The Changing American School*. Prepared by the Society's Committee. John I. Goodlad, Editor. Cloth...................... 5.00
Sixty-sixth Yearbook, 1967, Part I—*The Educationally Retarded and Disadvantaged*. Prepared by the Society's Committee. Paul A. Witty, Editor. Cloth........... 5.50
Sixty-sixth Yearbook, 1967, Part II—*Programed Instruction*. Prepared by the Society's Committee. Phil C. Lange, Editor. Cloth............................ 5.00
Sixty-seventh Yearbook, 1968, Part I—*Metropolitanism: Its Challenge to Education*. Prepared by the Society's Committee. Robert J. Havighurst, Editor. Cloth....... 5.50
Sixty-seventh Yearbook, 1968, Part II—*Innovation and Change in Reading Instruction*. Prepared by the Society's Committee. Helen M. Robinson, Editor. Cloth..... 5.50

Distributed by
THE UNIVERSITY OF CHICAGO PRESS, CHICAGO, ILLINOIS 60637
1968